AMERICAN MILITARY AIRCRAFT

AMERICAN MILITARY AIRCRAFT

A CENTURY OF INNOVATION

GENERAL EDITOR: JIM WINCHESTER

METRO BOOKS
New York

METRO BOOKS
New York

An Imprint of Sterling Publishing
387 Park Avenue South
New York, NY 10016

METRO BOOKS and the distinctive Metro Books logo are trademarks of Sterling
Publishing Co., Inc.

© 2005 by IMP AB.

Editorial and design by
Amber Books Ltd
74–77 White Lion Street
London N1 9PF
www.amberbooks.co.uk

ISBN 978-1-4351-5697-5

For information about custom editions, special sales, and premium and corporate
purchases, please contact Sterling Special Sales at 800-805-5489 or
specialsales@sterlingpublishing.com.

Manufactured in China

2 4 6 8 10 9 7 5 3 1

www.sterlingpublishing.com

CONTENTS

INTRODUCTION

This book features just some of the many hundreds of aircraft types developed for military use in the United States of America, and a few developed outside that have made a significant contribution to the US services.

The early years

The USA was one of the first nations to explore the use of heavier-than-air craft for military purposes; the Army testing a Wright biplane in 1908, and procuring their very first aircraft (another Wright) for $25,000 in 1909, a fortune at the time.

Progress was rapid, and in the years 1910–11 many firsts were achieved in military aviation. Aircraft were flown on and off ships, the first military gun was fired from an aeroplane (in the USA, 'aeroplane' and 'airplane' were more or less interchangeable in the early days), the first explosive bombs were dropped and the first successful 'hydroaeroplane' (seaplane) was operated.

In April 1914 Curtiss AB flying boats made the first wartime operations by American military aircraft during the Vera Cruz incident involving unrest in Mexico. An Army Aviation Section (of the Signal Corps) was formed just before the outbreak of World War I

▲ *A trio of F-4B Phantom IIs of VF-102 prepares for launch from one of the bow catapults on the USS Enterprise.*

▲ *Flown for decades on atomic alert, the Boeing B-52 has only seen action in conventional bombing campaigns in Southeast Asia and the Persian Gulf.*

that August. Active US involvement in the war began in 1917, but US pilots had flown with the Escadrille Américaine (later Lafayette Escadrille) since early 1916.

Despite the aforementioned pioneering developments and ample time to prepare for war, the USA developed very few effective combat aircraft before 1918. The Navy did useful work in European waters with a number of US-built flying boats and seaplanes but the US Army Air Service in France was exclusively equipped with foreign aircraft, including French SPAD and Nieuport fighters and British Airco DH.4 light bombers. The DH.4 was the first military machine mass-produced in the United States. The Thomas Morse MB-3 scout (or 'Tommy Morse') was the first American-designed fighter built in large quantities, but it did not appear until 1919.

During the 1920s and early 1930s funding for the US armed forces was kept at a very low level by successive administrations. General 'Billy' Mitchell's demonstrations of the ability of land-based aircraft to destroy ships at sea fostered interservice rivalries in an era when the Army and Navy had to fight for every budget dollar.

▲ *A Boeing B-17 of the 7th Bomb Group carries the olive drab and grey camouflage scheme applied to USAAC aircraft after the US entered World War II.*

▼ *Douglas SBD-5 Dauntlesses returning from a mission. The furthest aircraft has its aft defensive guns deployed from the rear cockpit.*

Proponents of strategic airpower and the Italian General Douhet's theory that 'the bomber would always get through' debated whether giant strategic bombers or larger numbers of fast, lightly armed aircraft were the way ahead. Several huge one-off aircraft were constructed and impressed crowds at interwar air races (as did many Army Air Corps 'pursuit ships', or fighters), but eventually two classes of bomber – 'Heavy' (such as the B-17) and 'Medium' (like the B-25) – were settled on.

Carrier air power

Following the Royal Navy's lead, the US Navy developed aircraft carriers more or less as we know them, although it would take further British inventions after World War I to make them the instruments of global power they are today. The same few ships went from decks packed with yellow and silver biplanes to blue and grey monoplanes able to carry useful and effective warloads, and paved the way

for the fleets of Essex-Class ships that would serve from World War II through to the Vietnam era.

Various different manufacturers dominated the supply of carrier-based aircraft in the years after World War II. 'All-Douglas' air wings equipped with the Skyraider, Skyhawk, Skyray and Skywarrior gave way to some 'all-Grumman' decks (Tomcat, Intruder, Prowler, Hawkeye, Greyhound). Today Boeing (through acquisition, merger and partnership) seems poised to dominate the near-to-mid future with the Hornet and Super Hornet in various configurations, and the V-22 Osprey tiltrotor.

World War II

The months between September 1939 and December 1941 allowed the USA to move its industry to a war footing and to replace its last biplanes with modern metal monoplanes. Although the best US fighters and bombers were somewhat behind the best British,

German and Japanese aircraft, new versions and new designs soon caught up. America's 'arsenal of democracy' built over 100,000 aircraft for itself and its allies, more than the output of all the Axis powers combined. The US

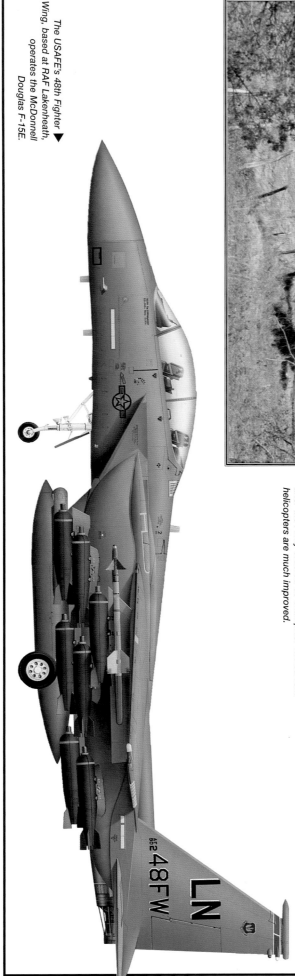

The USAFE's 48th Fighter Wing, based at RAF Lakenheath, operates the McDonnell Douglas F-15E.

Army Air Corps grew so large that it was all but a separate service by the time it actually became one in 1947.

Vietnam and the Cold War

The decades following World War II were a time of great advances and much experimentation. At any one time the US Air Force and Navy alone had numerous fighter and bomber aircraft types in service or development. The Army had many programmes for helicopters and other vertical lift vehicles. It was also a time in which the US sold or gave away thousands of aircraft to friendly nations. Soon the skies of Europe, Asia and Latin America were full of Mustangs, Sabres, Skyhawks or Starfighters, not to mention Dakotas, Hueys and Hercules. The particular subjects for illustration in this title reflect the success of American

▲ The Bell AH-1 Cobra first saw service in 1968 after the Army ordered 38 examples. The current helicopters are much improved.

combat aircraft in the world market. Vietnam proved that the most sophisticated aircraft intended for use against the cities and massed forces of the Warsaw Pact were unsuitable for use in 'limited wars', although they were all that was available to begin with. The next generation of aircraft and weapons were flexible enough (as was the doctrine) to prevail without great losses in two Iraq wars and elsewhere.

Mergers

Of the 20 or so major manufacturers of military aircraft active in 1950 and represented in this book, only four exist today under the same name. The others have either ceased to be, stopped making complete aircraft or have joined to form massive defence and aerospace conglomerates, responsible for everything from battle tanks to submarines and satellites. Douglas, McDonnell Douglas (itself the result of a huge merger in the 1960s), North American and Rockwell are just some of the companies absorbed by Boeing. In the realm of fighter aircraft they are challenged today only by Lockheed Martin within the US market, with Northrop Grumman one of the few large 'airframers' still competing for fixed-wing aircraft contracts.

The manufacture of certain classes of aircraft, such as military trainers, tactical transport aircraft and light helicopters, has just about slipped out of American hands altogether. The players in these fields are mainly European. What was once the aircraft division of the mighty Hughes Corporation is now Dutch-owned (although still building helicopters in

Arizona). International collaborative projects, such as the Lockheed/Alenia C-27J, Bell/Agusta BA 609 tiltrotor and Lockheed/Westand/Agusta US-101 (EH.101 Merlin) look like being the way forward in some areas to fulfil US military needs and satisfy laws about US content in arms purchases.

The most impressive of today's American warplanes, the B-2 Spirit, costs one hundred thousand times as much as the first US military aircraft. One way to cut costs is to eliminate the crew, their training and the space they take up. Sooner than in other countries, the future for America's combat, strike and reconnaissance platforms may lie in unmanned air vehicles, but for the bulk of military uses, the development and manufacture of piloted machines still has a long future.

▲ A US Marine Corps McDonnell Douglas TA-4F Skyhawk fires an unguided rocket while on a training sortie.

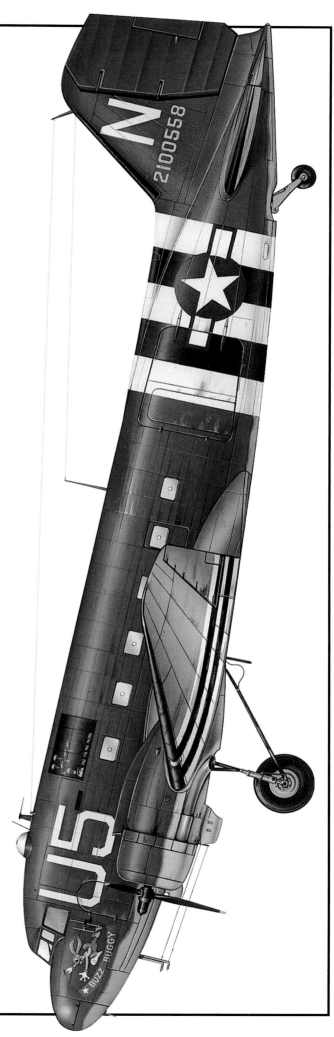

▼ During the D-Day landings this Douglas C-47 flew from a British base with the 81st Troop Carrier Squadron of the 436th Troop Carrier Group.

AIRCO
DH.4

● Day bomber ● British and US production ● Powerful engines

▲ After their success in France during World War I, British-built DH.4s and American-built DH.4s found further service in foreign air forces, including those of Belgium, Greece, Japan and Nicaragua.

The DH.4 was the first pupose-designed British bomber, and was one of the most successful aircraft of WWI. After its first flight in August 1916, the DH.4 was transformed by the Rolls-Royce Eagle engine, which enabled the aircraft's performance to match that of contemporary fighters. Nearly 7000 were built and production continued after the war, when several air forces, together with early airlines, retained the DH.4.

AIRCO DH.4

PHOTO FILE

▲ DH-4B air mail pioneer
Surplus DH-4s were converted for the US Postal Department to establish an air mail service; the front cockpit held mail bags. This aircraft has wingtip landing lights.

▲ 'Liberty Plane'
With hundreds of surplus DH-4s available after World War I, many found their way into civil operation. DH-4s were used not only as mail carriers, but also as airliners and crop-dusters.

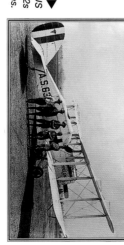

▲ Cabin-equipped DH-4A
DH-4As carried a pilot and two passengers. Nine were converted from DH-4s, serving with the RAF and on early routes across the English Channel.

Army air ambulance ▶
Among numerous DH-4 variants to enter US military service were a number of DH-4Amb-2s which were able to carry two stretcher cases.

▲ Steel-framed DH-4M-1
A.S.23007 was one of a number of American-built DH-4s rebuilt by Boeing and Atlantic Aircraft during the 1920s, with steel-tube fuselages. These aircraft were designated DH-4M-1s and -2s, respectively.

FACTS AND FIGURES

▼ Thirty aircraft were built for the US Postal Department, with increased-span wings and two 149-kW (200-hp) Hall-Scott engines.

▼ Total US DH-4 production reached 4846; 15 were built in Belgium; 1449 in the UK.

▼ DH.4s engines ranged in power output from 149 kW (200 hp) to 391 kW (524 hp).

▼ A DH.4 shipped to New Zealand became the first aircraft to fly over that country's highest mountain, 3760-m (12,336-ft) Mount Cook.

▼ The Airco DH.4 prototype flew in August 1916 from its base at Hendon, London.

▼ For coastal patrol tasks, the RNAS fitted floats to at least one DH.4.

PROFILE

de Havilland's day bombing master

Staggered wings were used on the DH.4 to give the pilot a good view of the ground for bombing. One or two Lewis guns were fitted in the observer's cockpit, and one or two forward-firing Vickers guns were mounted on the fuselage sides. In this form the DH.4 made an immediate impression over the Western Front in 1917.

Nearly 1500 were built in the United Kingdom, and almost 5000 with 298-kW (400-hp) Liberty 12 engines, in the United States, where the US Army used DH-4s until 1932. The US Navy and Marine Corps also used the type.

After the war, RAF aircraft were retired, and many were transferred to other countries. More than 1500 of the American aircraft were modified as DH-4Bs, while Boeing and Fokker Atlantic built 285 modernized DH-4Ms with steel-tube fuselages. There were more than 60 modified versions, including single-seaters, dual-

American interest in the DH.4 was high. Built by Dayton-Wright Aircraft, Fisher Body and Standard Aircraft, almost 5000 were built with 298-kW (400-hp) Liberty 12 engines fitted. In all, 1885 were shipped to France.

Originally meant to be powered by an uprated Beardmore engine of 119 kW (160 hp), the first DH.4 actually flew with a 172-kW (230 hp) BHP powerplant. However, it was Rolls-Royce's 186-kW (249-hp) (and later 280-kW/375-hp) Eagle 12-cylinder engine that took the DH.4 to fame.

engines, in the United States, where the US Army used DH-4s until 1932. The US Navy and Marine Corps also used the type.

DH.4

Type: light day bomber

Powerplant: one 280-kW (375-hp) Rolls-Royce Eagle VIII water-cooled 12-cylinder engine

Maximum level speed: 230 km/h (143 mph) at sea level

Endurance: 3 hours 45 min

Range: 700 km (435 miles)

Service ceiling: 6705 m (19,930 ft)

Weights: empty 1083 kg (2388 lb); maximum take-off 1575 kg (3472 lb)

Armament: (RNAS aircraft) two forward-firing 7.7-mm (.303-cal.) Vickers machine guns and one or two 7.7-mm Lewis machine gun(s) in the rear cockpit, plus up to 209 kg (460 lb) of bombs

Dimensions:
span	12.92 m (42 ft 5 in)
length	9.35 m (30 ft 8 in)
height	3.05 m (10 ft)
wing area	40.32 m² (434 sq ft)

COMBAT DATA

ENDURANCE

The DH.4 had a good range and endurance performance compared to the contemporary Albatros C.V/16. The post-war American-built DH-4M retained this ability.

DH.4
3 hrs 45 mins

C.V/16
3 hrs 15 mins

DH-4M
3 hrs 45 mins

ARMAMENT

While RFC DH-4s were equipped with three machine guns, RNAS aircraft used four, like the later US-built DH-4M. The Albatros was lightly armed by comparison, although it could carry a 'light bombload'.

DH.4
3 x 7. 7-mm (.303-cal.) machine guns
209-kg (460-lb) bombload

C.V/16
2 x 7.92-mm (0.311 in) machine guns

DH-4M
4 x 7.63-mm (.30-cal.) machine guns
209-kg (460-lb) bombload

POWER

The chief benefits of the post-war DH-4M were its more powerful engine and more robust steel-tube fuselage structure. With the Liberty 12 installed, it had twice the power of the C.V/16.

DH.4
280 kW (375 hp)

C.V/16
164 kW (220 hp)

DH-4M
313 kW (420 hp)

Above: The DH.4 was operational from April 1917. On 6 April, No. 55 Squadron flew from Fienvilliers on a mission to bomb Valenciennes. Its performance matched that of fighters of the time.

DH.4

N5977 was one of a batch of 50 DH.4s built by Westland Aircraft with Rolls-Royce Eagle engines. It carries the markings of No. 2 Squadron, RNAS, immediately prior to its redesignation in 1918 as No. 202 Squadron, RAF.

Above: In 1923, USAAC DH-4s conclusively demonstrated air-to-air refuelling for the first time. The receiver was aloft for over 37 hours.

control trainers and air ambulances. A total of 100 DH-4Bs were also used to establish the US air mail service, the aircraft serving until 1927.

The placement of the main fuel tank between the pilot and the gunner proved a disadvantage, as it hampered in-flight communication. It was also prone to catching fire if hit by enemy guns, earning the aircraft the nickname 'The Flaming Coffin'.

DH.4s were defensively and offensively well-armed. RNAS aircraft carried two forward-firing 7.7-mm (.303-calibre) Vickers machine guns above the engine (RFC machines carried only one) and one or two 7.7-mm Lewis machine guns in the rear cockpit.

The DH.4 was a conventional two-bay biplane with a wood and fabric structure, although its forward fuselage was skinned with plywood for strength. The tailplane was adjustable, allowing the pilot to trim the aircraft in flight.

Underfuselage/wing bomb racks on the DH.4 had a 209-kg (460-lb) capacity. As No. 55 Squadron, Royal Flying Corps received its first aircraft, Royal Naval Air Service examples were also being delivered. These aircraft undertook bombing, gun ranging (for ships), reconnaissance and photographic tasks.

British land-based bombers of World War I

■ **AVRO 504:** In November 1914, four modified RNAS 504 trainers from a base in France made a raid on Zeppelin sheds at Friedrichshafen.

■ **ROYAL AIRCRAFT FACTORY BE.2:** This two-seat reconnaissance type was adapted as a bomber, but was vulnerable to enemy fighters.

■ **SHORT BOMBER:** A land-based version of the Short 184 floatplane, the Bomber flew missions with the RNAS from late 1916.

■ **SOPWITH 1½ STRUTTER:** Armed with a forward-firing gun, this Sopwith design equipped RNAS and RFC units as a bomber and escort.

BEECH
C-12

● Multi-role turboprop light transport ● Derived from civil design

Initially supplied to the US Army and USAF in 1975 as a light transport, the Beech C-12 is today in service with all three US services and 18 other air arms (in some cases in its civil guise) in a wide variety of roles. The Beech B200 Super King Air, from which the C-12 is derived, was developed from the commercial Model 100 in the early 1970s. The new type featured a T-tail, longer wings and many internal refinements. Later versions have further improvements.

▲ Beechcraft's C-12F replaced the CT-39 Sabreliner as an operational support aircraft and featured more powerful engines, a cargo door and improved passenger facilities.

BEECH C-12

▼ **Special duties**
Not all C-12s supplied to air arms are used as transports. Some are camouflaged and used for aerial surveillance and other tasks.

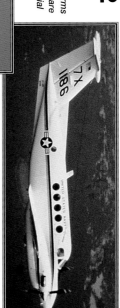

▲ **Navy transports**
A total of 78 Beech A200Cs was purchased by the US Navy and Marine Corps as UC-12Bs. They first entered service in 1980 as personnel and utility transports.

▼ **Mission support**
Designated UC-12J, this bigger and more powerful Beech 1900C is one of six used by the US Air National Guard for mission support from 1987.

Upgraded aircraft ▼
When the US Army took delivery of the more powerful C-12C/Ds with PT6A-41 turboprops it upgraded its large fleet of C-12As to the same standard. This C-12D features increased-span wings and cargo doors.

▲ **Army Hurons**
The US Army employs its C-12A/C/D Hurons in the utility role, supporting Army units and US embassies around the world.

FACTS AND FIGURES

▶ It took Beechcraft four years to develop the Model 200 Super King Air/C-12 with its large T-tail, from the Model 100.

▶ The first C-12 entered service with the US Army at Fort Monroe in July 1975.

▶ Two USAF C-12s are operated by US Customs for anti-smuggling surveillance.

▶ Extensive aerial arrays identify the RC-12 variants used by the US Army for electronics special missions.

▶ The Beech B200C/C-12F can fly faster, higher and further than the A200 model.

▶ Cargo doors and provision of wingtip fuel tanks are features of the C-12D.

PROFILE

Military utility 'off the shelf'

Beech developed its Super King Air 200 over a four-year period from 1969, using the successful King Air 100 executive turboprop transport as a basis. It had more powerful engines, a T-tail and increased wingspan as well as equipment changes.

It was bigger, faster and more capable than the King Airs already in service with the US Army as the U-21. A contract was placed for 34 of the new aircraft as C-12s, for the US Army and USAF.

In most respects these were standard Super King Airs from the production line, but with modified avionics and equipment to meet military requirements as staff transports.

In 1978 the US Navy bought the first of 78 C-12s for use as personnel and utility transports. In order to accommodate freight items these UC-12Bs had a large cargo door (1.32 x 1.32 m/52 x 52 in) on the port side. They also had 634-kW (850-hp) Pratt & Whitney PT6A-41 engines and a taller undercarriage assembly.

The US Army converted a number of its new C-12Ds for special electronic missions and battlefield surveillance as RC-12s. These have a large array of aerials and pods.

Below: This UC-12B was operated by the US Marine Corps headquarters and based at the Naval Air Facility at Washington, DC.

Above: A number of South American air arms, including that of Argentina, have purchased Super King Airs as affordable surveillance and maritime patrol platforms.

C-12F

Type: utility transport for USAF Operational Support Aircraft requirement

Powerplant: two 634-KW (850-hp) Pratt & Whitney Canada PT6A-42 turboprops

Maximum speed: 545 km/h (339 mph) at 7620 m (25,000 ft)

Initial climb rate: 747 m/min (2451 fpm) at sea level

Range: 3641 km (2262 miles) with maximum fuel at 10,670 m (35,000 ft)

Service ceiling: more than 10,670 m (35,000 ft)

Weights: operating empty 3656 kg (8060 lb); maximum take-off 5670 kg (12,500 lb)

Accommodation: two pilots, plus eight passengers or 1201 kg (2648 lb) of cargo

Dimensions:
span	16.61 m	(54 ft 6 in)
length	13.36 m	(43 ft 9 in)
height	4.52 m	(14 ft 10 in)
wing area	28.15 m²	(303 sq ft)

ACTION DATA

PASSENGERS

The usefulness of the C-12F as a liaison transport is limited by its size. This role is largely the preserve of larger, 19-seat machines like the C-12J (derived from the Beech 1900) and C-26A Metro, both civil designs that have been adapted for military roles.

C-12F 8 passengers

C-12J 19 passengers

C-26A METRO 19 passengers

MAXIMUM CRUISING SPEED

Though the C-12J is a larger aircraft it lacks the high cruising speed of the smaller C-12F. The Fairchild C-26A has a similar speed performance to the Beechcraft C-12F.

C-12F 536 km/h (333 mph)

C-12J 471 km/h (293 mph)

C-26A METRO 515 km/h (320 mph)

TAKE-OFF RUN TO 15 M (50 FT)

Both the 19-seaters here require almost 1000 m (3280 ft) in which to get airborne and attain a height of 15 m (50 ft). The smaller C-12F uses just under 800 m (2625 ft) of runway to do the same, making it more useful from smaller airports. Take-off performance varies according to the load being carried. Heavier loads need longer runways.

C-12F 786 m (2579 ft)

C-12J 991 m (3251 ft)

C-26A METRO 991 m (3251 ft)

SUPER KING AIR B200

Ireland's Air Corps is one of 18 air arms apart from the US services that has operated Beech C-12/Super King Airs. Three B200s were used for maritime patrol missions and as transports and multi-engine trainers.

The semi-monocoque fuselage structure of the Super King Air 200 is of light alloy. The cabin is air-conditioned and fully pressurized. Large windows along the fuselage and on the flight deck give good visibility.

Two Pratt & Whitney Canada PT6A turboprops each drive a three-bladed, metal, constant-speed fully-feathering and reversible propeller.

Accommodation is provided for two pilots and up to 10 passengers in the standard transport layout. When mission equipment is carried for maritime patrol, accommodation is reduced to a maximum of six, depending upon the duration of the flight.

The B200 has a cantilever T-tail structure of light alloy, with swept vertical and horizontal surfaces. The fixed incidence tailplane has de-icing 'boots' on the leading edges. Each elevator has a trim tab.

This standard Super King Air 200 has a passenger entry door at the rear of the cabin on the port side. It has integral steps built into the back of the door that lower to the ground. Some USAF, US Navy and US Army C-12s have large (1.32 m/52 in high and 1.32 m/52 in wide) cargo access doors.

The tricycle undercarriage has twin main wheels on each leg that retract forwards into the engine nacelle. The nose leg has a single, steerable nose wheel that retracts rearwards into the nose section.

IRISH AIR CORPS — AER CHÓR NA hÉIREANN

USAF/ANG light transports

■ **BRITISH AEROSPACE C-29A:** BAe's well-known 125 Series 800A executive jet was adopted by the USAF in the late 1980s for the Combat Flight Inspection and Navigation (C-FIN) role.

■ **FAIRCHILD C-26A:** When the US Air National Guard (ANG) needed a new operational support transport aircraft, the Metro 3, a 19-seater regional airliner was chosen in 1988.

■ **GATES LEARJET C-21A:** In the early 1980s the then Military Airlift Command operated the CT-39 Sabreliner for high-priority, time-sensitive cargos. The Learjet replaced these from 1984.

■ **SHORTS C-23:** For the distribution of spare parts around Europe, USAFE bought 18 Shorts 330 Sherpas (C-23As). Ten were later bought for the ANG, while the Army bought ex-civil C-23Bs.

BEECH

T-34 MENTOR/TURBO MENTOR

- Primary trainer ● Piston and turbine engines ● Armed versions

▲ Early T-34C Turbo Mentors entered service with the US Navy's Naval Air Training Command in November 1977, with student training commencing the following January.

Beech's T-34 Mentor and T-34C Turbo Mentor are much-loved and strikingly successful trainers which are used in several countries around the world. In its piston-engined guise, the Mentor was America's flying schoolroom of the 1950s and 1960s, and it remains in use training pilots in eight countries today. Instructors have used the advanced, turboprop-powered T-34C Turbo Mentor to train more than 10,000 US naval aviators.

BEECH T-34 MENTOR/TURBO MENTOR

Higher power ▼
General Motors offered this Allison 250B-engined AT-34 conversion to a number of users.

▲ USAF trainer
In 1953 the USAF adopted the Beech T-34A as its first post-war primary trainer.

▲ Navy T-34C
Powered by a Pratt & Whitney Canada PT6A-25 turboprop, the T-34C is still in US Navy service.

Canadian-built ▼
Canadian Car & Foundry built 100 T-34s for the USAF and 25 for the Royal Canadian Air Force.

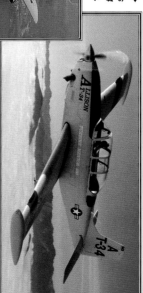

▲ Spanish E.17
This T-34A was one of 25 E.17s delivered to the Spanish air force. They were used for pilot training by the Academia General del Aire at San Javier until 1989.

FACTS AND FIGURES

► Developed from the V-tailed Beech Bonanza, the Model 45 Mentor was flown for the first time on 2 December 1948.

► T-34s were evaluated by the USAF as a possible light close-support aircraft.

► Fully aerobatic, the T-34 was strengthened to withstand +10/-4.5g.

► US Navy T-34C Turbo Mentors were intended to replace both the T-34B Mentor and North American T-28 Trojan.

► Beech offered an armament trainer, the T-34C-1, which carried 544 kg of weapons.

► Bell's X-14 VTOL research aircraft employed a T-34 tail section.

PROFILE

Beech's evergreen trainer

Simple and attractive aircraft, the Beech T-34 Mentor and T-34C Turbo Mentor are two of the most admired and practical flying machines in the sky.

The straightforward, low-wing T-34, with retractable tricycle landing gear, was designed in 1948 but is still going strong half a century later because it provides reliable service. The piston-engined Mentor was used to train US military pilots from 1954, as well as those of nations like Argentina, Canada and Japan, where the aircraft were built under licence. New air cadets continue to receive instruction in basic flying in the Mentor in Argentina, Colombia, the Dominican Republic, El Salvador, the Philippines, Turkey, Uruguay and Venezuela.

Dazzling in its orange and white high-visibility paint scheme, the T-34C Turbo Mentor, a T74 (PT6A) turboprop-engined derivative of the T-34B,

was first delivered in 1977. The T-34C will continue to train US Navy pilots until it is replaced by the Raytheon T-6A from 2004. Turbo Mentors were also exported.

Below: These three T-34Cs are used as armament trainers by Uruguay's Aviacon Naval at Montevideo.

Above: This Turbo Mentor, in sand camouflage, is one of 12 purchased by the Moroccan air force for pilot training at Marrakesh.

T-34C TURBO MENTOR

Fuerza Aerea Ecuatoriana operates the T-34C-1 weapons trainer. From 1979 a total of 14 T-34As and nine T-34C-1s were delivered to Ecuador to equip the Escuadron Entremaiento Aerea at Salinas.

The Pratt & Whitney Canada PT6A-25 turboprop is restricted to 298 kW (400 hp) in normal use to extend engine life and to provide constant performance over a wide range of temperatures and altitudes.

Two pilots sit in tandem with duplicated flight controls and instruments in the two cockpits. These are covered by separate one-piece, rearward-sliding canopies.

The tail unit is of light alloy cantilever structure. It has a fixed incidence tailplane with manually operated trim tabs on the elevators and rudder.

With the increased power of the PT6A turboprop, the T-34C required structural modifications to strengthen the rear fuselage and tail. These included twin ventral fins under the rear fuselage.

Beech increased the strength of the light alloy, semi-monocoque structure of the Turbo Mentor to permit higher speeds, aerobatics and a longer fatigue life in the primary training role.

T-34Cs have a low-set wing of conventional construction. It has no sweepback, but incorporates 4° of dihedral and single-slotted trailing-edge flaps. This version has underwing hardpoints with a pylon for air-to-surface weapons.

A Hartzell three-blade, constant-speed, fully-feathering metal propeller is used on the T-34C. A large hub-spinner is fitted to improve airflow.

Military trainers derived from civil designs

■ **CESSNA 526 CITATIONJET:** Derived from the CitationJet executive transport and first flown in 1983, this was Cessna's losing contender for the USAF/USN JPATS competition.

■ **ENAER T-35 PILLÁN:** Piper built the first two examples of this fully aerobatic trainer based on the Piper Saratoga cabin monoplane. Eighty were built by ENAER in Chile.

■ **NZAI CT-4 AIRTRAINER:** Based on the Australian-designed Victa Airtourer, the aerobatic and more powerful CT-4 first flew in 1972. Australia and Thailand were among its users.

■ **SCOTTISH AVIATION BULLDOG:** Derived from the Beagle Pup after Scottish Aviation acquired the Beagle company, the Bulldog still serves with the RAF. Production ended in 1982.

T-34C Turbo Mentor

Type: two-seat turboprop pilot trainer

Powerplant: one 533-kW (715-hp) (torque limited to 298 kW/400 hp) Pratt & Whitney Canada PT6A-25 turboprop

Maximum speed: 414 km/h (257 mph) at 5335 m (17,500 ft)

Maximum cruising speed: 397 km/h (246 mph)

Climb rate: 388 m/min (1273 fpm) at 3050 m (10,000 ft)

Range: 1205 km (745 miles) at 6100 m (20,000 ft)

Service ceiling: 9145 m (30,000 ft)

Weights: empty 1193 kg (2625 lb); maximum take-off 1938 kg (4264 lb)

Dimensions:
span	10.16 m (33 ft 4 in)
length	8.75 m (28 ft 8 in)
height	3.02 m (9 ft 7 in)
wing area	16.71m² (180 sq ft)

ACTION DATA

POWERPLANTS

Compared to the French SOCATA Epsilon and Chilean ENAER Pillán, the T-34A had a modest engine output. This was addressed in the 1970s when the design was modified to produce the turboprop-powered T-34C.

T-34A MENTOR 168 kW (225 hp)	TB 30B EPSILON 224 kW (300 hp)	T-35A PILLÁN 224 kW (300 hp)

MAXIMUM SPEED

Although the Mentor was not a particularly fast aircraft, it should be remembered that it entered service in the early 1950s and had a comparatively low power-to-weight ratio. Both the Epsilon and Pillán are powered by modern engines and use lightweight materials in their construction.

T-34A MENTOR	302 km/h (187 mph)
TB 30B EPSILON	378 km/h (234 mph)
T-35A PILLÁN	311 km/h (193 mph)

CLIMB RATE

A low power-to-weight ratio generally produces an inferior climb rate, thus the Mentor is left behind by the Epsilon and Pillán. Turboprop powerplants offer weight-saving and operating cost benefits compared to the older piston-engined designs, but the T-34 had the advantage of a low purchase price.

TB 30B EPSILON 564 m/min (1850 fpm)	T-35A PILLÁN 465 m/min (1525 fpm)	T-34A MENTOR 369 m/min (1210 fpm)

16

BEECHCRAFT
RC-12 GUARDRAIL

● Intelligence gathering ● US Army service ● Based on Super King Air

▲ Differing numbers of dipole and blade aerials distinguish RC-12 variants – this is an RC-12K. In common with other intelligence gatherers, comparatively little is known of their operations or equipment.

Based on the civil Super King Air 200 turboprop transport, the RC-12 Guardrail is indispensable in its mission of prying into an enemy's signals. This ordinary-looking Beechcraft machine is the US Army's most sophisticated spy aircraft. Henry L. Stimson, US Secretary of State in the 1930s, is quoted as saying: 'Gentlemen do not read each other's mail.' In the modern battlefield environment, however, such activities are a necessity.

BEECHCRAFT RC-12 GUARDRAIL

▼ Four-blade props
The four-blade propellers identify this aircraft as an RC-12K. This differs from the RC-12D in using the PT6A-42 engine.

▼ Stronger landing gear
Compared to the civil Super King Air the RC-12 has a strengthened undercarriage to cope with increased all-up weights and a port-side loading door.

▲ In the Gulf
The Gulf War saw extensive use of Sigint aircraft in the battlefield support role. This is an RU-21, based on the Beechcraft 90.

▲ Antennas farm
This RC-12N has perhaps the most extensive collection of receiving aerials of any of the RC-12 family due to its dual Elint and Comint roles. It is based on the RC-12K.

Bases in Germany ▼
85-0155 is an RC-12K attached to the 1st Military Intelligence Battalion in Germany, one of eight with the unit. Before the end of the Cold War there were two battalions in West Germany equipped with RC-12s: one at Stuttgart, the other at Weisbaden.

FACTS AND FIGURES

▼ In common with other US Army aircraft, the C-12 family is named after a native American tribe – Huron.

▼ About 200 of the 5000 King Airs delivered by the mid-1990s have been RC-12s.

▼ Over two dozen RU-21s and RC-12s served in Operation Desert Storm.

▼ The US Army's Chief of Staff called the Guardrail: 'One of our most important weapons on the battlefield.'

▼ The first civil Super King Air 200 made its maiden flight on 27 October 1972.

▼ US Navy RC-12Fs and RC-12Ms are used to clear missile ranges before test firing.

PROFILE

Eavesdropping over the battle

Guardrail is the codename given by the US Army to the Comint aircraft programme dating from the Korean War. Guardrail began as an effort to pinpoint an enemy's radio transmitters. First used in the 1960s in Korea, RU-21s (Beech King Air 90s) ascertained the location and intentions of an adversary from his radio transmissions.

In the mid-1970s, Beechcraft's enlarged Super King Air 200 was chosen to form the basis of 'Improved Guardrail V'. These aircraft served in Korea and Germany in various versions. RU-21Hs and RC-12Ds in particular saw service in the Gulf War.

Although up to six systems operators can be accommodated behind the pilots in some configurations, the RC-12 generally relies on automation to intercept enemy communications and often carries no equipment operators at all.

Guardrail's receivers locate, identify and intercept hostile communications and relay data via a downlink to ground vehicles for analysis. The latest versions, RC-12K, -12N and -12P, have extra equipment fitted to carry out the electronic intelligence (Elint) role formerly entrusted to the RV-1D Mohawk.

Above: The first of the Guardrail family were the RU-21 series based on the King Air 90. This RU-21E wears early US Army colours.

Below: The later RC-12 was based on the larger Super King Air 200. Low-visibility markings, as on this RC-12K, are standard today.

RC-12D Guardrail

Type: twin-engined communication intelligence (Comint) aircraft

Powerplant: two 634-kW (850-hp) Pratt & Whitney Canada PT6A-41 turboprop engines

Maximum speed: 481 km/h (299 mph) at 4265 m (13,993 ft)

Cruising speed: 438 km/h (272 mph) at 9145 m (30,000 ft)

Range: 2935 km (1825 miles) at maximum cruising speed

Service ceiling: 9420 m (30,900 ft)

Weights: empty 3327 kg (7335 lb); maximum take-off approx. 5885 kg (12,974 lb)

Accommodation: two pilots; Comint, data relay and self-protection equipment

Dimensions:
span 17.63 m (57 ft 10 in)
length 13.34 m (43 ft 9 in)
height 4.57 m (15 ft)
wing area 28.15 m² (303 sq ft)

INTELLIGENCE GATHERERS

ANTONOV An-12 'CUB': Western transport aircraft often form the basis of Elint machines, and the same is true in the former Eastern Bloc countries. This An-12 turboprop has been converted for intelligence gathering. Note the extra radomes on the fuselage and the bogus civil registration.

ILYUSHIN Il-20 'COOT': The Il-20 is a multisensor reconnaissance aircraft used mainly for Elint and Sigint duties, but with a side-looking airborne radar (SLAR) fitted under the forward fuselage. The Il-20 uses the airframe and engines of the Il-38 turboprop airliner and carries about 20 electronic systems operators.

BOEING RC-135: The USAF's C-135 tanker and transport aircraft family has been used extensively in the reconnaissance and electronic intelligence-gathering role. This is an RC-135V converted with an SLAR installation and much other equipment. The exact nature of their operations is shrouded in secrecy.

An obvious difference between the RU-21 (King Air) and the RC-12 (Super King Air) is the T-tail, which improves low-speed handling.

The low-visibility colour scheme used on the RC-12 fleet is predominantly matt grey, with matt black lettering.

Secondary electronic systems include a secure airborne relay facility and radio data-link, and an ALQ-156 missile detection system.

RC-12s are usually operated on a 'minimally manned' basis (note the faired-over cabin windows), the bulk of the onboard equipment functioning automatically and relaying gathered information to ground commanders.

The heart of the RC-12 is the AN/USD-9/V2 'Guardrail V' signals intelligence (Sigint) system. This intercepts enemy radio communications and incorporates a direction-finding system.

ALQ-136 and -162 electronic countermeasures equipment is contained in the RC-12D's wingtip pods. These increase the wing span of the aircraft by more than a metre (three feet).

233 75

U.S. ARMY

RC-12D GUARDRAIL

80-23375 is a Beech RC-12D, one of 13 built mostly for the US Army's 1st and 2nd Military Intelligence Battalions in Germany. This aircraft was lost in an accident during Operation Desert Storm.

Like civil Super King Airs, the RC-12 is fitted with the widely-used Pratt & Whitney PT6A engine, the RC-12D being powered by two -41 variants, rated at 634 kW (850 hp) each.

US Army battlefield support aircraft

INTELLIGENCE GATHERING: In order to fight effectively the US Army is heavily reliant on intelligence gathered about the enemy's capabilities, collected by a variety of aircraft types and passed to ground commanders.

MOHAWK AND 'QUICK FIX': Electronic intelligence was the job of the Grumman RV-1D Mohawk and EH-60A 'Quick Fix' helicopters.

GUARDRAIL IN THE GULF: During fighting with Iraq, US Army RC-12s filled the communications intelligence role, usually from a stand-off position for safety.

18

BEECH
T-1A JAYHAWK

● Civil design ● Tanker-trainer ● Military 'biz-jet'

▲ Despite its civilian origins the Beech T-1 Jayhawk has proved suitable for the rigours of military training. Crews have found the aircraft a forgiving teaching tool.

C utting an unusual shape in the sky with its all white colour scheme and swept-back wings, the T-1 Jayhawk is fast becoming the standard training tool for the United States Air Force. The shortage of T-38 Talon trainers coupled with a shrinking defence budget saw the United States Air Force undertake the unusual step of purchasing a civilian business jet for its training purposes. The aircraft required only minor modification.

BEECH T-1A JAYHAWK

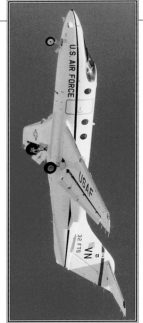

▲ Classic lines
The Jayhawk displays the low-set wings and the rear-mounted engines that have become the hallmarks of current 'biz-jets'.

▲ Bright future
Having been in service for only a relatively short period of time, the Beech Jayhawk is expected to have a long military career with the USAF.

Japanese use ▼
By early 1994 Japan's Air Self-Defence Force had also purchased the improved American Jayhawk to use as a light utility transport aircraft.

▲ Improved design
One of the military modifications specified involved the wings of the Jayhawk being strengthened in order to withstand the damaging effects of a heavy birdstrike. The pilot's cockpit glazing was also improved as a precaution.

▲ Training for all
The type passed its trials with 'flying colours', leading to the USAF quickly ordering 148 Jayhawks. A final total of 180 examples was acquired.

FACTS AND FIGURES

▼ The T-1A Jayhawk provides the USAF with an advanced trainer for instructing future tanker/transport pilots.

▼ A shortage of T-38 Talons saw the adoption of the Jayhawk in US service.

▼ Increased fuel capacity is one of the major changes to military Jayhawks.

▼ During training flights a senior instructor pilot is accompanied by at least four students to reduce operating costs.

▼ Jayhawks are the first aircraft delivered under the new pilot training programme.

▼ The Jayhawk is based on the civilian Beech Jet 400.

America's pilot provider

The Beech T-1 Jayhawk is now entering service in increasing numbers and providing the USAF with a unique training tool. In line with the current trend of using civilian aircraft for military applications, future USAF tanker and transport pilots now receive training at Reese AFB at a much reduced cost to the American taxpayer. One source of economies is that several trainees can be taken on each sortie under the guidance of one senior instructor pilot.

Alterations to the aircraft were required before it entered military service. These saw an increase in the strength of the wing leading edges and a revised cockpit windscreen. To reduce maintenance demands a single refuelling point was also installed on the aircraft. USAF examples are limited to the training role and therefore feature six fewer windows in the cabin area because of their reduced seating capacity.

In a somewhat ironic move given the original Mitsubishi design of the Jayhawk, the Japanese Air Self-Defence Force (JASDF) followed the American example and bought the aircraft for the training role. Beginning in early 1994, the JASDF took delivery of three Beech 400Ts (equivalent to the T-1A) to use for pilot training. These aircraft are equipped with extra fuel tanks and thrust reversers to simulate the handling of large transport aircraft for their pupil pilots.

Above: America's training fleet has worn a host of colour schemes, but the overall white is now used.

Above: Having completed another sortie, a student enters the landing circuit at Reese AFB, where the first aircraft was delivered in 1992.

T-1A Jayhawk

Type: advanced jet trainer/utility jet

Powerplant: two 12.9-kN (2900-lb-thrust) Pratt & Whitney Canada JT15D-5B turbojets

Maximum speed: 854 km/h (531 mph) at 8840 m (29,000 ft); cruising speed 828 km/h (514 mph) at 11,890 m (39,000 ft)

Range: 3575 km (2221 miles) with four passengers and maximum internal fuel load

Service ceiling: 12,495 m (41,000 ft)

Weights: empty 4588 kg (10,115 lb); maximum take-off 7157 kg (15,778 lb)

Accommodation: one instructor pilot; four students

Dimensions:
span	13.25 m	(43 ft 6 in)
length	14.75 m	(48 ft 5 in)
height	4.19 m	(13 ft 9 in)
wing area	22.43 m²	(241 sq ft)

T-1A JAYHAWK

This T-1A Jayhawk is based at Reese AFB in Texas, operating under the TTTS (Tanker/Transport Trainer System), The aircraft is proving to be an extremely practical training tool. Future orders for additional aircraft are currently being considered by the USAF.

Avionics equipment in the nose of the aircraft was relocated to the cockpit, also added was a turbulence-detection radar.

Pilots destined for the vast transport and tanker fleet of the US Air Force are instructed on the Jayhawk in an effort to develop the necessary skills required for handling large aircraft. This has resulted in a huge saving in training costs.

To improve the safety record of the aircraft the wings of US Air Force Jayhawks were strengthened, along with the pilot's windscreen.

A high-set tail allows the Jayhawk excellent handling qualities at high altitudes where most operational training takes place. Very few modifications were made to the flight control systems of the aircraft.

Positioned high on the rear fuselage are the Pratt & Whitney Canada JT15D turbofan engines. These received little modification prior to the entry of the Jayhawk into military service. Maintenance personnel have found the aircraft to be extremely reliable.

A distinguishing feature of the aircraft is its small undercarriage. This was seen as a weight-saving measure but also allows the aircraft to be maintained without requiring gantries.

U.S. AIR FORCE

10078

ACTION DATA

MAXIMUM SPEED

Matched against other military trainers the T-1 Jayhawk offers a maximum speed that is far in excess of its propeller-powered equivalents. Despite this performance, high speed is seldom used on training flights.

T-1A JAYHAWK — 854 km/h (531 mph)

C-12F — 545 km/h (339 mph)

KING AIR C90A — 457 km/h (284 mph)

RANGE

Additional fuel tanks were a requirement before the USAF would accept the Jayhawk into service. Despite the addition of wing tip tanks to the Beech C-12 variants the huge range of the Jayhawk cannot be equalled by its contemporaries.

T-1A JAYHAWK 3575 km (2221 miles)

C-12F 3641 km (2262 miles)

KING AIR C90A 2336 km (1452 miles)

MAXIMUM TAKE OFF WEIGHT

In its role as a training aircraft the Jayhawk requires a large take-off weight. Despite its relatively small size the Jayhawk matches this need surprisingly well. Compared to the King Air, which is also used in the utility role, the Jayhawk compares very favourably.

T-1A JAYHAWK 7157 kg (15,778 lb)

C-12F 3641 kg (8027 lb)

KING AIR C90A 2336 kg (5150 lb)

Serving their country

■ **CESSNA CITATION:** Operational with the Spanish Navy, the Citation is used as a navigation trainer and light transport aircraft. One model is used for reconnaissance duties.

■ **GRUMMAN GULFSTREAM:** The large dimensions of the Gulfstream III have made it an ideal platform for liaison and VIP duties. This example serves with the Danish air force.

■ **NORTH AMERICAN SABRELINER:** Currently reaching the end of its service with the United States armed forces, the T-39 Sabreliner continues to serve with South American air arms.

BELL

P-39 AIRACOBRA

● Tricycle undercarriage ● Mid-engined design ● Soviet service

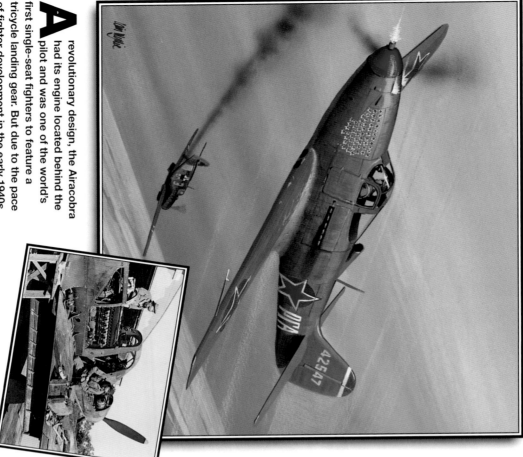

A revolutionary design, the Airacobra had its engine located behind the pilot and was one of the world's first single-seat fighters to feature a tricycle landing gear. But due to the pace of fighter development in the early 1940s the P-39 was rapidly outclassed. It fought well against heavy odds in the early days of World War II in the Pacific and later won high praise from Russia, which used its cannon to destroy German ground targets.

▶ The most remarkable feature of the P-39 was its mid-mounted engine, which drove the propeller via a long driveshaft. The main reason for adopting this layout was so that the aircraft could carry the massive 37-mm cannon.

BELL P-39 AIRACOBRA

P-39 in the Pacific ▶
The Airacobra performed well in the Pacific against Japanese opposition. It was mainly used for ground-attack missions.

▶ **Post-war racer**
At the end of World War II, several P-39s were snapped up at rock-bottom prices and modified for air racing.

▶ **Cannon armed**
The barrel of the mighty M4 37-mm cannon protruded through the propeller spinner.

▶ **Car door**
Another unusual feature of the P-39 was the side-opening, car-style door.

▶ **USAAF fighter**
When the US entered the war in 1941, the P-39 was the best fighter they had available. A few flew in Europe with the USAAF, but they were outclassed by German fighters and were replaced by Spitfires.

FACTS AND FIGURES

▶ The Airacobra was the first US single-seat fighter with a nosewheel to enter service.

▶ The prototype Bell XP-39 made its first flight on 6 April 1939.

▶ Russian forces took delivery of about 5000 P-39s during World War II.

▶ Although designed as a fighter, Soviet forces used the P-39 for ground attack, with great success.

▶ The RAF ordered 675 Airacobras, but only one squadron was ever equipped.

▶ P-39s were operated by the Italian Co-Belligerent Air Force during 1944.

PROFILE

Mid-engined attacker

One of many pre-war innovations explored by the Bell Aircraft Company, the Airacobra appeared when it was first produced. Its engine, 'buried' in the fuselage behind the pilot's seat, was fitted with an extension shaft to the propeller running under the cockpit. A tricycle undercarriage and a 37-mm cannon were also incorporated.

When war came in 1939, RAF tests revealed that the P-39's overall performance did not match that of British fighters. This and the fact that the Airacobra's unusual systems could prove unreliable caused it to be rejected for service.

In the Pacific, the USAAF had to use any available fighters and the outclassed Airacobras were thrown into war sorties against the Japanese during 1942/43. American pilots also flew it during the early combat operations in the Middle East. Bell improved the aircraft, and when US fighter groups re-equipped with other types

many Airacobras were passed to the Red air force, where the 'Little Shaver' proved very popular. 'Shaving' was Russian pilot slang for ground strafing, and the P-39 soon earned great respect as a destroyer of German tanks and vehicles.

Airacobra pilots stencilled dozens of tiny stars on their machines to show how adept the 'Lend-Lease' American fighter was at this deadly and dangerous task. The P-39 was also flown by Italian and French pilots during the war.

Above: Although its performance could not match that of fighters such as the Spitfire, the P-39 had respectable figures and good manoeuvrability.

Left: If the RAF had only retained the P-39 with its original turbocharged engine, it might have found a winner. Instead, it was discarded due to chronic unreliability.

P-39N Airacobra

Type: single-seat fighter and ground-attack aircraft with tricycle undercarriage

Powerplant: one 895-kW (1200-hp) Allison V-1710-63 liquid-cooled engine

Maximum speed: 642 km/h (399 mph)

Range: 1207 km (750 miles)

Service ceiling: 11,735 m (38,500 ft)

Weights: empty 2566 kg (5657 lb); loaded 3702 kg (8162 lb)

Armament: one 37-mm firing through airscrew plus two 12.7-mm (.50-cal.) machine guns in nose and four 7.62-mm (.30-cal.) machine guns in wings; bombload of up to 227 kg (500 lb)

Dimensions:
span	10.36 m (34 ft)
length	9.19 m (30 ft 2 in)
height	3.78 m (12 ft 5 in)
wing area	19.79 m² (213 sq ft)

COMBAT DATA

MAXIMUM SPEED

The late-model P-39N restored some of the lost performance of the early P-39s by having a more powerful engine. It was no better than a Bf 109, however, and grossly inferior to the excellent Yak 9.

P-39N AIRACOBRA	642 km/h (399 mph)
Bf 109G	623 km/h (387 mph)
Yak 9	700 km/h (435 mph)

SERVICE CEILING

Soviet fighters were almost invariably better at low altitude, and the P-39 was thus markedly superior to the Yak 9 at altitude. It was equivalent to the Bf-109G, which was a good performer at height.

P-39N AIRACOBRA	11,735 m (38,500 ft)
Bf 109G	11,750 m (38,550 ft)
Yak 9	10,950 m (35,925 ft)

ARMAMENT

The P-39's cannon was a single-shot killer, even to tanks. The use of a single, large cannon and two smaller guns was popular with Soviet and German designers but not the British or Americans.

P-39N AIRACOBRA	4 x 7.62-mm (.30-cal.) machine guns 2 x 12.7-mm (.50-cal.) machine guns 1 x 37-mm cannon
Bf 109G	2 x 7.92-mm machine guns 2 x 20-mm cannon 1 x 30-mm cannon
Yak 9	2 x 12.7-mm (.50-cal.) machine guns 1 x 23-mm cannon

P-39N AIRACOBRA

The Airacobra played an important part in World War II, notably in the hands of Soviet pilots. The Soviet air force not only found the type ideal for tank busting but also in the air-to-air role.

A large percentage of the 9558 Airacobras built wore the Soviet red star. These were usually assigned to the elite Guards regiments.

The engine was mounted immediately behind the pilot's seat, and a long shaft ran under the seat, through the cockpit to a gearbox below the propeller shaft.

The pilot sat in an extremely well-protected cockpit, surrounded by armour to protect him from bullets. This was especially useful in the ground-attack role.

Due to the cannon and engine installation, Bell had to design a tricycle undercarriage, the first in an operational fighter.

Chief armament of the P-39 was the 37-mm M4 cannon, fed by a belt-type magazine holding 30 rounds. British Airacobras had a 20-mm cannon instead.

In addition to the main cannon, the Airacobra had a pair of 12.7-mm (.50-cal.) machine guns in the top of the forward fuselage. The P-39Q could carry two more 12.7-mm guns in underwing pods.

Modified Airacobras

■ **NAVAL XFL-1:** The XFL-1 Airabonita was a naval variant with a tailwheel, strengthened fuselage and arrester hook. It was not adopted by the US Navy due to unsuccessful trials.

■ **V-TAIL:** An experimental trial of tail surfaces combining elevator and rudder functions was not used in service, as it reduced the P-39's excellent handling.

■ **SQUARE TAIL:** This trials XP-39E's square-cut wing and tailfin was also not adopted. Powered by an Allison V-1710-47, its tail bore a strong resemblance to that of a Mustang.

■ **AIR RACER:** This P-39, registration N40A, was owned privately and based in Orange County, California. It was painted red and white with blue trim, and flew frequently.

BELL

P-63 KINGCOBRA

● Close-support fighter ● Huge exports ● Airacobra development

▲ Although not one of the most successful wartime fighters, the Kingcobra operated successfully in the close-support and attack roles. It saw most service with Soviet forces and was most formidably armed and armoured.

Created as an improved version of the Bell P-39 Airacobra, the P-63 Kingcobra retained the tricycle landing gear of the earlier type, a nose cannon and an engine mounted behind the pilot driving the propeller through a long shaft. Like the P-39, it also had a car-type door for access to the cockpit. Unfortunately, the P-63 never measured up to the top wartime fighters, like the P-51, Bf 109 and Zero.

BELL P-63 KINGCOBRA

▼ Silver Kingcobra
Of the few P-63s which remained in the United States, some were used for test and training duties. The majority of the rest went to the USSR.

▲ Nose guns
Most P-63s had twin 12.7-mm (.50-cal) machine guns installed in the upper engine cowling.

▼ Experimental variants
Two XP-63Ns were flown with 'butterfly' tails. One was modified after the war to L-39-1 standard and flew swept-wing tests for the US Navy.

▲ Lend-Lease to Russia
Fitted with underwing drop-tanks, this P-63A flying with the Soviet air force is typical of the 2400 or more delivered under the Lend-Lease programme.

Allison power ▶
Removal of the engine access panels from this preserved P-63A reveals the 12-cylinder Allison V-1710 engine mounted behind the cockpit.

FACTS AND FIGURES

▼ A Kingcobra on display in San Antonio, Texas, survived use as a frangible bullet target during 1946.

▼ More than 3300 Kingcobras, in half a dozen versions, were produced.

▼ The first Kingcobra prototype made its initial flight on 7 December 1942.

▼ During the Korean War, some American pilots said that they had encountered P-63s flown by North Koreans.

▼ Both prototypes were lost in mishaps early in the flight test programme.

▼ About 2400 Kingcobras were turned over to the Soviet Union.

P-63A Kingcobra

Type: fighter and ground attack aircraft

Powerplant: one 988-kW (1325-hp) Allison V-1710-93 liquid-cooled 12-cylinder Vee piston engine driving a four-bladed propeller

Maximum speed: 660 km/h (410 mph) at 7620 m (25,000 ft)

Cruising speed: 608 km/h (378 mph)

Range: 724 km (450 miles)

Service ceiling: 13,106 m (43,000 ft)

Weights: empty 2892 kg (6376 lb); maximum take-off 4763 kg (10,500 lb)

Armament: one 37-mm cannon and four (two wing-mounted and two nose-mounted) fixed forward-firing 12.7-mm (.50-calibre) machine guns, plus up to three 237-kg (522-lb) bombs or six rocket projectiles dependent on the subvariant

Dimensions:
span	11.68 m	(38 ft 4 in)
length	9.96 m	(32 ft 8 in)
height	3.84 m	(12 ft 7 in)
wing area	23.04 m²	(248 sq ft)

COMBAT DATA

MAXIMUM SPEED

The P-63A was much faster than the P-40N Warhawk, since the Curtiss fighter was nearing the end of its development potential. The P-63 was much slower than, arguably, the greatest US fighter of World War II, the North American P-51D Mustang.

P-63A KINGCOBRA	660 km/h (410 mph)
P-51D MUSTANG	721 km/h (448 mph)
P-40N WARHAWK	609 km/h (378 mph)

RANGE

North American achieved exceptional range with the P-51, while Curtiss always struggled with the P-40 design. The P-63 was optimised for the ground attack role and, as such, was unlikely to be required to fly long-range escort or fighter missions. It had adequate range for the close-support role.

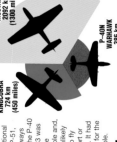

P-51D MUSTANG 2092 km (1300 miles)

P-63A KINGCOBRA 724 km (450 miles)

P-40N WARHAWK 386 km (240 miles)

ARMAMENT

Both the P-40 and P-51 adopted ground attack as a secondary role and were therefore able to carry fewer bombs than the P-63A. The Kingcobra also featured a powerful spinner-mounted cannon.

P-63A KINGCOBRA
1 x 37-mm cannon
4 x 12.7-mm (.50-cal.) machine guns
681-kg (1500-lb) bombload

P-51D MUSTANG
6 x 12.7-mm (.50-cal.) machine guns
454-kg (1000-lb) bombload

P-40N WARHAWK
6 x 12.7-mm (.50-cal.) machine guns
227-kg (500-lb) bombload

Close-support over Europe

A US Army Air Force (USAAF) order for two prototypes in June 1941 launched the P-63 Kingcobra. Further prototypes followed before deliveries of the first production version began in October 1943.

It quickly became clear that the P-63 was not advanced enough for front-line service, and the majority of Kingcobras were delivered to the Soviet Union under the Lend-Lease programme. A significant number also went to Free French forces, and a single example was

delivered to the RAF. Several were used as flying testbeds.

The P-63 was a low-wing design which served American forces well in a training capacity but was never used by them in combat. The Kingcobra was not an easy aircraft to fly, however, especially in the circuit pattern around an airfield, and pilots never bestowed on it the affection they extended to the Mustang, Thunderbolt and Hellcat.

Kingcobras were given a variety of second-line duties. In one of the most unusual, known

Below: All aircraft up to the P-63A-5 were fitted with a centre-section rack but had no wing racks. The four 12.7-mm (.50-calibre) machine guns were supplemented by a 37-mm cannon in the nose.

Above: At least 300 P-63s were delivered to the Free French Armée de l'Air. This is a P-63C with its distinctive ventral fin.

P-63A KINGCOBRA

One of a large number of P-63A and P-63C Kingcobras supplied to the Soviet air force during World War II, this P-63A-9 was fitted with an M10 (instead of an M4) hub cannon and additional armour.

as Project Pinball, modified, armoured Kingcobras acted as manned targets for gunnery exercises by fighters shooting frangible bullets.

The P-63 had a taller, more angular tail than the P-39 Airacobra. The P-63's configuration, including its laminar flow wing, was largely tested on the experimental XP-39E.

This large intake above the rear fuselage fed air to the carburettor. Placing the engine behind the pilot seemed, on paper, to offer many advantages. Instead it created a number of engineering problems and did not provide the hoped-for performance benefits.

An Allison V-1710 engine drove the four-bladed propeller of the P-63A via a long extension shaft. This ran forwards through the cockpit and between the pilot's legs.

Aircraft fitted with only the centreline hardpoint could carry a single 237-kg (522-lb) bomb. Alternatively, a 341-litre (75-gal) or 796-litre (175-gal) fuel tank could be fitted. Later aircraft carried more weapons; the A-9 and A-10 variants complementing this with 28 extra rounds of 37-mm ammunition.

Unlike other fighters, the P-63 did not have a hinged or sliding canopy. The pilot entered the cockpit via a car-type door on the port side.

Twin 12.7-mm (.50-calibre) machine guns were mounted in the upper nose.

The powerful nose armament was completed by the 37-mm cannon, which fired through the spinner. Subtypes up to the P-63A-8 carried only thirty 37-mm rounds.

Streamlined fairings covered the underwing machine guns. Starting with the P-63A-6, underwing hardpoints were fitted.

Bell fighters of the 1940s

■ **P-39 AIRACOBRA:** Designed as a highly manoeuvrable fighter, the radical P-39 proved to be a disappointment. It matured into an effective ground attack aircraft, however.

■ **P-59 AIRACOMET:** Planned as a contemporary of the Gloster E.28/39 and He 178, the P-59 did not in fact fly until after the Me 262 and Meteor. It was America's first jet fighter.

■ **XP-77:** Using pre-war racing aircraft design as a basis, Bell produced this lightweight wooden fighter prototype. It failed to achieve acceptable performance.

BELL
UH-1B/C IROQUOIS

● Airborne jeep ● Multi-role helicopter ● NATO workhorse

▲ A door-gunner rides 'shotgun' with his M60 as a pair of 'Hueys' fly over the Delta region in Vietnam. To many people, the war in Southeast Asia was symbolized by images of the UH-1.

Bell's Model 204 formed the basis for one of the most successful series of helicopters ever built. Flown for the first time in October 1956, it was designated XH-40, then HU-1 by the US Army (who called it the 'Huey'), before a designation change to HU-1A Iroquois. The HU-1B introduced a more powerful engine and the HU-1C had a new rotor system. Later still the HU- designation was changed to UH-. Variants were built by Agusta in Italy.

BELL UH-1B/C IROQUOIS

▲ Navy rescue
This TH-1L uses its sling hoist during a demonstration at Ellyson Field, Pensacola, Florida.

▼ Overseas success
Built under licence by Agusta in Italy as the AB 204, this 'Huey' serves in the anti-submarine role. Early versions of the UH-1 remain in service throughout Europe.

Anti-tank missiles ▶
The 'Huey' was employed in the development of the first air-to-ground missile for the US Army, which was used in Vietnam.

▲ Weapons platform
An Italian example demonstrates the offensive capabilities of the UH-1 by lifting off with two pylon-mounted machine guns and 21 rockets.

FACTS AND FIGURES

▶ Four prototype YUH-1Bs were ordered in June 1959, with the first flight taking place in the following April.

▶ A total of 1010 UH-1Bs were produced in Italy, Japan and the United States.

▶ The 'Huey' was the first helicopter to see widespread use as a gunship.

▶ Differences between the B and C models included a modified rotor system, wider rotor blades and a larger fin.

▶ The YUH-1B set an unofficial world speed record of 357 km/h (221 mph) in May 1964.

▶ The Royal Australian Air Force was the first non-US customer for eight UH-1Bs.

PROFILE

Bell's ubiquitous 'Huey'

The turbine engine was one of the keys to the Model 204's success. Mounted on the cabin roof just behind the gearbox, it left the cabin unencumbered and provided the performance required by the US Army. Early UH-1Bs retained the UH-1A's 716-kW (960-hp) T53 engine, but an 820-kW (1100-hp) power-plant was soon standard. The new model was delivered from March 1961 and could be armed with rocket pods and machine guns carried on the cabin's sides.

UH-1Bs were also built by Fuji in Japan and Agusta in Italy. Agusta models included the AB 204AS anti-submarine variant for the Italian and Spanish navies, plus civil AB 204Bs with Lycoming T53, General Electric T58 or Rolls-Royce Gnome engines.

The UH-1C, which flew in September 1965, used a new rotor system with 'door hinges' and wider blades. This provided more lift, enabling the fuel load to be increased and improving the machine's manoeuvrability

and speed. Variants of the UH-1C, with new designations, were used by the US Air Force, Navy and Marine Corps in the training, rescue and assault roles.

Above: This is one of six test YH-40s seen during a proving flight. There were few differences between these and the first production 'Hueys'.

Below: The glossy overall olive drab, with a yellow tail band and white lettering, soon gave way to dull green when the 'Huey' entered combat.

UH-1C

Type: single-engined multi-role utility helicopter

Powerplant: one 820-kW (1100-hp) Lycoming T53-L-11 turboshaft engine

Maximum speed: 238 km/h (148 mph) at sea level

Initial climb rate: 427 m/min (1400 fpm)

Range: 615 km (381 miles) with auxiliary fuel

Service ceiling: 3505 m (11,500 ft)

Weights: empty 2300 kg (5060 lb); maximum take-off 4309 kg (9480 lb)

Dimensions: rotor diameter 13.41 m (44 ft)
length 12.98 m (42 ft 7 in)
height 3.84 m (12 ft 7 in)
rotor disc area 141.26 m² (1520 sq ft)

COMBAT DATA

POWER

Although the Huey was the first practical transport helicopter to see widespread military use, the power of the early models was found to be lacking in the roles with which the helicopter was tasked. Later variants were fitted with improved engines.

UH-1C IROQUOIS 820 kW (1100 hp)

UH-1H IROQUOIS 1044 kW (1400 hp)

UH-60A BLACKHAWK 2302 kW (3087 hp)

MAXIMUM PAYLOAD

The early variants of the UH-1, although capable of lifting an acceptable load, required improvement. The advent of more powerful engines in later variants allowed an increased payload, although this was still restricted by the cabin size. The knowledge gained during the development of the 'Huey' was incorporated into the purpose-built Blackhawk.

UH-1C IROQUOIS 1361 kg (3000 lb)

UH-1H IROQUOIS 1759 kg (3900 lb)

UH-60A BLACKHAWK 3629 kg (8000 lb)

MAXIMUM SPEED

Because of its relatively light load the performance of the UH-1B was superior to that of later models which became much heavier, because of operational and design changes. The twin-engined Blackhawk offered improved performance in a streamlined fuselage while retaining the capability to carry large loads.

UH-1C IROQUOIS 238 km/h (148 mph)

UH-1H IROQUOIS 204 km/h (126 mph)

UH-60A BLACKHAWK 296 km/h (184 mph)

TH-1L

Pictured in red and white training colours, this TH-1L, the navy designation for the 'Huey', is used for pilot training. This involves flying from aircraft carriers and over-water navigation.

The cabin could hold nine passengers and crew, and offered excellent all-round visibility. The machine was often flown with the doors removed to allow rapid exit.

Two skids supported the UH-1 on the ground. Although less complex than wheeled landing gear, their use restricted the helicopter's movement once it had landed.

One Lycoming T53-L-5 engine powered the UH-1B, although its output was improved in later variants. Licence-built models were powered by Rolls-Royce engines.

The bulbous design of the fuselage allowed the carriage of stores on external pylons, so as not to restrict the internal load.

Originally on the left side of the tail boom, the tail rotor in later licence-built variants was positioned on the right-hand side. The tail size was also increased, because of the uprated engines.

Troop-carrying 'Hueys' were often called 'slicks' because their airframes were devoid of the external equipment which reduced performance; this name has been used throughout the UH-1's service.

A tail skid, designed to protect the rear rotor blades from striking the ground during landing, was positioned on the end of the boom.

Improving the breed

■ **UH-1H:** An improvement of the UH-1B design, advances included increased lifting capability and an enlarged cabin area. This variant serves with the Taiwan air force.

■ **MODEL 212:** Offering the reliability of an improved twin engine and a weather radar located in the nose, this Singaporean example serves with the local VIP flight.

■ **MODEL 214ST:** Possessing little commonality with earlier designs, this Venezuelan 'Huey' features a stretched cabin, improved performance and composite rotor blades.

BELL
AH-1 HUEYCOBRA (SINGLE)

● Gunship ● Tank killer ● Escort helicopter

arly Bell AH-1 HueyCobras opened a new era in warfare. From the dawn of rotary-wing aviation it was apparent that the helicopter could become a revolutionary weapon of war if it was armed. The HueyCobra was the first helicopter designed for armed battlefield duties. Although it had a number of features in common with the famous UH-1 'Huey', the AH-1 was the first of the real anti-tank helicopter gunships.

▲ The AH-1 HueyCobra received its baptism of fire in the jungles of Southeast Asia with the US Army. The AH-1 took over the role of premier tank-busting and specialised assault helicopter from the UH-1D.

BELL AH-1 HUEYCOBRA (SINGLE)

▲ Rocket strike
For the destruction of 'soft' targets the AH-1 carries up to four 70-mm LAU-68 pods, each containing seven unguided rockets.

Tank-busting missile ▶
The BGM-71A TOW used in Vietnam was a wire-guided anti-tank missile with a 3-km (2-mile) range.

▲ US Army Cobra
The Cobra first saw service in 1968 after the Army ordered 38 examples. The current helicopters are much improved.

Gun armament ▶
The AH-1's undernose turret contains a General Electric M197 three-barrelled 20-mm cannon which was aimed by the gunner in the front seat.

Slim lines ▶
The AH-1 (centre) was designed to present as small a target as possible to enemy ground fire.

FACTS AND FIGURES

▼ The AH-1 was designed with the rotor system, transmission and tailboom of the proven UH-1D 'Huey'.

▼ The AH-1 Cobra was first flown in prototype form on 7 September 1965.

▼ HueyCobras are equipped to carry TOW missiles.

▼ The US Army Aviation Association voted the AH-1 one of four 'most valuable weapons' of the Vietnam War.

▼ Bell produced more than 1600 first-generation, single-engine Cobras.

▼ AH-1s were often armed with two 'thumper' 40-mm grenade-launchers.

AH-1G/S HueyCobra

Type: attack/close-support helicopter

Powerplant: one 944-kW (1330-hp) Lycoming T53-L-13 or 1210-kW (1625-hp) T53-L-703 turboshaft engine

Maximum speed: 277 km/h (172 mph)

Cruising speed: 209 km/h (130 mph)

Range: 574 km (355 miles)

Service ceiling: 3530 m (11,600 ft)

Weights: empty 2754 kg (6059 lb); maximum take-off 4309 kg (9480 lb)

Armament: one M197 20-mm cannon in nose turret and 998 kg (2200 lb) of weapons (XM-18 Minigun pods and XM-157 70-mm rocket pods on four racks

Dimensions: main rotor diameter 13.41 m (44 ft)
length, rotors turning 16.26 m (53 ft 4 in)
height 4.17 m (13 ft 8 in)
rotor disc area 141.26 m² (1534 sq ft)

PROFILE

The world's first attack helicopter

In 1965 the US Army finalised its requirement for the world's first armed battlefield helicopter, the Bell AH-1 Cobra, often called the HueyCobra.

The idea had arisen before Vietnam, but the Cobra arrived on the scene just when it was needed in the Southeast Asia conflict. The AH-1 featured a streamlined, narrow-width fuselage that accommodated a two-man crew in tandem seats with the pilot above and behind the co-pilot/gunner.

The US Army progressively improved this fine helicopter. The engine power, performance and armament had all been enhanced by 1972 when the AH-1 proved especially valuable during the North Vietnamese offensive. Already successful using guns and rockets for direct support of ground troops, the Cobras were pitched against Communist PT-76 light tanks.

The early design was so effective that improved versions of the AH-1 Cobra were ordered for the Army and the US Marine Corps. Beginning in the 1970s, twin-engined versions replaced 'first generation' HueyCobras. These newer combat helicopters still remain with some units.

The HueyCobra unleashes a deadly BGM-71 TOW (Tube-launched Optically-tracked Wire-guided) missile towards an unsuspecting tank. It is guided to the target by a trailing wire.

The cockpit has bulletproof panels, but the forward fuselage is narrow and only lightly armoured.

Outboard a heavier load of 19-round LAU-69 rocket pods is carried. In total the AH-1G can deploy 52 unguided 70-mm rockets.

Both inboard pylons carry the classic armament of seven-round 70-mm LAU-68 unguided rocket packs for the destruction of light targets and unarmoured vehicles.

The tail and fuselage are very slender. This enables the helicopter to fly tight and low at tree-top level to help mask its presence.

The twin-bladed tail rotor is identical to that of the UH-1.

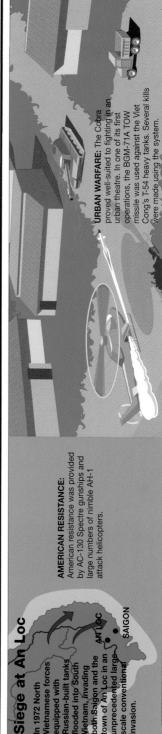

AH-1G HueyCobra

This HueyCobra is a US Army model in the three-colour camouflage used in the jungles of North Vietnam during the fighting of the early 1970s.

The AH-1 retained the UH-1's characteristically noisy two-bladed main rotor system and linkage.

The now common tandem seating of the gunner and pilot was first introduced into combat on a helicopter by the AH-1. In early Vietnam models, before the cannon was fitted, a single 40-mm grenade-launcher or twin 7.62-mm (.30-calibre) six-barrel Miniguns were carried.

Early Cobra's had a single Textron Lycoming T53 Turboshaft rated at 994kW (1330 hp). Later models have two.

The AH-1 was designed and developed in such a short period of time that, wherever possible, systems were kept either the same as those in the UH-1 or were made simple like this primitive tail bumper.

The HueyCobra has simple but very tough landing skids rather than a complex retractable undercarriage.

URBAN WARFARE: The Cobra proved well-suited to fighting in an urban theatre. In one of its first operations, the BGM-71A TOW missile was used against the Viet Cong's T-54 heavy tanks. Several kills were made using the system.

Siege at An Loc

In 1972 North Vietnamese forces equipped with Russian-built tanks flooded into South Vietnam, invading both Saigon and the town of An Loc in an unprecedented large-scale conventional invasion.

ANT LOC
SAIGON

AMERICAN RESISTANCE: American resistance was provided by AC-130 Spectre gunships and large numbers of nimble AH-1 attack helicopters.

COMBAT DATA

MAXIMUM CRUISING SPEED

Helicopters flying anti-armour missions often rely on stealth to ambush enemy columns. However, operating in enemy territory is very dangerous and these helicopters are among the fastest flying, using their speed to escape from threatening positions.

AH-1G HUEYCOBRA	277 km/h (172 mph)
LYNX AH.Mk 1	259 km/h (161 mph)
Mi-24 'HIND-A'	270 km/h (167 mph)

POWER

The 'Hind' is a far bigger helicopter as it is also designed as a troop carrier and is powered by two large engines. The AH-1G is at the other end of the spectrum, powered by a single, relatively small engine and relying on a streamlined shape and light construction for its performance.

AH-1G HUEYCOBRA
944 kW (1330 hp)

LYNX AH.Mk 1
1342 kW (1800 hp)

Mi-24 'HIND-A'
2238 kW (300 hp)

ARMAMENT

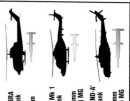

The main weapon used by all three helicopters is the anti-tank missile. The bigger 'Hind' can carry twice the number of missiles, but in reality would be more likely to carry a mixture of missiles and rockets. The cannon on the AH-1G and the gun on the Mi-24 are remote-controlled integrated systems. The gun on the Lynx can be fitted as required.

AH-1G
HUEYCOBRA
8 anti-tank
missiles
1 x 20-mm
cannon

LYNX AH.Mk 1
8 anti-tank
missiles
1 x 7.62-mm
(.30-cal.) MG

Mi-24 'HIND-A'
16 anti-tank
missiles
1 x 12.7-mm
(.50-cal.) MG

28

BELL

AH-1 HueyCobra (Twin)

● The first 'gunship' ● Close support ● Precision anti-armour

Bell's AH-1 HueyCobra was the first true attack helicopter.

Twenty-five years later, upgraded versions are still deadly weapons, reaching out with guns and missiles to halt the enemy in its tracks. Today the twin-engined HueyCobra is flown by Marine pilots, elite warriors who use the AH-1's speed and power to fight and win, no matter what the odds.

▲ In the front cockpit sits the HueyCobra gunner. At his disposal is a fearsome array of guns and missiles which he can bring to bear with frightening rapidity.

BELL AH-1 HueyCobra (Twin)

▲ Minigun
Early HueyCobras carried the Minigun, a six-barrelled machine gun which fired at rates of up to 100 rounds per second. Today the slower but harder-hitting M197 20-mm cannon is fitted.

▲ In the weeds
Like its serpentine namesake, the HueyCobra is designed to fight down among the trees and bushes, where it can lurk undetected until it is time to rear up and strike.

▲ Riding 'shotgun'
As well as taking out enemy tanks, the HueyCobra is charged with the vital task of escorting assault helicopters. These US Army helos are seen on exercise in Egypt during 1982.

▼ Rapid turnaround
When it is out of missiles, the HueyCobra can be re-armed in minutes by a well-drilled ground team. The TOW missiles are pre-packed in their launch tubes and are strapped straight on to the helicopter.

▲ SuperCobra
Derived from a project to supply the Shah of Iran with an upgraded version of the AH-1T, the SuperCobra prototype with its twin T-700 engines served as the basis for the development of the current Marine Corps AH-1W.

FACTS AND FIGURES

▶ The AH-1 first flew on 7 September 1965; new HueyCobras are produced today.

▶ Building a HueyCobra requires 38,500 hours of factory-worker time.

▶ The HueyCobra's stub wing provides some of the lift which keeps it in the air.

▶ HueyCobra pilots use night vision goggles and electronic sensors to fight in darkness and bad weather.

▶ In Operation Desert Storm, four Marine squadrons flew 1000 missions, including one which destroyed 60 tanks.

▶ The cannon of the AH-1W 'Whiskey Cobra' fires a depleted uranium shell.

PROFILE

Strike like a snake

The AH-1 HueyCobra evolved from the famous Bell UH-1 Huey. When the AH-1G model arrived in Vietnam it became the first rotorcraft designed specifically to carry arms to enter combat. With the helicopter's miraculous ability to leap in and out of tight places, and with a deadly powerhouse of weapons hanging under its stub wings, the HueyCobra is the infantryman's best friend.

New, hard-hitting Cobras are at work today. The US Army introduced TOW missiles to fight tanks. The Marines went a step further with the laser-guided Hellfire missile, fired from many kilometres away to kill a tank with pinpoint accuracy.

Today, Marines use the AH-1W 'Whiskey Cobra', a warrior for the hi-tech battlefield: as formidable in many situations as the Army's newer Apache, which came along years later. The 'Whiskey Cobra' excels at amphibious warfare, flying from ship decks or from land. Pilots of this thin, graceful ship praise its nimble flying qualities and its flexibility and fighting prowess.

AH-1W SuperCobra

Spearheading the Marine assault is the AH-1W, sweeping ahead of the ground troops to root out enemy armour and artillery before they can do any damage.

The two-man crew works as a team. The pilot is in the rear cockpit, sitting high up so he can get a good all-round view over the head of the gunner in the front seat. The gunner has a commanding view of the battlefield, and has night-vision sights to help him fire the weapons.

Above and below the pilot's cockpit are special blades which cut cables. Such obstructions are a very real danger at the altitudes at which Cobras normally work.

The stub pylons provide not only the means to carry a large weapon load but also act as miniature wings, providing valuable extra lift when the Cobra is in forward flight.

Under the AH-1W's chin is a General Electric turret which houses the deadly 20-mm M197 cannon. This weapon has three barrels, and can fire at a rate of 675 rounds per minute, although each burst is limited to just 16 rounds. The turret can swing through 110° either side of the nose.

AH-1W SuperCobra

Type: two-seat attack helicopter

Powerplant: two General Electric T-700 turboshafts, each rated at 1212 kW (1625 hp)

Maximum speed: 352 km/h (219 mph)

Range: 590 km (367 miles)

Hover ceiling: 4495 m (14,747 ft)

Weights: empty 4627 kg (10,200 lb); loaded 6690 kg (14,749 lb)

Armament: one M197 20-mm cannon in undernose turret and four underwing hardpoints for guided anti-armour or air-to-air missiles, Minigun pods, or unguided high explosive rockets

Dimensions: rotor diameter 14.63 m (48 ft)
fuselage length 13.87 m (45 ft 6 in)
height 4.11 m (13 ft 6 in)
rotor disc area 168.11 m² (1810 sq ft)

Helicopter killer – the HueyCobra can carry the Sidewinder missile on its stub pylons to shoot down other helicopters.

For use against 'soft' targets such as troops and trucks, the Cobra carries seven-round rocket pods on the stub pylons.

The Cobra's tail rotors are made from an aluminium honeycomb with a stainless steel skin and leading edge.

Cobras have been powered by a variety of engines over the years. Marine aircraft generally have two engines, as an added safety factor for long over-water operations.

Bell designed the Cobra before the days of modern composite materials. Its structure is conventional, with a semi-monocoque aluminium skin.

Marine Cobras fly in a bewildering variety of colour schemes, usually applied according to the type of terrain to be encountered. This strange sand-and-grey scheme was applied for the Gulf War.

COMBAT DATA

COMBAT RADIUS

Because of their unique abilities, helicopters do not need vulnerable fixed bases. Operating from hides very close to the battle area, they can get into action very quickly, and their lack of range when carrying a full load of fuel, troops and weapons is no handicap.

Mi-24F 'HIND' 160 km (99 miles)

AH.Mk 7 LYNX 270 km (168 miles)

AH-1W SUPERCOBRA 250 km (155 miles)

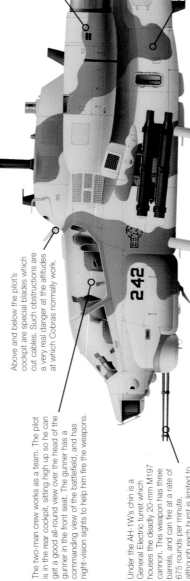

Firing the TOW

TOW stands for Tube-launched, Optically-sighted, Wire-guided, and is an admirably succinct explanation of how the missile is operated.

TARGET IN SIGHT

WIRE GUIDANCE: When it is fired, the TOW trails wires behind it which remain attached to the helicopter. These transmit guidance commands from the gunner, who literally 'flies' the missile to its target.

WIRE GUIDANCE

TRACKING: On the back of the missile are small flares which allow the gunner to follow its progress. He keeps the sight centred on target, and the missile is automatically guided to the point of aim.

TRACKING

BELL

OH-58 KIOWA/TH-57 SEARANGER

- JetRanger military variants ● USAF and Navy service ● Exports

J etRangers have been big sellers in civil markets throughout the Western world. The Model 206 has also found numerous military buyers, both in the US and abroad. With the US Army, as the OH-58 Kiowa battlefield observation helicopter, it saw service in Vietnam and has recently been re-ordered as the TH-67 Creek for primary rotary-wing training. The US Navy employs the same machine, designated TH-57 SeaRanger, for helicopter flight training.

▶ The versatility of the civil JetRanger has been exploited in the military variants. These are used by all three of the US services in a variety of training and offensive roles.

BELL OH-58 KIOWA/TH-57 SEARANGER

▼ SeaRangers of USN Training Squadron 8
All TH-57As have been replaced by newer TH-57Bs and TH-57Cs equipped as instrument trainers.

▲ Dual-control TH-57A trainer
Selected in January 1968, 40 Bell 206A JetRangers filled the Navy's rotary-wing trainer requirement.

▲ Blooded in Vietnam
The Kiowa was deployed in Vietnam from late summer 1969 and was used throughout the war. Although intended as an observation platform, it was in demand as a transport aircraft because of its size and agility.

▲ Down under Kiowas
Commonwealth Aircraft Corporation assembled 44 Model 206B-1 Kiowas (in addition to 12 built by Bell) for the Australian army and navy in the 1970s.

▲ Civil Bell 206s in military service
Numerous air forces, including Brunei's, operate civil 'off-the-shelf' JetRangers for training purposes.

FACTS AND FIGURES

▼ This helicopter traces its origins to a military prototype, the OH-4A, that first flew in December 1962.

▼ Bell claims that military Model 206s have flown over 17 million hours.

▼ US Army OH-58As, Cs and Ds were widely used during the Gulf War.

▼ According to Bell, the OH-58 surpasses all other machines, even the UH-1 'Huey', as the US Army's safest helicopter.

▼ Kiowas of the Canadian Armed Forces are designated CH-136; trainers are CH-139s.

▼ The Royal Australian Navy nicknamed its Kiowas 'Battle Budgies'.

JetRangers in uniform worldwide

Although it was not offered a production contract for a new observation and artillery spotting helicopter, Bell improved its OH-4 design and developed the civil Model 206 JetRanger. When, in 1968, the Army re-opened the competition, this design was selected by the Army as the OH-58 Kiowa to augment the Hughes OH-6 Cayuse that had won the original competition. Early examples of the Kiowa were sent immediately to the Vietnam War, where they distinguished themselves

as agile transports which could fly into areas the OH-6 could not.

The US Navy soon adopted the 206, but in a different role, as the TH-57 SeaRanger pilot trainer. Twenty years later, with the JetRanger still in civil production, the Army has ordered more machines, this time as TH-67 Creek trainers.

Exports to foreign air forces have been numerous, although many of these have been civil

machines. Training and liaison are common unarmed roles, but Sweden and Chile use armed Model 206s for anti-submarine work.

Below: Sweden's navy operates seven Italian-built Agusta-Bell AB 206A JetRangers as Hkp 6As. These can carry a torpedo or depth charges.

Above: The US Army has adopted the JetRanger as its New Training Helicopter (NTH), or TH-67 Creek.

TH-57C SeaRanger

Type: dual-control advanced training and transport helicopter

Powerplant: one 313-kW (420-hp) Allison 250-C20J turboshaft engine flat-rated to 236 kW (316 hp)

Maximum speed: 225 km/h (140 mph)

Maximum cruising speed: 214 km/h (133 mph)

Maximum rate of climb: 469 m/min (1538 fpm) at sea level

Range: 848 km (525 miles)

Service ceiling: over 6095 m (20,000 ft)

Hover ceiling: 3870 m (13,000 ft) in ground effect

Weights: empty 840 kg (1848 lb); maximum take-off 1520 kg (3348 lb)

Dimensions: main rotor diameter 10.16 m (44 ft 4 in)
fuselage length 9.49 m (31 ft 2 in)
height 2.91 m (9 ft 6 in)
rotor disc area 81.10 m² (882 sq ft)

ACTION DATA

MAXIMUM SPEED

Speed is not a major consideration in training, but the higher top speed of the Gazelle gives the student pilot useful lead-in training for the more powerful and faster types he or she is likely to fly.

TH-57C SEARANGER	225 km/h (140 mph)
GAZELLE HT.Mk 3	310 km/h (192 mph)
Mi-2T 'HOPLITE'	210 km/h (130 mph)

MAXIMUM RATE OF CLIMB

With a 30 per cent more powerful engine fitted into an airframe which is only 11 per cent heavier, the Gazelle has a better climb rate than the SeaRanger. The Mi-2 is a much older design and has a significantly inferior power-to-weight ratio than newer designs because of its smaller engine and heavier airframe.

GAZELLE HT.Mk 3	540 m/min (1771 fpm)
TH-57C SEARANGER	469 m/min (1538 fpm)
Mi-2T 'HOPLITE'	270 m/min (886 fpm)

RANGE

In the training role good range means greater endurance. This allows longer training flights to be undertaken further away from the training base. The Gazelle's shorter range is partly due to its proportionally smaller airframe. Smaller aircraft tend to be able to carry less fuel and thus have shorter range.

TH-57C SEARANGER	848 km (525 miles)
Mi-2T 'HOPLITE'	797 km (494 miles)
GAZELLE HT. Mk 3	670 km (415 miles)

OH-58A Kiowa

Beginning in May 1969, the US Army took delivery of 2200 OH-58As. Several hundred OH-58As and Cs have since been retired, and most remaining aircraft are operated by Air National Guard units. By the year 2000 as few as 300 are expected to remain in service.

A total of 435 OH-58As have been converted to OH-58C standard with a flat glass canopy to reduce glare, an uprated T63 engine, infra-red suppressed exhausts and internal improvements. Wire cutters are often fitted above and below the forward fuselage.

Between 75 and 84 OH-58As have been upgraded with forward-looking infra-red (FLIR) and communications links for civilian law enforcement agencies and are assigned to Army National Guard units in 27 states.

While the OH-58A was powered by a 236.5-kW Allison T63-A-700 turboshaft (a military derivative of the 250-C fitted to the JetRanger), the OH-58C introduced the improved 313-kW T63-A-700 variant. A common feature of the Kiowa is an exposed tail rotor driveshaft on the tailboom, which is covered on this example.

Many OH-58Cs can be fitted with Stinger air-to-air missiles on mountings on both sides of the fuselage behind the main cabin door. These provide protection from other helicopters, but are seldom carried.

A number of OH-58s were converted to OH-58D standard, radically changing the look of the aircraft and optimising it as a support helicopter to work with the AH-64 Apache anti-tank machine. OH-58Ds have since been armed as Kiowa Warriors.

US Army observation helicopters

- **BELL OH-13 SIOUX:** Famous for its exploits during the Korean War, Bell's Model 47 entered US service in 1946.

- **HILLER OH-23 RAVEN:** The first Ravens were air ambulances delivered to the Army in 1950. The last OH-23s were supplied in 1967.

- **HILLER YOH-5:** This turbine-engined light observation prototype was not put into production, but served as the basis for the civil FH-1100.

- **HUGHES OH-6 CAYUSE:** Later to become a big seller as the civil Model 500, the OH-6 'Loach' was awarded the first LOH contract.

BELL

OH-58D KIOWA

● Two-seat armed scout helicopter ● Special mast-mounted sight

▶ The OH-58D was originally an unarmed helicopter. In 1987, however, when Iran began to threaten ships in the Persian Gulf, armed Kiowas were used to protect oil tankers against gunboat attacks.

Bell's OH-58D Kiowa Warrior combines a proven design, increased power and hi-tech equipment in its important role as the US Army's main battlefield scout. The Kiowa Warrior goes into combat in careful co-ordination with ground commanders and heavier helicopters like the Apache. The OH-58D's main duty is to reconnoitre the enemy and pinpoint his forces, although it can also carry guns, rockets and guided missiles.

▲ Mast-mounted sight
The MMS is mounted on a non-vibrational bearing. It can swivel through 360° and tilt up or down 30°.

▲ Modern 'glass' cockpit
The OH-58D has a state-of-the-art cockpit with large multi-function displays (MFDs) for aircraft systems, navigation and targeting data. The MFDs are designed to be used at night when the crew wear night-vision goggles. These were not used in the First Gulf War because of smoke from burning oil wells.

▲ Dual-role scout
The OH-58D Kiowa Warrior has two main roles: as a scout helicopter for the army's land and airborne forces and, when required, as an armed attacker in its own right.

▼ Naval support
The 4th Squadron, 17th Cavalry, US Army, is trained to operate from US Navy vessels if necessary. OH-58D operations were mounted at sea during the 1991 Gulf War.

▶ Hellfire anti-tank missile launch
The MMS also contains a laser rangefinder and designator. The latter can be used to guide the OH-58D's own missiles or those of larger attack helicopters, like the AH-64 Apache.

FACTS AND FIGURES

▶ The US Army's 1/17th Cavalry flies a stealth version with a laser-proof windscreen and more pointed nose.

▶ Saudi Arabia's 15 Bell 406 Combat Scouts have a roof-mounted sight.

▶ The main rotor turns at 395 rpm and the tail rotor at 2381 rpm.

▶ The OH-58D is named after the native American Kiowa tribe. Other US Army helicopters are also named in this way.

▶ The stealth version of the Kiowa Warrior first flew on 6 August 1990.

▶ The first production unarmed OH-58D was delivered in March 1986.

PROFILE

The Cavalry's armed scout

The army uses the OH-58D to cope with the speed and complexity of modern warfare. Ground commanders need flexibility to stay on top of an enemy's manoeuvres, and the Kiowa Warrior uses a mast-mounted sight – a 'ball' above its whirling rotors – to spot the enemy, aim its own weapons and guide those of others.

In combat, the OH-58D hides beneath the horizon, using the contours of the ground to shield it, rising only to use its mast sight – known as 'nap of the earth', or NOE, flying. At the right moment, the OH-58D attacks on its own, or directs weapons from artillery batteries, larger attack helicopters or close air support fighter-bombers.

The Kiowa Warrior combines the aerodynamic shape of the earlier OH-58A/C spotter with a four-bladed rotor, a more powerful engine and a respectable weapons capacity. Bell also builds an export version of the OH-58D known as the 406 Combat Scout. In 1988 Saudi Arabia ordered 15 of these.

OH-58D KIOWA WARRIOR

Assigned to the 4th Squadron, 17th Cavalry, US Army, this OH-58D carries the unit's nickname ('Thugs').

High-tension wires can cause a helicopter to crash if its rotors become entangled. Wire-cutters are fitted above and below the cockpit to deal with these hazards.

The OH-58D's key sensors are located in the mast-mounted sight. Behind the two windows are a TV sensor and an imaging infra-red, which provide targeting and navigational information in all light and weather conditions.

Under the cabin, inboard of each main skid, a caving ladder is carried. This is dropped down for the rapid rescue of personnel.

The ALQ-144 IRCM turret provides protection against heat-seeking missiles.

Some Kiowa Warriors are intended to be air transportable, with collapsible skids, folding stabiliser and fin, removable wire-cutters and a support frame for the mast-mounted sight.

The exhaust is located in the upper panel of the engine fairing. Hot gases are ejected straight into the downwash, where they are rapidly diffused to reduce infra-red signature.

Two AGM-114C Hellfire anti-armour missiles are carried by this helicopter.

As well as the infra-red countermeasures turret on the tailboom, the Kiowa Warrior also uses two types of radar-warning receiver and a laser detection set for self-protection.

A Hydra-70 seven-tube 70-mm rocket pod is fitted on the port side weapons pylon.

Above: On 26 January 1991, during the First Gulf War, two OH-58Ds flying from a US Navy frigate liberated an Iraqi-held island in the Gulf and took 29 prisoners.

OH-58D Kiowa Warrior

Type: two-seat single-engined armed scout helicopter

Powerplant: one 485-kW (650-hp) Allison T703-AD-700 turboshaft

Maximum speed: 237 km/h (146 mph) 'clean' at 1220 m (4000 ft)

Maximum climb rate: 469 m/min (1540 fpm) at sea level

Range: 463 km (290 miles)

Hover ceiling: 3415 m (11,200 ft)

Weights: empty 1381 kg (3038 lb); maximum take-off 2041 kg (4490 lb)

Armament: 12.7-mm (.50 cal.) machine guns, seven-tube 70-mm rocket pods, plus provision for Stinger air-to-air missiles and Hellfire anti-armour missiles

Dimensions: main rotor diameter 10.67 m (33 ft 4 in)
length   12.85 m (31 ft 2 in)
height   3.93 m (9 ft 6 in)
main rotor disc area 89.37 m² (882 sq ft)

COMBAT DATA

MAXIMUM SPEED

Of these scout helicopters, the single-engined Kiowa Warrior is by far the best equipped. It is therefore heavier and slightly slower than the Gazelle and Bo 105.

OH-58D KIOWA WARRIOR	237 km/h (146 mph)
SA 341B GAZELLE	264 km/h (192 mph)
Bo 105M	242 km/h (130 mph)

RANGE

With the space in its fuselage taken up by avionics, the OH-58D does not have as much room available for fuel tanks as the other two less well-equipped helicopters. It therefore lacks their range.

SA 341B GAZELLE 670 km (415 miles)

OH-58D KIOWA WARRIOR 463 km (290 miles)

Bo 105M 658 km (408 miles)

HOVER CEILING

The ability to operate in most conditions is vital for a scout helicopter, especially the Kiowa Warrior. Rotor blade and engine design are important factors when flying in 'hot and high' conditions. Most OH-58 operations are flown below 1000 m (3280 ft).

Bo 105M 1615 m (5300 ft)

OH-58D KIOWA WARRIOR 3415 m (11,200 ft)

SA 341B GAZELLE 2000 m (6560 ft)

OH-58D scout mission

A major part of the Kiowa Warrior's job is to act as a scout working with gunship/anti-armour helicopters like the AH-64 Apache. In this role the OH-58D uses natural and manmade features as cover while scouting for targets.

HI-TECH SIGHT: The mast-mounted sight (MMS) contains a TV sensor, an infra-red imaging system and a laser designator/rangefinder.

INTO THE TRAP: Hiding behind a building, this OH-58D is using the extra height of its MMS to track the tanks beyond, without exposing itself to enemy fire.

APACHE SUPPORT: With the target in sight the scout can then radio for an anti-armour gunship helicopter to engage with rockets, missiles or gunfire.

DESTRUCTION: Using its laser designator, the scout can guide Hellfire anti-tank missiles from the gunship, without the latter being able to see the target.

BELL/BOEING

V-22 OSPREY

● Assault transport ● Vertical take-off ● Multiple roles

▲ The prototype V-22 Osprey is seen transitioning to horizontal flight. It is this unique ability which will revolutionize the speed of US Marine Corps amphibious assaults.

US Marines have a phrase for it: they call it 'Vertical Envelopment'. The idea is to bypass a defended coast by flying troops over the top, fast, landing them in the enemy rear before the foe can react. And nothing can move Marines as fast as the revolutionary V-22 Osprey, which flies like an aeroplane but takes off and lands like a helicopter.

BELL/BOEING V-22 OSPREY

▲ Sea trials
The Osprey has shown that it can operate from any deck large enough to give sideways clearance to the twin rotors.

▲ Osprey's forerunner
The Bell XV-15 was the culmination of a long line of experimental convertiplanes, and was the direct ancestor of the V-22.

Global reach ▶
The V-22 can be refuelled in flight. It can be deployed over intercontinental distances in less than a day – which is something that no helicopter can do.

▲ Marine assault
The most enthusiastic supporters of the V-22 are the US Marines, who see the aircraft as adding greatly to the ability with which they can carry out amphibious assaults.

▲ Folding wings
The Osprey takes up a lot of space, which is at a premium aboard even the largest carrier. To make more room, the rotors fold and the wing swivels in line with the fuselage.

▶ High-tech
The Osprey comes equipped with a modern 'glass' cockpit, dominated by multi-function controls and computerized video displays.

FACTS AND FIGURES

▶ The V-22 first flew on 19 March 1989, taking off vertically from Bell's research facility at Arlington, Texas.

▶ First transition from vertical to horizontal flight took place on 14 September 1989.

▶ The V-22 has twice the speed and twice the range of a comparable helicopter.

▶ V-22s can be deployed anywhere in the world within 36 hours.

▶ A typical helicopter needs three times as much maintenance as the V-22.

▶ Ospreys can carry a seven-tonne load slung beneath the fuselage at speeds of up to 375 km/h (233 mph).

High-speed assault

A Marine commander assaulting a defended shoreline needs to get his troops and equipment ashore fast. But landing craft are slow and make easy targets, and helicopters are horribly vulnerable to enemy fire. Until now, the only way to minimise the time the helicopters are at risk has been to launch them from as close to shore as possible, but that exposes the irreplaceable assault ships to danger from the enemy's long-range artillery and missiles.

The Osprey has changed all that. With its rotors pointing upwards, it can take off and land vertically on ship or ashore. But tilting the rotors forwards converts them into propellers, allowing the Osprey to fly twice as fast as the fastest helicopter.

Operating in conjunction with speedy air-cushion landing craft, the V-22 can deliver troops or weapons over much greater distances than a helicopter. An amphibious task force commander can now launch his attack from over the horizon, and still have his troops ashore in a shorter time than would have been possible with helicopters and landing craft.

XV-22 OSPREY

Although facing Congressional opposition, the V-22 has been described by senior Marine officers as 'our number one aviation priority'.

Test aircraft are often fitted with sensitive flight testing instruments to measure the aircraft's performance in all areas of the flight regime.

The Osprey is manned by a pilot and co-pilot. They control the aircraft by means of an electronic fly-by-wire system.

The Osprey's engines are immensely powerful, in order to lift the aircraft free of the ground without any aerodynamic assistance.

The huge paddle-bladed prop-rotors are a compromise between long helicopter-type rotors and much smaller aircraft-type propellers.

The V-22's prop-rotors are 11.58 m (40 ft) in diameter. Immensely strong to resist combat damage, one provides enough lift to keep the aircraft in the air alone if necessary.

The wing is fitted on a pivot. Swung fore and aft and with the rotors folded, an Osprey takes up no more room than a large helicopter.

Osprey's twin tail is set high on a boom, in order to leave room for the rear door and loading ramp.

The extensive use of composite material means that the V-22 is about 25 per cent lighter than a metal aircraft of comparable size and lifting power.

The tremendous width of the Osprey's rotor blades is clear in this photo of a landing on a 'Wasp'-class assault ship.

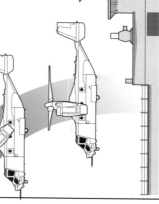

MV-22A Osprey

Type: two-crew multi-role convertiplane transport

Powerplant: two 4593-kW (6159-hp) Allison T406-AD-400 turboprops

Maximum speed: 556 km/h (345 mph) at sea level

Combat radius: 1880 km (1168 miles) search and rescue; 1000 km (632 miles) amphibious assault

Rate of climb: 332 m/min (1089 fpm) vertically

Service ceiling: 8000 m (26,250 ft)

Hovering ceiling: 4300 m (14,100 ft)

Weights: empty 14,433 kg (31,819 lb); loaded 24,948 kg (55,000 lb)

Payload: up to 25 fully equipped troops or 4500 kg (9920 lb) cargo internally, or 6800 kg (14,990 lb) external load

Dimensions: span (rotors turning) 25.76 m (84 ft 6 in)
    length   17.32 m (56 ft 10 in)
    height   6.63 m (21 ft 9 in)
    rotor area   210.00 m² (2260 sq ft)

ACTION DATA

TAKE-OFF PROCEDURE

Osprey can take off vertically or with a short take-off run. Transition from vertical flight to horizontal is automatic. As the aircraft's forward speed increases, control is switched from the aircraft's rotors (as in a helicopter) to the conventional flaps and ailerons (as in an aircraft).

PAYLOAD EFFICIENCY

A CH-53 helicopter can carry up to 55 troops in the assault role.

Although its capacity is only 25, the V-22 can make three trips to a helicopter's one, landing 75 troops in the same time that the CH-53 lands 55.

Landing comparison

MARINE ASSAULT: An amphibious assault using Ospreys and air-cushion landing craft can stand offshore a safe distance from enemy defences, and still land troops more quickly than helicopters and landing craft.

ENEMY THREAT: Most modern artillery pieces have a range of between 17 and 30 km (11 and 19 miles), putting any vessel coming within that range.

CLOSE RANGE: Conventional assaults are limited by the slow speed of conventional landing craft. To get troops ashore in under an hour, the assault fleet has to be within a few thousand metres of the coast, well within artillery range.

LARGE ASSAULT SHIP
60 KM (37 MILES) OFFSHORE

V-22 OSPREY

AIR-CUSHION LANDING CRAFT

ASSAULT SHIP
5 KM (3 MILES) OFFSHORE

CH-53

LANDING CRAFT

OBJECTIVE:
THE BEACH

36

BOEING

F4B/P-12

● Biplane fighter ● Inter-war defender of the US Fleet

Serving the US Navy at the end of the biplane era, the classic F4B was the star of a family of famous Boeing fighters which included the US Army Air Corps' P-12 and the export Model 100. The F4B was a super ship to fly and was the most capable carrier-based fighter of its time. For all its elegance and manoeuvrability, the F4B triumphed successfully for only a brief time before being eclipsed by the arrival of the monoplane in the late 1930s.

▶ Pilots loved the F4B for its superb manoeuvrability, massive strength and impressive performance. But by the end of the 1930s the days of open-cockpit biplane fighters were numbered.

BOEING **F4B/P-12**

▶ **Still going strong**
This P-12C is a rare survivor of the 568 built. A Boeing F4B-4 that also survived is on display at the Naval Aviation Museum at NAS Pensacola, Florida.

▶ **Last of the line**
A late-model P-12F above Hensley Field, Texas. This model was the equivalent of the Navy's F4B-4, and often had radio fitted.

▶ **Fabric fighter**
Early P-12s had a fabric-covered fuselage, but by 1930 Boeing was building P-12Es with a stressed metal skin for better strength.

Streamlining ▼
Early P-12 models had uncowled Wasp engines. The Townend ring cowling fitted to later models streamlined the engine and helped increase speed.

▶ **Line abreast**
P-12Es of the 27th Pursuit Group practise their immaculate precision formation flying above Selfridge Field, Michigan.

FACTS AND FIGURES

▶ The first F4B-1 went on duty aboard the carrier *Lexington* on 8 August 1929.

▶ A special F4B-1A served as a 'taxi' for Assistant Secretary of the US Navy Douglas Ingalls.

▶ The first prototype in this great fighter series flew on 25 June 1928.

▶ The F4B landed on a carrier deck at about 60 km/h, or about one-third the speed of the modern F-14 Tomcat.

▶ Many F4B-4 fighters served as unmanned target drones during World War II.

▶ The F4B was the favourite aeroplane of stunt pilot hero Frank Tallman.

F4B-4

Type: single-seat carrier-based fighter

Powerplant: one 410-kW (550-hp) Pratt & Whitney R-1340-16 radial piston engine

Maximum speed: 300 km/h (186 mph) at 1830 m (6000 ft)

Range: 600 km (373 miles)

Service ceiling: 8200 m (26,903 ft)

Weights: empty 1068 kg (2355 lb); loaded 1638 kg (3611 lb)

Armament: two 7.62-mm (.30-cal.) fixed forward-firing Browning machine guns or one 7.62-mm and one 12.7-mm (.50-cal.) Browning machine guns, five 12-kg (25-lb) bombs or one 227-kg (500-lb) bomb or one 208-litre (46-gal.) drop tank

Dimensions:
span	9.14 m	(30 ft)
length	6.12 m	(20 ft 1 in)
height	2.84 m	(9 ft 4 in)
wing area	21.13 m²	(227 sq ft)

COMBAT DATA

RANGE

Even in the early days of carrier aviation, naval aircraft were expected to operate over greater distances than their land-based equivalents – after all, emergency landing fields are few and far between in the vast ocean spaces – and the F4B comfortably outranged the contemporary British Bulldog.

BULLDOG
475 km
(295 miles)

F4B
600 km
(373 miles)

FLYCATCHER
500 km
(311 miles)

MAXIMUM SPEED

The F4B was one of the fastest fighters around when it went into service in the late 1920s. It had the edge on land-based machines like the Bristol Bulldog and was much quicker than the Fairey Flycatcher, the standard British carrier fighter of the time.

BULLDOG
280 km/h (174 mph)

F4B
300 km/h (186 mph)

FLYCATCHER
214 km/h (133 mph)

ARMAMENT

Aircraft armament in the biplane era had not advanced much in the decade since the end of World War I. Two forward-firing machine guns was the norm for most fighters of the early 1930s. However, the F4B's powerful radial engine meant that it could carry a fairly heavy bombload for a fighter.

BULLDOG
2 x 7.7-mm (.303-cal.) machine guns
4 x 10-kg (22-lb) bombs

FLYCATCHER
2 x 7.7-mm (.303-cal.) machine guns
4 x 10-kg (22-lb) bombs

F4B
2 x 7.62-mm machine guns
1 x 227-kg bomb

Boeing's great Navy biplane

In early days of carrier aviation, the F4B was the hottest thing with wings. Boeing's Model 83 and 89 prototypes led to four principal versions of this superb biplane fighter, numbered F4B-1 through F4B-4; the final version is the best remembered among the 200 or so of these aircraft which saw active service with the Navy between 1930 and 1938.

These great fighters were exciting and colourful: most had grey fuselage and wings; a brilliant yellow upper wing surface, and squadron colours on fuselage and cowling.

Part of the success of the F4B belongs to the Wasp engine, or R-1340, which was this period's finest technical achievement. But the real measure of the F4B was its prowess as a fighting plane.

Touchdown landing on the wooden deck of the USS Lexington. Landing and take-off accidents were common.

In the heyday of the biplane, this air-to-air dogfighter could not be defeated. Unfortunately, the romance of this era was all too brief. By the late 1930s, faster monoplane fighters had consigned biplanes to history.

US military aircraft generally sported bright colour schemes in the inter-war period. The vivid yellow wings aided recognition over the sea.

The 'Felix the Cat' insignia was the squadron badge of fighter squadron VF-6, operating from USS *Saratoga* in 1935. The badge is still being used today on the F-14 Tomcats of VF-31.

The nine-cylinder Pratt & Whitney Wasp radial was the forerunner of a family of engines that would power US Navy fighters throughout World War II.

A compartment in the headrest housed a dinghy in case the pilot was forced to crash-land in the sea. This version also had a radio fitted.

The undercarriage of the F4B needed to be strong. Even with the low speeds of biplane fighters, landings on carrier decks were often very hard.

The fuselage frame of all F4Bs was built of welded steel tube for strength. Stressed metal skins replaced fabric on the fuselage of the later versions, but all F4Bs retained a fabric-covered wing.

F4B-4

This F4B-4 was one of about 200 used by the US Navy between 1929 and 1938. The F4B-4 was similar to the Army's P-12E, with a 410-kW (550-hp) Wasp engine but with the essential arrester hook and wing bomb racks.

Carrier Air Power – then and now

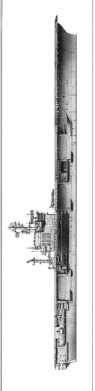

■ USS *KITTYHAWK* has been in service since 1961 and displaces more than 90,000 tonnes. It carries an air wing of 85 advanced combat jets, and with its nuclear arsenal deploys more firepower than the entire US Navy of the 1930s, and is able to project power on a global basis.

■ USS *RANGER* was laid down in 1931. It displaced only 14,500 tonnes, but it too could carry more than 80 aircraft. Most were tiny biplanes, however, and five or six could be stored in the space a single modern F-14 Tomcat occupies.

BOEING

P-26 PEASHOOTER

● Pioneering all-metal monoplane ● China war veteran ● Dogfighter

The Boeing P-26 Peashooter was an incredibly bold new venture: the first monoplane fighter to enter squadron service. Progress was rapid in the 1930s, however, so the P-26 enjoyed glory only briefly. When Pearl Harbor was attacked a decade after the P-26 was conceived, Peashooters remaining in the hands of a few Filipino pilots became easy pickings for the Japanese Zero.

▲ The P-26 was a major advance in fighter design, blending old features like fixed undercarriage and open cockpit with modern metal construction and powerful engine, including fuel injection.

BOEING P-26 PEASHOOTER

▲ Fastest fighter
For a short time, the P-26 was the fastest fighter in service. The P-26s of the Philippine Army Air Corps even managed to shoot down some faster Japanese fighters in December 1941.

▲ Open cockpit
The P-26 was the last open fighter in US service. The roomy cockpit was well liked by pilots.

▲ In stripes
This P-26 wears a typical inter-war colour scheme, with yellow wings and stripes. This type of scheme was abandoned before the start of World War II, when less visible toned-down colours were adopted.

◀ On parade
Pilots and ground crew of the 17th pursuit group on review at their base in March Field, California.

▲ Echelon formation
Stepped upwards away from the photographer, a P-26 pursuit squadron poses for the camera.

FACTS AND FIGURES

▼ The XP-936 prototype for the P-26 series first flew on 20 March 1932.

▼ Boeing in Seattle manufactured 136 Peashooters of all versions.

▼ On 12 December 1941, six Philippine P-26s battled 54 Japanese aircraft, shot down three, and suffered three losses.

▼ Twelve Boeing Model 281s, identical to the P-26, were built for export to China.

▼ The last flight of a P-26 occurred in 1964 when a restored 'warbird' went aloft in the United States.

▼ The modern Boeing 747-400 weighs much as 300 'Peashooters'.

PROFILE

Last of the old, first of the new

The P-26 had fixed landing gear with heavy, high-drag wheel pants, and was festooned with bracing wires. So although it was modern when introduced in 1931, it also marked the end of an era; it was the last open-cockpit fighter accepted by the US Army, the last with a fixed undercarriage, and the last with an externally braced wing. The P-26 was also

the final production fighter from Boeing.

Based on three XP-936 prototypes, the P-26A, B and C served with all US Army fighter groups in the 1930s. Variants were employed overseas by Guatemala, China and the Philippines (which employed a few P-26s in early days of World War II). In one of its few combat engagements Philippine P-26s

managed to down three Japanese aircraft despite being outclassed in every area of performance. American P-26s also put up futile resistance at Pearl Harbor.

Called a 'sport roadster' by Army pilots, the P-26 went into production in 1932. The last ship built was delivered in 1936. The last American Peashooter left service in 1943, but P-26s flew in Guatemala until 1957.

P-26A Peashooter

Type: single-seat pursuit aircraft

Powerplant: one 373-kW (500-hp) Pratt & Whitney R-1340-27 Wasp nine-cylinder air-cooled radial engine driving a two-bladed propeller

Maximum speed: 377 km/h (234 mph) at 2250 m (7382 ft)

Range: 580 km (360 miles)

Service ceiling: 8500 m (27,887 ft)

Weights: empty 996 kg (2196 lb); loaded 1340 kg (2954 lb)

Armament: one 7.62-mm (30-cal.) and one 12.7-mm (.50-cal.) or two 12.7-mm machine guns; provision for two 45-kg (100-lb) or five 13.60-kg (30-lb) bombs

Dimensions:
span 8.52 m (27 ft 11 in)
length 7.19 m (23 ft 7 in)
height 3.07 m (10 ft 1 in)
wing area 13.89 m² (150 sq ft)

COMBAT DATA

RANGE

The P-26 was smaller than contemporary canvas and wire biplanes, and as a result could not carry as much fuel. This, allied to the high drag caused by its bulky radial engine, had a slightly adverse effect on the Peashooter's range. Even so, it was more than enough for the short range interception missions it was designed for. The bigger Gauntlet could carry a much larger fuel load, increasing its range.

GAUNTLET	740 km (460 miles)
P-26 PEASHOOTER	580 km (360 miles)
He 51	400 km (249 miles)

MAXIMUM SPEED

Although fast for the time, the P-26 had only a slight speed advantage over the best of contemporary biplanes. It was tough and manoeuvrable, however, and gave the US Army Air Corps valuable monoplane experience.

GAUNTLET	370 km/h (300 mph)
P-26A PEASHOOTER	377 km/h (234 mph)
He 51	330 km/h (205 mph)

ARMAMENT

By the 1930s aircraft armament had not progressed beyond World War I levels, with two forward-firing machine guns as a standard fit. The P-26 had a slight advantage over its contemporaries in being armed with a pair of the classic Browning '50-calibre' heavy machine guns, which packed a hefty punch. It could also carry two 45-kg (100-lb) bombs.

P-26A PEASHOOTER 2 x 12.7-mm (.50-cal.) machine guns

GAUNTLET 2 x 7.7-mm (.303-cal.) machine guns

He 51 2 x 7.92-mm machine guns

The P-26B of 1935 featured a fuel-injected engine, revised controls and landing flaps. The flaps were fitted to reduce the landing speed, which had been excessively high in the P-26A.

The wide-chord wing and chunky tail of the P-26 were reminiscent of earlier Boeing designs such as the P-12.

The P-26's major contribution to aviation technology was its sturdy, all-metal construction.

The headrest helped protect the pilot if the aircraft rolled over on the ground.

The bracing wires showed that the P-26 was still halfway between the days of biplanes and more modern monoplanes.

The fairing over the undercarriage reduced drag. Fixed undercarriages were vanishing by the late 1930s.

The P-26 used the Pratt & Whitney radial engines common to most US fighters. They were strong and powerful, but had a large frontal area, which meant high drag.

The nickname 'Peashooter' came from the aircraft's tubular gunsight.

P-26A PEASHOOTER

This P-26A carries the badge of the 95th Pursuit Squadron, known as the 'Kicking Mules'. The squadron used the P-26 in the ground-attack role.

Monoplane fighters of the 1930s

DEWOITINE D.510: Developed from the D.500 of 1932, the D.510 was the mainstay of French fighter strength in the mid 1930s.

MITSUBISHI A5M 'CLAUDE': This Japanese carrier fighter first flew in 1935. It was one of the most manoeuvrable fighters ever built.

POLIKARPOV I-16: Flying only two years after the P-26 entered service, the Soviet I-16 was the true herald of fighters to come. A powerful engine and retractable undercarriage made it at least 100 km/h (60 mph) faster than the P-26.

BOEING

B-17 FLYING FORTRESS (EARLY)

- Heavy bomber ● Maritime defence ● Early wartime service

▶ The B-17 was designed to meet an exacting USAAC specification calling for an aircraft which was capable of 400 km/h (250 mph) over a range of 3540 km (2000 miles) when carrying a 907-kg (2000-lb) bombload.

Rolled out in 1935, the B-17 Flying Fortress represented something very new at a time when many bombers in service with the world's air forces were either biplanes, twin-engined monoplanes or slow, lumbering types. The B-17 was sold to the US Congress as a coastal patrol aircraft to guard approaches to isolated North America. However, America was not isolated for long and the B-17 was soon to develop into a crucial weapon.

BOEING B-17 FLYING FORTRESS (EARLY)

▶ **In war paint**
From March 1941 army depots applied olive drab and grey paint to their B-17Cs and Ds. By the time the US entered World War II, all the aircraft had been painted. These early versions were relegated to training duties by 1944.

▲ **The $432,034 gamble**
For Boeing, a company of just 600 employees, the money spent in building the revolutionary Model 299 prototype represented a huge gamble.

▲ **Flying Fortresses over the 'Big Apple'**
Six of the 13 YB-17 (later redesignated Y1B-17) test airframes are seen here over New York. Although similar to the Model 299 prototype, they had different engines and carried six crew.

▼ **Newly delivered D-model**
The third B-17 production model was the B-17D, which differed from the B-17C only in having engine cowling flaps and an extra crewmember. Forty-two were built in all.

▼ **RAF Fortress Mk I**
This RAF Fortress carries the serial AM528, erroneously applied at the Boeing factory in place of the intended AN528. Twenty of 38 Fortress Mk Is, which were ordered as training aircraft, were delivered in 1941.

FACTS AND FIGURES

▶ RAF Fortresses later flew anti-shipping missions in the Middle East and with Coastal Command in the UK until 1943.

▶ The first B-17s were delivered to the 2nd Bomb Wing at Langley Field in 1937.

▶ RAF experience over Europe resulted in better armament on later variants.

▶ On 8 December 1941, 30 B-17Ds were wrecked on the ground in the Philippines by Japanese bombers.

▶ A famous early B-17, Swoose ('half swan, half goose'), is preserved in Washington.

▶ Total Fortress production amounted to 12,731 aircraft.

PROFILE

First Fortresses for the Air Corps

When Boeing unveiled its Flying Fortress, critics argued that the world was not ready for such a big bomber. Despite its lofty name and good flight performance, the B-17 was not equipped for modern warfare. Early models, with their smooth lines and smaller fin, did not have a tail gunner.

In 1940 the Army Air Corps began receiving aircraft with a broader fin and tail gun position, although newly delivered B-17s on the

West Coast in 1941 lacked guns or ammunition.

To deter Japanese aggression, America planned to add four bomber groups to the one that was already in the Philippines by April 1942. Had the plan been implemented, the Pacific war could have been a very different story.

The first dozen B-17s detailed by the plan departed California for a stop in Hawaii on the night of 6 December 1941, and arrived 12 hours later during the Japanese attack on Pearl Harbor.

Many of the aircraft in the Philippines and Hawaii were destroyed on the ground.

The survivors of the Pearl Harbor attack became the first US aircraft in offensive action in World War II, attacking Japanese shipping from 10 December. The following month, the better armed B-17E started to enter service. No. 90 Squadron, RAF, took the B-17C to war (as the Fortress Mk I) over Germany in 1941 and later in the Mediterranean, but with little success.

The Flying Fortress was so-named for its original intended role – protecting North America's coast lines from maritime attack.

Many of the USAAC's B-17Cs were later modified to B-17D standard. The RAF was supplied with 20 C-models in 1941 on the understanding that the USAAC would be supplied with complete information on its combat performance.

B-17C FLYING FORTRESS

Aircraft 10 of the 7th Bomb Group carries the olive drab and grey camouflage scheme applied to USAAC aircraft after the US entered World War II.

The nose position had three gun sockets, one on either side and one in the centre, for a single 7.62-mm (.30-cal) machine gun. The 12.7-mm (.50-cal.) gun was said to break the Plexiglass if used from the nose positions.

Apart from the B-299 prototype, which used four Pratt & Whitney Hornet engines, four Wright Cyclones were the standard B-17 powerplants. The C-model's four R-1820s produced 895 kW (1200 hp) each.

Self-sealing wing fuel tanks were among the improvements introduced on the B-17C. Armour protection for the crew was also fitted.

Both the dorsal and ventral gun positions on the B-17C were equipped with twin 12.7-mm (.50-cal.) machine guns. The bomb-bay, situated below the wing centre section, carried a typical load of 2177 kg/4800 lb (eight 272-kg/600-lb bombs).

In place of the fuselage blisters on previous models, the B-17C had a simple oval opening for the twin waist gun positions. Each was usually equipped with a 12.7-mm (.50-cal) machine gun.

The B-17C and D featured the so-called 'tin bathtub' beneath the fuselage in place of the ventral 'blister' gun position.

Early bomber types of World War II

■ **AVRO MANCHESTER:** The Manchester of 1940 was judged to be a failure, thanks to its unreliable engines, but was developed into the RAF's most successful four-engined bomber, the Lancaster.

■ **JUNKERS Ju 86:** The Luftwaffe did not field a true four-engined bomber during World War II. The Ju 86 was an early twin-engined type, which was later used for high-altitude reconnaissance.

■ **VICKERS WELLINGTON:** This twin-engined aircraft was in RAF service when war broke out in 1939 and formed the backbone of Bomber Command until 1943.

Fortress Mk I

Type: heavy bomber and maritime patrol aircraft

Powerplant: four 895-kW (1200-hp) Wright R-1820-G205A Cyclone radial piston engines

Maximum speed: 515 km/h (320 mph)

Cruising speed: 373 km/h (232 mph) at 4267 m (14,000 ft)

Range: (normal) 3380 km (2100 miles); (maximum) 5085 km (3160 miles)

Initial climb rate: 396 m/min (1300 fpm)

Weights: empty 14,129 kg (31,149 lb); loaded 20,624 kg (45,468 lb)

Armament: one 7.62-mm (.30-cal.) machine gun in the nose, two 12.7-mm (.50-cal.) machine guns in each of the dorsal and ventral positions and two 12.7-mm machine guns through waist positions, plus up to 4761 kg (10,496 lb) of bombs

Dimensions:
span   32.23 m (105 ft 9 in)
length   20.97 m (68 ft 10 in)
height   4.68 m (15 ft 4 in)
wing area   125.45 m² (1350 sq ft)

ACTION DATA

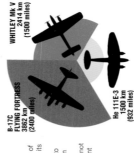

SERVICE CEILING

The USAAC's bomber specification was a demanding one, which required better speed, range and armament than that possessed by twin- and four-engined types then in service. Its service ceiling requirement, for example, was greatly increased.

B-17C FLYING FORTRESS 10,973 m (36,000 ft)	He 111E-3 7500 m (24,600 ft)	WHITLEY Mk V 7925 m (26,000 ft)

RANGE

Range was an important attribute of the Fortress, given its role as a maritime bomber designed to defend the US from attack. The RAF's bomber force was not able to reach distant targets until four-engined types entered service.

B-17C FLYING FORTRESS 3862 km (2400 miles)	WHITLEY Mk V 2414 km (1500 miles)	He 111E-3 1500 km (932 miles)

ARMAMENT

The Flying Fortress was well armed compared to other bombers of the period. However, its lack of rearward-facing guns proved to be a handicap, and was addressed on later versions. Its four engines allowed a bigger bombload to be carried than the others.

B-17C FLYING FORTRESS 6 x 12.7-mm (.50-cal.) machine guns, 1 x 7.62-mm (.30-cal.) machine gun, 4761-kg (10,496-lb) bombload
He 111E-3 3 x 7.9-mm machine guns, 2000-kg (4400-lb) bombload
WHITLEY Mk V 5 x 7.7-mm (.303-cal) machine guns, 3175-kg (7000-lb) bombload

42

BOEING

B-17 FLYING FORTRESS (LATE)

● Long-range heavy bomber ● Backbone of the US 8th Air Force

▲ The Flying Fortress was America's main strategic weapon in Europe during World War II. From the summer of 1943, huge numbers of Boeing's great silver bird were to be found on English airfields.

Boeing's Flying Fortress was one of the most important bombers in history. B-17s fought in every theatre of World War II, but won immortality in their epic daylight battles against the Luftwaffe in which thousands of young American flyers lost their lives transforming the impotent United States Army Air Force of early 1943 into a force of devastating, destructive power just 12 months later.

BOEING B-17 FLYING FORTRESS (LATE)

▲ Mass production
Nowhere was America's huge industrial might more visible than in the aircraft factories which turned out hundreds of B-17s each month.

Daring missions ▼
During the long bomb-run into the target area the bomb-aimer controlled the B-17. Losses were extremely high as the aircraft was forced to fly straight and level.

▼ A hard-fought battle
The Fortress was tough, but the skies over Germany were filled with experienced fighter pilots and flak bursts, leading to heavy losses.

▲ **Silver machines**
The B-17 soldiered on after World War II in some oddball roles. This is a rescue aircraft with a lifeboat carried under the fuselage.

▲ The young man's war
It was a rare B-17 pilot who was older than 30: most of the men who took the big bombers into battle were barely into their 20s.

FACTS AND FIGURES

➤ A B-17 shot down by Japanese Zeroes on the way to Pearl Harbor was the first American combat loss in World War II.

➤ The Boeing 299, the Flying Fortress prototype, first flew on 28 July 1935.

➤ 12,731 B-17s were built, with production of the B-17G model reaching 8680.

➤ At the height of the war in Europe, B-17s occupied more than 25 airfields in the south and east of England.

➤ More than 47,000 US 8th Air Force crew died in daylight raids over Germany.

➤ A search and rescue SB-17 flew the first American sortie of the Korean War.

Castles in the sky

In the mid 1930s, Boeing engineers suggested a big bomber to the US Army Air Corps. The best American bomber at the time was an inadequate, twin-engined adaptation of the DC-3 transport. The decision to go ahead with the B-17 Flying Fortress was a courageous leap forward; it gave the United States an embryonic bomber

force by the time of the attack on Pearl Harbor. Early B-17s did not have enough guns and were not available in sufficient numbers, but as the war progressed the Flying Fortresses took command of the skies.

B-17 crews faced unspeakable horror, pressing ahead into Luftwaffe fighters and flak while blinded by smoke, beaten by turbulence,

plagued with mechanical mishaps and paralysed by numbing cold. On the first Berlin mission, B-17 crewmen killed in the air numbered the same as Germans killed on the ground by bombs (about 400). As the bombing campaign wore on casualties aboard the B-17s remained high, but the bombing became more effective.

Right: B-17s were used to make precision daylight attacks on German industrial centres.

B-17F 'FAST WOMAN'

'Fast Woman' was one of the first American B-17s to arrive in Britain during World War II. Attached to the 359th Bomb Squadron of the 303rd Bomb Group, it was based at Molesworth in Huntingdonshire.

The 'Mighty Eighth' Force was the premier user of the B-17 Flying Fortress.

The Norden bombsight with which the B-17 was reputed to be able to 'drop a bomb into a pickle barrel' from 4000 m (13,120 ft).

The B-17 was powered by reliable Wright Cyclone radial engines. They were turbocharged, which enabled the Fortress to operate at higher altitudes than its European contemporaries.

Boeing were among the pioneers of stressed-skin design, and the B-17 was among the earliest all-metal monoplane heavy bombers to enter service.

The bomb-bay was relatively small, and although the B-17 could fly with an eight-tonne bombload it generally carried a quarter of that amount on operations.

Fortresses were defended by as many as 13 heavy machine guns. The vulnerable undersides were covered by a ball turret and by the two waist gunners.

The B-17 was immensely strong. Aircraft managed to return to base with severe battle damage, and the big bomber could still fly even with large sections of the huge vertical tail shot away.

B-17s were not originally fitted with tail guns. A tail gunner's position was added to the B-17E and all subsequent models.

Left: Hit by flak, a burning B-17 falls away from the protection of its fellows.

B-17G Flying Fortress

Type: 9- or 10-seat long-range bomber

Powerplant: four 895-kW (1200-hp) Wright R-1820-97 Cyclone turbocharged radial piston engines

Maximum speed: 462 km/h (287 mph)

Service ceiling: 10,850 m (35,600 ft)

Range: 3220 km (2000 miles)

Weights: empty 16,391 kg (36,136 lb); loaded 29,710 kg (65,499 lb)

Armament: 13 12.7-mm (.50-cal.) machine guns; 8000-kg (17,637 lb) maximum bombload

Dimensions:
span 31.62 m (103 ft 9 in)
length 22.66 m (74 ft 4 in)
height 5.82 m (19 ft 1 in)
wing area 131.92 m² (1420 sq ft)

■ **SIDE VIEW** □

3rd COMBAT BOX (7900 m/25,920 ft)
Each box contained 18 bombers, which could amass more than 200 heavy machine guns.

LEAD COMBAT BOX (7600 m/24,934 ft)
The formation commander flew in the lead bomber, with responsibility for navigation and ordering simultaneous release of bombs.

2nd COMBAT BOX (7300 m/23,950 ft)
Combat boxes manoeuvred in unison, always keeping in close formation for mutual support against fighters.

■ **PLAN VIEW**

Layered defences

Every B-17 aircraft contributed to the defence of the whole formation. Each squadron of six aircraft moved in unison in formations called boxes, and squadrons were layered and staggered horizontally and vertically, to allow simultaneous release of bombs.

COMBAT DATA

DEFENCES

Originally relatively lightly armed, the Flying Fortress entered combat in armour plate and with an all-round machine-gun fit. A box of 18 bombers could bring tens or even hundreds of guns to bear on an attacker coming from any direction.

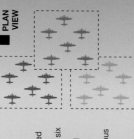

STIRLING
8 x 7.7-mm (.303-cal.) machine guns

B-17 FLYING FORTRESS
13 x 12.7-mm (.50-cal.) machine guns

B-24 LIBERATOR
10 x 12.7-mm (.50-cal.) machine guns

RANGE

Designed at a time when other air forces still thought twin-engine machines were heavy bombers, the B-17 was revolutionary with its ability to carry more bombs over much greater distances than its contemporaries.

STIRLING
3200 km (1988 miles) with 1600-kg (3527-lb) bombload

B-17 FLYING FORTRESS
3300 km (2051 miles) with 2500-kg (5512-lb) bombload

B-24 LIBERATOR
3000 km (1864 miles) with 2300-kg (5071-lb) bombload

44

C/KC-97 STRATOFREIGHTER

● B-29 development ● In-flight refuelling tanker ● Transport

B y combining major sections of the B-29 with an all-new upper fuselage, Boeing produced the Model 367, which first flew on 9 November 1944. Known to the USAF as the XC-97 Stratofreighter, this aircraft was to be the first in a long line of transports, tankers and tanker/transports based on the C-97. The refuelling techniques adopted from the KB-29P and refined on the KC-97 remain much the same on Boeing's modern KC-135.

▲ Using the wings and other major components of the B-29, Boeing was able to develop a large transport which was to become the basis of the USAF tanker fleet.

BOEING C/KC-97 STRATOFREIGHTER

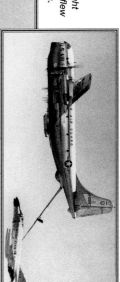

▼ Israeli transport
A YC-97 was supplied to Israel as payment for the cost of maintaining US aircraft, and one KC-97F and eight KC-97Gs were delivered later. They flew military missions in civilian markings.

Tanker transport versatility ▼
The KC-97G gave the USAF an aircraft which was capable of carrying freight or passengers without removing its refuelling system. This was the most common model.

▲ Fast-jet refuelling
KC-97Ls remained in US Air National Guard service until 1977. Many of them were fitted with auxiliary J47 turbojet engines so that they could reach the speeds required for refuelling fighters.

▼ Nose radome
When the C-97A entered service it introduced a distinctive chin radome, which housed an AN/APS-42 search radar. All subsequent aircraft featured radar.

▲ Wartime prototype
The first of three XC-97s flew in 1944. Its clamshell rear cargo doors and ramp can be clearly seen in this picture.

FACTS AND FIGURES

▼ On 9 January 1945 the first XC-97, carrying a 9072-kg (20,000-lb) payload, flew from Seattle to Washington DC in 6 hours and 3 minutes.

▼ With its pressurized cabin, the XC-97 was able to cruise at 9144 m (30,000 ft).

▼ The YC-97 used engine nacelles developed for the B-29.

▼ A single YC-97A flew in the Berlin airlift, carrying cargo such as coal, which was loaded by conveyor belt.

▼ MC-97C was the designation of casualty evacuation aircraft in the Korean War.

▼ New systems allowed the KC-97G to dispense with a radio operator.

Booming success for Boeing

Boeing chose the simplest structural route to produce the C-97. The lower fuselage lobe was of similar diameter to that of the B-29, while the upper fuselage also had a circular cross-section but was of greater diameter. Combining these gave Boeing two circular section cabins to pressurise, which was a much easier proposition than producing an elliptical pressurised fuselage of the same size.

In January 1942 a US Army Air Force order resulted in the construction of three XC-97 prototypes, which led, in turn, to the production of 10 YC-97 service test aircraft. These were to prove the C-97 concept and eventually led to production of 50 C-97As.

Although the C-97A proved to be an exceptional freighter, various efforts were made to improve it, including trials with three experimental KC-97As fitted with refuelling booms

taken from KB-29Ps. The aircraft proved to be a highly capable tanker, with the KC-97G becoming the most widely built model of the series.

Several KC-97 variants were made and the ultimate KC-97L served with Air National Guard units until 1977.

KC-97G Stratofreighter

Type: long-range transport and in-flight refuelling tanker

Powerplant: four 2610-kW (3500-hp) Pratt & Whitney R-4360-59B radial piston engines

Maximum speed: 604 km/h (400 mph)

Cruising speed: 483 km/h (300 mph)

Climb rate: 50 min to 6096 m (20,000 ft)

Range: 6920 km (4300 miles)

Operating ceiling: 9205 m (30,000 ft)

Weights: empty 37,421 kg (70,000 lb); maximum take-off 79,379 kg (130,000 lb)

Accommodation: 96 troops or 69 stretcher patients, plus refuelling system

Dimensions: span 43.05 m (141 ft 3 in)
length 33.63 m (110 ft 4 in)
height 11.66 m (33 ft 3 in)
wing area 164.34 m² (1768 sq ft)

Below: Ten service test aircraft were ordered in July 1945 for US Army Air Force trials. They had a larger fuel capacity than the XC-97.

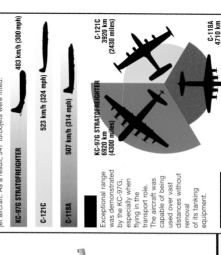

Above: Between March and August 1965, the KC-97Gs of the Wisconsin Air National Guard were brought up to KC-97L standard.

CRUISING SPEED

The KC-97G had a slower cruising speed than contemporary transport aircraft in USAF service. This proved to be a problem when the Stratofreighter was required to refuel fighters and other jet aircraft. As a result, J47 turbojets were fitted.

KC-97G STRATOFREIGHTER	483 km/h (300 mph)
C-121C	523 km/h (324 mph)
C-118A	507 km/h (314 mph)

Exceptional range was demonstrated by the KC-97G, especially when flying in the transport role.
The aircraft was capable of being used over vast distances without removal of its tanking equipment.

KC-97G STRATOFREIGHTER 6920 km (4300 miles)

C-121C 3920 km (2430 miles)

C-118A 4710 km (2920 miles)

Lockheed's C-121C and Douglas' C-118A, based on the Super Constellation and DC-6 airliners respectively, were able to fly only as transports. The C-121C had greater seating capacity than the KC-97G. The Stratofreighter retained all of its tanking equipment, however, and allowed the extra flexibility of combined transport and tanking missions with reduced payload.

KC-97G 96 PASSENGERS

C-121C 106 PASSENGERS

C-118A 74 PASSENGERS

KC-97L STRATOFREIGHTER

J47 turbojets were introduced under the wings of the KC-97L by the Illinois Air National Guard. This aircraft belonged to the 108th Air Refueling Squadron (ARS) and was the first conversion from KC-97G standard.

Each of the 28-cylinder Pratt & Whitney radials provided 2610 kW (3,500 hp) and turned a four-bladed propeller. The C-97A was able to transport two propellers on special racks beneath the forward fuselage.

Like the KC-97G from which it was converted, the KC-97L had additional fuel cells on the main cabin floor, as well as a substantial freight capacity.

ILLINOIS AIR GUARD

U.S. AIR FORCE

O-22697

This high B-50-style fin was introduced from the YC-97A onwards. The aircraft also introduced other changes, including a lighter wing, larger flaps and reverse pitch propellers.

General Electric J47-GE-25 turbojets became available for the KC-97 when the jet-augmented B-50 models went out of service. The modified version was originally known as the JKC-97G.

Most KC-97Gs and Ls were used almost exclusively in the tanker role. Their rear clamshell doors were replaced by the boom operator's position and observation windows.

Many KB-50s relinquished parts of their fuel pumping system as well as their jet engines to the KC-97L. The aircraft had a refined version of the Boeing-developed flying boom used on the KB-29P. The boom of the modern KC-135 has changed very little.

Boeing tanker chronology

■ **KB-29P SUPERFORTRESS:** Boeing pioneered the use of the flying-boom refuelling system on the KB-29P.

■ **KB-50:** Some 136 B-50s were modified to tanker configuration. Here an early conversion from a B-50D refuels two F-100 Super Sabres.

■ **KC-135 STRATOTANKER:** Boeing's KC-135 has become a classic military aircraft design and will be in service for many years.

■ **MODEL 707:** As secondhand 707 airliners became available, several air arms cheaply converted them into tankers.

BOEING

B-47 STRATOJET

- All-jet bomber ● Swept-wing design ● Bicycle undercarriage

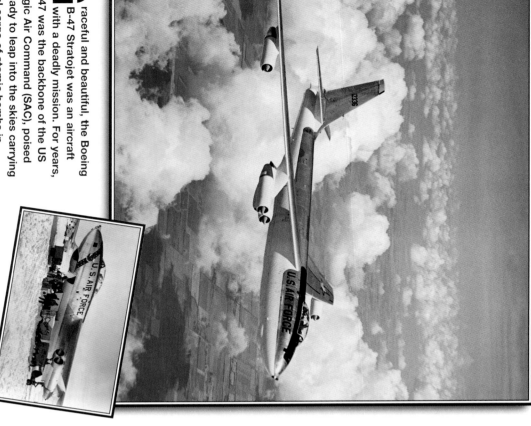

▲ Operating from distant bases was part of the SAC requirement; to some crews of the B-47 it meant the cold conditions of Alaska. Here a crew prepare its aircraft for take-off.

Graceful and beautiful, the Boeing B-47 Stratojet was an aircraft with a deadly mission. For years, the B-47 was the backbone of the US Strategic Air Command (SAC), poised and ready to leap into the skies carrying a lethal cargo of atomic bombs in response to a nuclear attack. SAC had nearly 2,000 Stratojets in service in the mid-1950s, the most potent bomber force ever assembled.

BOEING **B-47 STRATOJET**

Constant vigil ▶
With the need to launch at a moment's notice, B-47 crews were required to maintain a 24-hour alert. Here a Stratojet pilot waits for the call that will launch his bomber into the night's sky. Practice operations were undertaken at all hours.

▲ Combined operations
The nose of a KC-97 tanker partly obscures a B-47 positioned behind. These aircraft operated in close co-operation: the tanker supplied fuel to the bomber, allowing the Stratojet to strike targets at a greater distance. SAC pioneered routine IFR operations.

Long range ▼
A B-47 commander brings his aircraft in to formate with a KC-97 tanker. The refuelling receptacle was positioned on the nose of the bomber.

▲ Fighter handling
B-47 pilots found the bomber had exceptional handling for formation flying. It was also able to accomplish loops and rolls.

Late variants ▶
A late production Stratojet displays the bomber's unusual undercarriage design.

FACTS AND FIGURES

▶ The first B-47 flew on 17 December 1947, the anniversary of the Wright Brothers' first powered flight in 1903.

▶ A Stratojet set a transatlantic speed record from the US to England.

▶ The first B-47 production contract was for 10 aircraft, costing $30 million in all.

▶ Production of the B-47 had amounted to 2041 of all variants when assembly work ended in February 1957.

▶ Some 440 Stratojets were built for non-bombing duties such as reconnaissance.

▶ The B-47 strongly influenced the design of the Boeing B-52 Stratofortress.

PROFILE

SAC's first jet bomber

The Boeing B-47 Stratojet defeated several rivals to become the US Air Force's choice as its principal strategic bomber of the 1950s. Stratojets began to arrive at SAC bases in October 1951. The Stratojet was the first swept-wing jet bomber ever produced. It was appealing to the eye and had breathtaking performance, but the cramped cockpit arrangement was awkward and crew fatigue on long missions was a problem.

Many B-47s stayed on nuclear alert, ready to launch with their deadly cargo of atomic bombs. Some participated in Reflex deployments between the United States and Great Britain in support of worldwide strategic readiness. In 1959, Stratojets participated in Operation Oil Burner, practising low-level strike runs to penetrate below enemy radar detection while still accurately delivering nuclear weapons to their strategic targets.

Though it was stressful on crews, the B-47 was much-loved by nearly all who maintained and flew it.

Eventually replaced by the B-52 Stratofortress, the B-47 remained in operation with SAC until the 1960s. The last bomber version was retired on 11 February 1966, but the reconnaissance RB-47 variants remained on duty with the 55th SRW until 29 December 1967.

Above: A sight repeated right across the continental United States: two SAC Stratojets await their alert call to action.

B-47 Stratojet

Type: long-range strategic bomber

Powerplant: six General Electric J47-GE-25/25A turbojets, each developing 32.03 kN (7207 lb thrust) with water injection

Maximum speed: 975 km/h (606 mph) at 4970 m (16,306 m)

Cruising speed: 806 km/h (501 mph) at 11,735 m (38,500 ft)

Ceiling: 12,345 m (40,500 ft)

Range: 6437 km (4000 miles)

Weights: empty 36,630 kg (80,755 lb); maximum take-off 89,893 kg (198,180 lb)

Armament: two M24A1 20-mm cannon, each with 350 rounds of ammunition, in radar-directed, remotely-controlled tail turret, plus up to 9071 kg (20,000 lb) of bombs carried internally

Dimensions: span 35.36 m (116 ft)
length 33.48 m (109 ft 11 in)
height 8.51 m (27 ft 11 in)
wing area 132.66 m² (1428 sq ft)

Stratojet bombing mission

A possible mission planned from Kadena AB, Okinawa could have been against the strategic bomber base at Andyr in the Soviet Eastern District. This would have meant a round trip of 9656 km (6000 miles) over a duration of 11 hours with two in-flight refuellings by a KC-97. The mission profile would have been a simple climb to optimum cruising altitude of around 9750 m (32,000 ft) followed by a flight more or less direct to the target. However, no evasive action was deemed necessary. Similar attack profiles would also have been flown in Europe.

ANDYR

KADENA AB

B-47E-I STRATOJET

This B-47 Stratojet displays the late scheme of white anti-flash undersides, used to protect aircraft from the explosion of their own atomic bombs. SAC's blue ribbon insignia is painted on the nose.

The two pilots sat in tandem under a Plexiglass canopy. Visibility was excellent although the second pilot's forward view was restricted.

A tandem or 'bicycle' arrangement was used for the main undercarriage, each set of wheels being installed either side of the bomb bay.

Outrigger wheels were positioned within the outer engine pylons to provide some degree of lateral stability on the ground. They were vital during landings in cross-winds.

Located at the rear of the fuselage were twin 20-mm cannon. They replaced the earlier 12.7-mm (.50-cal) machine guns which had offered little protection.

The 35° swept-back wing was thin and had an extremely high aspect ratio. It proved to have very fine aerodynamic efficiency. The wings were constructed so that, during manoeuvres, they could flex up to 3 m (10 ft), allowing the bomber to accomplish loops and barrel rolls during certain attack procedures.

Because of the thin wings, fuel was carried in two main tanks positioned above and to the rear of the weapons bay. After testing, the bomb bay was made smaller than that of the early A models, reflecting advances in bomb design.

Later B-47E models did away with the internal jet-assisted take-off (JATO) units. Instead, the units were incorporated on an external rack which could be jettisoned following take-off. By using this procedure a larger bombload could be carried.

3 Bomb run: Capable of delivering a vast range of weapons, the Stratojet would use a variety of manoeuvres to avoid nuclear blast when dropping its ordnance.

2 High performance: In its day the B-47 was able to outrun enemy fighters, although some SAC reconnaissance versions did return to base after missions having received damage from MiG-15s.

Stratojet bombing mission

1 In-flight refuelling: So that the B-47 Stratojet could attack targets at great distance, the aircraft would refuel from a KC-97 tanker aircraft.

BOEING

RB-47E/H STRATOJET

● Reconnaissance duties ● Communist confrontations

Although the Stratojet is better known as a bomber, the B-47's most important work was done by aircraft that were operated as spy planes, using cameras, radar and snooping devices to keep tabs on communist nations. The Boeing RB-47 Stratojet was thus the backbone of the United States' reconnaissance effort against the Soviet Union. The work involved genuine danger. Four hundred RB-47s were engaged in these, still-classified, missions.

▲

PHOTO FILE

BOEING RB-47E/H STRATOJET

▼ Intelligence-gathering
Some aircraft were modified for Elint-gathering duties and received the somewhat confusing designation, ERB-47H. They carried a crew of five.

▲ Rare birds
For specialist photo-mapping and weather reconnaissance duties, 15 aircraft designated RB-47K were built. These served with the 55th Strategic Reconnaissance Wing at Forbes AFB.

▲ International incident
Seen on the ramp, this aircraft is an RB-47H, one of the last to remain in active service. This variant gained notoriety when one was intercepted and shot down by a Soviet MiG over the Barents Sea on 1 July 1960.

Last and first ▼
Although among the last aircraft to leave the production lines, the RB-47Es were also among the first to be withdrawn from service. Representing a tremendous improvement over the RB-50G Superfortress, the type was prematurely retired after changes were made to SAC's operational requirements.

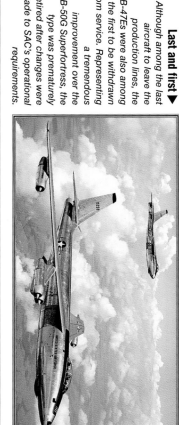

FACTS AND FIGURES

▶ Because of its undercarriage layout, the B-47 was sometimes referred to as the 'Middle River Stump Jumper'.

▶ The last Stratojets in service were the WB-47Es of the Air Weather Service.

▶ RB-47H 53-4296 is significant in being the last Stratojet used by SAC.

▶ Crews stationed with the 55th SRW's Detachment 3 at Eielson, Alaska, often flew sorties over the North Pole.

▶ In Britain, RB-47Hs flew from RAF Brize Norton and Upper Heyford.

▶ Aircraft belonging to the 55th SRW were often re-serialled to confuse observers.

PROFILE

SAC's Cold War sky spy

On 15 October 1952, two B-47s took off from Alaska, heading towards Soviet territory where a MiG-15 squadron was in a position to challenge them, and then flew over Siberia photographing strategic targets.

It was the first American 'overflight' of the Soviet Union, and it marked the beginning of a long campaign for the Boeing RB-47 Stratojet. For more than a decade afterwards, 'recce' RB-47 Stratojets poked at the fringes of, and sometimes flew over,

the USSR and other Soviet bloc countries.

Inside the Stratojet, within large bomb bays once configured to hold thermonuclear weapons, teams of reconnaissance specialists did their sinister work. Some 'electronic' and 'recce' Stratojets relied on electronic black boxes to ferret out secrets. Although aerial espionage was the principal mission, some of these special Stratojets had other duties: one functioned as a radio-relay ship with the sole job

of passing the 'go code' in the event of the US president authorising American forces to go to war. When Soviet fighters shot down an RB-47 over the Barents Sea in July 1960, the type still had a few years left to serve. Some flew sorties in Vietnam before the career of this aircraft ended in 1967.

Above: Once in the air, the Stratojet could be an unforgiving machine and pilots had to be constantly alert.

Above: Besides stateside bases, RB-47s were often deployed overseas, to RAF Brize Norton and Upper Heyford in Europe, Incirlik in the Middle East and Yokota in the Far East.

RB-47E Stratojet

Type: five-seat strategic reconnaissance aircraft

Powerplant: six 32.03-kN (7200-lb-thrust) General Electric J47-GE-25A turbojets

Maximum speed: 975 km/h (605 mph)

Initial climb rate: 1420 m/min (4660 fpm)

Range: 6437 km (3990 miles)

Service ceiling: 12,345 m (40,500 ft)

Weights: empty 36,630 kg (80,586 lb); loaded 89,893 kg (197,765 lb)

Armament: two M24A-1 20-mm cannon, each with 350 rounds

Dimensions:
span 35.36 m (116 ft)
length 33.50 m (109 ft 10 in)
height 8.51 m (27 ft 9 in)
wing area 132.66 m² (1427 sq ft)

COMBAT DATA

MAXIMUM SPEED

Although able to outperform a number of fighter interceptors, the RB-47H was not quite as fast as the smaller and more nimble Tu-16P. It was however quicker, though perhaps less versatile, than the lumbering turboprop-driven Tu-95RT 'Bear'.

RB-47H STRATOJET	956 km/h (593 mph)
Tu-16P 'BADGER-F'	991 km/h (614 mph)
Tu-95RT 'BEAR-D'	830 km/h (515 mph)

RANGE

Decent endurance made the B-47 ideal for the strategic reconnaissance role. In-flight refuelling was, however, essential for long-range sorties. The 'Bear' could cover vast distances, gathering intelligence.

RB-47H STRATOJET	4890 km (3032 miles)
Tu-16P 'BADGER-F'	6292 km (3900 miles)
Tu-95RT 'BEAR-D'	13,460 km (8345 miles)

SERVICE CEILING

Cruising at altitudes of nearly 13,000 m (41,000 ft), the B-47 Stratojet was considered to be virtually immune from fighter attack during its early years. However, two incidents involving interception by enemy MiGs and one shoot-down soon confirmed otherwise.

RB-47H STRATOJET	12,345 m (40,500 ft)
Tu-16P 'BADGER-F'	12,298 m (40,340 ft)
Tu-95RT 'BEAR-D'	10,300 m (33,780 ft)

RB-47H STRATOJET

Probably the most mysterious of all the Stratojets, the RB-47H was employed on strategic reconnaissance tasks by the 55th SRW for a number of years before finally being supplanted by the RC-135 in late 1967.

The large swept-back tail held the tailplanes away from the fuselage. Both vertical and horizontal units had large control surfaces with tabs set close inboard.

Located along the underside of the fuselage were the numerous blisters that housed the radar equipment.

Positioned at the rear of the fuselage was a pair of 20-mm cannon in a remote-control barbette. During spy flights, MiGs often engaged during running battles across the Soviet borders. Later 'recce' models saw the removal of this installation to add more radar equipment for spying purposes.

Further electronic equipment associated with signals intelligence was held in a pod attached to the lower starboard fuselage; this was added during the 'Silver King' modification programme.

Confined within the cramped quarters of the bomb bay, the radar operators were often referred to as 'crows'. When operating away from their home base, crews removed all their unit patches.

The bulge under the nose housed the antenna and associated equipment for the K-4A bombing radar. This was retained on the 'recce' variants to provide accurate navigation during spying missions.

Crews selected to fly spy missions with the RB-47 Stratojet were some of the best available within SAC. Most had already flown hundreds of hours on standard bomber variants.

Watchers and gatherers

■ **LOCKHEED EC-121 WARNING STAR:** With huge radomes mounted above and below the fuselage, the EC-121 was an airborne early warning variant of Lockheed's Constellation.

■ **VICKERS VALIANT B.(PR) MK 1:** First of the RAF's 'V-bombers', the Valiant was also employed in the photographic reconnaissance role, with cameras fitted in the weapons bay.

■ **GENERAL DYNAMICS RB-57F CANBERRA:** These heavily-modified Canberras were used for high-altitude reconnaissance duties over the Iron Curtain.

50

BOEING

KC-135 STRATOTANKER

● USAF tanker ● Passenger and cargo capability ● Long serving

Taking a huge risk, Boeing proposed, built and funded a military jet tanker/transport prototype in 1954. The aircraft was ordered into production as the KC-135, and one of the greatest success stories in military aviation had begun. Stratotankers have since served around the world, supporting all types of USAF missions, and have been involved in combat operations over Vietnam and in the Gulf War.

▲ Flying the KC-135 requires great skill and courage. The crew must either rendezvous with receivers at long range and at high altitude, or maintain an accurate course so that the receiver aircraft can fly to them.

BOEING KC-135 STRATOTANKER

▲ **Producing Stratotankers**
KC-135 production was a priority as the USAF was equipped with increasing numbers of fast, jet-powered bombers which were supported by propeller-driven tankers that could not keep up with them.

▲ **New developments**
A KC-135A in its original natural metal colour is refuelled by the KC-135R development aircraft. New engines gave the 'R' improved performance.

▼ **A-7D top-up**
Tactical jets are able to fly much longer attack missions with pre- and post-strike refuellings.

▲ **French tanker**
French C-135Fs were adapted to the probe-and-drogue system of refuelling.

▼ **Flying 'gas station'**
A pristine KC-135A, with its large cargo door visible on the forward fuselage, is seen early in its life.

FACTS AND FIGURES

▶ When the 93rd Air Refuelling Squadron of the 93rd Bomb Wing received the KC-135 in 1957, each tanker cost $3,670,000.

▶ KC-135s powered by the old J57 turbojet are nicknamed 'stovepipe' aircraft.

▶ A 54,000-piece kit is required to convert a KC-135A to KC-135R standard.

▶ On 19 November 1988, 'Cherokee Rose', a KC-135R, established 16 time-to-height records in four weight classes.

▶ New refuelling pods allow KC-135s to support probe-equipped receivers.

▶ The US Air National Guard received its first jet tankers, KC-135As, in 1975.

PROFILE

Boeing's immortal jet tanker

Boeing and the USAF confidently expect that the KC-135 will be refuelling bombers, fighters, reconnaissance aircraft and transports beyond the year 2025.

The aircraft, which began as the private-venture Boeing Model 367-80 (or 'Dash-Eighty'), has been constantly updated, keeping pace with modern technology and remaining as safe and efficient now as it was on 15 July 1954 when the 'Dash-Eighty' first flew.

The addition of a Boeing-developed refuelling boom and a slightly wider fuselage

produced the Model 717, known to the USAF as the Boeing KC-135 Stratotanker. Few modifications, the most important being a taller fin, were needed during the production of 732 aircraft. All of the surviving airframes have undergone a continuous evolution.

A host of special variants was produced, including the KC-135Q, a specialized supporter of the SR-71A; the KC-135E, a KC-135A re-engined with TF33 engines from old 707 airliners; and the KC-135R, which was powered by F108 engines and had a 150 per cent increase in the

fuel available for transfer at a radius of 4630 km (2877 miles). France was the only export customer for the Stratotanker and bought 12, designated the C-135F, to support its Mirage IV fleet. In USAF service the KC-135 will fly for many more years performing its unglamorous, but vital, role.

Below: The amount of time spent on station for a vital asset such as the E-3 Sentry may be increased from hours to a few days with regular KC-135 refuellings.

Above: These Early Strategic Air Command KC-135As maintain operational readiness. They have the original short fin.

KC-135A Stratotanker

Type: long-range tanker transport

Powerplant: four 61.16-kN (13,761-lb-thrust) Pratt & Whitney J57-P-59W turbojets

Maximum speed: 982 km/h (610 mph)

Cruising speed: 856 km/h (532 mph) at high altitude

Initial climb rate: 393 m/min (1290 fpm) at sea level

Range: ferry range 14,806 km (9200 miles); radius to offload 10,886 kg (24,000 lb) of fuel 5552 km (3450 miles); radius to offload 54,432 kg (120,000 lb) of fuel 1850 km (1150 miles)

Service ceiling: 13,715 m (44,997 lb)

Weights: operating empty 48,220 kg (106,307 lb); maximum take-off 143,335 kg (316,000 lb)

Dimensions:
span	39.88 m (130 ft 10 in)
length	41.53 m (136 ft 3 in)
height	12.70 m (41 ft 8 in)
wing area	226.03 m² (2433 sq ft)

Boeing's air-refuelling boom has control surfaces similar to those of an aircraft. It is also telescopic, so that a safe distance may be maintained between the tanker and the receiver.

Upgraded aircraft, beginning with the KC-135E programme, have increased-span tailplanes which were taken from 707 airliners.

Using a small control column the boom operator 'flies' the boom towards the receiver aircraft. The 'boomer' lies on his or her stomach on a couch.

In order to keep the KC-135 in service for as long as possible, a programme was initiated in 1975 to re-skin the lower wings. The airframe fatigue life was increased by 27,000 hours.

All of the Stratotanker's refuelling systems are mounted below floor level, which gives the aircraft great flexibility by allowing the carriage of cargo or up to 80 passengers, or any combination of the two.

KC-135R STRATOTANKER

Strategic Air Command began to receive the KC-135R in July 1984 and it represented a big leap in performance over earlier variants. The grey colour of this early delivery aircraft has largely been replaced by a dark-green over grey or overall mid-grey scheme.

A large door on the left forward fuselage hinges upwards to allow cargo or passengers to be loaded. Up to 37,650 kg (83,000 lb) of palletized freight may be accommodated.

CFM International F108-CF-100 turbofans, each of 97.86-kN thrust, power the KC-135R. This extra thrust provides an all-round performance improvement, including an impressive take-off, with the KC-135R becoming airborne 61 m (200 ft) before the KC-135A has left the runway.

ACTION DATA

MAXIMUM FUEL LOAD

Although the Stratotanker carries less fuel than the other two, it retains a useful cargo capability. The TriStar K.Mk 1 is restricted to the carriage of passengers, while 'Midas' has no transport capability.

KC-135R STRATOTANKER	II-78 'MIDAS'	TRISTAR K.Mk 1
92,212 kg (203,293 lb)	118,000 kg (260,145 lb)	142,111 kg (313,301 lb)

Tanking tactics

TWO RACE TRACKS: Flights of fighters set up a race-track at 90° to the track of the tankers. Each flight waiting its turn to refuel.

ACTIVE LEVEL: A series of tankers stack at 325-m (1066-ft) intervals above an active refuelling level. When the active tanker can give no more fuel it leaves the pattern and the remaining tankers all move down by one level.

LAST TANKER, LAST FLIGHT: If all goes according to plan, the last tanker in the stack should refuel the last flight of fighters and still have enough fuel remaining for the return to base.

TANKERS RETURN, FIGHTERS FLY ON: As the tankers return to base, the fully fueled fighters are free to penetrate deeply into enemy territory. A similar operation may be mounted to get them home.

BOEING

EC/RC-135

- Strategic reconnaissance ● Intelligence gatherer ● Command post

F
or decades the Boeing RC-135, the
aerial espionage cousin of the KC-135
tanker, has been vanguard of the
secret world of reconnaissance, giving its
crews hours of boring routine interrupted
by seconds of sheer terror. During tensions
with the Soviet Union, the 'spy in the sky'
RC-135 often flew within a kilometre of
Moscow's territory. The EC-135 is similar,
but is packed with radios to act as a flying
command post during a nuclear war.

▲ The EC-135 is based on the
same aircraft as the RC-135, but contains
different equipment. Most of this is for
communications with other US military
forces. There is usually a General on board
who can control the war from the air.

BOEING EC/RC-135

▲ High-tech
telephonist
The job of most of
the crew on the
EC-135 is to make
communication
connections with
ground stations or
other aircraft.

▲ Missile watchers
The two RC-135S Cobra Ball aircraft specialise in
tracking and photographing missiles. A unique
feature is the black painted wing, which reduces
glare for photography of re-entry vehicles. Aerials
are used to gather data from missile launchers.

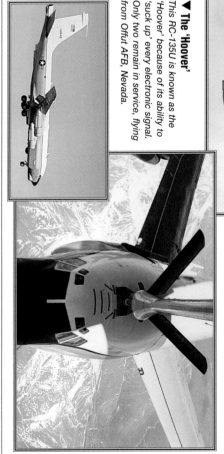

▼ The 'Hoover'
This RC-135U is known as the
'Hoover' because of its ability to
'suck up' every electronic signal.
Only two remain in service, flying
from Offutt AFB, Nevada.

▼ Command post
The airframe of the
EC-135 is festooned
with antennas for
the many radios.

▼ Inflight refuelling
Tanking is vital to the RC-135's ability to stay on
station for many hours at a time.

FACTS AND FIGURES

▶ The systems operators in the RC-135
are known as Ravens.

▶ The first RC-135 reconnaissance craft
became operational in August 1966.

▶ EC-135s have a trailing antenna which
can be reeled out to a length of 10 km
(6 miles) for communication with
submarines.

▶ Strategic Air Command RC-135s flew
more than 6200 intelligence-gathering
sorties during the Vietnam War.

▶ Several EC-135s carried a special nose
radome to track the Apollo spacecraft.

▶ The RC-135S can hunt for enemy mobile
missile launchers in wartime.

PROFILE

America's super snooper

The Boeing RC-135 strategic reconnaissance aircraft is the offspring of the Boeing KC-135 Stratotanker and is closely related to the spectacularly successful Boeing 707 airliner. Designed as an electronic eavesdropper, the RC-135 collects SIGINT (signals intelligence), including an enemy's radar emissions, radio communications or missile telemetry.

The closely related EC-135 was an airborne command post for Strategic Air Command, and

the E-6 Mercury still provides the same service for the US Navy's missile submarines. RC-135s of the US Air Force's 55th Wing deploy worldwide to snoop on potential adversaries in global trouble spots. During the Cold War, they flew closer to the USSR more often than any other Western aircraft. During Operation Desert Storm, the RC-135 gathered vital intelligence on Saddam Hussein's forces.

Using radios, radar and electronic equipment to spy

on potential opponents, the RC-135 continues to be vital to the overseas interests of the United States.

Below: The nose of the RC-135 is covered with bulges containing intelligence-gathering equipment.

Above: Despite the end of the Cold War, the RC-135 fleet is as important as ever to the United States. During the wars in Vietnam and the Gulf it proved it was just as good at collecting intelligence in a tactical war, as it was in the type of superpower stand-off for which it had been designed.

RC-135V

Type: multi-engine long-range reconnaissance aircraft

Powerplant: four 80.07-kN (18,016-lb-thrust) Pratt & Whitney TF-33-P-9 (JT3D-3B) turbojets

Maximum speed: 990 km/h (615 mph) at 10,000 m (32,800 ft)

Operational radius: 4300 km (2672 miles)

Service ceiling: 12,375 m (40,600 ft)

Weights: empty 47,650 kg (105,050 lb); loaded 144,000 kg (317,4666 lb)

Accommodation: reconnaissance versions of the Stratotanker carry electronic sensors and monitoring crews of up to 35

Dimensions: span   39.88 m (130 ft 10 in)
              length   41.53 m (136 ft 3 in)
              height   12.70 m (41 ft 8 in)
              wing area 226.00 m² (2433 sq ft)

COMBAT DATA

MAXIMUM SPEED

Compared to the main British and Russian intelligence gatherers, the RC-135 is faster. Although in the deadly game of strategic reconnaissance, endurance and equipment capability are the telling factors.

RC-135V	990 km/h (615 mph)
NIMROD R.Mk 1	925 km/h (575 mph)
Tu-95 'BEAR'	815 km/h (506 mph)

SERVICE CEILING

The three aircraft have similar ceilings. Operations are normally undertaken at around 10,000 m (32,800 ft), at which height they are high enough to 'peer' a long way into the target territory.

NIMROD R.Mk 1 12,800 m (41,995 ft)
Tu-95 'BEAR' 12,000 m (39,370 ft)
RC-135V 12,375 m (40,600 ft)

RANGE

Designed as a long-range bomber, the Tu-95 'Bear' has exceptional endurance. For longer missions RC-135s are supported by aerial tankers providing inflight refuelling to prolong the sorties.

RC-135V 8600 km (5344 miles)
NIMROD R.Mk 1 9200 km (5717 miles)
Tu-95 'BEAR' 13,000 km (8078 miles)

RC-135V

Known collectively by the codename Rivet Joint, the US Air Force has a fleet of 14 RC-135Vs and RC-135Ws for gathering electronic intelligence. Together they keep watch on potentially hostile nations on a global basis from bases around the world.

The elongated nose contains a side-looking radar, which provides an accurate picture of the coastline for precise navigation. This is very important when snooping close to a hostile country's airspace.

Large cheek fairings on either side of the fuselage contain flat antennas. These 'listen out' across a wide range of frequencies for signals which are analysed by the onboard crew.

The crew of the RC-135 is large: there are two pilots and two navigators on the flight deck, with about 17 systems operators in the cabin.

As well as 'listening' with extraordinary sensitivity, the RC-135 can also 'talk' thanks to satellite communications aerials fitted on the spine.

This bulge is inherited from the KC-135 tanker from which the RC-135 is derived. In the tanker it is used to mount the refuelling boom, but in the RC-135 it incorporates yet more antennas. Some RC-135s also have a downward-facing camera in the bulge.

The RC-135V has a mass of large aerials under the fuselage. These are highly sensitive to electronic signals, and are used to pick up and record radars and communications.

Four Pratt & Whitney TF-33 turbofans provide adequate power and economic operation, but will be replaced in the next few years by more modern engines. Missile warning/jamming gear is often carried just above the engines to protect the RC-135.

RC-135 missions

COMINT: Communications intelligence is the interception and recording of military communications. RC-135s may carry foreign language specialists to help in this work.

ELINT: Electronic intelligence gathering is the detection, location and classification of radars. The information may be passed to attack aircraft which can steer around potentially dangerous radars.

TELINT: The Cobra Ball aircraft gather telemetry intelligence. This entails recording signals from foreign missile tests and photographing the re-entry vehicles.

54

BOEING
OC-135W

- WC-135B conversion ● Treaty verification ● Three examples

A s the latest of the USAF's long line of C-135 variants, the small fleet of OC-135Ws plays a vital role in the post-Cold War era. Operating under the Open Skies agreement, the OC-135W is tasked, along with aircraft from 27 other nations, with flying arms verification flights. With the scaling down of conventional and nuclear arsenals, OC-135Ws, equipped with various cameras and sensors, help ensure that treaty obligations are complied with.

▶ Aircraft from participating nations, such as the Czech Republic, Russia, UK and the USA, carry the words 'Open Skies' along with other insignia to emphasise their peaceful role.

BOEING OC-135W

Operations from Offutt ▶
Controlled by the 55th Wing, Offutt AFB's assets include RC-135 reconnaissance aircraft, EC-135 and E-4B command posts, weather research WC-135Bs, OC-135s and various training versions of the C-135.

◀ Sensitive equipment
Cameras are the most important equipment aboard the OC-135. A bulge under the fuselage contains the cameras which are operated from the cabin.

White topped ▶
Like many aircraft based at Offutt AFB, the OC-135 contains much hi-tech equipment. To help keep this equipment and the aircraft cool, the upper fuselage is painted white to reflect solar radiation.

▲ Modified Andover
The RAF's Open Skies aircraft is a modified Andover designated C.Mk 1(PR). It is operated by MoD(PE) from Boscombe Down.

▲ Czech flights
Both the Czech Republic and Russia have been operating the Antonov An-30 'Clank' survey aircraft as their dedicated Open Skies verification equipment.

FACTS AND FIGURES

▶ Signatories of the Open Skies treaty include all NATO countries in Europe, the US, Canada and ex-Warsaw Pact nations.

▶ Some of the OC-135's cameras were removed from surplus RF-4C Phantoms.

▶ Modifications were made by the 4950th Test Wing at Wright-Patterson AFB, Ohio.

▶ A single TC-135B was converted from a WC-135B to train personnel destined to implement the Open Skies treaty.

▶ The first Open Skies demonstration flight was by a Belgian Hercules in April 1992.

▶ Originally called OC-135B, the aircraft were redesignated OC-135W in 1995.

OC-135W

Type: four-engined arms treaty verification aircraft

Powerplant: four 80.07-kN (18,016-lb-thrust) Pratt & Whitney TF33-P-5 turbofan engines

Maximum speed: 965 km/h (600 mph)

Cruising speed: 901 km/h (560 mph)

Initial climb rate: 393 m/min (1289 fpm)

Range: 7445 km (4626 miles)

Weights: operating empty 46,400 kg (102,294 lb); maximum take-off 124,960 kg (275,490 lb)

Accommodation: crew of 38

Dimensions: span   39.88 m (130 ft 10 in)
         length   41.00 m (134 ft 6 in)
         height   11.68 m (38 ft 3 in)
         wing area 226.03 m² (2433 sq ft)

Ensuring weapons destruction

With the falling of the Berlin Wall and the new relationship between NATO and ex-Warsaw Pact countries, arms reduction treaties have been agreed. Despite the improved relationships it is vital that adherence to the details of the treaties is independently verified by teams of observers from these nations.

The initial treaty was signed in March 1992, with each signatory permitted 42 annual flights to monitor the destruction of weapons and aircraft.

The aircraft the USAF uses for the task is the OC-135W. Three examples are operated by the

24th Reconnaissance Squadron, 55th Wing, based at Offutt AFB, Nebraska. The aircraft were produced by modifying three former WC-135B weather reconnaissance planes and are equipped with a number of photographic sensors including a panoramic camera for high-level photography, two oblique-mounted cameras and a vertically mounted camera for low-level work.

This modification and evaluation were completed in late 1993 and since then the OC-135s have been operational monitoring arms reductions.

The OC-135Bs (as they were originally designated) have been

upgraded to OC-135W standard and the first conversion has been relegated to training duties, leaving two operational aircraft.

The OC-135W carries a variety of aerial cameras, most of them positioned in the bulge beneath the fuselage. They include a KA-91A vertical-mounted panoramic camera for photography above 7925 m (26,000 ft), two KS-87B oblique-mounted framing cameras and a KS-87 vertical-mounted camera for low-altitude imagery.

Below: The fuselage of the OC-135W is almost devoid of windows, allowing the crew of analysts to operate their equipment free from reflections.

Above: Although the OC-135 is highly capable, it has proved more expensive to operate than originally anticipated and could possibly be replaced by the P-3 Orion.

OC-135W

Three OC-135s were converted, serialled 61-2670, 61-2672 and 61-2674. This aircraft was the last of the three to be upgraded to OC-135W standard and it is operated by the 24th Reconnaissance Squadron.

To make the treaty verification OC-135Ws easily identifiable, they carry the words 'Open Skies' along with the Open Skies logo on the tailfin.

The OC-135s were converted from WC-135s which were themselves modified from C-135B transports. This version is powered by the Pratt & Whitney TF33 turbofan engine.

The OC-135 accommodates 38 crew members including maintenance personnel, foreign representatives and members of the On-Site Inspection Agency (OSIA). This agency provides the sensors and linguists for all operational Open Skies sorties, and escorts foreign observation aircraft conducting missions over the United States.

Unlike the aircraft from which it was derived, the KC-135 Stratotanker, the OC-135 has the original refuelling boom faired into the fuselage.

OPEN SKIES

AF 61 2670 OF

UNITED STATES OF AMERICA

2670

Verifying arms treaties

RUSSIAN BOMBER DESTRUCTION: Long-range strategic bombers have been reduced by various treaties. The OC-135 overflies Russian military air bases, ensuring the specified number of strategic bombers have been destroyed. This is normally achieved by cutting through the rear fuselage, severing the tail.

NUCLEAR SILO CHECKS: Reductions in the number of ICBMs (intercontinental ballistic missiles) also have to be verified by flights over the sites to check the status of the silos.

Tu-154 'CARELESS': Germany currently uses the Tu-154 as its Open Skies aircraft. Russia is also planning to replace its An-30s with this type.

ACTION DATA

CRUISING SPEED

The tri-jet Tu-154 cruises at the highest speed of the three types, but it is actually more useful to be flying slower over a photographic target, allowing more time to accumulate the necessary photographs. Most participating nations use slower turboprop aircraft such as the Andover.

OC-135W	901 km/h (560 mph)
ANDOVER C.Mk 1	415 km/h (258 mph)
Tu-154M 'CARELESS'	950 km/h (590 mph)

BOEING

B-29 SUPERFORTRESS

● Long-range bomber ● Largest of World War II ● Assault on Japan

Boeing's talent for turning out huge aircraft paid a super dividend with the Superfortress: the B-29 became the 'big stick' of the final campaign of World War II. Feared by those who fell beneath its shadow, this giant brought war home to Japan's cities and people and ushered in the atomic age. The B-29 also fought in Korea, it was converted into a key post-war transport and tanker, and was even copied without permission by the Russians.

▲ Sting in the tail: in Korea, B-29 gunners were so good at shooting down enemy aircraft that it became the second highest-scoring Allied type, after the F-86 Sabre.

BOEING **B-29 SUPERFORTRESS**

▲ Fire from the sky
In the last days of World War II B-29s poured a deluge of incendiary bombs onto Japanese cities, which were built largely of wood. The resulting conflagration consumed most of the residential areas.

▲ The bomb ends the war
Many people believe that dropping the atomic weapons brought the war to a swift conclusion.

X-plane ▲ mother ship
Several B-29s and the improved B-50 were modified for special missions. Among the most important was carrying early supersonic X-planes to altitude.

▼ Atomic bomber
Immortalised in song, 'Enola Gay' was the Superfortress which dropped the first atomic bomb on Japan, hitting the port city of Hiroshima on 6 August 1945.

▲ Bomber over Korea
Just as the B-29 had flattened Japan, the Superfortress relentlessly crushed Communist resistance in Korea.

▶ Flying gas station
In its KB-29 form the Superfortress was the world's first true service tanker aircraft, pioneering the inflight refuelling that has become vital to modern air combat.

FACTS AND FIGURES

➤ On the night of 9-10 March 1945, 324 B-29s attacked Tokyo at low level in the most destructive air raid in history.

➤ $3 billion had been invested in the B-29 before the first aircraft flew – more than any other aircraft project to that time.

➤ Russia's Tupolev design bureau copied the B-29 as the Tu-4 bomber.

➤ After the war, KB-29s were the USAF's first aerial refuelling tankers.

➤ Crew members travelled from nose to tail of the B-29 through a 'personnel tunnel' above the bomb-bay.

➤ B-29s were used to drop the first atomic bombs on Japan, and in post-war tests at Bikini atoll.

PROFILE

The first strategic bomber

The B-29 was the first pressurized bomber to enter service, and was therefore able to operate over vast distances and at safe heights to deliver huge bombloads onto the enemy.

Originally designed to bomb Germany from America during World War II, the B-29 entered service only at the end of the European war. This massive, revolutionary bomber was transferred to the fight against Japan, where it devastated cities in huge firebomb raids.

Without the reach of the B-29, America would have had to fight for much longer to recover the Pacific islands from Japan. And it was the B-29 that delivered the final, catastrophic blow in the form of two atomic bombs, dropped onto the cities of Hiroshima and Nagasaki.

Post-war, the B-29 joined the Royal Air Force as the Washington, and inspired the Russian Tu-4. Its final battle was in Korea, where it carried out night bombing raids and shot down many enemy aircraft.

B-29 Superfortress

Type: 10/11-seat long-range strategic bomber

Powerplant: four 1641-kW (2200-hp) Wright R-3350 Cyclone 18 turbocharged radial piston engines

Maximum speed: 576 km/h (358 mph)

Range: 6598 km (4100 miles)

Service ceiling: 9170 m (30,085 ft)

Weights: empty 31,815 kg (70,000 lb); loaded 56,245 kg (141,000 lb)

Armament: two 12.7-mm (.50-cal.) machine guns in each of four remotely controlled turrets and three 12.7-mm guns or two 12.7-mm guns and one 20-mm cannon in the tail; bombload 9072 kg (20,000 lb)

Dimensions: span 43.05 m (141 ft 3 in)
length 30.18 m (99 ft)
height 9.02 m (29 ft 7 in)
wing area 161.27 m² (1735 sq ft)

In RAF service the B-29 served as a nuclear bomber, and as a secret reconnaissance aircraft which probed Soviet airspace for electronic signals.

The Superfortress represented one of the biggest technological leaps ever achieved by one aircraft type. Even today, its technology turns up in Russia's nuclear bombers.

It took 11 men to fly the B-29 on operations. There were two pilots, a bombardier, navigator, flight engineer, radio operator, radar operator, central fire control gunner, left gunner, right gunner and tail gunner.

Sitting alone in the tail compartment, the tail gunner had two machine guns and a 20-mm cannon at his fingertips.

Under its tail the Superfortress had a retractable tail bumper, which protected the rear fuselage when the aircraft took off.

The gunners all sat in the rear compartment, looking out for enemy fighters through domed windows and firing the guns via an early computer system.

Two enormous weapons bays carried the B-29's bombload. Each bay had winches inside to hoist the bombs up into the aircraft.

Most B-29s had a sophisticated radar under the belly which allowed them to bomb accurately even through cloud.

WASHINGTON B.Mk 1

The mighty Superfortress was a war-winning weapon, and went on to become one of the main forces in the Cold War. The RAF operated the type in the late 1940s and early 1950s, calling it the Washington.

The forward cabin was connected to the rear cabin by a crawlway. In the back sat the gunners, and there were also bunks for resting on long missions.

Superfortress superbomber

B-29 SUPERFORTRESS: The B-29's two bays held over 9000 kg (20,000 lb) of bombs, the biggest standard load of any wartime bomber.

B-17 FLYING FORTRESS: Although it theoretically could carry 7900 kg (17,400 lb) of bombs, the B-17 rarely flew combat missions with more than 2300 kg (5000 lb).

AVRO LANCASTER: The RAF's main bomber had a normal combat load of about 6300 kg (14,000 lb).

HEINKEL He 177: In theory, Germany's heaviest bomber could carry 6000 kg (13,200 lb), but in practice 2000 kg (4400 lb) was a more realistic load.

COMBAT DATA

The Boeing B-29 was a revelation when it first flew. Easily the biggest bomber of World War II, it flew faster than any of its predecessors, and at altitude it could outpace most of the Japanese fighters which were its principal foes.

MAXIMUM SPEED

B-29 SUPERFORTRESS	576 km/h (358 mph)
LANCASTER	462 km/h (287 mph)
B-24 LIBERATOR	467 km/h (290 mph)

BOEING

B-50/KB-50 SUPERFORTRESS

● Nuclear role ● Boeing's last piston-engined bomber ● Tanker conversions

For a brief period the Boeing B-50 Superfortress was the backbone of the US Strategic Air Command (SAC). A heavy bomber, tasked with the delivery of the first nuclear bombs in the US Cold War arsenal, it was developed from the B-29 but incorporated new materials and much more powerful engines. In 1949 the B-50 set a record by flying nonstop around the world, and in the 1950s it stood alert, armed with nuclear weapons, for several years.

▲ As the ultimate development of the B-29, the B-50 was the last of the USAF's piston-engined bombers. It also performed pioneering work as a tanker, but was rapidly overtaken by the jet age.

BOEING B-50/KB-50 SUPERFORTRESS

Triple-point tanker ▶
An F-100 Super Sabre, an F-101 Voodoo and a B-66 Destroyer refuel simultaneously from the three hoses of a KB-50.

▲ Tanker conversions
Replacing the underwing fuel tanks with jet engines and adding hose units produced the KB-50.

▲ The first B-50
Boeing changed the B-29D designation to the B-50A to ensure funding for the 'new' bomber.

Pure bomber ▶
The B-50 D had a single-piece nose section and 2650-litre (1640-gallon) underwing fuel tanks.

▲ Final role
All KB-50Ks (like the one pictured above) were converted from TB-50Hs.

FACTS AND FIGURES

▼ The B-50 can be distinguished from the similar B-29 by its taller tailfin and underwing fuel tanks.

▼ In total, 350 production B-50s and one prototype were built for the USAF.

▼ Boeing's B-50 made its maiden flight on 25 June 1947.

▼ After being delivered to SAC, more than 6000 work hours were needed to modify the B-50 to accommodate nuclear bombs.

▼ The B-50 began reaching SAC squadrons in June 1948.

▼ B-50s were briefly grounded because of rudder hinge problems.

PROFILE

Boeing's last piston-engined bomber

The Boeing B-50 began life as an improved B-29. Too late for World War II but just in time for the Cold War, the B-50 was capable of hauling atomic bombs and was expected to fly long-range missions. On 2 March 1949 the B-50 'Lucky Lady II' completed the first nonstop round-the-world flight, covering 37,742 km (23,500 miles) in 9¼ hours and 1 minute.

The B-50 was plagued by early problems. As initially designed its bomb-bay was inadequate for the heavy,

plutonium-based Type III nuclear bombs of the 1940s. It had the largest and most powerful reciprocating engine ever installed in an operational warplane and was prone to engine malfunctions. Early B-50s also suffered from metal fatigue. All of these problems were eventually solved, but, by this time, SAC was receiving the more capable B-36, B-47 and B-52 bombers.

Many B-50s undertook reconnaissance missions around the periphery of the Soviet

Union, while others were used to train SAC crews, or acted as weather reconnaissance machines. The majority of B-50s were converted into tankers, and the last aircraft flew during the Vietnam War.

RB-50B

All of the B-50Bs, except the first, were converted to RB-50B reconnaissance platforms. All of these ended their days as KB-50J tankers after 43 had been modified for even more specialised reconnaissance operations.

Like its B-29 predecessor, the B-50 had four remotely controlled gun turrets. The upper nose turret was fitted with four 12.7-mm (.50-cal.) machine guns and each of the other turrets contained two similar weapons. The tail position was fitted with two machine guns and a 20-mm cannon.

Four-row 28-cylinder R-4360 engines produced a 59 per cent power increase over those of the B-29.

B-50 in action

IN-FLIGHT REFUELLING: Early methods of air-to-air refuelling were complicated and could often be dangerous.

AROUND THE WORLD: By refuelling from a KB-29P tanker, the 'Lucky Lady II' flew nonstop around the world. Many RB-50Bs used this hose method of refuelling as standard.

B-50A Superfortress

Type: four-engined heavy bomber

Powerplant: four 2610-kW (3500-hp) Pratt & Whitney R-4360-35 Wasp Major turbocharged radial piston engines

Maximum speed: 620 km/h (384 mph)

Cruising speed: 378 km/h (234 mph)

Range: 7483 km (4640 miles)

Service ceiling: 11,278 m (37,000 ft)

Weights: empty 36,764 kg (80,880 lb); maximum take-off 76389 kg (168,056 lb)

Armament: 12 12.7-mm (.50-cal.) machine guns and one 20-mm cannon; 9072-kg (19,958-lb) bombload

Dimensions:
span	43.05 m	(141 ft 3 in)
length	30.18 m	(99 ft)
height	9.96 m	(32 ft 8 in)
wing area	161.55 m²	(1738 sq ft)

COMBAT DATA

MAXIMUM BOMBLOAD

A 9979-kg (22,000 lb) 'earthquake' bombload for the Lincoln represented an unusual mission. Its bombload was usually similar to that of the B-50A. The Tu-4 was a Soviet copy of the B-29.

B-50A
SUPERFORTRESS
9072 kg (19,958 lb)

LINCOLN B.Mk II
9979 kg
(22,000 lb)

Tu-4 'BULL'
8000 kg
(17,600 lb)

SERVICE CEILING

Both the Avro Lincoln and B-50A represented extreme developments of wartime designs. They offered good performance but could not match that of all-new designs.

B-50A
SUPERFORTRESS
11,278 m (37,000 ft)

LINCOLN B.Mk II
9295 m (30,500 ft)

Tu-4 'BULL'
11,200 m (36,740 ft)

RANGE

Although the B-50A offered long range, the range of the 'D' version was exceptional. The Lincoln could achieve the figure shown only when carrying a reduced bombload of 3000 kg. Tupolev could not match the range of the B-50 with its Tu-4.

LINCOLN B.Mk II
7162 km (4440 miles)

B-50A SUPERFORTRESS
7483 km (4640 miles)

Tu-4 'BULL'
5100 km (3160 miles)

Above: Serial number 49-391 was the last B-50D to be built and is seen here after being converted to a KB-50J. Even with jet boost the KB-50 struggled to keep up with contemporary military jets. The last KB-50 left service in 1965.

Above: Seen in February 1955, this WB-50D is one of 36 B-50D bombers stripped of weapons systems and used for weather reconnaissance. The last one was replaced by a WB-47 in 1967.

As it was heavier than the B-29, the B-50 required a larger fin to maintain directional stability. The vertical tail could be folded down so that the aircraft could be stored in an average-sized USAF hangar.

An internal pressure bulkhead between the rear cabin and bomb-bay was situated at the position of this fuselage band. Crewmembers moved between the front and rear pressure cabins via a pressurised tunnel above the bomb-bay.

As a range-improving feature, 57 B-50As and all RB-50Bs were equipped with the British hose refuelling system. The receptacle for the tanker's hose was situated in a fairing on the right-hand side beneath the tailplane. The system facilitated the nonstop B-50A circumnavigation of the world.

Constructed from a new type of aluminium known as 75 ST, instead of the 24 ST used on the B-29, the B-50's wing was nearly identical to that of the B-29 but 16 per cent stronger and more than 272 kg (600 lb) lighter.

After conversion to RB-50B standard, the rear bomb-bay could accommodate extra crewmembers, plus cameras and electronic equipment.

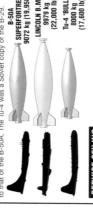

NUCLEAR BOMBING: The primary role of the B-50A/D was the long-range delivery of free-fall nuclear weapons. The aircraft were soon considered obsolete in this role, however.

THREE-POINT TANKER: KB-50J/K aircraft could trail three hoses and simultaneously refuel three probe-equipped aircraft. Here two FJ4 Furies and an F-8 Crusader are being refuelled.

BOEING

B-52 STRATOFORTRESS (SAC)

- Eight-engined nuclear bomber ● Still in service after 40 years

▶ By 1958 the B-52 was the most important component in the world's most powerful military force. US foreign policy was based on deterrence; SAC could deliver a nuclear weapon anywhere.

Stratofortresses were the mighty sword of the USAF's Strategic Air Command (SAC). From 1955 until 1991 the B-52 was on 'nuclear alert', sitting at the end of the runway armed with nuclear bombs and with crew poised nearby. SAC crews knew that a ballistic missile launched by a Soviet submarine could reach their base within 25 minutes. If they were to fight back, this was all the time they had to get into the air on what could be a one-way mission.

PHOTO FILE

BOEING B-52 STRATOFORTRESS (SAC)

▼ **Hound Dog carrier**
As ICBMs (intercontinental ballistic missiles) became more important, the B-52 took on the role of launching stand-off weapons like the jet-powered AGM-28 Hound Dog missile.

▶ **Air-to-air refuelling**
SAC also operated a large fleet of Boeing KC-135 tankers, which provided its 'anywhere in the world' capability.

▼ **Tandem seating**
The first two B-52s had a tandem two-seat cockpit unlike production aircraft, which had a side-by-side arrangement.

Nuclear deterrence ▼
B-52s eventually lost their primary role in the SAC deterrent to ICBMs. This B-52 is pictured flying over an Atlas missile in California.

▲ **Tailless but airborne**
On loan to Boeing at the time, this B-52H lost most of its 12-m (40-ft) tailfin on a low-level test flight. Amazingly, it landed safely.

FACTS AND FIGURES

▶ The second B-52 built, YB-52 serial number 49-23, was the first to fly and is now at the USAF Museum in Ohio.

▶ The prototype for the B-52 series made its first flight on 15 April 1952.

▶ B-52Ds over Vietnam carried a load equivalent to eight World War II B-17Gs.

▶ In January 1957 three B-52Bs flew nonstop around the world (a distance of 39,147 km/24,300 miles) in 45 hours and 19 minutes.

▶ The three pre-production B-52As built in 1954 cost a huge $29 million each.

▶ The 744th and last B-52 bomber entered service with SAC on 26 October 1962.

PROFILE

SAC's ultimate nuclear bomber

Boeing's B-52 Stratofortress was designed to drop atomic bombs from the stratosphere. The biggest USAF bomber of its era, the eight-engine B-52 dropped real 'nukes' during atmospheric tests in the Pacific in 1956 and 1962. For nearly four decades B-52 crews stood ready to drop nuclear bombs in anger if necessary. Indeed, until the late-1960s aircraft equipped with live nuclear weapons were maintained on airborne alert.

With the advent of surface-to-air missiles in the 1960s the

B-52 successfully shifted from high- to low-level weapon delivery, but the war in Vietnam brought a different mission – high-level tactical bombing with old-fashioned 'iron' bombs.

Built in seven production versions, the B-52 has been in service for more than 40 years and has outlived Strategic Air Command itself. Although its importance as a weapon system has been steadily downgraded, a number are expected to still be in operation at the end of the century, making it the longest-serving warplane in history.

B-52F STRATOFORTRESS

Phased out in the early-1970s, B-52Fs were the first SAC bombers to serve over Vietnam. 57-1069 of the 320th Bomb Wing flew 68 missions over Vietnam from Guam and is shown here after its return to the States.

Early production B-52s had a conventional side-by-side cockpit for the two pilots with two other crewmembers seated behind facing aft. The fifth and sixth crewmen sat on a lower level facing forward.

All B-52s except the 'H' model are powered by eight Pratt & Whitney J57 turbojets as fitted to numerous other types, like F-8 and F-100 fighters, A-3 bombers and U-2 reconnaissance aircraft.

The radome under the cockpit contains the bombing radar scanner.

The crew of a B-52 during the 1960s consisted of a pilot and co-pilot, route navigator and bombardier, defensive systems operator and tail gunner. All except the gunner were equipped with upward- or downward-firing ejector seats.

Introduced on the B-52G and later fitted to earlier aircraft was the capability to carry the AGM-28 Hound Dog nuclear surface-to-air missile. Its turbojet engine could be used by the aircraft to increase thrust on take-off. Hound Dog was phased out in the 1970s.

The tail turret on the B-52F is fitted with four 12.7-mm radar-guided machine guns. Some early models were built with a pair of 20-mm cannon instead. The ultimate 'H' model used a Vulcan 20-mm rotary cannon in this position. Tail guns were deleted from the remaining B-52s in the mid 1990s.

In an emergency the tail gunner is able to jettison the complete turret to escape. In the B-52G and H the gunner was moved from the turret to a cockpit position, firing his guns remotely.

External fuel tanks of varying sizes are fitted to most B-52s. The B-52F has two of the largest type, each holding 11,356 litres (3000 gallons). Those on the 'G' model hold a mere 2650 litres (70 gallons).

B-52s carry an enormous amount of fuel – around 147,112 litres (38,870 gallons) – in large internal tanks in the fuselage and wings. The J57-powered models also carry water tanks for the water injection system used by the engines during take-off to increase thrust.

The main undercarriage is made up of four two-wheel steerable trucks, which may be slewed in unison to allow cross-wind landings. Outriggers support the wings.

Twenty-seven RB-52Bs were built from 1955 and were able to carry a pod in the bomb-bay with four to six camera positions and/or electronic reconnaissance equipment and two operators. The 'convertible' concept was abandoned in 1956.

B-52D Stratofortress

Type: six-seat strategic bomber

Powerplant: eight 53.82-kN (12,075-lb-thrust) Pratt & Whitney J57-P-19W turbojet engines

Maximum speed: 893 km/h (554 mph) at altitude

Climb rate: 750 m/min (2460 fpm)

Combat range: 11,730 km (7275 miles)

Service ceiling: 11,600 m (38,000 ft)

Weights: empty 74,893 kg (164,765 lb); maximum 204,117 kg (449,057 lb)

Armament: four 12.7-mm (.50-cal.) machine guns in tail turret and up to 27,215 kg (59,875 lb) of bombs internally and on external racks

Dimensions:		
span	56.39 m	(184 ft 11 in)
length	47.73 m	(156 ft 7 in)
height	14.73 m	(48 ft 4 in)
wing area	371.60 m²	(3998 sq ft)

COMBAT DATA

UNIT COST

The rising cost of military aircraft was largely a result of advancing technology. The larger the order for a new aircraft, the lower the unit cost. The three experimental B-52As cost a huge $29 million each, while the mass-produced B-52Es were a 'mere' $6 million.

B-52E STRATOFORTRESS $6.00 m

B-29A SUPERFORTRESS $0.64 m

B-47E STRATOJET $1.87 m

RANGE

Interestingly, the B-47E actually had a shorter range than the World War II-vintage B-29. However, the B-47 was a much faster aircraft and could be refuelled in the air. The much larger B-52 had a considerably enhanced fuel capacity compared to the others.

B-52E STRATOFORTRESS 11,730 km (7275 miles)

B-29A SUPERFORTRESS 6600 km (4090 miles)

B-47E STRATOJET 6437 km (3990 miles)

MAXIMUM SPEED

At the end of World War II the B-29 was one of the fastest four-engined bombers. The jet age increased speeds considerably, the B-47 being able to hold its own against fighters in the early 1950s. Speed was less important by the time the B-52 was produced; range and load-carrying capacity being paramount.

B-52E STRATOFORTRESS 894 km/h (554 mph)

B-29A SUPERFORTRESS 576 km/h (357 mph)

B-47E STRATOJET 975 km/h (605 mph)

Boeing's strategic bombers

■ **B-17 FLYING FORTRESS:** Taking to the air in 1935, the B-17 was built in enormous numbers after the US entered World War II. Most of its missions took place over Europe.

■ **B-29 SUPERFORTRESS:** The B-29 was an advanced aircraft when it first flew in 1942. It was to bear the brunt of the bombing campaign over Japan; one delivered the first atomic bomb.

■ **B-50 SUPERFORTRESS:** Production of this more powerful development of the B-29 began in 1945. Although they saw action over Korea, most were converted to tankers as the KB-50.

■ **B-47 STRATOJET:** Predecessor of the B-52 and the first swept-wing jet bomber built in any numbers, the six-engined B-47 served SAC from 1951. At its peak 1,800 were in service.

BOEING

B-52G/H STRATOFORTRESS

● Strategic bomber ● Nuclear/conventional weapons ● Global reach

C onceived as the giant silver sword of the United States Air Force Strategic Air Command the B-52 Stratofortress was the biggest purely jet-powered bomber of its time, and has been flying for almost 50 years. Flown for decades on atomic alert, its only combat use has been the massive conventional bombing campaigns in Southeast Asia and the Persian Gulf.

▲ Displaying its enormous wingspan a B-52 gets airborne trailing a thick plume of smoke as its eight turbojet engines strain at full power to lift its 229,000 kg (504,859 lb) into the air.

BOEING B-52G/H STRATOFORTRESS

▲ Sting in the tail
Most versions of the B-52 had a fearsome rear defence of four '50-calibre' guns. These were aimed using the radar mounted above.

▲ Extending the range
By using inflight refuelling, the B-52 can cover any part of the globe from just a few bases. This veteran is seen on its way to Vietnam in 1972.

Modern-day warrior ▶
Two fully laden B-52Gs launch from Riyadh in Saudi Arabia for another mission against massed Iraqi armoured divisions during the Gulf War of 1991.

▲ Nuclear deterrence
The B-52 has an important role as a launch platform for nuclear missiles. Here a SRAM is launched from the massive weapons bay.

A fistful of throttles ▶
The B-52's cockpit is dominated by the central engine control panel. Every dial and lever is multiplied eightfold.

FACTS AND FIGURES

▶ The B-52 has a crew of five, including two pilots, navigator, electronic warfare officer and bombardier.

▶ Boeing manufactured 744 'Buffs' and finished the last aircraft in October 1962.

▶ A B-52 can reach any target in the world within 18 hours.

▶ During Operation Desert Storm, B-52s flew 1624 missions, and dropped 5,829,000 kg (12,850,744 lb) of bombs.

▶ Each B-52 contains 90 km (56 miles) of electrical wiring.

▶ In 1959, three B-52Bs flew nonstop around the world in under 50 hours.

B-52H Stratofortress

Type: five-seat long-range strategic bomber

Powerplant: eight 75.62-kN (17,014-lb-thrust) Pratt & Whitney TF33-P-3 turbofans

Maximum speed: 958 km/h (595 mph) at 3096 m (10,157 ft)

Range: 16,000 km (1000 miles)

Service ceiling: 16,765 m (55,000 ft)

Weights: empty 138,799 kg (30,600 lb); loaded 229,000 kg (504,859 lb)

Armament: one 20-mm M61A1 tail cannon; 81 454-kg (1000-lb) bombs, or 20 AGM-86 or AGM-129 cruise missiles, or four to six nuclear bombs

Dimensions:
span	56.39 m (176 ft 2 in)
length	49.05 m (160 ft 11 in)
height	12.40 m (40 ft 8 in)
wing area	271.60 m² (2923 sq ft)

COMBAT DATA

BOMBLOAD

The B-52H can carry a vast array of weaponry. Its load can include up to 20 nuclear cruise missiles or 81 free-fall bombs as well as anti-ship missiles or conventional cruise missiles. Designed during the Cold War, the B-52 carries its bombload over a great range and would have penetrated into the heart of the Soviet Union if necessary.

VICTOR 16,000 kg (35,274 lb)

B-52H STRATOFORTRESS 38,250 kg (84,327 lb)

Tu-95 'BEAR' 20,000 kg (44,092lb)

America's 'Big Stick'

The longest-serving front-line warplane in history, the B-52 Stratofortress was the right aircraft at the right time. It first flew on 15 April 1952 and became the backbone of the West's nuclear preparedness; had the need arisen, hundreds of B-52s would have headed for Russia to drop hydrogen bombs on key strategic targets.

The special 'Big Belly B-52D' could also carry 108 conventional bombs, and during the Vietnam War 129 B-52s, of several models, carried out the December 1972 'Christmas bombing', designed to force North Vietnam to the conference table.

Since then, the B-52 has been extensively modified. New engines and electronics have extended the life of the 'Buff' (Big Ugly Fat Fella) into the 1990s. B-52Gs flew the longest combat missions in history during Operation Desert Storm, from Louisiana to the Middle East. Today, B-52Hs have both nuclear and conventional roles.

The 'Buff' is one of the best-loved of all aircraft and can operate at high level or at very low level on terrain-avoidance under-the-radar missions.

'Buffs' can mount up to 24 340-kg (750 lb) or 454-kg (1000 lb) bombs on external wing pylons.

During both Gulf Wars B-52s pounded Iraqi targets from as far afield as England and Diego Garcia in the Indian Ocean.

The immensely strong wings of the B-52 not only support the eight engines but are also filled with fuel, giving the 'Buff' enormous range.

The B-52's wings can flex several metres up and down. Outriggers under the wingtips stop them from hitting the runway when carrying a full load of fuel and weaponry.

The radar-directed rear guns are controlled remotely by a gunner who aims via a screen in the forward cockpit.

B-52H STRATOFORTRESS

Known in the USAF as the 'Cadillac', the B-52H is significantly upgraded compared to the early Stratofortresses. With more modern turbofan engines it outperforms its predecessors in both range and payload. Built to carry nuclear-tipped ballistic missiles, it is still a vital weapon in the USAF arsenal.

On the lower level, facing forwards, are two navigators. One handles the route navigation, while the other operates the upgraded radar and weapon control systems.

The enormous bomb-bays of the B-52 can accommodate clips of a wide range of armament, ranging from 227-kg (500-lb) bombs to giant nuclear weapons.

The flight deck of the B-52 has two levels. The upper deck houses the two pilots. Behind them sit the electronic warfare officer, who handles all the countermeasures equipment, and the tail gunner, who fires by remote control.

The B-52 has a bicycle-type main undercarriage. This caters for crosswind landings and take-offs by crabbing, so that the aircraft's fuselage slews down the runway.

Launching from northern Saudi airspace, the B-52s attacked key military targets in northern Iraq, around the oil centres of Kirkuk and Mosul.

The Mediterranean flight path was chosen to avoid overflying other countries as much as possible.

The B-52s were refuelled by tankers flying from Lajes in the Azores.

The longest raid in history

On the first night of the First Gulf War, B-52Gs took off from Barksdale AFB in Louisiana, flew to northern Saudi Arabia and launched cruise missiles against Iraqi targets. They then flew all the way back to their base, having flown nonstop for more than 35 hours.

Barksdale AFB is a major Strategic Air Command facility, and is the location of the USAF 8th Air Force headquarters.

BARKSDALE AFB

BOEING

E-3 AWACS SENTRY

● Flying radar station ● Commands and controls the air battle

Boeing's E-3 Sentry is a flying radar station. This aerial headquarters patrols the skies and scans the military situation below, monitoring friendly and hostile aircraft. Inside the metal cocoon of the E-3's fuselage, technical experts work magic with radar and electronics to detect enemy warplanes, plot their course, and guide friendly fighters to shoot them down.

▲ A number of E-3 AWACS are assigned to NATO. Radar operators, communications technicians and battle analysts from each member state serve aboard each Sentry aircraft.

BOEING E-3 AWACS SENTRY

▲ **Giant radar**
This is the huge antenna for the APY-2 radar. On one side is the radar itself; on the other is the IFF equipment for detecting whether aircraft are friendly or hostile.

▲ **Flight deck**
E-3 pilots may expect to spend a good deal of time at their stations: AWACS missions often last 10 hours or more, flying basically a racetrack orbit.

▲ **Operator station**
The cabin of the E-3 is packed with consoles. From here, operators monitor air traffic on large screens which display output from the long-range radar.

▲ **Long endurance**
Inflight refuelling allows the E-3 to stay aloft for a day or more. On very long missions extra flight crew are carried to avoid over-exhaustion.

▲ **NATO's air force**
In addition to American, British and French E-3s NATO also has its own AWACS squadron, crewed by airmen from the member nations.

FACTS AND FIGURES

▶ The Boeing E-3 Sentry took to the air for the first time on 5 February 1972.

▶ Originally, the Sentry was expected to be an eight-engined aircraft.

▶ The AWACS radar can see over the horizon, detecting enemy aircraft hundreds of kilometres away.

▶ In all, 68 AWACS were built for the US, NATO, Saudi Arabia, Britain and France.

▶ The disc-shaped radar dome atop the AWACS is larger than many aircraft.

▶ The Sentry was the last version of the Boeing 707, which went out of production in 1991 after 37 years.

PROFILE

Eye in the sky

Getting the edge over the enemy by using a large aircraft for surveillance was a hot idea in 1955 when the Lockheed Super Constellation became the first Airborne Warning and Control System (AWACS). Today's E-3 is a modern AWACS aircraft which flies at jet speeds carrying up to 17 technicians who use the latest hi-tech wizardry.

To the pilots up front, the E-3 is an upscale version of the great Boeing 707, the great

and beautiful aircraft which revolutionised air travel. But to the technicians who sit out back, the E-3 AWACS is the eyes and ears of the battlefield commander, watching, analysing and directing.

During Operation Desert Storm, 30 air-to-air victories were

scored by Allied fighters who were guided into action by AWACS crews. With its long range and endurance, the E-3 AWACS can spy on an entire battlefield or, if necessary, an entire nation – as they did keeping tabs on the conflict in Bosnia.

E-3A AWACS SENTRY

Introduced into USAF service in 1977, the Sentry was selected to equip a multinational NATO unit based in Germany under Luxembourg registration. The first of 18 aircraft was delivered to the NATO Airborne Early Warning Force in 1981.

E-3s generally carry a mission crew of 16, under the overall mission commander. These include radar operators, communications specialists and weapons controllers.

AWACS has a flight deck crew of four, comprising pilot/aircraft commander, co-pilot, navigator and flight engineer.

USAF and NATO Sentries are powered by four Pratt & Whitney TF-33 turbofans. British, French and Saudi E-3s are powered by larger and more fuel-efficient CFM-56 engines.

Versions of the Sentry built for the UK, France and Saudi Arabia have much fatter and far more fuel-efficient engines than their USAF cousins.

British and French aircraft have a refuelling probe above the flight deck. The standard American boom receptacle is also retained.

The APY radar operates in various modes, including over-the-horizon, pulse-Doppler, passive and maritime.

Royal Air Force Sentries are equipped with wingtip ESM pods which house a Loral passive radar detection system.

Key to the E-3's capability is the Westinghouse AN/APY-1 or -2 radar. Its huge antenna, mounted above the fuselage, rotates six times per minute.

In order to control the air battle, AWACS is fitted with 13 HF, VHF and UHF communications links controlled by the computerized and digitized J-TIDS (Joint Tactical Information Distribution System).

Multi-mode radar control

PDNS: Pulse-Doppler Non-elevation Scan is the basic radar mode, used to measure the distance of airborne targets several hundred kilometres away.

MARITIME: Advanced signal processing systems allows AWACS to pick-out ship-sized targets amid the chaotic clutter of radar returns from the surface of the sea.

INTERLEAVED: AWACS can switch between modes several times per second. This allows the big aircraft to scan for aircraft and surface targets simultaneously.

E-3A AWACS Sentry

Type: airborne warning and control system

Powerplant: four 93.36-kN (21,000-lb-thrust) Pratt & Whitney TF-33-P-100/100A turbofans (USAF and NATO) or four 102.97-kN (23,168-lb-thrust) CFM-56 turbofans (UK, France and Saudi Arabia)

Maximum speed: 853 km/h (530 mph) at 6096 m (20,000 ft)

Normal operating speed: 563 km/h (350 mph) at 12,192 m (40,000 ft)

Endurance: six hours, flying at 12,192 m (40,000 ft) a distance of 1609 km (1000 miles) from base for a total mission time in excess of 11 hours

Service ceiling: 8850 m (29,035 ft)

Weights: empty 77,966 kg (171,996 lb); loaded 147,420 kg (325,000 lb)

Dimensions:
span	44.42 m	(145 ft 9 in)
length	46.61 m	(152 ft 11 in)
span	12.73 m	(41 ft 9 in)
wing area	283.30 m²	(3049 sq ft)

COMBAT DATA

ENDURANCE

The E-3 Sentry's exceptional endurance means that it is capable of flying unrefuelled surveillance missions lasting six hours at distances in excess of 1600 km (100 miles) from its home base.

E-2 HAWKEYE
6.25 hours

E-3 AWACS SENTRY
More than 11 hours

A-50 'MAINSTAY'
8 hours

OPERATING ALTITUDE

The Sentry has a surprisingly modest service ceiling, being bettered by the smaller propeller-driven Hawkeye. Even so, at its working operating heights above 8000 m (26,250 ft) the E-3 can 'see' for several hundred kilometres.

E-2 HAWKEYE
9000 m (29,525 ft)

E-3 AWACS SENTRY
8000 m (26,250 ft)

A-50 'MAINSTAY'
10000 m (32,680 ft)

RADAR RANGE

The Sentry's most important attribute is its amazing radar. Capable of detecting several thousand targets at extremely long range, it can also simultaneously direct and control 100 or more allied aircraft making intercepts.

E-3 AWACS SENTRY
650 km (404 miles)

E-2 HAWKEYE
550 km (342 miles)

A-50 'MAINSTAY'
350-400 km (217-249 miles) estimated

BOEING

E-3D/F SENTRY

● Airborne Early Warning (AEW) ● Improved systems ● Fighter control

▶ Both the British and French air arms received a significant boost to their capabilities with the introduction of the Sentry. All the aircraft see intensive operations.

After trying to develop an airborne early warning version of the Nimrod maritime reconnaissance aircraft, the UK finally gave up in 1986 and decided to buy a version of the Boeing E-3 instead. France followed suit. Deliveries of seven E-3Ds for the UK and four E-3Fs for France, were completed in May 1992. These aircraft are operated in conjunction with the E-3A Sentrys of the multinational NATO AEW Force (NAEWF).

BOEING E-3D/F SENTRY

▶ Eighty year Sentry
During 1995, No. 8 Squadron, RAF, applied special markings to one of its aircraft, in honour of the unit's 80th anniversary. A second Sentry squadron has since been formed.

Night ops ▶
Such is the importance of the Sentry's mission, that operations are flown around the clock.

707 lineage ▶
Even though it is a thoroughly modern, high-technology aircraft, the Sentry still has the unmistakable lines of the Boeing 707. France and the UK specified CFM56 engines which give more power and lower fuel consumption, but require larger nacelles than those of NATO E-3s.

▲ Waddington home
RAF Waddington is the base for RAF Sentry AEW.Mk 1s. The colours of No. 8 Squadron are worn on the port side, those of No. 23 to starboard.

▲ Extended endurance
In-flight refuelling is able to extend the E-3D/F's endurance to the limits of crew fatigue. Hose and drogue-equipped RAF VC10s or Tristars are the most likely tankers for the Sentry AEW.Mk 1.

▼ French visitor
French E-3Fs are frequent visitors to Waddington, as are NAEWF E-3As, as seen to the rear.

FACTS AND FIGURES

▶ Britain originally ordered only six Sentrys, but later exercised an option on a seventh aircraft.

▶ RAF Sentrys began constant patrols over Bosnia in November 1992.

▶ Maritime surveillance is an important secondary role for RAF E-3Ds.

▶ France ordered three E-3Fs, confirmed an option on a fourth, but cancelled options for its fifth and sixth Sentrys.

▶ Britain ordered its first six aircraft in December 1986.

▶ Initial French orders were placed in February 1987.

PROFILE

Anglo-French Sentry service

Compared to the original E-3A, both the RAF's E-3D Sentry AEW.Mk 1 and the French air force's E-3F are powered by quieter, more powerful and more fuel-efficient CFM56 turbofans. Mission systems have also been upgraded, with expanded computer memory and processing, colour displays to reduce operator workload and fatigue, and better jam-resistant radios. The RAF aircraft also have wingtip pods for integrated electronic warfare systems. These allow the E-3D's electronic support measures (ESM) equipment to detect and classify any target which is using a radar. Both the E-3D and the E-3F are fitted with

refuelling probes for use with hose-equipped tankers as well as the standard receptacle for USAF-style booms.

The aircraft are flown by a crew of two pilots, an engineer and a navigator. They also carry a communications operator and three technicians trained to test, operate and carry out limited airborne maintenance of the communications, computer and radar systems.

The main cabin houses nine mission specialists. The tactical director is in overall charge of the three fighter intercept controllers, three surveillance operators, a data link manager and an ESM systems operator.

In-flight refuelling probes are fitted to the E-3D and E-3F, allowing compatibility with the RAF's tanker fleet. The USAF-style refuelling receptacle is retained, however, giving added operational flexibility.

SENTRY AEW.MK 1

All seven RAF aircraft are pooled between two squadrons. No. 8 Squadron was the original unit and was joined by No. 23 Squadron on 1 April 1996, giving the Sentry fleet much greater manpower.

Commitments to Bosnia, Operation 'Warden' over Northern Iraq and constant exercises, mean that the E-3D fleet is stretched to the limit.

An array of high-lift devices, including leading-edge slats, trailing-edge flaps and over-wing spoilers are retained by the E-3 from its airliner origins.

For most missions a crew of 17 is carried. The work of the systems operators is very intense and demanding, with each person managing a bewilderingly large amount of data.

All RAF aircraft feature distinctive wingtip fairings which house Loral 1017 'Yellow Gate' ESM equipment. These sensors allow passive detection of enemy radar transmissions and are not fitted to E-3Fs.

Measuring 1.83 m (6 ft) in depth and 9.14 m (30 ft) in diameter, the rotodome houses the antenna array of the Westinghouse APY-2 radar. It rotates at six revolutions per minute when the radar is in use.

Modifications to the airframe of the basic 707 airliner are few. The most obvious are the large rotodome support struts and the lack of cabin windows.

CFM56 engines give the E-3D/F improved performance. With their bulbous cowlings, the engines are carried much closer to the ground than those of earlier Sentry variants. RAF aircraft have provision for two underwing hardpoints, which are apparently not used.

E-3D Sentry AEW.Mk 1

Type: airborne early warning and control and communications aircraft

Powerplant: four 106.8-kN (24,030-lb-thrust) CFM International CFM56-2A2 turbofans

Maximum speed: 853 km/h (530 mph) at 10,973 m (36,000 ft)

Endurance: more than 11 hours unrefuelled, or six hours on station at 1609 km (1000 miles) from base

Service ceiling: 12,192 m (40,000 ft)

Weights: empty 77,213 kg (170,256 lb); maximum take-off 147,417 kg (32,500 lb)

Accommodation: usual crew of 17, consisting of a flight crew of four, four support and nine mission crew members

Dimensions:
span	44.42 m (145 ft 9 in)
length	46.61 m (152 ft 11 in)
height	13.00 m (42 ft 8 in)
wing area	268.67 m² (2892 sq ft)

COMBAT DATA

TOTAL THRUST

With its extra thrust, the Sentry AEW.Mk 1 has better performance than the E-3Cs of the US Air Force. This allows hot-and-high missions to be flown with greater safety. Beriev's A-50 'Mainstay' has greater power still and is able to reach higher altitudes. This gives its radar the potential for increased range, but it is likely to be considerably inferior to its Western equivalents.

SENTRY AEW.Mk 1
427.2 kN (96,120 lb thrust)

E-3C SENTRY
373.6 kN (84,060 lb thrust)

A-50 'MAINSTAY'
470.7 kN (105,908 lb thrust)

Post-war British and French Boeings

■ **B-17 FLYING FORTRESS:** Free French forces were presented with a single B-17F, which served as a transport after the war.

■ **C-135F STRATOTANKER:** Delivered to KC-135A standard, surviving French C-135s have been re-engined as C-135FRs.

■ **WASHINGTON B.Mk 1:** Some 88 B-29s and B-29As were delivered to the RAF as Washingtons. They served from 1950-58.

■ **CHINOOK:** A modernisation programme and orders for new aircraft, have bolstered the strength of the RAF's Chinook fleet.

BOEING
E-4

- Airborne command post ● Four built ● Based on the 747 airliner

K nown as the AABNCPs (Advanced Airborne National Command Posts), or National Command Airborne Command Posts (NEACPs or 'Kneecaps'), the E-4 'Doomsday Planes' were always associated with the prospect of nuclear attack during the Cold War. The four USAF E-4Bs continue to provide an aerial command centre for US leaders in the event of not only nuclear war, but any major conflict or crisis.

▲ Boeing received its first E-4 contract in 1973, and delivered the first aircraft the following year after an internal refit by E-Systems. The first upgraded E-4B was redelivered in 1980.

BOEING E-4

▼ Continuing role
Despite the end of the Cold War, the E-4 has a continuing role during national emergencies.

▲ Communications gear
In terms of its communications systems, the E-4B is the world's best-equipped aircraft. Thirteen external communications systems, covering seven wavebands, use power from a 1200-kVA electrical system powered by an engine-driven generator.

▼ 'Air Force One'
The most recent 747s delivered to the USAF were two VC-25A Presidential transports based on Boeing's 747-200B airliner. The callsign 'Air Force One' is used when the President is aboard.

▲ Advanced technology
The E-4B's highly advanced range of communications systems are optimised for maximum reliability.

▲ Maximum endurance by IFR
The E-4s have in-flight refuelling capability via a receptacle above the nose of the aircraft.

FACTS AND FIGURES

▼ Four E-4Bs belong to the 1st Air Command and Control Squadron of the 55th Wing at Offutt AFB, Nebraska.

▼ E-4s are limited to 72 hours' endurance by their engines' lubricating oil capacity.

▼ The E-4 made its first flight without mission equipment on 13 June 1973.

▼ Including the VC-25s, the USAF operates six 747s; plans to buy ex-airline 747s for the National Guard were cancelled.

▼ Originally, the airborne command post requirement called for six E-4s.

▼ The E-4's systems are held in 1,613 'black boxes' – three times the number in an E-3.

PROFILE

Presidential 'Doomsday Plane'

U ntil recently an E-4 was kept on alert at Andrews Air Force Base, Maryland – a short helicopter journey from the White House. In the event of an attack on the United States, the President and his staff would have boarded the E-4 to direct American forces from the comparative safety of the air.

The E-4 uses the familiar Boeing 747 airliner's fuselage to accommodate the President (in his role as Commander-in-Chief of US forces) and key members of his battle staff. They reside in the flying equivalent of the White House's Situation Room. This 'war readiness aircraft'

is equipped with nuclear thermal shielding, protection against EMP (electromagnetic pulse) and a large variety of communications systems, covering seven wavebands from super-high to very-low frequency. If necessary, the aircraft can broadcast to the US population over the national radio network or link up to commercial telephone networks to send emergency messages.

Initially, the E-4As of the mid-1970s used equipment from

EC-135J Project 'Looking Glass' command post aircraft. But when the current E-4B entered service in 1980 it had considerably more equipment, including SHF (super-high frequency) satellite communications gear in a distinctive dorsal blister. The result was a command post and flying 'situation room' aircraft.

Although the Cold War has ended, the E-4 remains available for deployment worldwide in times of crisis.

Right: Three of the four E-4Bs were delivered as E-4As, without the dorsal antenna.

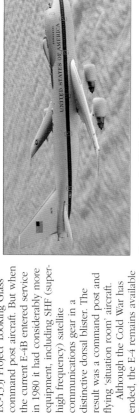

Above: Whenever the US President travels abroad, an aircraft from the E-4 fleet accompanies 'Air Force One' at a discreet distance in case an emergency situation arises.

E-4B

73-1676 was one of three E-4As delivered in the mid-1970s and was upgraded shortly after delivery to E-4B standard. All equip the 1st Air Command and Control Squadron, based at Offutt Air Force Base, Nebraska.

The E-4B carries two flight crews on potentially long missions, each consisting of an aircraft commander (pilot), co-pilot, navigator and flight engineer. A special navigation station and crew rest area are provided on the upper deck, behind the cockpit.

The most obvious external identification feature of the E-4B is the dorsal fairing on top of the forward fuselage. This contains the satellite/super-high frequency (SHF) antenna. The aircraft has nuclear thermal shielding and protection against EMP weapons.

E-4Bs are powered by four General Electric CF6 turbofans (military designation F103); The first two aircraft were delivered with Pratt & Whitney JT9Ds (F105s).

The main deck is divided between a flight crew section and four operating compartments for the President and his battle staff. These are the NCA (National Command Authority) area (similar in role to the White House Situation Room), conference room, battle staff area and C³I (command, control, communications and intelligence) area.

When the Boeing 747 was selected to fill the SS-481B Support System requirement in 1973, it was chosen because of its size and the fact that it was an 'off-the-shelf' design. Airframe costs were therefore kept to a minimum. The E-4s are painted in this all-over anti-flash white finish.

One of the 46 external antennas is an 8-km long, retractable very-low frequency (VLF) aerial trailing behind the aircraft. VLF is used to communicate with submerged submarines.

E-4B

Type: national emergency airborne command post (NEACP)

Powerplant: four 233.53-kN (52,544-lb-thrust) General Electric F103-PW-100 (CF6-50-E2) turbofans

Cruising speed: (typical) 933 km/h (580 mph) at 6096 m (20,000 ft)

Endurance: 12 hours (without in-flight refuelling); 72 hours (with in-flight refuelling)

Ferry range: 12,600 km (7829 miles)

Cruise ceiling: 13,715 m (45,000 ft)

Weights: maximum take-off 362,874 kg (800,000 lb)

Accommodation: two flight crews, each of four plus; total accommodation for 94 crewmembers, including a battle staff of 30

Dimensions:
span	59.64 m (195 ft 8 in)
length	70.51 m (231 ft 4 in)
height	19.33 m (63 ft 5 in)
wing area	510.95 m² (1676 sq ft)

EARLY COMMAND POSTS

BOEING EC-135C/J: E-4s replaced various versions of the EC-135 (itself based on the KC-135B tanker), which had performed the Project 'Looking Glass' task since 1961. 'Looking Glass' was the Strategic Air Command's (SAC) commitment to have a command post in the air at all times to direct SAC's manned and ballistic missile assets in time of war.

In times of crisis

THE PRESIDENT AND THE NCA: If the US was attacked, some leaders would be taken to the underground command centre in Virginia, while others, including the President, would board an E-4B in order to direct American forces. A National Command Authority (NCA) would coordinate the army, navy and air force.

72 HOURS' ENDURANCE: The E-4 can remain airborne for three days and nights, refuelled by USAF tankers. The key to its capability is the extensive array of communications systems fitted, covering seven wavelengths.

EMP AND NUCLEAR SHIELDING: In order to perform its role as a communications centre, the E-4 is protected against nuclear thermal damage and electromagnetic pulse weapons.

E-6 MERCURY

- Global mission ● Submarine communications ● Last of the 707s

M aintaining communication links with American missile submarines at sea is the unique job of the Boeing E-6 Mercury. The E-6, formerly the 'Hermes', was the final version of the Boeing 707 off the production line in Renton, Washington. The 707 airframe, originally designed in the 1950s, encloses the hi-tech comms system known as TACAMO (Take Charge and Move Out).

▲ Equipped with the latest communications systems, the E-6 Mercury will remain a vital component in the US chain of command well into the next century. A crew of 18 operators is required to control the systems.

BOEING E-6 MERCURY

▲ Mercury roll-out
An admiring crowd gives scale to the first production E-6, showing the huge size of this special communications aircraft.

▲ On the flightdeck
Cockpit systems are similar to those of the standard 707, except for the F108-CF-100 engine controls and the highly accurate navigation equipment. Air-refuelled missions may last up to 72 hours, and a relief aircrew is carried for these extended flights.

▲ Communicating from Mercury
Relief systems operators may also be accommodated, since the E-6 has eight bunks. An area is also set aside for the in-flight repair of faulty systems.

▲ Winging through the clouds
Missions are carried out at high altitude and over long ranges. The CFM engines are more powerful than the similar units fitted to the E-3 Sentry.

Wingtip sensor array ▶
High-frequency communication probes are fixed under the wing, and the wingtips are fitted with pods containing ultra-high frequency satellite receivers.

FACTS AND FIGURES

▶ The maiden flight of the series prototype aircraft took place on 19 February 1987; the aircraft have seen combat.

▶ On 2 August 1989 the first operational E-6 Mercury entered service.

▶ Two squadrons, each with eight E-6s, are operated by the US Navy.

▶ The E-6 carries extra bunks for relief crewmembers because of its long endurance flights of up to 72 hours.

▶ Boeing manufactured 18 E-6s for service with the US Navy.

▶ Training for Mercury pilots is carried out in Waco, Texas, by civilian contractors.

E-6A Mercury

Type: strategic communications aircraft

Powerplant: four 106.76-kN (24,021-lb-thrust) CFM International F108-CF-100 (CFM56-2A-2) turbofan engines

Maximum speed: 981 km/h (608 mph)

Maximum cruising speed: 842 km/h (522 mph)

Range: 11,760 km (7291 miles)

Service ceiling: 12,800 m (42,000 ft)

Weights: empty 78,378 kg (172,431 lb); maximum take-off 155,128 kg (341,281 lb)

Dimensions:
span	45.16 m (148 ft 2 in)
length	46.61 m (152 ft 11 in)
height	12.93 m (42 ft 5 in)
wing area	283.35 m² (3049 sq ft)

Above: Just visible at the extreme rear of this E-6's fuselage is the orange tip of the VLF trailing wire antennas. A tight orbit is flown to keep the wires vertical during use.

62782

Very low-frequency (VLF) trailing wire aerials are stowed in the rear fuselage. One retracts into the tailcone while the other is stored within the rear fuselage.

COMBAT DATA

RANGE

Aircraft of this type are often required to fly long distances on detachment to various parts of the world. Once there, they use air-to-air refuelling to stay airborne for long periods.

E-4B
12,600 km
(7812 miles)

E-6A MERCURY
11,760 km
(7291 miles)

Tu-142MR 'BEAR-J'
6400 km
(3968 miles)

PROFILE

Co-ordinating the submarine fleet

For several years the US Navy used the EC-130Q Hercules in the TACAMO role, which maintains low-frequency communications between American commanders and their nuclear submarines. However, a more modern aircraft, especially one that could provide extra space and improved crew comfort, was required as a replacement for the ageing Hercules. Navy experts decided that the Boeing 707-320 airliner offered the most suitable basis for the new aircraft, and issued a contract in 1983.

The 707 airframe, from which the E-6 was developed, provided maximum commonality with the E-3 Sentry AWACS (Airborne Warning and Communications System) aircraft, for ease of servicing. The huge CFM56 engines, chosen because of their outstanding fuel efficiency, resulted in ultra-long endurance while on patrol. In fact, since it can be refuelled aloft, the endurance of the Mercury is limited only by its engine oil capacity.

To communicate with submarines, the Mercury uses two trailing wire antennas which are hardened against the effects of nuclear blast and are deployed from its tailcone (1220 m/4000 ft long) and underfuselage (7925 m/26,000 ft long). When the aircraft flies a tight orbit these antennas hang vertically down and allow communications to be transmitted

to submarines towing their own aerial array.

After defence cuts in the 1990s, and as the threat of nuclear war becomes increasingly unlikely, the Navy has more E-6s than it needs and may assign some of them to secondary duties such as training or transport.

Above: Departing Renton for the short flight to Boeing Field in Seattle, the US Navy's first Mercury flew in 1987. The first two operational aircraft flew into NAS Barbers Point, Hawaii in August 1989 to serve with VQ-3 squadron in the Pacific theatre.

E-6A MERCURY

Some US Navy E-6s have been seen in this grey and white colour scheme, but most operational aircraft are painted an overall white. All Mercurys carry minimum markings.

Five communications stations are situated in the fuselage above the wing. A vast array of radio equipment is carried, including secure voice communications, which even allow secure communication between crew members via the intercom.

In addition to the satellite communications downlink equipment, the wingtip pods also contain electronic support measures systems.

Efficiency and reliability were the main factors behind the choice of CFM International engines. Internal fuel capacity is an enormous 70308 kg (154,678 lb), enough for a 10½-hour mission at 1850 km (1150 miles) from base.

NAVY

The crew rest areas, with bunks, galley and a toilet, are housed in the forward section of the fuselage. Such amenities are vital if the crew is to remain efficient on missions of up to three days.

A flight crew of four is standard, and they are the only crewmembers who have an outside view. The fuselage has no windows, apart from tiny portholes in the emergency escape doors.

Airborne relay station

TALKING TO SUBS: The E-6 is primarily tasked with providing communication links with the US Navy's ballistic missile-firing submarine fleet in a post-nuclear strike environment.

SECONDARY ROLE: As well as the wartime submarine communications role, the E-6 fleet has a secondary task of providing back-up VLF communications in parts of the world out of the range of ground-based transmitters.

RELAYING MESSAGES: Supported by the USAF's KC-135 tanker fleet, the Mercury can relay communications between ground stations, satellites, an E-4 command post aircraft and the submerged submarine fleet.

BOEING/GRUMMAN

E-8 J-STARS

- Stand-off surveillance ● Battlefield intelligence ● Gulf War veteran

Grumman's E-8 is a command post in the sky, able to detect, locate, track and classify enemy ground formations at long range. Flying for 12 hours at a time near the battlefield, this modified Boeing 707 uses Joint STARS (Surveillance Target Attack Radar System) to watch events unfold and to gather data. Rushed into service in the First Gulf War, the contribution made by the E-8 was enormous.

▲ Seventeen mission crew-members operate consoles displaying colour-coded images of enemy terrain and vehicles. A mission crew commander is usually a lieutenant colonel or colonel.

BOEING/GRUMMAN E-8 J-STARS

▲ Tested in action
The two E-8A prototypes saw active service in the First Gulf War despite still being only part-way through their test programme. Production E-8Cs have improved avionics.

▲ Gulf War operations
In the Gulf the two E-8A prototypes were flown by the 4411th Joint STARS Squadron and were useful in locating 'Scud' missile sites.

▲ Production deliveries
Production E-8C serial number 90-0175 is one of a fleet of E-8s ordered by the USAF/US Army.

▼ Ground Station
The US Army truck-mounted Ground Station Module relays data from J-STARS to tactical operations centres on the ground for use by Army commanders.

▲ Fighter escorts
With no weapons or defensive systems, E-8 J-STARS are usually escorted by F-15 Eagles on HVACAP (high-value asset combat air patrol) during a mission.

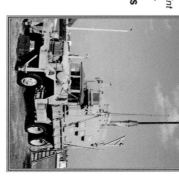

FACTS AND FIGURES

▶ USAF plans call for Joint STARS aircraft to be assigned to the 93rd Airborne Surveillance Control Wing at Robins AFB.

▶ The first production E-8 (the third ship, an E-8C) appeared on 22 March 1996.

▶ An eight-hour sortie can cover one million square kilometres (385,000 sq miles).

▶ The first two E-8s were not modified to receive air-to-air refuelling, though later aircraft will be equipped for this.

▶ The two Desert Storm E-8s flew 54 missions and logged 535 flight hours.

▶ One E-8B airframe was delivered before the cheaper E-8C version was chosen.

PROFILE

Army eyes over the battlefield

Although still being developed, two E-8 Joint STARS aircraft were rushed to Riyadh, Saudi Arabia, in 1990. Their job was to provide Operation Desert Storm commanders with a 'real-time' method of tracking the enemy's armour and other military vehicles.

The sophisticated SLAR (side-looking airborne radar) aboard this converted Boeing 707 airliner is able to distinguish even stationary objects on the ground over a distance of 250 km (155 miles), giving military

leaders an unprecedented ability to follow the enemy's every move on the battlefield.

E-8 development began in the late 1980s when advances in radar technology made it possible to design this 'air-to-ground' equivalent of the already proven E-3 AWACS (Airborne Warning and Command System) 'air-to-air' command centre.

Operated jointly by the USAF and US Army, improved versions of this Grumman-modified airframe have also been on duty over the Balkans

on behalf of United Nations forces. Cruising at 800 km/h, the E-8 Joint STARS aircraft maintain continuous C³I (command, control, communications and intelligence) operations monitoring hundreds of ground targets at a time.

The USAF and US Army have a requirement for 20 E-8Cs. Whether all these aircraft will be funded remains to be seen. One factor in the progress of the conversion programme has been the availability of suitable secondhand 707 airframes.

E-8A J-STARS

N8411 was the second E-8A airframe and was allocated the military serial number 86-0417. Production machines are designated E-8C and are converted from Boeing 707 ex-airliners.

E-8As carried a flight crew of four: a pilot, co-pilot, flight engineer and navigator/self-defence suite operator.

E-8A J-STARS

Type: multi-crew battlefield command and control aircraft

Powerplant: four 84.53-kN (19,019-lb-thrust) Pratt & Whitney JT3D-7 turbofan engines

Maximum cruising speed: 973 km/h (605 mph) at 7620 m (25,000 ft)

Endurance: 11 hours, or 20 hours with one inflight refuelling

Range: 9266 km (5758 miles)

Service ceiling: 12,800 m (42,000 ft)

Weights: maximum take-off 151,315 kg (333,592 lb)

Accommodation: pilot, co-pilot, flight engineer, navigator, plus 10 mission crewmembers

Dimensions:
span	44.42 m	(145 ft 9 in)
length	46.61 m	(152 ft 11 in)
height	12.93 m	(42 ft 5 in)
wing area	283.35 m²	(3050 sq ft)

The E-8 airframe is that of the Boeing 707-320C, the final version of the famous airliner. These lack the ventral fin of earlier models.

E-8Bs were to be powered by new GE/SNECMA F108 turbofan engines, as fitted to re-engined KC-135R tanker aircraft. However, efforts to cut costs have resulted in the E-8C with rebuilt TF33 engines.

The plan to use newly constructed Boeing 707-320C airframes for the production E-8B was changed on cost grounds; converted airliners are being used instead, the result being the E-8C.

The teardrop fairing known as the 'fiddle' was only fitted to E-8As. It contained the Flight Test Data Link used over long distances during Desert Storm to convey information to central command in Riyadh.

E-8As carried ten operator consoles. E-8Cs have 17 consoles and one dedicated to defensive electronics. The standard mission crew is 21, but this can be increased to 34 for longer missions.

The 7.93-metre 'canoe' fairing below the fuselage contains the Norden synthetic aperture radar that forms the heart of the J-STARS system.

COMBAT DATA

MISSION ENDURANCE

The E-8 can stay aloft for 11 hours before needing to refuel using the standard USAF air-to-air refuelling system. Flights of up to 72 hours' duration are possible, onboard supplies and crew fatigue being the governing factors. All three types are also capable of air-to-air refuelling.

E-8 J-STARS 11 hours	**E-6 MERCURY** 10½ hours	**E-4** 12 hours

---

J-STARS surveillance

QUICK DEPLOYMENT: Based in Riyadh, the E-8's deployment proved invaluable during Desert Storm. The Norden radar set is able to cover an area of 50,000 km² (19,300 sq miles).

TARGETS: Flying 54 missions, the E-8s targeted oil facilities, assembly areas, missile sites, tanks and other vehicles. Data was passed on to air forces which had been assigned an attack role.

GROUND STATION MODULE: The US Army's GSM receives relayed information from the J-STARS about the enemy's movements and passes this on to ground forces.

74

BOEING HELICOPTERS

CH-47 CHINOOK

- Tactical airlift ● Twin-rotor helicopter ● Heavy lifter

From Vietnam to the Gulf War, the Boeing Chinook has been the most successful Western tactical medium-/heavylift helicopter. Fast, massively powerful and with a large rear loading ramp and long interior, the Chinook takes loads that other helicopters cannot: it can transport heavy guns, light vehicles and even other helicopters. Now uprated with better engines and new avionics as the CH-47D, the Chinook remains in production over 30 years after it first flew, and remains unbeatable.

▲ The Chinook is an extremely capable helicopter. If a new variant is produced to replace the CH-47D, the Chinook will still be around 50 years after its introduction in 1962.

BOEING HELICOPTERS CH-47 CHINOOK

▼ **Trucking flight**
The first Chinook (CH-47A) had only a single cargo hook, but the modern versions have three, allowing safer carriage of heavy loads like this five-tonne truck.

▲ **Ladder climb**
The large rear door is very useful for special forces insertion techniques, using ropes or ladders to land troops.

▲ **Battle wagon** ▼
Transporting troops and their gear to the front is the Chinook's main role. The twin-rotor layout has the advantage of not needing a vulnerable tail rotor and allows a long cabin section.

▲ **Huey rescue**
In Vietnam the Chinook was one of the few machines capable of lifting downed aircraft. The wrecked Huey's rotor blades have been tied to stop them rotating in the wind.

▼ **Oil rig support**
With its large capacity and range, civil versions of the Chinook were very useful heli-liners in offshore locations like the North Sea. One Chinook was lost in a ditching incident in 1984 after the gearbox failed in flight.

FACTS AND FIGURES

▶ In the Falklands War in 1982, a British Chinook carried 82 paratroopers in a single lift and survived a minor crash.

▶ The MH-47E is a special operations version, with night-flying capability.

▶ A Chinook pilot was killed in the Gulf War after flying into a tower.

▶ The new CH-47D has triple hooks, night goggle-compatible cockpit, advanced rotors and improved crash protection.

▶ The lower fuselage is completely sealed to allow emergency ditching in water.

▶ RAF Chinooks inserted teams of SAS commandos into Iraq in the Gulf War.

PROFILE

Boeing's twin-rotor heavy helicopter

Designed to meet a US Army requirement for a heavylift helicopter, the CH-47 Chinook first flew in 1962. It remains one of the few helicopters to successfully use the 'twin-rotor' layout. Each engine can drive both rotors if one fails, and a synchronisation unit keeps the intermeshing rotors clear of each other.

Vietnam proved that the Chinook was a superb performer. It could lift artillery pieces, trucks, fuel bladders and even shot-down UH-1 Hueys, as well as performing routine troop lifts and medevac missions.

Good though it was, the war showed that it could be improved, and many foreign buyers specified new equipment, including pressure refuelling and improved crash

resistance. The US Army ordered an upgrade of its fleet in the 1980s to CH-47D standard, and also ordered the highly sophisticated MH-47E for special forces operations. These are equipped with Stinger missiles, laser and missile warning kit, inertial navigation

systems and an air-to-air refuelling probe. Chinooks were widely exported, and are operated by several nations including Argentina (which lost some in the Falklands War), Australia, Egypt, Iran, Italy, Japan, Libya and Taiwan.

CH-47C CHINOOK

The Royal Moroccan air force received 12 CH-47Cs built by Meridionali in Italy. The Chinook is also operated in North Africa by Libya and Egypt.

The crew consists of a pilot and co-pilot with full dual controls, and a loadmaster in the rear compartment.

The CH-47D has glass fibre rotors in place of the original metal ones. The projected future Chinook will have even more advanced 'swept-tip' blades, possibly of carbon-fibre composite construction.

A flexibly mounted machine gun can be fitted to the small starboard door for the loadmaster to give covering fire when operating in hostile landing zones.

The CH-47's maximum payload of more than 10 tonnes can be slung from one, two or three cargo hooks beneath the fuselage.

Fuel is carried in the long bulged fairings along the fuselage sides.

Fifty-five equipped troops or 24 litters can be accommodated in the main cabin. Small vehicles can also be carried inside the main fuselage.

The Lycoming T-55 turboprop is powerful and reliable. It is likely to be replaced by an engine in the 3500-kW (4690-hp) class if an advanced future Chinook is built.

The rear pylon carries both engines and the gearbox synchronisation unit. Chaff and flare dispensers and infra-red jammers can be mounted on the pylon.

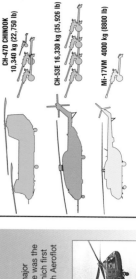

Below: Chinooks can carry armament like these rocket pods, but the best defence is speed and low-level flight.

Above: Helikopter Service is one of many North Sea operators who value the Chinook for its range and capacity, although its large size prevents it using small heli-decks.

CH-47D Chinook

Type: medium-/heavylift battlefield helicopter

Powerplant: two 3264-kW (4372-hp) Textron Lycoming T55-L-712 SSB turboshafts

Maximum speed: 298 km/h (185 mph) at sea level

Maximum cruising speed: 256 km/h (159 mph)

Combat radius: 190 km (118 miles) with maximum internal load; 60 km (37 miles) with maximum external load

Service ceiling: 6735 m (22,091 ft)

Weights: empty 10,151 kg (22,332 lb); maximum take-off 22,679 kg (49,894 lb)

Payload: internal 6300 kg (13,860 lb); external 10,340 kg (22,750 lb)

Dimensions: rotor diameter 30.14 m (99 ft)
fuselage length 15.54 m (51 ft)
height 5.77 m (19 ft)
rotor disc area 525.34 m² (5653 sq ft)

COMBAT DATA

CARGO CAPACITY

The Chinook is only beaten in the West by the even larger CH-53E, which has three engines. The Chinook can carry the same number of troops, thanks to its cabin shape. The Russian Mil Mi-17VM, a modified version of the Mi-8, is much smaller than these two helicopters, although other Russian helicopters dwarf the Chinook; the Mi-26, for example, can carry a C-130 Hercules.

CH-47D CHINOOK
10,340 kg (22,750 lb)

CH-53E 16,330 kg (35,926 lb)

Mi-17VM 4000 kg (8800 lb)

Twin-rotor helicopters

■ **BOEING VERTOL:** Piasecki became Vertol, which was taken over by Boeing. The highly successful CH-46 Sea Knight is still in service with the US Navy and US Marine Corps.

■ **BRISTOL:** The slender Bristol Belvedere was developed from the Bristol 173, Britain's first multi-engine helicopter, and served in the UK, the Middle East and the Far East.

■ **FOCKE-ACHGELIS:** The first practical twin-rotor helicopter was the Focke-Achgelis Fa 223 Drache, which was used operationally in the last years of World War II.

■ **PIASECKI:** Twin rotors were a trademark of the Piasecki company, and their naval HUP Retriever and military H-21 'Flying Banana' saw service in the 1950s and 1960s.

■ **YAKOVLEV:** The only major Soviet helicopter of this type was the Yakovlev Yak-24 'Horse', which first flew in 1955 and served with Aeroflot and the Soviet military.

BOEING HELICOPTERS

MH-47E CHINOOK

● Special operations ● In-flight refuelling ● Amphibious

▲ Designed to operate behind enemy lines, the MH-47 is packed with fire power in the form of two window-mounted machine guns, and Stinger air-to-air missiles.

With the Boeing MH-47E, the US Army enhanced its ability to carry out secret missions deep in enemy territory at night and in foul weather. The dark, dangerous-looking MH-47E is today's special operations version of the much-admired Chinook of the Vietnam era. With high-tech terrain-following radar and an infra-red sensor, the MH-47E is the trump card of the US Army's famous 'Night Stalkers'.

▼ All weather
The MH-47 cockpit is fully compatible with night vision goggle (NVG) systems.

▲ Weekend warriors
Smaller saddle tanks identify this as an early MH-47D operating with an Oklahoma unit of the Army National Guard.

Missile attack ▼
The avoidance of enemy missiles relies on low flying and a series of chaff dispensers situated on each side of the fuselage.

▼ Night vision
Situated in the nose is an AAQ-16 forward-looking infra-red (FLIR) turret, which is essential for low-level night operations.

▲ Special Ops kit
The MH-47E features numerous additions to the standard model CH-47, including radar, an in-flight refuelling probe, a complete set of defensive modifications and additional fuel tanks.

FACTS AND FIGURES

▶ Fifty-one MH-47Es are in production; all will be operated by the Special Operations Aviation Regiment.

▶ Operational equipment includes terrain-following and mapping radar.

▶ The contract for development of the MH-47E was awarded to Boeing in 1987.

▶ Missions include global clandestine, long-range airlift infiltration/exfiltration into hostile territory.

▶ A platoon of Rangers can be airlifted in one mission.

▶ The Chinook can be completely refuelled in less than 4 minutes.

PROFILE

Special Forces hauler

The special operations MH-47E can quickly be distinguished from other Chinooks by the air-refuelling probe extending from its nose. Other vital changes in the MH-47E lie beneath the skin – the latest avionics allow this clandestine warrior to fly behind enemy lines at night and in almost any adverse weather conditions.

According to US Army experts, the primary objective of the MH-47 is to give a 90 per cent probability of successfully completing a five-hour, deep-penetration, clandestine mission over a 560-km (350-mile) radius. Special Operations Forces (SOF), including the Army's elite 160th 'Night Stalkers', routinely train

for agent drops, counter-terrorist work, combat rescue, and sabotage. The capabilities of the MH-47E make these difficult jobs much easier.

Operating with specialised Hercules refuelling aircraft, the transfer of fuel – although difficult – can be accomplished in under four minutes in all weathers, thereby extending the striking reach of the SOF raiders.

Although in service with the US Army, Chinooks often support Navy SEAL special forces. The MH-47E is the only remaining American military helicopter that is capable of landing on water to launch or recover SEAL teams.

Below: This MH-47E is seen during maintenance. The type has proved to be very reliable and looks set to equip special operations units into the next century.

Above: The main transport assets of the SOF are seen here: a Chinook taking off on an exercise with an accompanying CH-53E.

Establishment of forward arming and refuelling points is another role assigned to the MH-47, for which three 3028-litre (800-gallon) fuel tanks are carried internally; these are known as 'fat cow' operations.

MH-47E Chinook

Type: Special Forces support helicopter

Powerplant: two Textron Lycoming T55-I-714 turboshaft engines

Maximum speed: 285 km/h (177 mph) at sea level

Maximum cruising speed: 259 km/h (161 mph) at sea level

Endurance: 5 hr 30 min

Combat radius: 560 km (350 miles)

Range: ferrying 2224 km (1380 miles); typical 1136 km (704 miles)

Weights: empty 12,210 kg (26,862 lb); maximum take-off 24,494 kg (53,887 lb)

Armament: two 12.7-mm (.50-cal.) machine guns; Stinger air-to-air missiles

Dimensions: rotor diameter   18.28 m (60 ft)
length   15.87 m (52 ft 1 in)
height   5.59 m (18 ft 4 in)
rotor area   282.60 m² (3041 sq ft)

COMBAT DATA

MAXIMUM SPEED

The twin-rotor design of the CH-47 means it will never have the performance to match others in its class, although this is more than compensated for by the operational equipment.

MH-47E CHINOOK	285 km/h (177 mph)
CH-47D CHINOOK	298 km/h (185 mph)
MH-53J PAVE LOW III ENHANCED	315 km/h (195 mph)

HOVERING CEILING

The extra equipment needed by the Special Operations Forces has meant that the MH-47E's performance is reduced when compared to cargo versions. The larger MH-53J is used where longer range is required, as the internal fit is similar.

MH-47E CHINOOK 2990 m (9800 ft)	**CH-47D CHINOOK** 3215 m (10,550 ft)	**MH-53J PAVE LOW III ENHANCED** 3565 m (11,700 ft)

INITIAL CLIMB RATE

Operational requirements have left the Special Forces helicopters with reduced climb performance also, but the ability to operate anywhere in adverse conditions outweighs any disadvantage.

CH-47D CHINOOK 669 m/min (2190 fpm)	**MH-53J PAVE LOW III ENHANCED** 631 m/min (2070 fpm)
MH-47E CHINOOK 561 m/min (1840 fpm)	

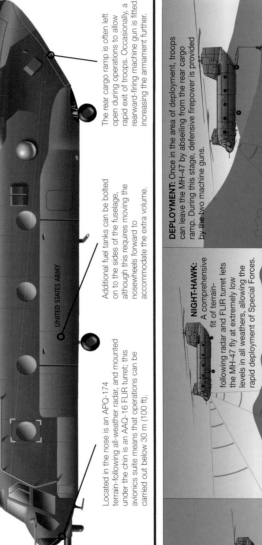

Operational requirements specified an up-rated version of the Lycoming engine to improve handling at low level and when hovering.

The rear cargo ramp is often left open during operations to allow rapid exit of troops. Occasionally, a rearward-firing machine gun is fitted, increasing the armament further.

UNITED STATES ARMY

Additional fuel tanks can be bolted on to the sides of the fuselage, although this requires moving the nosewheels forward to accommodate the extra volume.

Located in the nose is an APQ-174 terrain-following all-weather radar, and mounted under the chin is an AAQ-16 FLIR turret; this avionics suite means that operations can be carried out below 30 m (100 ft).

MH-47E CHINOOK

Developed in response to a request from the Special Operations Forces, the MH-47E was derived from the standard CH-47D, but is fitted with extremely sophisticated avionics.

To undertake long-range operations, the Chinook was the first helicopter to be fitted with an in-flight refuelling probe, allowing refuelling from a C-130 Hercules. With a length of 11 m (36 ft), it is the longest probe attached to any aircraft.

Special Forces operations

EXTENDED RANGE: To operate behind enemy lines, the MH-47 is fitted with a telescopic in-flight refuelling probe which extends forward. This enables contact with a Hercules tanker aircraft which trails a drogue behind its fuselage.

NIGHT-HAWK: A comprehensive fit of terrain-following radar and FLIR turret lets the MH-47E fly at extremely low levels in all weathers, allowing the rapid deployment of Special Forces.

DEPLOYMENT: Once in the area of deployment, troops can leave the MH-47 by abseiling from the rear cargo ramp. During this stage, defensive firepower is provided by the two machine guns.

BOEING-VERTOL
CH-46 SEA KNIGHT

● Assault transport ● Medium-lift helicopter ● US Marine Corps

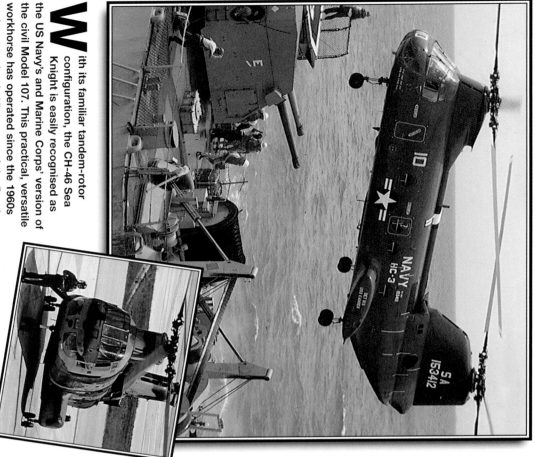

With its familiar tandem-rotor configuration, the CH-46 Sea Knight is easily recognised as the US Navy's and Marine Corps' version of the civil Model 107. This practical, versatile workhorse has operated since the 1960s and saw action in Vietnam and the Persian Gulf. The Navy relies upon the Sea Knight to supply its warships at sea, while the Marine Corps uses it as an assault helicopter. Despite its age, the CH-46 is still in service.

▲ Twin-rotor lifting power gives the old CH-46 impressive performance, and the aircraft will be more than 35 years old when it retires. The Sea Knight has notched up a good combat record.

▲ Resupply at sea
Transporting stores at sea is the UH-46's main task, ferrying loads from replenishment ships to warships. HH-46s serve in a similar role, but have a winch for search-and-rescue duties.

▼ Frozen North
In support of US Marine Corps detachments CH-46s are deployed to Norway. This is especially challenging as crews have to fly over the mountainous terrain in extreme weather.

▼ Shot down
This CH-46 was shot down during the American intervention in Grenada. One of the weaknesses of the Sea Knight is that it has little armour and is vulnerable to small arms fire.

▼ Jeep carrier
The CH-46 can even carry a light vehicle in its hold, thanks to its integral rear loading ramp. This can be opened in flight to allow paratroop drops, or while the Sea Knight is on the water for rescue duties.

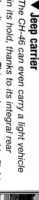

Storm service ▶
The biggest deployment for the CH-46 in recent years was Operation Desert Storm. Sixty were used for such varied tasks as casualty evacuation, resupply and vertical replenishment.

FACTS AND FIGURES

➤ The prototype flew on 22 April 1958, with the first production CH-46 following on 16 October 1962.

➤ The US Army tested a version of the CH-46 but decided not to operate it.

➤ In 1965 the Sea Knight replaced the Sikorsky H-34 with Marine units in Vietnam.

➤ Some 669 Sea Knights were built; US Navy and Marine Corps models served in Operation Desert Storm.

➤ Other military versions of this helicopter are employed in Canada, Japan and Sweden.

➤ The V-22 tilt rotor will begin replacing the CH-46 in the year 2000.

PROFILE

The Marine Corps' 'flying bullfrog'

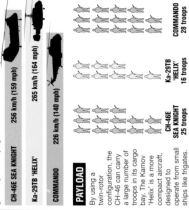

The CH-46 has earned a good reputation with the US Marine Corps despite its tendency to turn upside down when ditched at sea.

W hen the twin-turbine CH-46 Sea Knight was introduced it provided a new standard of performance to the Navy and Marine Corps. Both needed a strong, roomy, versatile helicopter for combat support. To the Navy, this meant 'vertical replenishment' – using helicopters to haul cargoes to ships at sea. The Marine Corps used the CH-46 to carry combat troops directly into battle, and many who served in Vietnam are alive today because the

Sea Knight snatched them to safety from the battlefield.

After more than three decades of service many Sea Knights are now approaching their limit of 10,000 flying hours. A number of improvements have been made to these valiant warriors, but the fleet is now ready to be replaced.

The US Navy is evaluating

the Kaman K-Max helicopter to take over the CH-46's supply mission, while the Marine Corps is planning to buy 425 Bell-Boeing V-22 Ospreys to replace its 238 remaining Sea Knights.

CH-46E Sea Knight

Type: troop-carrying military helicopter

Powerplant: two 1394-kW (1870-hp) General Electric T58-GE-16 turboshaft engines

Maximum speed: 256 km/h (159 mph)

Cruising speed: 225 km/h (140 mph) at sea level

Range: 996 km (618 miles)

Service ceiling: 5180 m (16,990 ft)

Weights: empty equipped 5100 kg (11,200 lb); maximum take-off 9707 kg (21,355 lb)

Accommodation: two pilots, up to 25 troops or up to 1415 kg (3113 lb) of cargo internally, plus up to 1000 kg (2200 lb) in an external sling

Dimensions: rotor diameter 15.24 m (50 ft)
length, rotors turning 25.40 m (83 ft)
height 5.09 m (17 ft)
rotor disc area 182.41 m² (1963 sq ft)

Another improvement retrofitted to the CH-46E is the use of glassfibre rotor blades. All CH-46s have a powered blade folding system.

CH-46E SEA KNIGHT

The CH-46 is still in service with 15 front-line units and two training squadrons in the US Marine Corps.

The cockpit seats two pilots and a loadmaster. Improved avionics were fitted to the CH-46F.

Provision exists for fitting 12.7-mm machine guns in the side doors. Troops usually exit through the rear door, with the side doors only used for crew exit and in emergencies.

Painted in a high-visibility orange paint scheme, this Sea Knight is an HH-46 variant; 38 of these aircraft were modified to this standard. Many are based at Point Mugu, California, for search-and-rescue duties.

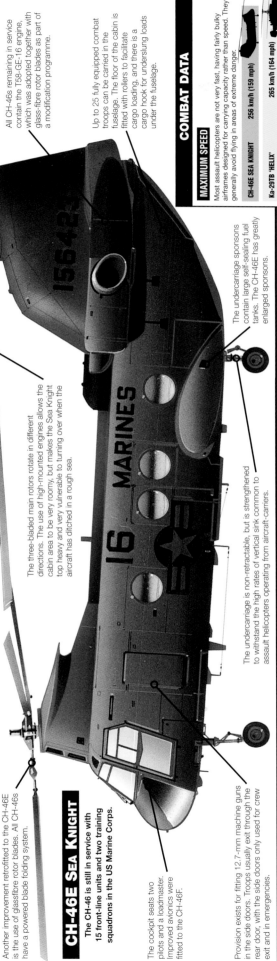

All CH-46s remaining in service contain the T58-GE-16 engine, which was adopted together with glass-fibre rotor blades as part of a modification programme.

Up to 25 fully equipped combat troops can be carried in the fuselage. The floor of the cabin is fitted with rollers to facilitate cargo loading, and there is a cargo hook for underslung loads under the fuselage.

The three-bladed main rotors rotate in different directions. The use of high-mounted engines allows the cabin area to be very roomy, but makes the Sea Knight top heavy and very vulnerable to turning over when the aircraft has ditched in a rough sea.

The undercarriage is non-retractable, but is strengthened to withstand the high rates of vertical sink common to assault helicopters operating from aircraft-carriers.

The undercarriage sponsons contain large self-sealing fuel tanks. The CH-46E has greatly enlarged sponsons.

COMBAT DATA

Most assault helicopters are not very fast, having fairly bulky airframes designed for carrying capacity rather than speed. They generally avoid flying in areas of extreme danger.

MAXIMUM SPEED

CH-46E SEA KNIGHT 256 km/h (159 mph)

Ka-29TB 'HELIX' 265 km/h (164 mph)

COMMANDO 226 km/h (140 mph)

PAYLOAD

By using a twin-rotor configuration, the CH-46 can carry a large number of troops in its cargo bay. The Kamov 'Helix' is a more compact aircraft, designed to operate from small ships like frigates.

| CH-46E SEA KNIGHT 25 troops | Ka-29TB 'HELIX' 16 troops | COMMANDO 28 troops |

Rescue under fire in Grenada

COBRA DOWNED: During the American assault on Grenada, a Cobra gunship was shot down at the Tanteen sports field near St Georges. The pilot, Captain Jeb Seagle, dragged his wounded co-pilot Tim Howard to safety and called for help on the emergency radio.

SEA KNIGHT RESCUE: A Marine Corps CH-46 from USS *Guam* landed and picked up Howard. The crew then waited on the ground for Captain Seagle despite the incoming gunfire. However, unknown to his rescuers, Seagle had been shot and killed.

ESCAPE TO SAFETY: Under the cover of suppressive fire from a Cobra, the Sea Knight returned to base, having suffered damage to its stabilising equipment. Tim Howard survived but lost his forearm in the incident.

CESSNA

O-1 BIRD DOG

- US light observation aircraft ● Korea and Vietnam veteran

One of the greatest observation and general-purpose aircraft ever to serve the military was the Cessna Bird Dog. Known as the L-19 during the Korean War and later as the O-1, the Bird Dog was developed from the Cessna 170 of the 1940s. A number still fly today, operated by small air arms around the world. The Bird Dog enjoyed a long and successful career with the US Air Force, performing many tasks such as pinpointing enemy troops, spotting targets for fighter-bombers, or undertaking attack, liaison and communications duties.

▲ Based on the civilian Model 170, the Cessna L-19/O-1 Bird Dog was a highly successful light observation aircraft in both US and foreign service. It flew during the Korea and Vietnam Wars.

CESSNA O-1 BIRD DOG

▼ Army trainer
During the 1950s, the US Army acquired 310 Model 305Bs for use as trainers. In military service they were known as TL-19Ds and had dual flight instruments.

▲ First of the many
Seen here in its original natural metal finish, the model 305 first flew in 1949 and was the eventual contest winner for the US Army's new light observation aircraft in 1950.

▲ Foreign orders
Widely exported, the Bird Dog served with several European nations, notably Austria and France. An example belonging to the French Armée de Terre (Army) is seen here.

Service in Southeast Asia ▼
Former French O-1s were transferred to the South Vietnamese air force and used extensively during the Vietnam War.

▲ Specialist Bird Dogs
This particular aircraft, with a redesigned tail and other modifications, was used by the US Army for Boundary Layer Control studies, in the southern United States.

FACTS AND FIGURES

▼ The name Bird Dog was chosen by US Army General Mark Clark after Cessna held a contest for names.

▼ Bird Dogs played a significant role in the conflicts in Southeast Asia.

▼ Efforts to promote a turboprop-powered Bird Dog were unsuccessful.

▼ In addition to the US, many other air arms around the world acquired the ubiquitous Bird Dog.

▼ In the secondary support role many Bird Dogs have been used for pilot training.

▼ Cessna built 3105 Bird Dogs for the US Army in their factory at Wichita, Kansas.

Widely used FAC and observation aircraft

When the US Army needed a plane to fly President-elect Dwight D. Eisenhower over the Korean battlefield in 1952, it chose the Cessna L-19 Bird Dog. This high-wing, all-metal aircraft achieved an unprecedented record of service in Korea, Vietnam and in many other parts of the world. Seen at first as simply a light observation craft, the Bird Dog proved indispensable to many varied military operations.

By the 1960s the Bird Dog was one of the slowest aircraft in military service. Nevertheless, its 159-kW (213-hp) Continental piston engine made it ideal for low flying in areas such as Vietnam, where the enemy would often lurk in the undergrowth.

In Vietnam, both the US Air Force and the South Vietnamese employed the Bird Dog in the perilous forward air control (FAC) role. The slow, low-flying Bird Dog was just the aircraft to succeed in finding the Viet Cong on the ground, using smoke, rockets or grenades to mark targets, and allow the fast, high-flying warplanes to swoop down and strike with bombs. FAC pilots flew some of the most dangerous and difficult missions of the war in the Bird Dog. Today, the aircraft still serves several air forces in the FAC/light observation and communications roles.

Below: Two early L-19s in flight. Originally delivered in natural metal, US Army aircraft began to adopt an overall dark green camouflage in 1951. Markings were toned down in the 1960s during the Vietnam War.

Above: Late-mark Bird Dogs could be fitted with both floats and wheels, making them amphibious.

O-1E Bird Dog

Type: two-seat light observation aircraft

Powerplant: one 159-kW (213-hp) Continental O-470 air-cooled piston engine

Maximum speed: 185 km/h (115 mph)

Maximum cruising speed: 209 km/h (115 mph)

Initial climb rate: 351 m/min (1150 fpm)

Range: 853 km (530 miles)

Service ceiling: 5640 m (18,500 ft)

Take-off run: 171 m (560 ft)

Weights: empty 732 kg (1610 lb); loaded 1088 kg (2394 lb)

Armament: four target-marking rockets

Dimensions:
span	10.97 m (35 ft)
length	7.85 m (25 ft 9 in)
height	2.22 m (7 ft 3 in)
wing area	16.16 m² (170 sq ft)

COMBAT DATA

POWER

Light observation aircraft were never very powerful, yet in comparison with the Auster AOP.Mk 9 and the older Piper L-4 Cub, the Cessna O-1 had a distinct performance advantage.

O-1E BIRD DOG	159 kW (213 hp)
AOP.Mk 9	134 kW (180 hp)
L-4H CUB	48.5 kW (65 hp)

SERVICE CEILING

Post World War II aircraft could out-perform their predecessors in just about every respect, the Bird Dog and AOP.Mk 9 being no exception. They could fly twice as high as the old L-4 Cub.

L-4H CUB	2834 m (9300 ft)
AOP.Mk 9	5640 m (18,500 ft)
O-1E BIRD DOG	5640 m (18,500 ft)

RANGE

These aircraft possessed excellent range. The 1950s-era Bird Dog could fly further than some contemporary jets. The old Piper Cub (or Grasshopper as it was christened) could loiter for long periods, but its very poor ceiling made it extremely vulnerable to ground fire and easy to spot. By the 1950s, this was a severe handicap in combat operations.

AOP.Mk 9	395 km (245 miles)
O-1E BIRD DOG	853 km (530 miles)
L-4H CUB	306 km (190 miles)

O-1E BIRD DOG

Although now more than 40 years old, an estimated 200 Bird Dogs are still in service with several countries. Italy continues to operate the type, three examples serving with the army.

Like many World War II-era aircraft, the O-1 Bird Dog incorporated large, ribbed control surfaces. They gave the aircraft a surprising level of agility in the air and enabled it to avoid ground fire from hostile forces.

O-1s were usually unarmed, though FAC aircraft often had mountings for target designator rockets under the wings.

A fully metal aircraft, the Bird Dog was light, simple and tough in construction, perfect for operations in Third World countries.

One variant of the Bird Dog, the TO-1E, had full dual flight controls for training. These aircraft were modified from existing O-1Es.

The cabin had seating for two, normally comprising a pilot and observer. During the Vietnam War, forward air control (FAC) missions were often flown solo.

A high-set wing gave the Bird Dog excellent STOL (Short Take-Off and Landing) ability, allowing it to operate from very small and awkward airstrips.

Most Bird Dog undercarriages had single main wheels, though four aircraft were delivered to the US Army as floatplanes. Later aircraft were compatible with both floats and wheels.

Cessnas in military service

■ **C-78/T-50 BOBCAT:** These aircraft were used both as conversion trainers and light transport aircraft during World War II. The latter wore this rather drab camouflage.

■ **T-41B MESCALERO:** Entering US Army service in 1966, these aircraft were used as primary flight trainers, though some served as hacks. Most have now been retired.

■ **O-2 SKYMASTER:** Developed, like the O-1, from a civil design, the unusual Skymaster supplanted USAF Bird Dogs in Vietnam, performing FAC duties.

■ **A-37B DRAGONFLY:** An attack derivative of the T-37 Tweet trainer, the Dragonfly was used by the USAF and numerous small air forces around the world in the 1970s.

CESSNA
O-2 SKYMASTER

- Twin-engined push-pull design ● Action in Vietnam and Zimbabwe

▲ Cessna's 1960s design for an affordable, easy-to-fly twin-engined aircraft soon found favour with the USAF and other forces which were attracted by its spritely performance and maintainability.

W hen it required an aircraft to serve as a forward air control (FAC) spotter in Vietnam, the USAF turned to a proven private aircraft design, the Cessna 337 Super Skymaster. Given the military designation O-2, the twin-engined Skymaster went to Southeast Asia in 1967, supplanting the single-engined Cessna O-1. From the mid 1970s Skymasters were also in action in Rhodesia, as the government fought Popular Front guerrillas.

PHOTO FILE

CESSNA O-2 SKYMASTER

▲ Vietnam veteran
69-7624 is one of 501 O-2As (Cessna Model 337M) delivered to the USAF from April 1967 for use in Vietnam. Many were transferred to National Guard units post-war.

Underwing hardpoints ▼
Both the O-2A and Milirole have four hardpoints for a wide variety of light air-to-ground weaponry. This Haitian aircraft carries four bombs.

▲ Light striker
Reims Aviation called its armed military variant of the turbocharged F337G the FTB337G Milirole.

▲ Ecuadorian Super Skymaster
This example of a civil 337 in military use has an underfuselage cargo pallet.

▲ Zimbabwean Lynxes
Zimbabwe operates 15 survivors of 18 French-built FTB337G Miliroles which were purchased secretly by the Rhodesian air force in 1976. Known as the Lynx, the type was used for FAC, COIN and light strike missions during Rhodesia's long bush war.

FACTS AND FIGURES

▼ A few O-2s were transferred from the US Air Force to the Navy and then to the Army.

▼ The USAF received a total of 531 O-2s during the Vietnam War years.

▼ The first Skymaster was the Model 336 with a fixed undercarriage.

▼ Although the 337 was called the Super Skymaster by Cessna, the USAF's official name was simply Skymaster.

▼ Including civil aircraft, Cessna built 1,978 Model 336/337s; 66 were built in France.

▼ Two O-2s served with the US Army's Berlin Brigade at Tempelhof airport.

PROFILE

Push-pull twin in uniform

The unusual power arrangement of the Model 337, with both engines on the centreline of the aircraft, makes it easier for the pilot to maintain control if one engine is lost. The success of the civil Skymaster, with its clean lines and twin-boom configuration, led to the use of this concept in the military O-2, which was conscripted for FAC duty in Vietnam.

Forward air control O-2As flew 'low and close' to identify the enemy for 'fast-mover' fighter-bombers or friendly artillery. This often meant flying straight into the guns deep inside enemy territory, equipped with little more than target-marking rockets.

A small number of USAF O-2Bs were equipped for 'psy-war' roles, including leaflet-dropping and loudspeaker broadcasting.

Most US O-2s have been retired, many going to private operators and government agencies, and a few have been transferred to other air forces, mainly in Central America.

Other military variants of the Model 337 design include the Reims Aviation-built Milirole, with provision for underwing weapons, and the Summit Aviation's Sentry O2-337. Both French- and US-built 337s/O-2s remain in service on three continents.

Below: At the time that the O-2A was ordered, the USAF contracted for 31 'off-the-shelf' Super Skymasters designated O-2B. They were equipped with loudspeakers and advanced communications for a psychological warfare role.

Above: The military Sentry O2-337 was an adaptation of the pressurized and turbocharged T337G. Haiti took delivery of six O2-337s, the first in 1975.

Two of Continental's well-known flat-six configuration IO-360 engines powered the Skymaster. A common variation was the installation of turbocharged 168-kW (225-hp) TSIO-360 engines in pressurized versions in order to maintain engine power at altitude.

In designing the 337, Cessna wanted to build a low-cost, easy-to-fly, twin-engined aircraft for civil use. In standard configuration the Super Skymaster is a four-seater, although fifth and sixth seats could be fitted in an alternative layout. Skymasters can be fitted with dual controls.

Pressurised aircraft are distinguished by their smaller fuselage windows, which are necessary to maintain fuselage strength under pressurisation.

The Skymaster has a conventional all-metal twin-spar wing structure and the fuselage is also of conventional monocoque design. Two slim metal booms support a cantilever tail unit with twin swept-back tailfins/rudders.

USAF psychological warfare O-2Bs were fitted with a high-powered loudspeaker system and leaflet dispenser in the starboard side of the rear fuselage.

A common modification on military 337s was the addition of Robertson high-lift flaps and drooped wing-tips to improve STOL performance. Wing hardpoints are also commonly fitted.

O-2A Skymaster

Type: forward air control observation aircraft

Powerplant: two 157-kW (210-hp) Teledyne Continental IO-360-C/D flat-six piston engines

Maximum speed: 320 km/h (198 mph) at sea level

Maximum cruising speed: 232 km/h (144 mph) at 3050 m (10,000 ft)

Range: (typical) 1706 km (1060 miles)

Weights: empty 1292 kg (2840 lb); maximum take-off 2449 kg (5390 lb)

Armament: four underwing hardpoints for up to ten 70-mm marker rockets or other light ordnance, including 5.56-mm or 7.65-mm light machine guns pods

Dimensions:
span 11.58 m (38 ft)
length 9.07 m (29 ft 9 in)
height 2.84 m (9 ft 4 in)
wing area 18.81 m² (202 sq ft)

ACTION DATA

COMBAT RADIUS

Introduced in the late 1960s, the USAF's O-2 represented a leap in capability for the air force's FAC component. Greater range meant that missions in South Vietnam could be undertaken further from bases, and loiter times over a target were improved.

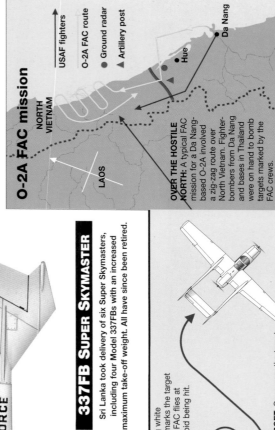

SUPER CUB 150
112 km (70 miles)

O-1E BIRD DOG
159 km (100 miles)

O-2A SKYMASTER
314 km (200 miles)

O-2A FAC mission

→ USAF fighters
→ O-2A FAC route
● Ground radar
▲ Artillery post

NORTH VIETNAM
LAOS
SOUTH VIETNAM

Da Nang
Hue

OVER THE HOSTILE NORTH: A typical FAC mission for a Da Nang-based O-2A involved a zig-zag route over North Vietnam. Fighter-bombers from Da Nang and bases in Thailand were on hand to bomb targets marked by the FAC crews.

337FB SUPER SKYMASTER

Sri Lanka took delivery of six Super Skymasters, including four Model 337FBs with an increased maximum take-off weight. All have since been retired.

SRI LANKA AIR FORCE

CC653

1 LORRY SPOTTED: A patrolling O-2 spots a lorry and informs a C-130 Hercules command post, which in turn alerts nearby USAF fighter-bombers in the area and directs them to the target.

2 MARKING THE TARGET: Once near the target, the bombers communicate with the O-2, which supplies more accurate targeting co-ordinates.

3 TARGET DESTROYED: Using white phosphorus rockets, the O-2 marks the target for the fighters. During strikes the FAC flies at right angles to the bombers to avoid being hit.

CESSNA
A-37 DRAGONFLY

● Light strike ● Counter insurgency ● Vietnam veteran

▶ Moving away from the trend of ever bigger, more expensive and faster strike aircraft, the Cessna A-37 has found great popularity with Latin American countries as well as with pilots in the United States. Many air forces have followed the trend of using armed trainer derivatives for attack missions.

Military trainers are usually developed from combat aircraft, but in the case of the A-37 the process occurred the other way round. Having built T-37A and B trainers for the USAF, Cessna developed a lightweight attack aircraft for the COIN – counter-insurgency – role. The A-37 saw combat in Southeast Asia, and has seen action in many wars, being almost mandatory in any South American coup attempt.

CESSNA A-37 DRAGONFLY

▶ **Jungle fighter**
Thailand's A-37s have seen extensive service in battles with insurgents along its jungle border areas.

▲ **Rocket strike**
Letting fly with 70-mm rockets, this YAT-37D gives an impressive firepower display. Only two YAT-37s were built, acting as prototypes. The jet proved to a sceptical USAF that such a small aircraft could work well.

▲ **Columbian striker**
Still very active in the Fuerza Aerea Colombiana (FAC), the A-37 has taken part in coup attempts. More normal duties for FAC's 20 Dragonflies are bombing drug plants and fighting the Communist insurgents in the north of the country.

Chilean 'fly' ▶
Since 1974 the Chilean air force has operated the A-37B as both a light strike aircraft and advanced trainer, helping pilots to convert to F-5s, Hunters, A-36 Halcons and Mirages.

▲ **Keep it simple**
Like any modified trainer, the A-37 has a simple cockpit which is barely more complicated than a propeller-driven Cessna. This is an advantage for this type of aircraft, as at low level it enables the pilot to concentrate on engaging the target.

▶ **Dragonfly sting**
By packing a GAU-2B 7.62-mm (.30-cal.) Minigun into the nose, the Cessna has a potent sting. The long refuelling probe is located in the centre of the nose. More gun pods can be carried if additional firepower is needed.

FACTS AND FIGURES

▼ Its distinctive engine sound led some pilots to nickname the A-37 'the 6000-pound dog whistle'.

▼ The prototype YAT-37D first flew on 22 October 1963, 11 years after the T-37.

▼ Vietnam captured some A-37s after the fall of South Vietnam in 1975.

▼ A-37s still fly in Chile, Colombia, Ecuador, Guatemala, Honduras, Peru, Salvador, South Korea and Uruguay.

▼ The single Minigun in the A-37's nose can fire 6000 rounds per minute.

▼ Some escaping South Vietnamese pilots flew their aircraft to safety in Thailand.

PROFILE

Striking hard in the Dragonfly

By carrying out a comprehensive update of the T-37 trainer, the USAF provided the beleaguered South Vietnamese air force with a seemingly viable alternative to more powerful strike aircraft. The A-37B first flew, as the YAT-37D, on 22 October 1963 and Cessna received a contract in August 1966 to modify 39 T-37s to attack configuration. The first A-37A was delivered in May 1967 and later that year was combat tested in Vietnam. Positive results from these tests led to the B model, with the J69-T-25 engine.

In February 1968 the first VNAF pilots went to the US to train, and by May 1969 A-37Bs equipped the 516th, 520th and 524th Fighter Squadrons. Seven other units subsequently converted to Dragonflies.

Despite its awesome firepower, the A-37 was vulnerable to ground fire and many were lost. US pilots remained 'in country' and flew many combat missions as the North Vietnamese Easter 1972 Offensive broke. A spirited defence of An Loc was the highlight of the Dragonfly's

deployment in Vietnam, but the small air force lacked the infrastructure to fight a decisive air campaign. When the war ended in 1975 a few A-37s were flown out, but many aircraft were abandoned to the Communists and, undoubtedly, flown by their new owners.

A-37B DRAGONFLY

The Fuerza Aerea de Chile uses its A-37Bs for light attack training. Grupo 12 operates around 20 of these aircraft from Punta Arenas. Chile also operates the similar Cessna T-37 trainer.

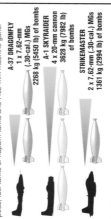

A-37B Dragonfly

Type: two-seat ground-attack aircraft

Powerplant: two 12.68-kN (1735-lb-thrust) General Electric J85-17A turbojets

Maximum speed: 816 km/h (506 mph)

Take-off distance: 471 m (1545 ft) to 30 m (50 ft) altitude

Range: 740 km (460 miles) with maximum load

Service ceiling: 12,730 m (41,750 ft)

Weights: empty 2817 kg (6197 lb); loaded 6350 kg (13,970 lb)

Armament: one GAU-2B 7.62-mm (.30-cal.) Minigun; 2268 kg (5450 lb) of bombs, rockets and napalm tanks

Dimensions:
span: 10.93 m (35 ft 10 in)
length: 8.62 m (28 ft 3 in)
height: 2.70 m (8 ft 10 in)
wing area: 17.09 m² (184 sq ft)

COMBAT DATA

Speed is something of a compromise in a light attack jet, as the aircraft becomes very expensive if it uses large powerful engines. But even these small jets are faster than an A-1.

MAXIMUM SPEED

A-37 DRAGONFLY	816 km/h (506 mph)
A-1 SKYRAIDER	518 km/h (321 mph)
STRIKEMASTER	834 km/h (517 mph)

ARMAMENT

Even the Cessna's hefty weapon load is dwarfed by the mighty A-1, which also had more powerful 20-mm cannon armament. Most light strike aircraft generally carry a pair of bombs or rocket pods, fuel tanks or napalm tanks and 7.62-mm machine guns.

A-37 DRAGONFLY
1 x 7.62-mm (.30-cal.) MGs
2268 kg (5450 lb) of bombs

A-1 SKYRAIDER
4 x 20-mm cannon
3628 kg (7982 lb) of bombs

STRIKEMASTER
2 x 7.62-mm (.30-cal.) MGs
1361 kg (2994 lb) of bombs

COMBAT RANGE

Jet engines gave the A-37 high speed, but they limited its range compared to old piston aircraft like the A-1. The extra fuel stored in the wingtip tanks and optional drop-tanks give it longer range than a Strikemaster, or the T-37 on which it is based. A-37s generally fly from bases close to their intended targets, but can refuel in flight.

A-1 SKYRAIDER
1840 km (1146 miles)

A-37 DRAGONFLY
740 km (460 miles)

STRIKEMASTER
466 km (144 miles)

Above: Although the A-37 was designed to be air-refuelled (a requirement for the USAF), few of the present operators actually use tankers. Fuel load can also be supplemented by four 378-litre drop-tanks, giving a maximum warload, the Cessna has a range of 740 km (460 miles).

Above: Dragonflies no longer operate with the USAF, the last aircraft being retired in 1992. The USAF now uses the OA-10A for forward air control.

The tailplane is relatively high mounted to keep it clear of the engine exhaust gases. The airframe is of conventional alloy construction and all control surfaces have electrically operated trim tabs.

To increase the power available to this modified trainer, the A-37 used a pair of General Electric J85 turbojets, producing more power than the Teledyne Continental J69s in the T-37. The A-37 was more than twice as powerful as a T-37.

Eight stores pylons were fitted under the wing. These could carry extra fuel tanks, napalm tanks, incendiary or cluster bombs, and gun and rocket pods.

Although the potential for armour was limited in such a light aircraft, the cockpit was fitted with layered nylon flak curtains to protect the crew from fragments.

One feature that distinguishes the A-37 from the T-37 is the wingtip fuel storage, giving the aircraft vital extra endurance and range.

To withstand the rigours of combat flying at low altitudes, the A-37 is stressed for 6g loading, and is a capable dogfighter.

Unlike most strike aircraft, the Cessna has no radar, infra-red, night-vision sights or TV system. The nose is the home of the GAU-2 Minigun, located to starboard.

Destroying cocaine farms in Colombia

Many Latin American countries use A-37s for bombing the remote jungle bases of drug cartels.

PROCESSING PLANT: The cocaine crop is turned into 'base' at processing plants using hydrochloric acid. These plants are the easiest target for the A-37.

OBSERVATION: Special forces observers hiding in the jungle call in the air strike, giving an accurate description of the target area.

AIR STRIKE: Using a mixture of incendiary napalm bombs and blast fragmentation rockets, the A-37s devastate the plant.

COCAINE CROP: The coca plants are a poor target, as they are difficult to destroy and their destruction alienates the peasant population.

CESSNA
T-37

- US Air Force primary trainer ● In service for over 40 years

Nicknamed the 'Tweet' or 'Tweety Bird' after an appealing cartoon character, the Cessna T-37 has been the USAF's primary training aircraft since the mid 1950s. The visually pleasing design has not changed externally in 40 years, although the instruments and equipment beneath its skin have been constantly improved. Genuinely loved and admired, the T-37 will still be training most USAF pilots well into the 21st century.

▲ Cessna stuck to conventional wisdom by designing its T-37 trainer with side-by-side seats. Like many air arms, the USAF is now turning to a tandem arrangement for basic training.

CESSNA T-37

▼ First jet experience
The T-37B is the first jet aircraft flown by most USAF pilots. Primary training takes between 80 and 85 hours of flight time, after which the student will graduate to advanced training on the T-38 Talon.

▲ Mass production
Around 1000 T-37s were built to meet the USAF's high demand for pilots during the 1950s and 1960s.

1980s upgrade ▼
Cancellation of the T-46A programme left the USAF without a successor to the T-37B and from 1989 it began to upgrade surviving Tweets for continued service.
The T-37 will be replaced by the T-6 Texan II from 2001.

▼ Foreign 'Tweets'
The T-37's excellent handling qualities make it the perfect mount for precision flying. T-37s are used by the Portuguese national aerobatic team.

▲ Trainer with teeth
Cessna developed an armed version of the T-37 for light attack as the A-37 Dragonfly. Sidewinder missiles were not part of the standard armament.

FACTS AND FIGURES

➤ Many student pilots briefly fly a propeller aircraft before advancing to primary training in the T-37.

➤ The USAF currently has about 550 T-37Bs in training squadrons.

➤ The prototype for the T-37 series made its first flight on 12 October 1954.

➤ Cessna began designing the T-37 as a private venture, aimed at introducing jet power to the primary training mission.

➤ In total, 1269 T-37s were manufactured for the US Air Force and for export.

➤ Cessna flew the first production T-37 on 27 September 1955.

T-37B

Type: two-seat primary trainer

Powerplant: two 4.56-kN (1026-lb-thrust) Continental J69-T-25 turbojet engines

Maximum speed: 685 km/h (425 mph)

Cruising speed: 612 km/h (379 mph)

Initial climb rate: 1027 m/min (3370 fpm)

Range: 972 km (600 miles)

Weights: empty 1755 kg (3860 lb); maximum take-off 2933 kg (6453 lb)

Accommodation: instructor (right) and student (left) in side-by-side seating

Dimensions:
span 10.30 m (33 ft 9 in)
length 8.92 m (29 ft 3 in)
height 2.68 m (8 ft 10 in)
wing area 17.09 m² (184 sq ft)

ACTION DATA

MAXIMUM SPEED

The single-engined Czech L-29, and the T-37B, have a comparable top speed, but both are out-paced by the French Magister. A higher top speed enables the French aircraft to transit to and from its training area more quickly, thus increasing training time.

T-37B	685 km/h (425 mph)
CM 170-1 MAGISTER	715 km/h (443 mph)
L-29 DELFIN 'MAYA'	679 km/h (421 mph)

CLIMB RATE

The twin-engined T-37B and Magister have a far superior climb rate to that of the L-29. The American trainer outclimbs the Magister on account of its more powerful engines which give a superior thrust-to-weight ratio.

T-37B 1027 m/min (3370 fpm)
MAGISTER 1020 m/min (3345 fpm)
L-29 DELFIN 'MAYA' 840 m/min (2755 fpm)

RANGE

With a standard fuel load, the T-37B can fly further or longer than either of its rivals. For a given flight condition, such as cruise, both twin-engined types can reduce their thrust settings to fly more economically than the single-engined L-29. Wingtip tanks were fitted to all three types to increase range.

T-37B 972 km (600 miles)
L-29 DELFIN 'MAYA' 640 km (400 miles)
CM 170-1 MAGISTER 925 km (575 miles)

Long-serving USAF trainer

Tens of thousands of USAF pilots have their first experience of jet flying in the T-37 'Tweet'. The T-37 was designed in 1952 to meet a USAF requirement for a jet-powered primary trainer and first flew on 12 October 1954. It was a very practical trainer design seating two side-by-side, with a low and wide-tracked undercarriage to ease landing and ground handling.

Cessna built 534 T-37As, and from 1959 switched production to the T-37B model with uprated J69 engines and improved navigation and communications equipment. Provision was also made for wingtip fuel tanks. In all, 466 T-37Bs were built, including some for export, and all surviving A-models were brought up to T-37B standard.

The T-37C was the ultimate 'Tweet' and was never used by the USAF. Built solely for export, some 269 T-37Cs were sold to 10 foreign operators.

'Tweets' were to have been replaced during the mid 1980s by Fairchild T-46As but this new design was abandoned, and instead Sabreliner Corporation began supplying modification kits to the USAF which allowed T-37s to be rebuilt for extended service. Now the USAF plans to replace the long-serving T-37 with the Raytheon T-6A Texan II turboprop from 2001.

Below: Most USAF T-37s are based in Texas where flying conditions are ideal for much of the year.

Above: The Pakistan air force is one of the eight current operators of the T-37C. The others are Chile, Colombia, Greece, Jordan, Peru, Thailand and Turkey.

T-37C

Turkey's air force, the Türk Hava Kuvvetleri (THK) received 20 ex-USAF T-37Bs and 50 new-build T-37Cs. Based at Cigli, they are operated by 122 Filo (squadron) of the Häva Okullari Komutanligi (Air Training Command).

Turkish student pilots commence their primary flying training with 123 Filo at Gazıemir with a 10/15-hour course on propeller-driven Cessna T-41Ds and Beech T-34As. At Cigli, they complete a 90/100-hour basic training course on the T-37 before moving to the co-located 121 Filo for advanced training on Lockheed T-33 Shooting Stars and Northrop T-38 Talons.

Four-digit codes on THK aircraft comprise the base identification number, followed by a three-number suffix which repeats the last three digits of the aircraft's serial.

The T-37's tailplane is set one-third of the way up the vertical fin to clear the efflux from the jet engines. As angle of attack increases, the tailplane remains in the relatively undisturbed airstream, thus preventing the aircraft from entering a deep stall.

Wide track undercarriage makes the T-37 easy and stable to taxi. However, its relatively short stroke means that a tail bumper is necessary to protect the rear fuselage during take-off rotation and landing.

T-37Cs have an armament training and limited light attack capability thanks to a single hardpoint under each wing. This can carry a multi-purpose pod containing a 12.7-mm (50-cal.) machine gun, two 70-mm folding-fin rockets and four 136-kg (316-lb) practice bombs.

Power is provided by two small J69 engines, which are licence-built versions of the French Turboméca Marboré used in the Fouga Magister. Buried in the wingroots and built by Continental, they deliver a total of over 9 kN (2050 lb thrust).

'Tweet' operators: American and export

■ **USA:** Since 1991 surviving USAF T-37Bs which numbered 632 in 1989) have been cycled through an upgrade for continued service, until their eventual replacement in 2001.

■ **CHILE:** Chile received 22 ex-USAF T-37Bs and 12 T-37C trainers during the 1960s. Some 20-plus survivors serve with the training school 'Capitán Avalos' at Santiago-El Bosque air base.

■ **PAKISTAN:** Pakistan's air force received a total of 37 new-build T-37Cs and 28 ex-USAF T-37Bs. Two are used by instructors for the 'Sherdils' ('Lionhearts') aerobatic team.

CONSOLIDATED

B-24 LIBERATOR

● Heavy bomber ● Long-range maritime patrol ● Transport

▲ The B-24 was a product of American bombing philosophy, which called for precision attacks from high altitude by well-defended aircraft using the Norden bombsight.

Consolidated's B-24 Liberator is often compared unfavourably to the more famous B-17 Flying Fortress.

But the B-24 was newer, more efficient and much more versatile than the Boeing design; and with nearly 20,000 aircraft completed, more Liberators were built than any other military aircraft in American history. It was a good bomber, serving on every front, but its most valuable work may have been the war against the U-boats.

CONSOLIDATED B-24 LIBERATOR

▲ **Not so lucky**
After raiding southern Germany, this B-24 fought a running battle with Luftwaffe fighters all the way through Italy, crashing just after the crew bailed out.

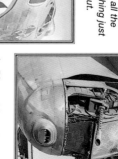

▲ **Blasted but alive**
Although not as strong as the B-17, the Liberator was tough enough to bring its crews home in spite of severe damage.

▶ **Snarling beasts**
Garishly painted B-24s were used as 'lead ships', acting as markers on which the huge Eighth Air Force bomber formations would assemble before setting off on raids over Europe.

▲ **Nose turret**
Late-model B-24s, from the 'G' onward, were fitted with powered nose turrets after experience had shown that Luftwaffe fighter pilots often attacked head-on.

▼ **Tactical strike**
After the Allied landings in France in 1944, Liberators were used to bomb tactical targets in support of the advancing armies. Railways, bridges and troop concentrations were heavily attacked.

▼ **Work of art**
'Alley Oop' was the nickname for this B-24, which sported typically bright nose art. USAF bombers were rarely camouflaged after 1943, going into action in a natural metal finish.

FACTS AND FIGURES

▶ Liberators were manufactured by Consolidated, Douglas, Ford and North American.

▶ The all-silver B-24 prototype made its first flight on 29 January 1940.

▶ The Luftwaffe used a captured B-24 for special covert operations.

▶ A B-24 crew crashed near Gyantse in Tibet while flying over the Himalayas on a supply mission to China.

▶ Winston Churchill used a modified B-24 as his personal transport.

▶ 19,256 Liberators and Privateers were manufactured between 1940 and 1945.

PROFILE

America's long-range bomber

The B-24 Liberator was built around the Davis wing; a long, thin, large-area structure mounted high on the fuselage. Its twin bomb-bays used 'roller shutter' doors which retracted within the fuselage when opened, reducing drag. The twin tail, like the wing, was a Consolidated trademark. All this resulted in an excellent long-range bomber which had other applications; there were cargo, tanker, patrol, training and reconnaissance variants. Some were armed with even more guns as bomber escorts.

A B-24 caught on the ground at Hickam Field, Hawaii, on 7 December 1941 produced the first American casualties of the war. Liberators fought in the Pacific and China-Burma-India theatres. From the Middle East they attacked their most famous target – Romania's Ploesti oilfields. They also joined with the B-17 in the Eighth Air Force's three-year aerial campaign over Europe. The B-24 was never as popular with its crews as the B-17, as it was quicker to catch fire in battle and sometimes suffered

hydraulic problems, but it was in some ways a better aircraft, with more modern systems.

The mighty armada of B-24s went to pasture in just a few years. Soon after the war, Liberators began to disappear from the skies. Today, only a couple of surviving examples are airworthy.

B-24 Liberator

Type: heavy bomber with a crew of 10

Powerplant: four 895-kW (1200-hp) Pratt & Whitney R-1830-43 Twin Wasp radial piston engines

Maximum speed: 488 km/h (300 mph)

Range: 2896 km (2850 miles)

Service ceiling: 9900 m (32,500 ft)

Weights: empty 15,413 kg (34,000 lb); maximum 27,216 kg (60,000 lb)

Armament: one 12.7-mm (.50-cal.) nose gun (some with additional 12.7-mm fixed nose guns), two more each in dorsal turret, tail turret, retractable ball turret, and waist positions, plus maximum internal bombload of 3629 kg (8800 lb)

Dimensions:
span	33.52 m	(110 ft)
length	20.22 m	(66 ft 4 in)
height	5.46 m	(17 ft 11 in)
wing area	97.36 m²	(1048 sq ft)

Left: Although the Liberator did not carry as many bombs as some other Allied aircraft, it had exceptional performance and massive defensive armament.

Below: The need for tight formation flying was vital for daylight bombing, where mutual cover meant survival.

B-24D LIBERATOR 'TEGGIE ANN'

'Teggie Ann' was the command ship for the 'Liberandos', the 376th Bomb Group. This unit was severely mauled following attacks on the Romanian oilfields at Ploesti in 1944.

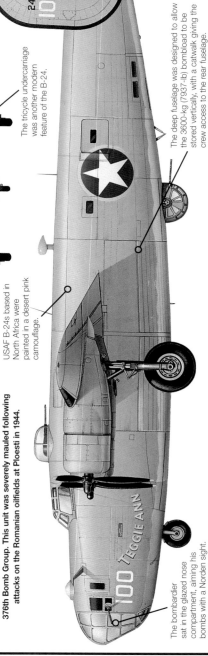

Some late-model B-24s could carry bombs on racks under the inner wing. Anti-submarine versions in RAF service carried rockets.

The very-long-span wing gave the B-24 long range and excellent performance at high altitude.

USAF B-24s based in North Africa were painted in a desert pink camouflage.

The tricycle undercarriage was another modern feature of the B-24.

The rear gunner fired a pair of 12.7-mm (.50-cal.) machine guns from a powered turret. This was replaced by manually controlled guns in the B-24L.

The deep fuselage was designed to allow the 3600-kg (7937-lb) bombload to be stored vertically, with a catwalk giving the crew access to the rear fuselage.

The bombardier sat in the glazed nose compartment, aiming his bombs with a Norden sight.

240664 | 100

'TEGGIE ANN' | 100

Closing the Atlantic Gap

BRITAIN'S SURVIVAL LIFELINE: Britain depended on America for war material and food to support its densely packed population, and those supplies came by convoy across the Atlantic.

CONVOY ESCORTS: Although most convoys were escorted by warships, the most effective weapon against the U-boat threat was continuous air cover.

THE ATLANTIC GAP: In the first years of conflict, aircraft lacked the range to cover the whole crossing, leaving a gap in the mid-Atlantic in which convoys were vulnerable.

WOLF PACKS: U-boats based in western France could be intercepted by British flying-boats in the first stage of their journeys, but once clear they were free to attack the convoys in mid-Atlantic.

CLOSING THE GAP: The deployment of very-long-range variants of the Liberator meant that the window of vulnerability was closed, and the U-boat menace was considerably reduced.

CONVOYS

SUNDERLAND

B-17 FLYING FORTRESS

B-24 LIBERATOR

U-BOATS

COMBAT DATA

MAXIMUM SPEED

The World War II generation of big four-engined bombers was reasonably fast by pre-war standards, but speed alone was never going to to get them away from marauding enemy fighters. The American solution to survival was to fly in large formations that were able to bring hundreds of guns to bear on interceptors.

B-24D LIBERATOR	488 km/h (300 mph)
HALIFAX	500 km/h (310 mph)
He 177	472 km/h (290 mph)

BOMBLOAD

Although the B-24 had, like other American bombers, a smaller load on paper than its contemporaries, some variants could carry up to six tonnes of weaponry. The Heinkel, by contrast, rarely carried more than half its stated capacity, and sometimes much less. The B-24 could carry its load higher and farther.

B-24D LIBERATOR	3629 kg (8000 lb)
HALIFAX	5900 kg (13,000 lb)
He 177	6000 kg (13,200 lb)

SERVICE CEILING

American bomber tactics called for precision strikes from high altitude. The B-24 had a long, very efficient wing, together with extremely powerful turbocharged two-row radial engines, and it customarily operated at greater heights than its European rivals. This lessened its vulnerability to fighters in the Pacific, where Japanese aircraft had to struggle to reach such high operating altitudes.

HALIFAX	7300 m (24,000 ft)
B-24D LIBERATOR	9900 m (32,500 ft)
He 177	7000 m (23,000 ft)

CONSOLIDATED

B-24 (US NAVY)

● Land-based bomber ● Anti-submarine patrols ● Surface radar

L osses of Allied shipping in the Atlantic to German submarines hunting in 'wolf-packs' highlighted the urgent need for a long-range patrol aircraft for the US Navy. With British Coastal Command already having demonstrated the suitability of the Liberator, the US Navy received its first aircraft in August 1942. Designated PB4Ys, these Liberators – with their exceptionally long range – saw extensive service in Europe and the Pacific.

▲ Naval Liberators were instrumental in closing the area of ocean known as the 'Atlantic Gap', where German U-boats preyed on Allied convoys delivering vital supplies to Britain.

PHOTO FILE

CONSOLIDATED B-24 (US NAVY)

▲ Great white bird
High over the Atlantic a PB4Y-1 Liberator flies an anti-submarine patrol. Operating far from its land base, the Liberator was one of the few forms of protection for convoys against the hunting 'wolf-packs' of German U-boats.

Proven design ▶
Early model Liberators operated by the US Navy differed very little from their Army Air Force counterparts.

Coastal Command ▶
Its radar lowered, a British-operated Liberator searches the ocean for German submarines. In addition to guns bristling from all angles, armament could include rockets mounted on either side of the nose on pylons, which were very effective against ships.

▲ Gear up
Undercarriage dangling, a Liberator takes off from Guadalcanal in 1943. The fighting around the Solomon Islands was some of the heaviest of the war.

Twin tails ▶
A distinctive feature of all Liberators was their twin tails, said to offer better handling at high altitude. Later aircraft were fitted with a single tail, and the type, renamed Privateer, had extensive post-war service.

FACTS AND FIGURES

➤ The B-24D served in every theatre, and in 1942-43 was the most important bomber in the Pacific.

➤ By 1942 the Liberator equipped 15 anti-submarine squadrons.

➤ More than 977 examples of the Liberator were operated by the United States Navy.

➤ Early Navy Liberators were particularly vulnerable to head-on machine-gun attacks by enemy fighters.

➤ The first operational unit of naval Liberators was based in Iceland.

➤ Reconnaissance versions remained in naval service until 1951.

PROFILE

Consolidated's convoy protector

Despite having already been supplying Britain with the essential materials for war by way of convoys across the Atlantic, America entered World War II still struggling to come to terms with the requirements of combat. In no area was this shortfall clearer than in the need for long-range patrol aircraft for the US Navy.

Initially denied, the request for Liberators was eventually granted after the huge losses of Allied shipping in the Atlantic. Operated under the naval designation PB4Y, the aircraft

were equipped with air-to-surface radar and depth-charges. After only a short period of service, shipping losses were greatly reduced. With its exceptionally long range, the Liberator replaced the B-17 Flying Fortress in the Pacific. It was used for bombing and patrol duties, bringing havoc to Japanese land installations and naval vessels.

After the end of World War II, Liberators remained in service for reconnaissance duties until 1951, when they were replaced by another Consolidated product: the

Privateer. Although this variant had seen limited combat use in World War II, it went on to play a key role in the Korean War as a patrol aircraft and continued to serve into the 1960s.

Below: After combat losses, a nose turret was installed on later variants of naval Liberators.

Above: Long range and the ability to carry a heavy warload let the Liberator roam the skies of the Pacific searching for enemy ships. Conventional bombing of land targets was still possible.

PB4Y-1 LIBERATOR

Adopted from the USAAF bomber versions, the blue coloured Liberators of the United States Navy saved countless lives by destroying enemy submarines. This example wears a late-war camouflage scheme.

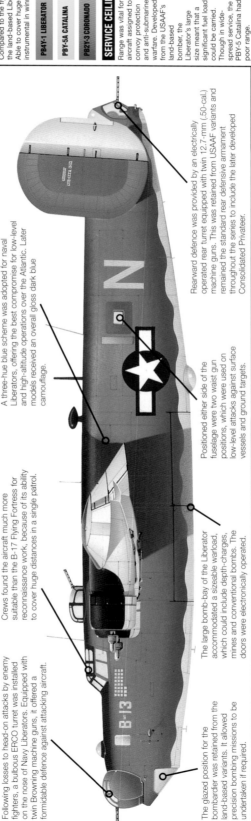

A three-hue blue scheme was adopted for naval Liberators, offering the best compromise for low-level and high-altitude operations over the Atlantic. Later models received an overall gloss dark blue camouflage.

Crews found the aircraft much more suitable than the B-17 Flying Fortress for reconnaissance work, because of its ability to cover huge distances in a single patrol.

The large bomb-bay of the Liberator accommodated a sizeable warload, which could include depth-charges, mines and conventional bombs. The doors were electronically operated.

Following losses to head-on attacks by enemy fighters, a bulbous ERCO turret was installed on the nose of Navy Liberators. Equipped with twin Browning machine guns, it offered a formidable defence against attacking aircraft.

The glazed position for the bombardier was retained from the land-based variants. It allowed precision bombing missions to be undertaken if required.

Positioned either side of the fuselage were two waist gun positions, which were used on low-level attacks against surface vessels and ground targets.

Rearward defence was provided by an electrically operated rear turret equipped with twin 12.7-mm (.50-cal.) machine guns. This was retained from USAAF variants and remained the standard rear defensive armament throughout the series to include the later developed Consolidated Privateer.

PB4Y-1 Liberator

Type: land-based maritime patrol aircraft

Powerplant: four 895-kW (667-hp) Pratt & Whitney R-1830-43 twin Wasp radial piston engines

Maximum speed: 488 km/h (303 mph)

Cruising speed: 225 km/h (140 mph)

Operational radius: 1730 km (1075 miles)

Service ceiling: 8540 m (28,000 ft)

Weights: empty 15,413 kg (33,980 lb); maximum take-off 27,216 kg (59,803 lb)

Armament: nine 12.7-mm (.50-cal.) machine guns, plus a maximum internal bomb load of 3692 kg (8139 lb)

Dimensions:
span	33.53 m	(110 ft)
length	22.73 m	(74 ft 7 in)
height	9.17 m	(30 ft 1 in)
wing area	97.36 m²	(1048 sq ft)

COMBAT DATA

MAXIMUM SPEED

Compared to the flying-boats operated by the US Navy in WWII, the land-based Liberator offered a vast improvement in speed. Able to cover huge areas of ocean in a single patrol, the type was instrumental in winning the war in the Atlantic.

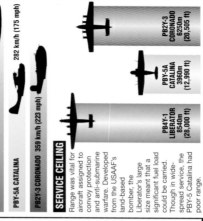

PB4Y-1 LIBERATOR 488 km/h (303 mph)

PBY-5A CATALINA 282 km/h (175 mph)

PB2Y-3 CORONADO 359 km/h (223 mph)

SERVICE CEILING

Range was vital for aircraft assigned to convoy protection and anti-submarine warfare. Developed from the USAAF's land-based bomber, the Liberator's large size meant that a significant fuel load could be carried. Though in widespread service, the PBY-5 Catalina had poor range.

PB2Y-3 CORONADO 6250m (20,505 ft)

PBY-5A CATALINA 3960m (12,990 ft)

PB4Y-1 LIBERATOR 8540m (28,000 ft)

MAXIMUM TAKE-OFF WEIGHT

Largest of the patrol aircraft in service with the US Navy was the Coronado flying-boat, which was also used as a heavy transport. Previously given to a bomber, the Liberator easily carried a large load of mines, depth-charges and rockets.

PB2Y-3 CORONADO 30,844 kg (68,000 lb)

PBY-5A CATALINA 16,067 kg (35,422 lb)

PB4Y-1 LIBERATOR 27,216 kg (59,803 lb)

■ **PB4Y PRIVATEER:** The final development of the navalised Liberators was the single-tailed Privateer. Operational in the final stages of World War II, the aircraft remained in post-war use.

■ **PB2Y CORONADO:** Costing five times more than a Catalina, Consolidated's Coronado gave only limited service as a transport and casualty-evacuation aircraft.

Ocean patrolling in World War II

■ **PBY CATALINA:** Achieving legendary fame for its exploits in World War II, the Consolidated Catalina saw extensive combat with RAF Coastal Command and the US Navy in the Pacific.

CONSOLIDATED
PB4Y-2 PRIVATEER

- Naval B-24 derivative ● War service ● 1950s spy flights

▲ By 1944 1370 PB4Y-2s were on order; although only 736 were delivered. US naval use of the B-24, as the PB4Y Liberator and Privateer, extended the design's front-line service by eight years.

T he PB4Y-2 Privateer was developed from America's most numerous warplane, the B-24 Liberator.

Redesigned for the demanding job of flying long-range maritime patrols, the Privateer differed from the Liberator in having a prominent single fin, an Erco nose turret, a lengthened fuselage, and revised engines and cowlings. A success in its own right, the Privateer saw combat with the American and French navies.

CONSOLIDATED PB4Y-2 PRIVATEER

▼ Post-war PB4Y-2
Named Our Baby, this PB4Y-2 is seen in Shanghai in 1945. The Privateer saw little wartime service, but the US Navy operated the type until 1951.

▲ RAF transport
Designated C-87C, the transport version of the B-24N was built in small numbers, all USAAF examples being delivered to the US Navy as the RY-3. The RAF used a few as Liberator C.Mk IXs.

▼ Longer fuselage and new tail
Flown in September 1943, the PB4Y-2 had a single fin, lengthened fuselage and revised engine nacelles.

▲ Search and rescue
PB4Y-2G was the designation of those Privateers converted post-war for search and rescue and weather reconnaissance duties.

▲ Aéronavale PB4Y-2
Among a large number of American aircraft received post-war, Privateers of the French navy saw active service in a number of 1950s and 1960s conflicts, notably those in the colonies of Algeria and Indo-China and during the Suez crisis.

FACTS AND FIGURES

- Loudspeaker-equipped PB4Y-2s were used in the Marianas to encourage Japanese soldiers to surrender.

- Total Privateer production was 736; the last was delivered in October 1945.

- The first flight of a Privateer took place on 20 September 1943.

- The last ever US Navy PB4Y-2 mission saw a PB4Y-2K drone shot down during missile tests on 18 January 1964.

- Anti-submarine radar was fitted to some USN PB4Y-2s, which became PB4Y-2Ss.

- PB4Y-2Ks carried a wing-mounted camera to record a missile hit.

PB4Y-2 Privateer

Type: long-range maritime patrol bomber and reconnaissance aircraft

Powerplant: four 1007-kW (1350-hp) Pratt & Whitney R-1830 Twin Wasp radial piston engines

Maximum speed: 380 km/h (236 mph) at 4200 m (14,000 ft)

Cruising speed: 225 km/h (140 mph)

Initial climb rate: 332 m/min (1090 fpm)

Maximum range: 4500 km (2800 miles)

Service ceiling: 6310 m (20,700 ft)

Weights: empty 17,003 kg (37,407 lb); maximum take-off 29,483 kg (64,863 lb)

Armament: twelve 12.7-mm (.50-cal.) machine guns in nose, twin dorsal and tail turrets and in two fuselage blisters, plus up to 5806 kg (12,780 lb) of bombs or other stores, including two ASM-N-2 Bat radar-homing anti-ship missiles

Dimensions: span   33.52 m
length   21.24 m
height   8.95 m
wing area   97.36 m²

COMBAT DATA

POWER

The Pratt & Whitney R-1830 Twin Wasps fitted to the Privateer were more powerful than the boosted engines fitted to the earlier wartime Liberator from which the Privateer was developed. Unlike earlier versions fitted with Bristol Pegasus engines, the Sunderland Mk V also used Pratt & Whitney Twin Wasps although they were of an earlier less powerful mark.

PB4Y-2 PRIVATEER
4028 KW (5400 hp)

PB4Y-1 LIBERATOR
3580 KW (4800 hp)

SUNDERLAND Mk V
3580 KW (4800 hp)

RANGE

The PB4Y-2 was equipped with enough fuel tank capacity for the maritime patrol missions envisaged for the type. It therefore lacked the outer wing tanks found in the Liberator, which consequently had a slightly longer range. The RAF's Short Sunderland flying-boat was Coastal Command's primary long-range maritime type for most of World War II. The RAF also operated Liberators.

PB4Y-2 PRIVATEER   4506 km (2800 miles)

PB4Y-1 LIBERATOR   4764 km (2950 miles)

SUNDERLAND Mk V   4329 km (2680 miles)

'Two by Four': the navy's Liberator

Privateers could travel almost twice as far with almost twice the bombload of the Navy's North American PBJ Mitchell. When it became operational on the islands of Midway and Tinian in January 1945, the Privateer enabled American naval aviators to dominate the Pacific approaches to the Japanese home islands. They were flying the ideal plane to sink Japanese ships and bottle up Japanese naval bases.

Redesignated P4Y-2 in 1950 and P-4B in 1962, the PB4Y-2 Privateer (nicknamed 'Two by Four' by navy personnel)

became a spy plane in the Cold War. The intrepid pilots and crews of this big plane found themselves caught up in some of the most adventurous flying of the era. In April 1950, Soviet MiG-15 fighters shot down a PB4Y-2 over the Baltic Sea in one of many dark moments during the jousting between the superpowers. This was the first casualty of the electronic intelligence (Elint) 'war' which was waged for over 30 years.

In 1961 a Chinese Nationalist PB4Y-2 was shot down by Burmese air force Hawker Sea Fury fighters while engaged in a

secret supply drop to Chinese-supported rebels in Burma's Shan state. The Privateer also saw combat in the Korean War and, in French service, in Suez and Indo-China.

The last Privateers in US service were later QP-4B drone aircraft retired in the early 1960s. Others served in Latin America.

Left: Intended for low- and medium-altitude use, the PB4Y-2s lacked turbo-superchargers on their Pratt & Whitney R-1830 radial engines.

Right: The lengthened fin and rudder planned for the cancelled B-24N were adopted for the PB4Y-2 Privateer development of the B-24 Liberator.

PB4Y-2 PRIVATEER

This aircraft of US Navy patrol squadron VP-871 was based at K-14 (Kimpo), Korea during 1952. Among their roles was target illumination (using flares) for Marine Corps night intruders.

The fuselage 'stretch' carried out to create the PB4Y-2 totalled 2.13 m (7 ft) and consisted of two plugs added fore and aft of the wings.

Late-production PB4Y-1s (equivalent to the B-24J) and most PB4Y-2s were fitted with the distinctive Erco nose turret which carried two 12.7-mm (.50-cal.) machine guns. In all, 12 defensive machine guns were carried.

Standard PB4Y-2s carried a crew of 11. Among these personnel was a radar operator. The PB4Y-2 carried an extensive search radar fit, which accounted for the various blisters on the forward fuselage. During the early Cold War years US Navy Privateers were engaged in 'ferreting' missions over Eastern Europe, the exact nature of which remains classified.

Though rarely carried in service, eight 726-kg bombs could be held in the Privateer's bomb bay. During the last months of World War II, PB4Y-2Bs were equipped to carry an ASM-N-2 Bat radar-homing anti-shipping bomb beneath each wing.

Each Erco 260TH Tear Drop carried two 12.7-mm (.50-cal.) machine guns. The single tailfin allowed a much improved field of fire for the waist gunners, compared to that of the PB4Y-1 Liberator.

US Navy units received 736 Privateers, the transport version of which (originally ordered by the USAAF as the C-87C) was known as the RY-3. This variant featured a cargo door and cabin windows.

Intended to operate at medium to low altitudes, the PB4Y-2 had non-turbo-supercharged Pratt & Whitney R-1830-94 radials in redesigned nacelles. Outer wing fuel tanks were deleted, as the four bomb bay tanks of 15,550-litre (4100-gallon) capacity were sufficient.

USN/USMC aircraft over Korea

■ **DOUGLAS AD SKYRAIDER:** Skyraiders flew against North Korean targets within three days of the start of the 'war'. Mainly carrier-based, they were used throughout the conflict.

■ **GRUMMAN F9F-2/-5 PANTHER:** The first US Navy jets to see combat service were Panthers from the USS *Valley Forge*. Fighter and attack missions were carried out.

■ **MARTIN PBM MARINER:** Japan-based Mariners undertook long-range patrols of up to 12 hours duration off the Korean coast, searching the sea for Communist infiltrators.

■ **McDONNELL F2H BANSHEE:** As well as carrier-borne fighter operations, Banshees were engaged in land-based reconnaissance duties with the Marine Corps, using F2H-2Ps.

CONSOLIDATED
PBY CATALINA

● Flying-boat and amphibian ● Search-and-rescue aircraft ● War service

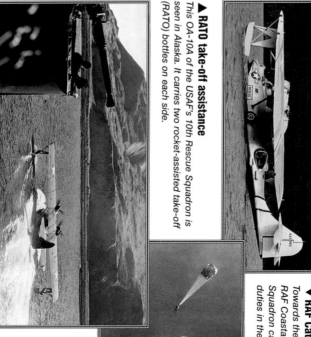

▲ The approach of a PBY Catalina was a welcome sight for many Allied sailors or downed airmen as they bobbed on the vast ocean in a dinghy awaiting rescue.

N ear the end of the war, an American Consolidated PBY Catalina flying-boat took off from Okinawa, flew to hostile waters within sight of the Japanese shoreline and rescued seven men from a ditched B-29 bomber. The mission involved flying over a long distance in bad weather, touching down on the water in full view of the enemy and filling the aircraft to capacity. It was a tough challenge, but the PBY Catalina was up to the demand.

CONSOLIDATED PBY CATALINA

▲ Navy 'non-specular sea blue'
This matt-blue finish was typical of that applied to US Navy aircraft in 1943. The PBY-5A amphibian was developed from the PBY-5 flying-boat to give the aircraft greater flexibility.

▼ Parasol wing
The Catalina's wing lifted the engines well clear of spray from rough waters.

▼ RAF Catalina operations
Towards the end of World War II RAF Coastal Command's No. 240 Squadron carried out air-sea rescue duties in the Far East.

▲ RATO take-off assistance
This OA-10A of the USAF's 10th Rescue Squadron is seen in Alaska. It carries two rocket-assisted take-off (RATO) bottles on each side.

▲ In the Aleutians
At the northernmost extremities of the Pacific Ocean, Catalinas were used for offensive and rescue roles in the campaigns along the Aleutian archipelago.

FACTS AND FIGURES

▶ When landing on open sea, the pilot brought the Catalina to a full stall just before touchdown.

▶ The first PBY flew in 1936 and the type stayed in production until 1945.

▶ Some PBYs carried the AR-8 airborne lifeboat, fitted under the wing.

▶ PBYs for Britain were the first military aircraft delivered by trans-Atlantic flight during the war.

▶ The US Coast Guard used PBYs for rescue duties from World War II until the 1950s.

▶ PBYs saved 161 airmen in the first eight months of 1943 in the Solomon Islands in the first eight months of 1943.

PROFILE

Search-and-rescue by 'Dumbo Cat'

No one knows how many men were rescued in combat by the courageous pilots who flew the Consolidated PBY Catalina into dangerous situations – but the number is in the thousands.

This twin-engined, parasol-wing flying-boat and amphibian was one of the slowest aircraft of the war; it was said that it was in danger of being struck by birds from behind. But, despite its unimpressive speed, the PBY was a sturdy, well-armed and versatile flying machine that could land in some of the most difficult conditions to rescue men in peril.

More Catalinas were built than any other flying-boat in history. Designed to a US Navy requirement for a long-range patrol bomber, the PBY proved to be a highly successful anti-shipping and anti-submarine aircraft in a number of theatres, and served with several Allied air forces. PBYs also rescued more survivors from ships and aircraft than any aircraft of the war.

Perhaps the most famous of all Catalinas were the US Navy's 'Black Cats', which operated against the Japanese in the Pacific in 1942. US Navy and USAAF 'Cats' were used for the search-and-rescue (SAR) role until the late 1940s.

Above: The USAAF received 75 ex-US Navy PBY-6As for the SAR role. These were designated OA-10B (A-10B after 1948) and were distinguished by their taller tails.

Below: After 1945 USAAF OA-10As remained in the Air Rescue Service, along with converted C-47s, B-17s and B-29s.

The antennas on the wings are part of the Catalina's ASV (air-to-surface vessel) radar which was developed during World War II for maritime patrol aircraft hunting enemy shipping and submarines. The radar was also useful for finding downed aircraft. The radome above the cockpit contains an additional centimetric-wavelength radar.

OA-10A CATALINA

Canadian Vickers built 230 PBY-5A amphibians for the US Navy, and all were transferred to the USAAF as OA-10A search-and-rescue craft. 44-33924 was one of this batch and is seen in post-war markings.

With the Catalina's ungainly appearance and performance and in honour of the Walt Disney cartoon character of the 1940s, SAR PBY aircraft were nicknamed 'Dumbo' by USAAF and Navy personnel.

Cupolas on both sides of the fuselage, which each carried a 12.7-mm (.50-cal.) machine gun in wartime, were introduced on the PBY-5 and were ideal for observers on the look-out for downed aircraft or personnel awaiting rescue.

Built by Canadian Vickers, the PBY-5A was known as the PBV-1A. The same company built 139 for the Royal Canadian Air Force, which called it the Canso. In RAF service the PBY-5A was known as the Catalina Mk III.

High-visibility markings distinguished USAF SAR aircraft, especially after World War II.

Catalina rescue off Japan

29 MAY 1945: An OA-10A on station with a US Navy lifeguard submarine shadowing a B-29 bombing raid on Japan was called to rescue the crew of a ditched aircraft.

CREW LOCATED: Having located the men, the Catalina landed and picked them up. However, on take-off the aircraft slammed into three large swells and the port engine was torn from its mount and smashed into the cockpit. The pilot was badly injured and the co-pilot radioed the rescue submarine.

SAVED BY THE SUB: The following morning the submarine delivered the crews from the B-29 and OA-10 to Iwo Jima. Between November 1944 and 14 August 1945, the 21st Bomber Command lost 3125 crewmen in attacks on Japan. Of these, 1424 went down at sea. Air Force and Navy units rescued 687, nearly half of those who ditched.

PBY-5A Catalina

Type: long-range maritime patrol bomber and air-sea rescue aircraft

Powerplant: two 895-kW (1200-hp) Pratt & Whitney R-1830-92 Twin Wasp radial piston engines

Maximum speed: 288 km/h (179 mph) at 2135 m (7000 ft)

Range: 4096 km (2545 miles)

Service ceiling: 4480 m (14,698 ft)

Weights: empty 9485 kg (20,911 lb); loaded 16,066 kg (35,419 lb)

Armament: two 7.62-mm (.30-cal.) machine guns in bow, one 7.62-mm machine gun firing aft from the hull step and two 12.7-mm (.50-cal.) machine guns in beam position, plus air-sea rescue equipment including life rafts

Dimensions:
span	31.70 m (104 ft)
length	19.47 m (63 ft 11 in)
height	6.15 m (20 ft 2 in)
wing area	130.06 m² (1400 sq ft)

ACTION DATA

CRUISING SPEED

USAAF Catalinas survived in the SAR role after World War II alongside the converted Douglas C-47 transports and B-17 and B-29 bombers of the Air Rescue Service. By the late 1940s, when the USAF became the USAAF and took overall responsibility for SAR, the Catalina was outmoded. The Albatross which replaced it had a higher cruising speed plus other improvements.

OA-10A CATALINA	182 km/h (113 mph)
SA-16A ALBATROSS	241 km/h (150 mph)
Do 24T-3	249 km/h (155 mph)

RANGE

Until the SA-16A Albatross was modified to SA-16B (later HU-16B) standard, with greatly increased fuel capacity and a longer wing span, it had only modest range. The Do 24 was a wartime German design capable of flying 1000 km (620 miles) further than the Albatross – but not as far as the OA-10.

OA-10A CATALINA	3782 km (2350 miles)
Do 24T-3	2897 km (1789 miles)
SA-16A ALBATROSS	1850 km (1150 miles)

ENGINE POWER

The Dornier Do 24 had more power than the other two types because of its three engines. Piston engine technology advanced in the years after World War II, and the Albatross had twin engines of appreciably more power than those fitted to the Catalina. Reliability was important for maritime patrol aircraft. Engines tuned to run at less than peak power were less likely to fail in service.

OA-10A CATALINA	1790 kW (2400 hp)
SA-16A ALBATROSS	2125 kW (2850 hp)
Do 24T-3	2238 kW (3001 hp)

CONVAIR

B-32 DOMINATOR

● Strategic bomber ● Late wartime service entry ● Crew trainer

▲ Beginning life almost as a scaled-up B-24 Liberator, progressive changes through the three prototypes of the B-32 led to the ultimate design, minus the initial round nose and twin fins.

Consolidated built the B-32 Dominator as an 'insurance' against any possibility that Boeing's B-29 project might fail. Had events turned out differently, the big, powerful B-32 might have led the 1944/45 bombing campaign against the Japanese home islands. But the B-32 was delayed in development, and the B-29 succeeded. This meant that the Dominator became little more than a footnote in aviation history, with only a handful flying operationally.

PHOTO FILE

CONVAIR **B-32 DOMINATOR**

▼ **Cyclone power**
Wright's 1641-kW (2198 hp) R-3350-23 Cyclone engine, unrivalled at altitude, powered both the B-32 and Boeing B-29.

▲ **Long-range mission master**
In standard form, the B-32 Dominator had provision for a crew of eight, and defensive armament of five twin-gun manned turrets. Teething problems meant the B-32 Dominator would see little action.

▼ **Prototype Dominator**
Consolidated built just three XB-32 prototypes before receiving a joint order with Boeing, who also built three XB-29 prototype aircraft.

▲ **Service entry**
Only 15 B-32s were to become operational before VJ-Day, all equipping the USAAF's 386th Heavy Bombardment Squadron. A total of 40 TB-32 crew trainers was also built, but withdrawn post-war.

FACTS AND FIGURES

► The 386th Bomb Group moved from the Philippines to Okinawa, bombing Japan during the last week of the war.

► Convair's B-32 beat the B-29 into the air by 14 days, flying on 7 September 1942.

► A double tail in the style of the B-24 was featured on the first two Dominators.

► The first mission was flown from Clark Field on 29 May 1945 against a Japanese Army depot deep in the Cagayan Valley.

► Some 118 Dominators were built before further development was cancelled.

► Consolidated's chief test pilot was killed when a prototype crashed on 10 May 1943.

Heavy bombload ▼
Each of the B-32's bomb-bays could carry 4536 kg (10,000 lb) of iron bombs. Had it not been beaten by the B-29, the Dominator might have made the nuclear strikes on Japan.

Superfortress understudy

When it first flew in 1942, the B-32 was one of the biggest and most capable bombers ever built. This high-winged, four-engined giant had many of the innovative features of its competitor, the B-29, including pressurisation and remote-controlled gun turrets.

Consolidated (which became Convair in the mid 1940s) had many problems developing the B-32 and was not able to begin delivery of production bombers until November 1944, almost eight months after B-29s had been deployed to begin their campaign against Japan. Even

then, production B-32s had the intended pressurisation and armament deleted.

Although this was an impressive aircraft, only 15 became operational before the war's end, equipping the 386th Bombardment Squadron on Okinawa. Forty TB-32s were also used for training, out of a total B-32 production run of 118.

While the B-32 saw very little combat, one B-32 flew the final US bombing mission of World War II. Between 15 and 18 August 1945, Dominators flew 'reconnaissance' missions over Tokyo, encountered hostile

ground fire and attacks by Japanese pilots who rebelled against the 15 August surrender. On 18 August, an engagement with fighters caused the death of a crewman, a significant event in history since he was the last American to be killed in World War II.

Below: The second XB-32 was an 'in-between' stage, with the twin fins of the first and glazed nose of the third.

Above: By the time the first production B-32 had taken to the air, it was a different machine altogether, incorporating the stepped glazed nose and conventional tail unit of the second and third XB-32 prototypes, respectively.

B-32 DOMINATOR

Seeing only limited service in the Pacific theatre, the B-32's life as a US Army Air Force heavy bomber was brief. A few flew as navigation trainers, but these aircraft were soon surplus to requirements.

One of five gun turrets, each with two 12.7-mm (.50-cal.) machine guns, was located in the nose. Originally, the B-32 was intended to carry advanced, remote-controlled gun turrets, like those of the B-29.

Like the B-29, the Dominator utilised four powerful Wright Cyclone radial piston engines, driving large-diameter, four-bladed propellers.

The B-32 usually carried its bombload in vertical stacks within the two capacious bomb-bays. Only the 386th Bombardment Squadron became operational on the type, and this machine carries 11 mission symbols.

The Dominator's enormous tail was a necessity in order to replicate the surface area of the two separate tails of the prototype aircraft. Because of hurried manufacture, the fuselage pressurisation system was deleted.

Like most heavy bombers of the period, the B-32 had a manned tail turret. In later machines, the tail and nose twin machine guns were replaced with single 20-mm cannon.

Late-war bomber projects

■ **AVRO LINCOLN:** Initially known as the Lancaster Mk IV, the Lincoln was too late to fly operationally in World War II but became an important RAF heavy bomber after the war.

■ **HEINKEL He 277:** A four-engined development of the He 177 Grief, eight production machines had been completed when manufacturing priority turned to fighters in 1944.

■ **NAKAJIMA G8N1 RENZAN:** Coming too late to enter service as the Japanese navy's first four-engined heavy bomber, the Renzan ('Rita') was tested in America after the war.

■ **VICKERS WINDSOR:** This experimental bomber was notable for its main undercarriage, which consisted of four separate units. Its skin was an unusual woven steel wire/fabric composite.

B-32 Dominator

Type: long-range strategic bomber

Powerplant: four 1641-kW Wright R-3350-23 Cyclone radial piston engines

Maximum speed: 575 km/h (357 mph) at 7620 m (25,000 ft)

Range: 1287 km (800 miles) with maximum bombload

Maximum range: 6115 km (3800 miles)

Service ceiling: 10,670 m (35,000 ft)

Weights: empty 27,339 kg (60,272 lb); maximum take-off 50,576 kg (111,500 lb)

Armament: provision for 9072 kg (20,000 lb) of bombs in two bomb-bays; 10 12.7-mm (.50-cal.) machine guns in five barbettes, but 14 weapons in seven barbettes were planned

Dimensions:
span	41.15 m (135 ft)
length	25.32 m (83 ft 1 in)
height	10.06 m (33 ft)
wing area	132.10 m² (1422 sq ft)

COMBAT DATA

ARMAMENT

Designed and built to the same specification as the B-29, the B-32 had a very similar weapons load. The German He 277 had a greater emphasis on defensive guns, and like many German bomber types had only a limited bombload.

B-32 DOMINATOR
10 x 12.7-mm (.50-cal.) machine guns
9072-kg (20,000-lb) bombload

B-29 SUPERFORTRESS
11 x 12.7-mm (.50-cal.) machine guns
9072-kg (20,000-lb) bombload

He 277B-5/R2
6 x 20-mm cannon, 4 x 13-mm cannon
3000-kg (6614-lb) bombload

SERVICE CEILING

Although unpressurised, the B-32 had a greater ceiling than the rival Superfortress. From the outset, the He 277 was also designed for high-altitude missions in order to escape fighters.

He 277B-5/R2
15,000 m (49,213 ft)

B-32 DOMINATOR
10,670 m (35,000 ft)

B-29 SUPERFORTRESS
9710 m (31,857 ft)

RANGE

Although smaller than the B-29, the B-32 had a considerably greater range. It also had a slightly longer range than the Heinkel He 277. Had its development been smoother, it may well have been the Dominator, not the Boeing B-29, that went on to be remembered as one of the most successful heavy bombers of all time.

B-29 SUPERFORTRESS
5230 km (3250 miles)

B-32 DOMINATOR
6115 km (3800 miles)

He 277B-5/R2
6000 km (3728 miles)

98

CONVAIR
B-36 FICON

● Giant strategic bomber ● Reconnaissance mother-ship

The B-36 was the 'Big Stick' of Cold War deterrence; 383 of these stupendous bombers were the backbone of the mighty Strategic Air Command from 1948 to 1959. The largest warplanes ever to fly in the West, they carried the biggest hydrogen bombs ever built and girdled the globe on nuclear alert or highly dangerous spying missions. At one stage they even carried their own fighter aircraft.

▶ The B-36 was massive, yet its incredible weight rested on just single mainwheels. These weren't quite the biggest wheels ever carried by an aircraft, but they dwarfed ground crew.

CONVAIR B-36 FICON

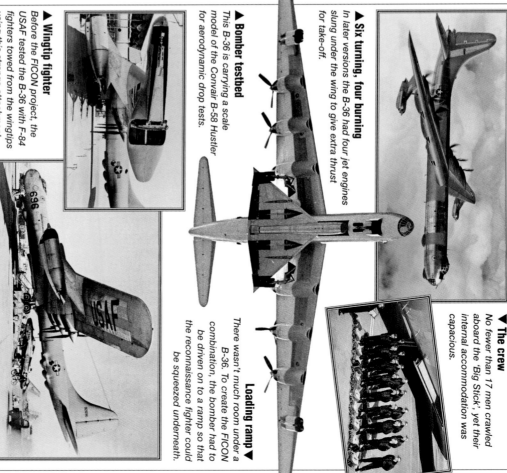

▶ **The crew**
No fewer than 17 men crawled aboard the 'Big Stick', yet their internal accommodation was capacious.

▶ **Six turning, four burning**
In later versions the B-36 had four jet engines slung under the wing to give extra thrust for take-off.

▶ **Bomber testbed**
This B-36 is carrying a scale model of the Convair B-58 Hustler for aerodynamic drop tests.

Loading ramp ▼
There wasn't much room under a B-36. To create the FICON combination, the bomber had to be driven on to a ramp so that the reconnaissance fighter could be squeezed underneath.

▶ **Wingtip fighter**
Before the FICON project, the USAF tested the B-36 with F-84 fighters towed from the wingtips using this strange attachment.

FACTS AND FIGURES

▼ A few B-36s were modified to carry a fighter in the bomb-bay.

▼ Convair developed a huge airlifter from the B-36, the experimental XC-99, but the giant transport never entered service.

▼ The B-36's radar and communications systems used 3000 vacuum tubes.

▼ To the men who flew it, the B-36 never had a name. The appropriate nickname 'Peacemaker' was assigned to this mammoth bomber years after it went out of service.

▼ B-36 missions lasted for so long that it was said to be equipped with a calender rather than clocks.

A deadly combination

Originally designed to drop bombs on Germany from bases in America, the big B-36 began as a six-engined bomber but soon had four jets added, making it a 10-engine behemoth by the time it entered service in 1948. It was tasked to rip out the heart of the Soviet Union with a retaliatory attack, using hydrogen bombs like the Mk 17, which weighed more than a DC-3 transport and was the largest bomb ever deployed by the US military.

When the B-36 flew overhead, it blotted out the sun.

In slang, it was called the 'aluminum overcast'. The bomber was so long that crewmen used a powered dolly to transport themselves through the middle of the aircraft between nose and tail.

At high altitude, the vast wings of the B-36 clawed so much air that the bomber was more manoeuvrable than jet fighters. Missions in this incredible giant lasted as long as 40 hours. No other American bomber ever approached the B-36's size, weight, and bomb-carrying capacity.

The NB-36H carried a nuclear reactor to test its effect on the aircraft. The next step would have been a nuclear-powered bomber.

GRB-36 FICON

With its enormous size, the B-36 was a natural to act as a mother-ship for a secret strategic reconnaissance programme. A small reconnaissance fighter was carried over a long distance to its target, dropped off to go in and get the pictures, and then hauled back home to the US.

The FICON (Fighter Conveyor) combination went operational in 1955, but only a handful of missions were flown. The operating unit was the 91st Strategic Reconnaissance Squadron.

The aircraft carried by the GRB-36 was the Republic GRF-84F, a special version of the USAF's main tactical camera ship.

The Thunderflash fighter was held on a complicated trapeze which swung down from the bomb-bay. The doors of the bomb-bay were cut away so that the fighter could fit in snugly.

To give the huge bomber an extra burst of speed over the target area, the B-36 was fitted with four J47 turbojets to augment the six huge piston engines driving the propellers.

Operational bombers had two pairs of gun turrets in the rear fuselage, operated remotely from observation posts by dedicated gunners. When not threatened by the enemy, the guns were retracted and covered by sliding panels.

The B-36 was covered with aerials and radomes for electronic equipment and bombing radars. Many variants had huge reconnaissance cameras wedged into the bomb-bays.

B-36s were normally festooned with defensive guns, the standard bomber featuring no less than 16 20-mm cannon, including two in the tail. The FICON aircraft had them all removed to save precious weight.

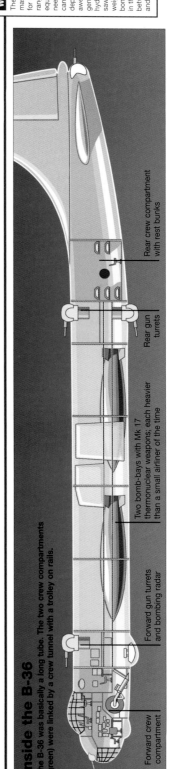

Inside the B-36

The B-36 was basically a long tube. The two crew compartments (green) were linked by a crew tunnel with a trolley on rails.

Forward crew compartment

Forward gun turrets and bombing radar

Two bomb-bays with Mk 17 thermonuclear weapons; each heavier than a small airliner of the time

Rear gun turrets

Rear crew compartment with rest bunks

B-36D Peacemaker

Type: intercontinental strategic bomber

Powerplant: six 2834-kW (3800-hp) Pratt & Whitney R-4360-53 radial piston engines and four 23.13-kN (5204-lb-thrust) General Electric J47-GE-19 turbojets

Maximum speed: 700 km/h (435 mph) at 11,000 m (36,000 ft)

Range: 10,944 km (6800 miles) with a 4500-kg (9921-lb) bombload

Service ceiling: 14,780 m (48,490 ft)

Weights: empty 77,581 kg (171,037 lb); loaded 185,976 kg (410,007 lb)

Armament: 16 20-mm cannon in nose, tail and six fuselage turrets, plus bombload of up to 39,000 kg (85,980 lb)

Dimensions:
span 70.10 m (230 ft)
length 49.40 m (162 ft 1 in)
height 14.22 m (46 ft 8 in)
wing area 443.32 m² (4772 sq ft)

COMBAT DATA

MAXIMUM SPEED

B-52 STRATOFORTRESS (1952) 965 km/h (600 mph)

B-36 PEACEMAKER (1946) 700 km/h (435 mph)

B-29 SUPERFORTRESS (1942) 570 km/h (354 mph)

Less than a decade spanned the first flights of the Boeing B-29, the Convair B-36 and the Boeing B-52, yet in that time maximum speed almost doubled. All three bombers used their big wings and immense engine power to outperform interceptors at height.

SERVICE CEILING

16,750 m (54,954 ft) **B-52 STRATOFORTRESS**

14,780 m (48,490 ft) **B-36 PEACEMAKER**

9750 m (31,998 ft) **B-29 SUPERFORTRESS**

Bombing from high altitude was seen as the only protection against fighters in the days before guided missiles. The B-36 FICON used another technique – its onboard fighter flew the last, most dangerous part of the mission.

WEIGHTS

B-36 PEACEMAKER 185,976 kg (41,007 lb)

B-52 STRATOFORTRESS 221,000 kg (487,222 lb)

B-29 SUPERFORTRESS 63,500 kg (139,993 lb)

Maximum take-off weights

The need for massive fuel loads for intercontinental range, and the equally pressing need for huge carrying capacity to deploy the awesome first-generation hydrogen bombs, saw the maximum weights of heavy bombers skyrocket in the decade between the B-29 and the B-52.

CONVAIR

B-58 HUSTLER

● Supersonic strategic bomber ● Delta wing ● Nuclear-armed

Brilliant but brief – that was the career of the Convair B-58 Hustler of the USAF's Strategic Air Command. From area-rule fuselage through crew escape capsules to its revolutionary J79 engines, everything about the B-58 pushed back the frontiers; it was a towering engineering achievement. Had it gone into battle, the Mach 2-capable Hustler, with its immense performance and advanced podded weapons, would have been able to penetrate Soviet defences with impunity.

▶ The B-58 was a technological wonder, with blistering performance. But its operational flexibility was limited to the strategic role by its unusual combined fuel- and weapon-pod concept.

PHOTO FILE

CONVAIR **B-58 HUSTLER**

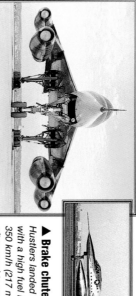

▶ Fast mover
Without its huge fuel and weapon pod the B-58 looked like a fighter, and performed like one too. With afterburner selected, the Hustler could climb at around 11,500 m (37,700 ft) per minute.

Flying capsules ▶
The three-man crew sat in individual cockpits. They liked their personal escape capsules, but disliked the lack of adequate air-conditioning.

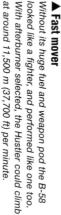

▶ Brake chute
Hustlers landed fast – a typical touchdown speed with a high fuel load remaining was around 350 km/h (217 mph). A braking parachute was often used to prolong the life of the wheelbrakes.

▶ Big delta
The B-58 was the biggest delta ever to enter USAF service and followed Convair's delta fighters, the F-102 and F-106 series.

▶ High altitude
Hustlers performed very well at altitude, and could climb to around 20,000 m (65,000 ft). This enabled them to escape the attentions of most fighters, but the shooting down of the U-2 spyplane in 1960 by a surface-to-air missile showed high altitude did not guarantee safety.

FACTS AND FIGURES

▶ The B-58's first flight took place on 11 November 1956, and it became operational in 1960.

▶ A B-58 carried a five-tonne bombload to a record height of 26,018 m (85,339 ft).

▶ The Hustler could fly at 1128 km/h (698 mph) at low level, never climbing above 155 m (500 ft).

▶ The first SAC Hustler wing set 19 world records, including supersonic flights to or from London, Tokyo and Paris.

▶ A fully loaded Hustler had to exceed 400 km/h (250 mph) before it could get aloft.

▶ To test the escape system a bear was ejected from a B-58 at 1400 km/h (868 mph).

PROFILE

Twice the speed of sound – in a bomber!

The Convair B-58 Hustler was the world's first supersonic strategic bomber. Designed around the same delta wing shape used on Convair's highly successful F-102 and F-106 fighters, the Hustler could fly non-stop for 18 hours – carrying a nuclear weapon to any target on the globe. This aircraft was, very simply, the most sensational in its category.

The B-58's four afterburning turbojets could maintain the big bomber at top speed for more than an hour before throttling back. The Hustler's refinements included pilot, bombardier-navigator and systems operator seated in tandem in three

cockpits; a two-component droppable weapons/fuel pod under the fuselage that housed any of three weapon systems; and an air-to-surface missile, nuclear bombs or electronic countermeasures gear.

When the advent of the surface-to-air missile brought aerial warfare down to sea level, the high-flying B-58 dropped successfully to low-altitude operations. But one feature stayed up in the stratosphere – its operating costs. The type was retired for economy reasons in 1970 after a decade during which the Hustler equipped two of the USAF's Strategic Air Command bomber wings.

B-58A HUSTLER

The 116 B-58s equipped two wings of Strategic Air Command, serving from 1960 to 1970, during which time the type set several speed and payload records.

The crew sat in individual cockpits, with the navigator behind the pilot and the defensive systems operator in the rear cockpit.

A powerful attack radar system was mounted in the nose. The navigator also had a computerised navigation system.

The Hustler had a short operational career, but it must have been a considerable headache for Soviet air defence planners. It was the most advanced bomber to enter service in the 1960s, since the Myasishchev M-50 and North American XB-70 Valkyrie failed to proceed beyond trials.

Refuelling in the B-58 was much easier than in most aircraft, as the delta wing gave excellent stability and the refuelling port was straight in front of the pilot's canopy.

The J79 turbojet was a mainstay of the inventory in the 1960s; it also powered the F-4 Phantom, the F-104 Starfighter and the Navy's RA-5 Vigilante.

Four external hardpoints could be fitted with 8820 kg (19,450 lb) of nuclear or conventional bombs.

The B-58 fleet usually had a natural metal finish, as camouflage was not needed for an aircraft that would rarely be seen from above in action.

The huge delta wing had no flaps. Control was provided by elevons – combined elevators and ailerons.

The rocket-powered BLU-2/B-2 and MB-1C pods contained fuel and weapons. The pod weapons bay could carry five nuclear bombs.

Since B-58 landings were usually fast and hard, the 16 tyres were filled with high-pressure nitrogen.

Chasing a B-58 was a dangerous business, because a Vulcan M61 20-mm cannon was mounted in the tail. This was radar-controlled and remotely operated by the defensive systems operator in the third cockpit.

Supersonic strikers

■ **MYASISHCHEV 'BOUNDER':** Roughly contemporary with the Hustler, the Soviet jet was larger but slower, and had limited range.

■ **NORTH AMERICAN XB-70:** First flown in 1964, the XB-70 was a Mach 3 bomber. Astronomical costs meant that it never entered production.

■ **GENERAL DYNAMICS FB-111:** Entering service in 1969, the FB-111 replaced the B-58. It was faster except when carrying a full load.

■ **TUPOLEV Tu-22M 'BACKFIRE':** Very similar in performance to the B-58, the swing-wing 'Backfire' became operational 20 years after the Hustler.

■ **ROCKWELL B-1:** The original B-1A prototype could reach Mach 2.5. The B-1B, which entered service in 1985, could fly at only half that speed.

B-58A Hustler

Type: three-seat supersonic bomber

Powerplant: four 69.39-kN (15,567-lb-thrust) General Electric J79-GE-5B afterburning turbojets

Maximum speed: 1128 km/h (700 mph) at sea level; 2218 km/h (1375 mph) or Mach 2.1 at high altitude

Range: 8250 km (5115 miles) on internal and pod fuel

Service ceiling: 17,336 m (56,862 ft) with operational load

Weights: empty 25,202 kg (55,440 lb); take-off 73,937 kg (163,003 lb) (80,250 kg/176,920 lb) after inflight refuelling

Armament: up to 8823 kg in underfuselage pod with any six types of nuclear bomb including B43 and B61; one 20-mm General Electric T-171 (M61A1) tail gun

Dimensions:
span	17.32 m (57 ft)
length	29.49 m (97 ft)
height	9.58 m (31 ft)
wing area	143.35 m² (1542 sq ft)

COMBAT DATA

MAXIMUM SPEED

The B-58 was the fastest bomber of its time, and was quicker than the Soviet 'Backfire' which appeared two decades later. The strategic bomber version of the F-111 fighter which entered service in the late 1960s was faster, but it could maintain its top speed for only a few minutes; the Hustler could keep going at Mach 2 for more than an hour.

B-58A HUSTLER   2218 km/h (1375 mph)

FB-111   2600 km/h (1612 mph)

Tu-22M 'BACKFIRE'   2125 km/h (1318 mph)

UNREFUELLED RANGE

The Hustler had superb range for such a powerful machine. It could strike considerably further than the FB-111 which replaced it in the supersonic wings of the USAF Strategic Air Command, and outperformed the 'Backfire' which entered service 10 years after the last B-58 landed for good.

FB-111   4700 km (2914 miles)

B-58A HUSTLER   8250 km (5115 miles)

Tu-22M 'BACKFIRE'   8000 km (4860 miles)

BOMBLOAD

The massive power which ensured great supersonic performance could be used to hoist heavy loads of conventional weapons. The B-58 was never envisaged as a conventional bomber, however, and lacked the fittings to carry the kind of immense loads the other two bombers could, in theory, manage.

Tu-22M 'BACKFIRE'   24,000 kg (52,800 lb)

FB-111   17,000 kg (37,400 lb)

B-58A HUSTLER   8823 kg (19,410 lb)

CONVAIR

F-102 DELTA DAGGER

● Supersonic fighter ● Delta-wing pioneer ● Long service career

▲ With its first attempt at the F-102, seen here, Convair could not get the aircraft to fly with anything like the required performance. A radical redesign followed, turning the aircraft into a world-class interceptor.

No spectacle in aviation was more dramatic than the F-102 taking off. Hurtling down the runway and lifting off with its afterburner throwing back a stabbing tongue of fire, the F-102 shattered the eardrums with its deafening roar. Once aloft, the F-102 climbed like a homesick angel, blazing into the stratosphere to intercept enemy bombers and shoot them down.

CONVAIR F-102 DELTA DAGGER

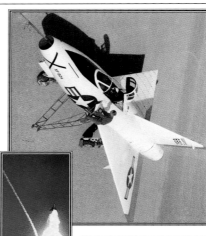

▲ Delta X-plane
To test the delta wing of the F-102, Convair built the XF-92 as a pure research craft. It was a hasty lash-up to get captured German delta-wing technology into the air as fast as possible.

Target drone ▲
Most surviving F-102s were turned into pilotless drones and blown up in missile tests.

▲ Pure delta
The wing of the F-102 was almost a perfect triangle, although the wingtip was very slightly cropped. Here a Falcon missile is being fired from the internal weapons bay.

▲ Deuce on guard
The F-102 enjoyed a successful career as the USAF's main interceptor in the late 1950s. This aircraft was one which guarded German skies.

▼ Sad end for a noble warrior
Still wearing the camouflage which it had worn on combat duty in Vietnam, this F-102 is a drone, about to meet its fate in a missile test.

▲ Atlantic defenders
The F-102 lasted in service in Iceland until 1973. Much of its time it shadowed Soviet 'Bear' reconnaissance aircraft over the unwelcoming waves of the North Atlantic.

FACTS AND FIGURES

▼ 990 Convair F-102s were built, including 111 two-seat TF-102As.

▼ The YF-102 prototype first flew on 24 October 1953.

▼ The Delta Dagger planned to use nuclear-tipped Falcon air-to-air missiles to stop Soviet bombers.

▼ The F-102 was one of the first jet aircraft to use onboard computers.

▼ With its afterburner lit, the Convair was more than 80 times as powerful as a Bf 109 fighter of World War II.

▼ F-102s went to Turkey and Greece as part of assistance programmes to NATO.

Defender of America's skies

The Convair F-102 was the first supersonic warplane with a delta- or triangle-shaped wing. Designed to defend North America against the bomber attack dreaded by so many during the Cold War, the F-102 combined a 'wasp waist' fuselage shape, technically called 'area rule', with blade-like wings and tail to become one of the fastest fighters of its era.

Though it was a fighter, the F-102 carried no gun. It was armed with an almost unbelievable battery of rockets, including a Falcon missile with an atomic warhead intended to break up bomber formations.

Pilots called this magnificent ship the 'Deuce'. It was huge and powerful, and a pleasure to fly. F-102s served briefly in Vietnam where, late in its career, this great plane was miscast in a limited war setting. A few F-102s flew with Greece and Turkey, the only foreign users of one of the best-loved and most memorable aircraft in history which led to the highly successful F-106 Delta Dart fighter.

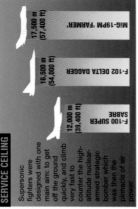

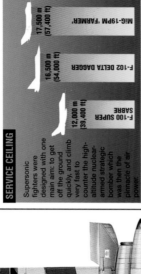

Left: Along with its successor, the F-106 Delta Dart, the Delta Dagger was regarded as one of the most beautiful fighters ever built.

Not so beautiful was the TF-102A trainer, which had two seats side-by-side in a cumbersome new front end.

F-102A Delta Dagger

Type: single-seat interceptor

Powerplant: one 49.72-kN (11,700-lb-thrust) Pratt & Whitney J57-P-23 turbojet, increasing to 76.51 kN (17,200 lb thrust) with afterburning

Maximum speed: 1328 km/h (825 mph) at 12,190 m (40,000 ft)

Combat radius: 870 km (540 miles) with full weapons load

Service ceiling: 16,500 m (54,000 ft)

Weights: normal loaded 12,565 kg (27,700 lb); maximum 14,290 kg (31,500 lb)

Armament: three Falcon heat-seeking missiles and one Nuclear Falcon, or three radar and three heat-seeking air-to-air missiles; up to 24 unguided 70-mm rockets

Dimensions:
span   11.62 m (38 ft 1 in)
length   20.84 m (68 ft 4½ in)
height   6.46 m (21 ft 2½ in)
wing area 61.45 m² (662 sq ft)

COMBAT DATA

SERVICE CEILING

Supersonic fighters were designed with one main aim: to get off the ground quickly, and climb very fast to counter the high-altitude nuclear-armed strategic bomber which was then the pinnacle of air power.

F-100 SUPER SABRE — 12,000 m (39,400 ft)
F-102 DELTA DAGGER — 16,500 m (54,000 ft)
MiG-19PM 'FARMER' — 17,500 m (57,400 ft)

INTERCEPT ARMAMENT

The F-102 was designed as a bomber interceptor, and was possibly the first fighter designed without a gun. Instead, it was armed with Falcon air-to-air missiles, the earliest successful weapons of their type. The MiG-19 could not match the F-102's firepower.

F-102 DELTA DAGGER — 6 x AIM-4 Falcon missiles or 2 x AIM-26 Falcons with nuclear warheads
F-100 SUPER SABRE — 4 x 20-mm cannon 2 x AIM-9 Sidewinder missiles
MiG-19 'FARMER' — 4x AA-1 Alkali missiles

MAXIMUM SPEED

MiG-19 'FARMER' — 1450 km/h (900 mph)
F-100 SUPER SABRE — 1390 km/h (864 mph)
F-102 DELTA DAGGER — 1328 km/h (825 mph)

The first generation of supersonic jets were capable of flying at speeds between 1.3 and 1.4 times the speed of sound. Although never achieving the kind of performance which had been expected of it, the delta-winged F-102 was nevertheless in the same league as its contemporaries.

F-102 DELTA DAGGER

The needle-nosed 'Deuce' was the first interceptor to be developed as part of an overall air defence weapon system, known as WS201A. The F-102 was considered just the airframe portion of this system, to which was added the radar and missile subsystems.

The radar component of the Hughes MG-10 fire-control system could track several airborne targets simultaneously at ranges of up to 50 km (30 miles), and lock-on to individual aircraft at around 25 km (15 miles).

The 'Bulldog' badge was for the 525th Fighter Interceptor Squadron, based at Bitburg AB.

The first F-102 design was disappointing in service, and was revised to incorporate 'area rule'. This produced a pinched waist, or 'Coke bottle' shape. To make the tail fatter in area to conform with the new design, large bulges were added each side of the rear fuselage. These were known, for obvious reasons, as 'Marilyns'.

Putting the weapons in an internal bay was a vital factor in the F-102's speed. If they had been on outside pylons, the drag would have degraded performance.

In addition to the Falcon missiles, the F-102 carried 24 unguided rockets. These were carried in tubes buried within the weapon bay doors. They were rarely used and eventually deleted.

The addition of drop-tanks gave the F-102 greatly increased range. It could now make ferry flights of over 2000 km (1250 miles).

Falcon missiles usually had a high-explosive warhead, but some F-102s also carried a nuclear-tipped version.

Most F-102s wore this gull-grey camouflage, although some adopted a green and brown scheme for service in the Vietnam War.

Launching the Falcon

ENCLOSED WEAPONS BAYS: To reduce drag to the barest minimum, the missiles were all carried internally. The capacious bays could hold up to six air-to-air missiles. This fashion has recently been revived with the F-22, albeit to make the aircraft more stealthy.

WEAPONS DEPLOYED: The F-102 had three weapon bays, each holding two Falcons in tandem. Here one of the side bays is opened. Usually three heat-seeking Falcons were carried with three radar-homing missiles.

MISSILE LAUNCH: With the bays open, the missile trapezes were lowered into the airstream to allow the weapon to fire straight off the rail. The doors to the bay would reclose immediately after.

CONVAIR
F-106 DELTA DART

● Interceptor ● Nuclear rocket armed ● Air defender

T hough it never fired a shot in combat, the F-106 Delta Dart is one of the most fondly remembered fighters to serve in the US Air Force. Building on experience from its predecessor, the F-102A Delta Dagger, the F-106 carried the flame as the guardian of North America at the height of the Cold War. Its job was simple: as an all-weather interceptor it was to detect, identify and destroy Russian bombers carrying atomic weapons to American cities.

▲ Convair's Delta fighters were extremely capable, complex and costly machines. The Dart was far more useful than the Dagger, which had grave development problems and was never reliable.

PHOTO FILE

CONVAIR F-106 DELTA DART

▼ Sharp shape
In the quest for all-out speed and climb rate, the F-106 was designed with sharp lines and a thin wing section. Variable air intake geometry was also used.

▲ Red defender
Operating at altitude, with little need for concealment, the F-106 was often painted in bright colours, including orange and red schemes. These colours were designed to make them more conspicuous when operating over Polar icefields.

▼ Delta wing
The Delta Dart's only similar feature to the Delta Dagger was its wing. The fuselage had to be considerably revised to cope with the 50 per cent extra thrust of its afterburning J75 engine. The cockpit was moved forward and the tailfin and rudder were redesigned.

▲ Genie launch
The nuclear-tipped Genie was an unguided rocket, intended to be fired into bomber formations.

Taking on gas ▲
The Pratt & Whitney J75 engine was powerful but thirsty, and tanking from KC-135s was a common task for F-106 pilots when on distant patrols.

FACTS AND FIGURES

➤ The J75 turbojet was chosen after plans to use the Wright J67 Olympus were sidetracked by technical problems.

➤ The YF-106A prototype made its first flight on 26 December 1956.

➤ The F-106B had a second crewmember seated behind the pilot.

➤ The last of 277 F-106As and 63 two-seat F-106Bs was delivered to the US Air Force in 1961.

➤ An advanced version with new radar, the F-106C, was only evaluated.

➤ The final operator was the 177th Fighter Group in Atlantic City in 1987.

PROFILE

America's delta defender

When it was introduced in the late 1950s, the F-106 was one of the fastest fighters in the world. It had twice the speed of the preceding F-102, and met all requirements of Aerospace Defense Command for a manned interceptor to defend North America. Linked via its complex MA-1 electronic fire-control system through a digital data-link into the nationwide SAGE (semi-automatic ground environment) air defence system, the F-106 was more than the sum of its 'black boxes'

and missiles. Improvements to the F-106 included the addition of a gun in a neat installation in the missile bay, causing a slight bulge.

From the time it entered service at Geiger Field, Washington, in 1959, the F-106 was the backbone of North American air defence and was the favourite of many pilots who flew it. The Delta Dart served for much longer than intended and was never actually replaced despite a continued threat by bombers and cruise missiles. Retirement of the last

Below: Patrols over Alaska were an important task for F-106 crews, as Soviet bombers could have threatened the USA by flying from bases in north-eastern Siberia.

Above: Despite its age, the F-106 remained in the USAF's inventory long after more modern tactical fighters entered service.

F-106 by the New Jersey Air National Guard in 1988 marked the end of the F-106 as a fighter. However, 200 airframes have been converted into QF-106 unmanned target drones.

F-106A DELTA DART

The F-106 was the primary air defence aircraft of the USAF between 1959 and the late 1970s, when the F-15C Eagle began entering service in numbers. Air National Guard Delta Darts were replaced by the F-16 Fighting Falcon.

A highly advanced avionics suite was integrated with the ground-based NORAD air defence system.

One of the main features from the Dagger required redesign was the air intake, which was insufficient to cope with the mass flow of the huge J75 engine.

The F-106 had a powerful search radar and also an infra-red search-and-track system, a feature lacking on many of today's fighters.

Delta wings were a common feature of late-1950s fighters such as the MiG-21 and Mirage. The delta offers good performance in transonic flight, but is often less useful at low airspeeds and high alpha.

The Delta Dart carried its weaponry in an internal bay, a most unusual feature. A semi-retractable M61 cannon, also fitted in the bay, was introduced in 1973 following the experience of fighter pilots in Vietnam.

The F-106 usually carried a pair of underwing fuel tanks.

The J75 engine was also used in the F-105 Thunderchief attack aircraft. It was one of the most powerful jet fighter engines of its day.

Air defence of North America

BOMBER ALERT: F-106s are scrambled to catch Soviet bombers out at sea before they can unleash their deadly cruise missiles. The area over the F-106 bases is defended by long-range Hawk and Nike missiles.

MISSILE DEFENCE: Air defence missiles handled most of the threat inshore.

FIGHTER CONTROL: The NORAD air defence controller vectors an F-106 towards the incoming bomber. The controller will give the pilot instructions, or the F-106's avionics will automatically compute an intercept solution.

BEAR ATTACK: At high altitude the long-range Tu-95 'Bear' was the main manned aircraft threat to the USA.

F-106A Delta Dart

Type: single-seat interceptor

Powerplant: one Pratt & Whitney J75-P-17 turbojet rated at 76.5 kN (17,212 lb thrust) dry thrust and 108.99 kN (24,523 lb thrust) with afterburning

Maximum speed: Mach 2.25 or 2400 km/h (1491mph) at 12,190 m (40,000 ft)

Range: 1850 km (1150 miles)

Service ceiling: 17,680 m (58,600 ft)

Weights: empty 10,800 kg (23,810 lb); loaded 16,012 kg (35,300 lb); maximum take-off weight 17,350 kg (38,250 lb)

Armament: one M61A-1 20-mm cannon, four AIM-4E and/or AIM-4G Falcon air-to-air missiles, plus two AIR-2B Genie nuclear rockets

Dimensions:
span	11.67 m (38 ft 3 in)
length	21.55 m (70 ft 8 in)
height	6.18 m (20 ft 3 in)
wing area	697.80 m² (7511 sq ft)

COMBAT DATA

MAXIMUM SPEED

All the interceptors of the 1960s could reach Mach 2 for a short time using afterburner. They could not go far beyond this speed because of kinetic heating causing damage to the alloy airframe.

F-106A DELTA DART	2400 km/h (1491 mph)
Su-15 'FLAGON'	2653 km/h (1648 mph)
LIGHTNING	2414 km/h (1500 mph)

RANGE

Interceptors are required to reach high altitude in a very short time, fire their weapons and return to base. These aircraft were designed for performance and not long range.

Su-15 'FLAGON' 1000 km (620 miles)

LIGHTNING14 1440 km (895 miles)

F-106A DELTA DART 1850 km (1150 miles)

CLIMB RATE

The Lightning and Su-15 'Flagon' could outclimb the heavier Delta Dart, which had more weapons and advanced avionics and carried a great deal more fuel. Most interceptors have to trade fuel load for rate of climb.

F-106 DELTA DART 12,131 m/min (40,000 fpm)

Su-15 'FLAGON' 13,700 m/min (44,950 fpm)

LIGHTNING 15,240 m/min (50,000 ft)

CURTISS
JN-4 'JENNY'

- Two-seat World War I trainer ● Barnstorming aircraft

T he JN-4 'Jenny' had a double career. It was America's universal aircraft of the 1920s, having been developed as a military trainer early in the Great War and then becoming the machine of post-war flying instructors and barnstormers. An open field, a nice day and a few heads cranked upwards in curiosity were all that were needed for the JN-4 to bring the thrill of aviation to ordinary people. Many of them learned about aircraft by watching the 'Jenny' perform.

▲ From 1919 to the late 1920s thousands of 'Jennys' were flown in what was known as the 'barnstorming era', introducing many Americans to aircraft for the first time. Surplus JN-4s were bought from the US Army for as little as $50 each.

CURTISS JN-4 'JENNY'

▲ JN-3 collision
The JN-4 was developed from the interim JN-3, 91 of which were sold to Britain and two were purchased by the US Army.

▲ Wartime Army JN-4D
Between November 1917 and January 1919 over 2800 JN-4Ds were built. To speed up delivery, six manufacturers built the D model.

Barnstorming in the 1920s ▶
Unhampered by regulations governing their use, post-war pilots used JN-4s for stunt flying.

▲ Half-scale Jenny
In 1961, F. A. Murray of Rockford, Illinois, built this half-scale replica of a JN-4D-2, and called it the JN-2D-1 'Jennette'. Power was supplied by a converted Ford Model 'A' 37-kW (50-hp) car engine.

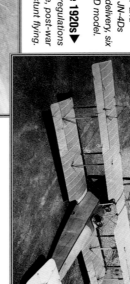

▲ In the Navy
Most of the US Navy's JN-4s were H models powered by112-kW (150-hp) engines. Thirty were purchased for advanced pilot training in 1918 and were followed by 90 JN-4HG gunnery trainers.

FACTS AND FIGURES

▼ The 'Jenny' first appeared in July 1916 when an initial batch of planes was sold to Britain and the US Army.

▼ After more than a decade, the last US Army JN-4s were retired in 1927.

▼ As well as pilot training, JN-4s were used for observation and bomber training.

▼ The contract to build 1,400 JN-4Ds for the US Army was worth $4,417,337 for the Curtiss Corporation.

▼ Approximately 7,280 JN-4s were built, including 4800 for the US Army.

▼ Of American and Canadian pilots in the World War I, 95 per cent trained on JN-4s.

PROFILE

From training to 'barnstorming'

A development of the 1915 JN-3 that flew combat reconnaissance with the US Army's expedition against General Pershing during the reconnaissance with Pancho Villa on the Mexican border, the Curtiss JN-4 'Jenny' was conceived to replace the antiquated pusher-type, open-to-the-wind trainers that had served the military until that time.

The military JN-4, a two-seater made of fabric, wood and wire, became the standard US Army trainer during

World War I and for about seven years after. In the air, the 'Jenny' seemed to have no vices. Even for the beginner it was an easy machine to fly.

After the war, 'Jennys' had a lively time in the civil world. Many pilots-turned-barnstormers purchased JN-4s from the government for very little and set out to earn their fortunes flying for fun, giving joy rides and displays. Stuntmen like Ormer Locklear were called the 'Flying Fools' for their wild

antics in the air – indeed, crashes were not infrequent.

The JN-4 gained immortality as a trainer aircraft and as a machine that brought aviation to the people.

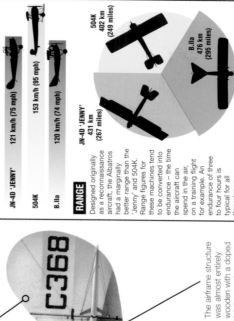

Below: Wearing Army JN-4H markings, this 'Jenny' was preserved in the US. As with the de Havilland Moth family, the numbers built ensured that examples still survive.

Above: This preserved 'Jenny' clearly shows the unequal-span wings. It carries the markings applied to US Army aircraft at the end of World War I.

JN-4D 'Jenny'

Type: two-seat military trainer

Powerplant: one 67-kW (90-hp) Curtiss OX-5 inline piston engine

Maximum speed: 121 km/h (75 mph)

Cruising speed: 97 km/h (60 mph)

Service ceiling: 1980 m (6500 ft)

Weights: empty 630 kg (1386 lb); maximum take-off 871 kg (1916 lb)

Accommodation: two pilots in tandem open cockpits

Dimensions:
span	13.30 m (43 ft 8 in)
length	8.33 m (27 ft 4 in)
height	3.01 m (9 ft 10 in)
wing area	32.70 m² (352 sq ft)

ACTION DATA

MAXIMUM SPEED

The Avro 504 used a more powerful engine than the early JN-4s, giving the aircraft improved performance; it was also more aerodynamically streamlined. The Albatros B.IIa was primarily an observation aircraft that was used for a secondary training role.

JN-4D 'JENNY'	121 km/h (75 mph)
504K	153 km/h (95 mph)
B.IIa	120 km/h (74 mph)

RANGE

Designed originally as a reconnaissance aircraft, the Albatros B.IIa had a marginally better range than the 'Jenny' and 504K. Range figures for these machines tend to be converted into endurance – the time the aircraft can spend in the air, on a training flight for example. An endurance of three to four hours is typical for all three types.

504K	402 km (249 miles)
B.IIa	476 km (295 miles)
JN-4D 'JENNY'	431 km (267 miles)

ENGINE POWER

The 504's rotary engine was the most powerful of those fitted to these three types; later versions of the JN-4 had bigger powerplants. The extra power of the 504 is reflected in its shorter range due to higher fuel consumption. All three aircraft had two-bladed propellers.

JN-4D 'JENNY'	67 kW (90 hp)
504K	82 kW (110 hp)
B.IIa	75 kW (100 hp)

JN-4CAN

The School of Aerial Fighting in Canada was equipped with the JN-4Can (for 'Canadian'). This was built by the Canadian Aeroplane Corporation of Toronto and known as the 'Canuck'.

The JN-4 had a larger tailfin and tailplane than earlier members of the JN family.

The airframe structure was almost entirely wooden with a doped fabric covering.

Control wires on aircraft of this era were often exposed, taking the shortest route between cockpit and the control surface.

The two-seat trainer aircraft was arranged to have an instructor in the rear seat and the pupil in the front. In civil aircraft the latter position was used for joy riders.

Privately owned, Canadian-built JN-4s remained in use into the 1930s. A few were built as late as 1927, using reconditioned parts. Some had a third cockpit and were known as the Ericson Special Three.

Underwing skids near the wingtip prevented the wing from touching the ground during a rough landing.

The Curtiss OX-5 inline piston engine drove a two-bladed wooden propeller on the JN-4Can. Later variants had a Wright-built Hispano-Suiza engine.

Behind the wheel covers were the spokes and wheel-rim, to which a rubber tyre was fitted. The undercarriage was of the cross-axle type.

Two-seaters of the inter-war years

■ **AVRO 504:** Famous as a trainer from World War I until the mid-1920s, the 504 started life as a bomber and reconnaissance aircraft.

■ **DE HAVILLAND DH.60 MOTH:** The first of the famous Moth family that ended with the Tiger Moth, DH.60s appeared in the early 1920s.

■ **HANDLEY PAGE GUGNUNC:** Designed for a US competition to find an aircraft that was 'safe' to fly, only one Gugnunc was built.

■ **HANRIOT H.433:** A dual-role observation and training aircraft of the late 1920s, the H.433 shared the JN-4's unequal-span wing layout.

CURTISS

P-1 & P-6 HAWK

● Interwar biplane fighter ● Classic US design ● Air racing heritage

Flying Curtiss biplane fighters was one of the great adventures in aviation. Powerful and nimble, the Curtiss P-1 and P-6 were the flagships of a family of great warplanes that equipped the US Army in the 1920s. The decade was called the 'Roaring Twenties' by Americans who celebrated the end of the Great War and the dawn of a new age of progress. Advances in aviation were happening quickly, with Hawk fighters at the forefront.

▲ Over a 10-year period, Curtiss developed a series of increasingly capable Hawk biplanes. Together with the Boeing P-12 they formed the backbone of the US Army's fighter force until the mid 1930s.

CURTISS P-1 & P-6 HAWK

▼ Six-gun fighter
A P-6E was returned to the manufacturers, where two extra 7.62-mm (.30-cal) machine guns installed in each wing; it was called the XP-6H.

▼ Aerobatics over Washington
With higher weights, larger landing wheels, an improved radiator and V-1150-3 engine, the P-1B was an improved, although slightly slower, development of the P-1A. Twenty-three P-1B Hawks were delivered from October 1926 and served alongside earlier aircraft.

▲ Ice-bound Hawk
Aircraft belonging to the 1st Pursuit Group, home-based in Michigan, often used a ski undercarriage for Arctic operations.

▲ Skis on P-1Cs
Curtiss received its first large Hawk order for the P-1C model. The aircraft was heavier and slower than earlier variants, but 33 were delivered. Some flew with this optional ski undercarriage.

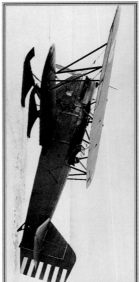

Prestone-cooled Conqueror ▶
Some of the original water-cooled YP-6 Hawks were re-engined with a Prestone cooling system and were designated P-6As. The system used much smaller radiators.

FACTS AND FIGURES

▶ A P-6 prototype, actually a converted P-1, won the 1927 National Air Races trophy at a speed of 320 km/h (198 mph).

▶ A US Army air pioneer, Lt Frank Tyndall, died in a P-1 crash on 15 July 1930.

▶ Curtiss manufactured a total of 239 Hawk biplane fighters.

▶ Curtiss Hawk biplanes served for exactly 10 years before giving way to the Boeing P-26 monoplane.

▶ Some Hawks had turbo superchargers for high-altitude performance.

▶ A single export Hawk was sold to Japan in the late 1920s.

End of the biplane era

Arriving at McCook Field, Dayton, Ohio, in August 1925, the Curtiss P-1 Hawk was the first aircraft in the US Army's 'P' for 'Pursuit' category, which later included immortals like the P-47 and P-51. A standard, single-seater biplane of the type which was popular in the 1920s, the P-1 was widely used. It was joined in 1928 by the P-6 Hawk, which had the same basic airframe but

many improvements. These included better all-round performance, spats on the wheels and machine guns mounted on the fuselage sides, rather than on top, to provide better visibility.

The best-known fighter in this series, the P-6E, began to reach the 17th Pursuit Squadron in 1932. But, by then, an era had ended: the first monoplane fighters were beginning to appear, and the biplane fighter soon disappeared for ever.

them in races, but the Curtiss Hawk never went to war.

The P-1 and P-6 were the greatest fighters of their brief moment in history, between the Great War and the Depression. Army pilots used them in aerobatic displays and entered

Eight P-6Es, in the flamboyant markings of the 17th Pursuit Squadron, demonstrate their highly polished formation flying skills. These formations were of no practical use in combat.

Curtiss studied the effects of wing flutter after one of its racers lost its wings. This research allowed them to use only two sets of main wing struts.

On the P-6E the tailskid of other models was replaced with a fixed tailwheel. This and other improvements produced a 13 km/h (8 mph) speed increase over the P-6A.

The most colourful of all Hawk markings were applied by the 17th Pursuit Squadron. The overall paint scheme was based on the Arctic snow owl which was the unit insignia.

Most P-6Es were fitted with three-bladed, variable-pitch propellers. The two machine guns fired through the propeller arc.

Moving the radiator back from its former chin position to a location just forward of the undercarriage legs, improved the aerodynamics of the P-6E. In addition, single-strut main landing gear units, with spatted wheels, were installed. The machine guns were moved from high on the nose to low on the fuselage sides.

P-6E HAWK

Wearing the distinctive black and white markings of the 17th Pursuit Squadron of the 1st Pursuit Group, this aircraft was delivered in 1932.

Curtiss Hawk evolution

- **R-6:** This specialist air racing machine set a new world speed record in 1922, and inspired the Hawk fighter designs.

- **P-2 HAWK:** Curtiss' own V-1400 engine powered the P-2, but it proved disappointing. The aircraft were therefore converted back to P-1As.

- **EXPORT HAWK:** Powered by Pratt & Whitney R-1340 radials, 16 of these aircraft were delivered.

- **HAWK P-3:** Only five production P-3A Hawks were built. This experimental aircraft has a retractable undercarriage.

P-6E Hawk

Type: single-seat pursuit biplane

Powerplant: one 522-kW (700-hp) Curtiss V-1750C Conqueror inline piston engine

Maximum speed: 317 km/h (198 mph)

Service ceiling: 7285 m (24,700 ft)

Range: 459 km (285 miles)

Weights: empty equipped 1224 kg (2693 lb); maximum take-off 1559 kg (3430 lb)

Armament: two synchronized fuselage-mounted 7.62-mm (.30-cal.) machine guns

Dimensions:
span	9.60 m	(31 ft 6 in)
length	7.06 m	(23 ft 2 in)
height	2.72 m	(8 ft 11 in)
wing area	23.41 m²	(252 sq ft)

COMBAT DATA

MAXIMUM SPEED

With its racing heritage and refined design, the P-6E was better than both of its contemporaries in terms of speed. British fighters had advanced little since World War I, hence the poor speed of the Siskin.

ARMAMENT

Boeing's P-12 was the US Army Air Corps' second fighter. It was more heavily armed than the P-6E but could not match its performance. The Siskin retained World War I standard armament.

P-6E HAWK
2 x 7.62-mm (.30-cal.) machine guns

P-12
1 x 12.7-mm (.50-cal.) machine gun
1 x 7.62-mm (.30-cal.) machine gun
1 x 227-kg (500-lb) bomb

SISKIN IIIA
2 x 7.7-mm (.303-cal.) machine guns
4 x 9-kg (20-lb) bombs

SERVICE CEILING

While the Armstrong Whitworth Siskin lagged behind in other areas, it did offer a good service ceiling. Without engine superchargers, however, none of these aircraft was capable of exceptional performance at high altitudes. The open cockpits of these machines also made flying at altitude very uncomfortable.

8230 m (27,000 ft)
8199 m (26,900 ft)
7285 m (24,700 ft)

CURTISS

SOC SEAGULL

- Scout aircraft ● Operated from battleships ● Seaplane

T he Curtiss SOC Seagull was the US
Navy's top observation aircraft in the
years just before World War II. The
battleship was still thought to be the most
important 'war wagon' on the high seas,
and the Seagull was the 'eyes' of the fleet's
battleships and cruisers. The pilot and
observer aboard were expected to spot
targets and direct the big guns of the huge
ships. Obsolete by the time war arrived, the
SOC was still in service in 1945.

▲ One of the last biplanes
to serve with the US Navy, the SOC
Seagull flew extensively from battleships
and cruisers during World War II. It
actually outlasted its replacement.

CURTISS SOC SEAGULL

▲ On dry land
When operating from shore
bases, Seagulls were fitted with a
wheeled undercarriage.

▼ Boss bird
Painted overall dark blue, this
aircraft was assigned to the
Commander of the Fleet.

▲ Use over North Africa
Although famous for their involvement in the Pacific war,
these aircraft also gave valiant service in other theatres,
flying in support of the Allied landings in North Africa in
1942 during Operation Torch, for example.

▲ Recovery
Seaplanes landed alongside their parent
ships and were hoisted aboard by cranes.

Start of a patrol ▶
Catapulted from a US Navy cruiser, an SOC
sets out on a mission during the Pacific war.

FACTS AND FIGURES

▶ In original configuration, the prototype
SOC was an amphibian that had wheels
incorporated into the floats.

▶ The 64 aircraft built by the Naval Aircraft
Factory were designated SON-1.

▶ Production of the SOC Seagull began in
1935 and ended in 1938.

▶ A proposed successor, the SO3C
Seamew, was unsatisfactory and was
replaced in service by Seagulls!

▶ SOCs featured prominently in most of
the major battles of the Pacific war.

▶ When the SOCs were finally withdrawn,
the era of the combat seaplane ended.

PROFILE

Long-serving naval scout

In the late 1930s, few aviation experts would have envisaged that this biplane scout would outlast several monoplanes in service.

The last of the Curtiss biplanes to be used operationally by the US Navy, the SOC Seagull originated in 1933. It was out of date by the time America entered World War II in 1941, but remained on duty until the war was over.

The SOC Seagull had folding wings and tail structure made of fabric-covered light metal alloy, and a welded, steel-tube fuselage. The pilot and observer/gunner were accommodated in tandem cockpits, enclosed by a continuous transparent canopy with sliding panels for access.

Very much a product of 1930s' technology, the Seagull appeared outmoded by rapid changes occurring in aviation as the war loomed; nevertheless, it performed admirably during World War II and was well loved by those who flew it.

Production Seagull floatplanes began to reach the fleet in 1935. In due course, about three dozen naval scouting squadrons were equipped with the type. A decade later, in 1945, when American Marines were landing on Iwo Jima in one of the final actions of the war, SOCs were still in front-line service.

Being a biplane, the SOC was blessed with remarkable agility, and in wheeled configuration could out-turn many faster monoplanes. To facilitate stowage in tight spaces on board battleships or aircraft carriers, the wings could be folded back.

Powering the SOC-3 was a Pratt & Whitney R-1340 engine, which churned out 447 kW (600 hp). It provided more than adequate performance for a seaplane, though the Seagull remained vulnerable to fighter attack.

SOC-3 SEAGULL

US aircraft operating in support of Operation Torch in North Africa had a distinctive yellow circle added outboard of their national insignia. This SOC-3 Seagull is quite unusual in that it carries no unit markings.

In the SOC, the standard crew consisted of a pilot and observer. A 7.62-mm (.30-cal.) machine gun was fitted in each cockpit and provided some defence. For take-off and landing, the canopies were often left in the open position.

Construction of this aeronautical anachronism consisted of a welded tubular steel fuselage with aluminum framed wings and tail surfaces, all covered in fabric.

A pair of small outrigger floats was fitted to the lower wings. Their purpose was only to provide stability for the aircraft while on the water.

In seaplane configuration, the SOC-3 was fitted with a single large centreline float. When the parent ship was in port, the aircraft were assigned to land bases and the floats were exchanged for a spatted wheeled undercarriage.

SOC-3 Seagull

Type: two-seat scout/observation aircraft

Powerplant: one 447-kW (600-hp) Pratt & Whitney R-1340-18 Wasp radial engine

Maximum speed: 266 km/h (165 mph)

Cruising speed: 214 km/h (133 mph)

Initial climb rate: 321 m/min (1050 fpm)

Range: 1086 km (673 miles)

Service ceiling: 4540 m (14,900 ft)

Weights: empty 1648 kg (3626 lb); loaded 2492 kg (5482 lb)

Armament: two 7.62-mm (.30-cal.) machine guns, plus external racks for two 147-kg (325-lb) bombs

Dimensions:
span	10.97 m (36 ft)
length	9.47 m (31 ft 1 in)
height	4.44 m (14 ft 7 in)
wing area	31.77 m² (328 sq ft)

COMBAT DATA

MAXIMUM SPEED

Dismissed as an anachronism at the start of the war, the SOC was slower than the two main rival enemy types, although, as a biplane, it had much greater agility and was a more flexible aircraft. The 'Jake' was its primary opponent in the Pacific war.

SOC-1 SEAGULL 266 km/h (165 mph)	
ARADO AR 196 310 km/h (192 mph)	
AICHI E13A 'JAKE' 375 km/h (233 mph)	

RANGE

An important criterion for naval seaplanes was an ability to range far from the parent ship to observe enemy activity. In the Pacific, the Seagull could roam extensively. The Japanese E13A could range even further and was one of the best scouts of World War II.

ARADO AR 196 1070 km (663 miles)

SOC-1 SEAGULL 1086 km (673 miles)

AICHI E13A 'JAKE' 2090 km (1296 miles)

BOMBLOAD

Scout aircraft were sometimes called upon to drop bombs, and here the Seagull received top marks, being able to carry a greater load than either of its main rivals. Bombs were mainly used to attack smaller warships, while leaving more specialized aircraft to attack larger capital ships.

AICHI E13A 'JAKE'	250 kg (550 lb)
ARADO AR 196	100 kg (220 lb)
SOC-1 SEAGULL	295 kg (650 lb)

Curtiss naval aircraft in World War II

■ **SBC HELLDIVER:** This early dive-bomber was obsolete at the start of the war, though some remained in service until late 1942.

■ **SB2C HELLDIVER:** Also named Helldiver, this monoplane dive-bomber replaced the Douglas Dauntless from 1943 onwards.

■ **SC SEAHAWK:** Designed in 1942, the Seahawk was really too late to see service; only 66 examples were delivered before VJ-Day.

■ **SO3C SEAMEW:** Intended as a successor to the SOC, these aircraft proved unsuccessful and had short careers in the Navy.

CURTISS

SBC HELLDIVER

● Dive bomber ● Combat trainer ● Complex development

► Although the SBC was a strong aircraft with very good handling characteristics, it was totally outclassed by new monoplanes by the time World War II started in Europe.

A s the second of three aircraft named Helldiver by the Curtiss company, the SBC was probably the least successful. Originally a parasol-winged fighter, the SBC went through major changes in design and role before becoming a carrier-based scout-bomber. The outbreak of World War II saw the Helldiver exported to France and Great Britain, but its only combat service was with the US Navy aboard the aircraft carrier USS Hornet.

CURTISS SBC HELLDIVER

Staggered wings ▼
After the failure of the initial parasol design, it was realized that a much stronger wing was needed to withstand the stresses of dive-bombing. The solution was a strong biplane arrangement with the upper wing further forward than the lower wing and a single sturdy interplane strut.

▲ Capable trainer
Although intended as a front-line aircraft, the SBC made a vital contribution to the US war effort as a combat trainer.

▼ French deliveries
In 1940 the US diverted 50 SBC-4s to beleaguered France although they arrived too late to be used in combat. This example is seen at the factory prior to delivery.

▼ Improved version
The last SBC-3 on the production line became the XSBC-4, with a more powerful Wright R-1820 engine and the ability to carry a 454-kg (1000-lb) bomb.

Diverted to Britain ▼
After the fall of France in 1940, five SBC-4s were acquired by the RAF as instructional airframes and were named Clevelands.

FACTS AND FIGURES

➤ The prototype XSBC-1 crashed in September 1934 when the wing folding mechanism failed in flight.

➤ British Clevelands differed from standard SBC-4s in having self-sealing fuel tanks.

➤ The SBC-4 was the last biplane combat aircraft ever ordered by the USA.

➤ In 1940, SBC-4s aboard a French aircraft carrier were diverted to Martinique where they were eventually scrapped.

➤ The SBC was the second of three Curtiss bomber types named Helldiver.

➤ US Marine Corps SBC-4s remained in service until June 1943.

Last American combat biplane

I n 1932 the US Navy ordered a new two-seat fighter prototype from Curtiss. Designated XF12C-1 and fitted with a parasol wing, the aircraft proved to be unsuitable in this role. However, it was decided to use the design as a scout aircraft and the XSBC-1 prototype was constructed. More problems followed as the aircraft suffered a structural wing failure during tests, and the parasol wing layout was abandoned.

The resulting XSBC-2 biplane was a far better aircraft and went into production for the US Navy with an uprated Pratt & Whitney Twin Wasp Junior engine as the SBC-3 Helldiver. Entering service in 1936, 83 SBC-3s were delivered before production switched to the SBC-4 fitted with a more powerful engine. The US Navy ordered 174 of this new model, but 50 were diverted to France as the situation in Europe worsened.

SBC-3 HELLDIVER

The brightly painted red tail is the marking carried by aircraft from USS _Yorktown_ in 1937. The black 'Man O'War Bird' emblem denotes that this aircraft is from VS-5.

The SBC-3 was fitted with a 615-kW (825-hp) Pratt & Whitney R-1535-82 Twin Wasp Junior piston engine.

After the failure of the parasol wing design a biplane unit was introduced. The wings were of metal frame covered with metal skin on the upper wing and fabric on the lower wing.

A forward-firing 7.62-mm (.30-cal.) machine gun was aimed by the pilot using a sight attached to the windshield. A second 7.62-mm machine gun could be fitted on a flexible mounting in the rear cockpit.

A large 'greenhouse'-type cockpit covered both crew members. It was situated behind the top wing and so gave the pilot poor vision above and forward.

The landing gear retracted into the all-metal monocoque fuselage in a similar fashion to the Grumman F2F and F3F. An arrester hook was fitted for aircraft carrier operations.

Below: During the early years of World War II many SBC-4s served with US Naval Reserve Units. This example was based in Chicago.

Above: SBC-4s of VS-8 and VB-8 from USS Hornet are seen engaged in manoeuvres days before the Japanese attack at Pearl Harbor.

The type saw brief wartime service with the US Navy and Marines before being withdrawn to second-line duties.

US Navy carrier aircraft of 1939

■ **DOUGLAS TBD DEVASTATOR:** Entering service in 1937, the TBD remained the US Navy's primary torpedo aircraft until 1942.

■ **GRUMMAN F3F:** Following on from the successful FF and F2F biplane fighters, the F3F served with both the US Navy and US Marines.

■ **GRUMMAN JF/J2F DUCK:** Being of amphibious design, the Duck was very versatile and was used in patrol, survey and rescue roles.

■ **VOUGHT SB2U VINDICATOR:** Operated as a scout and a bomber, the SB2U served with front-line units for six years from 1936.

SBC-4 Helldiver

Type: two-seat carrier-based scout-bomber

Powerplant: one 708-kW (950-hp) Wright R-1820-34 Cyclone 9 radial piston engine

Maximum speed: 381 km/h (236 mph) at 4635 m (15,000 ft)

Initial climb rate: 497 m/min (1630 fpm)

Range: 950 km (590 miles) with 227-kg (500-lb) bombload

Service ceiling: 8320 m (27,900 ft)

Weights: empty 2196 kg; maximum take-off 3462 kg

Armament: one forward-firing 7.62-mm (.30-cal.) machine gun and one 7.62-mm machine gun on a flexible mount plus up to 454 kg (1000 lb) of bombs

Dimensions:

span	10.36 m (34 ft)
length	8.64 m (28 ft 4 in)
height	3.84 m (12 ft 7 in)
wing area	29.45 m² (317 sq ft)

COMBAT DATA

MAXIMUM SPEED

Although the Skua was a more modern monoplane design, it was slower than the biplane SBC-4. A lack of speed with all early war scout bombers resulted in heavy losses to enemy fighters.

SBC-4 HELLDIVER	381 km/h (236 mph)
SKUA Mk II	362 km/h (224 mph)
SB2U-3 VINDICATOR	391 km/h (242 mph)

BOMBLOAD

Although the SB2U-3 Vindicator was a significantly more powerful aircraft, it could only match the earlier SBC-4 in bomb-carrying capacity. The Skua was less capable than either American design.

SBC-4 HELLDIVER	454-kg (1000-lb) bombload
SKUA Mk II	227-kg (500-lb) bombload
SB2U-3 VINDICATOR	454-kg (1000-lb) bombload

RANGE

With the large areas covered by a carrier group, long range is essential for naval aircraft. Again the Vindicator was far superior, allowing it to strike at targets beyond the range of most carrier-based bombers. The Skua had the shortest range but generally operated in the smaller North and Mediterranean Seas.

SKUA Mk II	760 km (471 miles)
SB2U-3 VINDICATOR	1802 km (1117 miles)
SBC-4 HELLDIVER	950 km (590 miles)

CURTISS

P-36/Hawk 75

● Monoplane fighter ● Exported widely ● Asian and European combat

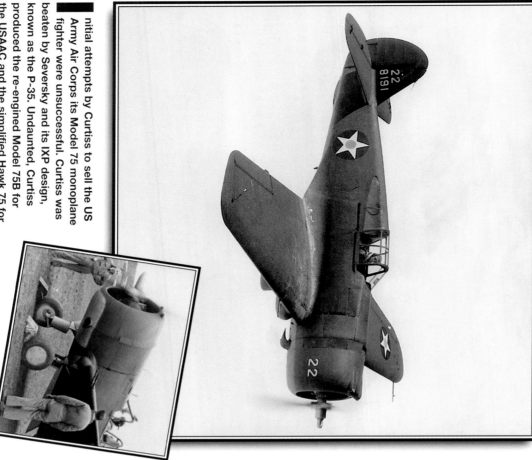

nitial attempts by Curtiss to sell the US Army Air Corps its Model 75 monoplane fighter were unsuccessful. Curtiss was beaten by Seversky and its IXP design, known as the P-35. Undaunted, Curtiss produced the re-engined Model 75B for the USAAC and the simplified Hawk 75 for export. Sales drives during the late 1930s were a great success, especially once the USAAC ordered 210 Hawk 75s (P-35As) – the biggest US fighter order placed since 1918.

▲ Most of the Model 75's World War II service was with the French, Dutch, British and Finnish forces, though a few US examples were used in the opening months of the Pacific War.

CURTISS P-36/HAWK 75

▲ RAF Mohawk
The RAF's Model 75s were known as Mohawks. All those delivered had been originally ordered by France.

▲ Fighting the Japanese
Twenty H75-A7s served in the Dutch East Indies from May 1940 and saw intensive fighting against the Japanese.

US Army P-36C ▶
The USAAC's few P-36Cs featured extra wing-mounted 7.62-mm (.30-cal) guns.

Preserved Hawk ▼
In the colours of a P-36C serving with the 27th Pursuit Squadron, USAAC in September 1939, this aircraft is preserved by the USAF Museum in Ohio. The colourful paint scheme was applied for participation in the National Air Races.

▲ Large French orders
France's Armée de l'Air ordered a total of 1130 Model H75s before World War II; only about 600 were completed and of these about 200 reached France. Some were diverted to Morocco; others escaped to Britain.

FACTS AND FIGURES

▶ China and Argentina were granted licences to build a simplified Model 75 with fixed landing gear.

▶ A few captured Hawks were impressed into service by the Luftwaffe.

▶ Most USAAC P-36As had been replaced by Curtiss P-40s by December 1941.

▶ In its infancy, Hindustan Aircraft Ltd (HAL) of India built at least five Hawk 75s. French Hawks diverted to Britain were fitted with British equipment and sent to Portugal, South Africa and India.

▶ The original USAAC contract for 210 aircraft was valued at US$4,113,550.

Exported Hawks go to war

It was the Hawk 75 export model that saw the most service and combat during World War II, and was destined to serve on both sides.

Though it was the main US Army fighter at the time of the Japanese attack on Pearl Harbor, US combat use was to be virtually confined to the few that managed to get airborne over Hawaii on 7 December 1941.

Sales to France, Norway and the Netherlands had followed the original US order; the 200 that entered French service were

their most effective fighters before the German invasion in 1940. However, though it was a sound aircraft with excellent manoeuvrability, the Hawk was outclassed in speed and firepower by more modern European designs such as the Messerschmitt Bf 109, often its main adversary.

Aircraft en route to France were delivered to the UK. A few later served with the RAF in the Burma campaign, while Dutch machines in the East Indies saw limited action against the

Japanese, as did a small number of H75Ns in Siam.

Apart from Finland's use of Hawks against the Russians, other Axis Hawks included Vichy French aircraft that briefly fought US forces in North Africa.

Below: Hawk 75s captured by the Nazis in 1940 were assembled in Germany and passed on to Finland for use against the Russians after the German invasion of the USSR in June 1941. Some remained in service as late as 1948.

Above: Registered NR1277, this is the second Hawk 75 demonstrator featuring fixed gear and bomb racks.

Hawk 75A-8 (P-36G)

Type: single-seat monoplane fighter

Powerplant: one 895-kW (1200-hp) Wright R-1820-G205A Cyclone radial piston engine

Maximum speed: 518 km/h (322 mph) at 4633 m (15,200 ft)

Cruising speed: 420 km/h (261 mph)

Initial climb rate: 6 min to 4572 m (15,000 ft)

Range: 1046 km (650 miles)

Service ceiling: 9860 m (32,350 ft)

Weights: empty 2121 kg (4676 lb); maximum take-off 2667 kg (5880 lb)

Armament: four wing-mounted 7.62-mm (.30-cal.) and two fuselage-mounted 12.7-mm (.50-cal.) machine guns

Dimensions:
span 11.27 m (37 ft)
length 8.68 m (28 ft 6 in)
height 2.81 m (9 ft 3 in)
wing area 21.92 m² (236 sq ft)

COMBAT DATA

MAXIMUM SPEED

Though it was a manoeuvrable aircraft, the P-36 lacked the speed of its European contemporaries. Some Japanese designs also had a superior top speed.

P-36C HAWK	501 km/h (311 mph)
HURRICANE Mk IIC	541 km/h (366 mph)
Ki-43-IIb 'OSCAR'	530 km/h (329 mph)

RANGE

While lacking in range compared to the Nakajima 'Oscar', the Hawk compared favourably with the Hawker Hurricane which was limited to 740 km in cannon-armed Mk IIC form. The four Hispano cannon imposed a weight penalty.

HURRICANE Mk IIC
740 km (460 miles)

P-36C HAWK
1320 km (820 miles)

Ki-43-IIb 'OSCAR'
3200 km (1988 miles)

ARMAMENT

The first Hawk 75/P-36 variants were fairly lightly armed, though the P-36C fared better than the 'Oscar'. Cannon armament featured prominently on British and other countries' aircraft later in the war; the Hurricane was a prime example, with four 20-mm Hispanos.

P-36C HAWK
1 x 12.7-mm (.50-cal.) machine gun
3 x 7.62-mm (.30-cal.) machine guns

HURRICANE Mk IIC
4 x 20-mm cannon

Ki-43-IIb 'OSCAR'
2 x 12.7-mm (.50-cal.) machine guns

HAWK 75A-8

Norway ordered 36 of these aircraft just prior to the German occupation. Six were delivered to Free Norwegian forces in Canada in February 1941 (including this aircraft based in Toronto), but the rest were requisitioned by the US Army as P-36Gs.

Though the Model 75 prototype was powered by a 671-kW (900-hp) Wright XR-1720 radial, the export models employed a large diameter R-1820 Cyclone 9. The Army's P-36s, on the other hand, had a Pratt & Whitney R-1830 Twin Wasp installed.

Among the improvements introduced with the Model 75B was the scalloped rear fuselage behind the cockpit to provide a rear view for the pilot.

When Curtiss engineers realised that the service life of the radial-engined P-36 would be limited, a P-36 was re-engined with a new 12-cylinder, liquid-cooled Allison V-1710. This became the XP-37 and led directly to the P-40 Warhawk fighter family.

Curtiss's Hawk 75 was a stressed-skin, cantilever low-wing monoplane with hydraulically-operated split flaps and main landing gear. Even the tail wheel retracted. However, manufacturers were also building advanced monoplane fighter aircraft, including Seversky.

By the time the H75A-8 appeared, the Hawks were fitted with much improved armament totalling six machine guns; four in the wings and two above the engine, firing through the propeller arc.

Model 75 Hawk colours

■ **FINLAND:** This Hawk 75A-3 was attached to LeLv 32 at Suulajärvi in September 1941. It was among a number assembled in Germany from captured French and Norwegian examples.

■ **NETHERLANDS EAST INDIES:** The 1st Squadron of the Royal Netherlands East Indies Army Air Corps operated Hawk 75A-7s against the Japanese until February 1942.

■ **UNITED STATES:** The US Army's P-36s were never officially named. The only operational finish carried by these aircraft was olive drab/neutral grey as applied to this P-36C.

■ **VICHY FRANCE:** Among the 200 examples delivered to the Armée de l'Air, this Hawk 75A-3 ultimately served in 'Vichy' French markings with the 2nd Escadrille of GC1/4 at Dakar in Senegal.

CURTISS

P-40 WARHAWK (EARLY VERSIONS)

● US Army fighter ● Widely used ● Fighter-bomber

Perhaps the best-known Curtiss aircraft of World War II, the P-40 was developed from the radial-engined P-36 fighter of 1936. Although considered by many to be obsolete when it first appeared, the P-40 went on to be built in very large numbers, as the US had no better fighter at the time. Despite poor performance at altitude, the P-40 distinguished itself in the North African theatre and became famous as the mount of the 'Flying Tigers' in China.

▲ Not one of the best American fighters of World War II, the early P-40 was nevertheless an effective aircraft and achieved everlasting fame with the American Volunteer Group.

CURTISS P-40 (EARLY VERSIONS)

Desert Tomahawk ▶
In RAF service, the early P-40 was known as the Tomahawk. Operating primarily as ground attack aircraft in the North African theatre, they were often seen with sharkmouth insignia, as here.

▲ Army fighter
Although outclassed even at the start of World War II, the P-40B acquitted itself well in US service.

◀ Evolutionary design
The fitting of an in-line engine gave much improved performance, but manoeuvrability remained mediocre.

▼ Armament removed
In RAF service, the two 12.7-mm (.50-cal.) machine guns were often mounted on top of the engine were often removed. This aircraft is an exception.

Early colour scheme ▶
When first delivered to US Army pursuit squadrons in 1940, P-40s originally wore this green paint scheme and had striped rudders. This aircraft is seen next to a huge Boeing XB-15.

FACTS AND FIGURES

➤ The first prototype P-40 was actually a production Curtiss P-36 fitted with a liquid-cooled Allison V12 engine.

➤ Early P-40s were built in three versions, known as the P-40, P-40B and P-40C.

➤ Based at Langley Field in Virginia, the 8th Pursuit Group was the first P-40 unit.

➤ During 1942 the P-40B-equipped 'Flying Tigers' shot down 286 Japanese army aircraft in just six months.

➤ Tomahawks were widely used by the RAF in North Africa.

➤ RAF P-40Cs were the slowest of all production Warhawks.

Slow but tough US fighter

B ehind the times when it first appeared, the Curtiss P-40 never did catch up. Factors such as its modestly powered engine and its light armament were compounded by very poor performance at altitude and mediocre manoeuvrability.

These shortcomings were not because of poor design, but were a reflection of the outmoded US Army specification which called for low-level ground-support fighters.

In 1940 the P-40 was placed into large-scale production for the US Army and found export customers in France and Britain, who were desperately seeking fighters in their struggle with Germany. Britain took over the French order after France fell to Germany. These aircraft, named Tomahawks by the RAF, were heavily committed to the fighting in North Africa. They performed bravely in this theatre and achieved good results at low level, but at high altitude suffered heavy losses to German Bf 109E fighters.

By 1941 the improved P-40B had entered service, and it was this model which was transferred to the famous American Volunteer Group, or 'Flying Tigers', in China. Under the skilful leadership of Claire Chennault, these aircraft achieved a remarkable kill-to-loss ratio against the Japanese.

Below: In RAF service, Tomahawk IIBs proved too slow as fighters to tackle Luftwaffe Bf 109s and were thus relegated to the ground attack role.

Above: An early USAAF P-40 in flight. This was among the last aircraft delivered to the US before late 1941.

P-40B Warhawk

Type: single-seat fighter-bomber and pursuit aircraft

Powerplant: one 776-kW (1040-hp) Allison V-1710-33 in-line piston engine

Maximum speed: 552 km/h (343 mph)

Initial climb rate: 6 min to 4500 m (14,764 ft)

Range: 386 km (240 miles)

Service ceiling: approx 10,000 m (32,800 ft)

Weights: empty 2724 kg (6005 lb); loaded 4010 kg (8841 lb)

Armament: two 12.7-mm (.50-cal.) machine guns mounted in the nose and four 7.62-mm (.30-cal.) machine guns in the wings

Dimensions: span 11.42 m (37 ft 6 in)
length 10.00 m (32 ft 10 in)
height 3.77 m (12 ft 4 in)
wing area 21.95 m² (236 sq ft)

COMBAT DATA

ARMAMENT

Both the P-40 and unusual Bell P-39 Airacobra were average fighters and not very effective or hard-hitting. The Messerschmitt Bf 109E was one of the best fighters of the early war years.

P-40B TOMAHAWK — 2 x 12.7-mm (.50-cal.) machine guns
4 x 7.62-mm (.30-cal.) machine guns

P-39N AIRACOBRA — 2 x 12.7-mm (.50-cal.) machine guns, 1 x 20-mm cannon
4 x 7.62-mm (.30-cal.) machine guns

Bf 109E-7 — 4 x 7.92-mm machine guns
1 x 20-mm cannon

EMPIRE OF THE RISING SUN: The Japanese captured many Allied airfields during their advance. By March 1942 the 'Flying Tigers' were effectively confined to operating from central China.

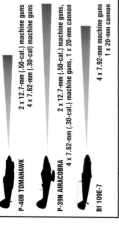

MANCHURIA

CHINA

FRENCH INDO-CHINA

THAILAND

BURMA

KEY:
Japanese advance between July 1937 and May 1944
American Volunteer Group bases

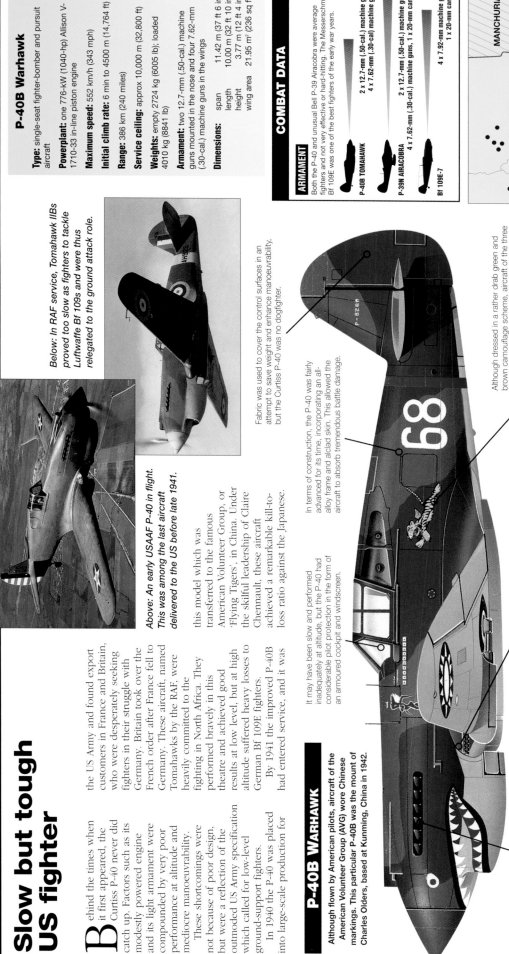

P-40B WARHAWK

Although flown by American pilots, aircraft of the American Volunteer Group (AVG) wore Chinese markings. This particular P-40B was the mount of Charles Olders, based at Kunming, China in 1942.

Early P-40s were powered by a liquid-cooled Allison V-1710 engine, which provided adequate performance, though the type was no real threat against Japanese fighters.

It may have been slow and performed inadequately at altitude, but the P-40 had considerable pilot protection in the form of an armoured cockpit and windscreen.

Original armament consisted of just four machine guns. On the P-40B this was increased to six, with an additional pair of 7.62-mm (.30-cal.) guns mounted in the wings.

Fabric was used to cover the control surfaces in an attempt to save weight and enhance manoeuvrability, but the Curtiss P-40 was no dogfighter.

In terms of construction, the P-40 was fairly advanced for its time, incorporating an all-alloy frame and alclad skin. This allowed the aircraft to absorb tremendous battle damage.

Although dressed in a rather drab green and brown camouflage scheme, aircraft of the three AVG squadrons were adorned with large, vicious-looking sharkmouths on the nose, complete with eyes. A tiger motif was located on each side of the fuselage, just behind the cockpit.

'Flying Tigers' combat tactics

ATTACKING BOMBERS: Long-range Japanese bombers had little armour and huge unprotected fuel tanks. A few bursts from the P-40s' guns was usually enough to turn a 'Betty' or 'Nell' into flames.

MINIMAL INVOLVEMENT: In order to destroy the maximum number of enemy aircraft for the fewest losses, pilots were instructed to avoid dogfighting at all costs. Once in a 'furball' with an A6M2 'Zero', an early P-40 was a sitting duck.

TIGERS' TACTICS: In order to mount the most effective attack against enemy fighters, AVG pilots would work in pairs, flying their lumbering P-40Bs in from the sun and diving through the Japanese formations.

CURTISS
P-40 WARHAWK (LATE)

- Single-seat fighter ● Desert fighter-bomber ● 'Flying Tiger' in China

Despite criticisms of its inferiority to Spitfires, Messerschmitts, Zeroes and Mustangs, the P-40 was important – if not critical – to victory in World War II. As the most numerous US Army fighter at the time of Pearl Harbor, the P-40 bred a generation of fighter pilots and won fame with General Chennault's 'Flying Tigers', who took it to the limit against superior Japanese forces.

▶ The P-40 was immortalised by the 'Flying Tigers' of the American Volunteer Group in China, who used the type with great success against the previously all-conquering Japanese.

CURTISS **P-40 WARHAWK**

▶ Still flying
This P-40 has been restored, and flew at a British air show in 1984. The shark mouth marking was used by No. 112 Squadron RAF, which flew ground-attack missions in Egypt in 1942.

▶ Lucky escape
A Zero fighter almost claimed this P-40, flown by John Wood of the USAAC, over Guadalcanal. The P-40 was better able to withstand a hit than a Zero, but was inferior to it in most other respects.

▲ Kittyhawk
The first Tomahawks lacked performance, but the improved Kittyhawk Mk III had a more powerful Allison engine and enlarged tailfin.

▲ Desert airstrip
Tactical air support meant using rough strips just behind the front line. The rugged P-40 did well in the severe conditions of the desert, where sand was a constant problem as engines wore out.

Scramble ▶
Pilots race for take-off as enemy aircraft approach. The P-40 was an excellent attack aircraft, but never really did well as an interceptor fighter.

Loading up ▲
The Warhawk family carried six powerful 12.7-mm (.50-cal.) machine guns, which were excellent weapons for the ground-attack role as well as for air combat.

FACTS AND FIGURES

▶ The prototype for the P-40 series was flown in October 1938.

▶ At Pearl Harbor on 7 December 1941, 73 P-40s were among 152 US Army aircraft destroyed by the Japanese attack.

▶ Production of all P-40s totalled 16,802, including 13,738 for US forces.

▶ The 'Flying Tigers' in China were credited with 286 aerial victories while losing 23 American P-40 pilots.

▶ P-40s served with Australia, Britain, China, the USSR and South Africa.

▶ When World War II ended, the US had only one P-40 group still in service.

PROFILE

Close air support in the Warhawk

K nown by many names, including Hawk, Kittyhawk, Tomahawk and Warhawk, 31 variants of the P-40 battled on every continent. The definitive P-40N entered production in 1943, and reached US Army Air Force squadrons in March 1944.

By then, the P-40 was not a world-class pursuit ship. To some extent it was purposely assigned to secondary theatres so that more advanced warplanes (P-38, P-47, P-51)

could fly where the US perceived its first priorities. But none of this meant much to American pilots slogging in the Aleutians, Australians in New Guinea, or South Africans in Libya; they took this solid, rugged fighter and made the most of what they had.

It was plenty. The P-40 excelled when primitive maintenance, terrible weather and heavy odds were the order of the day. It was not in the category of a Bf 109 or Zero

Like many imperfect or obsolete fighters, the P-40 came in very useful as a ground-attack machine. The Desert Air Force used the type extensively, often working alongside the equally rugged Hawker Hurricane.

as a dogfighter, but was superb at providing close support to ground troops. When production ended in September 1944 the P-40 had served almost everywhere and had been used for just about everything.

Early P-40s had a pair of 12.7-mm (.50-cal.) machine guns on top of the fuselage, but these were often deleted in RAF aircraft.

The only parts of the P-40 which were fabric-covered were the control surfaces. This was to save weight and to make flying easier.

RAF Desert Air Force P-40s all wore a two-tone brown camouflage scheme.

P-40N Warhawk

Type: single-seat interceptor and fighter-bomber

Powerplant: one 1015-kW (1360-hp) Allison V-1710-81 inline piston engine

Maximum speed: 609 km/h (378 mph) at 3210 m (10,530 ft)

Rate of climb: to 4500 m (14,670 ft) in 6 minutes 40 seconds

Range: 386 km (240 miles)

Service ceiling: 11,630 m (38,160 ft)

Weights: empty 2724 kg (6045 lb); loaded 4018 kg (8858 lb)

Armament: six 12.7-mm (.50-cal.) machine guns in wing; provision for 227-kg (500-lb) bomb or 197-litre (43-gallon) drop-tank under fuselage

Dimensions:
span	11.42 m (37 ft 6 in)
length	10.20 m (33 ft 6 in)
height	3.77 m (12 ft 4 in)
wing area	21.95 m² (236 sq ft)

COMBAT DATA

MAXIMUM SPEED

The original P-40 was as fast as its contemporaries, but it lacked the agility and acceleration of the Zero. It could dive very fast, however, and the American Volunteer Group in China used it to make quick slashing attacks on the Japanese, accelerating away to avoid a dogfight.

HURRICANE Mk II	540 km/h (336 mph)
TOMAHAWK Mk IIB	555 km/h (345 mph)
A6M5 ZERO	540 km/h (336 mph)

SERVICE CEILING

Allison-engined aircraft often had very good performance at low level, but unless boosted by a powerful supercharger they tended to be somewhat sluggish at high altitude. The early P-40s were no exception, and high-level performance was far from ideal.

A6M5 ZERO 11,000 m (36,000 ft)
HURRICANE Mk II 10,000 m (33,000 ft)
TOMAHAWK Mk II 9200 m (30,200 ft)

ARMAMENT

Originally fitted with 12.7-mm machine guns, the Tomahawks in British service usually carried 7.7-mm (.303-cal.) Brownings like other RAF fighters to ease logistic problems. Later aircraft switched back to 12.7-mm (.50-cal.) weapons, and although the aircraft could carry cannon these were never fitted.

TOMAHAWK Mk IIB 6 x 7.7-mm (.303-cal.) machine guns
A6M5 ZERO 2 x 20-mm cannon 2 x 7.7-mm (.303-cal.) machine guns
HURRICANE Mk II 8 x 7.7-mm (.303-cal.) machine guns

The 'shark mouth' was one of the most characteristic of all Warhawk markings. No. 112 Squadron aircraft was the first to wear it.

TOMAHAWK MK IIB

This Curtiss Tomahawk Mk IIB served with No. 112 Squadron RAF, based at Sidi Haneish, North Africa, in the autumn of 1941. The squadron later received Kittyhawks and took part in the Italian campaign.

The Allison V-1710 engine was fitted with a supercharger. The cowling was later changed, with an enlarged air scoop.

Wing armament was four Browning 7.7-mm (.303-cal.) guns. This was later changed to six 12.7-mm (.50-cal.) machine guns, with 235 rounds per gun.

The fuselage hardpoint could carry a single 227-kg (500-lb) bomb or a 197-litre (43-gallon) fuel tank.

The canopy was later improved to give better visibility. The front windscreen was bulletproof and the cockpit was armoured.

For an average performer, the P-40 had a good level of equipment fit, with effective cockpit heating, heat ducting to the guns, armour and self-sealing fuel tanks.

The fuselage was of modern construction, with all-alloy framework covered by an 'Alclad' skin. Additional fuel was contained in a fuselage tank.

The Kittyhawk Mk II (P-40F) had a lengthened fuselage. With the rudder hinge behind the elevator hinge, the pilot had increased manoeuvrability and better control.

Warhawk development

■ **CURTISS P-36 HAWK:** First flown in 1935, the radial-engined Hawk was an intermediate step between the great Hawk biplanes and the P-40.

■ **P-40B:** Fitting an Allison inline engine to the P-36 produced a better fighter, which was used by the Flying Tigers in China.

■ **TOMAHAWK:** Early P-40s were known as Tomahawks in RAF service, and flew with distinction in the desert campaigns of 1941 and 1942.

■ **KITTYHAWK:** Later P-40s with bigger engines were known as Kittyhawks. This example is a P-40F with a Rolls-Royce Merlin engine.

■ **WARHAWK:** The final P-40s were known as Warhawks, a name which the US Air Force applied to the whole Hawk series. This is a P-40N of 1943.

CURTISS
C-46 COMMANDO

● Biggest wartime twin ● Vital transport ● Long serving

The Curtiss C-46 Commando was one of the great transports of World War II and has proved to be a rugged and reliable workhorse in both military and civil service ever since. The twin-engine, double-bubble C-46 is best remembered, however, for hauling war supplies over the 'Hump'. This was the transport route from India to China that traversed the Himalayan range and contained some of the most difficult flying conditions anywhere in the world.

▶ First flown on 26 March 1940 the C-46 was ordered by the USAAF in September as a troop and cargo transport. Its cavernous fuselage was well used in the Far East and Pacific theatres.

CURTISS C-46 COMMANDO

▶ Air ambulance
The majority of C-46s built for the USAAF served in Asia. This Commando served in the role of air ambulance at Saipan in the Marianas in June 1944. It could carry up to 33 stretchers and additional medical staff.

▶ Flight deck
Unlike the contemporary bombers the C-46's cockpit was roomy and relatively uncomplicated for the pilots.

CW-20 prototype ▶
The first prototype was briefly used by the USAAF before being sold to British Overseas Airways Corporation and used for flights between Gibraltar and Malta in 1942.

▶ Para-dropper
In service with Troop Carrier Command, the C-46D dedicated troop carrier was adapted to, but saw little use as, a parachute aircraft.

▲ Production line
The main production line was established at Curtiss' plant in Buffalo, New York.

FACTS AND FIGURES

▶ The prototype CW-20 with twin fin and rudder first flew on 26 March 1940; the fuselage sides were also rounded.

▶ C-46s had carried 2.5 million kgs (2756 tons) of cargo over the 'Hump' by December 1943.

▶ Total production of the C-46 Commando numbered 3181 aircraft.

▶ US Air Force C-46 Commandos ended their service career at Howard Air Force Base, Panama, in 1968.

▶ C-46s fought a 'secret war' in Laos, flown by airlines that worked for the CIA.

▶ The Commando was built in 23 variants for the US Army, Navy and Marine Corps.

C-46 Commando

Type: medium-range passenger/cargo transport

Powerplant: two 1566-kW (2100-hp) Pratt & Whitney R-2800-34 Double Wasp 18-cylinder radial engines

Maximum speed: 435 km/h (270 mph) at 3048 m (10,000 ft)

Cruising speed: 378 km/h (235 mph) at 2745 m (9006 ft)

Range: 2897 km (1800 miles)

Service ceiling: 6705 m (21,998 ft)

Weights: empty 13,290 kg (29,299 lb); maximum take-off 22,680 kg (50,000 lb)

Dimensions: span   32.93 m (108 ft)
              length   23.27 m (76 ft 4 in)
              height   6.63 m (21 ft 9 in)
              wing area 126.16 m² (1358 sq ft)

COMBAT DATA

MAXIMUM SPEED

With its powerful Pratt & Whitney R-2800-34 Double Wasp engines, the C-46 had a top speed nearly 20 per cent faster than its main rival the Douglas C-47 and 40 per cent faster than the three-engined Ju-52 operated by the Luftwaffe.

C-46 COMMANDO	435 km/h (270 mph)
C-47	370 km/h (230 mph)
Ju-52	270 km/h (168 mph)

RANGE

Greater fuel capacity and a high all-up weight gave the C-46 an exceptional range which enabled it to fly over the 'Hump'. It could fly further than the C-47 and over three times as far as the Ju-52 which was designed for the European theatre.

Ju-52 917 km (570 miles)

C-47 2575 km (1600 miles)

C-46 COMMANDO 2897 km (1800 miles)

PAYLOAD

Although the C-47 could lift the same weight as the C-46 it only had the fuselage space to take 28 fully armed troops while the C-46 could take 50 troops. The smaller Ju-52 had less than half of the payload and could carry only 18 troops. All three flew vital supply missions to their troops.

C-46 COMMANDO	4536 kg (10,000 lb)/50 troops
C-47	4536 kg (10,000 lb)/28 troops
Ju-52	1202 kg (2650 lb)/18 troops

Heavylift hero of the Far East

To carry fuel, food, supplies and ammunition to Allied troops in China, C-46 Commando pilots braved the horrendous weather, terrible cold and dizzy altitude of the Himalayan mountain range, flying from bases in India.

The aircraft were loaded and flown under the most primitive conditions, their fuel pumped by hand from drums. On the Assam-Chunking route, which was typical, Commando pilots had to vault peaks of about

4000 m (13,100 ft), even though ice began to form on the aircraft's wings at 3050 m (10,000 ft).

The bulky, swollen-looking C-46 Commando never quite achieved the elegance of its near-contemporary the Douglas DC-3, but it had a greater capacity to carry people and freight. The Commando dropped in and out of airfields all over the world and they were used in action in the Korean War and for training for Vietnam. Hundreds of

Above: *C-46s were used after the war in glider towing experiments, using a solid towing link between the two aircraft. This C-46F is towing a WACO CG-15A.*

Commandos later became civil servants operating with airlines in dozens of countries.

C-46 COMMANDO

The Commando was the biggest and heaviest twin-engined US cargo transport aircraft of World War II which became famous for flying supply missions over the Himalayan mountains.

Power was provided by two 1566-kW (2100-hp) Pratt & Whitney Double Wasp 18-cylinder radial piston engines driving Hamilton Standard propellers.

The fuselage was formed from two partial rings, one above the other, which met at a tension diaphragm – the cabin floor. This gave the C-46 its double-bubble appearance.

The cantilever low wing was built in three main sections. The centre-section was built into the fuselage. Hydraulically-operated slotted flaps extended from the ailerons to the fuselage.

Similar in structure to the wings, the all-metal single fin, rudder and tailplane are of the cantilever monoplane type. Trim tabs are fitted on the elevators and rudder.

Above: *More than half a century after it was first flown by the USAAF, this C-46A, built by Curtiss-Wright, is still flying regularly with the Confederate Air Force in Texas.*

This C-46 is in the colours of the Japan Self-Defence Force in about 1973. It was being used for general transport and utility duties.

The crew of four comprised the pilot, co-pilot, navigator and radio operator. The flush windscreen was replaced by a stepped version in the C-46D.

Over the 'Hump'

To supply the Allied war against the Japanese a constant flow of food, ammunition and other vital supplies were lifted over the Himalayas by hardworking C-46s.

OVER THE HIMALAYAS: For the 805-km (500-mile) flight from Assam to Chunking the C-46s had to climb fully laden to 4265 m (13,993 ft), through the icing layer at 3050 m (10,000 ft), then land in appalling weather conditions.

Chunking

Assam

C-46 MAINSTAY: A massive air transport supply effort was undertaken from the Assam region of India to supply friendly forces fighting the Japanese in the south-west of China.

PRIMITIVE FACILITIES: The Assam airfields were largely unpaved and were transformed into boggy conditions by the monsoon rains for nearly half of the year. The aircraft were refuelled by hand from drums.

122

CURTISS
SB2C HELLDIVER

● Dive-bomber ● Carrier strike ● US Navy

Disadvantaged from the start by having to replace the highly capable SBD Dauntless, the Helldiver never quite won a similar place in the hearts of US naval aviators. It took time to prove itself in action and eventually became an effective carrier-launched dive- and torpedo-bomber in the war against the Japanese. But the SB2C did not win the reliability battle soon enough for some commanders and picked up the derogatory nickname 'Beast'.

▶ The Helldiver was a hard-hitting aircraft which gained many combat successes, but pilots hated it. The designation SB2C was said to stand for 'son of a bitch, second class' by aircrews.

CURTISS SB2C HELLDIVER

▼ **Hook down to land**
Ready to land, this SB2C pilot has lowered the tail hook of his aircraft. When landing, Helldivers often revealed their poor handling to careless pilots.

▲ **Weapons away**
Helldivers were built to carry a 726-kg (1600-lb) bomb internally, or two smaller 454-kg (1000-lb) weapons, or a torpedo.

▶ **Big bird**
Even with its wings folded, the Helldiver was a big aircraft. This was due to the requirement for an internal bomb-bay.

Rear gunner ▶
In combat, the Helldiver's rear gunner slid back the hood to fire a pair of 7.62-mm (.30-cal.) Browning machine guns.

▶ **Fleet strike force**
By 1944 hundreds of SB2Cs were in service with the carrier battle groups of the US Pacific Fleet.

FACTS AND FIGURES

▶ From an order for 450 Helldivers for the Royal Navy, only 26 reached Britain. None of them were used operationally.

▶ In total, 5,516 Helldivers were delivered to the US Navy during World War II.

▶ One of the prototype SB2Cs fell to pieces in a dive-bombing trial.

▶ The Helldiver specification was influenced by the Luftwaffe's success with the Ju 87 Stuka dive-bomber.

▶ SB2Cs first went to war with carrier squadron VB-17 on USS *Bunker Hill*.

▶ The USAAF used the SB2C as a trainer and target-towing aircraft.

Dive-bomber from hell

Taking its name from an earlier Curtiss type, the Helldiver was a powerful, modern dive-bomber designed to undertake a variety of combat missions. It was also tentatively required by the US Marines and the Army Air Forces which compromised the SB2C, giving the manufacturers the demanding task of creating a 'multi-role' aircraft in the middle of a war. There was no time to perfect the requirement and when the Army did not order the aircraft in quantity, it was left to the

Navy to sort out the teething troubles. A long list of 'fixes' was required, which delayed the Helldiver's deployment for some months.

But the job was done, and from November 1943 when Helldivers pounded the Japanese island garrison of Rabaul until the end of the war the Navy used the Helldiver in every major surface action as an integral part of its carrier air groups. Cannon armament, a relative rarity on World War II American aircraft, was fitted to the SB2C-1C, the

last suffix indicating the heavier, more powerful guns. One of the most effective models was the SB2C-4 which introduced the distinctive 'cheese grater' split flaps to aid stability during a dive.

Above: The SB2C was not a good marketing tool for Curtiss. The company boss, Guy Vaughan, called it 'one of the biggest crosses we had to bear'.

Below: The Royal Navy tested the Helldiver, but rejected it immediately because of its appalling handling, which was said to be even worse than the Fleet Air Arm's Barracuda.

SB2C Helldiver

Type: three-seat dive-/torpedo-bomber

Powerplant: one 1268-kW (1900-hp) Wright R-2600-8 Cyclone air-cooled engine

Maximum speed: 452 km/h (294 mph)

Range: 1786 km (1200 miles)

Service ceiling: 7530 m (29,100 ft)

Weights: empty 4990 kg (10,978 lb); loaded 7550 kg (16,610 lb)

Armament: two 20-mm cannon or four 12.7-mm (.50-cal.) machine guns in wings and two 7.62-mm (.30-cal.) machine guns in rear cockpit; up to 454 kg (1000 lb) of bombs in internal bay

Dimensions:

span	15.20 m (49 ft 6 in)
length	11.20 m (36 ft 8 in)
height	5.10 m (13 ft 2 in)
wing area	39.20 m² (422 sq ft)

The Battle of Leyte Gulf

3 DECOY FORCE: A third decoy force was sent in from the north to distract the Americans. Task Force 38 eventually gave chase. The decoy was not noticed for some time.

2 AMERICAN AIR RAIDS: Japanese efforts to thwart American landings failed after SB2Cs attacked and sank a battleship and damaged a cruiser.

1 JAPANESE STRIKE FORCES: The Japanese Plan Sho-1 operation was intended to stop American landings at Leyte. The First Striking Force ('A' and 'C') sailed from Brunei; a second fleet came from the north.

Japanese aircraft sink US carrier *Princeton*

SB2Cs attacked from here

PHILIPPINE ISLANDS

Force 'A'

Force 'C'

BRUNEI

Japanese Naval Forces

US Pacific Fleet

SB2C HELLDIVER

In June 1944, the US Navy changed the colour scheme of all its aircraft to overall gloss dark blue. The Helldiver served from 1943 to 1949 with the USN.

Tail buffeting was a constant problem, and despite a redesign it never entirely disappeared.

The arrester hook was connected to a large hydraulic damper to reduce the impact of catching the deck wire.

The gunner was protected by a large sheet of armour. Between him and the pilot was the radio bay, the life raft, the autopilot controls and a large fuel tank.

Unlike earlier dive-bombers, the SB2C had a large internal bomb-bay with displacement gear for the bombs and hydraulic doors over the bay. The wingroot contained additional fuel tanks.

Upper surface divebrakes were fitted to the wing, and the trailing-edge flaps were split. The leading-edge slat opened simultaneously with undercarriage operation.

Engine oil and hydraulic fluid tanks were fitted behind the engine, with an oil cooler at the bottom of the engine bay.

One early source of trouble was the Wright Cyclone engine and its Curtiss Electric four-bladed propeller. Many of the propellers, like this one, had the spinner removed in service. The carburettor intake was in the top of the cowling.

ACTION DATA

Dive-bombers were vulnerable to attack from enemy fighters due to their low speeds. The D4Y3 had fairly good speed and was a streamlined design compared to the SB2C, with its bulbous radial engine.

SB2C HELLDIVER	452 km/h (280 mph)
D4Y3 'JUDY'	575 km/h (357 mph)
BARRACUDA Mk II	367 km/h (228 mph)

RANGE

An important feature of a carrier-based aircraft was its range performance due to the fact that it operated over water. The D4Y3 traded range for a higher top speed, while the Barracuda had a superior range but a comparatively low top speed.

SB2C HELLDIVER	1786 km (1107 miles)
D4Y3 'JUDY'	1520 km (942 miles)
BARRACUDA Mk II	1850 km (1147 miles)

DOUGLAS
B-18 BOLO

● Twin-engined bomber ● DC-2 airliner development ● Foreign service

▲ Intended to replace the Martin B-10 as the USAAC's standard bomber, the DB-1 (Douglas Bomber 1) beat competition for orders from the Martin 164 and Boeing 299.

Incredible as it seems now, the Douglas B-18 was the US Army's standard bomber in 1940. At a time when Spitfires and Messerschmitts were duelling in the Battle of Britain, American bomber crews were training and preparing for war in this slow machine, with inadequate range, that was little more than a military adaptation of a transport aircraft. The B-18 (dubbed 'Bolo' officially, although the name was rarely used) was inadequate for modern warfare.

DOUGLAS B-18 BOLO

▼ Comparatively sluggish
With a top speed of just 346 km/h (215 mph), the B-18 soon found itself outclassed when the US entered World War II in 1941.

▲ RCAF Digby
Twenty general reconnaissance Digby Mk Is (as they were known in Canadian service) were delivered to the air force during 1939 and 1940.

▼ Wartime camouflage
Camouflage was soon applied to USAAC Bolos once war had broken out. This one crashed at Hickam Field, Hawaii, in 1943.

▲ Round nose B-18
The first production Bolos were designated B-18 and featured this round, turretless, but more aerodynamic, nose design.

Ready for action at March Field ▶
The 7th Bombardment Group's fleet of Bolos is seen at March Field, California, in 1940. The 7th BG was the first unit to receive production B-18s. By 1940 most USAAC bomber squadrons were equipped with B-18/B-18As, but a number were destroyed in Hawaii on 7 December 1941.

FACTS AND FIGURES

▶ The RAF investigated the purchase of B-18s in the maritime reconnaissance-bomber role as the Digby Mk I.

▶ Post-war, some surplus B-18s were used for crop-spraying and as freighters.

▶ Three air forces operated B-18s; Brazil received two B-18s in 1942.

▶ The USAAF's 7th Bombardment Group commander, Major Austin Straubel, was killed in a B-18 crash in Java in 1942.

▶ The first B-18s were evaluated by test pilots at Wright Field, Ohio, in 1935.

▶ The B-18 bomber's span was 1.37 m (4 ft 6 in) greater than that of the Douglas DC-2.

PROFILE

Bomber cousin of the DC-2

Douglas developed the B-18 in 1934 to provide the US Army Air Corps with an aircraft which had twice the bomb-carrying capacity of the Martin B-10. Douglas drew upon engineering work on the DC-2 airliner, the predecessor of the famous DC-3. The result was the utilitarian B-18 bomber, which was ready for examination by Army experts in 1935.

The Army ordered the B-18 into production in January 1936, even though fighters that were far faster than this low-wing, somewhat underpowered.

medium bomber were already appearing on the scene.

With its deep fuselage, the B-18 had space for two pilots and a crew totalling six men, including three gunners and a bombardier. B-18s participated in many realistic military exercises in the late 1930s.

Pilots were satisfied with the aircraft, but knew that it did not measure up to world standards.

By the time America entered the war, the B-18 was being used only to train bombardiers. As many as 122 were fitted with special equipment to hunt for

submarines. Few, if any, B-18s saw actual combat and by the end of the war none remained in service.

The B-18 was designed around the wings and engines of the DC-2 and proved adaptable to other roles, including maritime reconnaissance as the B-18B. For this role it was fitted with a nose-mounted search radar and a magnetic anomaly detector (MAD) in a tail 'stinger' and carried depth charges in its bomb-bay. Two B-18s were converted as unarmed transports, designated C-58.

Above: The 7th Bombardment Group fly from their California base in the late-1930s.

Right: This Bolo has spray booms fitted under its wings. A number were converted as 'ag' aircraft post-war.

B-18A BOLO

The 18th Reconnaissance Squadron was one of three reconnaissance units equipped with the B-18A Bolo. This example operated from Mitchell Field, New York, in 1940.

The retractable dorsal turret housed a 7.62-mm (.30-cal.) machine gun. When manned, it was extended upwards to allow the gunner to see the enemy. A ventral gun fired through a tunnel in the fuselage floor.

An internal bomb-bay below the B-18A's wing centre-section carried up to 2948 kg (6500 lb) of bombs. Its relatively spacious fuselage made the Bolo adaptable for other roles, such as transport.

In common with the DC-2 airliner, the Bolo was fitted with two Pratt & Whitney R-1820 Cyclone 9 radial piston engines. In their -53 form they produced 746 kW.

B-18As had a small globular turret mounting for a flexible 7.62-mm (.30-cal.) machine gun. Above this was the bomb aimer's position in an extended glazed nose.

The Bolo's crew consisted of a pilot and co-pilot, a bomb aimer/navigator and nose, dorsal and ventral gunners.

Douglas bombers for the USAAC

■ **B-7:** This monoplane, equipped with retractable undercarriage, was developed from the XO-35 reconnaissance aircraft of 1930.

■ **A-17/A-33:** In 1942 the USAAC took over 31 Douglas 8As (export derivatives of Northrop's A-17 attack-bomber) bound for Norway.

■ **B-23 DRAGON:** To address the B-18's shortcomings, Douglas developed the larger B-23. It first flew in 1939, but few were built.

■ **XB-19:** Douglas' response to a 1934 USAAC requirement for a large bomber, the B-19 was defeated by a lack of funding.

B-18A Bolo

Type: medium bomber, maritime patrol and training aircraft

Powerplant: two 746-kW (1000-hp) Wright R-1820-53 Cyclone 9 radial piston engines

Maximum speed: 346 km/h (215 mph) at 3050 m (10,000 ft)

Range: 1931 km (1200 miles)

Service ceiling: 7285 m (23,900 ft)

Weights: empty 7403 kg (16,321 lb); maximum take-off 12,552 kg (27,672 lb)

Armament: three hand-operated, flexible 7.62-mm (.30-cal.) machine guns in nose, ventral and dorsal positions), plus up to 2948 kg (6500 lb) of bombs carried in an internal bay

Dimensions:
span	27.28 m	(89 ft 6 in)
length	17.63 m	(57 ft 10 in)
height	4.62 m	(15 ft 2 in)
wing area	89.65 m²	(965 sq ft)

COMBAT DATA

MAXIMUM SPEED

Designed to fulfil an airliner role for Lufthansa, as well as a bomber role for the Luftwaffe, the He 111 possessed a respectable turn of speed, a healthy 75 km/h faster than the B-18. The RAF's Wellington was not far behind.

B-18A BOLO	346 km/h (215 mph)
WELLINGTON Mk I	394 km/h (245 mph)
He 111E-3	420 km/h (261 mph)

ARMAMENT

The B-18 had an excellent bombload for a medium bomber of the period – almost one tonne more than the He 111 and Wellington. Light defensive armament was typical of the late 1930s.

He 111E-3 3 x 7.9-mm machine guns 2000 kg (4409 lb) of bombs	**WELLINGTON Mk I** 4 x 7.7-mm (.303-cal.) machine guns 2041 kg (4500 lb) of bombs	**B-18A BOLO** 3 x 7.7-mm (.303-cal.) machine guns 2948 kg (6500 lb) of bombs

SERVICE CEILING

The early variants of the Wellington had an inferior ceiling to other medium bombers. This deteriorated further in the wartime Mk IC variant, although the problem was addressed in the Merlin-engined versions.

He 111E-3	7200 m (23,622 ft)
WELLINGTON Mk I	6584 m (21,600 ft)
B-18A BOLO	7285 m (23,900 ft)

DOUGLAS
C-47 SKYTRAIN

● Worldwide service ● Transport and glider tug ● Still flying

Based on the DC-3, the Douglas C-47 Skytrain became the most widely used transport of the war. This familiar and versatile military transport hauled cargoes, dropped paratroops and towed gliders. No airfield was too close to the front or too rough for the versatile Skytrain. Eisenhower called the C-47 one of the four most important weapons of the war, along with the bazooka, the Jeep and the atomic bomb.

▲ Many crewmembers owed their lives to the strength of the C-47, when the aircraft were caught by enemy fighters or anti-aircraft fire. Equally, many troops were saved by supplies and reinforcements delivered by the Skytrain.

DOUGLAS C-47 SKYTRAIN

▲ **Skytrain gathering**
Many hundreds of aircraft were involved in operations from the UK. Here, closely parked C-47s prepare for a mission in support of the D-Day invasion forces.

▲ **Floating transport**
A single XC-47C was built with floats and a few aircraft were converted to this configuration in the field.

▲ **'Gooney Bird'**
US Army Air Force personnel nicknamed the C-47 'The Gooney Bird'.

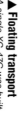

▼ **Last of the line**
Douglas built 10,691 C-47s, this aircraft being the last manufactured at the Long Beach factory. Some aircraft were built in Japan and the USSR.

▲ **Supply drop**
Troops in every theatre, from Europe through Africa to the Pacific, regarded the C-47 as a lifeline. All types of equipment, food and medical supplies were dropped by parachute to the front line.

FACTS AND FIGURES

► On 10 July 1943 Skytrains dropped 4,381 Allied paratroopers during the invasion of Sicily.

► The prototype for the DC-3/C-47 made its maiden flight on 17 December 1935.

► More than 1,000 C-47s participated in the D-Day invasion.

► Skytrains were fine glider tugs and were used to haul glider-borne troops into battle in France and Burma.

► Some C-47s were flown with floats, instead of their wheeled undercarriage.

► Skytrains were built in Japan by Nakajima and in the USSR by Lisunov.

PROFILE

Unsurpassed military transport

The qualities which made the DC-3 a fine airliner made the C-47 a superb military transport, which served in every theatre of the war.

The twin-engined C-47 was rugged and reliable, and could fly from primitive airfields in the midst of the war zone, carrying cargo, troops or towing gliders.

The Skytrain was in many respects the most versatile military aircraft ever built and

flew in a number of very important operations. The most memorable C-47 mission was the dropping of paratroopers in Normandy in the hours before the 6 June 1944 invasion of Europe by Allied armies.

But the C-47 was everywhere: in Burma, an enterprising Skytrain pilot poked a Browning automatic rifle out of his cockpit and shot down a Japanese Zero fighter. In the Aleutian Islands C-47s equipped with

skis brought supplies to American soldiers by landing on and taking off from ice-covered surfaces.

Many Skytrains survived being hit by gunfire and being attacked by fighters, and were deemed the 'most survivable' of all Allied transport aircraft.

C-47A SKYTRAIN

During the D-Day landings 'Buzz Buggy' flew from a British base with the 81st Troop Carrier Squadron of the 436th Troop Carrier Group.

Left: Gliders were too valuable to be used only once and therefore a system of retrieval was devised. The glider's towline was held above the ground between two poles and snatched by a long hook trailing from a low-flying C-47 Skytrain.

C-47A Skytrain

Type: cargo, troop or paratroop transport and glider tug

Powerplant: two 895-kW (1200-hp) Pratt & Whitney R-1830-92 Twin Wasp radial piston engines

Maximum speed: 365 km/h (227 mph) at 2285 m (7497 ft)

Range: 2414 km (1500 miles)

Service ceiling: 7070 m (23,196 m)

Weights: empty 8256 kg (18,201 lb); maximum take-off 11,794 kg (26,000 lb)

Accommodation: up to 28 paratroops or 14 stretchers or 4536 kg (10,000 lb) of cargo

Dimensions: span 29.11 m (95 ft 6 in)
length 19.43 m (63 ft 9 in)
height 5.18 m (17 ft)
wing area 91.69 m² (987 sq ft)

COMBAT DATA

PAYLOAD

Being a larger aircraft than the C-47, the Curtiss C-46 was able to carry more cargo. The capabilities of the C-46 were well suited to the Pacific theatre and most never saw the difficult combat action of the C-47. The Ju 52/3mg3e had a poor payload.

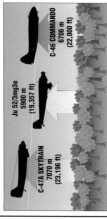

C-47A SKYTRAIN 4536 kg (10,000 lb)	
Ju 52/3mg3e 2000 kg (4409 lb)	
C-46 COMMANDO 7219 kg (15,915 lb)	

SERVICE CEILING

At higher altitudes an aircraft possesses better range. This is an important factor for long-distance flights or those over mountainous terrain.

C-47A SKYTRAIN 7070 m (23,196 ft)
Ju 52/3mg3e 5900 m (19,357 ft)
C-46 COMMANDO 6706 m (22,000 lb)

RANGE

Flying over 'the hump' into China was the main mission of the C-46, which had an extremely long range. The Junkers Ju 52/3mg3e served in a very similar, but more tactical, role to the C-47. Its range was much less than the American equivalent, however, and the Ju 52 was not a great glider tug. The Ju 52 was the only one with defensive guns.

Ju 52/3mg3e 1100 km (684 miles)
C-46 COMMANDO 7219 km (4486 miles)
C-47A SKYTRAIN 2414 km (1500 miles)

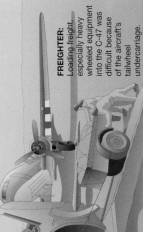

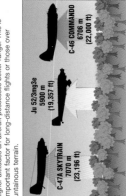

A three-man crew of pilot, co-pilot and radio operator flew the C-47. The radio operator sat in a separate compartment behind the cockpit and the aircrew entered by the small forward door.

Folding wooden seats along the cabin sides could accommodate up to 28 fully equipped paratroops. As well as cargo, standard internal fittings allowed 18 stretchers to be carried.

Two large cargo doors allowed cabin access, one opening forwards and the other backwards. A small door inset into the forward freight door was used for in-flight paratroop dropping.

Above: Although it was an exceptional airlifter, the C-47 was not very easy to load. All cargo had to be hauled through the left-hand side cargo doors.

Douglas designed the C-47 with a structure of metal stressed-skin and multiple spars, which produced a wing which was very resistant to fatigue.

Two Pratt & Whitney R-1830 14-cylinder air-cooled radial piston engines, each of 30-litre (6.6-gallon) capacity, drove the Hamilton Standard propellers of all the standard production Skytrains.

All Allied aircraft taking part in the D-Day operations were painted with these black and white 'invasion stripes' as a recognition aid.

FREIGHTER: Loading freight, especially heavy wheeled equipment into the C-47 was difficult because of the aircraft's tailwheel undercarriage.

Skytrain versatility

This highly versatile aircraft flew many types of mission, but its primary role was as a transport and glider tug.

GLIDER TUG: Several hundred gliders were used in the D-Day assault on Normandy. Packed with troops and equipment, the glider was released near the landing zone.

WACO CG-4A HADRIAN: Using gliders, the Allies were able to increase the capacity of their transport fleet quickly and cheaply.

DROPPING PARATROOPS: Several daring airborne raids would not have been possible without large numbers of C-47s; 28 troops could be dropped in quick succession.

DOUGLAS
TBD DEVASTATOR

- Carrier-based torpedo-bomber ● All-metal construction ● WWII service

This American torpedo bomber is remembered mostly for a tragic reason—the Douglas TBD Devastator fell in flames at Midway, where an entire squadron was lost in a matter of minutes. The Devastator was a perfectly acceptable aircraft by prewar standards, but it came on the scene when change was occurring rapidly. By the time men and machines were pitted in combat in the Pacific, the TBD was no longer an effective warplane.

▲ Though the Devastator represented the state of the art in the mid 1930s, it was to be tragically outclassed during the early battles of the Pacific in 1942.

PHOTO FILE

DOUGLAS TBD DEVASTATOR

▲ First squadron equipped
VT-3 was the first unit to receive the Devastator, in October 1937. Three more squadrons followed suit in 1938 and 1942. All four saw action against the Japanese.

▲ First Devastator
First flown in April 1935, the prototype had a lower cockpit canopy. This was raised on production aircraft to improve visibility on takeoff and landing.

▲ Devastator floatplane
The first production TBD was fitted with Edo floats and test flown from Newport, Rhode Island, in 1939.

Hydraulic wing folding ▼
TBDs were the first Navy aircraft with hydraulically powered wing folding. The wings' upward fold was also unusual.

California factory ▼
TBDs shown here are under construction at Douglas' Santa Monica factory. The aircraft on the left carries the markings of Navy unit VT-2.

▲ Aboard Enterprise before Midway
Only four of these TBDs from torpedo bomber squadron VT-6 returned from their next mission.

FACTS AND FIGURES

▼ One of the first Technicolor films to deal with Naval Aviation was Dive Bomber in 1941, which featured VT-3 TBDs.

▼ TBD carrier trials began in December 1935 aboard the USS Lexington.

▼ Devastators ended their career as communications and training aircraft.

▼ The Devastator was the Navy's first all-metal low-wing aircraft, and its first carrier-based monoplane.

▼ The first TBD was delivered to the Navy just nine days after its initial flight.

▼ Douglas built 129 production TBD-1s while also developing the SBD Dauntless.

The devastated Devastator

onald Douglas's fine aircraft company developed the TBD Devastator in 1934 to give the Navy a much needed torpedo bomber able to fly from aircraft-carrier decks. The low-wing, tailwheel-equipped Devastator was able to carry a torpedo or bomb beneath its fuselage, or bombs under its fuselage and wings.

The crew of three consisted of a pilot, gunner and radio operator. All three men faced as much danger as anyone who ever flew. From the very beginning of World War II, it

was obvious that the Devastator was outclassed.

On June 4, 1942, at Midway, no fewer than 35 Devastators were shot down, including all of the Navy's Torpedo Squadron Eight (VT-8), with the exception of sole survivor Ensign George Gay.

Having succumbed to Japanese fire and bobbing in a life raft, Ensign Gay had a front row view of the battle as Japanese guns blasted his squadron out of the sky. Many were victims of withering fire from the ships' guns; others were shot down by fighters.

Below: This prewar view shows Devastators of VT-5. By early 1942, TBDs from this unit, aboard USS Yorktown, were raiding Japanese targets in the Gilbert Islands.

TBD-1 Devastator

Type: three-seat torpedo bomber

Powerplant: one 671-kW (900-hp) Pratt & Whitney R-1830-64 Twin Wasp radial piston engine

Maximum speed: 332 km/h (205 mph) at 2440 m (8000 ft)

Cruising speed: 206 km/h (128 mph)

Range: 1152 km (415 miles)

Service ceiling: 6005 m (19,700 ft)

Weights: empty 2804 kg (6169 lb); maximum take-off 4624 kg (10,173 lb)

Weapons: two 7.62-mm (.30-cal.) machine guns, one forward-firing and one on flexible mounting; plus one 454-kg (1000-lb) torpedo or up to 680 kg (1500 lb) of bombs.

Dimensions:
span	15.24 m (50 ft)
length	10.67 m (35 ft)
height	4.60 m (15 ft)
wing area	39.20 m² (422 sq ft)

ACTION DATA

SPEED

The Avenger, which also suffered losses during the Battle of Midway, had a top speed about 60 m.p.h. higher than the TBD. This, combined with its better defensive armament, made it less vulnerable to Japanese fighters.

TBD-1 DEVASTATOR 332 km/h (205 mph)

TG-2 204 km/h (126 mph)

TBF-1 AVENGER 436 km/h (270 mph)

RANGE

Range was an important feature for a torpedo-bomber, allowing it to fly missions over longer distances from the carrier, lessening the risk to the ship. The TBD's range bettered that of the TG-2 by 100 percent.

TBD-1 DEVASTATOR 1152 km (714 miles)

TG-2 531 km (329 miles)

TBF-1 AVENGER 1955 km (1212 miles)

WEAPONS

As the Devastator was a huge improvement over the TG-2, so the Grumman Avenger was a much better armed aircraft, both defensively and offensively, with more machine guns and a high-capacity weapons bay.

TBD-1 DEVASTATOR 2 x 7.62-mm (.30-cal.) machine guns 1 torpedo or 680 kg (1500 lb) of bombs

TG-2 1 x 7.62-mm (.30-cal.) machine gun 1 torpedo

TBF-1 AVENGER 2 x 7.62-mm (.30-cal.), machine guns 1 x 12.7-mm (.50-cal.) machine gun 1 torpedo or 726 kg (1600 lb) of bombs

Above: Seen over Wake Island in 1942, this TBD from the Enterprise carries a fresh coat of sea green and pale gray paint. In May, a USN dispatch ordered the red in national insignia and tail markings.

Soon afterward, the Devastator was withdrawn from combat, left behind by a war that moved faster than it did.

TBD-1 DEVASTATOR

TBD-1 0322 carries the prewar markings of Torpedo Squadron 6 (VT-6), one of four units equipped with the Devastator from 1937.

Though fitted on the production line with wing flotation bags to allow the crew time to escape the aircraft if it ditched, these were removed in wartime. This ensured that the TBD would sink, taking its advanced Norden bombsight with it.

Carried under the fuselage, a 454-kg (1000-lb) torpedo was the TBD's usual load. However, an alternative often used in 1942 against Japanese targets in the Gilbert and Marshall Islands was up to three 227-kg (500-lb) bombs or 12 45-kg (100-lb) bombs, six under each wing.

At the beginning of their service TBDs suffered a number of crashes after pilots, not used to folding wings, failed to check that their wings were locked in position.

The R-1830 variant of Pratt & Whitney's well-known Twin Wasp powered the TBD. This powerplant was also widely used in other types, such as the C-47 Skytrain.

While the TBD boasted a powered wing folding mechanism, this lacked sufficient power to move the wings in a strong cross wind, necessitating a 'group effort' by ground handlers.

Devastators were manned by three crew: a pilot, navigator/torpedo officer and gunner. The latter sat at the rear of the cockpit "glasshouse" and fired a 7.62-mm (.30-cal.) machine gun. A forward-firing machine gun was also fitted in the inner port wing.

Navy aircraft at Midway

■ **CONSOLIDATED PBY CATALINA:** Catalina patrol bombers based at Midway and endowed with a 2,790-mile range gave the Navy prior warning of the approaching Japanese fleet.

■ **DOUGLAS SBD DAUNTLESS:** Carrier-based Dauntless dive-bombers inflicted the bulk of the damage on the Japanese fleet, helping sink four of its carriers.

■ **GRUMMAN F4F WILDCAT:** Fighter escort for the bombers came from carrier-based Wildcats. In all, 79 were deployed aboard three carriers: *Enterprise*, *Hornet* and *Yorktown*.

■ **GRUMMAN TBF AVENGER:** Some of the Navy's first Avengers were deployed to Midway, flying missions against the Japanese in which they suffered huge losses.

Douglas
SBD DAUNTLESS

● Carrier-borne dive-bomber ● Hero of the Pacific war

f it had done nothing else but fight at Midway – where a handful of carrier pilots turned the tide of the Pacific war – the Douglas SBD Dauntless would be counted among important aircraft of the 20th century. But the SBD did more than wreck the Japanese fleet in that battle on 4 June 1942. From its conception in 1938 until late-1944 the SBD showed itself to be the most important American dive-bomber ever built.

▲ Deck and air crew prepare for a mission. No aircraft did more to win the Pacific war than the SBD Dauntless: it sank more Japanese ships than any other type.

Douglas SBD DAUNTLESS

PHOTO FILE

Dive attack ▶
The leader of a section of SBDs rolls into the attack. Dive strikes were usually made from between 4500 and 6000 m (15,000 and 20,00 ft), with the dive angle reaching about 70°. This gave great accuracy.

▲ Dauntless 'Leathernecks'
Although best known as a US Navy warplane, the Dauntless also served in large numbers with the US Marine Corps, operating from land bases.

▲ Difficult Dauntless
Despite its successes, the SBD Dauntless was underpowered, vulnerable and, above all, exhausting to fly for any length of time.

Carrier launch ▶
An SBD gets the signal to take off from its carrier. The air wing was carefully arranged on the deck in the order in which the aircraft were due to fly.

▲ In North Africa
Atlantic Fleet SBDs got their first taste of major action in November 1942, during the Allied landings in North Africa, known as Operation 'Torch'.

FACTS AND FIGURES

▶ Pilot Lieutenant Robert Dixon signalled "Scratch one flat-top" after his attack on the Japanese carrier Shoho.

▶ The first Dauntless, a modified XBT-2, was test-flown on 22 April 1938.

▶ At the battle of Midway, Dauntlesses sank Japan's four main aircraft-carriers.

▶ One US Navy Dauntless gunner was credited with shooting down seven Mitsubishi Zero fighters in two days.

▶ SBDs sank more Japanese shipping than any other US aircraft in the Pacific.

▶ The last Dauntless, an SBD-6, was rolled out on 22 July 1944.

PROFILE

Douglas' deadly dive-bomber

The Douglas SBD Dauntless pounded the Japanese at Coral Sea, Midway and in the Solomons, and supported US Navy and Marine Corps actions until late 1944. This was a fair achievement for an aircraft that was underpowered, vulnerable, short on range and exhausting to fly. For all its flaws, the Dauntless, designed by Jack Northrop and Ed Heinemann, was a dramatic success.

Pilots of the SBD Dauntless sat high in a relatively 'clean'

aircraft optimized to hurl bombs at targets while flying straight down into the enemy's midst. The pilot aimed the aircraft, and a crutch-like trapeze threw forth a centreline bomb that narrowly cleared the propeller arc before boring downwards. The SBD roared, rattled and required constant attention on stick, throttle and rudder, but pilots took pride in mastering it and praised its achievements as a dive-bomber. The US Army Dauntless, the A-24, was outfought on Java in

1942 and was later used mostly for training. By the end of the war, Navy Dauntlesses were replaced by the Curtiss SB2C Helldiver, but this aircraft never won the affection routinely bestowed on its predecessor.

Above: Until mid-1942, US aircraft wore highly visible red and white rudder stripes.

Left: In the dive the Dauntless used 'Swiss cheese' divebrakes to keep the speed down.

Above: Three SBD-5s return from a mission. The furthest aircraft has its aft defensive guns deployed from the rear cockpit.

SBD-5 Dauntless

Type: two-seat carrier-based scout and dive-bomber

Powerplant: one 895-kW (1200-hp) Wright R-1820-60 Cyclone air-cooled radial piston engine

Maximum speed: 410 km/h (254 mph) at 3050 m (10,000 ft)

Initial climb rate: 518 m (1700 fpm) per minute

Range: 730 km (453 miles) on a bombing mission; 1244 km (771 miles) on a scouting mission

Service ceiling: 7400 m (24,275 ft)

Armament: two 12.7-mm (.50-cal.) fixed machine guns in the nose and two 7.62-mm (.30-cal.) manually aimed machine guns in the rear crewman's position, plus up to 725 kg (1600 lb) of bombs under the fuselage and 295 kg (650 lb) of bombs under the wings

Dimensions:
span 12.66 m (42 ft)
length 10.09 m (33 ft)
height 4.14 m (14 ft)
wing area 30.19 m² (325 sq ft)

COMBAT DATA

MAXIMUM SPEED

The Dauntless was a neat design, but the lack of power did not give it a blistering turn of speed. However, compared to its early-war rivals it was well placed. Its intended replacement in the US Navy, the Curtiss SB2C Helldiver, was not much faster at about 470 km/h (292 mph).

SKUA Mk II	362 km/h (224 mph)
SBD-5 DAUNTLESS	410 km/h (254 mph)
D3A1 'VAL'	385 km/h (239 mph)

BOMBLOAD

Compared to its rivals the Dauntless carried an exceptional load, due largely to the high stressing of the centreline cradle. This in turn allowed it to carry bombs of true ship-killing size. The small wing bombs gave added firepower, notably in attacks against land targets.

SBD-5 DAUNTLESS	1020 kg (2240 lb)
SKUA Mk II	330 kg (7245 lb)
D3A1 'VAL'	370 kg (814 lb)

RANGE

One area where the Dauntless did not perform well was range, certainly compared to its main rival in the Pacific, the D3A. This gave Japanese carrier commanders a slight advantage: they could position their ships so that the D3As could just reach the Americans, but were themselves out of range of the Dauntless force.

D3A1 'VAL'	1470 km (911 miles)
SBD-5 DAUNTLESS	1244 km (771 miles)
SKUA Mk II	1223 km (758 miles)

Power for the Dauntless came from the trusty Wright R-1820 Cyclone engine. Even at 746 kW (1000 hp) in the SBD-3/4 this was not really enough, so the SBD-5 introduced an uprated Cyclone offering 895 kW (1200 hp).

The bomb armament consisted of a single weapon of up to 726 kg (1600 lb) on the centreline, with 295 kg (650 lb) of bombs under the wings.

The pilot had a telescopic bombsight projecting through the windshield. This tended to fog over because of the change in temperature during the dive.

SBD-4 DAUNTLESS

Clutching a bomb to its belly, this Dauntless served with the US Marine Corps in July 1943, flying in New Guinea. The US Navy and USMC SBDs exacted a huge toll on the Japanese shipping fleet.

The centreline bomb was carried on a special double-armed cradle. When the bomb was released by the pilot, the cradle swung forwards so that the bomb would clear the propeller arc.

In the rear cockpit sat the radio operator. It was also his task to operate the rear defensive armament, which consisted of a pair of 7.62-mm (.30-cal.) Browning machine guns. In transit these weapons were stowed in the fuselage behind hinged doors. On entering the combat zone, the rear canopy was stowed in the fuselage and the guns deployed from their bay, giving the gunner a wide field of fire.

The wings had a strange brake assembly which extended on both the upper and lower surfaces. On the undersides the brake surfaces were located right the way across the fuselage. All the surfaces had large holes in them, hence the name 'Swiss cheese' divebrakes, to avoid buffeting problems.

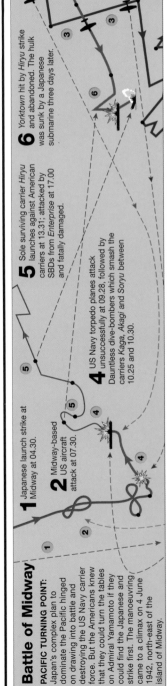

Battle of Midway

PACIFIC TURNING POINT:
Japan's complex plan to dominate the Pacific hinged on drawing into battle and destroying the US Navy carrier force. But the Americans knew that they could turn the tables on Admiral Yamamoto if they could find these aircraft and strike first. The manoeuvring came to a climax on 4 June 1942, north-east of the island of Midway.

1 Japanese launch strike at Midway at 04.30.

2 Midway-based US aircraft attack at 07.30.

3 Main US Navy carrier strikes launched between 08.00 and 09.00.

4 US Navy torpedo planes attack unsuccessfully at 09.28, followed by Dauntless dive-bombers which smash the carriers *Kaga*, *Akagi* and *Soryu* between 10.25 and 10.30.

5 Sole surviving carrier *Hiryu* launches against American carriers at 13.31; attacked by SBDs from *Enterprise* at 17.00 and fatally damaged.

6 *Yorktown* hit by *Hiryu* strike and abandoned. The hulk was sunk by a Japanese submarine three days later.

DOUGLAS
A-20 BOSTON/HAVOC

● Multi-role light bomber ● Low-level strike attack

▲ The A-20 was greatly feared by the enemy as it combined speed, agility and a hard-hitting weapon load. It successfully fulfilled many roles that it was never designed to undertake.

D uring World War II the Douglas A-20 Havoc, called Boston by the RAF, fought on every continent and in every theatre of the war. It was not the fastest plane in its class, but it was extremely tough, handled well and was a popular and effective fighting machine, especially in the low-level attack role. Pilots knew they could fly the A-20 much like a fighter, inflicting considerable damage on their adversaries in the process.

PHOTO FILE

DOUGLAS A-20 BOSTON/HAVOC

Slim profile ▶
The narrow fuselage of the A-20 is apparent when seen from ahead. The shape gave speed and agility, but restricted the movement of the navigator and gunner.

▼ Boston bomber
The RAF was one of many satisfied foreign users. The Boston Mk III was used as a light bomber, but other Bostons served as radar night-fighters.

▲ Formation flying
Swarms of A-20s ranged at will over north-west Europe both before and after the invasion of Normandy.

Precision bomber ▶
Bombing with deadly accuracy, Bostons and Havocs were used to attack communications targets in France and Belgium.

▲ Rocket-launcher
The hard-hitting Boston Mk III could be armed with 27-kg (60-lb) rockets. The great strength of all the A-20 variants was their versatility in accepting almost any armament.

FACTS AND FIGURES

▶ The prototype for the A-20 Havoc series, the DB-7, first flew on 23 January 1939.

▶ One A-20 was evaluated by the US Navy as the BD-1, and eight reached the Marine Corps, designated BD-2.

▶ The first American A-20s used in combat flew from England in 1942.

▶ Russia received 3125 A-20s, Britain 1800 and the United States 1962.

▶ The final A-20 was rolled out at Santa Monica on 20 September 1944.

▶ An F-3A Havoc photo ship was the first Allied aircraft to land at Itazuke, Japan, after the August 1945 surrender.

PROFILE

The all-purpose attack bomber

When designers Jack Northrop and Edward Heinemann designed the Douglas DB-7 in 1938, the idea of a twin-engined attack bomber with tricycle gear seemed futuristic. Although considered very advanced when it was purchased by Britain in 1940, it was no match for top fighters such as the Spitfire and Bf 109. Known as the Boston in

RAF service, it was used as a bomber and as a carrier for Turbinlite, a searchlight used to illuminate Luftwaffe warplanes by night for RAF Hurricanes to stalk.

As the A-20 Havoc the aircraft entered service with US Forces as a heavily-armed attack bomber. Havocs saw a lot of service. They ranged far and wide over the Pacific, strafing

and bombing in the war against Japan, and supplied devastating fire support for the Normandy landings of June 1944. They were also popular with the Soviet air force, which was the largest user of the type. The P-70 night-fighter version and the F-3 Havoc reconnaissance craft were used mostly for training and saw limited combat.

A-20G HAVOC 'QUEEN JULIA'

The A-20G was an attack variant, with improved armour, navigation equipment and bomb-aiming controls. It saw action in the Pacific and with Soviet forces on the Eastern Front.

Emergency flight controls were fitted to the rear crew compartment of early A-20s.

The Wright Cyclone was a powerful and dependable radial engine, fitted with superchargers.

The pilot enjoyed a good view ahead from the small cockpit.

A-20s had a variety of different noses. Attack variants had a heavy gun armament in place of the original glazed bomb-aimer's position.

The Havoc's long, slim bomb-bay usually carried small bombs suitable for attacking tactical targets.

Additional underwing bomb racks increased the A-20G's warload by 1000 kg (2200 lb).

The A-20's tricycle landing gear was an extremely unusual feature in a pre-war aircraft design.

The A-20G carried a pair of 12.7-mm (.50-cal.) guns in a power-operated rear turret. The Soviets put their own turrets onto A-20s.

Early DB-7 had sometimes shown a lack of directional stability, therefore the fin and rudder were enlarged to cope with increased engine power.

Havocs flew some extremely dangerous missions. This raid on a Japanese anchorage in New Guinea resulted in the loss of one of the attacking A-20s.

Havocs around the world

■ **FRANCE:** The first user of what was to become the Boston and then the Havoc was the French air force. Some were operated by the Vichy air force and others diverted to the RAF after the defeat of France in 1940.

■ **ON THE EASTERN FRONT:** The Soviets flew more A-20s than anybody else, receiving more than 3000 under Lend Lease. This Soviet navy A-20B served with the Northern Fleet in the Arctic late in 1943.

■ **DEFENDER OF THE EMPIRE:** British and Commonwealth air forces operated large numbers of Douglas bombers. This Boston Mk III was in action in March 1943 in New Guinea with No. 22 Squadron, Royal Australian Air Force.

A-20G Havoc

Type: two-/three-seat light-attack bomber

Powerplant: two 1193-kW (2625-hp) Wright R-2800-23 Double Cyclone radial piston engines

Maximum speed: 546 km/h (340 mph) at 3780 m (12,400 ft)

Range: 1754 km (1087 miles)

Service ceiling: 7865 m (25,800 ft)

Weights: empty 7250 kg (14,950 lb); loaded 12,338 kg (27,144 lb)

Armament: six forward-firing 12.7-mm (.50-cal.) machine guns in nose; two 12.7-mm machine guns in power-operated dorsal turret; one manual 12.7-mm machine gun in the ventral position; up to 1814 kg (3990 lb) of bombs

Dimensions:
span	18.69 m	(61 ft)
length	14.63 m	(48 ft)
height	5.36 m	(18 ft)
wing area	43.11 m²	(464 sq ft)

COMBAT DATA

MAXIMUM SPEED

The Douglas DB-7 from which the A-20 was developed was one of the fastest bombers in service at the beginning of World War II. The Bristol Blenheim was, like the Douglas design, intended to be a light, fast bomber, but proved far more fragile. The Dornier Do 17 was classed as a medium bomber, but had similar performance to the smaller American machine.

A-20B HAVOC	475 km/h (295 mph)
Do 17Z	425 km/h (264 mph)
BLENHEIM Mk IV	470 km/h (291 mph)

RANGE

The A-20's range was sufficient for most tactical purposes, although the advanced Douglas design had less of a reach than its British equivalent. But the Blenheim had been developed from a record-breaking light transport, and had exceptional long-distance performance.

A-20B HAVOC	1600 km (992 miles)
Do 17Z	1100 km (682 miles)
BLENHEIM Mk IV	2500 km (1550 miles)

BOMBLOAD

Early versions of the Havoc had a relatively small weapons load, although the Dornier, classified as a medium bomber, could carry very little more. By the end of the war A-20s were routinely carrying nearly two tonnes of bombs.

A-20B HAVOC	907 kg (2000 lb)
Do 17Z	1000 kg (2200 lb)
BLENHEIM Mk IV	454 kg (1000 lb)

DOUGLAS

A-26 INVADER

- Twin-engined bomber ● European and Pacific service

P erhaps better known for its post-war exploits, the Douglas A-26 Invader first served in the European and Pacific theatres of World War II from September 1944. Designed by Ed Heinemann to replace the A-20 Havoc, the A-26 was very similar to the Havoc in configuration. The roles of bomber, night-fighter and ground-attack aircraft were envisaged for the type, but it was for air-to-ground roles that production aircraft were ordered.

▲ Almost too late for combat during World War II, the Invader was destined for service during the Korean War and even flew, in refurbished form, during the Vietnam conflict.

134

DOUGLAS A-26 INVADER

DOUGLAS A-26 INVADER

▲ XA-26 prototype
In an olive drab finish and fitted with large propeller spinners, the XA-26 prototype 41-19504 runs its engines. The serial '219504' was erroneously painted on its fin.

Wheels up on Okinawa ▼
This eight-gun Invader of the 89th Bomb Squadron, 3rd Bomb Wing, made a belly landing on Okinawa after one of the last strikes of the war on 11 August 1945.

Early gun nose ▼
This 'gun nose' B-model has four 12.7-mm (.50-cal) machine guns on the starboard side and two to port.

▲ Flak damage
A direct hit by German flak took off the port wing of this A-26B over Europe.

▼ First Invaders in Europe
In heavily overcast conditions at Beaumont-sur-Oise, A-26Bs of the 552nd Bomb Squadron, 386th Bombardment Group, share the apron with B-26 Marauders in May 1945.

FACTS AND FIGURES

➤ In all, 67 A-26s were lost in operations in the European theatre. Seven air-to-air victories by A-26s were confirmed.

➤ Douglas 'mocked-up' a 14-gun version of the A-26B; it failed to enter production.

➤ A-26s were known as B-26s in 1948, after the last Martin Marauders were retired.

➤ Unlike other bomber types, most A-26s were retained after 1945, and many became staff transports and target tugs.

➤ As well as A-20s, the A-26 was also used to replace B-25 Mitchells in some units.

➤ Of 2452 Invaders built, 2446 were A-26Bs and A-26Cs.

PROFILE

Just in time for the war

X A-26 41-19504, the Invader prototype, first took to the air on 10 July 1942. This aircraft had the glazed nose of the projected A-26C bomber variant. The A-26A night-fighter would have had a radar set in the nose, with four 20-mm cannon in a ventral pack.

For attack missions, the A-26B had six 12.7-mm (.50-cal.) machine guns in its nose (later increased to eight), remotely controlled dorsal and ventral turrets, each with two 12.7-mm machine guns, and up to 10 more in underwing and under-

fuselage packs. The night-fighter was cancelled, but the A-26B and A-26C models were rushed into production. The first Invaders in combat were four A-26Bs used in New Guinea, where the aircraft proved unpopular on low-level sorties. Clearly, all the type's 'bugs' had yet to be ironed out.

In September 1944 the 553rd Bomb Squadron at Great Dunmow, England received 18 machines. Their results were more promising. Eventually, 11,567 missions were flown, delivering 18,344 tonnes (18,054 tons) of bombs. One aircraft was

even credited with a probable 'kill' of an Me 262 jet fighter.

In the Pacific, air-to-ground and anti-shipping strikes were typical. Three USAAF bomb groups used A-26s against targets in Okinawa, Formosa and mainland Japan; A-26s were active near Nagasaki when the second A-bomb was dropped on 9 August 1945.

Left: *With eight extra machine guns guns in four underwing two-gun packs, the two A-26s nearest the camera are a glazed-nose A-26C (in the foreground) and an A-26B.*

Above: *A mixed complement of A-26s within the squadrons of a bomb group was not unusual. The 386th Bombardment Group operated both A-26Bs and Cs.*

A-26B INVADER

Stinky was an A-26B built at Douglas's Tulsa, Oklahoma plant. Attached to the 552nd Bomb Squadron, 386th Bombardment Group, it was based at Beaumont-sur-Oise in April 1945.

As well as a pilot, A-26s were crewed by a bombardier/navigator, who normally sat next to the pilot but also had a work station in the nose, and a gunner.

Nose gun armament fitted to the B-model Invader varied from batch to batch. Six or eight 12.7-mm (.50-cal.) machine guns were typical. Some carried cannon.

Poor visibility was a problem on early-build Invaders. The original heavily-framed canopy was hinged at the front and was difficult to open into the airstream during an in-flight emergency. Later aircraft had a two-section 'clam shell' canopy, hinged at the sides and meeting in the middle. These greatly improved visibility and made emergency exits easier.

Pratt & Whitney's R-2800 Double Wasp 18-cylinder radial engine powered the A-26 Invaders. During the production life of the B model, the oil cooler air intakes were redesigned, which accounted for 80 per cent of the later improvement in the aircraft's performance. The inside of the engine cowlings were painted in an olive drab anti-dazzle finish to reduce glare problems encountered by pilots.

The Invader's gunner reached his position via a bomb bay entry hatch and remotely controlled the dorsal and ventral turrets, each of which held two 12.7-mm (.50-cal.) machine guns. In the 'gun-nose' C-model, the navigator also served as a gun loader for the nose armament.

A bomb bay with capacity for up to 1814 kg (4000 lb) of bombs filled the space between the cockpit and the gunner's position. Large two-piece bomb bay doors were even longer, stretching from the cockpit almost as far as the ventral turret.

Douglas's famous wartime designs

■ **A-20/P-70 HAVOC:** Immediate predecessor of the Invader, the A-20 was built in bomber and attack versions; the P-70 was a night-fighter.

■ **C-47 SKYTRAIN:** Known by the RAF and Commonwealth as the Dakota, the C-47 was the Allies' standard wartime transport aircraft.

■ **DB.7 BOSTON:** The RAF employed a bomber variant of the A-20 known as the Boston and a night-fighter version called the Havoc.

■ **SBD DAUNTLESS:** This carrier-borne scout bomber served the US Navy in large numbers in the Pacific theatre.

A-26C Invader

Type: three-seat light attack bomber

Powerplant: two 1419-kW (1900-hp) Pratt & Whitney R-2800-79 Double Wasp radial piston engines

Maximum speed: 600 km/h (373 mph)

Initial climb rate: 619 m/min (2031 fpm)

Range: 2253 km (1400 miles)

Service ceiling: 6735 m (22,096 ft)

Weights: empty 10,365 kg (22,850 lb); maximum take-off 15,876 kg (35,000 lb)

Armament: six 12.7-mm (.50-cal.) machine guns (two each in nose, dorsal and ventral positions), plus 1814 kg (4000 lb) of bombs internally

Dimensions:
span	21.34 m (70 ft)
length	15.62 m (51 ft 5 in)
height	5.56 m (18 ft 3 in)
wing area	50.17 m² (540 sq ft)

COMBAT DATA

MAXIMUM SPEED

Among the improvements introduced with the A-26 was an increased top speed. The A-26C had a speed advantage of close to 100 km/h over its predecessor, the A-20 Havoc. The Havoc's contemporary, the B-26 Marauder, was slower still.

A-26 INVADER	600 km/h (373 mph)
A-20G HAVOC	510 km/h (317 mph)
B-26 MARAUDER	454 km/h (282 mph)

CEILING

The Invader had a lower service ceiling than the A-20, of about 6700 m, just 300 m more than that of the B-26. The Invader's initial operations in the Pacific theatre were at low level. Bomb-release altitudes were higher in Europe.

A-26C INVADER 6735 m (22,096 ft)	
A-20G HAVOC 7865 m (25,804 ft)	
B-26 MARAUDER 6400 m (21,000 ft)	

RANGE

One of the greatest improvements to come with the Invader was range. The A-26C had a 400–500 km (250–310 mile) advantage over the types it was to replace. This added to the versatility of the type, and was especially useful in the 'over-water' operations carried out in the Pacific.

A-20G HAVOC 1754 km (1090 miles)	
A-26C INVADER 2253 km (1400 miles)	
B-26 MARAUDER 1851 km (1150 miles)	

DOUGLAS
C-54 SKYMASTER

- Transoceanic transport ● Airliner derivative ● Fifty years' service

H aving proven itself during World War II and the Berlin Airlift, the Douglas C-54 Skymaster continued to soldier on with military forces into the 1950s. Much of the supply work done from Japan to Korea during the Korean War was accomplished by this sleek, four-engined design. Relegated to the Reserve forces from front-line duty, C-54s served the US military in support roles well into the 1960s. Others served foreign air forces even longer.

▲ Like the C-47, the C-54 was derived from an airliner design and built in large numbers on commandeered production lines during World War II. After 1945 surplus aircraft equipped new airlines.

DOUGLAS C-54 SKYMASTER

PHOTO FILE

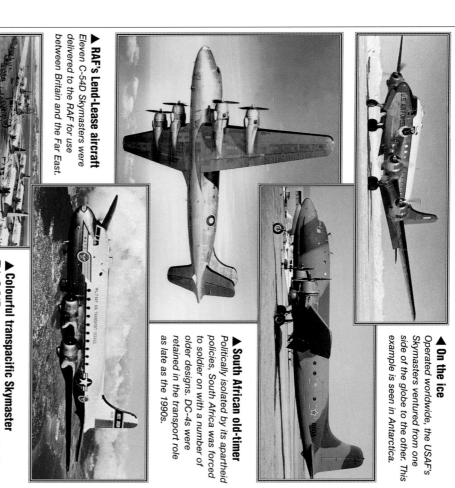

▲ On the ice
Operated worldwide, the USAF's Skymasters ventured from one side of the globe to the other. This example is seen in Antarctica.

▲ South African old-timer
Politically isolated by its apartheid policies, South Africa was forced to soldier on with a number of older designs. DC-4s were retained in the transport role as late as the 1990s.

▲ RAF's Lend-Lease aircraft
Eleven C-54D Skymasters were delivered to the RAF for use between Britain and the Far East.

▲ Colourful transpacific Skymaster
This C-54E was operated post-war by the Pacific Division of the USAF's Military Air Transport Service.

▲ Airlifter extraordinaire
Though many USAF C-54s were disposed of to airlines after 1945, several hundred were retained.

FACTS AND FIGURES

▶ The first US aircraft destroyed in the Korean War was a C-54, attacked by North Korean Yaks at Kimpo in 1950.

▶ The last C-54s in US military service were retired in the early 1970s.

▶ During a high speed turn-around, a C-54 can be refuelled in eight minutes.

▶ The law creating the USAF was signed by President Harry Truman aboard the presidential VC-54C in June 1947.

▶ One XC-114 was built with a lengthened fuselage and Allison liquid-cooled engines.

▶ USAF aerobatic team the 'Thunderbirds' employed a C-54D as a support aircraft.

USAF's master of the skies

C louds of smoke and the familiar cough of propeller engines on start-up remained a part of the USAF's story into the 1950s and beyond. Development of jet-powered transports (known as 'airlifters' in today's jargon) fell far behind that of other kinds of aircraft. Douglas's C-54 Skymaster continued to carry people and cargo long after age had caught up with them.

At the time of the Pearl Harbor attack in 1941, Douglas had its four-engined DC-4

transoceanic passenger transport in production for United and American Airlines. Thus, when it commandeered the production line in early 1942, the USAAF had a ready-made long-range transport ready for service.

More than 1000 were built for the USAF and 200 for the Navy, most during World War II; they saw service in several theatres. After VJ-Day many were declared surplus and sold to airlines and foreign air forces. However, hundreds remained and went on to provide sterling

service during the Berlin Airlift and the Korean War. Others served into the 1960s in a range of roles including air-sea rescue and missile range support.

Left: R5D-2 was the US Navy's designation for the C-54B. This heavily modified example was flown by the US Naval Research Laboratory as a radar laboratory. Each of the underwing pods carried a radar set and the fuselage-mounted mast held meteorological gear.

Right: A USAF C-54D demonstrates a rocket-assisted take-off (RATO), reducing the necessary runway length.

C-54G Skymaster

Type: long-range transport

Powerplant: four 1081-kW (1450-hp) Pratt & Whitney R-2800-9 Twin Wasp radial piston engines

Maximum speed: 442 km/h (274 mph) at 6095 m (20,000 ft)

Cruising speed: 306 km/h (190 mph) at 3050 m (16,000 ft)

Range: 6435 km (4000 miles) with 4535-kg (10,000-lb) payload

Ceiling: 6795 m (22,300 ft)

Weights: empty 17,659 kg (38,850 lb); maximum take-off 33,113 kg (72,850 lb)

Accommodation: flight crew plus up to 50 troops in canvas bucket seat, 44 passengers (in staff transport role) or 14,742 kg (32,430 lb) of freight

Dimensions:
span	35.81 m (48 ft)
length	28.60 m (38 ft 4 in)
height	8.38 m (27 ft 6 in)
wing area	135.64 m² (1460 sq ft)

COMBAT DATA

MAXIMUM SPEED

The Skymaster was the USAF's fastest transport at the beginning of World War II. Both the Douglas C-47 and Fairchild C-82A were twin-engined designs.

C-54A SKYMASTER	**427 km/h (274 mph)**
C-47A SKYTRAIN	**365 km/h (226 mph)**
C-82A PACKET	**399 km/h (247 mph)**

POWER

Skymasters had twice the power of Skytrains, thanks to their four engines. Though also a twin-engined design the C-82 was equipped with considerably more powerful engines.

C-54A SKYMASTER	**3848 kW (5800 hp)**
C-47A SKYTRAIN	**1790 kW (2400 hp)**
C-82A PACKET	**3132 kW (4200 hp)**

RANGE

C-54s (and civil DC-4 airliners) introduced higher speeds and transoceanic range performance to transport aviation. The post-war Fairchild C-82A had much improved range for a twin-engined design. Its fuselage and 'twin boom' design also allowed larger, heavier items to be carried more easily.

C-54A SKYMASTER	**4828 km (3000 miles)**
C-47A SKYTRAIN	**2575 km (1600 miles)**
C-82A PACKET	**6236 km (3870 miles)**

Designed in the late 1930s, the DC-4 was an all-metal aircraft apart from its fabric-covered control surfaces.

Search-and-rescue aircraft often sport high-visibility markings for peacetime operations. Large areas of Dayglo orange/red on the tail and wings of rescue aircraft were a feature of the USAF's post-war rescue types.

Another modification made to the aircraft for the SAR role was the installation of an observation blister in the rear fuselage, on the starboard side opposite the main cargo door.

Rescue aircraft carried associated equipment in the main cabins, but the standard C-54D transport was able to accommodate up to 50 troops in canvas seating. In the freight role, maximum payload was 14,742 kg (32,430 lb).

SC-54D SKYMASTER

Aircraft 42-72566 is one of 36 C-54Ds modified by Convair in 1955 for use by the Air Rescue Service, Military Air Transport Service. In 1962 surviving aircraft were redesignated HC-54D.

The C-54D was the Skymaster variant built in the largest numbers. Including the 86 delivered to the US Navy as R5D-3s, 380 were built, all at Douglas's Chicago plant.

Essentially similar to the C-54B, the D-model differed in having four Pratt & Whitney R-2000-11 Twin Wasp 14-cylinder radials, rated at 1007 kW (13250 hp) for take-off.

Among the modifications made to SC-54Ds by Convair for the air-sea rescue role was the fitting of a search radar in a nose-mounted radome.

U.S. AIR FORCE

US military transports from Douglas

■ **C-47/R4D SKYTRAIN:** One of the most famous transports of all time, the well-known DC-3 was built by the thousand during World War II, serving in every theatre.

■ **R3D/C-110:** This short-haul feeder liner was intended, as the DC-5, for airline use in the late 1930s. The US Navy used a few as R3Ds; the USAAF impressed several Dutch civil aircraft as C-110s.

■ **R6D LIFTMASTER/C-118:** Effectively an enlarged, pressurised development of the DC-4, the DC-6 was employed in relatively small numbers by the USAAF and Navy.

■ **C-74 GLOBEMASTER:** Design of this long-range heavy transport began during World War II. Derived from the DC-4, it had such novel features as an autopilot. Only 14 were built.

DOUGLAS

A-1 SKYRAIDER (KOREA)

- Strike fighter ● Piston-engine attack ● Carrier aircraft

A
ble to deliver an incredible array of ordance, the Skyraider's origins began with the Douglas Dauntless of World War II fame. Incredibly strong with a good performance, the A-1 long outlived its anticipated life until people believed that the only replacement for the Skyraider was another Skyraider! It was in the Korean War that the early models of the aircraft began to prove that carrier- or land-based, the Skyraider had few equals in combat.

▲ Nicknamed the 'Spad' by its adoring pilots, the Skyraider proved that the age of the jet was not complete. Delivering ordnance with pinpoint accuracy long after the last jets had gone home, the Skyraider also proved better able to absorb massive battle damage.

DOUGLAS A-1 SKYRAIDER

▼ Airfield beat-up
Even with a load of bombs and rockets, the Skyraider could still thunder less than 30 m (100 ft) above the runway at around 550 km/h (350 mph). Pilots loved it for its low-level performance.

First of many ▶
A few early Skyraiders were finished in bare metal, but most were painted dark blue.

▶ Rocket raider
A favourite Skyraider tactic was unguided rocket attacks. Up to a dozen 127-mm (50-in) rockets could be carried, or two of the massive 30-cm (12-in) 'Tiny Tim' weapons, as well as the 20-mm cannon.

▼ Hooking up
With the ability to make lower speed approaches than a jet, the AD-1 was easier to land on deck.

'Tiny Tim' ▶
With its speedbrakes deployed just behind the wing, this AD-1 reveals its load, including a pair of huge 'Tiny Tim' rockets. The AD-4 could carry more than its own weight.

FACTS AND FIGURES

▶ In a raid in May 1951, AD-1s flying from USS Princeton used aerial torpedoes to burst a North Korean dam at Hwachon.

▶ The XBT2D of 1945 was the first US single-seater dive/torpedo bomber.

▶ The Skyraider was able to carry more ordnance than a wartime B-17 Fortress.

▶ In 1952, a US pilot successfully landed his Skyraider after having been blinded by a shell hit.

▶ Skyraiders were also used in Vietnam, where two aircraft shot down MiG-17s.

▶ In Korea, the Skyraiders carried every weapon in the US Navy arsenal.

PROFILE

'Spad' goes to war in Korea

Making its maiden flight on 18 March 1945 as the XBT2D-1, the aircraft that became the Skyraider was designed by the legendary Ed Heinemann. In 1946 it looked set for a peaceful and probably brief career as an 'old-fashioned' piston-engined attack aircraft in the new jet age. The Skyraider's career was in fact anything but mundane, thanks to its fine showing in the Korean War. Proving that 'low and slow' still produced results in ground-attack work, the AD squadrons of the US Navy and

Marine Corps gave outstanding air support to United Nations ground forces.

By integrating air strikes with the faster jets which acted as escorts, the Skyraider pilots flying off Task Force 77's carriers could go in unmolested by enemy air attack. The main hazard was from ground fire, a fact of life faced equally by land-based Marine Corps AD units. Combat flying in the Skyraider gave pilots the reassurance that their aircraft could take a great deal of punishment and still fly home. The AD-1 first entered Navy

service in November 1946 and it soon became clear that the basic design was immensely versatile. Being such a large aircraft (for a single-seater), the Skyraider could accommodate a second seat and the necessary equipment inside the fuselage for a radar/ECM operator. This version, the AD-1Q, covered 35 airframes out of the total 242 AD-1 Skyraiders built.

Left: The Skyraider was also fitted with underwing radar. A few XBT2D destroyers were completed with an underwing searchlight and room for a second crewmember.

Above: Although it was considered obsolete just after its inception, the Skyraider was still fighting in Chad as late as 1979.

AD-1 Skyraider

Type: single-seat ground-attack aircraft

Powerplant: one 2252-kW (3020-hp) Wright R-3350-26W Cyclone radial engine

Maximum speed: 498 km/h (310 mph)

Range: 1448 km (900 miles)

Service ceiling: 9753 m (32,000 ft)

Weights: empty 4577 kg (10,070 lb); loaded 8178 kg (17,992 lb)

Armament: four 20-mm cannon in wings, plus mixed ordnance including bombs, napalm and unguided folded-fin aircraft rockets on centreline and wing stores stations

Dimensions:		
span	15.24 m	(50 ft)
length	11.63 m	(38 ft)
height	4.7 m	(15 ft)
wing area	37.16 m²	(400 sq ft)

COMBAT DATA

MAXIMUM SPEED

For a piston-engined fighter-bomber, the AD-1 was quite fast, however, even the early jets could outrun it. The wartime Il-10 could not match post-war aircraft.

AD-1 SKYRAIDER	518 km/h (310 mph)
F9F PANTHER	846 km/h (525 mph)
Il-10 SHTURMOVIK	476 km/h (295 mph)

ARMAMENT

Few jet fighters could match an AD-1's weapon load until the mid 1960s, and most did not have the same firepower from their guns either. The Il-10 was designed for anti-armour attack and usually carried eight rockets in addition to its powerful cannons.

AD-1 SKYRAIDER	4 x 20-mm cannon / 3628 kg (7982 lb) of bombs
Il-10 SHTURMOVIK	2 x 37-mm cannon / 2 x 29-mm cannon / 600 kg (1352 lb) of bombs
F9F PANTHER	4 x 20-mm cannon / 907 kg (1995 lb) of bombs

RANGE

The bulky airframe of the AD-1 held a good reserve of fuel, like many naval aircraft. The Il-10 was designed for tactical support from front-line airfields and had short range. Early jets usually had short range and most were inferior to the AD-1.

Il-10 SHTURMOVIK	1070 km (665 miles)
F9F PANTHER	2180 km (1352 miles)
AD-1 SKYRAIDER	1840 km (1140 miles)

AD-1 SKYRAIDER

The mainstay of the US Navy's carrier-borne attack force in Korea, the AD-1 entered service in 1946 and was only finally retired in 1968 during the Vietnam War.

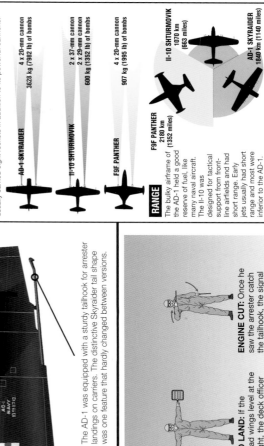

The large cockpit was a typical feature of late American piston fighters. Topped by a bubble canopy offering excellent visibility, it had no ejector seat and pilots 'bailed out' manually.

The single 1470-litre (730-gallon) fuel tank was located just behind the pilot, next to the radio and avionics racks. The large twin speedbrakes were located on the fuselage sides just behind it.

The AD-1 was equipped with a sturdy tailhook for arrester landings on carriers. The distinctive Skyraider tail shape was one feature that hardly changed between versions.

Massive strength was built into the wing. Several Skyraiders made it home after taking hits from flak shells of up to 37 mm (1.46 in).

Much of the Skyraider's success was due to the superb Wright R-3350 two-row radial engine, which was powerful and reliable.

Deck landing signals for carrier pilots

TOO LOW: The most dangerous condition was too low, as the pilot risked striking the carrier's stern.

TOO HIGH: Both hands raised told the pilot that he was too high to make a safe approach to the deck.

ONE WING HIGH: If the pilot had too much bank on, the deck officer gave a 'one wing high' signal to him.

WAVE-OFF: This signal told the pilot to terminate the approach as it looked unsafe to the deck officer.

SAFE TO LAND: If the aircraft had wings level at the right height, the deck officer gave the pilot this signal.

ENGINE CUT: Once he saw the arrester catch the tailhook, the signal 'cut engines' was given.

Douglas
A-1 SKYRAIDER (VIETNAM)

- Vietnam warbird ● Versatile strike fighter ● Rescue support

N ear the end of its long American career, the Douglas A-1 Skyraider became a Vietnam rescue craft, known by its call-sign 'Sandy'. The A-1 pilot's task was complex: he had to locate and protect shot-down air crew while directing rescue helicopters and other support aircraft to make a pick-up, all in the face of strenuous efforts by the North Vietnamese to prevent the rescue. In spite of the fact that it was old, noisy and rather slow, the hard-hitting Skyraider was more than able to do the job.

▲ Major Bernie Fisher carried out an amazing rescue in Vietnam in 1966, actually landing his A-1 in the A Shau valley to pick up his squadron buddy, Major Datford Myers.

Douglas A-1 SKYRAIDER (VIETNAM)

▲ Primed to fight
Rockets hang from the wings of a Skyraider. The red tapes are flags attached to safety pins, which prevented weapons being armed by accident during handling on the ground. The white phosphorus rockets were used as target-markers.

▲ Jungle colours
The jungle camouflage of this Skyraider had some chance of fooling North Vietnamese MiG fighters, but it was little protection against the main enemy – anti-aircraft fire.

▲ Rescue team
A pair of 'Sandys' escort an OV-10 Bronco. The OV-10 acted as a forward air-control station, co-ordinating the rescue and target-spotting. A-1 pilots and controllers worked very closely together.

▼ Built like a tank
Pilots also called the A-1 the 'Spad', as its chunky appearance was reminiscent of the robust biplane fighter used by America during World War I.

▲ Navy mission
Powerful piston engines roar into life as Navy A-1s prepare for a mission. The naval ancestry of the Skyraider can be seen in the folding wings, designed to take up less deck space on a carrier.

FACTS AND FIGURES

▶ Between 1945 and 1956, 3180 Skyraiders were built.

▶ The maiden flight of the A-1 was made at Mines Field, California, on 18 March 1945.

▶ The last wartime use of aerial torpedoes occurred when Skyraiders attacked the Yalu River dams in the Korean War.

▶ In Vietnam, propeller-driven A-1 Skyraiders shot down two jet-propelled MiG-17 fighters.

▶ Some Vietnamese air force pilots logged over 4000 combat hours in the Skyraider.

▶ Skyraiders were still engaged in a shooting war in Chad as late as 1979.

PROFILE

Pilot pick-up in Vietnam

American fliers rescued in Vietnam in 1969 were glad that Ed Heinemann designed the Douglas A-1 (AD) Skyraider in a hotel room in 1944. One of the last great piston-engined combat planes, the Skyraider was big, tough, and an incredible performer. Known by their callsign 'Sandy', Skyraiders were the key element in the US air force rescue organisation in Southeast Asia. Directing and protecting the rescue force, the ageing bombers also kept the enemy away from aircrew stranded on the ground.

The rescue mission in Vietnam was tailor-made for a heavy, sturdy combat aircraft which carried enough fuel to loiter for extended periods and enough bombs to wreck the enemy's day.

Two Skyraider pilots were awarded the Medal of Honor for Vietnam action. A 'Jolly Green' rescue helicopter escorted by A-1s became a familiar sight. 'Sandy' pilots managed 300 rescues from 1965 until turning the job over to the A-7D Corsair II in 1972.

The A-1E was a multi-role variant of the Skyraider. Originally designated AD-5, it was easily identifiable by its enlarged side-by-side cockpit. Fitted out for transport it could carry 12 passengers.

The original ground-attack Skyraider was fitted with a pair of 20-mm cannon, but by the end of the aircraft's production run four cannon were standard, and most aircraft involved in Vietnam had them.

A-1H SKYRAIDER

At the beginning of the Vietnam War the A-1 was still serving aboard US Navy carriers. This example was flown by the commander of VA-52 aboard the USS Ticonderoga in the early 1960s.

The 18-cylinder Wright R-3350 engine could survive serious battle damage. It kicked out a lot of oil, however, much of which was deposited on the fuselage.

In the early stages of the war Navy A-1s were used to bomb conventional targets in North Vietnam. For rescue missions, a wider range of weaponry could be carried.

Fuel was carried in one large tank in the fuselage behind the pilot. When external tanks were added, the A-1 could loiter over a rescue scene for several hours.

With 14 underwing hardpoints, the Skyraider could carry a fearsome variety of weaponry. Typical loads included bombs, rockets and smoke markers up to a total weight of more than 3600 kg (7937 lb).

Designed as a torpedo- and dive-bomber, the Skyraider was fitted with huge divebrakes on the sides of and below the fuselage.

The folding wings, tailhook and sturdy undercarriage were naval features that were found on all Skyraider variants.

A-1H Skyraider

Type: single-seat carrier-based attack bomber

Powerplant: one 2013-kW (2700-hp) Wright R-3350-26WA 18-cylinder radial piston engine

Maximum speed: 518 km/h (322 mph)

Range: 2000 km (1243 miles)

Service ceiling: 8685 m (28,494 ft)

Weights: empty 5429 kg (11,969 lb); loaded 11,340 kg (25,000 lb)

Armament: four wing-mounted 20-mm M3 cannon with 200 rounds per gun plus up to 3629 kg (8000 lb) of bombs or rockets on one under-fuselage and 14 underwing hardpoints

Dimensions:
span	15.25 m (50 ft)
length	11.84 m (38 ft 10 in)
height	4.78 m (15 ft 7 in)
wing area	37.19 m² (400 sq ft)

COMBAT DATA

MAXIMUM SPEED

The Skyraider was a World War II aircraft, and in terms of pure speed was no match for the jet-powered A-4 of the early 1950s, let alone the sheer Mach 2 power of the Phantom II of 1960. But speed is not everything in combat, and the A-1 had virtues the other two classic fighters lacked.

A-1 SKYRAIDER	518 km/h (322 mph)
A-4 SKYHAWK	1040 km/h (646 mph)
F-4 PHANTOM	2300 km/h (1429 mph)

MISSION FLEXIBILITY

The Skyraider may not have been able to carry as much weight of ordnance as the more powerful jets, but with 14 hardpoints under the wings and one under the fuselage it could carry and deliver a greater variety of weapons on a single mission than almost any other fighting plane giving the A-1 the flexibility to fly different missions.

A-1 SKYRAIDER	15 hardpoints
A-4 SKYHAWK	5 hardpoints
F-4 PHANTOM	5 hardpoints

LOITER TIME

Compared to a jet, piston engines are extremely economical. The Skyraider might have been slow, but it could fly out to a rescue site, call in some fast jets to make an attack, direct the rescue helicopters to make the pick-up while the jets refuelled, call in the fast movers again, and then escort the whole force clear of enemy territory – all on a single load of fuel.

A-1 SKYRAIDER	7 hours
A-4 SKYHAWK	4 hours
F-4 PHANTOM	3 hours

Directing the rescue

MAKING CONTACT: The downed pilot contacts the 'Sandy' flight leader via his survival radio. The rescue pilot then establishes his ground location and calls in the helicopters.

DRIVING OFF THE ENEMY: The 'Sandy' Skyraider deliberately draws fire to locate enemy positions. Any enemy troops approaching too close to the person to be rescued are engaged with cannon, bombs and rockets.

RESCUE: As the 'Jolly Green Giant' rescue helicopter makes the pick-up, 'Sandy' stands guard from above, ensuring that enemy ground forces cannot interfere.

DOUGLAS

C-124 GLOBEMASTER II

- Long-range strategic transport ● Heavy-lifter ● Missile transport

▲ The C-124 fleet spent most of its life hauling freight and passengers across the globe. It could carry a huge payload, especially when compared to its predecessors.

They used to call it 'Old Shaky'. Liked by its crews, loathed by the soldiers transported in it, the Douglas C-124 Globemaster II was the giant airlifter of the Cold War. Part of its unpopularity was due to an unwarranted reputation among non-airmen for being crash-prone. In fact, the C-124's overall safety record was good, and it continued to give sterling service until replaced by the massive Lockheed Galaxy in the late 1960s.

DOUGLAS C-124 GLOBEMASTER II

▲ Turboprop test
A single C-124 was the testbed for the Pratt & Whitney YT-57 turboprop. This immense engine, rated at no less than 11,190 kW (15,000 hp), was intended for the Douglas C-132, but was cancelled in 1957.

▲ Breaker's yard
With the introduction of the C-5 Galaxy in 1970, the C-124 fleet was taken out of service. The aircraft ended their days in the 'graveyard' at Davis-Monthan Air Base in Arizona.

▼ Biggest of them all
The C-124 could not be compared with any other transport. It was the first to combine features such as split-level decks and internal hoists.

▲ Mercy mission
The C-124 was always on hand in disasters. These victims were airlifted to safety after the terrible 1958 earthquake in Armenia.

SAC nuclear missile transporter ▲
The C-124 fleet was used by Strategic Air Command to deploy 60 Thor intermediate-range ballistic missiles to bases all over eastern England, and 'Honest John' short-range tactical nuclear missiles to Cold War hot-spots.

FACTS AND FIGURES

▶ The prototype Globemaster II flew on 27 November 1949. Douglas built 204 C-124As and 243 C-124Cs.

▶ The Globemaster's payload was three times that of other large transports.

▶ The C-124 suffered only two serious accidents, in 1950 and 1951.

▶ Though in production for only five years (1951-55), C-124s served operationally until the C-5 Galaxy arrived in 1969.

▶ The C-124C model introduced APS-42 weather search radar in a 'thimble' nose.

▶ The turboprop YC-124B flew on 1 February 1954, but was not produced.

PROFILE

The first strategic transporter

When the C-124 entered service in May 1950 it was able to carry more supplies and equipment, faster and farther, than any previous transport. Evolved from the less successful C-74 Globemaster I, which served in the immediate post-war era, it had been inspired by the war against Japan, where the vast expanses of the Pacific had stretched the capabilities of existing air transports. In five

years from 1951 the 447 Globemaster IIs which were built gave the US Air Force a far greater reach than it had ever before possessed.

The C-124 was one of the first and greatest challenges for the C-124 was the building of Thule air base in northern Greenland in 1952 – possibly the toughest construction project ever undertaken, which was supplied entirely from the air.

(77-ft) long cargo hold. The C-124's ability to carry large items (such as heavy tractors) was perhaps more important than its ability to handle great weight.

One of the first aircraft in which cargo loading and handling had been considered from the start. It was equipped with clamshell nose loading doors, a loading ramp, an electric hoist and two overhead cranes in the 23.47-m

The Globemaster family had a busy life. The original C-74 was heavily used in the Berlin Airlift. Subsequently, the C-124 served in the Korean and Vietnam Wars, until replaced by the mighty Lockheed C-5 Galaxy.

C-124C GLOBEMASTER II

The Military Air Transport Service of the USAF was the main user of the C-124, though it was also operated by Strategic and Tactical Air Commands, Air Materiel Command and Far East Air Forces.

The crew compartment was located behind the flight deck. It contained a galley, toilet and bunks for six people. The initial design for its predecessor, the C-74, had twin fighter-type canopies for the two pilots.

The wingtip pods generated hot air for de-icing the leading edges of the wing and tailplane. This modification was retrofitted to all C-124s.

An APS-42 weather radar was fitted in a nose 'thimble' mounting.

The huge fuselage cross-section allowed the C-124 to carry cargoes such as heavy guns, light tanks and radars, which no previous transport could manage.

The C-124 tailplane was one of the features taken from the original C-74 design.

MATS
30035

Twin rows of portholes show the two deck levels of the C-124.

Internal electric hoists, located in the cargo bay just aft of the wing, could lift cargo up to seven tonnes in weight.

MILITARY AIR TRANSPORT SERVICE

U.S. AIR FORCE

30035

American heavyweights

- **DOUGLAS C-74 GLOBEMASTER I:** Originally built for Pan American but used by USAF, the C-74 was cancelled after 14 had been built.

- **LOCKHEED R6O CONSTITUTION:** Also designed for Pan Am, the two 168-seat R6O Constitutions were used by the US Navy until they were decommissioned in 1955.

- **CONVAIR XC-99:** A cargo version of the Convair B-36 bomber, the single example of the double-deck C-99 was the largest and heaviest transport of its time.

- **DOUGLAS C-133 CARGOMASTER:** Although much more powerful than the C-124, the turboprop C-133 could not handle such enormous loads.

- **LOCKHEED C-5 GALAXY:** It was not until this phenomenal heavy-lifter – for years the world's largest aircraft – flew in the late 1960s that the C-124 finally became obsolete.

C-124C Globemaster II

Type: heavy cargo transport

Powerplant: four 2834-kW (3800-hp) Pratt & Whitney R-4360-63A radial piston engines

Maximum speed: 490 km/h (304 mph) at 6350 m (20,800 ft)

Range: 6486 km (4020 miles) with 12-tonne payload

Service ceiling: 6600 m (21,650 ft)

Weights: empty 45,888 kg (100,954 lb); loaded 83,915 kg (184,613 lb)

Accommodation: two pilots, navigator, flight engineer, two loadmasters; up to 200 troops or 123 troops plus 45 ambulatory patients and 15 medical attendants; maximum payload 33,565 kg (66,000 lb)

Dimensions:
span	53.07 m	(174 ft 2 in)
length	39.75 m	(130 ft 5 in)
height	14.72 m	(48 ft 3 in)
wing area	232.81 m²	(2505 sq ft)

COMBAT DATA

PAYLOAD

Key to the C-124's longevity was its ability to carry large loads, half again as much as even the best of contemporary freighters like the C-97. The British Beverley could likewise lift outsize loads, but was a smaller and much less capable aircraft.

BEVERLEY	94 troops or 20 tonnes
C-124 GLOBEMASTER II	200 troops or 33 tonnes
C-97	134 troops or 24 tonnes

MAXIMUM SPEED

The Globemaster and the C-97 were both powered by immense Pratt & Whitney Wasp engines. The C-97 was derived from a high-performance passenger airliner, however, and its lower drag meant that it was much faster than the block-like C-124. The Beverley was even less streamlined than the Globemaster, and had less powerful engines.

C-124 GLOBEMASTER II	490 km/h (304 mph)
C-97	600 km/h (327 mph)
BEVERLEY	383 km/h (237 mph)

RANGE

Post-war American aircraft designers were always aware of the vast distances encountered in the Pacific conflict which had just ended, and their aircraft generally had much better range than transports from other countries. The Beverley was a tactical machine, and had a much smaller range.

C-124 GLOBEMASTER II
6486 km (4020 miles)

C-97
6800 km (4220 miles)

BEVERLEY
2100 km (1300 miles)

144

DOUGLAS

C-133 CARGOMASTER

- Heavy freighter ● Intercontinental missile transporter ● Civil airlift

▲ In US Air Force service, the C-133 was the undisputed master when it came to the long-range transportation of heavy and outsized loads, including ballistic missiles, fighter fuselages or spacecraft.

One of several Douglas transports of its era, the C-133 served for a decade hauling supplies (some for US forces in Vietnam) and transporting nuclear warheads and Atlas, Thor, Titan and Jupiter ballistic missiles. The Cargomaster was the first USAF aircraft specified for turboprop engines. This big aerial freighter was produced at the same time as the Lockheed C-130 Hercules, although the 'Herc' flew first.

DOUGLAS C-133 CARGOMASTER

Turboprop powerplants ▶
Four Pratt & Whitney T34s made the C-133 the first USAF strategic transport to feature turboprop power.

▲ Global transporter
Part of the US Air Force's commitment was to deploy soldiers and freight around the world at short notice, with the C-133 becoming a vital asset.

▲ Multi-cargo capability
The Cargomaster could carry up to 200 fully equipped troops as an alternative to military vehicles and their crews.

▲ Vietnam delivery
The C-133 made a significant contribution to the US war effort before the arrival of the C-5 Galaxy.

Dedicated missile mover ▼
The improved C-133B was designed specifically for the transport of missiles.

FACTS AND FIGURES

➤ The first C-133, built to be operational and not as a prototype, made its maiden flight on 23 April 1956.

➤ The Cargomaster's interior was pressurised, heated and ventilated.

➤ Vehicles up to 3.66 m (12 ft) in height could be driven into the C-133 via rear doors.

➤ The Cargomaster's multi-wheel landing gear folded into blisters on the side of the fuselage.

➤ Total production was 50 Cargomasters, including 15 advanced models.

➤ Efforts to use veteran C-133s in civilian roles met with little success.

America's mighty Cargomaster

Seemingly the ideal successor to the Douglas C-124 Globemaster II, the C-133 had a tube-like fuselage and high, slender wing. Handling the majority of the large hauling for the US Air Force in the mid-1960s the Douglas C-133 Cargomaster was extremely practical: its circular interior accommodated 96 per cent of all types of US Army vehicles. In addition, it had the 'reach' to span oceans and it was easy to load and unload through the rear loading ramp.

The transportation of the first-generation ballistic missiles was a special challenge. Because of the size of the large missiles and nuclear warheads, the C-133 was the chosen aircraft to carry

them. This was an unpublicised but high-priority function at the height of the Cold War.

Unfortunately, the C-133 was expensive to operate and had a short fatigue life. After the US build-up in Vietnam in the mid-1960s, the Cargomaster was retired from service in 1971 in favour of the jet-powered C-5 Galaxy.

A total of 35 production C-133As were completed before manufacture was switched to the improved C-133B, which had more power and improved structural strength. Fifteen of these aircraft were used to transport Strategic Air Command's intercontinental missile systems throughout the 1960s.

After their military retirement in the early-1970s, a small number of C-133s which had low flying hours and whose airframes were in good condition were sought by civil operators, but their use was short-lived.

C-133B Cargomaster

Type: strategic heavy freighter

Powerplant: four 4847-kW (6500-hp) Pratt & Whitney T34-P-9W turboprop engines

Maximum speed: 558 km/h (346 mph) at 2740 m (9000 ft)

Normal cruising speed: 500 km/h (310 mph)

Range with full payload: 3620 km (2245 miles)

Service ceiling: 6125 m (20,000 ft)

Weights: empty 54,595 kg (120,109 lb); maximum take-off 129,730 kg (285,406 lb)

Payload: up to 49,895 kg (109,770 lb) of cargo such as Atlas, Thor or Jupiter ballistic missiles, two 18,144-kg (39,917-lb) excavators or 16 loaded Jeeps

Dimensions: span 54.75 m (179 ft 7 in)
length 48.0 m (157 ft 5 in)
height 14.70 m (48 ft 3 in)

C-133B CARGOMASTER

USAF C-133Bs served with the 1,501st Air Transport Wing of MATS, based at Travis AFB, California, the first aircraft being delivered on 21 March 1960.

The all-metal fuselage could accommodate most vehicles, pallets and heavy missile systems. For heavy loads a roller conveyor system could be fitted in less than five minutes.

The Cargomaster's four Pratt & Whitney T34 turboprops each drove a 5.5-m (18-ft), three-blade Curtiss-Wright propeller.

The C-133B introduced larger sized four-piece clam-shell rear-loading doors with an integral ramp. All doors were sealed as the whole of the fuselage was pressurised.

Fuel was carried in the wing tanks and in centre-section bladder tanks. The total capacity was 68,557 litres (18,113 gallons).

For high-altitude and cold-weather missions, the C-133 used thermal anti-icing.

For emergencies the C-133 had four automatically ejected and inflated life-rafts on either side of the inner fuselage.

The port landing gear pod held an AiResearch auxiliary gas turbine for pressurisation, ventilation and engine starting.

For the loading of trucks and Jeeps the C-133 had large doors in the port forward and starboard rear fuselage sides.

The Cargomaster's normal crew was four or five, but this could be doubled for long-range operations.

USAF strategic transports

■ **DOUGLAS C-74 GLOBEMASTER:** Design of this development of the C-54 began during World War II. Only 14 were built, the first in 1945.

■ **DOUGLAS C-124 GLOBEMASTER II:** A development of the C-74, the C-124 had a deeper fuselage and clam-shell nose doors.

■ **LOCKHEED C-141 STARLIFTER:** The first jet strategic transport aircraft for the USAF, the C-141 flew in 1963. Most are still in service.

■ **LOCKHEED C-5 GALAXY:** The USAF's largest transport, and for years the world's largest aircraft, in total 130 Galaxies were built.

ACTION DATA

PAYLOAD

The C-133 was the largest American heavylift transport before the C-5 Galaxy. However, even the C-5 Galaxy could not match the awesome lifting capability of the Ukrainian An-22.

C-124 GLOBEMASTER II 31,070 kg (68,355 lb)

C-133B CARGOMASTER 49,895 kg (109,770 lb)

An-22 ANTEI 'COCK' 80,000 kg (176,000 lb)

146

DOUGLAS
F3D SKYKNIGHT

● Naval fighter ● All-weather night interceptor ● Korean victories

On November 2, 1952, over Korea, the F3D Skyknight recorded the first ever night-time downing of a jet by another jet fighter. The Marine Corps aircraft had succeeded in downing what they believed was a Yak-15. Conceived in 1946, the Skyknight was, from the outset, designed exclusively as a night and all-weather fighter. Later in its career the F3D would go on to receive missile armament, and see action in Vietnam.

▲ The Skyknight destroyed more enemy aircraft over Korea than any other Navy or Marine type. However, its near-vintage design meant it was withdrawn as a fighter by 1959.

DOUGLAS F3D SKYKNIGHT

PHOTO FILE

DOUGLAS F3D SKYKNIGHT

▲ Improved fighter
The follow-on F3D-2 served only with the Marines. Its intended J46 engines were problematic, and its pilots had to make do with the earlier F3D-1's J34s.

▲ Skyknight in Korea
A great success in the night-time air war, the F3D proved its worth and paved the way for a new generation of all-weather fighters.

Electronic Skyknight ▼
After retirement from front-line duties, the F3D went on to serve as a trainer, electronic warfare aircraft and a trials platform.

▲ Missile armament
Sixteen missile-armed F3D-2Ms were converted from existing Marines F3D-2s. Four underwing pylons could each carry an early-model Sparrow medium-range radar-guided air-to-air missile.

▲ First production version
The F3D-1 with underpowered Westinghouse J34 turbojets was not a success, and production ended with only 28 delivered.

FACTS AND FIGURES

▼ Rather than using expensive and heavy ejection seats, Skyknight crews escaped from the aircraft via a fuselage chute.

▼ Skyknights originally wore a dark-blue color scheme, later replaced by black.

▼ The F3D-1 is the only side-by-side seat fighter to have served with the Navy.

▼ In Vietnam the EF-10B electronic warfare aircraft was regularly used until the introduction of the Grumman EA-6A.

▼ Operating from Da Nang with VMCJ-1, the EF-10B flew strike protection duties.

▼ In Vietnam, the Marines lost a total of four EF-10Bs in combat, one to a SAM.

F3D-2 Skyknight

Type: two-seat carrier-based all-weather night fighter and (later) electronic warfare aircraft

Powerplant: two 315,87-kN (3400-lb-thrust) Westinghouse J34-WE-36 turbojets

Maximum speed: 964 km/h (599 mph) at 6096 m (20,000 ft)

Initial climb rate: 1372 m/min (4500 fpm)

Range: 1931 km (1200 miles)

Service ceiling: 12,192 m (40,000 ft)

Weapons: four 20-mm cannon and underwing pylons stressed for two 454-kg (1000-lb) bombs or eight air-to-ground rockets

Weight: 12,154 kg (26,794 lb) loaded

Dimensions:
span	15.24 m (50 ft)
length	13.72 m (45 ft)
height	4.88 m (16 ft)
wing area	37.16 m² (400 sq ft)

ACTION DATA

SPEED

These early naval all-weather fighters featured straight wings and non-afterburning power units. Out of the three, the British Sea Venom comes out on top with light weight and good aerodynamics. The Skyknight still has an edge over the rival American Banshee.

F3D-2 SKYKNIGHT	964 km/h (599 mph)
F2H-4 BANSHEE	853 km/h (530 mph)
SEA VENOM FAW.Mk 22	1011 km/h (628 mph)

RANGE

F3D-2 SKYKNIGHT 1931 km (1200 miles)	
SEA VENOM FAW.Mk 22 1802 km (1120 miles)	
F2H-4 BANSHEE 2414 km (1500 miles)	

WEAPONS

The three fighters all carry typical mid 1950s fighter armament of four hard-hitting 20-mm cannon. Later, the Skyknight would carry missiles, but in Korea the Marines' F3Ds scored with cannon alone.

F3D-2 SKYKNIGHT 4 x 20-mm cannons

SEA VENOM FAW.Mk 22 4 x 20-mm cannons

F2H-4 BANSHEE 4 x 20-mm cannons

The Marines' 'Flying Nightmare'

Under the 1962 change in U.S. aircraft designations, the then obsolete Skyknight fighter became the F-10. The F3D-2Q electronic warfare aircraft that served in Vietnam was known as the EF-10.

The Skyknight began as a Douglas aircraft project, launched on April 3, 1946, under the request of the Navy. In fact, time would see the F9F-2 Panther and F2H-4 Banshee, while the Skyknight would see success with the Marines, alongside the veteran F4U-5N Corsair and F7F-3N Tigercat night fighters. The Navy evaluated 28 F3D-1s, which first flew on 13 February 1950, but this machine never saw frontline service. The only Navy unit to

go aboard the carriers was VC-4, a training squadron. The F3D-2 introduced slightly improved engines, the J34-WE-36 rather than WE-22, and made its maiden flight on 14 February 1951. Intended to power the aircraft was the Westinghouse J46, but this proved too problematic, consequently making the Skyknight a little underpowered. The Marine Corps took all 237 production F3D-2 models, and in Korea, the most famous Marines were

The Douglas F3D had hydraulically-powered folding outer wings for deck storage, though they continued to be used to save space on the Marines' South Korean airfields.

VMF(N)513, the 'Flying Nightmares', whose F3D pilots made six air-to-air night kills, taking on the superior MiG-15, as they escorted B-29s deep into enemy territory.

Two underwing pylons usually carried drop tanks, but could lift 454-kg (1000-lb) bombs or be replaced with air-to-ground rocket racks.

The Skyknight had sturdy, single-wheeled undercarriage units. Originally designed for carrier operations, the tough F3D was at home on rough Korean airfields.

As well as conventional landing equipment, the naval-designed F3D had an arrestor hook and an unusual retractable wheeled tail-bumper for nose-up landings.

F3D-2 SKYKNIGHT

This VMF(N)513 was flown by Major Jack Dunn and RO Sergeant Larry Porton when they scored the squadron's second MiG-15 kill, during a routine bomber escort mission on 12 January 1953.

The F3D carried a primitive APQ-35 radar in the nose, with 300 vacuum tubes and three separate radar sets: for search, gun lock-on and tail warning.

Rather than using ejection seats, the Skyknight's two crew escaped via a vaulting bar and escape chute which exited below the rear fuselage. A flap opened as a windbreak to protect the two. In Korea, two VMF(N)513 aircraft and their crew were lost to unknown causes.

Power came from two Westinghouse J34 turbojets, without afterburners. Although slightly underpowered, the F3D was quicker than any other Korean-based Marine aircraft.

In Korea, VMF(N)513, the 'Flying Nightmares' flew the F3D-2 alongside veteran F4U-5N and F7F-3N fighter-bombers.

The F3D had four fixed forward-firing 20-mm cannon below the nose, with 800 rounds of ammunition.

The first jet air-to-air night kill

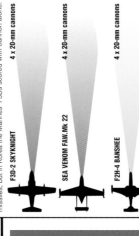

NOVEMBER 3, 1952: Pilot Major W. T. Stratton, Jr. and his radar operator, MSgt. H. C. Hoglind of VMF(N)513 were on a routine patrol when contact was made with a target at about the same altitude.

YAK-15: What was believed to be a Yak-15 was picked up, though contact was lost before it was picked up again, the F3D then closing for a visual identification.

HIT WITH CANNON FIRE: After the visual contact had been obtained, Stratton opened fire at about 11,000 ft) altitude. The first burst hit the port wing, the second and third the fuselage. Explosions followed and the Yak went down on fire.

DOUGLAS

F4D SKYRAY

● Tail-less design ● Fleet defence

Designed at the height of the Cold War, the bat-winged, fast-climbing Douglas F4D Skyray's mission was to guard the US Fleet against attack by Soviet bombers. Today, those who flew this great jet, one of the most advanced interceptors of its time, praise the Skyray as a little-appreciated legend. Only a few hundred US Navy and Marine pilots actually flew the 'Ford', but it was much-loved and performed its duties superbly.

▲ The Skyray was typical of the second generation of jet fighters, possessing exceptional performance but being tricky to fly. The accident rate was high, especially during carrier operations.

▲ Lippisch delta
The configuration of the Skyray owed much to the German aerodynamics' expert Dr Lippisch, who had devised the layout of the Me 163.

▼ Fleet defender
The first line of the fleet's defence was the Skyray. The early Sidewinder missile was just coming into service with the F4D.

▼ Deck approach
Coming in slow with the hook down, the F4D was quite a handful. Early naval jets approached the deck at twice the speeds of wartime fighters.

▼ Clean design
Although the Skyray looked beautiful and handled well, the design had control and powerplant problems.

▲ Mixed weapons
Late in its career the F4D was cleared to carry the Sidewinder heat-seeking missile, while retaining rocket and gun armament. The underfuselage pod was the NAVPAC, containing extra navigation equipment.

FACTS AND FIGURES

► Skyrays of Navy squadron VF(AW)-3 twice won the NORAD (North American Air Defense Command) Trophy.

► The first XF4D-1 Skyray prototype made its maiden flight on 23 January 1951.

► The Westinghouse XJ40 turbojet engine was powerful but unreliable.

► The XJ40-powered 'Ford' set a world speed record of 1211.746 km/h (751 mph on 3 October 1953.

► The Skyray was also flown with the Allison J35 turbojet engines.

► In May 1958, US Marine Colonel Edward LeFaivre seized five world climb records.

148

PROFILE

The tail-less wonder

Douglas' star designer Ed Heinemann used German tail-less delta research when he created this carrier-based interceptor, even though the manta-like wing was not a genuine delta. The sleek, unorthodox Skyray had a fantastic rate of climb – just what was needed to 'scramble' against high-flying bombers. The F4D Skyray was the only Navy aircraft to serve in the US Air Force's Air Defense Command, charged with fending off the first blows of the Third World War that never came.

Just 419 F4Ds (redesignated F-6A in 1962) were built. Technical problems and rapid advances in technology limited the aircraft's service life to the period between 1956 and 1962, but 11 US Navy, six Marine and three Reserve squadrons used this remarkable interceptor during its brief tour of duty. Navy pilots operated this aircraft from carriers, flew it under difficult operational conditions, and found it to be a superb performer with fine handling qualities.

F4D-1 Skyray

Type: single-seat all-weather interceptor fighter

Powerplant: one Pratt & Whitney J57-P-8A turbojet rated at 45.38 kN (10,180 lb thrust) dry and 71.18 kN (15,968 lb thrust) with afterburner

Maximum speed: 1162 km/h (720 mph)

Cruising speed: 837 km/h (519 mph)

Range: 1930 km (1197 miles)

Service ceiling: 16,764 m (54,986 ft)

Weights: empty 7268 kg (15,990 lb); normal loaded 9983 kg (21,963 lb); maximum take-off 12,300 kg (27,060 lb)

Armament: four internal 20-mm cannon, plus up to 1814 kg (3990 lb) of bombs, rocket pods, AIM-9 Sidewinder air-to-air missiles or auxiliary fuel tanks mounted on seven external hardpoints

Dimensions:
span	10.21 m (33 ft)
length	13.79 m (45 ft)
height	3.96 m (13 ft)
wing area	51.75 m² (557 sq ft)

COMBAT DATA

MAXIMUM SPEED

The Skyray was closely matched by contemporary fighters, all of which had limited power from their engines. A few years later, fighters were flying at Mach 2 with afterburner engaged.

MIG-17 'FRESCO' 1145 km/h (710 mph)
SCIMITAR 1143 km/h (709 mph)
F4D-1 SKYRAY 1118 km/h (693 mph)

ARMAMENT

The Scimitar and Skyray both outgunned the MiG-17, which was designed with a relatively light armament in typical Russian fashion. The era of missile armament was just beginning.

MIG-17 'FRESCO' 3 x 23-mm cannon 500 kg (1100 lb) of bombs
SCIMITAR 4 x 30-mm cannon 1814 kg (3990 lb) of bombs
F4D-1 SKYRAY 4 x 20-mm cannon 1814 kg (3990 lb) of bombs

RANGE

Unusually for a Russian fighter, the MiG-17 had quite long range. The F4D was not far behind thanks to its capacious fuselage fuel tanks, a necessity for a naval fighter.

SCIMITAR 966 km (600 miles)
F4D-1 SKYRAY 1930 km (1197 miles)
MIG-17 'FRESCO' 2250 km (1398 miles)

Below: The tail-less delta was a short-lived phenomenon in US aircraft design, also appearing in the F-102.

Above: Like most contemporary fighters in the 1950s, the F4D had no end of minor problems. The inlets had to be extensively redesigned to prevent compressor stalls.

The outer wing folded up to allow the Skyray to fit onto aircraft carrier lifts. The cannon were mounted in pairs in the wing, with 70 rounds per gun.

The trailing-edge control surfaces acted as combined elevators and ailerons for roll and pitch. The outer stores pylon could carry a 19-round 70-mm rocket pod.

Unusually, the Skyray also had a tailhook as well as a tailwheel, to compensate for its high nose attitude on landing and take-off.

Large fuel cells were mounted in the blended wing and fuselage junction, with 1200 litres (300 gallons) in each side.

Inlets in the wingroots were a common feature of early 1950s aircraft, notably the Hawker Sea Hawk, a British contemporary, and the large 'V' bombers.

F4D-1 SKYRAY

VF-162 'Hunters' was the shortest lived F4D unit, receiving the type in September 1962 and turning to the new F-8 Crusader only two years later, after a single cruise deployment aboard USS *Intrepid*.

Like many early jet fighters, the F4D had particularly poor cockpit visibility, especially to the rear.

The Skyray was equipped with an APQ-50 radar system, giving limited target range information. An Aero 13F weapon fire-control package was located behind the radar scanner dish.

Naval fighters of the 1950s

■ **HAWKER SEA HAWK:** The straight-wing Sea Hawk was a conservative design, but served as late as the 1970s in Indian service.

■ **MCDONNELL F3H DEMON:** Plagued by problems with low engine power, the Demon was armed with early series Sparrow missiles.

■ **NORTH AMERICAN FJ-4 FURY:** Effectively a navalised F-86, the FJ4 was powered by a licence-built version of the British Sapphire turbojet.

■ **SUPERMARINE SCIMITAR:** The Fleet Air Arm's first swept-wing jet, the Scimitar could carry nuclear weapons and Bullpup missiles.

150

DOUGLAS
A-3 SKYWARRIOR

● Largest carrier aircraft ● Nuclear bomber ● Long service

N icknamed the 'Whale' by its crews, the Douglas A-3 Skywarrior was an impressive aircraft by all accounts. It began to enter service in the mid 1950s and, ultimately, enjoyed a colourful and long service career; the final examples were retired from the US Naval Reserve during the early 1990s. Skywarriors proved their worth during the Vietnam War, and were among the first aircraft to drop bombs in anger over the North in 1965.

▲ Designed as a carrier-borne nuclear bomber, the A-3 achieved only modest success in its intended role. However, it blossomed as a tanker, reconnaissance and Elint aircraft.

DOUGLAS A-3 SKYWARRIOR

PHOTO FILE

▲ Aboard ship
Folding wings were an absolute necessity for operations at sea, and enabled the massive A-3s to be 'parked' on deck with relative ease.

Assisted take-offs ▶
This early A3D-1, seen in 1954, was equipped with JATO (Jet-Assisted Take-Off) bottles in an effort to improve the type's short-field performance.

Rear gun turret ▶
As originally delivered, the bomber variants had a twin cannon mounted in a tail turret designed by Westinghouse. In service the guns were often removed, and, on later versions, the turret was omitted entirely.

▲ Skywarrior up North
This rare picture shows an A-3B attacking a ground target over North Vietnam.

▲ Dual-role variant
Identified by the distinctive blister fairing below the cockpit, the EKA-3B was a combined electronic warfare/tanker variant which saw extensive service in Vietnam.

FACTS AND FIGURES

▶ In 1957 two Skywarriors flew from San Francisco to Hawaii in a record time of four hours and 31 minutes.

▶ The first operational cruise of the A-3 was with VAH-1 on USS Forrestal in 1957.

▶ As late as 1987 EA-3Bs were still serving with front-line US Navy units.

▶ During the Cuban missile crisis in 1962, a single A-3 unit, VAP-62, flew a variety of missions and later received an award.

▶ The A-3 actually outserved its intended replacement, the A-5 Vigilante.

▶ Many examples served as testbeds at NAS Point Mugu in California.

EA-3B Skywarrior

Type: carrier-borne and land-based electronic reconnaissance platform

Powerplant: two 55.16-kN (12,411-lb-thrust) Pratt & Whitney J57-P-10 turbojets

Maximum speed: 982 km/h (610 mph)

Cruising speed: 837 km/h (520 mph)

Range: 4667 km (2900 miles)

Service ceiling: 12,495 m (41,000 ft)

Weights: empty 17,856 kg (39,366 lb); loaded 33,112 kg (73,000 lb)

Accommodation: crew of seven: pilot, co-pilot and navigator, plus four electronic systems operators

Dimensions:
span	22.10 m	(72 ft 6 in)
length	23.27 m	(76 ft 4 in)
height	6.95 m	(22 ft 10 in)
wing area	75.43 m²	(812 sq ft)

COMBAT DATA

MAXIMUM SPEED

Early examples of the A-3 were originally powered by anaemic Westinghouse J40s, although these were soon replaced by more powerful engines. At maximum speed, the A-3 was slower than its B-66 cousin and its electronic warfare successor, the EA-6B.

EA-3B SKYWARRIOR   982 km/h (610 mph)

EB-66C DESTROYER   1032 km/h (641 mph)

EA-6B PROWLER   1003 km/h (623 mph)

MAXIMUM THRUST

As the largest aircraft ever to operate from carrier decks on a regular basis, the A-3 needed as much thrust as it could get. It was thus more powerful than the very similar USAF Douglas B-66 Destroyer, which was purely land-based. The EA-6B Prowler was not as large or as heavy and did not require as much thrust.

EA-3B SKYWARRIOR   110 kN (24,750 lb thrust)

EB-66C DESTROYER   91 kN (20,475 lb thrust)

EA-6B PROWLER   100 kN (22,500 lb thrust)

SERVICE CEILING

Intended as a nuclear bomber, the Skywarrior was designed to fly at high altitudes where it would be immune to attack from ground forces. All three aircraft – the A-3, Destroyer and Grumman EA-6B Prowler – served in Vietnam and, ironically, were often casualties of ground fire.

EA-3B SKYWARRIOR 12,495 m (41,000 ft)

EB-66C DESTROYER 10,880 m (35,696 ft)

EA-6B PROWLER 11,460 m (37,598 ft)

PROFILE

'Whales' in the Navy

E legant but having a deadly purpose, the A-3 was designed as a carrier-borne nuclear bomber but the Skywarrior did not serve for long in its intended role. By the time it had entered service the US Navy had begun to relinquish the strategic mission, instead preferring to concentrate on using its air assets in the context of limited wars.

When war broke out in Southeast Asia, 'Whales' flew round-the-clock sorties from carrier decks. They initially acted as conventional bombers,

attacking targets in North Vietnam. Designer Ed Heinemann had campaigned from the start to keep weight to a minimum and this proved advantageous; the large A-3s could operate from both the bigger carriers and the small World War II vintage 'Essex'-class wooden-decked ships. From late 1966, front-line A-3s began to adopt other roles such as tanking, reconnaissance and intelligence gathering. As the war in Southeast Asia continued, the Skywarriors still performed sterling work, and many crews

returning from sorties over the North welcomed the sight of a KA-3B tanker. The advent of specialist Intruder variants caused the A-3 slowly to disappear from carrier decks.

Above: When first delivered to US Navy heavy attack squadrons, A-3s were painted overall dark blue. This soon changed to the familiar grey and white scheme.

Above: With its landing gear and tail hook deployed, this A-3B is just about to 'trap' aboard the USS Forrestal. The weight of the A-3 meant that the arrester gear had to be very strong.

A-3B SKYWARRIOR

Seen wearing the markings of VAH-2, this Skywarrior is shown as it would have appeared in 1965, on board the USS Coral Sea in the Gulf of Tonkin. At this time, it was configured as an A-3B bomber/tanker.

Above the refuelling probe, this A-3 carries the unit insignia of Heavy Attack Squadron (VAH) 2. This unit had the distinction of being the first to take 'Whales' to Vietnam, and commenced flying bombing missions on 29 March 1965.

As the largest aircraft ever to be deployed aboard ship, the Skywarrior took up a substantial amount of space. The wings folded outboard of the engines to lie almost flat, and the tail hinged to starboard for stowage below deck.

Twin speed brakes were fitted to the rear fuselage, directly below the horizontal tailplane and were hydraulically actuated.

Under the rear fuselage was the buddy refuelling pack, with a single hose reel. US Navy aircraft used the British-developed probe-and-drogue refuelling system in Vietnam.

The raised cockpit included seating for three crew. Only one set of flight controls was fitted, at the pilot's station on the port side. Next to him sat the bombardier/navigator. Behind the pilot, facing aft, was a third seat, originally occupied by a gunner who operated the twin cannon on early variants.

Skywarriors converted for the in-flight refuelling role had a fuel tank fitted into the rear section of the bomb bay. Most converted A-3s retained bombing capability.

Over the years, A-3s were seen with a variety of different nose profiles. Later aircraft had a flat-tipped radome housing the AN/ASB-12 radar system.

Douglas carrier aircraft of the 1950s

■ **DOUGLAS A-1H SKYRAIDER:** One of the best loved of all aircraft, the venerable 'Spad' was the US Navy's principal medium attack aircraft during the 1950s and 1960s.

■ **DOUGLAS A-4C SKYHAWK:** Designed as the smallest aircraft to carry a nuclear weapon, the A-4 served with both the US Navy and Marines and was exported to many countries.

■ **DOUGLAS F4D (F-6) SKYRAY:** Nicknamed the 'Ford', the Skyray entered service in 1951, but was already obsolescent. By 1962 only three frontline units remained equipped with the type.

DOUGLAS

EA/KA/RA-3 SKYWARRIOR

● Tanker ● Electronic warfare aircraft ● Reconnaissance

T he Douglas A-3 Skywarrior was created to give the US Navy a carrier-based nuclear bomber, but the aircraft grew to brilliance while it was performing unplanned duties in reconnaissance and air refuelling. This warplane was designed by Edward H. Heinemann, one of the world's most accomplished aircraft designers and a man whose name was synonymous with decades of achievement by Douglas.

▲ Flying from the US Navy's supercarriers, the A-3 was one of the heaviest aircraft ever to go to sea. It was also one of the most adaptable, and was still in regular use 30 years after entering service. It has been replaced by the smaller Grumman A-6 family.

DOUGLAS EA/KA/RA-3 SKYWARRIOR

▲ Land based
Not all A-3 variants went to sea. The RA-3B and EA-3B were developed specifically for reconnaissance and electronic warfare and were land based.

Buddy 'tanker' ▶
The A-4 Skyhawk, the Navy's smallest jet carrier aircraft, is seen tanking an EA-3B with the aid of a buddy pack. Both aircraft were based on the USS Saratoga in 1967.

▲ Tonkin Gulf
This EKA-3B of VAQ-130 is seen over the Gulf of Tonkin in support of a strike mission over North Vietnam. The unit operated from the attack carrier USS Bon Homme Richard.

VAQ-33 warrior ▶
The EKA-3B was fitted with a powerful ALQ-126 defensive avionics system, ALQ-86 electronic countermeasures and a side-looking ALQ-100 radar. Three operators sat behind the flight deck.

▲ Bomber original
Originally, the A-3 series were heavy attack bombers tasked with long-range strike, carrying large bombs (including nuclear weapons); tail guns were deleted in later attack variants. These aircraft were based on the USS Forrestal.

FACTS AND FIGURES

▶ The twin 20-mm cannon on early A-3s had 500 rounds per gun in a Westinghouse Aero 21B turret.

▶ Production of this aircraft totalled 283 A-3s, plus 294 similar US Air Force B-66s.

▶ In 1959 a Skywarrior at a weight of 38,102 kg (83,825 lb) took off from USS Independence.

▶ In July 1956 a Skywarrior flew from Honolulu to Albuquerque, covering 5150 km (3193 miles) in 5 hours 40 minutes.

▶ Reconnaissance RA-3s in Vietnam often shot 3000 rolls of camera film.

▶ The A3D-T2 was a crew trainer with a crew of student navigators.

Jamming, tanking and reconnaissance

First flown on 28 October 1952, the resplendent, deep-blue Skywarrior was equipped to handle an atomic or hydrogen bomb weighing up to 5805 kg (12,800 lb). The Skywarrior introduced advanced equipment, including a Westinghouse AN/ASB-1A bombing system.

The prototype aircraft was powered by two 34.14-kN (6985-lb-thrust) Westinghouse XJ40-WE-3 turbojet engines. The US Navy had invested heavily in this disastrous engine, but the Skywarrior's underwing pylon arrangement made it easy to substitute Pratt & Whitney J57s.

The Skywarrior's blue paint scheme was replaced by the grey-white adopted by the Navy in 1955, and it abandoned its nuclear mission for electronic warfare (EA-3), reconnaissance (RA-3), radar training, executive transport and air refuelling (KA-3). In Vietnam, from 1965, the Skywarrior was used briefly as a conventional bomber, before being shifted to the additional duties.

Nicknamed the 'Whale', the Skywarrior was the US Navy's standard tanker in the 1980s. The A-3 Skywarrior finally began its retirement from US Navy service in 1992.

This EKA-3B made one of its final public appearances at the Fairford Air Show in 1991. The last EKA-3Bs were retired as late as 1992, after completing a remarkable length of service.

ERA-3B SKYWARRIOR

This aircraft was an ECM 'aggressor' trainer version, converted from the RA-3B. Four examples of this variant were completed in the early-1970s, and four more later, for training the fleet in ECM conditions.

Power for the Skywarrior was supplied by two Pratt & Whitney J57 turbojets similar to those fitted to the single-engined Douglas A-4 Skyhawk.

The Soviet-style red star on the fin of VAQ-34 aircraft referred to their role of simulating an enemy ECM threat.

With a wing span of over 22 m (72 ft), wing folding outboard of the engines was necessary to aid stowage aboard a carrier.

The ERA-3B flew with VAQ-34, or Tactical Electronic Warfare Squadron 34, then known as the 'Electric Horsemen'.

Carrier-based aircraft must have an immensely strong undercarriage able to withstand heavy landings aboard an aircraft-carrier.

The rear fuselage fuel tanks held over 4 tonnes of fuel. Over 2 tonnes (nearly 2½ tons) of fuel was also carried in each main wing.

To operate the ECM equipment the ERA-3B carried a crew of electronic warfare officers (EWO), seated in a fuselage compartment behind the cockpit.

The cockpit had room for two crew – a pilot and co-pilot/navigator. Ejection seats were not fitted.

Like some other versions of the A-3 Skywarrior family, the ERA-3B was equipped with an inflight refuelling probe.

Reconnaissance aircraft of the 1960s

■ **RF-8 CRUSADER:** The RF-8 was a specialist reconnaissance version of this fine fighter. They carried many vital missions over North Vietnam. This example served with the 192nd Tactical Reconnaissance Squadron.

■ **RF-101H VOODOO:** Different variants of the RF-101 flew many vital missions over North Vietnam. This later example served with the 192nd Tactical Reconnaissance Squadron.

■ **CANBERRA PR.Mk 9:** The highly versatile Canberra was converted into a photo-reconnaissance craft. This example is a PR.Mk 9, a number of which still serve with RAF No. 39 Squadron.

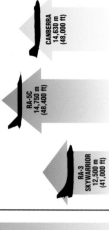

EA-3B Skywarrior

Type: naval electronic warfare aircraft

Powerplant: two Pratt & Whitney J57-P-10 turbojets rated at 46.71 kN (10,480 lb thrust) dry and 55.16 kN (12,375 lb thrust) with water injection

Maximum speed: 982 km/h (609 mph) at 3050 m (10,000 ft)

Range: 4667 km (2895 miles)

Service ceiling: 12,495 m (41,000 ft)

Weights: empty 17,876 kg (39,327 lb); loaded 31,752 kg (69,854 lb); maximum overload take-off 37,195 kg (81,830 lb)

Armament: twin 20-mm tail cannon were deleted in the 1960s

Dimensions:
span	22.10 m (72 ft 6 in)
length	23.27 m (76 ft 4 in)
height	6.95 m (22 ft 9 in)
wing area	75.43 m² (812 sq ft)

ACTION DATA

WEIGHT

The Skywarrior and the RA-5 are two of the heaviest types to serve regularly from aircraft-carriers. Such large aircraft took up a large amount of space on the crowded flight decks.

RA-3 SKYWARRIOR
37,195 kg (81,830 lb)

RA-5C
36,133 kg (79,493 lb)

CANBERRA
24,925 kg (54,835 lb)

RANGE

Reconnaissance aircraft need good range to penetrate deep into enemy airspace without requiring 'tanker' aircraft. The Canberra has been so successful it has recently been operating over Bosnia.

RA-3 SKYWARRIOR
3380 km (2095 miles)

RA-5C
2414 km (1495 miles)

CANBERRA
5840 km (3620 miles)

SERVICE CEILING

The RA-5 and Canberra both have a very impressive ceiling, allowing them to 'peer' deep into enemy territory. The RA-3 is heavier and therefore cannot reach such altitudes.

CANBERRA
14,630 m
(48,000 ft)

RA-5C
14,750 m
(48,400 ft)

RA-3
SKYWARRIOR
12,500 m
(41,000 ft)

154

DOUGLAS

B-66 DESTROYER

● Bomber/reconnaissance aircraft ● Radar jammer ● Used in Vietnam

Although conceived as an atomic-age medium bomber, the B-66 Destroyer earned its spurs as a Vietnam-era electronic warrior. With the same pleasing lines as the Douglas A3D Skywarrior, the B-66 impressed everyone with its dramatic performance when it first took to the air. Although its tour of duty in the bomber role lasted for only a couple of years, the B-66 was repeatedly revived in a variety of other roles, including electronic jamming in Vietnam.

▲ The B-model of the B-66 was the only version to serve as a bomber. Outmoded by the 1960s, many B-66s were converted to jammers for use in the Southeast Asian conflict.

PHOTO FILE

DOUGLAS B-66 DESTROYER

▼ The first Destroyer
Five pre-production RB-66As were built instead of a B-66 prototype. They were equipped with four cameras, and photo-flash bombs and cartridges for night-time work. Aircraft 52-2828 was the first of the five.

▲ Primary reconnaissance variant
The RB-66B variant, featuring a removable in-flight refuelling probe, was produced in the largest numbers. Of the 145 RB-66Bs built, 52 were converted to EB-66E standard for use in Southeast Asia.

Radar test machine ▼
The first WB-66D, 55-0390, was modified in the early 1970s to test the Hughes APG-63 radar that was intended for the F-15 Eagle.

Jamming in Southeast Asia ▼
Seen at Takhli Air Base, Thailand, at the height of the Vietnam War, this RB-66C is typical of B-66 jammer aircraft in Southeast Asia.

▲ Tactical bomber
The B-66's bomb-bay beneath the centre-section could hold over 6800 kg (15,000 lb) of bombs. The Destroyers were intended to replace B-26 Invaders.

FACTS AND FIGURES

➤ In March 1956 two RB-66Bs averaged 1127 km/h (700 mph) on a flight from Tucson, Arizona, to Crestview, Florida.

➤ The first flight of a Destroyer (an RB-66A) was made in California on 28 June 1954.

➤ The first RB-66A tested engines for the Convair 880 and 990 airliners.

➤ A Destroyer shot down near Hanoi was the second largest warplane downed in the Vietnam War – a B-52 was the largest.

➤ In 1957 B-66Bs flew through H-bomb mushroom clouds over Bikini Atoll.

➤ In 1966 B-66Bs used in-flight refuelling to fly non-stop from the US to Europe.

RB-66B Destroyer

Type: all-weather day/night reconnaissance aircraft

Powerplant: two 45.4-kN (10,200-lb-thrust) Allison J71-A-10 or -13 turbojet engines

Maximum speed: 1015 km/h (629 mph)

Initial climb rate: 1475 m/min (4840 fpm)

Combat radius: 1490 km (925 miles)

Maximum range: 3975 km (2465 miles)

Service ceiling: 13,700 m (45,000 ft)

Weights: empty 19,720 kg (43,384 lb); maximum take-off 37,648 kg (82,826 lb)

Armament: two 20-mm cannon in radar-controlled General Electric tail turret

Dimensions: span 22.10 m (72 ft 6 in)
length 22.91 m (75 ft 2 in)
height 7.19 m (23 ft 7 in)
wing area 72.46 m² (780 sq ft)

COMBAT DATA

MAXIMUM SPEED

The B-66, with its swept wings, was capable of higher speeds than other light-to-medium bomber types of the period. The B-57 was a Martin-built development of the British Canberra and had a similar top speed of around 900-950 km/h (560-590 mph) at altitude.

B-66B DESTROYER	1015 km/h (629 mph)
B-57B	962 km/h (596 mph)
CANBERRA B.Mk 2	917 km/h (569 mph)

RANGE

The Destroyer's range of nearly 4000 km (2500 miles) compared well with that of the B-57, but was a little less than that of the RAF's Canberra. However, the B-66 had the advantage of being capable of air-to-air refuelling.

B-66B DESTROYER 3975 km (2465 miles)
B-57B 3701 km (2298 miles)
CANBERRA B Mk 2 4281 km (2659 miles)

ARMAMENT

The B-66 was a large aircraft and was capable of lifting a bombload of almost seven tonnes. The B-57B was able to carry around four tonnes of ordnance, which was considerably more than early-model Canberras.

B-66B DESTROYER 6804-kg (15,000-lb) bombload 2 x 20-mm cannon
B-57B 4173-kg (9200-lb) bombload 4 x 20-mm cannon
CANBERRA B.Mk 2 2722-kg (6000-lb) bombload

Heinemann's USAF heavyweight

Few combat aircraft had a more impressive record for versatility than the Douglas B-66 Destroyer. This high-wing, twin-engined medium-bomber came from the design shop of Douglas's fabled engineering chief Edward Heinemann (with major design work by John C. Buckwalter) and was an offspring of the Navy A3D Skywarrior.

The B-66 excelled first in the photo-reconnaissance and weather reconnaissance roles (as the RB-66 and WB-66, respectively) and latterly as an electronic warfare (EW) platform. In the EW role, the B-66 became a veteran of difficult missions over North Vietnam.

Although at first glance the B-66 may appear to have been designed for two pilots, it is, in fact, a single-pilot aircraft with the aviator situated on the centreline behind a V-shaped windscreen. In its latter-day role of jamming communications and seeking out radars in North Vietnam, the RB-66C carried a busy crew of pilot, navigator and five sensor/jammer operators.

By 1970 only EB-66 variants were still in service, in Vietnam and Germany, and by 1974 the last Destroyer had been retired because of fatigue and maintenance problems.

Originally the B-66 was to be an 'off-the-shelf' aircraft for the USAF, incorporating minimal changes to the Navy's A-3 design. However, once the USAF's requirements had been satisfied, the B-66 was an almost entirely new design. Major changes centred on the engines, wings and control surfaces and internal layout.

Above: The B-66 was only briefly in service as a bomber. Thirteen Destroyers were converted to EB-66B standard and a further two to NB-66Bs. The latter were test aircraft.

Right: The second of the WB-66Ds is seen here in pristine condition after delivery from Douglas's Tulsa, Oklahoma, factory. This was the final production Destroyer variant.

B-66B DESTROYER

Beginning in 16 March 1956, 72 B-66Bs were delivered to the USAF. 54-0505 was one of these aircraft and is seen here in the markings of the 47th Bomb Wing based at RAF Sculthorpe in Norfolk.

Three crew manned the bomber version of the B-66: pilot, navigator and gunner/bomb-aimer. The RB-66As and Bs had only two crew and the navigator operated the cameras.

As the RB/B-66 was intended as a tactical light bomber and reconnaissance platform for day and night operations, it was equipped with APS-27 bombing and K-5 navigation radar sets.

The EB-66B and later electronic countermeasures Destroyers dispensed with bombing and camera equipment. The camera/bomb-bay was fitted with jamming equipment and an electronic warfare officer (EWO) replaced the gunner.

Two 45.4-kN (10,200-lb-thrust) Allison J71-A-10 or -13 turbojets powered the B-66 variants. Ex-USAF B-66s have been used as testbeds for other engine types. Douglas used a B-66 to test a pair of Pratt & Whitney TF33 turbofans, and nacelles, prior to fitting four, as the JT3D, to its DC-8 commercial transport.

The RB-66C (and upgraded EB-66C) jamming aircraft and WB-66D weather reconnaissance variants carried extra crew in a pressurised compartment in the former camera/bomb-bay.

A radar-controlled General Electric gun turret at the rear of the aircraft held two 20-mm cannon. Defensive armament of this type would soon disappear from Western bomber designs; Soviet designs continued to be so equipped for some years afterwards.

An internal bay could be configured to hold cameras in the RB-66A and B or as a bomb bay for up to 6804 kg (15,000 lb) of bombs in the B-66B.

Camera ship, bomber and jammer

RADAR BOMBING: Equipped with LORAN (long-range navigation) equipment, EB-66s in Vietnam were used to guide flights of bombers to their targets so that they could attack from high altitude. The success of these raids was debatable.

RADAR JAMMING: The Destroyer made its name as a radar-locating and jamming aircraft during the Vietnam conflict. RB-66 and EB-66 aircraft often flew unescorted, but they were also used to accompany air raids. Onboard sensor operators located and jammed enemy radar, and guided bombers around the threat.

RECONNAISSANCE: Using photo-flash bombs to illuminate targets, RB-66s were tasked with reconnaissance by day and by night in all weathers.

DOUGLAS
AC-47 'SPOOKY'

- C-47 conversion ● Vietnam War gunship ● Minigun armament

E arly 1960s, as a means of bringing
experiments with the 'gunship'
concept began in the US in the
enemy position from the air. Some USAF
generals were sceptical at first, concerned
that an aircraft in such a position would be
vulnerable to enemy fire. However, as soon
as the first armed C-47s began to fly
combat missions in Vietnam in late 1964,
the concept proved its worth.

accurate, concentrated fire to bear on an

▲ By the time C-47s
were undergoing conversion to 'Spooky'
standard in the mid 1960s, the
venerable but versatile Skytrains
were all at least 20 years old.

PHOTO FILE

DOUGLAS AC-47 'SPOOKY'

Widely employed ▶
Two units were equipped with
'Spooky' – 4th Air Commando
Squadron (at Da Nang, Pleiku,
Phu Cat and Nha Trang) and
14th Air Commando Squadron
(at Nha Trang, Phan Rang,
Bien Hoa and Binh Thuy).

◀ Eight crew members
'Spooky' missions were manned
by seven USAF personnel and a
Vietnamese observer.

▲ Southeast Asia camouflage
In common with most other tactical types in the
Southeast Asian theatre, the 'Magic Dragons' were
finished in three-tone colours with light-coloured
under surfaces.

Minigun pods ▶
General Electric's SUU-11 gun pods were intended
for underwing mountings on smaller COIN aircraft,
but were adapted for use in the AC-47. Each was
manned by a gunner.

▲ Psy-war operations
As well as AC-47s, the USAF
used a small number of EC-47s
for leaflet-dropping missions.

FACTS AND FIGURES

- ➤ The 'Puff the Magic Dragon' nickname
  came from a popular song of the same
  name released in the 1960s.

- ➤ In 1965 prices, the first 20 AC-47Ds were
  converted for US $4,288,975.

- ➤ For target illumination at night, each
  AC-47 carried 56 hand-dropped flares.

- ➤ During its first 11 days of use the first
  AC-47 flew seven training and 16 combat
  missions; 179,710 rounds were fired.

- ➤ The aircraft captain in the left-hand
  pilot's seat could aim and fire all the guns.

- ➤ By the end of 1965, AC-47s were based
  in Thailand for service over Laos.

PROFILE

'Puff the Magic Dragon'

Originally known as the FC-47 (suggesting a 'fighter' variant), the gun-toting version of the long-serving 'Gooney Bird' transport was soon known by the more appropriate AC-47 designation and by the codename 'Spooky'. The gunship concept, of which the AC-47D was the first example, was based on a large fixed-wing aircraft flying in a pylon turn to bring fire down on a target using fuselage-mounted sideways-firing rotary Miniguns. From the outset, 'Spooky' was

seen as a night weapon, flares being used to illuminate targets. The first night mission was flown on 23/24 December 1964 and was deemed successful. AC-47s were able to loiter for long periods over suspected Viet Cong ground positions.

Soon nicknamed 'Puff the Magic Dragon' after a song of the same name, the AC-47D paved the way for further gunship development, based on the C-119 and C-130. Once these were in service, most AC-47s were transferred to the VNAF.

AC-47D 'Spooky'

Type: counter-insurgency gunship

Powerplant: two 820-kW (1100-hp) Pratt & Whitney R-1830-90D Twin Wasp radial piston engines

Maximum speed: 257 km/h (159 mph)

Initial climb rate: 3050 m (10,000 ft) in 9.5 min

Normal range: 2575 km (1600 miles)

Service ceiling: (typical) 914 m (3000 ft)

Weights: empty 8226 kg (18,097 lb); maximum 14,061 kg (30,934 lb)

Armament: three fuselage-mounted 7.62-mm (.30-cal.) General Electric SUU-11A Miniguns, each with a 6000 round-per-minute rate of fire

Dimensions:
span   29.11 m (95 ft 6 in)
length   19.43 m (53 ft 11 in)
height   17.00 m (55 ft 9 in)
wing area   91.69 m² (987 sq ft)

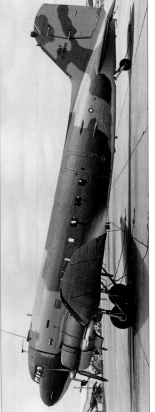

Above: Around 25 C-47s were converted to AC-47D standard, the first entering service with the 4th Air Commando Squadron in late 1965.

Right: Among other 'special mission' C-47s to serve in Southeast Asia were a small number of EC-47N electronic reconnaissance platforms.

AC-47D 'SPOOKY'

The USAF's 4th Commando Air Squadron based at Tan Son Nhut Air Base was charged with introducing the AC-47, doing so in late 1964. Delays had been experienced in the supply of Miniguns.

Fire control equipment in the AC-47D was almost non-existent. The pilot used a gunsight mounted in the port cockpit window through which he viewed the target.

On 8 February 1965 a 'Magic Dragon' was sent to the Bong Son area in the face of a Viet Cong offensive in the Central Highlands. In under five hours, the gunship poured 20,500 rounds of 7.62-mm (.30-cal.) ammunition into a hilltop where the VC were dug in. Over 300 soldiers were killed.

Gunship aircraft operated at relatively low altitudes and were camouflaged to reduce their vulnerability in their new role. By the late 1960s, aircraft were carrying a three-tone green and brown Southeast Asia colour scheme with white unit codes on the tailfin.

For night operations, 'Spooky' was fitted with a flare dispensing system to illuminate targets for the attentions of the gunners and their Miniguns. Originally it had been intended to convert Convair C-131s for the role, but the Douglas transport was available in larger numbers.

Initial AC-47 conversions were fitted with four air-cooled 12.7-mm (.50-cal.) machine guns. These were soon replaced by three far more effective General Electric SUU-11A six-barrelled rotary Miniguns of 7.62-mm (.30-cal.) calibre. One of these was mounted in the cargo doorway, the other two in the rearmost cabin windows.

GUNSHIP FIREPOWER

'SHADOW' and 'STINGER': To increase the firepower available to gunship units, the USAF chose the C-119 Packet as the basis for their next generation of 'Magic Dragon'. The first of 52 were delivered in 1968, the AC-119G featuring four Minigun pods and new sensors, including a illuminator light set and night observation gear. More conversions followed: 26 AC-119Ks had underwing jet booster engines and two 20-mm rotary cannon added.

'SPECTRE': During 1967 an AC-130A prototype was converted and tested in Vietnam. Night flying aids and improved sensors helped guide the aircraft, which boasted no fewer than four Miniguns and four 20-mm rotary cannon. Successful trials led to seven more C-130A conversions. These were put to work 'truck hunting' along the Ho Chi Minh Trail. Later examples carried a 40-mm Bofors cannon, side-looking radar and a laser designator.

Special missions transports over Vietnam

■ **DOUGLAS EC-47:** As well as the gunship role, C-47s in Southeast Asia were assigned electronic intelligence and 'psy-war' tasks.

■ **FAIRCHILD UC-123K PROVIDER:** Fitted with spray bars, C-123s were used on Ranch Hand defoliant-spraying missions.

■ **LOCKHEED DC-130E HERCULES:** USAF C-130s (like this USN example) launched and directed spy drones over targets in the North.

■ **LOCKHEED HC-130H HERCULES:** Specially equipped 'Herks' coordinated combat rescue missions to retrieve downed aircrew.

EUROCOPTER
HH-65A DOLPHIN

● Search and rescue ● Coastal patrol ● Utility helicopter

41104

COAST GUARD

▲ A stretcher can be attached to the Dolphin's winch cable, which is particularly useful when picking up a casualty from a ship. The HH-65A is the US Coast Guard's most numerous asset, with nearly 100 examples currently in service.

Speeding to the rescue with the US Coast Guard, the HH-65 Dolphin has saved hundreds of lives since its was introduced in 1987. Serving in coastal locations across America, this short-range recovery version of the Eurocopter Dauphin multi-role helicopter has demonstrated impressive versatility. Fitted with advanced avionics and search equipment, the Dolphin is first to the rescue whatever the weather.

EUROCOPTER HH-65A DOLPHIN

COAST GUARD

▼ **High-visibility paint scheme**
The US Coast Guard has replaced its Dolphin's original white and red colour scheme (shown left) with an all-over high-visibility red, reflecting the helicopter's dedicated civil rescue role.

▲ **Short-range rescue**
The HH-65A is the short-range component of the modernised Coast Guard fleet, operating alongside the longer ranged HH-60J Jayhawk and fixed-wing HU-25 Guardian, a version of the French Dassault Falcon 20.

Advanced cockpit ▶
The Dolphin's modern cockpit is designed for minimum effort all-weather operations and includes comprehensive radio systems and datalink. The flight deck normally houses two, but it can be flown by a single pilot.

▼ **Safety record**
The HH-65A has a reputation as a very safe helicopter, thanks to its automatic flight control system, airspeed regulator, flotation bags, Rockwell-Collins navigation and Northrop SeeHawk FLIR.

▲ **Rescue equipment**
In addition to a winch and searchlight, the cabin contains first-aid gear, a removable stretcher and a sliding seat for the engineer.

FACTS AND FIGURES

▶ The Dolphin was criticised for lacking power in hot and high conditions, but a re-engining programme was cancelled.

▶ The crew can be supplemented by a rescue diver for special missions.

▶ Dolphins were purchased to replace the elderly Sikorsky HH-52.

▶ Israel purchased two HH-65s, and in trials operated them from the navy's fleet of fast patrol craft.

▶ Two HH-65s are used by the US Navy test centre at Patuxent River, Maryland.

▶ Flotation bags allow waterborne ditchings in bad weather – up to sea state five.

PROFILE

Coast Guard rescue helicopter

A round the coast of America, the United States Coast Guard waits patiently for calls for help. Teams of swimmers and boat crews are used for inshore rescues, and fixed-wing and larger rotary-wing aircraft, such as the Sikorsky HH-60J 'Jayhawk' and special versions of the C-130 Hercules transport, carry out the long-range work. The responsibility of the HH-65A Dolphin, a modernised

version of the Eurocopter SA 366 Dauphin purchased in 1987 to replace the elderly single-engined Sikorsky HH-52, is to undertake rescues at ranges up to 760 km. Although built in France, the new HH-65A incorporates 70 per cent American components.

A total of 96 Dolphins serve around the United States from Astoria to San Diego. Fitted with advanced infra-red search systems, a winch, all-weather

avionics and a searchlight, the HH-65A is ideal for short-range rescue work.

Although the Dolphin has been a success, there was controversy over complaints voiced by the US Coast Guard that the aircraft lacked power, especially in the hot conditions around the coastlines of California and Florida in the summer. Re-engining the helicopter was considered, but rejected on the grounds of cost.

The HH-65A is seen here with its stablemate, the improved Eurocopter Panther 800. A more powerful and upgraded development, the Panther seems unlikely to serve with the USCG, which was not entirely satisfied with the Dolphin.

HH-65A DOLPHIN

The Eurocopter SA 366G Dolphin has been employed by the US Coast Guard since 1982, replacing the larger amphibious Sikorsky HH-52A in most units.

Typically, the HH-65's crew will consist of a pilot, co-pilot and flight engineer/winch operator. The helicopter has a winch stressed to 1200 kg (2646 lb) mounted above the starboard door.

The Dolphin carries a sophisticated Planar array weather and search radar, plus equipment to allow joint missions with Coast Guard HU-25s, HH-60Hs, RG-8s and C-130s.

The HH-65's twin engines drive 11.68-m (38-ft 4-in) four-bladed rotors. Like the Gazelle and Panther, the tail rotor is the fenestron 'fan-in-fin' type.

The Coast Guard refit their French Dolphins with more powerful American-built Textron Lycoming LTS101 turboshafts, making the aircraft capable of a maximum speed of 324 km/h (201 mph).

If the HH-65 is unfortunate enough to suffer a double engine failure over the sea, a successful ditching will be aided by the helicopter's pop-out inflatable floats.

The Dolphin's tailboom is sealed for enhanced buoyancy and contains an increased size all-composite Fenestron tail rotor. The aircraft's mainly composite structure leads to its nickname of 'plastic puppy'.

On patrol with the US Coast Guard

■ **HC-130H:** With a large APS-137 radar on the fuselage sides, the HC-130H can search large areas of ocean with great accuracy.

■ **HH-52 SEAGUARD:** The single-engined predecessor to the HH-65, the old HH-52 could land on the water, unlike the HH-65.

■ **HU-25 GUARDIAN:** Derived from the Dassault Falcon 20, the HU-25 can fly counter-smuggling or long-range rescue missions.

■ **SCHWEIZER RV-8:** For covert spying against smugglers, the low-light TV-equipped RV-8 wears a low-visibility paint scheme.

HH-65A Dolphin

Type: short-range coast guard search-and-rescue helicopter

Powerplant: two 507-kW (680-hp) Textron Lycoming LTS101-750 turboshaft engines

Maximum speed: 324 km/h (201 mph)

Operational radius: 760 km (472 miles) with maximum fuel and 400 km (249 miles) with maximum passenger payload; no external fuel carried

Endurance: 4 hours

Hover ceiling in ground effect: 2290 m (7513 ft)

Hover ceiling out of ground effect: 1627 m (5338 ft)

Weights: empty 2718 kg (5992 lb); loaded 4050 kg (8929 lb)

Dimensions:
span	11.94 m (39 ft 2 in)
length	13.88 m (45 ft 6 in)
height	3.98 m (13 ft 1 in)
rotor disc area	119.90 m² (1291 sq ft)

ACTION DATA

MAXIMUM SPEED

A generation ahead of the HH-3 or the Wessex and with considerably more streamlining, the HH-65A is capable of high speeds. SH-3s held speed records in the early-1960s.

HH-65A DOLPHIN	324 km/h (210 mph)
HH-3F	267 km/h (166 mph)
WESSEX HC.Mk 2	212 km/h (132 mph)

RANGE

With its much bigger fuselage, the HH-3 has greater fuel capacity and longer range. This allowed it to fulfil the long-range rotary search-and-rescue role in support of the inshore HH-65.

HH-65A DOLPHIN	760 km (472 miles)
HH-3F	1005 km (624 miles)
WESSEX HC.Mk 2	770 km (478 miles)

HOVER CEILING

Hover ceiling is a theoretical figure measured during the first flights of the prototype. It can be affected very significantly by high temperature (this figure is calculated at a standard temperature of 15°C). The HH-65 often flies in hot weather at sea level.

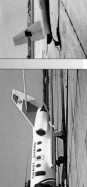

HH-65A DOLPHIN	1627 m (5338 ft)
HH-3F	2500 m (8202 ft)
WESSEX HC.Mk 2	1220 m (4003 ft)

FAIRCHILD

AC/C-119 FLYING BOXCAR

- Twin-engined transport ● Korean War action ● Vietnam gunship

▲ As well as serving with the USAF and Marine Corps, the C-119 was also operated by the air forces of Belgium, Brazil, Ethiopia, France, Italy, India, Nationalist China and South Vietnam.

F airchild's C-119 Flying Boxcar was the standard US military cargo transport of the 1950s, seeing action during the Korean War. This distinctive twin-engine, 'twin boom' transport hauled cargoes all over the world until superseded by the C-130 Hercules in the 1960s. Vietnam brought a final curtain call when the AC-119 'Shadow' and 'Stinger' gunships made their presence felt during the night-time missions over Viet Cong positions.

FAIRCHILD AC/C-119 FLYING BOXCAR

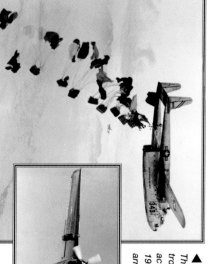

▲ Supplying the troops
This C-119 drops supplies to United Nations troops near Chungju. The C-119 first saw action in the Korean War starting in August 1950, when the 314th Troop Carrier Group arrived in Japan.

▲ Twin-boom layout
Following on from the C-82 Packet, the Flying Boxcar used a similar layout but with a redesigned fuselage and more powerful Wright Duplex Cyclone engines.

▼ Indian jet booster conversion
India's air force fitted a HAL-built Bristol Orpheus turbojet take-off booster engine to a number of C-119s.

▼ Arctic markings
Aircraft intended for service in the Arctic carried dayglo paint for improved visibility.

▲ C-119J with 'beaver' tail
A number of C-119s were modified by the USAF with this flight-operable door and ramp known as the 'beaver tail'.

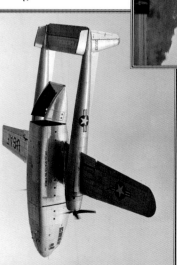

FACTS AND FIGURES

➤ A number of USAF Flying Boxcars were used to retrieve satellite capsules descending from space by parachute.

➤ The C-119 prototype was a modified C-82 and first flew in November 1947.

➤ Surplus C-119s are employed today as aerial fire-bombers in the United States.

➤ The C-119 was the third transport type to undergo gunship conversion; the others being the C-47 and C-130.

➤ The last USAF Boxcars were AC-119s in Air National Guard Service until late 1975.

➤ The first C-82, on which the C-119 was based, was delivered in 1945.

PROFILE

Boxcar, Shadow and Stinger

Twin-boom cargo planes were the trademark of Fairchild after World War II. These heavylift transports helped the United States in supporting its armed forces in its post-war foreign commitments.

The C-82 Packet was a modest success. The XC-120 Packplane of 1950 with its detachable cargo pod flew as an experiment only. Fairchild really hit the mark, however, with its C-119. This aircraft was a development of the Packet and its capacious interior

led soldiers to call it the Flying Boxcar. The unofficial name stuck.

In the Korean War C-119s provided a lifeline between Japan and Korea, and in 1954 they hauled supplies for the French in Indochina. In both Asian conflicts the Flying Boxcar air-dropped supplies while under fire, and in Korea they delivered paratroops. C-119s formed the backbone of USAF air transport in the 1950s, and the US Marines Corps also operated the type as the R4Q Packet. The Vietnam conflict

brought a new lease of life for the C-119 when a number were urgently converted to AC-119 gunships for interdiction and close support; these aircraft were named AC-119G 'Shadow' and AC-119K 'Stinger'.

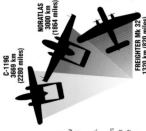

Below: To speed up deliveries of the C-119C during the Korean War, another production line was set up by Kaiser Manufacturing.

Above: C-119s served in a number of roles with the USAF, including satellite tracking and recovery and medical evacuation.

AC-119K 'STINGER'

'The Super Sow' was one of 26 AC-119K 'Stinger' gunships converted from C-119G Flying Boxcars and placed in service from late 1969 with the 18th Special Operations Squadron.

The AC-119K was used for interdiction rather than fire support and therefore carried more sensors than the AC-119G 'Shadow'.

Extra power for the 'Stinger' was supplied by two J85 turbojets in pods under the outer wings. These improved performance at higher gross weights.

While the AC-119G carried only four 7.62-mm (.30-cal.) Miniguns in the port side of the fuselage pod, the AC-119K was more heavily armed with an additional pair of M61 20-mm rotary cannon. As war in Vietnam continued some aircrew dispensed with the Miniguns in favour of more cannon.

Intended to operate at night, the AC-119s had black undersides and vertical tail surfaces, with camouflage on the upper surfaces and a small national insignia.

An AVQ-8 Xenon searchlight was fitted in the port side rear doorway for illuminating potential targets.

Sensors included an APQ-133 side-looking beacon-tracking radar in the rear of the aircraft. This complemented the APQ-136 search radar in the nose.

In addition to armament and sensors the AC-119 gunships were fitted with armour plating to provide some protection from ground fire.

AC-119K 'Stinger'

Type: twin-engined interdiction gunship

Powerplant: two 2610-kW (3500-hp) Wright R-3350-85 Duplex Cyclone 18-cylinder radial piston engines and two 12.67-kN (2851-lb-thrust) General Electric J85-GE-17 turbojets

Cruising speed: 391 km/h (243 mph)

Combat range: 1595 km (991 miles)

Weights: empty 20,300 kg (44,754 lb); loaded 34,925 kg (76,996 lb)

Armament: four 7.62-mm (.30-cal.) GAU-2 Miniguns and two 20-mm M61 cannon

Accommodation: 10 crew including flight crew, sensor operators and gunners

Dimensions:
span 33.29 m (109 ft 3 in)
length 26.36 m (86 ft 6 in)
height 8.08 m (26 ft 6 in)
wing area 134.43 m² (1447 sq ft)

COMBAT DATA

RANGE

The C-119 possessed a good range performance for an aircraft in its class. The very similar Nord Noratlas was also able to cover distances of around 3000 km (1860 miles). Few other aircraft of the period had the load-carrying capacity of these two types. The Bristol Freighter was another design dating from World War II, and although it could carry a reasonable load it lacked range.

NORATLAS 3000 km (1864 miles)
C-119G 3669 km (2280 miles)
FREIGHTER Mk 32 1320 km (820 miles)

CRUISING SPEED

Again, the Noratlas and C-119 shared similar performance, with the C-119 having a slightly lower cruising speed. The power-to-weight ratios of these two types are therefore similar. The smaller Bristol Freighter is significantly slower.

C-119G 322 km/h (200 mph)
NORATLAS 335 km/h (208 mph)
FREIGHTER Mk 32 262 km/h (163 mph)

MAX TAKE-OFF WEIGHT

The larger C-119 had a significantly higher take-off weight and load-carrying capacity than the Noratlas. The maximum take-off weight of the Noratlas was, in fact, only just over one tonne more than that of the smaller Bristol Freighter.

C-119G 33,747 kg (74,399 lb)
NORATLAS 21,000 kg (46,297 lb)
FREIGHTER Mk 32 19,958 kg (44,000 lb)

RISKY LANDING: Fuel consumption dropped and the aircraft slowly climbed to 3000 m (9843 ft) as it attempted to make it back to base. Electing to land the aircraft and uncertain whether there was damage to his controls, the 'Stinger' captain skilfully made a 'no flap' approach. Only when they had landed did the crew realize that the C-119 had lost a third of its right wing.

PULLED OUT OF DIVE: The AC-119 dropped more than 300 m (980 ft) in just a few seconds, and the flight crew struggled with the controls to bring it out of the dive. The use of full throttle, however, increased the fire and other damage meant fuel was running low. To maintain height the crew jettisoned every possible item from the cabin, including guns and sensor equipment!

Mayday over Laos!

8 MAY 1970: After destroying several enemy trucks on an armed reconnaissance mission over a heavily defended road in Laos a 'Stinger' was hit by anti-aircraft fire. The aircraft's right wing burst into flames.

FAIRCHILD

C-123 PROVIDER

● Assault transport ● Vietnam combat record ● Special missions

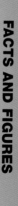

A fter a difficult development phase, the Fairchild C-123 Provider became the flying supply truck of the Vietnam War. It was a rugged and versatile cargo aircraft that could land and take off in the middle of a combat zone. The Provider has is now retired from US service but is still flying in Korea, Thailand and El Salvador – achieving remarkable longevity for a transport that owes its origins to a World War II glider.

▲ When the C-123 was put in to production the large and distinctive dorsal fin was added. Providers served with great distinction in Vietnam and also flew lifeline missions supporting personnel based at Arctic radar stations.

162

FAIRCHILD C-123 PROVIDER

▼ Three-engined take-off
Fairchild fitted its own J44 turbojets to the wingtips of a test aircraft. It was able to take-off with one main engine out and its initial climb rate was improved by 300 per cent.

Pantobase ▶
Michael Stroukoff formed his own company, specialising in the manufacture of experimental C-123 designs. The company built two such aircraft, including this machine with a pantobase undercarriage. It could operate from ice, snow, water and land.

▲ Thunderbird transport
Wearing a scheme to match the display aircraft, this C-123 backed up the USAF aerobatic team.

▲ Vietnam Provider
Standard C-123Ks served widely in Vietnam, but it was the UC-123B/K aircraft used to spray Agent Orange defoliant which received the most publicity.

▼ On top of the world
Ten C-123Bs, fitted with wingtip J44s and a ski-undercarriage, were redesignated C-123Js. They were used to support Arctic-based distant early warning radar stations and served until 1976.

FACTS AND FIGURES

▶ During the 78-day siege of Khe Sanh in Vietnam, C-123s made 179 landings and 105 airdrops.

▶ In all, 312 C-123s were built by three manufacturers.

▶ Among newly-built Providers were 24 aircraft for Saudi Arabia and Venezuela.

▶ A C-123 pilot was awarded the Medal of Honor for landing at a Vietnamese airstrip to rescue men under fire.

▶ The first flight of a Fairchild-built C-123 was on 1 September 1954.

▶ C-123s were used to spray defoliants over the South Vietnamese jungle.

PROFILE

From glider to tactical transport

Michael Stroukoff designed the C-123 while working for Chase Aircraft company. One of many innovative aircraft designs produced just after World War II, the C-123 began life as the XG-20 cargo glider. This all-metal glider was designed with conversion to a powered assault transport in mind, and first flew as the XC-123 Avitruc on 12 April 1951. Five pre-production C-123Bs were ordered from Chase and production of these was passed to the car manufacturer Kaiser-Frazer.

Kaiser-Frazer experienced difficulties with the contract, however, and it was therefore

given to Fairchild, who produced 302 aircraft and called them Providers. The aircraft entered service with the USAF's 309th Troop Carrier Group in July 1955.

The Provider served around the world, but the shining moment of its career was the conflict in Vietnam. Here a transport was needed that could land on a crude runway, near the fighting, sometimes under fire. The C-123 Provider filled this role with distinction.

The C-123K was fitted with two J85 turbojets, which provided additional boost, and this model formed the basis of a number of special mission variants.

Above: Early natural-metal finishes were over-painted with camouflage when the Provider went to war. C-123s set new standards in assault tactics.

Right: Eleven C-123B Providers were transferred to the US Coast Guard. They were sometimes known as HC-123Bs and were fitted with a search radar mounted in a thimble radome on the nose.

C-123J PROVIDER

Only one Air National Guard (ANG) squadron flew the ski- and jet-equipped Provider. The 144th Tactical Airlift Squadron of the Alaska ANG received its first aircraft in June 1960.

A 4.45-kN (1001-lb-thrust) Fairchild J44 turbojet engine was mounted on each wingtip of the C-123J. C-123Ks had their more powerful jet engines mounted on underwing pylons.

When ski equipment was added the maximum payload of the C-123J was reduced to 3785 kg (8344 lb).

A fairing was fitted ahead of the nose to accommodate the front of the retracted nose-ski.

Equipped with the classic rear-loading ramp/door, the C-123 was a superb tactical airlifter.

Arctic flying can be hazardous and most aircraft which regularly fly over large areas of ice and snow carry some form of day-glo marking to make them highly visible in the event of a forced landing.

For operations from ice and snow, skis were attached to the undercarriage legs. The skis surrounded the wheels, which were left partially exposed so that the C-123J could use normal runways with skis still attached. The skis did not retract into the fuselage.

O-64394
ALASKA
ALASKA AIR GUARD
U.S. AIR FORCE

Provider versatility
The Provider could be adapted to fly a wide range of missions.

DEFOLIANT SPRAYER (UC-123B/K): To deny the Viet Cong cover in the jungle, defoliant was sprayed which caused the trees to shed their leaves.

FLYING FROM ICE (C-123J): Take-off performance was improved by the use of auxiliary turbojets, although skis added considerable weight to the airframe. Ski-equipped C-130s replaced these aircraft.

AMPHIBIAN (YC-123E): This special machine had a very flexible undercarriage, combining water, ice, snow, hard runway and rough-field capability in one system. The aircraft was not adopted for service, however.

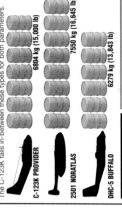

C-123K Provider

Type: twin-engined assault transport

Powerplant: two 1865-kW (2500-hp) Pratt & Whitney R-2800-99W Double Wasp piston engines and two 12.69-kN (2855-lb-thrust) General Electric J85-GE-17 turbojet engines

Maximum speed: 367 km/h (228 mph) at 3050 m (10,006 ft)

Cruising speed: 278 km/h (173 mph) at 3050 m (10,006 ft)

Range: ferry range 5279 km (3280 miles); with maximum payload 1666 km (1035 miles)

Service ceiling: 9560 m (31,365 ft)

Weights: empty 16042 kg (35,367 lb); maximum take-off 18,288 kg (40,318 lb)

Accommodation: two pilots and two loadmasters; 60 fully equipped combat troops or 50 stretchers or up to 6804 kg (15,000 lb) of cargo

Dimensions: span   33.53 m (110 ft)
length   23.92 m (78 ft 6 in)
height   10.39 m (34 ft 1 in)
wing area 113.62 m² (1223 sq ft)

COMBAT DATA

MAXIMUM PAYLOAD

Finding the balance between payload and STOL performance was difficult with the technology available to these contemporaries. The C-123K falls in-between these types for both parameters.

C-123K PROVIDER — 6804 kg (15,000 lb)
2501 NORATLAS — 7550 kg (16,645 lb)
DHC-5 BUFFALO — 6279 kg (13,843 lb)

TAKE-OFF DISTANCE

Although it can carry a much larger payload than the DHC-5 Buffalo, the C-123K requires less than 100 metres of extra runway to become airborne. The 2501 Noratlas has a greater payload but is not an outstanding STOL performer.

C-123K PROVIDER — 551 m (1808 ft)
2501 NORATLAS — 630 m (2067 ft)
DHC-5 BUFFALO — 470 m (1542 ft)

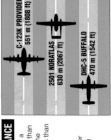

RANGE

The DHC-5 excels in the range category compared to its rivals, due to the efficiency of its turboprop powerplants. Being a larger aircraft than the C-123K, the Nord Noratlas has a better range, but in the tactical/assault transport role the C-123K's range is more than adequate.

C-123K PROVIDER — 1666 km (1035 miles)
2501 NORATLAS — 2600 km (1616 miles)
DHC-5 BUFFALO — 3493 km (2170 miles)

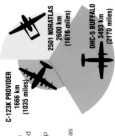

FAIRCHILD

AU-23 PEACEMAKER

- Short take-off and landing ● Turboprop power ● Multi-role

▲ Developed as a mini-gunship in response to the USAF's Credible Chase programme, the AU-23A also proved itself to be a useful transport and multi-role aircraft. Late in 1996, 22 Thai aircraft remained in service.

Fairchild Hiller Corporation discovered the brilliant, Swiss-built Pilatus PC-6 Turbo Porter almost by accident. Stunned by the ability of the Turbo Porter to land and take off in as little as 182 m (600 ft), Fairchild's managers started, in 1964, to build the aircraft for civil and military use. Over one-third of the examples built were delivered as AU-23A Peacemakers, able to carry a variety of weapons for jungle warfare.

FAIRCHILD AU-23 PEACEMAKER

▼ Well-armed
The counter-insurgency (COIN) version of the AU-23 had one underfuselage and four underwing hardpoints with a combined maximum capacity of 908 kg (2000 lb) of mixed stores, as well as a door-mounted machine gun.

▲ Counter-insurgency
Under the Credible Chase programme, the AU-23A was first called the Armed Porter.

▼ Warplane modifications
The Peacemaker, as it was subsequently named, had a full military nav/com avionics installation and a weapons control system for operations in the hostile environment of Southeast Asia.

▲ STOL utility
To complement its short take-off and landing performance, the AU-23A had low-pressure tyres for rough field operations.

▲ US Army UV-20
The US Army had two PC-6 Turbo Porters for use in Berlin. These UV-20 Chiricahuas were painted in gloss olive green with white tops and were flown by the Berlin Brigade.

FACTS AND FIGURES

▶ An AU-23A Peacemaker was able to carry almost its own weight in weapons or other stores.

▶ Edward Uhl, Fairchild president, used a PC-6 for commuting from 1966 to 1986.

▶ Fairchild manufactured 92 Turbo Porters, including 35 military Peacemakers.

▶ The Peacemaker normally had four underwing hardpoints and one fuselage station, for bombs or rockets.

▶ Up to 11 passengers or eight fully equipped paratroops could be carried.

▶ The last Thai AU-23 delivered was the final single-propeller Fairchild aircraft.

PROFILE

Armed US-built Swiss STOL design

During an unplanned landing at the Fairchild factory in 1962, the strange-looking, long-nosed Turbo Porter demonstrated its STOL (Short Take-Off and Landing) ability. Company officials saw a demand for an aircraft with this sort of performance, and gained permission to produce the Swiss aircraft in the USA. The best known US-built version was the Minigun- and cannon-armed AU-23A Peacemaker, built as a small gunship for the US Air Force (USAF) and Thai police forces.

After Peacemakers began appearing in Southeast Asia with the CIA airline Air America, Fairchild began promoting the aircraft for military purposes. The US Navy version (OV-12 Riverine) was ordered in 1968, but later cancelled. Strangely, although the AU-23A was intended to be flown by American forces in Southeast Asia, most went directly to Thailand's police forces. When the US Army needed a couple of these aircraft a decade later for use with the Aviation Detachment of the

Berlin Brigade (UV-20 Chiricahua), it had to turn to Pilatus, since Fairchild's factory space was by then dedicated to the A-10 production. The company had discontinued Peacemaker production at a time when many additional aircraft could have been sold.

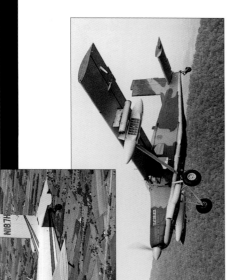

Above: Design work on the Fairchild Hiller PC-6 Heli-Porter, which led to the AU-23A, began in November 1964. The first aircraft flew in October 1965.

Above: As operated in Southeast Asia, the AU-23A was fitted with reconnaissance cameras and a 'Skyshout' public address propaganda system with 20 speakers, in an underwing pod.

The unusually shaped all-metal cantilever tail unit had a rectangular rudder with a small dorsal fillet. The even larger rudder had a corrugated metal surface, while the low-set variable incidence tailplane had Flettner trim tabs.

One passenger could be seated in the starboard side of the cockpit and a further 10 people in a high-density layout behind. There was a large sliding door on the starboard side and double doors with no central pillar on the port side.

AU-23A PEACEMAKER

In addition to those delivered to the USAF, a large number of AU-23 Peacemakers were supplied to the Royal Thai Police for anti-insurgent and smuggler patrols as well as casualty evacuation duties.

Most production AU-23As were powered by a 430-kW (577-hp) Garrett AiResearch TPE331 turboprop which drove a three-bladed Hartzell HC-B3TN/ metal variable-pitch propeller.

The AU-23 had a single-spar all-metal structure wing of constant chord. The whole trailing edge was hinged, the inner sections forming double-slotted flaps and the outer section single-slotted ailerons.

The robust fixed undercarriage had large oleo shock absorbers and oversize low-pressure tyres on the main wheels. The tailwheel was steerable.

Special operations in Southeast Asia

■ **CESSNA O-2 SKYMASTER:** The armed Cessna O-2 was used for FAC (forward air control) and special missions in Vietnam.

■ **DOUGLAS A-1E SKYRAIDER:** Loaded with munitions, the A-1E was successfully operated for counter-insurgency in Southeast Asia.

■ **NORTH AMERICAN AT-28D TROJAN:** Specially converted T-28D Trojans were used for Vietnam COIN operations.

■ **HELIO U-10 COURIER:** With an even better STOL performance than the AU-23A, the U-10 was used by the US Army for special operations.

AU-23A Peacemaker

Type: single-engined mini-gunship and counter-insurgency (COIN) aircraft

Powerplant: one 430-kW (577-hp) Garrett AiResearch TPE331-1-101 turboprop

Maximum speed: 264 km/h (164 mph) at 3050 m (10,006 ft)

Climb rate: 490 m/min (1608 fpm)

Combat range: 1100 km (684 miles)

Service ceiling: 8500 m (27,887 ft)

Weights: empty 1185 kg (2612 lb); maximum take-off 2200 kg (7218 lb)

Armament: one 20-mm XM-197 cannon, plus two 7.62-mm (30-cal.) SUU-11A/A Miniguns and one underfuselage and four underwing hardpoints with combined maximum capacity of 907 kg (2000 lb) of mixed stores including bombs, cannon pods, flares, Minigun pods, napalm, rockets and smoke grenades, or reconnaissance and Skyshout pods

Dimensions:

span	15.13 m (49 ft 8 in)
length	10.90 m (35 ft 9 in)
height	3.20 m (10 ft 6 in)
wing area	28.80 m² (310 sq ft)

COMBAT DATA

ARMAMENT

Intended for use as a small gunship, the Peacemaker was heavily armed with multi-barrelled Miniguns and a 20-mm cannon. Its armament was not as heavy as that of the Argentinian Pucara or the OV-10E Bronco, both of which carry a heavier ordnance load. Typical stores include rockets and gun pods.

AU-23A PEACEMAKER 1 x 20-mm cannon
2 x 7.62-mm (.30-cal.) Miniguns
907-kg (2000-lb) ordnance load

IA-58A PUCARÁ 2 x 20-mm cannon
4 x 7.62-mm (.30-cal.) machine guns
1500-kg (3307-lb) ordnance load

OV-10E BRONCO 4 x 7.62-mm (.30-cal.) machine guns
1633-kg (3600-lb) ordnance load

TAKE-OFF RUN

Short-field performance was not a primary requirement for the FAMA/FMA IA-58A Pucara. Rockwell's OV-10 is now appearing in several smaller air forces, who appreciate its short take-off capabilities. The AU-23A offers true STOL performance, however.

IA-58A PUCARÁ — 300 m (984 ft)

OV-10E BRONCO — 226 m (741 ft)

AU-23A PEACEMAKER — 155 m (509 ft)

FAIRCHILD

A-10 THUNDERBOLT II

● CAS and anti-armour aircraft ● Gulf War veteran ● Forward air control

Built to attack the Warsaw Pact's main battle tanks, the Fairchild A-10 Thunderbolt II was named after a Fairchild Republic product from another era, the P-47 Thunderbolt of World War II. The twin-engined, single-seat A-10 'Warthog' showed its excellent air-to-ground capability in the unlikely setting of the Middle East during the Gulf War. Despite this success, the end of the Cold War and changes in USAF

▲ Plans for the withdrawal of the A-10 from the USAF inventory were well advanced by 1990, but events in the Persian Gulf meant that the retirement of the 'Warthog' was postponed.

FAIRCHILD A-10 THUNDERBOLT II

▲ Second prototype
The two YA-10A prototypes flew for the first time in 1972. The second one is seen here carrying 'dumb' iron bombs. Service aircraft carry the Maverick air-to-surface missile as their primary anti-tank weapon.

▼ Vulnerability issue
Since the A-10's introduction debates have raged about the vulnerability of this relatively slow aircraft. As a result, the F-16 was chosen to replace it.

▲ Camouflage
Since the Gulf War, all-over grey paintwork has replaced the grey/green scheme.

▲ Avenger cannon
The cannon is so powerful that it can be fired only in short bursts as it dramatically slows down the aircraft.

Countermeasures ▼
Even though it is relatively unsophisticated, the A-10 carries an electronic jamming pod.

FACTS AND FIGURES

▼ A-10s entered service in April 1976; 144 aircraft were committed to the Persian Gulf war zone in 1990/91.

▼ The first A-10 prototype made its initial flight on 10 May 1972.

▼ A-10s shot down two Iraqi helicopters during the Gulf War.

▼ Although almost as large as the multi-crewed B-25 Mitchell bomber of World War II, the A-10 is flown by a single pilot.

▼ In 1994 plans to export 50 surplus A-10s to Turkey were cancelled.

▼ At its maximum rate of fire, a 30-round burst from the GAU-8 takes half a second.

Forward air control in the 'Warthog'

More than 100 A-10s were committed to the 1991 Gulf War and performed admirably in the air-to-ground and FAC roles.

The need for a close air support (CAS)/anti-armour aircraft was one of the lessons learned in the Vietnam conflict. The machine needed to be able to fly from rough forward airstrips, carry heavy weapon loads and withstand battle damage. Speed was not a major consideration.

Fairchild's A-10A was the design chosen to fill this 'A-X' requirement. A sturdy, somewhat heavy, single-seat attack aircraft, the A-10 was said to be too slow; it flew at subsonic speeds in an era when fast anti-aircraft missiles were rapidly appearing on the scene. Despite this, 713 A-10s were built, and the first entered service in 1976. Units in the continental US, Alaska, Europe and Korea were equipped with the type.

However, the end of the Cold War meant that this specialist aircraft was no longer a vital requirement, and it was to be replaced by the Lockheed Martin F-16. Surplus A-10s began to take over from the well-worn Rockwell OV-10 Broncos in the forward air control (FAC) role, with a number being redesignated OA-10A.

A-10A THUNDERBOLT II

The 706th Tactical Fighter Squadron, 926th Tactical Fighter Group, operated A-10As during Operation Desert Storm. After the Gulf War, the unit took on squadron/wing status and F-16C/Ds.

In its original 'tank-busting' role the A-10's main weapon was the General Electric GAU-8/A Avenger 30-mm seven-barrelled Gatling-type cannon.

For the FAC role the OA-10 carries few weapons apart from two rocket pods for target marking and AIM-9 Sidewinder air-to-air missiles. The pilot is provided with NVG (night-vision goggles) for a night-fighting capability.

Survivability was one of the key considerations of the A-10's designers. The aircraft is able to fly on one engine or with one tailfin missing. The pilot sits in a titanium 'tub' as protection from ground fire.

Two General Electric TF34 turbofans power the A-10 and are high-mounted in pods to the rear of the aircraft to avoid debris when using rough airstrips. The nacelle design results in a low infra-red signature, which reduces vulnerability to heat-seeking missiles. This design also makes maintenance easier as access to the engine is less restricted than in other types.

The main undercarriage retracts forwards into an underwing bay. In theory, once the aircraft's weapon load has been dropped, a safe wheels-up landing can be made with minimal wing damage.

This A-10 carries the 'NO' tailcode of the 926th Fighter Wing, based in New Orleans. In September 1996 it received A/OA-10As once again to take on the attack/FAC training role.

Dozens of A-10As have been redesignated OA-10A without undergoing any modifications. Some have received changes to cockpit lighting to make them compatible with NVG equipment.

An AN/ALQ-184 electronic countermeasures (ECM) pod is a common fitting on both FAC OA-10s and tank-busting A-10s.

Split ailerons give the A-10 an exceptional rate of roll for the rapid low-level manoeuvres required for the anti-tank and FAC roles.

AGM-65 Maverick anti-tank strike

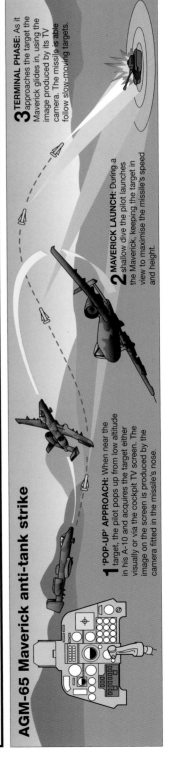

1 'POP-UP' APPROACH: When near the target, the pilot pops up from low altitude in his A-10 and acquires the target either visually or via the cockpit TV screen. The image on the screen is produced by the camera fitted in the missile's nose.

2 MAVERICK LAUNCH: During a shallow dive the pilot launches the Maverick, keeping the target in view to maximise the missile's speed and height.

3 TERMINAL PHASE: As it approaches the target the Maverick glides in, using the image produced by its TV camera. The missile is able follow slow-moving targets.

OA-10A Thunderbolt II

Type: single-seat anti-tank and FAC aircraft

Powerplant: two 40.3-kN (9068-lb-thrust) General Electric TF34-GE-100 turbofan engines

Maximum speed: 682 km/h (424 mph) at sea level

Maximum climb rate: 1828 m/min (5997 fpm) at sea level

Combat radius: 885 km (550 miles)

Service ceiling: 10,575 m (34,695 ft)

Weights: empty 10,977 kg (24,200 lb); loaded 21,500 kg (47,399 lb)

Armament: one General Electric GAU-8/A 30-mm cannon, plus up to 7258 kg (16,000 lb) of weapons; forward air control load consists of up to 12 LAU-68 seven-tube rocket pods, two AIM-9 Sidewinder air-to-air missiles and an ECM pod

Dimensions:
span	17.53 m (57 ft 6 in)
length	16.25 m (53 ft 4 in)
height	4.47 m (14 ft 8 in)
wing area	47.01 m² (506 sq ft)

ACTION DATA

WEAPON LOAD

The A-10A had an unmatched load-carrying ability in the CAS role, almost twice that of the Soviet's equivalent aircraft, the Sukhoi Su-25. The V/STOL Harrier is able to lift heavier loads with a short take-off than it can when taking off vertically.

7258 kg (16,000 lb) A-10A THUNDERBOLT II	
4400 kg (9700 lb) Su-25K 'FROGFOOT-A'	
4173 kg (9200 lb) HARRIER GR.Mk 7	

MAXIMUM SPEED

The Thunderbolt II has been criticised throughout its operational career as being too slow and vulnerable for its CAS role. Both the 'Frogfoot' and Harrier are capable of speeds of around 1000 km/h (620 mph) at sea level without a load.

A-10A THUNDERBOLT II	682 km/h (424 mph)
Su-25K 'FROGFOOT-A'	975 km/h (606 mph)
HARRIER GR.Mk 7	1065 km/h (662 mph)

TAKE-OFF DISTANCE

The STOL ability of the Harrier gives it an unbeatably short take-off run, although this limits the aircraft's load-carrying ability. At maximum take-off weight both the A-10 and Su-25 require about 1200 m (3937 ft) of runway to get airborne.

HARRIER GR.Mk 7	405 m (1329 ft)
Su-25K 'FROGFOOT-A'	1200 m (3937 ft)
A-10A THUNDERBOLT II	1220 m (4003 ft)

GENERAL DYNAMICS/MARTIN

RB-57F

● High altitude reconnaissance ● Active service life

▲ A dedicated high-altitude reconnaissance version of the Anglo/American Canberra with huge wings, the RB-57F became one of the most enduring symbols of the Cold War.

F lying at high altitude, photographing and observing activity behind the Iron Curtain in the 1960s, were the General Dynamics RB-57Fs of the 7907th Combat Support Wing, USAF. Developed to replace the grounded RB-57Ds, the new aircraft were built by General Dynamics and were all converted from earlier variants. They operated from bases around the world and provided Strategic Air Command with a highly capable reconnaissance platform.

GENERAL DYNAMICS/MARTIN RB-57F

▼ Spy in the sky
All specialist equipment, including cameras and sensors, was contained in a huge tray which fitted into the cavernous bomb bay. All of the RB-57s had been withdrawn by late 1974.

▲ Little in common
Although it retained the basic profile of earlier B-57 variants, the RB-57F was in essence an entirely new aircraft, with new wings, tail surfaces and engines. Only the original fuselage was retained.

▲ Cold War warriors
In their heyday, these aircraft were primarily employed on long-range missions probing the Iron and Bamboo Curtains.

▼ Extra power
The increased weight of the aircraft required greater thrust, RB-57s thus incorporated twin Pratt & Whitney P60 auxiliary turbojets outboard of the main turbofan engines.

▼ Massive wing
The enormous wing, which had a span of 37.31 m (122 ft) is evident in this shot of an early example.

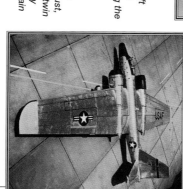

FACTS AND FIGURES

▶ The first RB-57Fs were used for intelligence gathering missions over Eastern Europe and the Soviet Union.

▶ The TF33 turbofans which powered the RB-57F were also used on 707 airliners.

▶ The podded auxiliary engines often seen under the wings were not always fitted.

▶ Serious wing fatigue problems on the earlier RB-57Ds resulted in the need for the improved reconnaissance variant.

▶ Later in their careers, the aircraft were used for Weather Reconnaissance.

▶ All crews who flew with the 58th WRS from Kirtland AFB were volunteers.

PROFILE

Sentinel Supreme

During the 1960s, at the height of the Cold War, strategic reconnaissance was seen as a vital instrument in the development of new national defences by both superpowers. A specialised version of the Canberra, the RB-57D began to enter service with Strategic Air Command (SAC) in 1956, and with its long span wings could fly at altitudes similar to those reached by the Lockheed U-2.

Structural problems with the wings resulted in the grounding of the D models in 1963, however, and as a result, a new version known as the RB-57F was developed to replace them. These aircraft were more

extensively redesigned and had huge Pratt & Whitney TF33 engines and longer noses, housing special radar equipment. The new variant began to enter service in 1964 and was operated primarily by the USAF 56th and 58th Weather Reconnaissance Squadrons. The former unit was stationed in Japan for several years and used its aircraft for air sampling and weather reconnaissance duties.

Besides their normal roles, RB-57Fs were also used to monitor contamination levels in the air in the aftermath of atomic test explosions. The last active USAF unit to fly the B-57 was the 58th Weather

Above: On the ground the RB-57F looked ungainly with the wings drooping considerably at rest. Wing bending loads at the wing roots were immense and, as for the D models, structural fatigue was always a problem during operations.

Right: Among the last examples in service, were the WB-57Fs (the 'W' signifying 'Weather') of the 58th WRS. Some RB-57Fs were in use as late as 1993, several examples serving with NASA's test fleet at Edwards AFB.

Reconnaissance Squadron (WRS). Later operated on behalf of various government agencies these aircraft soldiered on until the mid 1990s.

Throughout their career with Strategic Air Command the RB-57Fs remained in natural metal finish. Markings were large and colourful, unlike the TR-1s of recent times.

The cockpit was not very different from the standard B-57B bomber variant, both crew members sitting on upward-firing ejection sheets. Canopy shields helped to keep out sunlight at high altitude.

Forward- and side-mounted X-band radars were housed in the elongated nose. Different nose sections could be fitted depending on the role.

The special passive sensors were housed in the bomb bay. These included a large and powerful HIAC (High Altitude Camera) and various electronic devices.

A single Pratt & Whitney J60 auxiliary turbojet was fitted outboard of the main engine on each wing, and provided a useful 12.9 kN (22,900 lb thrust) of extra thrust.

Like the wings, the tail surfaces were massive, with the vertical stabiliser nearly double the size of that fitted to other variants. High altitude operations required a larger control surface area for effective directional stability.

WB-57F

By the late 1960s, the RB-57Fs were being used primarily for air sampling and weather reconnaissance duties and were thus re-designated as WB-57Fs. This example flew with the 58th WRS.

R/WB-57Fs were the only Canberra variants to be powered by these huge Pratt & Whitney TF33 turbofans. These were quieter and more economical than contemporary turbojets.

R/WB-57F

Type: two-seat high-altitude reconnaissance aircraft

Powerplant: two 71.17-kN (16,010-lb-thrust) Pratt & Whitney TF33-P11a turbofan engines, plus two 12.9-kN (2900-lb-thrust) Pratt & Whitney turbojets

Maximum speed: 777 km/h (482 mph)

Initial climb rate: 2316 m/min (7600 rpm)

Range: 5133 km (3180 miles)

Service ceiling: 19,507 m (64,000 ft)

Weights: empty 16,726 kg (36,797 lb); loaded 28,576 kg (62,867 lb)

Accommodation: one pilot and one navigator

Dimensions: span 37.31 m (122 ft)
length 21.03 m (69 ft)
height 5.79 m (19 ft)
wing area 185.8 m² (2000 sq ft)

ACTION DATA

RANGE

Long range enabled these aircraft to fly deep into foreign airspace and gave them excellent endurance. This range was achieved by placing huge fuel tanks in the wings or fuselage, thus considerable skill and effort from the pilot was required to get these leviathans into the air.

RB-57F 4830 km (3180 miles)
U-2C 6440 km (4000 miles)
Yak-25 'MANDRAKE' 7242 km (4490 miles)

MAXIMUM SPEED

Adding the TF33 engines, considerably improved the performance of the B-57, especially at high altitude where it was most needed. The Yakovlev Yak-25 was faster than both the U-2 and RB-57F and was an amazing aircraft, though it remains little known to this day.

RB-57F 805 km/h (482 mph)
U-2C 850 km/h (527 mph)
Yak-25 'MANDRAKE' 870 km/h (540 mph)

SERVICE CEILING

These aircraft flew at extreme altitudes and the crew were required to wear special high pressure g-suits and helmets. The U-2 flew so high, it could almost have been in orbit, though one was shot down during a spy flight over the Soviet Union in 1960.

U-2C 24,384 m (80,000 ft)
Yak-25 'MANDRAKE' 20,426 m (67,000 ft)
RB-57F 19,507 m (64,000 ft)

MASSIVE AREAS COVERED: The aircraft came from the 58th Weather Reconnaissance Squadron at Kirtland AFB, New Mexico. It repeatedly covered 116,550 km² (45,000 square miles)of ground using both colour and infra-red film.

Keeping an eye on the corn belt

DEADLY FUNGUS: America's midwestern 'corn belt' was badly effected by a fungus (known as corn blight) which destroyed 15 per cent of the US corn (maize) crop in 1970. To monitor the problem, radical measures were used.

RB-57 DRAFTED IN: Unsure of the extent of the problem, the US Department of Agriculture established the Corn Blight Watch Experiment in 1971. Using a number of aircraft types, large areas were photographed and huge amounts of data gathered for analysis. The most effective of the platforms used was an RB-57 of the USAF's Air Weather Service.

GENERAL DYNAMICS

F-111F

● Swing-wing strike fighter ● Gulf War precision laser-bomber

T he F-111F was the ultimate combat variant of the amazing General Dynamics F-111. Known to its pilots as the 'Aardvark', the F-111 has a slender fuselage, side-by-side seating and 'swing' wings. In its day it was a revolutionary warplane of unrivalled all-weather striking power, and the modern F-111F, with a Pave Tack targeting device bulging in its belly, could hit targets with uncanny accuracy.

▲ A Gulf War F-111 pilot checks the mighty TF30 turbofan. The F-111 was a superb performer in the Gulf, showing that after 20 years it remained almost unique in its long-range strike capability.

GENERAL DYNAMICS F-111F

▲ In-flight refuelling
The F-111 was designed to strike deep into Russia from bases in England. Fuelling in flight extended its range still further.

▲ Massive payload
Few attack aircraft had as many armament options as the 'Aardvark'. Together with the F-15E, it was the only aircraft capable of delivering the GBU-28 'bunker buster' used to devastating effect in the Gulf War.

▲ Precision strike
Key to the F-111's performance is its ability to carry a heavy load of laser-guided bombs, which are able to strike to within centimetres of a designated target.

Desert strike ▲
Carrying a large load of 'iron bombs', an F-111F heads for a target somewhere in Iraq.

▼ Capsule cockpit
Instead of having ejection seats, the entire cockpit of the F-111 detaches as a parachute-retarded escape capsule.

▲ Take-off position
The F-111's wings sweep forward for take-off and landing.

FACTS AND FIGURES

➤ The first F-111A made its maiden flight on 21 December 1964.

➤ The F-111 was originally called the TFX (Tactical Fighter Experimental).

➤ After a tragic start, F-111s returned to Vietnam in 1972 and flew 4,030 successful sorties in five months.

➤ The F-111F, with more powerful engines, improved avionics and Pave Tack, served with the USAF until July 1996.

➤ One F-111F was lost during the air attack on Libya in April 1986.

➤ The 66 F-111Fs at Taif in Saudi Arabia flew 4,000 sorties during the Gulf War.

PROFILE

'Aardvark' – the laser-bomber

The F-111 supersonic fighter-bomber was the world's first operational aircraft with a variable-sweep wing, and for two decades was the most advanced strike bomber. Introduced in 1968, it has flown in a number of versions, including the nuclear-armed FB-111A strategic bomber. Today, only the EF-111 electronic warfare model remains in US service.

The complex F-111 suffered a tortuous development process,

culminating in the F-111F. Although the earlier F-111D had more advanced electronics, the 'F' model was much more reliable. Above all, it had more powerful and fuel-efficient engines than previous variants.

The F-111F has seen more action than other 'Aardvarks'. It performed well in a long-range counter-terrorist strike against Libya in 1986. During Operation Desert Storm the F-111F was a workhorse, accurately delivering more precision ordnance than

any other warplane.

When they were retired in 1996 the F-111Fs were replaced by F-15E Eagles. The remaining airframes are in storage and could be returned to operational status in a time of crisis.

F-111F

The F-111Fs of the 48th Tactical Fighter Wing, based at RAF Lakenheath, were sent to the Taif airfield in Saudi Arabia during the 1991 Gulf War. They were arguably the most accurate and lethal bombers of the war.

The F-111 is still one of the fastest aircraft in the world at low level. The main factor limiting an F-111 pilot who wishes to run his aircraft flat-out is that the canopy would melt due to air friction heating after 10 minutes.

The multimode APQ-144 attack radar and the APQ-146 terrain-following radar allow the aircraft to fly terrain-hugging attacks at low level day or night, whatever the weather.

The Pave Tack pod housed in the weapons bay has a stabilised turret containing an infra-red sensor and a laser designator. It enabled the F-111F to drop laser-guided munitions autonomously at night.

Paveway III bombs have an advanced proportional guidance system, and are distinguishable from earlier laser-guided weapons by their long fixed noses.

The wing is swept to the forward position of 16° for landing and back to 72.5° for high speed.

The F-111F could carry up to 14,228 kg (31,367 lb) of ordnance on its underwing and under-fuselage hardpoints, including air-to-air missiles and Vulcan cannon pods.

A typical mission load included a pair of 'Paveway' 1000-kg (2200-lb) laser-guided bombs, two AIM-9 'Sidewinder' missiles for self-defence, and the huge AVQ-26 Pave Tack laser-designation turret mounted under

The F-111 may have a fighter designation, but it is an out-and-out attack aircraft. Pilot visibility to the rear is poor, but thanks to the downward slope of the nose the forward visibility is excellent for a fast strike aircraft.

The complex system of moving wing glove and variable inlets are designed to cope with the conflicting requirements of Mach 2 flight and variable-geometry wings.

The F-111 has a fuel emergency jettison pipe between the afterburner nozzles. Dumping fuel with afterburner on results in a spectacular 'torch'.

The GBU-24 is a BLU-109 907-kg (2000-lb) steel-jacketed penetration bomb fitted with a Paveway III laser-guidance kit.

The ALQ-131 jamming pod mounted on the rear fuselage gives the F-111F additional defence against hostile radar.

Chaff and flare dispensers are fitted on the underside of the tail. These were designed to decoy enemy radar-guided and heat-seeking missiles.

Pave Tack attack

DETECTION: An F-111F crew could detect their target visually via the infra-red sensor mounted in the Pave Tack turret under the fuselage. This allowed the attackers to acquire aiming points by day or by night at ranges of several kilometres.

WEAPONS RELEASE: The fire-control computer calculated the optimum point for dropping weapons. Releasing the bomb in a climb 'tossed' it further than would be possible in a level release or a diving attack.

ILLUMINATION: As the bomber turned away, the Pave Tack turret swivelled to keep the target in sight. Just before the weapon arrived, the F-111F illuminated the target with a laser beam onto which the bomb steered with deadly accuracy.

F-111F

Type: two-seat tactical strike fighter

Powerplant: two 111.65-kN (25,050-lb-thrust) Pratt & Whitney TF30-P-100 afterburning turbofans

Maximum speed: Mach 1.2 or 1468 km/h (910 mph) at sea level; 2655 km/h (1646 mph) clean at altitude

Radius of action: more than 2200 km (1365 miles)

Service ceiling: 18,300 m (60,000 ft)

Weights: empty 21,500 kg (47,300 lb); loaded 45,360 kg (99,792 lb)

Armament: up to 14,228 kg (31,302 lb) of ordnance, including bombs, missiles or gun pods. Normal tactical load of two or four precision-guided weapons plus AIM-9 Sidewinder missiles

Dimensions:
span   19.20 m (63 ft)
length   22.40 m (73 ft 6 in)
height   5.21 m (17 ft)
wing area   48.77 m² (525 sq ft)

COMBAT DATA

SPEED AT LOW LEVEL

The F-111F had one of the longest operational service lives of any modern combat jet and was also one of the world's fastest jets, especially at low level. With its wings swept back it could penetrate the air more cleanly, suffering less turbulence than most of its rivals.

F-15E EAGLE
1400 km/h (1678 mph)

F-111F
1468 km/h (910 mph)

Su-24 'FENCER'
1320 km/h (818 mph)

RANGE ON INTERNAL FUEL

The F-111F was designed at the height of the Cold War, and from the start was tasked with penetration missions. These involved flying very fast and very low through enemy air defences, striking at key command and communications targets deep inside enemy territory.

F-111F
4700 km (2914 miles)

Su-24 'FENCER'
2000 km (1240 miles)

F-15E EAGLE
2500 km (995 miles)

WEAPONS LOAD

The F-111F's internal bomb-bay was designed to carry two nuclear bombs or missiles. However, it usually housed a cannon pod or a Pave Tack guidance pod. But the bomb-bay was only part of the story. More than 14 tonnes of weaponry could be carried on six swivelling underwing pylons.

F-111F

F-15E EAGLE

Su-24 'FENCER'

GRUMMAN
J2F Duck

- Early Grumman amphibian ● Pacific rescue missions ● USCG service

T his new family of single-engined biplane amphibians was among Grumman's first designs. The US Navy of the mid-1930s immediately found them ideally suited to utility duties aboard aircraft-carriers. Grumman Ducks were somewhat awkward-looking, but highly functional flying machines. Built by Grumman and Columbia, JF and J2F Ducks served with distinction in the Pacific island-fighting campaign during World War II, and around the world.

▲ Grumman's G-20 Duck design paved the way for a number of monoplane amphibian designs, beginning with the twin-engined G-21 Goose of 1937. Examples of each are still flying today.

GRUMMAN J2F DUCK

▼ Coast Guard JF-2
Grumman's first amphibious design, the JF, made its maiden flight in 1933. From 1936, the type equipped US Navy utility squadrons aboard US Navy aircraft-carriers. The JF-2 rescue variant was built for the USCG.

▲ Preserved J2F-6
This preserved airworthy example of the J2F-6, built by Columbia Aircraft, wears the pre-war markings of Navy utility squadron VJ-4.

US Navy photo-ship ▲
Seen in 1942 colours, this J2F-5 also carries the markings of an Atlantic Fleet air photographic unit.

▲ First US Navy deliveries
BuNo. 0162 was the first J2F-1 delivered to the US Navy, arriving at Naval Air Station, Anacostia, in April 1936.

▲ Duck!
J2F tasks included target-towing, for which this Duck is equipped.

FACTS AND FIGURES

► The Duck was the first aircraft built after Leroy Grumman left Loening Aircraft to form his own company.

► Columbia Aircraft was still building these amphibians when World War II ended.

► Argentina, Colombia and Mexico received Ducks in the 1930s and 1940s.

► Between 1942 and 1945, US Navy and Marines Ducks rescued downed aircrew from the battle for Guadalcanal.

► A J2F-5 and five J2F-6s were operated by the USAF as OA-12s for air-sea rescue.

► As the Japanese invaded the Philippines, US Navy J2F-5s rescued VIPs.

PROFILE

First of the Grumman amphibians

After the attack on Pearl Harbor on 7 December 1941, a lone Grumman Duck set forth to search for the Japanese fleet, its radio operator armed with a bolt-action Springfield rifle. The single-engined Grumman Duck biplane was neither a fighter nor a bomber, but it found itself in action more than once in the Pacific. And, at the time of the US entry into World War II in 1941, the Duck was unique as the only biplane still in production for a US Navy operational role.

When originally ordered into production in 1932, these amphibians (JF-1 to JF-3 and

J2F-1 to J2F-6) were deemed quite advanced, with their all-metal construction and relatively clean lines. The US Navy, Marines and Coast Guard employed them for a variety of utility missions. Under pressure to deliver naval fighters and attack aircraft, Grumman transferred production to the nearby plant of the Columbia Aircraft Corporation.

Post-war, Ducks saw limited use and some were assigned to US Army Air Forces. A few have been preserved.

Above: USCG JFs and J2Fs served until the early 1950s, when they were phased out after some 17 years of service.

Below: At the US Navy's request, J2F-6 production was transferred to Columbia Aircraft on Long Island.

The first JF-1 Ducks were powered by a Pratt & Whitney R-1830 Twin Wasp 14-cylinder radial engine driving a three-bladed propeller. However, JF-2s for the Coast Guard were fitted with Wright R-1820 Cyclone 9s. This engine became the standard Duck powerplant, the J2F-6 having a 783-kW (1050-hp) R-1820-54.

Ducks shared airframe design features, such as a semi-monocoque fuselage, with Grumman's first fighter design, the XFF-1.

As the US Navy's Ducks were intended for utility transport duties aboard aircraft-carriers, providing a ship-to-shore link, they were fitted with arrester hooks for deck recovery.

The large central amphibian float was faired into the J2F's fuselage. The fuselage had sufficient room for two passenger seats. The seats could be replaced with a stretcher in the casualty evacuation role.

Two or three crewmembers were carried aboard the US Navy's Ducks – apart from the pilot, there was an observer and, if required, a radio operator. The rear cockpit had provision for a 7.62-mm (.30-cal) machine gun, but this was seldom fitted. Two wing bomb racks were installed from the outset; in the J2F-5 and J2F-6, they were each able to carry a 147-kg (325-lb) depth charge or bomb.

J2F-6 Duck

Columbia Aircraft built 330 J2F-6s, production ending in August 1945. In World War II, Pacific-based US Navy and Marine Corps J2Fs flew air-sea rescue missions.

Grumman's amphibian family

■ **G-44 WIDGEON:** Grumman's first twin-engined design, the G-21, flew in May 1937. In all, 345 were built for military and civil users. Wartime aircraft served with the USN, USCG and RAF.

■ **G-21 GOOSE:** Grumman flew the Widgeon, which was cheaper than the Goose, in June 1940. Early examples saw military service; some civil G-44s remain airworthy today.

■ **G-73 MALLARD:** An enlarged variation of the G-21 Goose design, the Mallard, first took to the air in 1946. All 59 built went to civil users, except for two received by the Egyptian air force in 1949.

■ **G-64/G-111 ALBATROSS:** Large numbers of this air-sea rescue amphibian, first flown in 1947, were delivered to the USN and USAF. Anti-submarine warfare versions were exported.

J2F-6 Duck

Type: two/three-seat utility amphibian

Powerplant: one 783-kW (1050-hp) Wright R-1820-54 Cyclone 9 nine-cylinder radial piston engine

Maximum speed: 306 km/h (190 mph)

Cruising speed: 249 km/h (154 mph)

Initial climb rate: 405 m/min (1328 fpm)

Maximum range: 1370 km (850 miles)

Normal range: 1085 km (673 miles)

Service ceiling: 8140 m (26,700 ft)

Weights: empty 2470 kg (5430 lb); maximum take-off 3307 kg (7290 lb)

Armament: usually unarmed, although provision was made for one 7.62-mm (.30-cal.) machine gun in rear cockpit and up to 294 kg (647 lb) of bombs or depth charges

Dimensions:
span	11.89 m	(40 ft)
length	10.36 m	(34 ft)
height	3.76 m	(12 ft 4 in)
wing area	38.00 m²	(409 sq ft)

ACTION DATA

CRUISING SPEED

Grumman's Duck had a good turn of speed, although this was marginally less than that of the Arado Ar 196. Aichi's 'Jake' was a significantly slower machine.

J2F-6 DUCK	249 km/h (165 mph)
Ar 196A-3	267 km/h (166 mph)
E13A1a 'JAKE'	222 km/h (138 mph)

POWER

Duck amphibians and 'Jake' floatplanes had a similar power rating. The Arado had a smaller engine, but was a smaller, lighter machine without the need for a powerful engine.

J2F-6 DUCK	783 kW (1050 hp)
Ar 196A-3	716 kW (960 hp)
E13A1a 'JAKE'	790 kW (1060 hp)

RANGE

The Japanese Aichi E13A design had a healthy 2000-km (1300-mile) range, useful for its naval reconnaissance role. Like the Duck and Ar 196, the E13A was employed from both ships and shore bases. Both the Arado and Aichi were float-plane designs; the J2F was a more versatile amphibian, able to operate from aircraft-carriers and land.

Ar 196A-3	800 km (496 miles)
J2F-6 DUCK	1207 km (748 miles)
E13A1a 'JAKE'	2090 km (1296 miles)

GRUMMAN
F2F/F3F

- Single-seater ● Carrier based ● Last USN biplane fighter

A natural development of the FF1 two-seat naval fighter of 1931, Grumman proposed a single-seat fighter, the F2F, in 1932. The larger F3F followed in 1934 and was destined to be the last biplane fighter ordered by the US Navy for delivery in 1937/38. These tubby biplanes, with their characteristic retractable landing gear (a Grumman patented design), were to keep the biplane era alive in the American fleet until late in 1940.

▲ The famous 'Fighting Two' squadron based on the USS Lexington flew F2F and F3F 'Flying Barrels' continuously from 1935 until 1940.

174

GRUMMAN F2F/F3F

▼ **Fleet fighter**
When the last F3F-2 was accepted in May 1938, all seven US Navy and Marine Corps fighter squadrons operated Grumman single-seaters. This situation lasted until December 1939.

▲ **Top guns**
The Mk III Mod 4 telescopic gunsight was mounted on top of the cowling, projecting forward from the small windscreen, for the two fixed, forward-firing (through the propeller) 7.62-mm (.30-cal.) Browning machine guns that were fitted in the upper fuselage.

▼ **Last US Navy biplane fighter**
The bigger and more powerful F3F was the US Navy's basic carrier-borne fighter until the early-1940s. This F3F-2 served with VMF-2 Squadron.

▲ **New factory**
When 27 FF-1s were ordered, Grumman rented a new factory at Farmingdale to build them.

▼ **Red Rippers**
Production of 55 F2F-1s ended in October 1935, with nine aircraft going to VF-5B 'Red Rippers'.

FACTS AND FIGURES

▶ The F2F and F3F were stressed to 9g, similar to that of the F-16 and F/A-18.

▶ Grumman's unique undercarriage design on the F2F/F3F became a distinctive feature of the F4F Wildcat carrier fighter.

▶ The first aircraft-carrier to have the F2F on board was the USS Lexington in 1935.

▶ Grumman delivered the last F2F in August 1935 and F3F in May 1939.

▶ The first two XF3Fs were destroyed in high-speed dives, the airframe being strengthened for production aircraft.

▶ A total of 140 F2Fs and F3Fs remained in service as station hacks in 1942.

PROFILE

The US Navy's 'Flying Barrels'

Taking the nickname 'Flying Barrel' on account of its deep forward fuselage and engine cowling, the Grumman biplane fighter was a legend in its time. The mainstay of the US carrier force immediately before World War II, it provided many young aviators, who would later hold command positions, with a sound training in shipboard fighter operations.

Starting life as the Grumman G-8 (later XF2F), the F2F-1 first entered service in 1935. One of the Navy's most illustrious fighter squadrons, VF-2B 'Fighting Two', helped prove the

aircraft, which had a production run of 54.

Before the F2F entered service, Grumman anticipated future Navy requirements and secured orders for its G-11 (F3F). Similar to its predecessor, it had a longer fuselage and increased wingspan to enhance handling qualities. The first two XF3Fs crashed during flight tests, but an order for 35 F3F-1s was confirmed.

A larger diameter Cyclone engine powered the F3F-2 and

this was the subject of an order for 81 aircraft for 1937/38 delivery. More engine power and other improvements produced the F3F-3, 27 of which were built. Few better tributes could be made to these biplanes than the longevity of service and late phase-out date of November 1943.

F3F-2s used the 708-kW (950-hp) Wright R1820-22 Cyclone nine-cylinder single-row radial air-cooled engine.

Two 7.62-mm (.30-cal) Browning machine guns were mounted forward of the cockpit and fired through the propeller arc

Left: This F3F carries the 'M' prefix to the squadron letter ('F') denoting a Marine Corps aircraft. In this case the aircraft belongs to Marine Fighter Squadron Two (VMF-2), indicated by the '2' prefix.

After front-line service the F3F-1s were used for pilot training at NAS Norfolk and Miami until February 1941.

F3F-2

With a more powerful Wright engine, the F3F-2 was the ultimate 'Flying Barrel'. This version had an improved speed, climb rate and performance range.

Compared to the F2F, the F3F's fuselage was nearly 0.5 m (1 ft 7 in) longer, the wingspan was increased by 1.07 m (3 ft 6 in) and it had a slightly bigger tail unit; improved handling was the goal.

F3F-2 '1009' was one of a relatively small number of F3Fs to serve with the US Marine Corps units, in this case VMF-1.

The tube ahead of the pilot's windscreen is a Mk III Mod 4 telescopic gunsight.

Grumman's patent undercarriage had the mainwheels retracting into the fuselage behind the engine.

Watertight compartments in the lower fuselage provided flotation during an emergency water landing.

Grumman's naval fighters

■ **SF-1:** The US Navy ordered 33 SF-1 (G-6) scouts in 1932, the first being delivered to Squadron VS-3B 'Scouting Three' based on USS *Lexington* on 30 March 1934.

■ **F2F-1:** The first single-seat fighter from Grumman, the all-metal F2F-1 entered service with VF-2 aboard USS *Lexington* in January 1935, serving until 1940.

■ **F4F WILDCAT:** One of the great naval fighters of World War II and the last monoplanes produced by Grumman, the XF4F was initially flown in February 1939 and was soon ordered.

F3F

Type: single-seat carrier fighter/bomber

Powerplant: one 708-kW (950-hp) Wright R1820-2Z Cyclone air-cooled engine

Maximum speed: 425 km/h (264 mph)

Initial climb rate: 701 m/min (2300 fpm)

Range: 1328 km (824 miles)

Service ceiling: 9205 m (30,200 ft)

Weights: empty 1478 kg (3252 lb); loaded 2042 kg (4492 lb)

Armament: two 7.62-mm (.30-cal.) Browning machine guns, plus two 52.6-kg (115-lb) bombs

Dimensions:
span	9.75 m (32 ft)
length	7.07 m (23 ft 3 in)
height	2.84 m (9 ft 4 in)
wing area	24.15 m² (260 sq ft)

COMBAT DATA

MAXIMUM SPEED

Grumman's reputation as a builder of fighters for the US Navy was just developing during the 1930s, the F3F going some way towards its enhancement. The F3F was a relatively quick aircraft, though the days of the biplane were numbered.

F3F	425 km/h (264 mph)
GLADIATOR	414 km/h (257 mph)
P-26 PEASHOOTER	377 km/h (234 mph)

RANGE

Naval aircraft must possess good range performance because of the nature of their operation, often some distance from an aircraft-carrier. Long range allows a good radius of operation and an increased time spent patrolling the skies on the lookout for enemy aircraft that may threaten the fleet. Both the P-26 and Gladiator were land-based machines.

GLADIATOR 710 km (440 miles)

P-26 PEASHOOTER 579 km (358 miles)

F3F 1328 km (825 miles)

ARMAMENT

By American standards the F3F was typically armed with two machine guns, while the British Gladiator demonstrates that fighter types of the period were generally better armed. This trend continued into the early years of World War II. Higher calibre machine guns then became the norm.

F3F 2 x 7.62-mm (.30-cal.) machine guns

GLADIATOR 4 x 7.7-mm (.303-cal.) machine guns

P-26 PEASHOOTER 2 x 7.62-mm (.30-cal.) machine guns

GRUMMAN
F4F WILDCAT

● Carrier-based fighter bomber ● Pacific War hero ● Royal Navy service

W ildcat squadrons used by the American Marines and Navy made their stand against Japan's superior Mitsubishi A6M Zero. While the Zero held the advantage in performance, the Wildcat achieved its greatness in part due to the exceptional men who flew it. As Foster Hailey of the *New York Times* said in 1943:

'The Grumman Wildcat, it is no exaggeration to say, did more than any single instrument of war to save the day in the Pacific.'

▲ The American F4F was exported to the Royal Navy for operation aboard its carriers, and was for a while designated the Grumman Martlet until the service returned to the name Wildcat.

PHOTO FILE

GRUMMAN F4F WILDCAT

▲ Carrier battlegroup protector
The Wildcat shared the decks of the US Navy's Pacific carriers in the early battles of the war with other classic types such as the Douglas Dauntless, Grumman Avenger and later the Vought Corsair.

Fleet Air Arm fighter ▶
The Royal Navy's first American fighter, the Wildcat was greatly respected.

▲ Carrier operations
With its folding wings and catapult gear the Wildcat was a dedicated carrier fighter both with the US Navy and the Royal Navy. However, the F4F also saw action from land bases.

▲ Grumman heritage
The Wildcat was one of a long line of Grumman-built naval fighters, from the F3F to today's F-14 Tomcat.

▲ Pacific warrior
Until it started being replaced by the Hellcat from 1943, the Wildcat was the US Navy's most important fighter. This example carries the markings of fighter squadron VF-41. The red centre of the national marking was deleted from late 1942.

FACTS AND FIGURES

▶ Total production was 7825 Wildcats, including 1988 Grumman F4Fs and 5837 General Motors FMs.

▶ The Wildcat was first flown by Robert L. Hall on 2 September 1937.

▶ Fleet Air Arm Wildcats were the remnant of orders by France and Greece.

▶ A long-range reconnaissance version of the Wildcat was effective but was quickly replaced by a photo-reconnaissance F6F.

▶ Top Wildcat ace was Major John L. Smith who shot down 19 Japanese warplanes.

▶ Wildcats were also used by the Royal Canadian Air Force and US Marines.

Grumman's fleet defender

In the 1930s the US Navy mistakenly chose the Brewster Buffalo over the Grumman F4F Wildcat. By the 1941 Pearl Harbor attack, however, the decision was reversed: the Wildcat replaced Navy biplane fighters and battled Japanese Zeros in the Pacific. A far better fighter than the Brewster, the Wildcat did not meet the standards of the Japanese Zero but it contributed mightily to the American war effort. Lieutenant Edward 'Butch' O'Hare, flying an

F4F, shot down five Japanese bombers in five minutes to become the first US Navy ace.

The Wildcat was sturdy and very manoeuvrable. It was not the easiest aircraft to fly but, once mastered, was incredibly responsive. Most Wildcats were manufactured by General Motors as the FM-2. Some went to Britain's Royal Navy, which called it the Martlet.

This portly, mid-winged fighter made a vital contribution:

A rugged and powerful Wright Cyclone engine gave the F4F a good power-to-weight ratio. The two-stage blower sometimes caused problems and was replaced by a single-stage model.

The F4F was heavily armed with no less than six wing machine guns. Although not as powerful as cannon, they were quite adequate against most Japanese opposition.

F4F-4 Wildcat

Type: single-seat carrier-based fighter

Powerplant: one 895-kW (1200-hp) Wright R-1830-36 Cyclone radial piston engine

Maximum speed: 512 km/h (317 mph)

Cruising speed: 249 km/h (154 mph)

Range: 1239 km (768 miles)

Service ceiling: 12,010 m (39,400 ft)

Weights: empty 2612 kg (5746 lb); maximum take-off 3607 kg (7935 lb)

Armament: six fixed 12.7-mm (.50-cal.) Browning air-cooled machine guns with 240 rounds per gun plus two 45-kg (100-lb) bombs

Dimensions: span   11.60 m (38 ft)
length   8.50 m (28 ft)
height   3.60 m (12 ft)
wing area   24.15 m² (260 sq ft)

COMBAT DATA

MAXIMUM SPEED

The power of engines and improved aerodynamics during the 1940s led to a consistently higher maximum speed of the F4F over its predecessor the F3F, and the F6F over the Wildcat which it replaced in US Navy squadron service.

F4F-4 WILDCAT	512 km/h (317 mph)
F3F	425 km/h (263 mph)
F6F HELLCAT	612 km/h (379 mph)

RANGE

Surprisingly, the F4F had less impressive range than the earlier F3F, due to its fuel thirsty and powerful engine and the efficiency of the F3F's wing. The F6F had greater range because of the addition of an underfuselage tank and new powerplant.

F4F-4 WILDCAT 1239 km (768 miles)

F6F HELLCAT 1674 km (1038 miles)

F3F 1577 km (978 miles)

ARMAMENT

The Wildcat introduced much improved armament over the F3F, the six Browning 12.7-mm machine guns (retained on the later Grumman Hellcat) having long range and a hard punch.

F4F-4 WILDCAT 6 x 12.7-mm (.50-cal.) machine guns

F6F HELLCAT 6 x 12.7-mm (.50-cal.) machine guns

F3F 2 x 7.62-mm (.30-cal.) machine guns

The pilot was protected by thick armour behind the cockpit, bulletproof glass ahead and the massive engine in front of him.

All-metal vacuum operated split trailing-edge flaps were fitted.

A US Navy Wildcat drops its tailhook in order to catch the wire aboard the deck of a carrier in the Pacific.

Wing tanks contained 606 litres (158 gallons) of aviation gasoline, and were self sealing.

outnumbered and outgunned, it held the line until the most successful naval fighter in history, the Grumman F6F Hellcat, became available to turn the tide of the Pacific War.

The cockpit was rather cramped and visibility was not great, but the problems were resolved on Grumman's F4F replacement, the F6F Hellcat. Immediately behind the pilot was a Mk 1A liferaft.

F4F-4 WILDCAT

The F4F was heavily involved in Operation Torch in November 1942, the codename for the important Allied invasion of French North Africa.

This F4F carries early intermediate markings. The red spot has been removed from the centre of the star, but the yellow recognition circle around the roundel has yet to be applied.

The undercarriage design was little changed from that on inter-war Grumman biplanes, with the mainwheels only half retracting to lie flat against the lower fuselage in a shallow well.

Wildcats over Wake Island

AERIAL PATROL: Flying in close formation on interception duties above the clouds, the Wake Island Wildcats did not catch sight of the attacking Japanese aircraft because of the bad weather.

AIRBASE ASSAULT: After evading the attentions of the defending F4Fs, the Japanese aircraft were free to bomb Wake's air base and destroy most of the island's 12 Wildcats before they had time to react.

REVENGE: The four Wildcats which had not been on the ground during the raid were able to attack the invading Japanese fleet, and managed to sink two destroyers.

GRUMMAN

TBF/TBM AVENGER

● Three-seat torpedo-bomber ● Battle of Midway veteran

Grumman's portly TBF Avenger (built by Eastern Aircraft as the TBM) was the most important American torpedo-bomber of World War II. Big, noisy and powerful, the Avenger flew from carrier decks and spanned vast Pacific distances to attack the Japanese Navy with its torpedo or bombs. The Avenger had staying power, with many Allied nations using the type long after the war. US Navy Avengers were still on hand for transport duty in the Korean War.

▲ Avengers saw their first combat in the Battle of Midway in June 1942. Although their losses were high, production was stepped up, with nearly 10,000 being built in several variants before the war ended.

178

GRUMMAN **TBF/TBM AVENGER**

▲ **Royal Navy Avengers**
This TBF-1 (Avenger Mk I) flew with the Fleet Air Arm's No. 846 Squadron. FAA aircraft were carrier and land based.

▲ **Flying on into the 1990s**
A number of Avengers have survived to be restored by enthusiasts. In service until the 1950s, some surplus aircraft were converted into water bombers and were used to fight forest fires for many years. Some of the restored aircraft are ex-fire bombers.

▲ **Barrel shaped**
For a single-engined aircraft the TBM was fairly big. The same engine was fitted to the B-25 Mitchell bomber.

▲ **Airborne early warning**
To provide early warning protection for USN carriers the TBM-3W, with its large radome, entered service after the war.

▲ **Carrier-borne**
A US Navy Avenger lumbers off the deck of a carrier. The bulk of Avengers were built by General Motors (Eastern Division) as Grumman was fully committed to building fighters for the Navy.

FACTS AND FIGURES

► US President George Bush was the youngest naval aviator when he flew Avengers in combat in the Pacific.

► Avenger production totalled 9,839; 7,546 by General Motors, the rest by Grumman.

► The TBF was initially called the 'Tarpon' in the Royal Navy and later the 'Avenger'.

► When used against submarines, Avengers destroyed or shared in the destruction of 42 U-boats.

► Avengers used the first high-velocity aircraft rockets (HVARs) in January 1944.

► Six TBFs saw action in the Battle of Midway on 4 June 1942; only one returned.

PROFILE

General Motors torpedo truck

Grumman Iron Works was a nickname for the company that designed the Avenger. Grumman created shipboard aircraft that were sturdy, heavy and tough. When it replaced the inadequate Douglas TBD Devastator as the US Navy's torpedo-bomber in the Pacific, the Grumman Avenger had the strength and power to do the job.

However, as Grumman was busy fulfilling large orders for fighters, the job of constructing the bulk of the Avenger order

was subcontracted to the Eastern Aircraft Division of the General Motors Corporation.

Despite a poor start at the 1942 Battle of Midway, the Avenger performed superbly through to the end of the war and, in addition to torpedo bombing, took on other roles including close air support of ground troops.

The Avenger was pleasant to fly, although spinning was prohibited. When flown with determination by a strong pilot, it could almost turn like a fighter,

hence its single, and later twin, forward-firing gun armament.

Britain (921 aircraft) and New Zealand (63) also used Avengers during the war. Canada, France, Japan and the Netherlands employed it after 1945.

TBM-1 (AVENGER Mk II)

As well as the US Navy, Britain's Fleet Air Arm and the Royal New Zealand Air Force operated Avengers during World War II.

Power for the Avenger was supplied by Wright's big R-2600 Cyclone 14 radial engine. Three main fuel tanks were fitted with a total capacity of 1248 litres (330 gallons).

TBF-1 Avenger

Type: three-seat carrier-based torpedo-bomber

Powerplant: one 1268-kW (1700-hp) Wright R-2600-8 Cyclone 14-cylinder radial piston engine

Maximum speed: 436 km/h (270 mph) at 5030 m (15,000 ft)

Climb rate: 435 m/min (1425 fpm)

Range: 1778 km (1100 miles)

Service ceiling: 6830 m (22,400 ft)

Weights: empty 4788 kg (10,534 lb); maximum take-off 7876 kg (17,327 lb)

Armament: (TBF-1C) two fixed forward-firing 12.7-mm (.50-cal.) machine guns; one 12.7-mm machine gun in rear turret, one 7.62-mm (.30-cal.) machine gun in ventral position; 907 kg (2000 lb) of bombs or one torpedo in internal bomb-bay

Dimensions: span   16.51 m (54 ft 2 in)
         length   12.20 m (40 ft)
         height   5.00 m (16 ft 5 in)
         wing area   45.52 m² (490 sq ft)

COMBAT DATA

ARMAMENT

The Avenger was in every way an improvement over the TBD. Its gun armament was significantly greater and it could deliver twice the weight of bombs or a larger torpedo. The B6N was lightly armed.

TBD-1 DEVASTATOR
2 x 7.62-mm (.30-cal.) machine guns
454 kg (1000 lb) of bombs/torpedoes

TBF-1 AVENGER
3 x 12.7-mm (.50-cal.) machine guns
1 x 7.62-mm (.30-cal.) machine gun
907 kg (2000 lb) of bombs/torpedoes

B6N TENZAN
2 x 7.7-mm (.303-cal.) machine guns
800 kg (1760 lb) of bombs/torpedo

MAXIMUM SPEED

The TBF had a 100 km/h speed advantage over the TBD. The more streamlined B6N was faster still, due to its more powerful engine and lighter weight. The B6N was intensively used in the last two years of the war, latterly as kamikaze aircraft.

TBD-1 DEVASTATOR   332 km/h (206 mph)
TBF-1 AVENGER   436 km/h (270 mph)
B6N TENZAN   480 km/h (298 mph)

RANGE

With well over twice the range of the TBD, the TBF still lagged far behind the equivalent Japanese design. Range is a very important attribute for a carrier-based aircraft. The B6N's long range allowed it to strike first in a carrier battle.

TBD-1 DEVASTATOR 669 km (415 miles)
TBF-1 AVENGER 1778 km (1100 miles)
B6N TENZAN 3045 km (1890 miles)

Above: The Avenger's weapons bay was big enough for a torpedo or 907-kg bomb. The prototype first flew on 1 August 1941.

Above: A Royal Navy Avenger aboard HMS Illustrious. Thirty-three first- and second-line FAA squadrons were equipped with the Avenger, which served from numerous carriers and shore bases from Canada to the Far East.

Avenger Mk II serial number JZ490 was based in Britain in mid 1944 and carried the black and white identification stripes worn by Allied aircraft during the invasion of Europe.

The ventral machine-gun position was occupied by the bomb-aimer. The hydraulically operated bomb-bay doors could be controlled by the bomb-aimer or the pilot.

To ease stowage aboard aircraft-carriers the Avenger had hydraulically folding wings. The main undercarriage retracted into the wings; the rear wheel also retracted. The arrester hook was electrically operated.

Two crewmembers sat in the long cockpit 'glasshouse': the pilot, who also fired the wing guns and released the torpedo, and the radio operator, who also manned the rear gun turret.

NAVY 490

Post-war Avengers

■ **CANADIAN NAVY TBM-3E:** The Canadian navy was one of several to receive Avengers under the Mutual Assistance Program after World War II. Another was the former enemy, Japan.

■ **FIRE BOMBER:** As the TBF/TBM was retired by the US Navy in the 1950s, surplus aircraft found other uses. This example is one of a number used as water bombers in Canada and the US.

■ **CROP SPRAYER:** Another role for the civilian Avenger in Canada was that of forest or agricultural crop sprayer. In New Zealand experimental crop dusting was tried with Avengers.

GRUMMAN
F6F HELLCAT

- Fleet carrier aircraft ● Naval strike-fighter ● Used by US Navy aces

T he Hellcat is one of the few aircraft in history which was right from the start. Designed after Pearl Harbor, the Hellcat required almost no testing or development work before being rushed into production. Swarms of these beefy, gloss-blue fighters wrested control of Pacific skies from the vaunted Japanese Zero and chalked up a record of success in air combat that has rarely been matched.

▲ Most of the US Navy's wartime aces notched up their kills using the tough and manoeuvrable F6F. Lieutenant Hanks was a Hellcat ace, shooting down five Japanese aircraft in just one month.

▼ **Take-off flag**
Lieutenant John Clarke gives the take-off signal flag to an F6F pilot. Taking off with the canopy open meant that it was easy to escape if the aircraft ditched after leaving the ship.

▲ **Radar goes to sea**
Later Hellcats had advanced instruments such as radio altimeters and radar.

▲ **Strike Hellcat**
Hellcats served on with France after the war, and saw extensive action in Indochina.

▼ **Crowded decks**
The US Navy's carriers carried more aircraft than could be hangared, and many Hellcats were parked on deck alongside Avengers and SBDs.

▲ **Spreading wings**
Like most naval fighters, the Hellcat had folding wings. They used the typical Grumman feature of swivelling back to lie each side of the fuselage.

FACTS AND FIGURES

▶ The XF6F-1 prototype made its first flight on 26 June 1942.

▶ Of 6,477 aerial victories claimed by US Navy pilots during World War II, 4,947 were credited to F6F Hellcat pilots.

▶ On 3 April 1944, Royal Navy Hellcats attacked the *Tirpitz* at Kaafjord, Norway.

▶ Grumman made 12,275 Hellcats at its New York plant between June 1942 and November 1945, the largest number of fighters ever produced at a single factory.

▶ F6F-3K drones gathered particles from atomic clouds during the 1946 nuclear tests at Bikini atoll.

PROFILE

King of the carrier fighters

The sturdy, powerful F6F Hellcat is one of the few fighters developed after the outbreak of World War II to succeed in that conflict. A big, heavy machine in an age when experts lauded small, light fighters, the Hellcat was fast enough and agile enough to become the outstanding dogfighter of the Pacific war.

Pilots also praised the strength of the F6F, which they jokingly called a product of the 'Grumman Iron Works' because they knew that sustaining damage in combat no longer meant certain death. The Hellcat could and did bring its pilot home.

This remarkable aircraft also proved its merit as a night-fighter

(using early radar) and a reconnaissance aircraft. Britain employed the Hellcat throughout the East Indies, Malaya, Burma and in the final assault on Japan. Half a decade later, the Hellcat was all but gone from U.S. service when the final examples were used as unmanned flying bombs – the Korean War's equivalent of today's cruise missile.

Two of the elements which won the Pacific War: the F6F Hellcat aboard an 'Essex'-class carrier.

F6F-5 HELLCAT

This Hellcat was flown by fighter squadron VF-27 from the light carrier USS *Princeton*, sunk during the Battle of Leyte Gulf in October 1944.

The F6F was powered by the 18-cylinder Pratt & Whitney Double Wasp engine, one of the largest piston powerplants available during World War II.

This VF-27 fighter is armed for a ground-attack mission, with bombs and 127-mm (5-in) high-explosive rockets.

The fin and tailplanes were built around very strong central spars. The aircraft itself was extremely strong, and could survive substantial battle damage.

The F6F was strongly built. For added protection, it was equipped with a self-sealing fuel tank and a tough sheet of armour to protect the pilot.

On internal fuel the F6F had a combat radius of 800 km (500 miles), but this could be extended by the use of external tanks.

Like the rest of the fighter, the undercarriage was extremely tough to withstand repeated carrier landings.

Battle of the Philippine Sea

Fought on 19 and 20 June 1944, the Battle of the Philippine Sea saw the final elimination of Japanese carrier air power as a factor in the Pacific war. An American invasion fleet was approaching the Mariana Islands; capture of the islands would give the USA air bases from which its bombers could strike direct at the Japanese homeland. It was the task of the Imperial Navy to stop the landings and defeat the US Pacific fleet.

FIRST MOBILE FLEET: On 15 June three fleet carriers and six light carriers sail from Japanese bases in the Philippines 800 km (500 miles) west.

INVASION FORCE: On 11 June the American amphibious fleet approaches from the east, guarded by the massive Task Force 58 – seven battleships and no less than 15 carriers. After destroying the Japanese fighters on the islands, TF 58 moves to guard the landings from the Japanese fleet approaching from the Philippines.

HEAVY LOSSES: Japanese aircraft are shot out of the sky by F6F Hellcats. 253 Japanese fighters lost for 30 American.

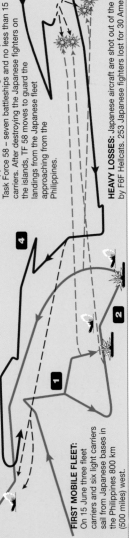

SAIPAN

TINIAN

GUAM

1. **19 JUNE** Japanese fleet divides to launch air attack

2. **19 JUNE** Carriers *Taiho* and *Shokaku* sunk by US submarines

3. **19 JUNE** Japanese air power annihilated, fleet withdraws

4. **20 JUNE** Pursuing US fleet launches air strike

5. **20 JUNE** US aircraft sink one carrier and damage three

F6F-5 Hellcat

Type: single-seat carrier-based fighter

Powerplant: one 1492-kW (2000-hp) Pratt & Whitney R-2800-10W Double Wasp 18-cylinder radial piston engine

Maximum speed: 620 km/h (380 mph) at medium altitude

Range: 1675 km (1040 miles)

Service ceiling: 11,500 m (37,500 ft)

Weights: empty 4191 kg (9200 lb); loaded 6991 kg (15,400 lb)

Armament: six 12.7-mm (.50-cal.) Browning M2 machine guns with 400 rounds each; two or three bombs up to maximum of 907 kg (2000 lb); and six 127-mm (5-in) HVAR (High-Velocity Aircraft Rockets)

Dimensions: span   13.08 m (42 ft 10 in)
length   10.23 m (33 ft 7 in)
height   3.99 m (13 ft 1 in)
wing area   31.03 m² (334 sq ft)

COMBAT DATA

MAXIMUM SPEED

F6F-5 HELLCAT	620 km/h (380 mph)
A6M5 ZERO	570 km/h (355 mph)
P-38J LIGHTNING	666 km/h (415 mph)

The Hellcat was not particularly fast by European standards, and it was outperformed by US land-based fighters like the P-38. But it had a significant advantage over its main rival in the Pacific, the previously all-conquering Mitsubishi Zero.

ARMAMENT

F6F-5 HELLCAT
6 x 12.7-mm (.50-cal.) machine guns

A6M5 ZERO
2 x 20-mm cannon
2 x 13-mm machine guns

P-38J LIGHTNING
1 x 20-mm cannon
4 x 12.7-mm (.50-cal.) machine guns

American fighters were always fairly lightly armed, especially compared to their opponents. But the USA more than made up for any inferiority by the ruggedness of its aircraft, the superior training of its pilots, and the accuracy of their shooting. The A6M5 Zero was equipped with cannon giving more deadly firepower but it lacked defensive armour.

GRUMMAN
F7F TIGERCAT

● Post-war fighter ● Night-fighter variants ● Korean War service

Although developed too late to fight in World War II, the Grumman F7F Tigercat was an outstanding carrier-capable fighter which served valiantly in Korea. This was one of several twin-engined fighters designed by Grumman engineers during the war and combined a slim, streamlined fuselage with a pair of powerful engines. While it rarely flew from carriers, the F7F proved to be a fine land-based fighter in US Marine Corps service.

▲ After a short but highly distinguished service career, most importantly over Korea, the Tigercat found its way into a number of civilian roles such as air racing and fire-bombing.

GRUMMAN F7F TIGERCAT

Torpedo attack ▶
As a naval fighter-bomber, one of the Tigercat's primary roles would have been anti-shipping strike using torpedoes.

▶ Changing times
Although the F7F was designed to fly from the US Navy's new 'Midway'-class carriers, by the time the first prototype flew it was ordered into urgent production for the Marine Corps.

▶ Fighting fires in the US
Extensively modified Tigercats have proved to be quite successful in the fire-bombing role. The aircraft's rugged design, high-power, rapid transit speed and manoeuvrability at low level make it ideal for the task.

▲ Two-seat night-fighters
Post-war production included 60 F7F-3N and 13 F7F-4N night-fighters.

Folding fighter ▶
In between initial F7F-1 and F7F-3 production, Grumman built a number of two-seat F7F-2N night-fighters. All Tigercats retained the wing-folding mechanism designed for naval use.

FACTS AND FIGURES

▶ The Tigercat's first flight was made inadvertently during taxi tests on 2 November 1943.

▶ Grumman lost the Tigercat prototype in an accident on 1 May 1944.

▶ In the late 1940s Tigercats served with Marine Corps squadrons in China.

▶ The Tigercat scored its first night air-to-air victory by downing a Po-2 'Bedcheck Charlie' biplane on 1 July 1951.

▶ Grumman manufactured 364 Tigercats of all models.

▶ Five Tigercats are flying in the United States as restored warbirds.

PROFILE

Cats eyes over Korea

During the Korean War enemy biplanes operating at night were far more than just a nuisance: they inflicted considerable damage. A small number of US Marines, flying Grumman F7F Tigercats equipped with airborne radar and machine guns, fought these Po-2 biplanes during the nocturnal hours. Air-to-air fighting was both dangerous and demanding, but the Tigercat proved up to the job.

Conceived as a Navy shipborne fighter, the attractive

F7F Tigercat made its mark with the Marine Corps in the 1940s and 1950s. There were single- and two-seat day- and night-fighter versions.

Although the Tigercat was as fast and nimble as smaller, single-engined fighters (under most circumstances it was faster than the Grumman F6F Hellcat), it was not a difficult machine to fly. Pilots remarked upon the speed with which the F7F reacted to the controls and its superb handling qualities.

In addition to their wartime mission, Tigercats served as

target drone controllers and as unmanned drones. Once released from military service, a small number of the aircraft enjoyed success in civilian hands as aerial fire-bombers.

Tigercats arrived in Korea under the command of VMF(N)-542 and flew alongside Corsairs on night interdiction raids against supply routes. By 1953 the aircraft had been absorbed by VMF(N)-513.

A radar operator sat in the cramped rear cockpit behind the pilot. Heating was inadequate for the Korean winter.

An advanced radar set was housed in the elongated nose of the F7F-3N and -4N variants.

R-2800-34W engines gave the Tigercat blistering performance, even when carrying a weapon-load.

With a suitably cat-like face painted on its nose, this radar-equipped F7F night-fighter makes a sprightly take-off.

In general, the F7F was of conventional configuration, although in plan view the narrowness of the fuselage is apparent. The aircraft was all metal.

Only night-fighting Tigercats flew in Korea and all arrived in a gloss dark blue colour. They were quickly repainted in a matt black scheme, which was less visible to searchlights.

Korean theatre F7F-3Ns were rarely seen without a centreline store. This was usually a 568-litre (150-gallon) napalm tank – a useful 'area' weapon. The Tigercat often flew in support of ground forces.

For night interdiction work the F7F-3N was well armed. A typical load consisted of eight 127-mm rockets under the wings and four 20-mm cannon, two in each wingroot.

All Tigercats had the pilot's cockpit in the same position, parallel to the engines. In the single-seat variants a fuel tank was installed behind the pilot but this was moved in the night-fighters.

A distinctive feature of the F7F was its stalky nose gear unit. The Tigercat was the first US Navy carrier-borne aircraft to be equipped with a tricycle undercarriage.

Advanced twin-prop fighters

- **DE HAVILLAND HORNET:** Of the twin-engined fighters which emerged at the very end or just after World War II, the British Hornets and Sea Hornets were some of the most graceful.

- **DORNIER Do 335 PFEIL:** As the war situation worsened, the German aircraft industry became ever more innovative, as exemplified by the radical Do 335.

- **LOCKHEED XP-58 CHAIN LIGHTNING:** Based on the P-38 Lightning, this specialised escort and ship-busting fighter never entered squadron service.

- **NORTH AMERICAN P-82 TWIN MUSTANG:** Having flown in early 1945, the excellent Twin Mustang missed World War II but served alongside the F7F in Korea.

F7F-3 Tigercat

Type: twin-engined naval fighter and fighter-bomber

Powerplant: two 1566-kW (2100-hp) Pratt & Whitney R-2800-34W Double Wasp 18-cylinder radial piston engines driving three-bladed propellers

Maximum speed: 700 km/h (434 mph) at 6765 m (22,000 ft)

Cruising speed: 357 km/h (221 mph)

Initial climb rate: 1380 m/min (4525 fpm)

Range: 1931 km (1200 miles)

Service ceiling: 12,405 m (40,700 ft)

Weights: empty 7380 kg (15,236 lb); maximum take-off 11,666 kg (25,665 lb)

Armament: four 20-mm cannon in wingroots and four 12.7-mm (.50-cal.) machine guns in nose, plus one torpedo beneath the fuselage or up to 454 kg (1000 lb) of bombs or rockets under each wing

Dimensions:
span	15.70 m (51 ft 6 in)
length	13.83 m (45 ft 4 in)
height	5.05 m (16 ft 7 in)
wing area	42.27 m² (455 sq ft)

COMBAT DATA

MAXIMUM SPEED

Late-war naval fighters marked the pinnacle of piston-engined fighter design. A few of these machines served after the war, but were quickly replaced by jets.

F7F-3 TIGERCAT	700 km/h (434 mph)
SEA HORNET F.Mk 20	752 km/h (466 mph)
F8F-1B BEARCAT	678 km/h (420 mph)

ARMAMENT

With the fighter-bomber role in mind, the F7F was given considerable firepower with its nose-mounted machine-gun battery and wing cannon.

F7F-3 TIGERCAT	4 x 20-mm cannon, 4 x 12.7-mm (.50-cal.) machine guns, 908-kg (1000-lb) bombload
SEA HORNET F.Mk 20	4 x 20-mm cannon, 908-kg (2000-lb) bombload
F8F-1B BEARCAT	4 x 20-mm cannon, 908-kg (2000-lb) bombload

CLIMB RATE

These high-performing fighters all offered exceptional climb performance. The two new Grumman designs outperformed the de Havilland Sea Hornet, which was a developed version of the World War II Mosquito.

F8F-1B BEARCAT	1395 m/min (4575 fpm)
F7F-3 TIGERCAT	1380 m/min (4525 fpm)
SEA HORNET F.Mk 20	1219 m/min (4000 fpm)

GRUMMAN
F8F BEARCAT

● Carrier fighter ● Air racer ● Vietnam fighter-bomber

A lthough US Navy pilots never flew the Grumman F8F Bearcat in combat, they all had a special affinity for this 'hot rod' of the late-1940s. For sheer performance, the Bearcat was one of the greatest piston-engine fighters ever flown. But the Bearcat was a victim of the jet-age, and although it was a superb aircraft the new generation of jets left it standing. It finally saw action with the French, as a fighter-bomber over the jungles of Vietnam.

▲ The military lost interest in the Bearcat in the 1940s, but civil interest has gone from strength to strength. The massive piston engine made the F8F a formidable racer and fighter.

GRUMMAN F8F BEARCAT

▲ Small but deadly
The Bearcat was the smallest fighter Grumman could design around the Double Wasp engine. The performance gained this way was at the expense of range.

▲ More armour
The early Bearcat required extensive modifications, and the F8F-2 had more armour, a variable ratio supercharger, revised engine cowling and a taller tail fin.

Night fighter ▼
The F8F-1N night-fighters had a small pod under the right wing housing a 3-cm (1-in) wavelength radar set. The pilot's display was mounted under the instruments.

▲ Ground attack stores
Bearcats could carry a 454-kg (1000-lb) bomb under each wing, or a 378-litre (100-gallon) drop-tank or Mk 9 HVAR 127-mm (5-in) rockets. The four cannon had 200 rounds of ammunition each. Some Bearcats had a modified fuel system with large 567-litre (150-gallon) centreline fuel tanks.

FACTS AND FIGURES

▶ In 1946 a Bearcat climbed to 3050 m (10,000 ft) in 1 minute 34 seconds, a feat no jet of that era could equal.

▶ Bob Hall piloted the prototype on its maiden flight on 31 August 1944.

▶ When production ended in 1949, the Navy had 24 squadrons of F8Fs.

▶ A civil Bearcat flown by Darryl Greenamyer set a piston speed record of 776.449 km/h (481.4 mph) on 16 August 1969.

▶ Between 1951 and 1954 French Bearcats flew over 120,000 sorties in Indochina.

▶ Bearcat production, planned to be several thousand, was cut to 770.

PROFILE

Final growling Grumman

The last of the great piston-engined Grummans, the F8F was the best seaborne piston fighter belonging to the US Navy. It was faster than the preceding F6F Hellcat despite being slightly smaller. Designed and flown in trials during 1944, the Bearcat did not see active service in World War II. Huge orders for versions built by General Motors were cancelled after the war, and the Grumman order sharply reduced. The F8F-1B entered service in 1946,

featuring four cannon, and a small number of F8F-1N night-fighters was also procured.

The F8F flew in the photographic reconnaissance role and remained in service with the US Navy until 1952. By 1950, the Bearcat was obsolescent as a fighter but still saw service with the French air force as a fighter-bomber in Indochina, dropping napalm bombs at Dien Bien Phu. The Royal Thai Air Force was another Bearcat operator.

Above: Grumman built a single civil Bearcat for company use from spare parts, which did not cost the Navy or the company anything. Basically an F8F-1 but with the later model tall tail, the aircraft, N700A, was equipped with a full avionics fit for airways flying. It was used by Field Service Representative Roger Kahn to tour the US Navy's F8F squadrons.

Above: As an air racer, the Bearcat was hard to beat. Only similar aircraft like the Hawker Sea Fury could compete with it on speed.

A favourite use of the Bearcat was in post-war air racing, with a modified F8F called 'Rare Bear' setting a record speed at Reno.

F8F-1 Bearcat

Type: single-seat carrier-based fighter/bomber

Powerplant: one 1566-kW (2100-hp) Pratt & Whitney R-2800-22W/34W 18-cylinder piston engine

Maximum speed: 680 km/h (421 mph)

Cruising speed: 402 km/h (250 mph)

Initial climb rate: 300 m/min (1000 fpm)

Range: 1780 km (1103 miles)

Service ceiling: 10,575 m (34,690 ft)

Weights: empty 3207 kg (7055 lb); maximum (combat) 4387 kg (9651 lb); maximum with external stores 5873 kg (12,921 lb)

Armament: four 12.7-mm (.50-cal.) Colt-Browning machine guns (later, four 20-mm cannon) plus one 725-kg (1600-lb) or two 454-kg (1000-lb) bombs and four 127-mm (5-in) HVAR rockets

Dimensions:
span	10.92 m (35 ft)
length	8.61 m (28 ft)
height	4.23 m (14 ft)
wing area	22.67 m² (244 sq ft)

COMBAT DATA

F8F-1B BEARCAT
1780 km
(1103 miles)

MAXIMUM SPEED

The last piston fighters were approaching the limiting speeds which could be achieved with piston engines and propellers. A civil Bearcat was timed unofficially at 805 km/h (499 mph) in 1947, but jets were soon in service, making such speeds seem relatively slow.

LA-9	690 km/h (428 mph)
SEA FURY	740 km/h (459 mph)
F8F-1B BEARCAT	680 km/h (421 mph)

RANGE

Range was vital to naval fighters, but the demand for greater performance meant bigger engines, which used more fuel and left less space for it. The La-9 was much lighter than the F8F or the Sea Fury, its small engine providing it with greater range.

SEA FURY	1130 km (700 miles)
La-9	2550 km (1581 miles)

ARMAMENT

Four cannon were fairly standard for fighters by the end of World War II and for the following 10 years. Early La-9s often had a cannon deleted from the port wing. Sea Furies and Bearcats actually flew more ground-attack missions than air defence.

F8F-1B BEARCAT
4 x 20-mm cannon

SEA FURY
4 x 20-mm cannon

La-9
4 x 23-mm cannon

F8F BEARCAT

About 120 Bearcats were used by the Armée de l'Air in Indochina in support of ground forces fighting the Vietminh. Between July 1951 and 1954, French Bearcat units flew no less than 120,000 missions.

Stability was marginal in the prototype Bearcat and the tailfin height was increased in production versions. The fuselage contained a fire extinguisher below the tailfin and a shock absorber for the tailwheel.

The high bubble canopy offered a superb view. The F8F had reduced cockpit armour compared to the F6F.

Grumman were famous for their strong airframes and the Bearcat was no exception. Radios and avionics were fitted just behind the cockpit, with a fire extinguisher below. The large main fuel tank (700 litres/180 gallons)) was under the cockpit.

A 64-litre oil tank and a 60-litre (17-gallon) water injection tank were crammed into the small forward fuselage. An armoured bulkhead protected the pilot.

Powerful and reliable, the massive Double Wasp radial was an 18-cylinder air-cooled engine, also used in the Grumman Guardian anti-submarine aircraft.

The pilot aimed his weapons through a Mk 8 illuminated reflector gunsight.

Armament consisted of four 20-mm cannon, although early F8F-1s were fitted with four 12.7-mm (.50-cal.) machine guns. Rockets, bombs and napalm tanks were used by the French air force in Vietnam.

Last of the piston fighters

■ **GRUMMAN F7F-3 TIGERCAT:** The Tigercat was a night-fighter, but was also used by the Marine Corps in Korea for close support. Some were modified for reconnaissance duties.

■ **HAWKER SEA FURY:** The last piston-engined fighter in Royal Navy service, the Sea Fury was a superb aircraft with very high speed. One even shot down a MiG-15 in Korea.

■ **LAVOCHKIN La-9:** Like the F8F, the La-9 was basically a derivation of a wartime design (the La-5/7) built in small numbers. The La-9 had a new duralumin skin and improved cooling.

■ **NORTH AMERICAN F-82 TWIN MUSTANG:** Designed to meet the need for a long-range escort fighter for B-29s in the Pacific, the F-82 also fought briefly in the Korean War as a night-fighter.

GRUMMAN

F9F COUGAR

● Swept wing ● Carrier jet ● Target drone

T he F9F Cougar was created by a simple expedient: Grumman took its proven, straight-wing Panther, which had been among the US Navy's first jet fighters, and redesigned it with swept-back wings. The result was two generations of Cougars which arrived late, long after the swept-wing North American F-86 Sabre was already in combat. Cougars served briefly as carrier-based fighters and were also used for training assignments.

▲ The first production Cougar came off the Bethpage line in 1952, as the last of the straight-wing Panthers was leaving the factory. Cougars went to Korea just in time for the armistice.

GRUMMAN F9F COUGAR

▲ Rocket test
F9Fs were among the first fighters to be armed with Sidewinder missiles. Up to four could be carried on the wings.

▼ Atlantic fleet
Four Cougars of VF-81 squadron fly over the Atlantic in August 1958. This view clearly shows the width of the wingroot.

▼ Wing sweep
The wing had a sweepback of 35° and was fitted with prominent fences inboard.

Folded up ▼
The F9F-8 featured a dogtooth in the wing, a stretched fuselage, more fuel and a reprofiled canopy offering the pilot a better view.

Wing vortex ▼
As this Cougar pulls into a turn, the vortexes spiralling from the wingtips are clearly visible.

FACTS AND FIGURES

▶ The F9F-8 was flown supersonic in a dive, a rare event for an aircraft with centrifugal compressor engines.

▶ In total, 1988 Cougars were built between 1951 and February 1960.

▶ The second-generation F9F-8 was first flown on 18 January 1954.

▶ Cougars were tested on the US Navy's 'flex deck', an experiment in landing on carriers without wheels.

▶ The last Cougar two-seat trainers were retired from service in February 1974.

▶ Some 110 examples of the reconnaissance F9F-8P Cougar were built.

F9F-8 Cougar

Type: carrier-based fighter and trainer

Powerplant: one 32.03-kN (7185-lb-thrust) Pratt & Whitney J48-P-8A turbojet engine

Maximum speed: 1135 km/h (704 mph) at sea level

Climb rate: 24 m/sec (79 fps)

Range: 1610 km (998 miles)

Service ceiling: 15,240 m (50,000 ft)

Weights: empty 5555 kg (12,222 lb); normal loaded 8356 kg (18,383 lb); maximum take-off 9433 kg (20,753 lb)

Armament: four 20-mm cannon (or camera installation in F9F-8P), plus up to 1816 kg (3990 lb) of bombs, napalm tanks, or external fuel tanks on underwing hardpoints

Dimensions:
span	10.52 m (34 ft)
length	13.54 m (44 ft)
height	3.73 m (12 ft)
wing area	31.31 m² (337 sq ft)

COMBAT DATA

MAXIMUM SPEED

The US started producing swept-wing fighters in the early-1950s. The Cougar was a direct development of the Panther and had much improved performance over its straight-wing contemporaries.

F9F-8 COUGAR	1135 km/h (704 mph)
F9F-5 PANTHER	932 km/h (578 mph)
SEA HAWK FGA.Mk 6	901 km/h (559 mph)

RANGE

Naval fighters were very dependent on good range performance as combat often took place far from the carriers. The larger engine on the Cougar used more fuel than the Panther, providing more power but reducing the range. The Sea Hawk was a smaller design and often carried external fuel tanks to help increase the range. The Panther carried extra fuel in wingtip tanks.

F9F-8 COUGAR	1610 km (998 miles)
F9F-5 PANTHER	2092 km (1297 miles)
SEA HAWK FGA.Mk 6	1191 km (740 miles)

ARMAMENT

Typical of the period, all three types carried heavy cannon armament for air-to-air combat. A secondary ground-attack role was important and the Cougar could carry a fair bombload.

F9F-8 COUGAR	4 x 20-mm cannon 1816 kg (3990 lb) of bombs
F9F-5 PANTHER	4 x 20-mm cannon 908 kg (1998 lb) of bombs
SEA HAWK FGA.Mk 6	4 x 20-mm cannon 454 kg (1000 lb) of bombs

Grumman's first swept-wing jet

Swept-back wings were the key to the success of the Grumman F9F Cougar, permitting higher speeds and better performance to be derived from the earlier F9F Panther design. Throughout the Korean War, pilots of straight-winged F9F Panthers watched helplessly as swept-wing Sabres and MiG-15s fought at higher speeds than they could reach. Naval aviators were delighted when Grumman went ahead with the much improved Cougar in 1951.

Cougars served aboard aircraft-carriers from 1953, but the combat role for this aircraft was short-lived. The F9F-8P was a special photographic reconnaissance version, and the F9F also displayed with the 'Blue Angels' aerobatic team. F9F-8 fighters even had a small ranging radar.

Most US Navy pilots remember the Cougar because it was the US Navy's advanced pilot trainer for more than two decades, some flying until 1974. A few were converted to serve as unmanned drones.

Above: With more space in the nose than the F9F-5P, the F9F-8P contained a large battery of cameras. It was unarmed, relying on speed alone to elude enemy fighter aircraft.

Above: In addition to its four 20-mm cannon, the F8F could carry a hefty bombload. The Cougar never went to war, being marginally too late for Korea and too old to serve in Vietnam.

This QF-9J served as a target drone from 1969-70. The aircraft was built as the second in the final block of F9F-8s and became an F9F-8B before conversion to a drone aircraft.

Operational fighter Cougars had four 20-mm cannon in the nose, but drones and F9F-8Ps had no guns.

A simple ranging radar was fitted in an undernose bulge. This modification was retrofitted to many early model Cougars, and the bulge remained on many drones.

Visibility from the F9F's cockpit was very good, and was improved in the F9F-8. The two-seat TF-9J was one of the first fighter trainers with a properly designed tandem dual cockpit.

Air for the J48 was fed through two intakes in the wing roots. This configuration was somewhat inhibiting, as the intakes were hard to modify if a more powerful engine requiring a larger mass flow of air was to be installed.

In the lengthened wingroots of the F9F-8, 95 litres (25 gallons) of extra fuel could be stored, and 252 litres (67 gallons) extra in the longer fuselage. This was the result of stretching the centre fuselage.

Most operational F9F fighters were painted in a gloss white scheme, or gloss dark blue in the early years. Trainers were painted white with orange panels, and drones received many colour schemes.

The tailhook retracted into a neat fairing and was almost invisible when not in use.

The F9F's broad fuselage was the result of using the centrifugal compressor Pratt & Whitney J48 engine, which was much wider than later axial-flow jet engines.

Grumman's jet fighters

■ **F9F-2 PANTHER:** Famous for producing superb naval fighters, the Panther marked Grumman's debut in the field of jet fighters, and they fought in the early part of the Korean War.

■ **F10F JAGUAR:** Continuing the theme of naming its fighters after 'big cats' Grumman produced the Jaguar. It failed because too much advanced technology was introduced at once.

■ **F11F TIGER:** The Tiger was the US Navy's first supersonic aircraft. It was, however, produced in small numbers due to engine problems and was soon replaced by the F-8 Crusader.

■ **F-14 TOMCAT:** The US Navy's primary interceptor entered service over 25 years ago. Yet it is such a fine fighter that it is still one of the most capable combat aircraft flying.

GRUMMAN

F9F PANTHER

● Early navy jet ● Korean War MiG-killer ● Tactical fighter-bomber

T he F9F Panther brought the jet age to the US Navy. Although not the first to reach widespread service and to win real popularity among the Navy and Marine pilots who flew in it. There were reconnaissance and target-drone Panthers too, but this superbly tough warplane is best remembered as the most important carrier-borne jet fighter of the Korean War.

▲ The Panther gained many 'firsts' for the US Navy. It was the first Navy jet to go to war, the first to use a blown flap and the first to try an inflight-refuelling system.

GRUMMAN F9F PANTHER

▼ Wingtip tanks
Besides being useful perches for the deck crews, the Panther's tip tanks helped to improve the aircraft's rather poor rate of roll.

▲ Swinging guns ▶
This experimental Emerson gun installation was tested, but, like similar projects in Russia by MiG, it was not used in squadron service.

Prototype ▶
Despite being lost in an accident, the first Panther prototype showed promise.

▼ Rocket ship
A favourite armament of Korean War Panthers was six high-velocity aircraft rockets, used against surface targets.

▼ Carrier operations ▶
Although the Panther was basically sound, it had a high landing speed and poor control in certain conditions, providing the US Navy with valuable experience of jet operations at sea.

FACTS AND FIGURES

▶ The first flight by a Panther prototype was an inadvertent 'hop' during taxi tests on 21 November 1947.

▶ The Navy's first jet-versus-jet 'kill' was a MiG-15 downed on 9 November 1950.

▶ Panthers flew 78,000 combat sorties in the Korean 'police action'.

▶ The only foreign air arm to receive F9Fs was the Argentine air force, which acquired 24 Panthers in 1958.

▶ Panthers shot down two North Korean Yak-9 prop-driven fighters.

▶ 1385 Panthers were built by Grumman between 1947 and 1953.

The first Navy jet to go to war

The F9F Panther was the most successful of the first generation of US Navy jets. Originally proposed as a four-jet combat craft, which the Navy sensibly rejected, the single-engine Panther was a sturdy warplane which performed well but required nurturing over time.

Panthers flew in Navy squadrons with three choices of powerplant (J33, J42 and J48) before the Navy settled on the F9F-5 propelled by a J48, based on the Rolls-Royce Tay.

The Panther flew for the first time in 1947, and was the first carrier-based jet fighter to see combat. Extensively used on ground-attack duties in Korea, the Panther was a fine warplane in the hands of a trained pilot. Its structural strength, a trademark of the 'Grumman Iron Works', helped Marines enormously when they flew Panthers through gunfire to attack ground troops in Korea. But in spite of the fact that a

Panther gained the US Navy's first jet kill, a MiG-15 in November 1950, the F9F was seriously outclassed by the swept-wing F-86 Sabre and MiG-15 which were entering service.

The last operational Panther was retired in October 1958, but the old fighter continued as a training machine and target tug well into the 1960s.

Panthers were usually finished in an all-midnight blue paint scheme. This colour was used on all versions of the aircraft, including the ground attack and reconnaissance variants.

F9F-2 PANTHER

This Grumman F9F Panther was used by VMF-311, a US Marine Corps squadron flying ground-attack missions in support of UN forces in Korea.

The 'panther's head' paint scheme was a personal badge.

Four 20-mm cannon were mounted in the nose, which could be slid forward to gain access for reloading.

Panthers had two ventral airbrakes, mounted left and right on the front fuselage.

The Panther suffered instability problems which were never entirely cured. With the hydraulic control boost inoperative, aileron stick forces were very high.

The deep, sturdy fuselage was so shaped because the J42 engine was of centrifugal design. The shape was useful, however, as it gave a very large volume for internal fuel – twice as much as the British Hawker Sea Hawk.

An internal 95-litre (25-gallon) tank of water/methanol was fitted beneath the fin, to give extra engine thrust.

Although ostensibly a fighter, the Panther usually delivered air-to-ground munitions such as HVAR rockets or bombs.

The thick wingroot, with its engine intakes built into it, was typical of Grumman's famously strong engineering. The folding hinge was unusually close inboard to the fuselage.

The strong tailhook and high landing speed caused at least two Panthers to rip their tails off on landing.

Fighters from the 'Grumman Iron Works'

■ **F3F:** The first Grumman carrier fighters in the 1930s established all of the company's characteristics, with toughness and agility foremost.

■ **F6F HELLCAT:** Swarms of these big, beefy fighters wrested control of the Pacific skies from the fighters of Imperial Japan.

■ **F8F BEARCAT:** The last of the great Grumman prop-fighters, the Bearcat missed World War II. It served into the 1950s.

■ **F9F COUGAR:** A swept-wing adaptation of the Panther, the Cougar served well into the 1960s, ending as an advanced trainer.

■ **F-14 TOMCAT:** Possibly the last Grumman fighter, the Tomcat has been the US Navy's main airborne defender since the 1970s.

F9F-5 Panther

Type: single-seat carrier-based fighter and attack aircraft

Powerplant: one 31.14-kN (6985-lb-thrust) thrust Pratt & Whitney J48-P-6 turbojet (licence-built Rolls-Royce Tay)

Maximum speed: 932 km/h (578 mph) at 6706 m (22,000 ft)

Range: 2100 km (1300 miles)

Service ceiling: 13,000 m (42,650 ft)

Weights: empty 4603 kg (11,429 lb); loaded 8492 kg (18,682 lb)

Armament: four 20-mm Browning M3 cannon each with 190 rounds; up to 1360 kg (2992 lb) of underwing bombs or rocket projectiles

Dimensions:
span	11.58 m	(38 ft)
length	11.84 m	(39 ft)
height	3.73 m	(12 ft)
wing area	23.23 m²	(262 sq ft)

COMBAT DATA

MAXIMUM SPEED

Although heavy and very strongly-built to withstand the rigours of carrier operations, the Panther was not much slower than the first generation of straight-winged land-based jets. But by the early 1950s all had been outclassed by the new swept-wing fighters.

F9F-5 PANTHER
932 km/h (578 mph)

F-80C SHOOTING STAR
956 km/h (593 mph)

METEOR F.Mk 8
950 km/h (589 mph)

RANGE

Carrier aircraft generally have longer ranges than their land-based counterparts. This is an operational necessity: there are few conveniently placed diversionary fields in the wide expanses of the ocean. For the naval pilot the choice is simple: you make it back to the carrier, or you learn to swim.

F9F-5 PANTHER
2100 km (1240 miles)

F-80C SHOOTING STAR
1700 km (1054 miles)

METEOR F.Mk 8
1100 km (682 miles)

ARMAMENT

The US Navy was much quicker than the US Air Force to adopt the heavy cannon armament which had been accepted as standard elsewhere in the last years of World War II. In addition to its cannon, the Panther could carry a considerable load of air-to-ground ordnance.

METEOR F.Mk 8
4 x 20-mm cannon
900 kg (1980 lb)
of bombs or rockets

F9F-5 PANTHER
4 x 20-mm cannon
1360 kg (2860 lb)
of bombs or rockets

F-80C SHOOTING STAR
6 x 12.7-mm (.50-cal.) MGs
900 kg (1980 lb)
of bombs or rockets

GRUMMAN
S-2 TRACKER

- Hunter-killer aircraft ● Twin-engined ● Carrier based

Although the hunter-killer teams of AF-2S and AF-2W Guardians were serving the US Navy well in the anti-submarine role, navy planners were keen to acquire a single new aircraft type, capable of finding and killing a submarine. The Tracker was chosen out of 24 design proposals and the aircraft proved exceptional from the moment of its first flight, operating with US Navy units for 25 years and finding a ready export market.

▲ With 1269 aircraft having been produced, Trackers became a common sight with anti-submarine units around the world. They served with at least 14 air arms.

GRUMMAN S-2 TRACKER

▼ **MAD submarine hunter**
This S-2D (S2F-3 before 1962) has its MAD (Magnetic Anomaly Detector) boom deployed. This device locates disruptions in the earth's magnetic field, caused by a submarine's hull.

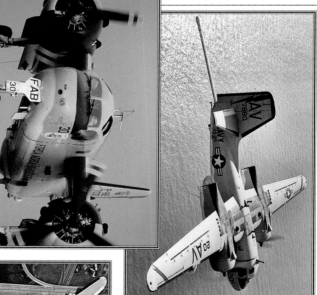

▲ **South American sub-hunter**
Eight ex-USN S-2Es were delivered to the Brazilian air force during the 1970s, to supplement 13 earlier machines. They are designated P-16E.

▲ **Flying from 'Melbourne'**
Australian Trackers deployed aboard HMAS Melbourne.

▲ **Tracker firepower**
Internal weapons of the S-2D included huge Mk 57 or Mk 101 special weapons or a Mk 52 mine.

▲ **Early Tracker**
This S2F-1 (S-2A) has its underfuselage AN/APS-33G radome deployed.

FACTS AND FIGURES

▶ Development of the Cougar, and continuing production of the Panther, delayed Grumman's work on the S-2.

▶ S2F-2 Trackers had enlarged bomb bays, able to carrying a nuclear depth charge.

▶ A Tracker with the Pacific Missile Range Facility served the USN until 1986.

▶ Nicknamed 'Stoof' in US Navy service (from S-two-F), the Tracker was originally officially named the Sentinel.

▶ S-2As were exported to Brazil, Italy, Japan and the Netherlands.

▶ De Havilland Canada built 100 CS2Fs between 1956 and 1958.

PROFILE

Carrier-borne sub-destroyer

Combining in one airframe the ability to handle the dissimilar tasks of finding and then sinking a submarine had distinct advantages. Employing one aircraft type saved space on the carrier deck and required a less complex support structure.

Grumman responded to the US Navy specification with the G-89, which was small enough to operate from escort carriers but accommodated a crew of four and all the necessary equipment. The aircraft was one

of the first twin-engined types to operate from a carrier and introduced several innovations to overcome related problems.

From the XSF-1, but Grumman's G-89 evolved the commitment to the Korean War effort caused delays in the programme. Two years elapsed between the Navy's signing of a contract and the first flight on 4 December 1952.

Testing proceeded quickly, and the first S-2A reached VS-26 in February 1954. Production quickly gained pace.

with 14 Avenger and Guardian squadrons re-equipping in the next 36 months.

As new, improved variants appeared throughout the Tracker's career, it proved itself to be highly capable and reliable and saw extensive carrier service during the Vietnam War.

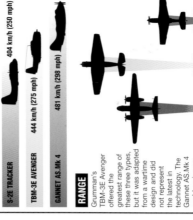

Pictured in 1963, this S-2E demonstrates the large searchlight fitted to the starboard wings of most Tracker variants, and the type's distinctive dihedral tailplanes.

Each R-1820 engine was closely cowled. The cowling extended beneath the wing to accommodate the main undercarriage. Aft of the trailing edge, each fairing ended in a battery of sonobuoy launch tubes.

Typical of the compact nature of the Tracker, the S-2 was the tail area, which housed the MAD 'stinger', arrester hook and a small-wheeled, tail-bumper unit.

S-2A TRACKER

Japan received this S-2A from US Navy stocks and it is seen in the colours of No. 11 Squadron, 1st Air Group, Japanese Maritime Self-Defence Force, when 30 years old.

Three weapons pylons were mounted beneath each wing, for the carriage of torpedoes, rockets or other stores.

AN/APS-38A search radar was carried within a large ventral radome. On the ground the radome was retracted to avoid scraping runways or carrier decks, and to avoid drag it was deployed in the air only when a search was being conducted.

Two flight crew handled the general operation of the Tracker, while a radio operator and MAD specialist sat in a compartment immediately behind the cockpit.

Early S2F-1 aircraft carried an inverted 'Y-shaped' antenna serving the AN/APA-70C ECM (Electronic Counter-Measures) system. Later machines used AN/APA-69A in a distinctive radome.

Japanese Trackers were never ship-based, but they retained the strongly built undercarriage of the naval machines and the tall nose-gear leg.

Trackers around the world

■ **ARGENTINA:** Various examples of the S-2A, S-2F and S-2E have been flown by the Argentine navy. S-2Es took part in the 1982 Falklands War.

■ **PERU:** During 1976, Peru replaced its nine S-2As with refurbished, ex-USN S-2Es. Four more were delivered in 1983.

■ **NETHERLANDS:** Twenty-six S2F-1s were delivered new to the Dutch navy in 1960-61, with more added from US and Canadian sources.

■ **UNITED STATES:** As the largest Tracker operator, the US was the only user of the rare Mk 90 nuclear depth charge capable S-2C.

S-2E Tracker

Type: four-seat anti-submarine warfare aircraft.

Powerplant: two 1137-kW (1525-hp) Wright R-1820-82WA piston engines

Maximum speed: 404 km/h (250 mph) at 1220 m (4000 ft)

Endurance: 9 hours

Maximum climb rate: 425 m/min (1394 fpm)

Range: 1480 km (920 miles) normal, 2090 km (2215 miles) maximum

Service ceiling: 6125 m (20,000 ft)

Weights: empty 8537 kg (18,780 lb), maximum take-off 13,501 kg (29,700 lb)

Armament: up to 2182 kg (4800 lb) of torpedoes, depth charges and rockets, including nuclear stores

Dimensions:

span	22.12 m	(72 ft 6 in)
length	13.26 m	(43 ft 6 in)
height	5.07 m	(16 ft 8 in)
wing area	46.08 m²	(496 sq ft)

COMBAT DATA

MAXIMUM SPEED

Anti-submarine warfare aircraft spend long periods flying at low speeds and low altitudes. A low cruising speed is therefore of benefit for long range and endurance, although a fast transit speed may also be desirable.

S-2E TRACKER	404 km/h (250 mph)
TBM-3E AVENGER	444 km/h (275 mph)
GANNET AS.Mk 4	481 km/h (298 mph)

RANGE

Grumman's TBM-3E Avenger offered the greatest range of these three types, but it was adapted from a wartime design and did not represent the latest in technology. The Gannet AS.Mk 4 could cruise on one engine, but still had less range than the Tracker.

S-2E TRACKER	1480 km (920 miles)
TBM-3E AVENGER	1820 km (1130 miles)
GANNET AS.Mk 4	1065 km (660 miles)

WEAPON LOAD

From the S-2C model onwards, the Tracker had an extended weapons bay allowing it to carry a wider range of ordnance. With underwing hardpoints also in use, the S-2E could engage several targets on each mission.

S-2E TRACKER	2182 kg (4800 lb)
TBM-3E AVENGER	907 kg (2000 lb)
GANNET AS.Mk 4	3219 kg (7080 lb)

GRUMMAN

S-2E/F/G/UP TRACKER

- 1950s design ● US and foreign service ● Turbine conversions

▲ While originally intended as a carrierborne aircraft, most S-2s that are still in service are land-based and equip the navies of smaller nations which require an affordable ASW platform.

T he first carrier-borne anti-submarine aircraft to combine the 'hunter' and 'killer' functions, detecting and tracking submarines and attacking them with bombs and depth charges, the S-2 Tracker entered US Navy service in 1954.

The Tracker seemed an ideal counter to the Soviet Union's vast fleet of attack submarines threatening US warships. Many were exported and a few remain in service, some fitted with new engines and avionics.

GRUMMAN S-2E/F/G/UP TRACKER

▼ Folding wings
Designed to operate aboard aircraft-carriers, the S-2 has folding wings to ease storage below deck. Until recently Canada operated its S-2s in this low-visibility dark grey colour scheme.

▲ Prototype Turbo Tracker
Built as an S2F-3S (S-2E after 1962) and retired by the US Navy years before its designation changed, this S-2T still carries US Navy markings. Taiwan's conversions were completed under a USN Foreign Military Sales contract.

▼ Argentine S-2A
Having retired its S-2As, Argentina is having its S-2Es refurbished by Israel Aircraft Industries.

▲ Republic of China naval service
Taiwan's original fleet of S-2Es and Fs has been retired or converted. This example has now received turbine engines.

▲ Fire-bomber S-2F1T
Marsh Aviation offers turboprop conversions for both civil fire-bomber and military aircraft.

FACTS AND FIGURES

- ▶ The first S2F Tracker completed its maiden flight from Long Island, New York, on 4 December 1952.

- ▶ Navy crews nicknamed the Tracker the 'Stoof' after its S2F designation.

- ▶ The first S-2G conversion was undertaken by Martin, the rest by the Navy using kits.

- ▶ In all, 1269 Trackers were built, including 100 under licence by de Havilland Aircraft of Canada.

- ▶ The S-2G variant was modified to carry Bullpup air-to-surface missiles.

- ▶ Marsh S-2 turboprop conversions employ a five-bladed propeller.

PROFILE

Breathing new life into the 'Stoof'

By the early 1960s, the S-2 had been in US Navy service for almost 10 years. In 1962 the new S-2E variant was introduced. This benefited from AQA-3 'Jezebel' passive long-range acoustic search equipment used in conjunction with a 'Julie' active acoustic echo-ranging by explosive charge device. The equipment was installed in the lengthened S-2D airframe, which offered more internal room than earlier versions. The S-2F (an S-2B with 'Jezebel' and 'Julie' fitted) followed. In 1972, 50 S-3Es were converted to the more

capable S-2G, an interim aircraft pending the introduction of the all-new Lockheed S-3 Viking. These were the last carrier-borne USN Trackers and made their final cruise in 1975.

The Tracker was eagerly snapped up by foreign navies, with surplus S-2Es and Gs going to Australia, Turkey and various Asian and South American nations. An affordable anti-submarine platform, the Tracker has become a candidate for major upgrades with new engines and avionics gear. Argentina, Brazil and Taiwan have taken delivery of rebuilt Turbo Trackers.

Tracker variants from the S-2D onwards had a lengthened forward fuselage with accommodation for two pilots and two radar operators. New navigation systems and radios are fitted as part of the S-2T conversion.

A key change made in the S-2T is the replacement of the original Wright R-1820 Cyclone 9 piston engines with 1227-kW (1645-hp) Garrett TPE331 turboprops, which produce about 10 per cent more power. Pratt & Whitney Canada PT6As have also been offered in other conversion packages.

S-2E Tracker

Type: carrier-borne anti-submarine warfare aircraft

Powerplant: two 1137-kW (1525-hp) Wright R-1820-82WA Cyclone radial piston engines

Maximum speed: 426 km/h (264 mph) at sea level

Patrol speed: 241 km/h (149 mph) at 455 m (1500 ft)

Endurance: 9 hours with maximum fuel and 10 per cent reserves

Weights: empty 8505 kg (18,711 lb); maximum take-off 13,222 kg (29,088 lb)

Armament: one Mk 47 or Mk 101 nuclear depth charge or similar weapon in weapons bay, 60 echo-sounding depth charges in fuselage, 32 sonobuoys in engine nacelles, plus a variety of bombs, rockets or torpedoes on six underwing hardpoints

Dimensions:
span   22.12 m (72 ft 7 in)
length   13.26 m (43 ft 6 in)
height   5.05 m (16 ft 7 in)
wing area 46.08 m² (496 sq ft)

The later versions of the Tracker (from S-2D) had a longer wing span, enlarged tail surfaces and greater fuel capacity.

Above: Taiwan's Trackers carry one of two colour schemes, either grey or two-tone blue and dark grey. All were surplus ex-US Navy aircraft.

Right: Brazil continues to fly S-2Es and re-engined S-2Ts from its carrier Minas Gerais. Operated by the air force, they are designated P-16E and P-16T.

S-2T TURBO TRACKER

Taiwan ordered 32 S-2T conversions, the first two of which were carried out by Grumman and delivered in 1989. The remainder were tackled in Taiwan using kit sets of parts.

The new engines and their Dowty advanced technology four-bladed propellers boost top speed to 500 km/h (310 mph) at 1525 m (5000 ft) and the payload by 500 kg (1100 lb). Cruising speed, field length, single-engined performance and time-between-overhauls are also improved.

As well as having new engines, the Tracker has improved avionics. These include the magnetic anomaly detector (MAD) and radar as well as the acoustic receivers and processors.

ACTION DATA

PATROL SPEED

Contemporary carrier-borne ASW types include the Fairey Gannet and Breguet Alizé, only the latter of which remains in service along with a small numbers of Trackers. A great deal of ship-borne ASW work is now carried out by helicopters like the Sea King.

S-2E TRACKER   241 km/h (149 mph)
BR.1150 ALIZÉ   232 km/h (144 mph)
SEA KING Mk 42B 90 km/h (56 mph)

ENDURANCE

Larger fixed-wing aircraft have a considerably longer endurance than helicopters and operate at greater distances from the carrier or land base. The Alizé is smaller than the Tracker and thus carries less fuel, hence its shorter endurance.

S-2E TRACKER 9 hours

BR.1150 ALIZÉ 7 hours 35 min

SEA KING Mk 42B 3 hours

CLIMB RATE

A better climb rate than any fixed-wing aircraft is inherent in the design of a helicopter, due to its ability to rise vertically. The Tracker and Alizé have comparable climb rates, which are fairly typical for this type and size of aircraft.

S-2E TRACKER 425 m/min (1400 fpm)
BR.1150 ALIZÉ 420 m/min (1380 fpm)
SEA KING MK 42B 661 m/min (2170 fpm)

Post-war US Navy ASW aircraft

■ **GRUMMAN AF GUARDIAN:** A replacement for the TBM Avenger, there were two versions of the AF, the radar-equipped AF-2W 'hunter' (below) and the weapon-carrying AF-2S 'killer'.

■ **GRUMMAN TBM-3E:** Famous during World War II as a torpedo-bomber, the TBM was used after the war by the US Navy as an anti-submarine aircraft equipped with radar.

■ **LOCKHEED S-3 VIKING:** The only carrier-borne type ever produced by Lockheed, the jet-powered Viking replaced the S-2 from 1974 and is still in service.

GRUMMAN
ALBATROSS

● Rescue and utility amphibian ● Widely exported ● War service

n Korea and Vietnam, downed combat fliers were plucked out of hostile waters by courageous and little-publicised air crews who flew the Grumman SA-16 Albatross (known to the US Navy as the UF, and across all services as the HU-16 from 1962). Their missions were fraught with danger. In more peaceful times, the SA-16 performed thousands more rescues; it was an 'angel of mercy' to thousands of survivors of accidents, crashes and shipboard fires.

▶ In the USAF, SA-16s replaced OA-10A Catalinas and supplemented land-based types like the SC-47 Skytrain. The last USAF Albatross was retired in 1973.

GRUMMAN ALBATROSS

▶ **Longer wings and more fuel**
The UF-2/SA-16B differed from the earlier UF-1/SA-16A, shown here, in having better range.

▶ **Air Rescue Service operational experience**
The modifications introduced in the SA-16B were a low-cost, highly successful way of improving the performance of ARS SA-16s.

▲ **Record breaker**
Coast Guard HU-16E 7255 set several world records including, in 1962, a straight-line distance record for amphibians.

▼ **Iberian Albatross**
Spain operated both SAR and ASW Albatrosses from 1954 until the late 1970s, including ex-Portuguese craft. Most Albatrosses were supplied under the Mutual Defense Assistance Program.

▲ **Triphibian Albatross**
Described by Grumman as the first aircraft in aviation history to be successfully operated from land, water, ice and snow in the same configuration, the Triphibian Albatross had a 4.57-m (15-ft) skid attached to the hull, and small skids below each float.

FACTS AND FIGURES

➤ The prototype JR2F-1 Pelican took to the air on 1 October 1947. Production aircraft were called UF-1 Albatrosses.

➤ A total of 466 Albatrosses was built by Grumman between 1947 and 1961.

➤ A Taiwanese SA-16A was shot down by a Chinese MiG during a 1966 rescue.

➤ Nine crew and four aircraft were lost in SA-16 operations in Vietnam, but in three years 47 US airmen were rescued.

➤ The USAF's last HU-16B Albatross is preserved at the USAF Museum.

➤ The hulls for 249 of the 466 Albatrosses were built by car manufacturer, Plymouth.

PROFILE

Life-saving seabird from Bethpage

Grumman already had plenty of flying-boat experience with designs like its World War II JRF Goose when, in 1944, it began design work on the bigger, faster Albatross. This high-winged, twin-engined aircraft has been used in several military roles since its debut in 1947 but it had always been intended for general-purpose and rescue duties.

Initially, the US Navy saw the UF Albatross as a utility aircraft to replace the JRF. However, the

USAF was first to order the type (as the SA-16) after it became responsible for worldwide air rescue operations upon its establishment in 1947.

The Albatross scored dozens of 'saves' during the 1950-53 Korean War, including the rescue of top US air ace, Captain Joseph McConnell. Ten years later, the Albatross (redesignated HU-16 in 1962) returned to active duty for a brief stint, between 1964 and 1967, carrying out combat rescue duty off the coast of Vietnam. More than a dozen other

countries have operated the Albatross, in South America, Europe and Asia. Many of these aircraft were refurbished former USAF and US Navy aircraft. A number have employed HU-16s for additional duties including anti-submarine work, for which they are radar-equipped.

The last examples were retired by the Greek air force in the mid-1990s, being replaced by ex-US Navy P-3B Orions. However, a number of preserved civilian examples remain airworthy.

Eighty-three UF-1Gs flew with the United States Coast Guard between 1951 and 1983 (most becoming UF-2Gs; HU-16Es from 1962) on rescue, fishery patrol and anti-pollution duties.

SA-16A Albatross

Type: search-and-rescue amphibian

Powerplant: two 1063-kW (1425-hp) Wright R-1820-76A or -76B Cyclone 9 nine-cylinder radial engines

Maximum speed: 383 km/h (237 mph) at sea level

Cruising speed: 241 km/h (149 mph)

Normal range: 1850 km (1150 miles)

Service ceiling: 7560 m (25,000 ft)

Weights: empty 9442 kg (20,772 lb); maximum take-off 13,381 kg (29,500 lb) (water operations), 14,969 kg (37,000 lb) (land operations)

Accommodation: two pilots, navigator, radio operator, plus two observers for search sorties. Provision also for up to 10 passengers 12 stretchers, 22 troops or 2268 kg (5000 lb) of cargo

Dimensions:
span	24.38 m (80 ft)
length	18.49 m (60 ft 8 in)
height	7.39 m (24 ft 3 in)
wing area	77.39 m² (833 sq ft)

ACTION DATA

MAXIMUM SPEED

The ASW version of the Albatross was offered to the US Navy as the PF-1 but was rejected in this role in favour of the more capable Marlin P5M. The larger and more powerful Marlin also had a slight speed advantage over the PF-1.

HU-16B ALBATROSS	383 km/h (236 mph)
Be-6 'MADGE'	377 km/h (234 mph)
P5M-2 MARLIN	405 km/h (251 mph)

CLIMB RATE

The Marlin and Albatross had closely comparable climb rates from sea level, both significantly better than that of the Soviet Beriev Be-6. All three were piston-engined designs. With a full load of anti-submarine weapons aboard, climb rates suffered.

P5M-2 MARLIN	366 m/min (1200 fpm)
HU-16B ALBATROSS	354 m/min (1160 fpm)
Be-6 'MADGE'	250 m/min (820 fpm)

RANGE

The HU-16B used much of the equipment intended for the PF-1. Space was limited in the modestly-sized Albatross, especially when compared to larger types like the Marlin and Be-6. This affected the amount of fuel carried and thus range performance.

HU-16B ALBATROSS	2760 km (1710 miles)
Be-6 'MADGE'	4800 km (2980 miles)
P5M-2 MARLIN	3300 km (2050 miles)

SHU-16B ALBATROSS

This Albatross, one of 11 ex-Norwegian aircraft, was among at least 13 Albatrosses operated by the Hellliniki Aeroporia (Greek air force). Its serial number is derived from its USAF identity, 51-7177.

Power was provided by two Wright R-1820 Cyclone 9s, as fitted to the S-2 Tracker. Most production Albatrosses employed the R-1820-76A or -76B variants rated at 1063 kW (1425 hp).

Many USAF SA-16As and Navy UF-1s were converted to SA-16B and UF-2 standard respectively. Wingspan was increased by 5.1 m (16 ft 9 in), the tailfin height was increased and each wing float had a 780-litre (206-gallon) fuel tank fitted.

An ASW Albatross carried a crew consisting of a pilot, co-pilot, flight engineer, navigator, ASW operator and weapons loader. Weapon options included high-velocity aerial rockets (HVARs), Zuni rockets, Mk 43 homing torpedoes or Mk 54 depth charges. These could be carried on the underwing pylons normally reserved for fuel tanks.

Many of the features intended for the PF-1 (a maritime patrol version offered to the US Navy, but rejected) were introduced in the SA-16B/ASW (later redesignated SHU-16B) for export.

Apart from a new nose radar, the SHU-16B had a retractable magnetic anomaly detector (MAD) 'sting' under the tail, a searchlight under the starboard wing and ECM antennae in the wingtips. An ASW operator was in charge of the latter mission equipment.

Among the changes made for the ASW role was the installation of an AN/APS-88 search radar in an enlarged nose radome. This replaced the AN/APS-31A fitted in the SAR version.

Among the airframe changes found in the HU-16B were lengthened wings, a taller fin, and fuel cells in each float to increase range.

Albatross on three continents

ITALIAN HU-16A: In the markings of 15° Stormo, Italian air force, this ex-USAF HU-16 carries the high visibility markings typical of the search-and-rescue Albatross.

AFReS HU-16B: Crewed by Air Force Reserve crews, several Albatrosses in this low-visibility paint scheme were used as 'command posts' for SAR operations off Vietnam.

US NAVY HU-16C: Originally designated UF-1, this HU-16C served as a SAR aircraft and 'station hack' at NAS Brunswick, Maine in about 1966. US Navy HU-16s did not carry unit markings.

GRUMMAN
C-1 TRADER/E-1 TRACER

● Tracker development ● Carrier transport ● Airborne early warning

A pioneer of AEW (Airborne Early Warning) operations using large over-fuselage radomes, the WF-2 Tracer (later designated E-1) was based on the Grumman TF Trader (later designated C-1). In turn the Trader was a development of the S2F-2 Tracker, with a deeper fuselage for use as a 'carrier onboard delivery' (COD) aircraft, flying important supplies, mail and personnel from bases ashore to aircraft carriers at sea.

▲ A welcome sight to US Navy aircraft carrier crews around the world, the Trader was often the bringer of vital supplies and news from home. The last Trader was retired in 1988.

GRUMMAN C-1 TRADER/E-1 TRACER

Fixed 'umbrella' ▶
Unlike more recent types, such as the E-2 and E-3, the radome of the E-1B was fixed. The aircraft was sometimes described as carrying its own umbrella.

◀ COD on Constellation
Traders played a vital role flying from carrier to carrier and from shore bases. They were particularly appreciated during the Vietnam War.

Tracer into service ▶
Here the first production WF-2 Tracer shows off its radome. Extending the fairing backwards caused less drag, but at the expense of radar efficiency.

▲ Limited testing
With its similarity to the Tracker, only limited testing of the Trader was required before its 1955 clearance for service. The first TF-1 was used for much of the testing and wore this dark colour scheme.

▼ Folded for stowage
Traders retained the wing-folding system of the Tracker, but Tracer wings folded backwards.

FACTS AND FIGURES

➤ The first TF Trader made its maiden flight on 19 January 1955 and the last was delivered on 30 December 1958.

➤ The prototype Tracer took to the air for the first time on 17 December 1956.

➤ Grumman completed a total of 87 Traders between 1955 and 1958.

➤ A C-1A Trader made the last US Navy carrier landing by a piston-engined aircraft on 21 September 1988.

➤ Between February 1958 and September 1961 Grumman built 88 Tracers.

➤ Grumman failed to win a Tracer order from Sweden for a much-modified E-1.

C-1A Trader

Type: twin-engined COD aircraft

Powerplant: two 1137-kW (1525-hp) Wright R-1820-82 or -82A radial piston engines

Maximum speed: 451 km/h (280 mph) at 1220 m (4000 ft)

Cruising speed: 269 km/h (167 mph)

Climb rate: 594 m/min (1950 fpm)

Range: 1785 km (1105 miles)

Ceiling: 7560 m (24,800 ft)

Weights: empty 7544 kg (16,600 lb); maximum take-off 11,158 kg (24,548 lb)

Accommodation: nine passengers on rearward-facing seats or up to 1588 kg (3495 lb) of freight

Dimensions:
span	21.23 m (69 ft 8 in)
length	12.80 m (42 ft)
height	4.97 m (156 ft 4 in)
wing area	45.06 m² (485 sq ft)

COMBAT DATA

CRUISING SPEED

Although it had little effect on flying characteristics, the E-1B's fixed radome caused considerable drag, which gave the aircraft a slow cruising speed.

E-1B TRACER 262 km/h (162 mph)

AD-4W SKYRAIDER 402 km/h (249 mph)

E-2C HAWKEYE 576 km/h (357 mph)

CREW

As AEW systems increased in complexity, the mounting airframes became larger. This in turn allowed the carriage of larger crews, who were better able to make use of the increased capability.

E-1B TRACER 4 persons

AD-4W SKYRAIDER 3 persons

E-2C HAWKEYE 5 persons

POWER

With its turboprop engines, the Grumman E-2 Hawkeye has more than enough power for carrier launches with its heavy load of AEW equipment. The Hawkeye was as worthy a replacement for the Tracer, as the Tracer was for the Douglas AD-4W/5W Skyraider.

E-2C HAWKEYE 7322 kW (9820 hp)

AD-4W SKYRAIDER 2013 kW (2700 hp)

E-1B TRACER 2274 kW (3050 hp)

COD and the 'Stoof with a Roof'

Douglas had been producing a COD version of its AD Skyraider for the US Navy since 1950, but concern was mounting that the aircraft was unable to accommodate large items such as engines or nuclear stores. Grumman used the S2F-2 Tracker airframe as a basis for its TF-1 Trader. It featured a deeper fuselage and could seat nine passengers or accommodate up to 1588 kg (3494 lb), which were loaded via a specially designed fuselage door. In 1953

the Navy showed keen interest in the aircraft. The type entered production on the same line as the Tracker, entering service late in 1955.

Two special variants of the TF-1 were produced: the TF-1Q (later EC-1A) Electronic Countermeasures (ECM) aircraft and the TF-1W which flight tested a mock-up of the WF-2's radar antenna fairing.

As with the Trader, Grumman pressed on with its WF-2 design with little Navy backing. The aircraft eventually appeared with its AN/APS-82 radar housed in a

large, strut-mounted radome and with modified tail surfaces and wing-fold mechanism. It served from 1960 to 1977.

Below: To many, the WF-2 was 'Willy Fudd' (a play on its designation), while others nicknamed it the 'Stoof with a Roof', from the S2F-2's 'Stoof' appellation.

Above: With a TF-1 Trader and S2F-2 Tracker (nearer the camera) in formation, the similarities are obvious.

Being based on the S2F-2 airframe, the Trader retained the increased-span tailplanes of this variant.

With their busy operational schedules, the C-1As made good use of their rear-mounted arrester hooks.

With all offensive equipment deleted, including the Tracker's nacelle-mounted sonobuoy launch tubes, the C-1A had long, streamlined fairings at the rear of its nacelles.

Wing folding is an important feature of many naval aircraft. The Trader's wings folded upwards across the upper fuselage, while those of the Tracer folded backwards to lie alongside the fuselage.

C-1A TRADER

All carriers (except for one training ship) lost their Traders during the 1980s. Previously, aircraft had been assigned to specific ships, such as USS Nimitz.

Crews found the C-1A an ideal carrier-based transport and the type achieved an excellent safety record.

Grumman's post-war pistons

■ **F7F-3N TIGERCAT:** Designed as a carrier-based fighter and fighter-bomber, the Tigercat saw only limited service aboard carriers. The night fighters were the only types to operate at sea.

■ **F8F BEARCAT:** While pilots adored the Bearcat for its performance, ground crew faced problems with maintenance. The F8F is often considered the best piston-engined fighter ever.

■ **S-2 TRACKER:** One of Grumman's most successful post-war designs, the S-2 led to the C-1A and E-1B. It was an outstanding anti-submarine warfare aircraft, and a few served into the 1990s.

GRUMMAN
F11F TIGER

● First US Navy supersonic fighter ● Sidewinder-armed ● 'Blue Angels'

F or several years the F11F Tiger was seen by millions during aerobatic performances by the US Navy's 'Blue Angels' team. The Tiger was the first supersonic fighter to enter US Navy service and had a brief moment of glory in the 1950s when it operated from American carrier decks. The Tiger was an interim aircraft, however, and was soon replaced.

▲ The Tiger's career in the US Navy was relatively short because of the appearance of the more capable Vought F8U Crusader and ongoing problems with the F11F's J65 engine.

GRUMMAN F11F TIGER

▲ Prototype Tiger
The Tiger prototypes were easily distinguished by their short noses; 138604 was the first.

▼ Into service
In all, six squadrons were equipped with the Tiger, including VF-21, whose aircraft wore 'shark's mouth' markings.

▲ Early production
The short nose of this F11F indicates that it is one of the first operational examples.

▲ Air-to-air missiles
This development F11F-1 is fitted with four early Sidewinder missiles.

▲ Reconnaissance variant
Grumman planned to build a photo-reconnaissance version of the Tiger, the F11F-1P (originally F9F-9P), but all 85 were cancelled.

▲ Panther/Cougar development
An F11F-1 of VF-33 'Squadron waits to leave the USS Intrepid via the port catapult. A development of the F9F Panther and Cougar, the F11F was first known as the F9F-8 and then the F9F-9.

FACTS AND FIGURES

➤ The US Navy's 'Blue Angels' aerobatic team used Tigers for longer than any other aircraft, from 1957 to 1969.

➤ One of the two F11F-1Fs was flown to a world altitude record of 23,449 m (76,913 ft).

➤ Tigers spent their last years in service as advanced pilot trainers.

➤ In 1962 the F11F-1 was redesignated F-11A; the J79-engined F11F-1F would have been known as the F-11B.

➤ The prototype Grumman G-98 Tiger first flew, as the YF9F-9, on 30 July 1954.

➤ Grumman manufactured 201 Tigers between July 1954 and December 1958.

Fast cat for the 'Blue Angels'

In 1953 the US Navy turned to its best-known warplane manufacturer, Grumman, to build a single-seat, high-speed fighter for carrier operations. The F11F Tiger had many advanced features, including a 'wasp-waisted', or 'area-ruled', fuselage for supersonic flying and an afterburner for its turbojet engine. However, the Tiger lacked an air-to-air radar and, in spite of its speed and manoeuvrability, had little potential for growth.

Entering service in March 1957, the F11F was a familiar sight on the aircraft-carrier decks of the US fleet for about three years. One aircraft gained notoriety in 1958 when a pilot making a gunnery run managed to fly into his own stream of cannon shells and had to eject and parachute to safety. He was widely reported as the first US test pilot ever to shoot himself down.

Always seen as a temporary expedient by the Navy, this attractive warplane was,

Below: After the 42nd Tiger had left the production line a longer nose was introduced to accommodate a radar set. This was never fitted, however.

Above: The first F11Fs were phased out as early as 1959, only months after production ended.

perhaps, best known for its role in equipping the Navy's 'Blue Angels' display team for several years. In squadron service it began to be replaced by Vought's F8U Crusader in the late 1950s.

F11F-1 Tiger

Type: single-seat carrier-based day-fighter

Powerplant: one 33.14-kN (7450-lb-thrust) Wright J65-W-18 afterburning turbojet engine

Maximum speed: 1207 km/h (748 mph) at sea level

Maximum cruising speed: 929 km/h (575 mph) at 11,580 m (38,000 ft)

Initial climb rate: 1565 m/min (5130 fpm)

Range: 2044 km (1267 miles)

Service ceiling: 12,770 m (41,900 ft)

Weights: empty 6091 kg (13,400 lb); maximum take-off 10,052 kg (22,114 lb)

Armament: four 20-mm cannon and up to four underwing AAM-N-1 (AIM-9) Sidewinder 1A or 1C infra-red air-to-air missiles

Dimensions:
span	9.64 m (31 ft 7 in)
length	14.31 m (46 ft 11 in)
height	4.03 m (13 ft 3 in)
wing area	23.23 m² (250 sq ft)

F11F-1 TIGER

This F11F-1 wears the distinctive markings of US Navy Fighter Squadron VF-21. The light grey upper and white under surfaces were typical of service Tigers during the 1950s.

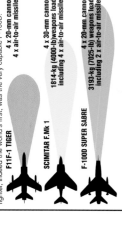

To improve the Tiger's air-to-air capability, it was intended to fit radar in the lengthened nose of later production aircraft. However, this plan was abandoned because of the F11F's short service career.

The Tiger's primary armament was four fixed forward-firing 20-mm cannon mounted under the engine air intakes. The F11F was also fitted with the newly-developed Sidewinder heat-seeking air-to-air missile.

The Tiger's thin wing (thinner than that of the F9F-6) introduced new structural techniques in its manufacture. The outer wing skins, which enclosed a boxed beam structure, were milled from solid aluminium slabs for strength.

Four underwing pylons were used to carry fuel tanks and early examples of the Sidewinder heat-seeking air-to-air missile. These pylons were redundant, and therefore removed, on 'Blue Angels' display aircraft.

The Wright J65 afterburning turbojet was a licence-built version of the British Armstrong Siddeley Sapphire engine. The prototype and first three F11F-1s were initially fitted with non-afterburning engines because the afterburning version was not ready. Later aircraft had afterburning J65-W-18 engines fitted from the outset, although these were de-rated compared to the intended W-6 version.

In an attempt to solve the Tiger's engine problems, two F11F-1Fs were built with the larger General Electric J79 engine. This powerplant gave the F11F Mach 2 performance. It was later used in McDonnell's F4H Phantom II.

COMBAT DATA

ARMAMENT

The Royal Navy's first supersonic fighter, the Scimitar, could carry an air-to-surface load, including bombs, rockets and missiles in addition to its air-to-air armament. The USAF's first supersonic fighter, indeed the world's first, was the very capable F-100D.

F11F-1 TIGER — 4 x 20-mm cannon / 4 x air-to-air missiles

SCIMITAR F.Mk 1 — 4 x 30-mm cannon / 1814-kg (4000-lb) weapons load, including 4 x air-to-air missiles

F-100D SUPER SABRE — 4 x 20-mm cannon / 3193-kg (7025-lb) weapons load, including 2 x air-to-air missiles

CLIMB RATE

All three types were fitted with afterburning turbojet engines – two in the case of the Scimitar and Super Sabre. The single-engined Tiger had a poorer climb rate because of its low power-to-weight ratio. It was also hampered by its trouble-plagued J65 engine.

F-100D SUPER SABRE — 5517 m/min (18,100 fpm)
SCIMITAR F.Mk 1 — 3658 m/min (12,000 fpm)
F11F-1 TIGER — 1565 m/min (5130 fpm)

RANGE

The Super Sabre's range of nearly 2500 km (1600 miles) was attained with the aid of drop-tanks. The F-100 and Scimitar could also be air-to-air refuelled, which added to their flexibility.

SCIMITAR F.Mk 1 — 2288 km (1546 miles)
F11F-1 TIGER — 2044 km (1267 miles)
F-100D SUPER SABRE — 2494 km (1419 miles)

'Blue Angels' manoeuvres

OPENER: At 2286 m (7,500 ft), the 'Blue Angels' roll on their backs and perform a 'Split-S' towards the ground. At a closing speed of 1900 km/h (1180 mph) the four F11Fs meet at the centre of the field and pass within feet.

FLEUR-DE-LYS: The 'Blue Angels', in diamond formation with a solo man below, perform the breathtaking Fleur-de-Lys. At the start of its climb the formation separates and rolls into place, and reforms in the diamond formation as it passes the crowd.

LEFT ECHELON ROLL: Approaching low in an echelon, in which each Tiger is stepped back and down to the left of the leader, the team rolls to the left. This difficult manoeuvre helped the team to establish its reputation.

GRUMMAN
A-6 INTRUDER

● Classic naval aircraft ● Three decades of service ● Many upgrades

▲ A familiar sight on US carrier decks in both Navy and Marine Corps markings, the A-6 proved a highly capable aircraft in many combat actions.

O n 28 February 1997 a ceremony was held at NAS (Naval Air Station) Whidbey Island to celebrate the retirement of the A-6 Intruder from the US Navy. The aircraft had provided more than three decades of service, most recently by A-6E variants equipped with advanced laser and infra-red (IR) targeting systems. In the course of its career the A-6 was involved in several combat actions and fought superbly during the Gulf War.

GRUMMAN A-6 INTRUDER

▲ **HARM compatibility**
From 1990 the A-6E was given AGM-88 HARM (High-Speed Anti-Radiation Missile) capability.

▲ **Into the storm**
Wearing mission symbols and heavily armed, this A-6E prepares for launch on a Desert Storm raid.

▲ **Protecting the Kurds**
After the First Gulf War Intruders were involved in Operation 'Provide Comfort' – the protection of Kurdish people returning to Northern Iraq.

▲ **Intruder's last war**
Both A-6E strike aircraft and KA-6D tankers were involved in the 1991 Gulf War.

▼ **Tacit Rainbow**
Designed to attack enemy radars, the AGM-136 Tacit Rainbow was tested on this A-6E.

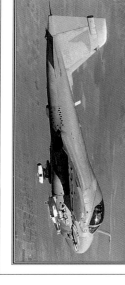

FACTS AND FIGURES

▶ VA-75 squadron introduced the Intruder into service in 1963 and was the last unit to fly the type in 1997.

▶ Neither the advanced A-6F nor the cheaper A-6G entered production.

▶ F/A-18C/D Hornets currently undertake the missions once flown by Intruders.

▶ Several US Marine Corps A-6Es were passed to the Navy when the Marines retired their A-6s.

▶ The US Navy and Marines Corps intend to replace their A-6Es with F/A-18E/Fs.

▶ Some 240 A-6As became A-6Es; 12 were built per year between 1972 and 1977.

A-6E Intruder

Type: all-weather shipborne attack aircraft

Powerplant: two 41.40-kN (9040-lb-thrust) Pratt & Whitney J52-P-8B non-afterburning turbojets

Maximum speed: 1037 km/h (643 mph) clean at sea level

Maximum climb rate: 2323 m/min (7620 fpm) at sea level

Range: 1627 km (1008 miles) with maximum military load; ferry range 5222 km (3240 miles)

Service ceiling: 12,925 m (42,400 ft)

Weights: empty 12,132 kg (26,690 lb); maximum take-off for catapult launch 26,580 kg (58,478 lb)

Armament: a maximum of 8165 kg (17,963 lb) of ordnance and external fuel

Dimensions:
span	16.15 m	(53 ft)
length	16.69 m	(54 ft 9 in)
height	4.93 m	(16 ft 2 in)
wing area	49.13 m²	(529 sq ft)

COMBAT DATA

THRUST

With its afterburning engines, the F/A-18C is a more powerful aircraft than the A-6E or A-7E which it replaced. It has shorter range than the A-6E, however.

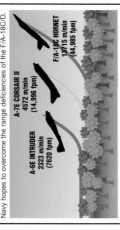

A-6E INTRUDER 82.80 kN (18,080 lb thrust)

A-7E CORSAIR II 66.60 kN (14,982 lb thrust)

F/A-18C HORNET 142.40 kN (32,034 lb thrust)

BOMBLOAD

As a dedicated attack aircraft, the A-6E could carry a formidable bombload. The A-7E was the US Navy's second attack platform, but did not have the weapons-carrying ability of the A-6E.

A-6E INTRUDER 8165 kg (17,963 lb)

A-7E CORSAIR II 6804 kg (15,000 lb)

F/A-18C HORNET 7031 kg (15,500 lb)

INITIAL CLIMB RATE

Comparing aircraft in clean condition, the F/A-18C has by far the most impressive climb rate. When the F/A-18E/F is introduced, the Navy hopes to overcome the range deficiencies of the F/A-18C/D.

A-6E INTRUDER 2323 m/min (7620 fpm)

A-7E CORSAIR II 4572 m/min (14,996 fpm)

F/A-18C HORNET 13715 m/min (44,985 fpm)

At the front line to the last

New avionics and radar were primary features of the A-6E Intruder when it first flew in 1970. In order to achieve rapid procurement of the new model within a limited budget, the US Navy began a programme of upgrading A-6As to the higher standard while new A-6Es were being built.

Further upgrades were added to the Intruder, including a navigation system that was used in the F-14A Tomcat. The most important modification, however,

was the addition of a Target Recognition Attack Multi-sensor (TRAM) turret beneath the nose. This contained laser, IR and video sensors, allowing accurate targeting and compatibility with smart, laser-guided munitions.

A programme to fit the A-6 fleet with new composite wings was started in 1988. In addition, the capability to fire stand-off missiles, including the AGM-84E SLAM, was added in the early 1990s, making the last of the Intruders highly capable attack platforms.

A-6E INTRUDER

In service with VA-42 'Green Pawns', this A-6E wears the low-visibility camouflage which was common at the end of the type's career. VA-42 was the Atlantic Fleet Replenishment Squadron.

A removable air-to-air refuelling probe was normally mounted on the centreline, aft of the nose radome. Refuelling was possible from KA-6Ds and other hose-equipped tankers.

Short-sighted US Navy officials cancelled the formidable A-6F in favour of the A-12. This was later scrapped.

Early in the Intruder programme, it was realised that the rear fuselage-mounted airbrakes interfered with airflow around the tail. Hence split airbrakes were employed at each wingtip.

For stowage aboard the carrier, the Intruder's wings were folded hydraulically at a hinge line just outboard of the outer pylon.

Single-piece, all-moving tailplanes provided pitch control and all flying controls were hydraulically powered. The rudder hinge line allowed fuel to be jettisoned from the fuselage tanks.

Intruders proved vulnerable to small-arms fire over Vietnam, a problem which was to surface again when the type was used at low level in the Gulf. The prominent exhausts could also attract heat-seeking surface-to-air missiles.

Shown here with a load of 18 Mk 82 227-kg (500-lb) bombs, the A-6E was also able to carry stand-off weapons such as the AGM-84E SLAM (Stand-off Land Attack Missile).

Both the pilot and navigator sat on Martin-Baker GRU-7 ejector seats. The bombardier/navigator was positioned to starboard, slightly below and behind the pilot, and was responsible for operating the attack systems.

FLIR and laser-designator systems were located in the TRAM turret, at the heart of the A-6E's attack avionics.

TRAM attack

Gyro-stabilisation allows the TRAM turret to remain locked on to the target, even as the aircraft overflies it.

1 TARGETING INFORMATION: Using its Forward-Looking Infra-Red (FLIR) and laser-targeting systems, the A-6E is able to calculate precise targeting information for dumb or laser-guided munitions.

2 OVER THE TARGET: FLIR allows the A-6E to attack the hottest parts of a target: the engine room of a ship or a moving tank. The TRAM turret rotates to keep the target designated and in view of the IR system.

3 POST-STRIKE ASSESSMENT: After the attack the FLIR is able to look backwards from the turret. TV-like pictures are produced, which are viewed in the cockpit and recorded by an onboard video recorder for damage assessment.

GRUMMAN
E-2 HAWKEYE

● Combat proven ● Airborne early warning ● Fighter controller

▲ Throughout 22 years of service the E-2 Hawkeye has become an indispensable part of US naval operations. The latest E-2C Group II aircraft are far more capable and are likely to remain in use for some time.

D esigned as a flying radar station, the Hawkeye is the US Navy's eye in the sky. Sometimes called 'the affordable AWACS' (Airborne Warning and Control System), it is just what the US Navy requires to guard its aircraft-carrier battle groups and to direct friendly warplanes when the action begins. This twin-engined aircraft, with its long, slender wing, huge tail, and saucer-shaped rotodome, is now a familiar sight in every US Navy carrier air wing.

GRUMMAN E-2 HAWKEYE

▼ Fuel venting
An anonymous E-2, probably flying a research and development mission, dumps fuel from the rear-mounted fuel vent pipe.

▲ Rotodome
An E-2C from USS Constellation shows off its enormous radar rotodome.

Catapult launch ▼
The Hawkeye runs its engines up to full power before the steam catapult hurls it from the carrier deck at take-off speed.

▼ Feet-dry Hawkeye
All US Navy E-2s have a permanent shore base and most export customers fly their E-2s solely from airbases. This aircraft flies from NAS Norfolk, Virginia.

▲ Folded Hawkeye
With its wings folded the Hawkeye presents a more compact shape for stowage aboard the crowded decks of an aircraft-carrier.

FACTS AND FIGURES

▸ The Hawkeye was the last propeller-driven naval aircraft built by Grumman, the world's primary naval aircraft builder.

▸ In December 1971 Israel purchased four Hawkeyes equipped with APS-125 radar.

▸ Other users of the Hawkeye include Egypt, Japan, Singapore and Taiwan.

▸ The Hawkeye made its first flight from Grumman's Peconic River, Long Island, facility on 21 October 1960.

▸ The Hawkeye is now back in production, equipped with the AN/APS-145 radar.

▸ Hawkeyes are launched ahead of other carrier aircraft and are the last to return.

PROFILE

Eyes of the fleet

Nicknamed the 'Hummer' by its crews, the E-2 Hawkeye was designed to replace the earlier E-1B Tracer, the first radar plane in the fleet. The Hawkeye, with turboprop engines, a higher speed and a higher ceiling, was a great improvement over its predecessor. The Hawkeye introduced a General Electric APS-96 radar, the antenna of which revolves at six revolutions per minute inside the disc-shaped radome.

Japan received the first of its E-2s in 1982 and it is known as Daya (kite) in Japanese service. Several countries fly the E-2, including Egypt, Israel and Singapore.

The first production Hawkeyes began reaching squadron VAW-110 'Firebirds' based at North Island, California, in 1964. In Vietnam, the Hawkeye performed its primary mission of protecting aircraft-carriers with its radar 'eyes', but it also served as a flying headquarters for F-4 Phantom IIs and F-8 Crusaders on combat air patrols.

The Hawkeye's radar unit has changed again, to APS-138, APS-139 and APS-145. The APS-145, now being retrofitted to aircraft in the fleet, offers better resistance to jamming. Although it is now getting old, the present E-2C Hawkeye is an up-to-date, state-of-the-art military fighting machine.

E-2C HAWKEYE

This aircraft belongs to VAW-126 'Seahawks', part of CVW-3, aboard the USS *John F. Kennedy*. The unit is home based at NAS Norfolk, Virginia, and proved invaluable during Operation Desert Storm.

A crew of five is normally carried, including pilot and co-pilot, a combat information centre officer, air control officer and radar operator.

E-2C Hawkeye

Type: carrier-based airborne early warning aircraft

Powerplant: two 3661-kW (4910-hp) Allison T56-A425 turboprop engines

Maximum speed: 598 km/h (374 mph)

Endurance: 6 hours 6 min

Ferry range: 2583 km (1602 miles)

Service ceiling: 9390 m (30,000 ft)

Weights: maximum take-off 23,556 kg (51,900 lb)

Accommodation: crew of five; fuel load of 5624 kg (12,399 lb)

Dimensions:
span	24.56 m (80 ft 7 in)
length	17.54 m (57 ft 7 in)
height	5.58 m (18 ft 3 in)
wing area	65.03 m² (2593 sq ft)

COMBAT DATA

SERVICE CEILING

The Hawkeye requires a good service ceiling because the higher the radar is, the further it can see. The E-2 is being fitted with the exceptional AN/APS-145 radar, giving it stunning performance.

E-2C HAWKEYE 9390 m (30,000 ft)

P-3 AEW ORION 8625 m (28,297 ft)

E-3C SENTRY 8840 m (29,003 ft)

RADAR RANGE

Using the latest AN/APS-145 radar the P-3 AEW will be able to locate low-flying aircraft targets at very long range. In its E-3D and E-3F variants the Sentry is much more capable than the E-3C.

E-2C HAWKEYE 480 km (300 miles)

P-3 AEW ORION 556 km (345 miles)

E-3C SENTRY 470 km (291 miles)

CREW

As it is a small aircraft the E-2C carries few crew. This means a necessary reliance on automation and a heavy workload for operators. In larger aircraft there are more crew to divide the work between.

E-2C HAWKEYE 5 crew

P-3 AEW ORION 16 crew

E-3C SENTRY 20 crew

Avionics systems create a vast amount of heat and must be kept cool to maintain their efficiency. A large dorsal radiator cools the fluid of the E-2's cooling system.

Remaining on station for four hours, 300 km (186 miles) from the carrier and without inflight refuelling, the Hawkeye requires long endurance. This is achieved by its long, slender wings.

A four-fin tail arrangement was required to give the Hawkeye sufficient directional stability, but the tail had to be small enough to fit in a carrier's hangar.

US Navy E-2Cs have been slow to take on the low-visibility markings of the rest of the fleet, retaining colourful squadron markings and grey and white camouflage.

With a diameter of 7.32 m (24 ft) the rotodome houses the AN/APS-139 radar and 'identification friend or foe' systems. It is lowered on jacks for parking on the carrier.

Very strong undercarriage units are features of all ship-borne aircraft designed to be launched by steam catapult. This bar on the nosewheel leg connects with the catapult shuttle on the deck.

Although the original E-2C model was powered by the 3661-kW (4910-hp) T56-A-425, the latest E-2C Group IIs are fitted with the even more powerful 3803-kW (5096-hp) T56-A-427.

AIRBORNE CONTROLLER: When the E-2 detects enemy aircraft or anti-ship missiles (ASMs) it alerts F-14 Tomcats, which are sent on barrier combat air patrol to intercept.

Controlling the air war

OVER THE HORIZON: Acting as an extension of the aircraft-carrier's own radar, the E-2C is able to monitor possible threats at greater distances.

9150 m (30,000 ft)

AIRCRAFT-CARRIER

RANGE km (miles)	900 (560)	800 (500)	700 (435)	600 (373)	500 (310)	400 (250)	300 (186)	200 (125)	100 (62)

Tu-22M

F-14

ASM

E-2

204

GRUMMAN
C-2A GREYHOUND

- COD aircraft ● Derived from the E-2 Hawkeye ● Twin turboprop

D uring the 1960s Grumman built the Greyhound for hauling supplies and people from land bases to the decks of the US Navy's aircraft-carriers. This is known in jargon as the COD (carrier on-board delivery) mission. The Greyhound draws its fundamental design features from the better-known Grumman E-2 Hawkeye airborne early-warning aircraft. It is a superb aircraft with a fine record of safety and performance.

▲ The US Navy's C-2 Greyhound fleet was delivered in two batches, beginning in the mid-1960s and ending in the late-1980s. Most of the original batch have now been retired.

GRUMMAN C-2A GREYHOUND

▲ **Atlantic and Pacific C-2s**
Two transport units are equipped with C-2s and are based in the US. A detachment is also stationed in Japan. Training is carried out at NAS Norfolk, Virginia.

▲ **Carrier on-board delivery**
COD squadrons are attached to Hawkeye-equipped airborne early warning wings.

▲ **Folding wings for easy stowage**
The Greyhound has the same wing as the E-2 Hawkeye. Wing folding is a necessity for aircraft moving within the confines of a fleet carrier.

▼ **Mail call**
One of the Greyhound's most important deliveries, at least from the sailors' point of view, is the cargo of mail for crews.

▼ **Different cargoes**
As well as ferrying personnel, the C-2 delivers weapons for the carrier's combat aircraft. Among the weapons shown here are three AIM-54 Phoenix air-to-air missiles for an F-14 Tomcat.

FACTS AND FIGURES

▶ The Greyhound prototype completed its maiden flight on 18 November 1964.

▶ Fifty-eight Greyhounds were produced in two batches – between 1964 and 1968 and between 1985 and 1989.

▶ A proposal to re-open the Greyhound production line was rejected in 1991.

▶ Plans to replace the Greyhound with a version of the Lockheed S-3A Viking met with only limited success.

▶ The C-2A replaced the Grumman C-1A Trader, which was based on the S-2.

▶ Grumman considered a jet-powered version of the C-2 but it was never built.

PROFILE

Delivery van of the US Fleet

The Grumman C-2A Greyhound was developed in the early 1960s by mating a deeper, more capacious fuselage to the basic wings and tail of the E-2 Hawkeye. The result was a highly effective transport for the essential task of delivering supplies to aircraft-carriers at sea.

Although it is equipped with a tailhook and folding wings for carrier operations, the Greyhound is not intended to be stationed aboard a carrier. Instead, it is operated by a shore-based squadron placed in a strategic location to resupply ships at sea. The C-2A Greyhound is also successful in its secondary duty as a training aircraft, and has been used for training Hawkeye crews.

Before the cockpits of combat aircraft were opened up to women in 1993, the Greyhound was one of the very few carrier-capable aeroplanes to be flown by female pilots. Unlike the crews of fighters and bombers, these transport pilots fly a real-world mission every time they take off and land. Great care has to be taken when landing the Greyhound on an aircraft-carrier because its large wingspan leaves little room for manoeuvre on a crowded deck. But, for its size, the Greyhound is relatively easy to fly.

C-2A GREYHOUND

Aircraft 155124 was one of the original batch of 19 Greyhounds delivered from the mid-1960s. 'JM' is the tailcode of Fleet Logistics Support Squadron 24 (VR-24), 'Lifting Eagles', based at Sigonella, Italy.

In all, including prototypes, 58 Greyhounds have been delivered to the US Navy. The 39 built in the 1980s differ from earlier C-2s in having uprated engines and an auxiliary power unit fitted.

The Greyhound's engines are the same 3663-kW (4900-hp) Allison T56-A-425 turbines as those fitted to the E-2C Hawkeye. This commonality between the two aircraft eases maintenance and reduces the need to carry different spare parts in the cramped confines of an aircraft-carrier.

Redesigned for the transport role, the Greyhound's fuselage is considerably larger than that of the Hawkeye. When configured for passengers, the Greyhound can carry up to 39 people. Twenty stretchers can also be installed.

Mission profiles for the Greyhound centre around its role for the delivery of high-priority cargo and passengers to and from carriers at sea. Its range of 1900 km (1180 miles) when fully loaded is far greater than that of land-based helicopters.

The tail design is another feature shared with the E-2. Four fins are required to provide sufficient tail area, but must still fit within the cramped confines of the carrier hangar. All except the port inner fin have a rudder fitted.

For the loading of bulky items like aircraft engines and weapons, the C-2 has a rear ramp. An arrester hook is fitted for carrier landings.

Below: This photograph of 162153, one of the batch built in the 1980s, shows the wing and tail design to good effect. These are shared by the E-2 Hawkeye.

Above: Carrying the 'RG' tailcode of the since-disestablished VRC-50, this Greyhound was based at Cubi Point in the Philippines.

C-2A Greyhound

Type: twin-engine carrier onboard delivery (COD) transport

Powerplant: two 3663-kW (4900-hp) Allison T56-A-425 turboprop engines

Maximum speed: 574 km/h (356 mph)

Range: 1930 km (1199 miles)

Service ceiling: 10,210 m (33,500 ft)

Weights: empty 16,486 kg (36,269 lb); maximum take-off 26,081 kg (57,378 lb)

Accommodation: two pilots, up to 39 passengers or 20 stretchers plus four attendants or up to 6800 kg (14,960 lb) of palletised cargo

Dimensions:
span	24.56 m (80 ft 6 in)
length	17.32 m (56 ft 10 in)
height	4.84 m (15 ft 10 in)
wing area	65.03 m² (700 sq ft)

ACTION DATA

LOAD CAPACITY

The tilt-rotor Osprey, if funded, will greatly enhance the COD capabilities of the fleet. It has almost twice the capacity of the C-2. For land-based operations the C-2 has a maximum load of 6800 kg. The Viking, based on the S-3 ASW aircraft, has a limited capacity.

C-2A GREYHOUND 6800 kg (14,960 lb)
V-22A OSPREY 9072 kg (19,958 lb)
US-3A VIKING 2600 kg (2068 miles)

RANGE

When fully loaded and making a short take-off, the Osprey has an impressive range performance – an improvement on that of the C-2. The US-3A also has an excellent range.

US-3A VIKING 3700 km (2294 miles)
C-2A GREYHOUND 1930 km (1199 miles)
V-22A OSPREY 3336 km (2068 miles)

TAKE-OFF RUN

The Viking has the shorter take-off distance of the two fixed-wing aircraft. The Osprey tilt-rotor has a vertical take-off capability, but uses a short take-off run when carrying all but the smallest payloads.

C-2A GREYHOUND 932 m (3057 ft)
V-22A OSPREY 152 m (499 ft)
US-3A VIKING 670 m (2198 ft)

Carrier on-board delivery aircraft

■ **GRUMMAN C-1 TRADER:** The Trader was a variant of the S-2 Tracker, which had its ASW equipment removed to make room for freight.

■ **GRUMMAN TBM-3R AVENGER:** As well as carrying personnel, COD Avengers delivered nuclear weapon components in times of crisis.

■ **GRUMMAN US-3A VIKING:** To supplement the C-2 fleet, a small number of anti-submarine S-3A Vikings have been converted for COD tasks.

■ **FAIREY GANNET COD.Mk 4:** In common with American COD designs, the British Gannet COD.Mk 4 was based on an existing design.

GRUMMAN
OV-1 MOHAWK

- Battlefield reconnaissance ● Electronic intelligence ● STOL aircraft

▲ Mohawk crews had an excellent view from the domed cockpit windows. The cockpit was also fitted with sensor systems and the crew had the ability to produce photographic prints.

Few combat aircraft can boast of a service career lasting more than 35 years. As the first turboprop-powered aircraft for the US Army, the OV-1 Mohawk entered service in 1961. A series of variants, modifications and upgrades has meant that it has remained the primary battlefield reconnaissance and liaison type for the army and has even flown in the attack role. The OV-1 served in the Vietnam War and, almost 30 years later, in the Gulf.

GRUMMAN OV-1 MOHAWK

▼ **Short take-off**
Demonstrating its STOL capabilities, this early Mohawk is finished in the original overall olive-drab US Army camouflage. The full-span leading-edge slats and large area flaps can also be seen.

▲ **SLAR pod**
Mapping out the ground on either side of the aircraft, the radar occupies a huge pod slung under the fuselage and is capable of tracking moving vehicles.

▲ **Bound for Argentina**
Seven OV-1Ds await the application of Argentine army markings before they are delivered.

▼ **Drop-tanks and camouflage**
Although underwing tanks were usual on the OV-1D, this four-tone paint scheme is very rare.

▲ **Odd pod**
This OV-1D has a highly unusual pod on the right outboard pylon, which may be some type of electronic countermeasures system.

FACTS AND FIGURES

➤ At least 16 EV-1E aircraft were built under the Quick Look III programme, but the US Army denies their existence.

➤ US OV-1s were replaced by Beechcraft RC-12K/N reconnaissance aircraft.

➤ A few OV-1Ds which were used in South Korea were given to the nation.

➤ Israel was the only export customer and may have used Israeli systems to update its aircraft to OV-1D standard.

➤ US military aid to Argentina in the 1990s has included at least 36 Mohawks.

➤ NASA used one OV-1, with a wing-mounted jet, for noise monitoring tests.

PROFILE

Battlefield surveillance platform

Grumman designed the G-124, which became the OV-1, in response to a joint US Army and Marines proposal of 1956. The requirement called for an aircraft which could carry a range of observation equipment and was capable of short take-off and landing (STOL) performance from rough airfields.

Nine development YOV-1A aircraft were ordered, and the first flew on 14 April 1959. That same year, the army, after the Marines had dropped out of the programme, placed orders for

OV-1A, -1B and -1C versions, and eventually received 64, 90 and 133, respectively. Each variant carried a different set of sensors, but the later OV-1D combined all of these systems in one airframe and had more powerful engines. Israel has converted its four OV-1Cs to OV-1D standard.

Cameras, side-looking airborne radar (SLAR) and infra-red systems were all available in the OV-1D, and the specialised RV-1D was developed to undertake electronic intelligence (ELINT) duties. In Vietnam,

armed Mohawks flew attack missions as JOV-1As, while OV/RV-1Ds provided vital local intelligence and a reliable back-up to other systems in the Gulf.

Left: Mohawks were painted in a grey colour scheme when they were retired from US Army service. Large numbers of OV-1s served in Europe, especially in Germany.

Right: A weather-worn OV-1D shows the extended radome ahead of the nose and the two-seat cockpit. The overwing position of the exhaust afforded some protection from heat-seeking missiles. A four-seat OV-1E variant was proposed but was never built.

OV-1D Mohawk

Type: two-seat reconnaissance, observation and liaison aircraft

Powerplant: two 820-kW (1100-hp) Textron Lycoming T53-L-15 turboprops

Maximum speed: 478 km/h (296 mph) at 1525 m (5000 ft)

Maximum cruising speed: 443 km/h (275 mph)

Maximum climb rate: 716 m/min (2350 fpm) at sea level

Take-off run: 177 m (385 ft) to 15 m (50 ft) altitude

Range: 1642 km (1020 miles)

Service ceiling: 9235 m (30,300 ft)

Weights: empty equipped 5020 kg (11,044 lb); maximum take-off 8722 kg (19,188 lb)

Dimensions:
span	14.63 m	(48 ft)
length	12.50 m	(41 ft)
height	3.86 m	(12 ft 8 in)
wing area	33.45 m²	(360 sq ft)

COMBAT DATA

MAXIMUM CRUISING SPEED

The Beechcraft RC-12D has replaced the OV-1 in US Army service. The types have similar cruising speeds but speed was more important for the OV-1 since it often flew dangerous missions.

OV-1D MOHAWK	443 km/h (275 mph)
RC-12D GUARDRAIL	438 km/h (272 mph)
MSSA	315 km/h (195 mph)

TAKE-OFF RUN TO 15 METRES (50 FEET)

Exceptional short-field performance was a feature of the OV-1. The MSSA is based on the Pilatus Britten-Norman Islander and shares its STOL capabilities. The RC-12D is not a STOL aircraft.

OV-1D MOHAWK	177 m (385 ft)
MSSA	381 m (1250 ft)
RC-12D GUARDRAIL	869 m (2850 ft)

RANGE

In the intelligence-gathering role range and endurance are important factors and in this area the RC-12D beats the much older OV-1 design.

OV-1D MOHAWK	1642 km (1020 miles)
MSSA	1348 km (835 miles)
RC-12D GUARDRAIL	2935 km (1820 miles)

OV-1D MOHAWK

Israeli Mohawks are fitted with locally-built avionics and, although details are scarce, are probably equivalent to the American OV-1D standard. The aircraft were delivered as OV-1Cs with infra-red surveillance systems.

The primary infra-red detection and observation system is the AN/AAS-24 scanner. A sensor for this is mounted in the extreme nose.

Two crewmembers (pilot and observer) sit side-by-side on Martin-Baker J5 ejection seats. The observer is responsible for operating and monitoring the observation systems, including the use of upwards-firing flares for night photography.

The wings can accommodate two stores pylons on each side. The inboard pair is usually fitted with 567-litre (150-gallon) drop-tanks while the outer pylons remain empty. In Vietnam, JOV-1As could carry 1225 kg (2700 lb) of rocket pods and other weapons.

Unusually for a turboprop aircraft, the Mohawk is fitted with two airbrakes, one mounted on each side of the rear fuselage. These would have been useful during diving attacks in Vietnam.

A distinctive feature of the Mohawk is its triple fin and rudder arrangement. De-icing boots cover the leading edges.

Mohawks can keep local commanders informed of enemy movements using the AN/APD-7 SLAR.

SLAR-equipped aircraft

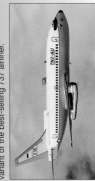

■ **BOEING 737 SURVEILLER:** Indonesia is the only country operating this maritime patrol variant of the best-selling 737 airliner.

■ **BOEING/GRUMMAN E-8 J-STARS:** The combat-proven E-8 combines Grumman systems and a Boeing airframe.

■ **ILYUSHIN Il-20 'COOT-A':** Dedicated to electronic intelligence and radar reconnaissance, the 'Coot-A' has an SLAR under the fuselage.

■ **FAIRCHILD (SWEARINGEN) MERLIN IVC:** Carrying an Ericsson Erieye SLAR, this machine tested systems for the Saab 340 AEW & C aircraft.

GRUMMAN

EA-6B PROWLER

● Electronic warfare aircraft ● In combat from Vietnam to the Gulf

Based on the Grumman A-6 Intruder, the EA-6B Prowler harnesses the electron to 'clean up' combat zones so that friendly warplanes can attack in safety. The Prowler takes a pilot and three operators into action with a powerhouse of 'black boxes', intent on jamming an enemy's radar. But it does more than jam; with its HARM missiles, the EA-6 is a fearsome radar-killer in its own right.

▲ The jamming systems of the EA-6B are some of the most sophisticated in the world. A handful of these aircraft can 'black out' an area the size of France with their powerful electronic systems.

GRUMMAN EA-6B PROWLER

▲ ADVCAP Prowler
In 1990 the advanced capability (ADVCAP) variant of the EA-6B was introduced. This is fitted with a global positioning kit for pinpoint navigation, and chaff, flare and self-protection jamming systems.

Folding wings ▼
With its wings folded up, the EA-6 has a narrow profile. Under the fixed wingroot is the massive TJS jamming pod, containing a high-powered noise generator and a tracking receiver. Operating power is generated by a wind turbine on the pod's nose.

▼ Electronic power
The Prowler's systems are never turned on when it is on deck, as they emit enough energy to microwave anyone passing by.

▲ Catapult launch
The EA-6B is a heavy machine, and a catapult launch is essential for it to reach flying speed. If for any reason the launch fails, the four-man crew will instantly eject as the aircraft clears the deck.

▼ Gulf strike mission
Prowlers were vital components in the Gulf, protecting the massive Coalition air offensive which destroyed Saddam Hussein's air defences.

FACTS AND FIGURES

➤ The first EA-6 Prowler flew at Calverton, New York, on 25 May 1968.

➤ The Prowler has a black radiation warning symbol on its nose so that deck crews do not get 'fried' inadvertently.

➤ Home port for Navy EA-6Bs is Whidbey Island Naval Air Station, north of Seattle.

➤ The Prowler has been through five electronics upgrade programmes.

➤ In 1995, Congress agreed to a US Air Force plan to retire the EF-111 and to fill the electronic 'gap' with EA-6Bs.

➤ The HARM missile used by some Prowlers has a launch weight of 361 kg (749 lb).

PROFILE

Jamming with the fleet

Prowlers are in short supply and are sorely needed. Modern air power demands electronic warfare aircraft, and the US Navy developed the Grumman EA-6B to give its Carrier Air Wings a trump card in today's hi-tech warfare. The Prowler fought in Vietnam (1972), and in every action since – Grenada (1983), Libya (1986), the Gulf War (1991) and Bosnia (1995). The final Prowler was delivered in 1991 and the final

'upgrade' programme curtailed two years later.

The Prowler is 1.37 m (4 ft 6 in) longer than the A-6 Intruder and substantially heavier. It sends out jamming transmissions from underwing pods, and analyses hostile signals received by equipment in a bulge on its tail.

Although well into middle age, the Prowler remains one of the best electronic warriors and will stay in service.

The Prowler is one of the most expensive aircraft in the US Navy inventory. The huge cost of the EA-6B is offset, however, by the lives and aircraft saved by the protection it can provide.

Prowlers have replaced the US Air Force's EF-111 Ravens, even though Prowlers are slower and lack the Raven's 'reach' to accompany strike aircraft on some missions.

The pilot sits in the front port cockpit, surrounded by three electronic countermeasures officers (ECMOs). ECMO one sits by his side and operates the navigation, radar and communications equipment, with ECMO two and three operating the tactical jamming suite.

ECMO two operates the ground-mapping Norden APS-130 radar system, a downgraded version of the A-6E's APQ-156 with attack functions deleted.

The ICAP-II improvement programme allows the pair of underwing TJS pods to jam in any one of seven frequency bands. They can also simultaneously interfere with more than one enemy radar, even when they are using widely different frequencies.

Self-protection jamming to decoy enemy radar-guided missiles is provided by a deception jamming suite. The antenna for this is located next to the refuelling probe.

EA-6B Prowler

Type: four-seat electronic warfare aircraft

Powerplant: two Pratt & Whitney 49.80-kN (9300-lb-thrust) J52-P-408 turbojets

Maximum speed: 1048 km/h (650 mph) in 'clean' condition at sea level

Range: 1770 km (1097 miles)

Service ceiling: 12,550 m (41,164 ft)

Weights: empty 14,588 kg (32,028 lb); loaded 24,703 kg (54,347 lb)

Payload: four AGM-88A HARM (High-speed Anti-Radiation Missiles), AN/ALQ-99 emitter pods, or Aero 1-D 1136-litre (300-gallon) drop-tanks; some with AN/ALQ-149 jamming system

Dimensions:
span	16.15 m (53 ft)
length	18.24 m (60 ft)
height	4.95 m (16 ft)
wing area	49.13 m² (529 sq ft)

EA-6B PROWLER

This EA-6B 'ICAP-II' Prowler flies with VMAQ-2, one of four US Marine Corps squadrons based at the Marine Corps Air Station, Cherry Point. The unit is fully carrier-capable and often deploys with the fleet.

The large HARM missile has a passive seeker head and can be used in standby or pre-programmed modes.

The EA-6B has wingtip speed brakes, similar to those of the Sukhoi Su-25 'Frogfoot'.

The Prowler has wing spoilers for primary roll control, assisted by flaperons at low speeds. The large flaps are almost full-span, and the wing has upper-surface blowing to increase lift at low airspeeds.

The large pod on top of the tail fin houses the system integration receiver, which detects hostile radar emissions and sends them to a central computer for threat analysis.

The aft-facing cylindrical pod on the tail is the ALQ-136 deception countermeasures system, known as the 'beercan' to crews.

A large avionics pallet and fuel tanks occupy the fuselage area behind the engines. The J52 turbojet was also used in the McDonnell Douglas A-4 Skyhawk.

The Prowler can carry an internal fuel load of 6995 kg (15,390 lb), with an additional 4547 kg (10,000 lb) in underwing tanks.

163031
VMAQ-2
MARINES

COMBAT DATA

MAXIMUM SPEED

The Prowler was derived from a subsonic carrier bomber which was able to fly and fight in all weathers, by day or night. The EA-6 lacks the Mach 2 performance of the EF-111, but since its main function as escort formations of heavily-laden strike aircraft at subsonic speeds this is no real handicap.

EF-111 RAVEN
2272 km/h (1049 mph)

EA-6B PROWLER
1048 km/h (650 mph)

Yak-28 'BREWER-E'
1200 km/h (744 mph)

RANGE

The EA-6 has a shorter range than its land-based equivalents. Nevertheless, thanks to its ability to launch from a carrier anywhere on the world's oceans it can reach a much greater range of potential targets than aircraft like the EF-111, which can only operate from a few high-tech air bases.

EF-111 RAVEN
3000 km
(1860 miles)

EA-6B PROWLER
1770 km
(1087 miles)

Yak-28 'BREWER-E'
1900 km (1078 miles)

ELECTRONIC WARFARE CAPABILITY

The Prowler and the EF-111 have a similar electronics fit, but the 'Spark Vark' is a more recent adaptation, and greater computerisation means that one electronic warfare officer can do the job of three aboard the 'Brewer'. Both are a great deal more sophisticated than the 'Brewer', which was operational with Soviet forces until the break-up of the USSR.

EF-111 RAVEN   100%
EA-6B PROWLER   90%
                40%
Yak-28 'BREWER-E'

Location of enemy radar transmitters

Prowlers will often operate in pairs, both to produce wider and more powerful jamming transmissions and, as depicted here, to locate and fix enemy radar sites.

LEAD PROWLER: ►
One aircraft flies close enough to the enemy to activate his radar. The 'senso' notes the exact bearing of the enemy transmitter.

◄ TRAILING PROWLER: Close enough to pick up the enemy radar, but far enough behind for any radar beams to be too weak to return an echo to the enemy, the second Prowler also notes the bearing of the radar site.

LOCATION FIXED: A simple triangulation calculation exactly fixes the location of the enemy radar.

MISSION ACCOMPLISHED: Once the two Prowlers have noted the radar's bearing, they can turn away before coming within range of enemy missile defences.

GRUMMAN
F-14A TOMCAT

● Long-range fleet interceptor ● Recon platform ● Fighter bomber

W ith its high speed and ultra-long-range weapons, the Tomcat is the main defender of the US fleet and can operate hundreds of miles away from the carrier. Its AWG-9 radar can engage six targets at once and its Phoenix missiles can kill hostile bombers 150 km away before they can launch their attacks. The Tomcat is one of the world's true 'Top Guns'.

▲ Tomcat aircrew are an elite within an elite. The pilot and backseat Naval Flight Officer act as a carefully co-ordinated team to wring the best from the awesome combination of performance, sophistication and firepower at their command.

PHOTO FILE

GRUMMAN F-14A TOMCAT

▲ **Fleet defender**
The main threat to US Navy carriers is posed by long-range bombers armed with sea-skimming missiles. Only the Tomcat can intercept the bombers before they get within lethal range.

▲ **Power to protect**
The F-14's high-thrust TF-30 turbofans and swing wing allow it to operate from short carrier decks. Take-offs are made using a powerful steam catapult.

▼ **Detecting the enemy**
As well as its own radar, the F-14 operates with an E-2 Hawkeye, a flying radar station with a huge rotating antenna above the fuselage.

Deadly performer ▼
The F-14 has Mach 2+ performance, a high rate of climb and good manoeuvrability – all the hallmarks of a great fighter.

▲ **Combat-proven**
The F-14 opened its score on 19 August 1981, when F-14 pilots Lt Larry Muszynski (above left) and Cdr Hank Kleeman of VF-41 'Black Aces' squadron destroyed a pair of marauding Libyan Sukhoi Su-22 'Fitters'. Two MiG-23s fell to F-14s in a similar incident during 1989.

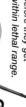

FACTS AND FIGURES

▼ The Tomcat's AWG-9 radar can detect, track and engage targets at ranges of more than 150 km (93 miles).

▼ One Tomcat can engage the same number of targets as three F/A-18 Hornets.

▼ The AIM-54C Phoenix is the world's longest-range air-to-air missile.

▼ The Tomcat's high magnification TV camera enables visual target identification at more than 50 km (30 miles).

▼ Forming the outer edge of a battle group's defences, the Tomcat can engage enemy bombers and missiles more than 800 km (500 miles) out from its home carrier.

PROFILE

Defender of the fleet

The Tomcat has been one of the great superfighters of the world since its first squadron took to the skies in 1972. It packs a massive punch, performs superbly and is the warplane of choice for many aspiring military pilots. Nothing is more calculated to worry an enemy than to know Tomcats are on his track.

And yet this tremendous fighting machine can operate from a 110-m (360-ft) strip of aircraft carrier deck, in all weathers and around the clock. Working with E-2C Hawkeye radar planes and using air-to-air refuelling, a squadron of Tomcats can sanitise the airspace 650 km out from the Carrier Battle Group, allowing no hostile aircraft to threaten the warships below.

Even sea-skimming missiles can be killed by Tomcats using their Phoenix and AMRAAM missiles.

The fact is that Tomcats and their aircrews have to be good – they are protecting a 10-warship, $15-billion battle group manned by 10,000 sailors projecting as much firepower as the United Kingdom's entire armed forces.

The F-14's swing wings allow it to combine high-speed performance and supersonic manoeuvrability with docile low-speed handling.

This Tomcat is armed with two short-range Sidewinder missiles outboard with four longer-range Sparrows inboard.

F-14A TOMCAT

An F-14A Tomcat of VF-143, an Atlantic Fleet fighter squadron nicknamed the 'Pukin' Dogs'. This world famous unit fought in Korea, Vietnam and the Gulf War, and has flown the Tomcat for 20 years.

The key to the F-14's success lies in its powerful Hughes AN/AWG-9 radar, which can detect fighter-sized targets at very long range, and even allows the F-14 to shoot down cruise missiles.

The Tomcat carries a crew of two – pilot up front and Naval Flight Officer behind, controlling the radar and weapons systems.

The 150-km (93-mile) ranged AIM-54 Phoenix missile steers itself towards the target using an onboard inertial navigation system, then homes in using its own onboard radar.

The Tomcat can extend its range or endurance by using inflight refuelling, or by carrying external fuel tanks.

The F-14's powerful TF-30 turbofans give the aircraft superb performance and economy, but have proved troublesome and unreliable.

Highly colourful squadron markings have given way to a subdued low-visibility grey camouflage on all US Navy aircraft.

Weapons of the Tomcat

■ **AIM-9 SIDEWINDER:** The highly agile Sidewinder is used against manoeuvring targets. It homes in on heat from the enemy's jetpipes. **Range 8 km (5 miles).**

■ **AIM-7 SPARROW:** The Sparrow homes on radar energy reflected from the target, which must be illuminated by the F-14's radar for the whole of its flight. **Range 45 km (28 miles).**

■ **AIM-54 PHOENIX:** Weighing in at almost 450 kg, costing $2m and with a range in excess of 150 km, the AIM-54 is the world's biggest, most costly and longest-ranged air-to-air missile. A Tomcat can launch six AIM-54s simultaneously against separate targets. The missile's onboard radar lets the F-14 turn away after launch. **Range 150 km (93 miles).**

■ **BOMBCAT:** The Tomcat can carry a range of 'dumb' (unguided) bombs for use against ground targets. Tomcat squadrons began training in the bombing role in 1991.

F-14A Tomcat

Type: two-seat long-range shipboard fleet defence interceptor, tactical reconnaissance aircraft and fighter-bomber

Powerplant: two 92.97-kN (20,918-lb-thrust) Pratt & Whitney TF-30 turbofans with afterburning

Maximum speed: 2485 km/h (1544 mph)

Combat radius: 525 km (326 miles) on internal fuel; 1210 km (752 miles) with two 409-litre (90-gallon) tanks

Service ceiling: 15,515 m (50,900 ft)

Weights: empty 18,191 kg (40,104 lb); maximum take-off 32,098 kg (70,764 lb)

Armament: one 20-mm Vulcan cannon, six AIM-54 Phoenix missiles or six AIM-7 Sparrow plus four AIM-9 Sidewinder missiles

Dimensions:

span	19.54 m (64 ft 1 in)
	(11.65 m/38 ft 3 in swept)
length	19.10 m (62 ft 8 in)
height	4.88 m (16 ft)
wing area	52.49 m² (565 sq ft)

COMBAT DATA

The MiG-29 'Fulcrum' has about the same radar and missile range as the F/A-18, which is much less than that of the Tomcat.

REACH

The Tomcat's fuel capacity and highly efficient turbofan engines allow it to operate further out from the carrier than its F/A-18 Hornet counterpart. Once at its patrol station it can see further and reach further with its Phoenix, destroying enemy fighters before they can launch their own missiles against the fleet or the Tomcat itself.

MiG-29 'FULCRUM' long-range radar (290 km/180 miles) and missiles (150 km/93 miles)

F/A-18 Hornet has relatively short-range radar (80 km/50 miles) and missiles (45 km/280 miles)

AIRCRAFT CARRIER

SIMULTANEOUS ENGAGEMENT

F-14 TOMCAT

F/A-18 HORNET

The F-14 can simultaneously engage up to six targets flying at different altitudes, airspeeds and in different directions. Because the Phoenix missile has its own radar it is independent after launch. The F/A-18 can fire only two Sparrows at a time against targets which are close together. Unlike the Phoenix, the Sparrow requires the Hornet to continue flying towards the enemy using its radar, making it vulnerable to a return missile shot.

GRUMMAN
F-14D TOMCAT

● New engines ● Improved digital avionics ● Ground attack

F ew aircraft typify America's dominance of the skies above the world's oceans like the Grumman F-14 Tomcat, flown by the US Navy. Projecting power far beyond the fleet, the Tomcat can track and destroy up to six targets at once. With such a capability, it would seem that there was little room for improvement, but the Tomcat's design had deficiencies and, after years of budget cuts and setbacks, the improved F-14D Super Tomcat finally emerged.

▶ Representing America's worldwide interests, the US Navy is often involved in potentially hazardous situations. For these Tomcat pilots, the threat of conflict is never far away.

PHOTO FILE

GRUMMAN F-14D TOMCAT

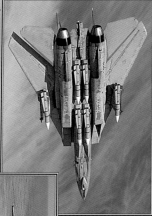

Thirsty bird ▶
Every fighter, no matter how advanced, requires fuel. Here an F-14D tanks from a Kansas ANG KC-135.

▲ Fleet defence
Overlapping circles of firepower allow the F-14D Tomcat to show its 'claws' to all who intrude into the carrier battle group zone. The aircraft is equipped with long-range Phoenix and short-range Sidewinder missiles.

▼ Who goes there?
The improved avionics include a nose sensor pod equipped with a long-range camera. This allows the Weapon Systems Operator to identify aircraft at great distances.

▲ All aboard
All carrier pilots have to endure the high tension of 'trapping' aboard the aircraft-carrier. The F-14D Tomcat, with its tough frame, is capable of making multiple landings on board ship.

▲ Partners
Two aircraft that play a key role in America's carrier fleets are the anti-submarine warfare S-3 Viking and the F-14D Tomcat air interceptor. Both have a long future ahead of them with the US Navy.

FACTS AND FIGURES

▶ The first F-14D Tomcat flew on 9 February 1990, and was actually a converted early F-14A variant.

▶ Martin-Baker ejection seats have been replaced by American NACES models.

▶ Only 37 new-build F-14Ds have been completed.

▶ Delivery to the Navy began in November 1990. Training Squadron VF-124 accepted its first example at Miramar.

▶ Squadrons operating the new aircraft include VF-1 and VF-14.

▶ The Department of Defense has withheld funding for additional F-14D Tomcats.

Protector of the fleet

In today's troubled world, conflicts can break out anywhere; gone are the well defined Cold War enemies, replaced by numerous volatile nations. The need to strike targets around the world has made the aircraft-carrier increasingly important as a versatile asset in the role of power projection.

Grumman's Tomcat is a key component in that role but, from its service introduction, US Navy pilots complained about its lack of agility in a dogfight and its dangerous tendency to enter a flat spin, both caused by the low-rated engines. Grumman undertook a series of modifications that would allow the Tomcat to remain at the cutting edge.

In the case of the Super Tomcat, improvements went far beyond the fitting of a new turbofan engine; this improved model also has new avionics and attack radar, embodying all-digital technology currently available to the latest generation of high-performance fighter.

One of the roles now performed by this air interceptor is that of ground attack. For these missions, the F-14D can carry a wide selection of laser-guided bombs and missiles.

Reductions in America's carrier fleet, coupled with cost-cutting measures, have resulted in the planned deployment of F-14Ds being limited to just a handful of squadrons.

Left: A Tomcat orbits high over the carrier battle group. The pilots are secure in the knowledge that their mount is one of the most potent fighters currently in service.

Above: Resplendent in its red and white prototype colours, the F-14D undergoes testing of its in-flight refuelling abilities with a tanker aircraft.

F-14D Tomcat

Type: two-seat shipborne interceptor

Powerplant: two 102.75-kN (23,1230 lb) General Electric F110-GE-400 turbofans with afterburner

Maximum speed: 2485 km/h (1543 mph)

Combat radius: 1994 km (1238 miles)

Range: 3220 km (2000 miles)

Service ceiling: 15240 m (50,000 ft)

Weights: empty 18191 kg (40,111 lb); maximum take-off 27086 kg (59,725 lb)

Armament: one internal 20-mm Vulcan cannon, AIM-54C Phoenix, AIM-9M air-to-air missiles

Dimensions: span (unswept) 19.54 m (64 ft 2 in)
length 19.10 m (62 ft 8 in)
height 4.88 m (16 m)
wing area 52.49 m² (565 sq ft)

FUTURE CARRIER AIR POWER

F/A-18E SUPER HORNET: Originally proposed in 1991 as a replacement for the abandoned A-12 Avenger project, extensively redesigned F/A-18E/F single- and two-seat Hornets are now in service. They feature a stretched fuselage and an enlarged wing coupled with larger horizontal tails. The internal fuel load has been increased by an extra 1360 kg (3000 lb). Two more weapons pylons and a new non-afterburning powerplant developed from the GE F412 give the Super Hornet a considerable extra warload, and extended range and endurance. First flying in 1996, the Super Hornet will fill the gap left by the retirement of the A-6 Intruder and will also replace the F-14 Tomcat.

ES-3A SHADOW: First flying in 1991, the ES-3A is a carrier-based Elint aircraft modified from the S-3A with OTH surveillance equipment. The co-pilot position has been replaced by a third sensor station and the bomb bays have been modified to accommodate avionics. The ES-3A has a new radome, direction-finding antenna, and other equipment in a dorsal 'shoulder', plus an array of seven receiving antennas on its fuselage. Two USN squadrons deploy eight ES-3As aboard each carrier.

F-14D SUPER TOMCAT

Despite the improvements made to the US Navy's F-14D Super Tomcat, budget constraints mean that operational examples are limited to a training unit and four fighter squadrons.

A large nose-mounted test boom was fitted to the prototype F-14D, providing information on the Super Tomcat's performance.

Production models are fitted with twin undernose sensor pods. They house a television camera set and infra-red sensor tracking pod. Although the television offers a narrow field of view, its image is directly displayed within the rear cockpit, greatly easing target acquisition.

Improvements to the cockpit include the installation of NACES ejection seats and upgraded digital cockpit displays. The crew can track and acquire targets more quickly than in previous models.

The 'punch' of the Tomcat is its sophisticated missile war load. With overlapping layers of defence, the F-14D is also able to dogfight 'in close' with its internal M61 cannon.

Variable-sweep wings give the Tomcat high speed in the swept configuration, and the ability to land aboard an aircraft-carrier at slow speed when unswept.

The F-14D Super Tomcat can undertake ground attack missions because of the adoption of specialised pylons under the fuselage. Weapons range from ordinary drop bombs to laser-guided munitions for specific targets.

The most significant modification to the F-14D was the adoption of the General Electric F110 turbofan, which removed all the engine problems that had hindered early Tomcat variants.

Tomcat trilogy

■ **COLOURED TAILS:** Reflecting an era when high-visibility markings were the order of the day, this F-14A Tomcat from VF-32 'Swordsmen' sported a bright yellow tail.

■ **DESERT CAT:** Iran purchased 79 Tomcats before the fall of the Shah. Their current status remains unknown, although they have been used in combat against Iraq.

■ **FADE TO GREY :** Reflecting the current low-vis colour scheme of overall grey is this F-14 from VF-143 'Pukin' Dogs'. The squadron now flies the improved F-14B variant.

HILLER

UH-12 RAVEN

● Lightweight 1950s design ● US Army's H-23 ● War veteran

F lagship for an exceedingly successful helicopter family which included the Model 360 and the military H-23 Raven, the UH-12 was created in 1948 by helicopter genius Stanley Hiller. As a test bed for his innovative 'Rotor-Matic' control system, it went on to be built in large numbers. At least 2300 examples have provided excellent service to civil and military users, and many are still on duty, from Britain to New Zealand.

▲ Popular with civil and military operators alike, the Hiller was produced throughout the 1950s and until the late-1960s. After Hiller was taken over by Fairchild, production was restarted in 1973.

PHOTO FILE

HILLER UH-12 RAVEN

▲ **Army H-23 Raven**
The US Army operated the UH-12 as the H-23 Raven from 1950. This H-23B carries the wing of an L-20 Beaver.

▲ **Powerful light helicopter**
Hiller billed the UH-12E as the most powerful US-built light helicopter.

Piston-engined ▶
The earliest Hiller UH-12s were powered by Franklin engines, while later models used more powerful Lycoming flat-six powerplants. The final UH-12E-4s had an Allison 250 turboshaft as fitted to machines like the Bell 206 JetRanger.

▲ **Over San Francisco Bay**
Hiller marketed the civil Hiller 12C for land- or ship-based port work, such as personnel transport and the off-loading of light priority cargoes.

Large US Army orders ▶
US Army Ravens were delivered for 17 years from 1950. The most common variant was the OH-23G; 793 were built.

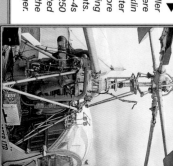

FACTS AND FIGURES

➤ An early UH-12 was the first commercial helicopter to log a transcontinental flight across the United States.

➤ Over 1600 UH-12s went to the US Army and were used in Korea and Vietnam.

➤ As a flying ambulance, the UH-12 can carry two stretcher cases.

➤ UH-12s were exported to at least 18 countries, many via the Mutual Defense Aid Program.

➤ The Hiller UH-12 was the US Army's primary trainer until 1965.

➤ UH-12s were manufactured by Hiller in Palo Alto, near San Francisco, California.

PROFILE

Light helicopters from Palo Alto

In 1971 the US Army held a celebration to mark 100,000 accident-free miles flown by one of its veteran Hiller H-23 Ravens (the military designation for the UH-12). This kind of satisfaction by those who rely on the UH-12 is far from unusual. For decades the versatile Hiller UH-12 has enjoyed a reputation for safety and reliability in roles like police work and agricultural spraying, as well as military operations.

The UH-12 is of simple construction, incorporating two-blade main and tail rotors with

a sturdy, upswept tailboom. Built in highly successful two-, three- and four-seat configurations, the type was fitted with a variety of Franklin and Lycoming piston engines. Aircraft built in the 1970s had almost twice the installed horsepower of the earliest models; there was even a turboshaft-powered version.

Production of what was at first known as the Model 360 began in the late 1940s and continued as the Fairchild-Hiller UH-12 and Model 12 until 1965. At least 300 Hillers were

exported to overseas customers, both military and civil.

Stanley Hiller's son, Jeffrey, took over the business in 1994. The company continues to develop the UH-12 in piston- and turbine-engined versions and as a new five-seater – a testimony to the soundness of the 1940s design.

Left: Numerous civil UH-12s have been used for agricultural tasks such as crop spraying. In New Zealand most UH-12s have undergone conversion and been fitted with Allison 250 turboshaft engines.

Below: A number of UH-12s in the US are employed in a major insect control campaign in the Atlantic coast states. Over 1000 UH-12s are still flying worldwide.

H-23D Raven

Type: three-seat light observation and training helicopter

Powerplant: one 186-kW (250-hp) Lycoming VO-450-23B flat-six air-cooled piston engine

Maximum speed: 153 km/h (95 mph) at sea level

Cruising speed: 132 km/h (82 mph)

Initial climb rate: 320 m/min (1050 fpm)

Range: 317 km (197 miles)

Service ceiling: 4023 m (13,200 ft)

Weights: empty 824 kg1817 lb); loaded 1225 kg (2700 lb)

Armament: normally none, although small arms were often carried by crew in active service

Dimensions: main rotor diameter 7.44 m (24 ft 5 in)
length 8.47 m (27 ft 9 in)
height 2.98 m (9 ft 9 in)
rotor disc area 91.51 m² (985 sq ft)

ACTION DATA

MAXIMUM SPEED

Speeds around 160 km/h (100 mph) were typical for the first mass-produced light helicopters. Bell's Sioux was widely used by US forces; the Mi-1 was an early product of the famous Mil factory.

H-23D RAVEN	153 km/h (95 mph)
H-13H SIOUX	161 km/h (100 mph)
Mi-1M 'HARE'	170 km/h (106 mph)

RANGE

The slightly larger Mi-1 had a considerably longer range than the two American types. This was largely due to the greater fuel capacity of the aircraft.

H-23D RAVEN	317 km (197 miles)
H-13H SIOUX	383 km (238 miles)
Mi-1M 'HARE'	620 km (385 miles)

CLIMB RATE

The Raven, which entered service after the Sioux, demonstrated a marginally better climb rate. A more powerful engine in both the Raven and 'Hare' was the main reason for this difference.

Mi-1M 'HARE'	390 m/min (1280 fpm)
H-23D RAVEN	320 m/min (1050 fpm)
H-13H SIOUX	235 m/min (771 fpm)

The 'goldfish bowl' cockpit of the Hiller features a bench seat which is able to accommodate three people, including the pilot. Dual controls are optional.

A two-bladed main rotor is fitted. These are interchangeable and are constructed of bonded stainless steel with an aluminium honeycomb core.

The first UH-12s were fitted with a 133-kW (178-hp) Franklin engine; the latest 1990s-built examples have a 227-kW (304-hp) Lycoming powerplant. A 224-kW (300-hp) Allison 250 turboshaft is also available.

The Hiller UH-12E was one of the most widely produced civil variants and has been built since 1959. Current production is based on this model.

A distinguishing feature of the UH-12 family is the tail rotor driveshaft running from the main gearbox to the low-slung tailboom.

The light-alloy tail rotor is protected from 'grounding' by a tail skid. The tail rotor, vital to the control of the aircraft, is one of the most vulnerable parts of a helicopter.

The simply constructed tailboom is made of beaded light-alloy sheet and does not contain internal stiffeners. The fuselage is also of light alloy.

Hiller vertical risers

■ **UH-5:** Hiller's first helicopter with a main rotor/tail rotor configuration, the UH-5 also saw the first use of its 'Rotor-Matic' control system.

■ **HJ-1 HORNET:** Twelve of these two-seat ramjet-powered helicopters were built, plus a further 12 for the US Army as the YH-32.

■ **FH-1100:** Hiller's attempt to build a machine to rival the Bell JetRanger and Hughes 500 was derived from the unsuccessful military OH-5.

■ **X-18:** This unusual machine was flown in 1959 to test the practicality of tilt-wing aircraft. It was short-lived and the results were inconclusive.

HUGHES
OH-6 CAYUSE

● Vietnam veteran ● Hundreds in service ● Top-secret missions

Hughes overcame competition from Bell and Hiller to win a contract for the US Army's new LOH (light observation helicopter). The OH-6 went on to become the US Army's primary observation helicopter in Vietnam. Although some problems were encountered during the OH-6's production, new variants based on the civil Model 500 found success. Recently, the aircraft has been tasked with a new role, flying special forces missions with the US Army.

▲ Well-armed, small and agile, the OH-6A performed well in Vietnam. Many Cayuses have been exported and the Model 500 has breathed new life into the series.

HUGHES OH-6 CAYUSE

▲ Post-war service
OH-6As which survived the Vietnam War were passed on to National Guard and Reserve units. Some were modified for special duties.

▲ 'People planks' and Special Forces
This MH-6H serves with the US Army's 160th Special Operations Air Regiment (SOAR). It is able to carry personnel on the 'people planks'.

▼ Testing time in the navy
Four ex-US Army OH-6As are on loan to the US Navy Test Pilots' School at Patuxent River. They are used to give students light helicopter experience.

No tail rotor (NOTAR) ▼
McDonnell Douglas' NOTAR concept allows operations from tight spots, but with the cost of diminished speed and increased fuel consumption.

▲ Armed for support
AH-6Gs are not used as traditional gunships. They are most likely to lend fire support to a covert mission if it is compromised and attacked.

FACTS AND FIGURES

▶ For observation duties the US Army received 1434 Cayuses from an originally planned 4000.

▶ The first service OH-6s were delivered to the US Army in September 1965.

▶ Soldiers nicknamed the OH-6 'Loach' because of its LOH role designation.

▶ Cayuse and Model 500 variants serve in Japan, where some are dubbed 'chisai baggu' (little bug).

▶ In Vietnam damaged Cayuses numbered 420; many were returned to flying status.

▶ McDonnell Douglas still produces civil helicopters inspired by the OH-6 design.

OH-6A Cayuse

Type: light observation helicopter

Powerplant: one 237-kW (320-hp) Allison T63-A-5A turboshaft engine derated to 160 kW (215 hp) for continuous running and 188 kW (250 hp) for take-off

Maximum speed: 241 km/h (149 mph)

Economic cruising speed: 216 km/h (134 mph) at sea level

Range: 611 km (379 miles) at 1525 m (5000 ft)

Service ceiling: 4815 m (15,800 ft)

Weights: empty equipped 557 kg (1225 lb); maximum take-off 1225 kg (2695 lb)

Armament: one XM27 7.62-mm (.30-cal.) machine gun or XM-75 40-mm grenade-launcher; provision for two M60 7.62-mm machine guns

Accommodation: one pilot and one observer plus up to four passengers, or one pilot and one medic and up to two stretchers

Dimensions: main rotor diameter 8.03 m (26 ft 4 in)
fuselage length 7.01 m (23 ft)
height 2.48 m (8 ft 2 in)
main rotor disc area 50.60 m² (544 sq ft)

COMBAT DATA

MAXIMUM SPEED

The OH-6A is faster than its close contemporary the Aérospatiale SA 318C Alouette II. Although the more recent Gazelle AH.Mk 1 has greater speed still, it is vulnerable in combat.

OH-6A CAYUSE — 241 km/h (149 mph)
GAZELLE AH.Mk 1 — 310 km/h (192 mph)
SA 318C ALOUETTE II — 205 km/h (127 mph)

CLIMB RATE

The OH-6A and Alouette II are closely matched in terms of climb rate. The Gazelle can climb faster, but over the battlefield agility and survivability are more important.

GAZELLE AH.Mk 1 — 540 m/min (1770 fpm)
SA 318C ALOUETTE II — 396 m/min (1300 fpm)
OH-6A CAYUSE — 381 m/min (1250 fpm)

RANGE

Comparatively short range is perhaps the one weak point of the OH-6A. In Vietnam the aircraft frequently flew from forward bases, so range was less of a problem. And in operations since then, the Army has operated them from US Navy ships and covert bases.

OH-6A CAYUSE — 611 km (379 miles)
GAZELLE AH.Mk 1 — 670 km (415 miles)
SA 318C ALOUETTE II — 720 km (446 miles)

Cayuse for the aerial cavalry

Seeking a replacement for its first-generation Bell and Hiller types, the US Army issued a requirement for a high-performance, easily maintained and cost-effective observation helicopter. After announcing the OH-6A Cayuse as the winner, the Army received its first in September 1965 and the helicopter soon went into combat in Vietnam.

Hughes struggled to meet the pressures of wartime

production and, with Bell offering its improved OH-58A Kiowa in a renewed competition, manufacture of the OH-6A was prematurely terminated after 1434 had been completed.

Hughes also developed a civilian variant of the OH-6A, the Model 500. This machine went on to spawn a range of new military helicopters, including a family of special operations variants. These

black-painted MH- and AH-6s were first used in the 1983 US invasion of Grenada and later in the Gulf. Their operations are kept highly secret.

Left: With its small-diameter, four-bladed main rotor, the OH-6A was ideal for riverine support operations in the jungles of Vietnam.

Right: A tight formation of four Cayuses flies before a setting sun. The aircraft is far from being in the twilight of its career.

OH-6A CAYUSE

'Loaches' served in huge numbers in Vietnam, where 658 were lost in combat and a further 297 in accidents. Non-standard markings were a feature of operations in Southeast Asia.

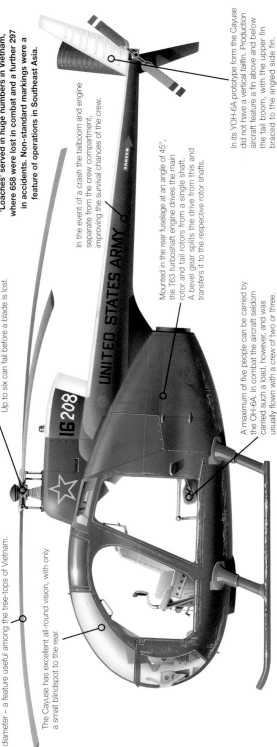

With its four-bladed main rotor, the OH-6A has excellent control response and little vibration at high speeds. The rotor is also of small diameter – a feature useful among the tree-tops of Vietnam.

The Cayuse has excellent all-round vision, with only a small blindspot to the rear.

In the event of a crash the tailboom and engine separate from the crew compartment, improving the survival chances of the crew.

Each of the rotor blades is attached to the one opposite by 15 flexible stainless steel straps. Up to six can fail before a blade is lost.

Mounted in the rear fuselage at an angle of 45°, the T63 turboshaft engine drives the main rotor and tail rotors from a single shaft. A bevel gear splits the drive from this and transfers it to the respective rotor shafts.

A maximum of five people can be carried by the OH-6A. In combat the aircraft seldom carried such a load, however, and was usually flown with a crew of two or three.

In its YOH-6A prototype form the Cayuse did not have a vertical tailfin. Production aircraft feature a fin above and below the tail boom, with the upper fin braced to the angled side fin.

Suppression and insertion

From Vietnam to the Gulf, the 'Loach' and its descendants have proved highly capable combat helicopters.

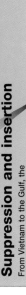

VIETNAM OPS: Operations in Vietnam typically involved engagements with Viet Cong troops at less than tree-top height.

FIRE SUPPORT: Rocket and gun-armed AH-6Gs of the US Army's 160th SOAR fly in support of insertion/exfiltration missions by the same unit's MH-6Hs. The AH-6Gs also provides support for pre-placed special forces teams.

INSERTION FROM THE PLANK: With a 'people plank' on either side of its fuselage, the MH-6H is able to drop or pick up two personnel extremely rapidly. Some sources claim that the 'plank' can also be used as a sniper platform.

HUGHES/SCHWEIZER
300/TH-55 OSAGE

● Lightweight helicopter ● Police operations ● Military trainer

n 1948 the Hughes Aircraft Company began specialising in helicopters. Its second design, the Model 269/300, served as the basis for one of the most successful families of light helicopters. Having evaluated five examples as potential observation aircraft in 1958, the US Army adopted this simply constructed two-seater as its standard primary helicopter trainer in the 1960s. Hughes went on to build nearly 3000 for both civil and military users.

▲ The success of the Model 269/300 family paved the way for the Model 369/500 design, which placed Hughes among the world's leading producers of light helicopters.

HUGHES/SCHWEIZER 300/TH-55 OSAGE

▼ Traffic watching
Robust and fuel-efficient, the 300 is an ideal machine for monitoring traffic conditions.

▲ Police service
More than 17 US city police departments have operated the Model 300 as a relatively economical surveillance platform. The 300 has also proved its military potential in the training role.

▼ In the US Army
The Osage provided experience for the first generation of US Army chopper pilots.

▲ Over California
A lieutenant from Whittier, California, keeps in touch with a police department 300.

▲ Schweizer production
By the time Schweizer began building Hughes 300s in July 1983, more than 2800 had been built.

FACTS AND FIGURES

➤ Schweizer Aircraft bought the entire Model 300 programme in 1986; its 500th 300C was delivered in 1994.

➤ In 1996 a Model 300C training helicopter was priced at $187,500.

➤ Iraq acquired 30 Model 300Cs for crop-dusting, but used them for pilot training.

➤ In 1996 12 nations operated military Model 269s, including Indonesia, North Korea, Pakistan, Paraguay and Honduras.

➤ Kawasaki assembled 38 TH-55As as TH-55Js for the JGSDF.

➤ Schweizer builds a turbine development of the Model 300 – the Model 330.

Hughes' first successful chopper

Designated TH-55A Osage, the Hughes Model 269A-1 was delivered to the US Army after being selected in 1964. The Osage was a refinement of the civil Model 200 Utility, which was derived from the original Model 269 that had first flown in October 1966.

The next major variant was the three-seater Model 300 (269B), which, with an uprated Lycoming engine, became the Model 300C in 1969. This was the most widely produced version, with more than 1000 being built by Hughes. Licence production was

also undertaken by BredaNardi in Italy, as the NH-300C.

Popular with civil operators, the Model 300 has being used for roles as diverse as crop-spraying and policing duties. For the latter, the Hughes 300C Sky Knight, with a public address system and an infra-red sensor, was introduced.

In military service, several countries have adopted the type, principally for pilot training. TH-55As were supplied to Algeria, Haiti, Nigeria, Spain (designated HE.20s) and Sweden (as Hkp 5Bs). Other nations have

acquired Model 300s, including Colombia and Japan.

Having acquired the programme from Hughes' new owners, McDonnell Douglas, in 1986, Schweizer introduced a new TH-300C trainer variant. Turkey was an early customer.

Above: This Hughes 300, based at Lakewood, Los Angeles, is fitted with a searchlight, a siren and warning light. Police versions often carry armour.

Below: For agricultural operations, the Hughes 300 often carries a crop-spraying or dry powder dispersal kit. Stretcher kits, cargo racks and slings may also be fitted.

Model 300C

Type: three-seat light utility/training helicopter

Powerplant: one 168-kW (225-hp) Textron Lycoming HIO-360-D1A piston engine derated to 142 kW (190 hp)

Maximum cruising speed: 153 km/h (95 mph)

Endurance: 3 hours 24 min at sea level

Initial climb rate: 229 m/min (751 fpm) at sea level

Range: 360 km (224 mph) at 124 km/h (77 mph) at 1220 m (4003 ft)

Service ceiling: 3110 m (10,200 ft)

Hover ceiling: 1800 m (5906 ft) in ground effect; 840 m (2756 ft) outside ground effect

Weights: empty 474 kg (1050 lb); maximum take-off 930 kg (2050 lb) (with external load 975 kg/2150 lb)

Dimensions: rotor diameter 8.18 m (26 ft 10 in)
fuselage length 9.40 m (30 ft 10 in)
height 2.66 m (8 ft 9 in)
rotor disc area 52.50 m² (565 sq ft)

ACTION DATA

NEVER-EXCEED SPEED

Never-exceed speed, or velocity (Vne), is greater than the true maximum safe speed of the aircraft. The older Series 300C is slower than its more recent, aerodynamically efficient and stronger counterparts, the Robinson R22 and Enstrom F-28F.

MODEL 300C 169 km/h (105 mph)

R22 BETA 190 km/h (118 mph)

F-28F FALCON 180 km/h (112 mph)

POWER

The Hughes 300 has more power than the smaller but more recent R22. Also flown by police forces, the Enstrom has the same powerplant as the Hughes, albeit turbocharged, and the 300C has its motor derated to 142 kW (190 hp).

F-28F FALCON 168 kW (225 hp)

R22 BETA 119 kW (160 hp)

MODEL 300C 168 kW (225 hp)

CLIMB RATE

The Hughes 300C lags behind in this category, but performed well against its 1960s contemporaries. For the military training role, as well as crop-dusting and observation, the practicality and economy of operation are more important factors.

F-28F FALCON 442 m/min (1450 fpm)

R22 BETA 366 m/min (1200 fpm)

MODEL 300C 229 m/min (751 fpm)

TH-55A OSAGE

Based at the Army Aviation Center at Fort Rucker, this TH-55A is one of 792 originally ordered by the US Army. The TH-55A is powered by a HIO-360-B1A engine. In 1996, 12 military users still operated the type; the US has retired its fleet.

The Hughes 300 series tail rotor is of the teetering type, with just two blades freely pivoted as one unit. Each comprises a steel tube spar with glass-fibre skin. A spring-mounted bumper protects the blades.

A simple pod and boom configuration on the 300 affords good handling characteristics. The light alloy tailboom has horizontal and vertical stabilizing surfaces.

The fully-articulated, three-bladed main rotor of bonded metal construction has an aluminium core spar. A main rotor tie-down kit is standard on the Osage.

The AVCO-Lycoming flat-four piston engine is mounted directly behind the crew. A crash-resistant aluminium fuel tank can be supplemented by an auxiliary tank of 72 litres.

TH-55As can accommodate three crewmembers side-by-side, typically two students and an instructor, within the Plexiglass cabin. On either side of the cabin there is a forward-hinged removable door. Police versions of the 300 carry a siren, a searchlight, safety mesh seats, night lights, first aid kits and uprated electrical systems.

Piston-engined military training helicopters

■ **BELL MODEL 47:** Bell's Model 47 Sioux first flew in 1945, was used by at least 30 air arms. It stayed in production until 1974.

■ **HILLER UH-12:** A contemporary of the 300, more than 2200 UH-12s were built. Military operators included the Royal Navy.

■ **ROBINSON R22:** Designed in the late 1970s, the R22 was bought by only one military customer, the Turkish army.

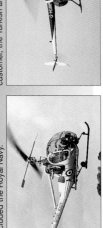

■ **SAUNDERS-ROE SKEETER:** Designed by Cierva, the two-seat Gipsy Major-engined Skeeter served with both Britain and Germany.

KAMAN

H-43 HUSKIE

● Intermeshing rotor ● Firefighter ● Rescue

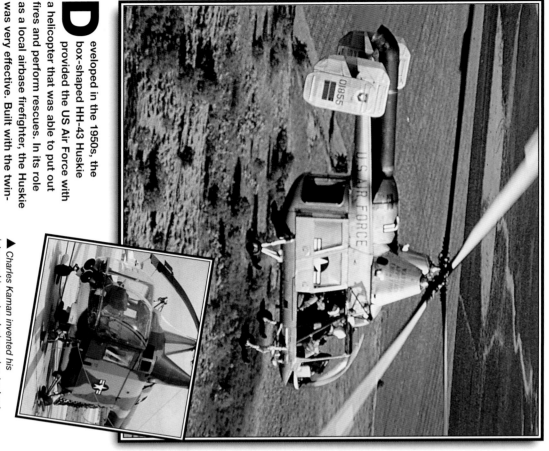

▲ Charles Kaman invented his intermeshing rotor design using tools at home, and the system remains unique. The concept has most recently been rejuvenated in the company's K-Max utility transport helicopter.

D eveloped in the 1950s, the box-shaped HH-43 Huskie provided the US Air Force with a helicopter that was able to put out fires and perform rescues. In its role as a local airbase firefighter, the Huskie was very effective. Built with the twin-meshing rotors that are the signature of inventor and entrepreneur Charles Kaman, the Huskie ended its career in the Vietnam War.

KAMAN H-43 HUSKIE

▼ Huskie rescue
When flying aircrew rescue sorties in Vietnam, the Huskie was painted in camouflage. Due to the H-43's limited range, it was generally used only over South Vietnam, although its small size allowed it to operate in small jungle clearings.

▲ Firefighter
With its underslung load of firefighting chemicals contained in a special tank and fully-equipped firefighters in the rear cabin, the Huskie was effective in the airfield firefighting role.

▲ Delta delivery
Huskies were used over the Mekong Delta area of South Vietnam, operating in a support role for the US Navy's inshore PBR (Patrol Boat, River) force.

▼ Red fins
Huskies based in friendly territory wore bright 'rescue' colours. The rotors could be stored in the 'fore and aft' position to save space.

▲ Box body
The advantage of the Kaman rotor system is that the helicopter does not require a tail rotor, so it can be designed with a capacious interior.

FACTS AND FIGURES

▶ Ex-US Huskies have served with the air forces of Burma, Colombia, Morocco, Pakistan and Thailand.

▶ The Huskie established seven world records using its T53-1 engine.

▶ The first flight of the prototype in this series took place on 13 December 1958.

▶ The USAF received 263 Huskies (18 H-43As, 203 HH-43Bs and 42 HH-43Fs) between 1958 and 1968.

▶ The Huskie's rescue hoist has a capacity of 272 kg (600 lb) for lifting personnel.

▶ A few civilian Huskies remain in use undertaking logging operations.

Two rotors are better than one

Best known for its service with the US Air Force, this fine helicopter began in the late-1950s as a US Navy training and observation craft.

The Huskie was created to help the Air Force to deal with accidents and fires on its airfields. Speed and range were not important. What mattered was the ability of this helicopter to spring quickly into action, to maintain a stable hover, and to carry firefighting and rescue equipment. The Huskie was also fitted with a pair of loudspeaker horns, which were used to transmit directions during a firefighting emergency.

The two pilots of the HH-43 had almost unprecedented visibility through the Plexiglass cockpit. And the Huskie gave the pilot a degree of responsiveness and stability not found on many helicopters.

Typically, the Huskie also carried two para-jumpers (known as PJs), who were trained in medical treatment and rescue work. As the US's role in Vietnam grew, the Huskie's job of local airbase rescue was expanded and a number flew missions behind enemy lines.

Left: The Huskie crew often had to operate under dangerous and terrifying conditions. This burning C-97 was part of a training session, but the H-43 tackled many other fires for real.

Right: One of the H-43's many unusual features was the exhaust boom that projected over the tail to keep the rear door area safe.

H-43 HUSKIE

Pakistan operated six Huskies, none of which remains in service. The H-43 was also exported to Burma (12), Columbia (six), Morocco (four) and Thailand (three).

Unusually, the Huskie had wooden main rotor blades. These were attached to the rotor head only by dragging hinges.

Despite its unorthodox rotor system, the H-43 had conventional helicopter controls consisting of cyclic and collective pitch levers. Visibility from the cockpit was excellent.

Huskies had an unusual undercarriage system of four struts fitted with wheels and skis. The forward struts were longer than the rear ones, giving the H-43 a tail-down appearance on the ground.

The H-43 was powered by a T53 turboshaft engine. When one of the first Kaman K-225s (developed from the H-43) was fitted with a Boeing YT 50 engine, it became the world's first gas-turbine-powered helicopter.

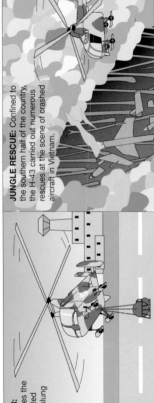

Each rotor blade has a servo-flap which makes the cyclic pitch changes by twisting the blade.

The H-43 had twin rotors on different shafts, with the rotors turning in an intermeshing pattern.

Similar to the Kamov twin-rotor designs, the H-43 had large, wide fins at the rear for directional control.

Fire crews or cargo could be loaded through the wide twin clamshell doors. The main fuel supply of 755 litres (166 gallons) of kerosene was stored under the cabin floor.

Huskie missions

NAVAL SUPPORT: Huskies were used in support of the 'brown water navy', the force of patrol craft deployed in the Mekong Delta area of South Vietnam. The helicopter usually carried door guns for these missions, as Viet Cong snipers were a threat.

FIREFIGHTER: For tackling fires the Huskie was fitted with an underslung container of firefighting chemicals.

JUNGLE RESCUE: Confined to the southern half of the country, the H-43 carried out numerous rescues at the scene of crashed aircraft in Vietnam.

COMBAT DATA

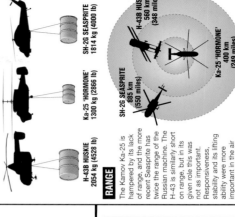

H-43B Huskie

Type: three-place rescue helicopter

Powerplant: one 615-kW (825-hp) Avco Lycoming T53-L-1B turboshaft engine

Maximum speed: 165 km/h (103 mph)

Range: 560 km (348 miles)

Service ceiling: 7740 m (25,394 ft)

Weights: empty 2095 kg (4619 lb) loaded 4150 kg (9149 lb)

Accommodation: useful load of 2054 kg (4528 lb) including crew, passengers and rescue/firefighting equipment; seating for eight passengers, 12 combat troops on folding seats, or four stretchers and a medical attendant

Dimensions: main rotor diameter 14.55 m (47 ft 9 in)
length 7.80 m (25 ft 7 in)
height 3.88 m (12 ft 9 in)
rotor disc area 52.49 m² (565 sq ft)

MAXIMUM SPEED

The Huskie has the least-impressive top speed of these three similarly sized aircraft. The Kamov Ka-25 is also a twin-rotor helicopter but uses two co-axial rotors. The SH-2G is the most modern of the three and, like the Ka-25, is turboshaft-powered.

H-43B HUSKIE	165 km/h (103 mph)
Ka-25 'HORMONE'	209 km/h (130 mph)
SH-2G SEASPRITE	256 km/h (159 mph)

PAYLOAD

The powerful H-43 has the most impressive load-carrying capacity. This is especially noteworthy given its modest power compared to the other types. Speed and range were never important considerations in the Huskie's design.

H-43B HUSKIE 2054 kg (4528 lb)	
Ka-25 'HORMONE' 1300 kg (2866 lb)	
SH-2G SEASPRITE 1814 kg (4000 lb)	

RANGE

The Kamov Ka-25 is hampered by its lack of range, and the more recent Seasprite has twice the range of the Russian machine. The H-43 is similarly short on range, but in its given role this was not as important. Responsiveness, stability and its lifting ability were more important in the air rescue role.

H-43B HUSKIE 560 km (348 miles)
SH-2G SEASPRITE 885 km (550 miles)
Ka-25 'HORMONE' 400 km (249 miles)

KAMAN

SH-2 SEASPRITE

- Anti-submarine ● Search and rescue ● Anti-patrol vessel

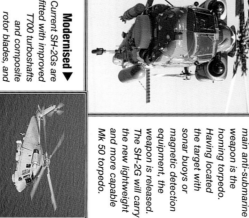

Kaman's SH-2F Seasprite and SH-2G Super Seasprite are the current models of a sturdy, versatile helicopter that has been a familiar sight on the world's oceans for four decades. Originally a Vietnam-era rescue helicopter hampered by limited range, this Kaman design has shown extraordinary growth potential. New engines and systems have kept the SH-2 up-to-date and make it a formidable anti-submarine weapon.

▲ Kaman's Seasprite is an unremarkable but enduring design that has given excellent service for nearly four decades. Fulfilling roles as varied as combat search and rescue and anti-submarine patrol, the Seasprite may still remain in service well past 2010.

PHOTO FILE

KAMAN SH-2 SEASPRITE

▼ **Watching the Soviets**
The SH-2 was often used to shadow Soviet naval auxiliaries, like this research vessel in the Sea of Japan. The SH-2 could detect ships with its own radar, or by homing on their radar.

LAMPS ▶
The original H-2 was upgraded to Light Airborne Multi-Purpose System standard in 1969/70 with major avionics improvements.

▶ **Torpedo attack**
The Seasprite's main anti-submarine weapon is the homing torpedo. Having located the target with sonar buoys or magnetic detection equipment, the weapon is released. The SH-2G will carry the new lightweight and more capable Mk 50 torpedo.

▲ **In the hangar**
With rotors stowed away the SH-2 could fit in the hangar of frigates such as the 'Knox' class, originally designed to carry a drone helicopter.

Modernised ▶
Current SH-2Gs are fitted with improved T700 turboshafts and composite rotor blades, and are painted grey.

FACTS AND FIGURES

▶ Early Seasprite models were rebuilt in Connecticut to become advanced SH-2Fs and SH-2Gs.

▶ The Seasprite helicopter known as HU2K-1 first flew on 2 July 1959.

▶ Egypt bought the SH-2F, and the SH-2G has been selected by the Australian navy.

▶ Kaman is flying an SH-2F with the company's Magic Lantern anti-ship mine detector housed in a pod.

▶ The first flight of the new SH-2G took place on 28 December 1989.

▶ Turkey received 14 surplus SH-2Fs under an agreement proposed in 1994.

Sub-chasing Seasprite

The Seasprite and SH-2G Super Seasprite are the only helicopters from Charles Kaman's Connecticut company that do not use the famous inventor's twin meshing rotors having instead a conventional single-rotor system.

The Seasprite first flew in 1959 and entered service in the 1960s as a ship-launched US Navy rescue and utility helicopter. An early Seasprite flew a dramatic mission on 19 June 1968, when Commander Clyde Lassen went deep into North Vietnam under heavy fire to rescue a downed Phantom crewman; he was one of only two US naval aviators to be awarded the Medal of Honor in that conflict.

In the 1970s and 1980s, the single-engine craft with three-bladed rotors evolved into a twin-engine helicopter with four-bladed rotors and considerable anti-submarine capability. Today's more powerful, better-equipped SH-2G Super Seasprite is perhaps not quite in the class of the newer Sikorsky SH-60B Sea Hawk, but it is a weapon that no submarine skipper can ignore. SH-2F and SH-2G helicopters serve with half-a-dozen air arms outside the United States.

SH-2F SEASPRITE

This SH-2F served with HSL-33 of the US Navy. The variant was replaced by the modified SH-2G aboard US Navy frigates and destroyers.

SH-2 Seasprite

Powerplant: two 1285-kW (1723-hp) General Electric T700-GE-401/403C; SH-2F has two 1007-kW T58-GE-8F turboshafts

Maximum speed: 265 km/h (165 mph) at sea level

Maximum cruising speed: 230 km/h (143 mph)

Range: 679 km (422 miles)

Service ceiling: 5670 m (18,602 lb)

Weights: empty 3193 kg (7039 lb); maximum take-off 6033 kg (13,300 lb)

Armament: up to two Mk 46 or Mk 50 lightweight torpedoes; 7.62-mm (.30-cal.) machine gun may be pintle-mounted in each doorway; the SH-2G can carry the AGM-65 Maverick air-to-ground missile

Dimensions: rotor diameter   13.51 m (44 ft 4 in)
length   16.08 m (52 ft 9 in)
height   4.58 m (15 ft)
rotor disc area   143.41 m² (471 sq ft)

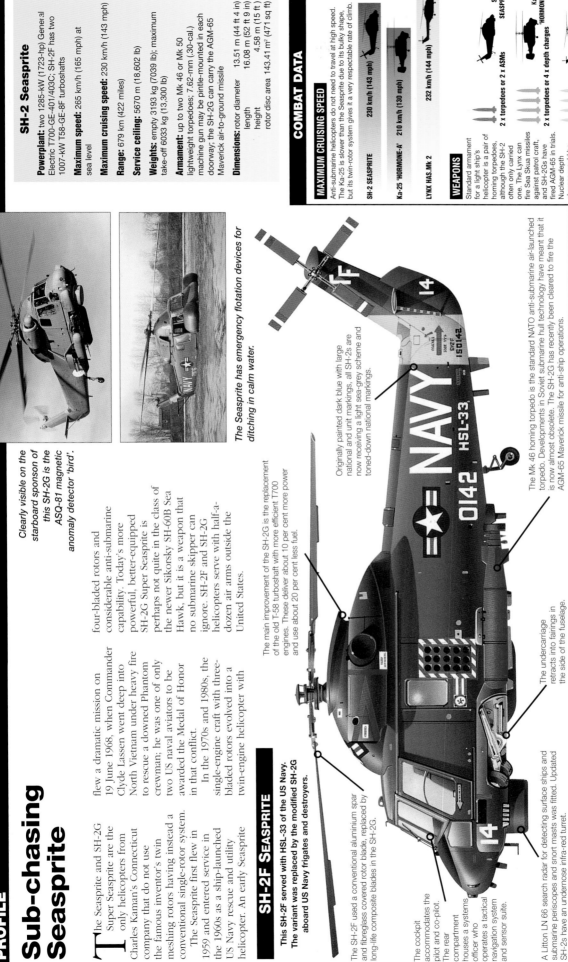

Clearly visible on the starboard sponson of this SH-2G is the ASQ-81 magnetic anomaly detector 'bird'.

The Seasprite has emergency flotation devices for ditching in calm water.

The main improvement of the SH-2G is the replacement of the old T-58 turboshaft with more efficient T700 engines. These deliver about 10 per cent more power and use about 20 per cent less fuel.

Originally painted dark blue with large national and unit markings, all SH-2s are now receiving a light sea-grey scheme and toned-down national markings.

The Mk 46 homing torpedo is the standard NATO anti-submarine air-launched torpedo. Developments in Soviet submarine hull technology have meant that it is now almost obsolete. The SH-2G has recently been cleared to fire the AGM-65 Maverick missile for anti-ship operations.

The undercarriage retracts into fairings in the side of the fuselage.

A Litton LN 66 search radar for detecting surface ships and submarine periscopes and snort masts was fitted. Updated SH-2s have an undernose infra-red turret.

The cockpit accommodates the pilot and co-pilot. The rear compartment houses a systems officer who operates a tactical navigation system and sensor suite.

The SH-2F used a conventional aluminium spar and fibreglass covered rotor blade, replaced by long-life composite blades in the SH-2G.

COMBAT DATA

MAXIMUM CRUISING SPEED

Anti-submarine helicopters do not need to travel at high speed. The Ka-25 is slower than the Seasprite due to its bulky shape, but its twin-rotor system gives it a very respectable rate of climb.

SH-2 SEASPRITE   230 km/h (143 mph)

Ka-25 'HORMONE-A'   210 km/h (130 mph)

LYNX HAS.Mk 2   232 km/h (144 mph)

WEAPONS

Standard armament for a light ship's helicopter is a pair of homing torpedoes, although the SH-2 often only carried one. The Lynx can fire Sea Skua missiles against patrol craft, and SH-2Gs have fired AGM-65 in trials. Nuclear depth charges would be used for extra deep diving submarines.

SH-2 SEASPRITE   2 x torpedoes or 2 x ASMs

Ka-25 'HORMONE-A'   2 x torpedoes or 4 x depth charges

LYNX HAS.Mk 2   2 x torpedoes or 4 x depth charges or 2 x ASMs

ENDURANCE

Mission endurance is vital to ASW helicopters, which must maintain long patrols at considerable distances from the ship.

SH-2 SEASPRITE   2½ hours

Ka-25 'HORMONE-A'   4 hours

LYNX HAS.Mk 2   3 hours

Attacking submarines from small ships

1 SHIP GUIDANCE: Having acquired a submarine with its onboard passive or active sonar, the ship guides the Seasprite towards the target area. The ship processes data from the Seasprite's sonobuoys or dipping sonar.

2 DETECTION AND ATTACK: The Seasprite makes a final check on the target location, usually by dropping sonobuoys or using MAD gear which reacts to the target's magnetic field. The crew launch a torpedo or depth charge when positioned near the target.

3 TARGET SUBMARINE: The Mk 46 torpedo makes a spiral search pattern to acquire the target, using active and passive homing.

LOCKHEED

P-38 LIGHTNING

- Twin-engine fighter ● Flown by top aces

M any believe the Lockheed P-38 Lightning was the finest American fighter of World War II. The twin-boomed P-38 was fast, heavily-armed and extremely versatile. While it had trouble matching single-engine fighters like the Messerschmitt 109 and Focke-Wulf 190, the Lightning was very manoeuvrable for such a big machine, and in capable hands it could hold its own. The P-38 more than held its own in the South West Pacific, where the aircraft was flown by Major Richard I. Bong and Major Thomas B. McGuire, America's top-scoring aces of all time.

▲ Lieutenant Murray J. Shubin was just one of the many aces to succeed in a Lightning. Shubin gained five kills in an hour in his P-38, which he named after his Australian girlfriend.

PHOTO FILE

LOCKHEED P-38 LIGHTNING

▼ Photo fighter
The F-5 reconnaissance Lightning performed dangerous lone missions without any armament.

▲ Napalm attack
Lightnings blast Japanese positions with napalm bombs near the Ipoh Dam in the Philippine Islands.

Night Lightning ▼
The P-38M was one of the fastest night-fighters of the war, despite the added weight of radar and a second crewmember.

▲ Clothes line
The Lightning served throughout the Solomons. It performed many tasks, including drying the clothes of 13th Air Force pilots!

Caught napping ▼
It wasn't all victories; this sad remnant of a P-38 at Tacloban was the result of Japanese bombing during the 1944 struggle for Leyte.

▲ Outdoor factory
Lightnings were built in the California sun while the Lockheed production line was modernised.

FACTS AND FIGURES

▼ The P-38 Lightning prototype made its first flight on 27 January 1939.

▼ The Lightning produced for the Royal Air Force was at first named the Atlanta.

▼ Experimental Lightning variants included the high-altitude XP-49 and XP-58 Chain Lightning bomber escort.

▼ To overcome tail buffeting in early P-38s, an aluminium fillet was added to the wingroot.

▼ F-4 and F-5 photo-gathering Lightnings were among the best reconnaissance aircraft of the war.

▼ Production of all versions of this great Lockheed fighter totalled 9924 aircraft.

The fork-tailed devil in the sky

As late as 1944, when Mustangs were sweeping the skies clear of foes, a poll in flying classes showed that student pilots' 'most wanted' aircraft was the Lockheed P-38 Lightning, the design of which dated back to 1937.

The P-38 was rugged and versatile, and because of its low-drag aerodynamic shape and heavy weight it accelerated to high speeds faster than any previous warplane. A potent

One 20-mm cannon and four heavy machine guns concentrated in the nose made the P-38 one of the hardest-hitting American fighters of the war. The battery of guns was also very useful in the ground-attack role.

fighter and a superb fighter-bomber, it also flew as a night-fighter, reconnaissance aircraft, ambulance, torpedo-bomber and target tug.

More than 100 US Army squadrons flew the P-38, which was produced in at least two-dozen versions. In the Pacific, P-38 pilots carried out the long-range intercept mission which downed and killed Japan's Admiral Isoroku Yamamoto, a planner of the Pearl Harbor

attack. In the Mediterranean, Luftwaffe pilots showed respect for the Lightning by calling it *der gabelschwanz Teufel* (the fork-tailed devil).

The ultimate P-38L model was flown by Dick Bong and Tommy McGuire, who with 40 and 38 victories, respectively, were the most successful American fighter pilots in history.

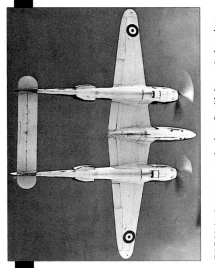

RAF Lightnings were early aircraft with low-rated engines, and had all the faults and none of the advantages of later machines. They were not popular with British pilots.

P-38J LIGHTNING

This Lockheed P-38J served with the 55th Fighter Squadron at Kingscliffe, Northamptonshire, and flew fighter escort for 8th Air Force bombers over Germany.

The turbo-charged Allison in-line engines were never the P-38's best feature, being prone to over-heating.

The Lightning's nosewheel undercarriage was a very welcome new feature for pilots. It made engine maintenance easy for the engineers, as well as reducing accidents on take-off and landing.

Early Lightnings were notoriously uncomfortable, having a cramped cockpit that lacked proper heating. The first attempts at flying at high altitude resulted in pilots getting frostbite.

Unlike British twin-engine aircraft such as the Mosquito, the P-38 was built with 'handed' engines turning in opposite directions. This eliminated engine torque reaction, making take-off extremely simple.

Early Lightning prototypes suffered severe buffeting around the tail from the airflow over the wings, but this was cured in production versions.

Turbo-charged engines with boom-mounted radiators gave the P-38 superb high-altitude performance. Early examples for Britain were delivered without turbos, which virtually crippled the aircraft as a fighting machine.

P-38L Lightning

Type: single-seat fighter and fighter-bomber

Powerplant: two turbo-charged 1194-kW (1600-lb-thrust) Allison V-1710-111/113 in-line piston engines

Maximum speed: 666 km/h (414 mph) at 7620 m (25,000 ft)

Range: 765 km (475 miles) on internal fuel

Service ceiling: 13,400 m (44,000 ft)

Weights: empty 5806 kg (12,800 lb); loaded 9798 kg (21,600 lb)

Armament: one 20-mm cannon and four 12.7-mm (.50-cal.) machine guns, plus up to 1450 kg (3197 lb) of ordnance – usually two 454-kg (1000-lb) or 726-kg (1600-lb) bombs or 10 127-mm (5-in) high-explosive rocket projectiles under wings

Dimensions:
span 15.85 m (52 ft)
length 11.53 m (37 ft 10 in)
height 3.00 m (9 ft 10 in)
wing area 30.42 m² (327 sq ft)

COMBAT DATA

MAXIMUM SPEED

The P-38 was the first American Army Air Force fighter capable of more than 650 km/h (400 mph). Its sensational high-altitude performance remained a feature of the type throughout its career, along with its superb climbing and diving ability.

P-38L LIGHTNING	666 km/h (414 mph)
A6M6 ZERO	557 km/h (346 mph)
Bf 109G	620 km/h (385 mph)

SERVICE CEILING

The P-38's twin turbo-charged engines gave it superb high-altitude performance, and at heights over 8000 m (26,240 ft) it was one of the best fighters in the world. At medium altitudes, however, the big fighter had less of an advantage, and could get into trouble against more agile German or Japanese machines which could out-turn the P-38L.

P-38L LIGHTNING 13,400 m (44,000 ft)

A6M6 ZERO 10,700 m (35,100 ft)

Bf 109G 11,500 m (37,730 ft)

ARMAMENT

Although on paper the P-38 had lighter armament than most of its opponents, the concentration of guns in the nose allowed it to bring an immense amount of fire to bear on targets at all ranges. Lightnings were known to 'saw Zeros in half' with a long burst of fire.

P-38L LIGHTNING
1 x 20-mm cannon
4 x 12.7-mm (.50-cal.) machine guns
1450 kg (3197 lb) of bombs

A6M6 ZERO
2 x 20-mm cannon
3 x 13.2-mm machine guns
1x 250-kg (550-lb) bomb

Bf 109G
1 x 30-mm cannon
2 x 20-mm cannon
1 x 454-kg (1000-lb) bomb

The Lightning's prey

■ **KAWANISHI N1K2:** Developed from a floatplane, the N1K2 was one of the most manoeuvrable fighters ever, let down by unreliable engines.

■ **MITSUBISHI A6M ZERO:** The great Japanese fighter was far more agile than the Lightning, but it was considerably slower.

■ **MITSUBISHI G4M:** The Japanese navy's main bomber proved horribly vulnerable to being set ablaze by the P-38's concentrated firepower.

■ **NAKAJIMA Ki-43:** The Japanese army's equivalent of the Zero was regularly shot down by Lightning pilots in the South West Pacific.

■ **NAKAJIMA Ki-84:** This was the best Japanese fighter of the war. Although slower, in competent hands it could sometimes outfly the Lightning.

LOCKHEED

HUDSON

● Maritime patrol ● Anti-submarine ● Light bomber transport

▲ Converted airliners often made rather indifferent warplanes, but the Hudson was an immediate success. Orders for it from Britain made Lockheed a big name in America's aircraft industry.

O ne of the few combat aircraft to have been developed from a civil transport, the Lockheed Hudson maritime patrol bomber (and navigator trainer) owes its basic design to the Lockheed Model 14 Super Electra of the late-1930s. The Hudson was a smooth-handling and popular aircraft which never quite had the performance needed in warfare. Nevertheless, it made a fine contribution to the Allies' war effort.

LOCKHEED **HUDSON**

▼ Rockets and radar
For anti-submarine patrol work, the Hudson was fitted with eight rockets and simple radar.

▲ Airliner lines
The Hudson's airliner heritage made it a good warplane. The capacious but sleek fuselage gave the aircraft long range and high speed, and the broad wings made it very stable in flight.

▲ Lifeboat carrier
This aircraft from No. 123 Squadron, Royal Canadian Air Force, carried a large lifeboat under the fuselage, which could be dropped to survivors at the scene of a disaster.

▲ American patrol
This immaculate Hudson, with the pre-1942 American markings and British camouflage, was one of the first A-29s repossessed by America.

▲ Hudson down
The crew walked away from this mishap in a Hudson Mk VI, which has a radio direction-finding loop aerial.

FACTS AND FIGURES

➤ A Hudson directed British naval forces to the German prison ship *Altmark* in February 1940.

➤ The prototype for the Hudson made its maiden flight on 10 December 1938.

➤ A single Hudson was used by the Sperry Gyroscope Company as a test aircraft.

➤ No. 280 Squadron, RAF, was the first to use Hudsons to drop airborne lifeboats over the North Sea in 1943.

➤ Some Hudsons were based in Manaos, Brazil, to patrol the South Atlantic.

➤ A total of 2941 Hudsons had been built when production ended in May 1943.

PROFILE

Airliner turned patrol bomber

B ased on the Super Electra civil transport, the Hudson was the first American-built aircraft to fly with the Royal Air Force during World War II. The airframe was instantly recognisable as a modified Electra, with more powerful engines, gun armament and internal bomb-bay. This bomber was rushed into production to meet Britain's requirement for a maritime patrol aircraft and navigation trainer. Search-and-rescue Hudsons were also built,

with a lifeboat stored under the fuselage.

After its early success in British use, the Hudson was employed by the US Army Air Forces in A-28 and A-29 attack variants, and as the AT-18 advanced trainer. The US Navy adopted the Hudson as a patrol bomber, and called it the PBO. US Navy Hudsons sank two U-boats on 15 March 1942. This was the first of several such successes in combat. An A-29 sank the German submarine *U-701* on 7 July 1942.

Right: In US Army Air Force service, the A-28 and A-29 series was never officially known as the Hudson, reflecting the fact that the aircraft was first and foremost designed to serve the RAF.

Above: This highly polished Hudson is an AT-18 gunnery trainer. These aircraft allowed trainee gunners to fire shots realistically from the turrets in peacetime conditions.

Hudsons were used by many Allied air forces, including the Soviet Union and South Africa. The aircraft continued to serve faithfully in support roles up until the end of the war.

HUDSON MK V

This Lockheed Hudson Mk V served with No. 48 Squadron of the Royal Air Force Coastal Command, based at Stornoway in the Outer Hebrides during 1941. Its main tasks were patrol and air-sea rescue.

The RAF's Hudson had provision for two forward-firing fixed machine guns in the upper fuselage, ahead of the pilot.

Standard accommodation was for a crew of four: pilot, navigator, bomb-aimer and radio operator.

The Hudson's fuselage was very similar to the Super Electra airliner from which it was developed. The lower fuselage, however, contained a large bomb-bay with provision for up to 635 kg (1400 lb) of offensive weapons or rescue life-rafts.

The upper surface of the fuselage contained a Perspex astrodome for visual observation, a large aerial mast with cables to the horizontal tailfin and a bullet-shaped fairing for the D/F loop antenna.

The Hudson's Boulton Paul dorsal turret provided good visibility and two hard-hitting 7.62-mm (.30-cal.) machine guns.

The tail unit featured twin vertical fins and rudders, enabling the gunner (generally the radio operator) to have an almost completely clear field of vision and the ability to engage fighters flying behind him.

The large internal space could be converted into a troop transport or for VIP work.

Coastal Command patrollers

■ **BRISTOL BEAUFORT:** Coastal Command's standard torpedo-bomber from 1940 to 1943, the prototype first flew in 1938.

■ **ARMSTRONG WHITWORTH WHITLEY:** Outmoded as bombers, Whitleys were the first to carry ASV.Mk II radar in Coastal Command.

■ **CONSOLIDATED LIBERATOR:** Late-model B-24s were used as VLR (very-long-range) patrol aircraft hunting for German U-boats.

■ **VICKERS WARWICK:** An enlarged variant of the famous Wellington, in the anti-submarine role the Warwick was just too late for war service.

Hudson Mk I

Type: maritime patrol-bomber

Powerplant: two 820-kW (1100-hp) Wright GR-1820-G-102A radial piston engines

Maximum speed: 396 km/h (245 mph) at 1980 m (6500 ft)

Range: 3154 km (1955 miles)

Service ceiling: 7620 m (25,000 ft)

Weights: empty 5275 kg (11,605 lb); maximum take-off 7938 kg (17,464 lb)

Armament: two 7.62-mm (.30-cal.) forward-firing machine guns and two similar weapons in a dorsal turret, plus up to 635 kg (1400 lb) of bombs or depth charges in internal bomb-bay

Dimensions:
span	19.96 m	(65 ft)
length	13.51 m	(44 ft)
height	3.61 m	(12 ft)
wing area	51.19 m²	(551 sq ft)

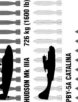

COMBAT DATA

Flying-boats, carrying the extra weight of a strong hull, tend to have a lower top speed than equivalent landplanes. The Hudson design was based on that of a small airliner and had a fairly good speed compared to its contemporaries.

MAXIMUM SPEED

HUDSON Mk IIIA	407 km/h (252 mph)
PBY-5A CATALINA	288 km/h (179 mph)
BV 138C-1	275 km/h (170 mph)

RANGE

To take advantage of the ability to land on water, flying-boats tend to have a good range performance. This also allows longer periods on patrol. Both the Catalina and BV 138 were renowned for range, especially compared to the Hudson.

HUDSON Mk IIIA	2494 km (1546 miles)
BV 138C-1	5000 km (3100 miles)
PBY-5A CATALINA	4096 km (2540 miles)

BOMBLOAD

In the anti-submarine role the Catalina was a great threat to the U-boat because of its armament capacity. For its size the Hudson was also well-equipped, hauling a similar load to the BV 138.

HUDSON Mk IIIA	726 kg (1600 lb)
PBY-5A CATALINA	1814 kg (3990 lb)
BV 138C-1	300 kg (660 lb)

LOCKHEED

PV-1 VENTURA/PV-2 HARPOON

● Light bomber/maritime patroller ● Built to an RAF requirement

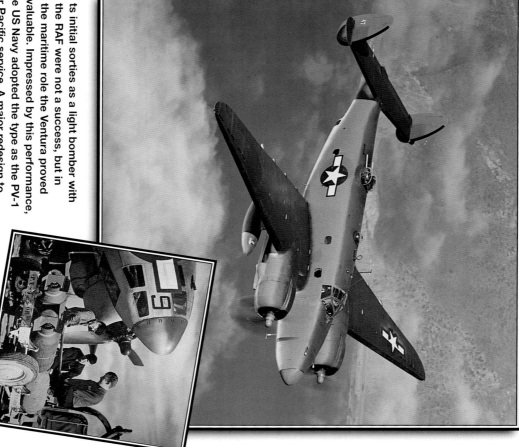

Its initial sorties as a light bomber with the RAF were not a success, but in the maritime role the Ventura proved invaluable. Impressed by this performance, the US Navy adopted the type as the PV-1 for Pacific service. A major redesign to increase range and load-carrying ability resulted in the PV-2 Harpoon. After war service, surplus aircraft flew with several air forces, while others were converted to crop sprayers and executive transports.

▶ Although designed to an RAF requirement for a light bomber, the Ventura was found to be more suitable for maritime patrol duties. When the US Navy took over ASW duties in spring 1942, it ordered the PV-1.

LOCKHEED PV-1 VENTURA/PV-2 HARPOON

▲ RAF Ventura Mk II
The RAF took delivery of 394 Ventura light bombers, which entered service in 1942. By 1943 all were with Coastal Command units.

▼ Post-war conversions
Harpoons were among a number of wartime aircraft converted into executive transports after 1945.

▼ North Atlantic livery
This all-white colour scheme was usually used over the North Atlantic and made the black rubber de-icer boots very prominent. The underwing tanks carried 587 litres (150 gallons) each and bomb-bay tanks increased range further.

▼ Improved war load
Successive versions of the Ventura carried between 1134 kg (2495 lb) and 1362 kg (2994 lb) of weapons. The Harpoon had 1816 kg (3900 lb) internally, with an extra 454 kg (1000 lb) under each wing.

▼ Post-war Reserve PV-2
This Harpoon, seen in post-war markings, has had its undernose 12.7-mm (.50-cal.) guns removed.

FACTS AND FIGURES

▶ The first Marine Corps night-fighter unit, VMF(N)-531, scored its first kill with a radar-equipped PV-1 in November 1943.

▶ A failure as an RAF bomber, all Venturas went to Coastal Command in 1943.

▶ PV-2 Harpoons saw limited war service, being phased out by the US Navy in 1948.

▶ On Christmas Eve 1943, a No. 1 Squadron, RNZAF, Ventura crew shot down three Japanese 'Zero' fighters.

▶ Venturas built on British contract and taken over by the US Navy were PV-3s.

▶ US Marine Corps PV-1 night-fighters had six forward-firing guns and British AI radar.

Lodestars in Allied uniforms

Pleased with the Hudson, the British Air Ministry was interested in Lockheed's proposal to modify the Lodestar in a similar way, as a replacement for both the Hudson (in the maritime reconnaissance role) and the Bristol Blenheim light/medium bomber.

The Ventura, as it was to be known, was larger than the Hudson, with more powerful engines, improved armament and a greater load-carrying capability. Large numbers went to the RAF, RAAF, RNZAF and SAAF. A few were retained by the USAAF for over-water patrols as B-34 and B-37 Lexingtons.

From 1942 the US Navy took over all ASW work from the army and obtained 1600 PV-1s. The improved PV-2 Harpoon followed, with major design changes to optimise it for the maritime role.

War surplus PV-1s and -2s were used after the war for a variety of roles. Some have been restored by warbird enthusiasts.

PV-2 HARPOON

This PV-2 wears the markings of US Navy Patrol Bomber Squadron VPB-142 based in the Marianas Islands in 1945. Wartime deliveries to Allied air arms included five to the Brazilian air force and four to the RNZAF.

As a maritime patrol bomber the PV-2 had a crew of four or five, comprising a pilot, navigator/bomb aimer, radio operator/gunner and turret gunner. When operated solely as a patrol aircraft a fifth crewmember was carried.

Harpoons (and most Venturas) were fitted with two Pratt & Whitney R-2800 Double Wasps, each rated at 1491 kW (2000 hp). These engines were also fitted to the Vought F4U and Douglas A-26.

The Harpoon was a major redesign of the Ventura to optimize it for maritime patrol. It had longer span wings to improve take-off performance with a full fuel load and enlarged vertical tail surfaces.

Initial PV-2 operations revealed a serious wing wrinkling problem. Attempts to solve this by reducing the span failed and a complete wing redesign was required, which slowed down production.

The Harpoon differed from the Ventura in almost every detail except for small sections of the fuselage, inboard wing ribs and engine cowlings.

This PV-2 carried eight 127-mm (5-in) high-velocity aerial rockets (HVAR) below the wings as well as two 587-litre (150-gallon) droptanks. An internal bomb-bay held up to 1816 kg (3990 lb) of bombs.

Armament consisted of eight 12.7-mm (50-cal.) machine guns, including three in an undernose pack, two above the nose, two in a dorsal turret and one in the ventral position.

Disaster over Amsterdam

1 OPERATION 'RAMROD 16': On 3 May 1943 twelve Venturas of No. 487 Squadron, a New Zealand-manned unit, set off on a daylight raid on Amsterdam. At 4.43 p.m. Squadron Leader Leonard Trent led his squadron skywards towards Amsterdam.

2 GERMAN WOLFPACK: Unknown to the Ventura force, two crack Luftwaffe fighter units were alerted to the trap. The Venturas lumbered into the trap and most were ripped to shreds by the 70 enemy fighters.

3 LONE SURVIVOR: Trent continued the bomb run with five remaining Venturas. Four of these were shot down, but Trent managed to release his bombs over the target before being shot down himself. He was awarded the Victoria Cross for his bravery.

PV-1 Ventura

Type: twin-engined maritime patrol/bomber

Powerplant: two 1491-kW (2000-hp) Pratt & Whitney R-2800-31 Double Wasp radial engines

Maximum speed: 518 km/h (321 mph) at 4205 m (13,800 ft)

Maximum range: 2670 km (1650 miles)

Service ceiling: 8015 m (26,300 ft)

Weights: empty 9161 kg (20,154 lb); maximum take-off 15,422 kg (33,924 lb)

Armament: two 12.7-mm (50-cal.) machine guns each in nose and dorsal turret, two 7.62-mm (.30-cal.) machine guns in ventral position, plus six 227-kg (500-lb) bombs or one torpedo in bomb-bay and up to two 454-kg (1000-lb) bombs under the wings

Dimensions:
span	19.96 m (65 ft 6 in)
length	15.77 m (51 ft 8 in)
height	3.63 m (11 ft 10 in)
wing area	63.73 m² (686 sq ft)

COMBAT DATA

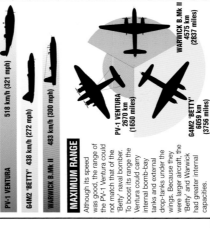

MAXIMUM SPEED

Based on the civil Lodestar, the Ventura was a relatively fast warplane, even with a typical weapon load aboard. The G4M 'Betty' first flew in 1939 and suffered at the hands of Allied fighters. Both the 'Betty' and Warwick were purpose-designed military aircraft.

PV-1 VENTURA	518 km/h (321 mph)
G4M2 'BETTY'	438 km/h (272 mph)
WARWICK B.Mk II	483 km/h (300 mph)

MAXIMUM RANGE

Although its speed was good, the range of the PV-1 Ventura could not match that of the 'Betty' naval bomber. To boost its range the Ventura could carry internal bomb-bay tanks and external drop-tanks under the wings. Because they were larger aircraft, the 'Betty' and Warwick had greater internal capacities.

PV-1 VENTURA	2670 km (1650 miles)
WARWICK B.Mk II	4575 km (2837 miles)
G4M2 'BETTY'	6059 km (3756 miles)

INTERNAL BOMBLOAD

Although it was a bigger aircraft than the PV-1, the G4M had a limited load capacity. The Warwick carried over two and a half tonnes of bombs and was intended as a replacement for the Wellington in the maritime reconnaissance role.

PV-1 VENTURA	1362 kg (2994 lb)
G4M2 'BETTY'	1000 kg (2200 lb)
WARWICK B.Mk II	2608 kg (5738 lb)

LOCKHEED

P-80 SHOOTING STAR

● Jet fighter ● European deployment ● Test flying

▲ Proudly wearing the Lockheed emblem on its nose, the P-80 Shooting Star was equipped with six forward-firing machine guns, a typical armament fit for fighters of the era.

I n 1944 the US Army Air Force began gunnery trials in Nevada with the Lockheed P-80 Shooting Star; this design promised to revolutionise air warfare. The P-80 was the first fully operational type in the US to have a jet engine – an innovation already familiar to German and British scientists. The US rushed four P-80s to Europe – two each to England and Italy – and they were hours from entering combat when World War II ended.

PHOTO FILE

LOCKHEED P-80 SHOOTING STAR

▼ Graceful lines
Before the addition of wingtip tanks and essential service equipment, the Shooting Star was one of the most elegant aircraft ever produced by Lockheed. Pilots marvelled at the design.

▲ Fighter testing
Known as Lulu Belle, this P-80 was flown against the conventionally powered fighters of the period to explore jet tactics.

▲ Future potential
With large test markings displayed on its fuselage, this particular P-80 undertook a series of developmental flights to try out future jet fighter equipment.

▲ Service entry
Seen high over California's foothills, this P-80A was assigned to the 412th Fighter Group at March Field in late 1945.

◀ Lakebed landings
Early flights were performed from the Muroc range in California, and made use of the many dry lakebeds.

FACTS AND FIGURES

▼ The Shooting Star was designed from the start to be the United States Army Air Force's first operational jet fighter.

▼ One of the first examples of the P-80 was completed in just 143 days.

▼ Early aircraft were given names like The Grey Ghost and Silver Ghost.

▼ Lockheed hoped to deliver 450 Shooting Stars per month during World War II, but this was never accomplished.

▼ Richard Ira Bong, America's highest-scoring ace, was killed testing a P-80.

▼ Many pilots found it hard to adjust to the new demands of jet flying.

PROFILE

Shooting for success

Work on the P-80 began in 1943 when famous engineer Clarence L. ('Kelly') Johnson persuaded his bosses at Lockheed to attempt to build the USAAF's first operational jet fighter in just 180 days. They actually completed the pace-setting first P-80 in 143 days.

The P-80 was a clean design with straight wings and tail surfaces, and a tricycle landing gear. Air intakes positioned on the lower fuselage forward of the wing leading edge fed the British-

designed de Havilland H.1B turbojet, which was replaced in production examples by the Allison/General Electric I-40 (J33).

Many pilots with propeller experience took to the jet-powered P-80 with enormous enthusiasm. An ambitious programme progressed toward the goal of getting the Shooting Star into combat. Several P-80s were lost in tragic mishaps, but the aircraft performed well, and the USAAF moved rapidly to finalise the configuration of this

fighter and to develop a photo-reconnaissance version. Had World War II lasted weeks longer, it is certain that the P-80 Shooting Star would have done battle with the top fighters developed by the Axis, including Germany's much-vaunted Messerschmitt Me 262.

Despite the early success of the Shooting Star, it was quickly overshadowed by more advanced designs from rival manufacturers. The type was retained for second-line duties, in which the Shooting Stars remained for a number of years until fatigue problems caused their withdrawal.

Below: Having just completed another test flight, an early P-80 is seen parked on one of Muroc's dry lakebeds. A major debrief followed each flight.

Above: After completing extensive test work, this Shooting Star was restored by ex-Lockheed employees.

XP-80 Shooting Star

Type: single-seat jet fighter

Powerplant: one 10.9-kN (2450-lb-thrust) de Havilland H.1B Goblin turbojet

Maximum speed: 808 km/h (557 mph); cruising speed 692 km/h (429 mph)

Initial climb rate: 914 m/min (3000 fpm) from sea level

Range: 1609 km (1000 miles)

Service ceiling: 12,497 m (41,000 ft)

Weights: empty 2852 kg (6274 lb); maximum take-off 4498 kg (9896 lb)

Armament: six 12.7-mm (.50-cal.) nose-mounted machine guns

Dimensions:
span	11.27 m (36 ft 11 in)
length	10.00 m (32 ft 9 in)
height	3.12 m (10 ft 3 in)
wing area	22.29 m² (240 sq ft)

FIGHTING JETS

BRITISH FIGHTERS: Entering service with the Royal Air Force in late 1944, the Gloster Meteor (pictured above) saw limited use, often on ground attack duties. After the end of World War II, a host of specialised variants were introduced into service, such as night-fighters, target-tugs and tactical photo-reconnaissance models. Widely exported to European and Middle Eastern countries, the Meteor remained in limited service until the late 1970s when it was finally replaced by more modern types. The Meteor had the distinction of being the first jet fighter in RAF service.

GERMAN GENESIS: Widely regarded as the best fighter of World War II, the Messerschmitt Me 262 was introduced into (limited) operational service before its rivals. After the end of the war, the Me 262 had remarkable agility and was able to outperform anything the Americans or British could offer. Hampered by a dwindling fuel supply, the Germans initially used the aircraft as a light bomber before pilots saw the full potential of the fighter. After the end of hostilities, Allied pilots flight-tested the aircraft and were thoroughly impressed. It had only limited post-war service, but the aircraft's design influenced fighter design for years to come. Other variants constructed were two-seat trainers, night-fighters, and precision attack bombers which were equipped with a glazed nose-section for an additional crew member.

RF-80A SHOOTING STAR

Many early model Shooting Stars were built for, or converted to, the photo-reconnaissance role. This example saw service in Korea, where the aircraft operated with an escort of fighters.

The pilot enjoyed exceptional visibility through a teardrop sliding canopy. The cockpits of reconnaissance versions differed very little from fighter variants. The only additions were camera switches, film counters and blinker lights to replace the K-14 gunsight.

An enlarged forward section housed the reconnaissance camera suite. Access to the camera bay installation was by way of an upward-hinging nose section. Camera film could be replaced in a few minutes by experienced personnel.

Mounted low on either side of the fuselage were the small intakes. They were prone to ingesting foreign objects when the aircraft operated from semi-prepared runways.

Though the aircraft were initially flown in their peacetime natural colour scheme, some RF-80s adopted olive-drab upper surfaces when they went to war in Korea. Despite this the retention of the large 'buzz' numbers compromised the end result.

A red fuselage band was painted on all early Shooting Stars. This denoted the turbine position within the engine. At this point the rear fuselage could be removed to allow maintenance personnel access to the engine.

To answer requests from USAF pilots for additional range, wingtip tanks were installed on the Shooting Star. They varied in size, and later models were fitted with additional fuel tanks under the wings.

Lockheed's adaptable lady

■ **T-33 SHOOTING STAR:** Developed into a highly successful trainer, the T-33 is operated by a number of countries. It provides the first experience of jet flight for many pilots.

■ **XF-90:** Offered to the USAF as a potential long-range bomber escort, the XF-90 was not successful and eventually lost out to the two-seat McDonnell F-101 Voodoo.

■ **F-94C STARFIRE:** A specialised variant of the T-33 was developed to intercept intruders at night. Fitted with an improved radar, the aircraft saw much service with the USAF.

LOCKHEED

T-33

● Trainer version of the F-80 ● Thousands built ● Still in service

ronically, it was the poor safety record of the P-80 that finally convinced Lockheed to proceed with a two-seat trainer version. The first TP-80C was converted from a P-80C airframe and flew in its new form on 22 March 1948. More than 6750 examples of the T-33A production aircraft were built, including almost 900 made under licence in Canada and Japan. Even though it is 50 years since the aircraft's first flight, several T-33As remain in service.

▲ Thousands of pilots gained their wings on the T-33A and its derivatives. Several also went to war in the type, usually as members of the world's smaller air arms.

PHOTO FILE

LOCKHEED T-33

▲ Ecuadorean formation
Many South American nations received AT-33As, which have a secondary attack role.

▲ Photographic T-bird
Lockheed launched the RT-33A as a low-cost reconnaissance platform.

Luftwaffe service▼
Germany received 192 T-33As, making the country the second-largest European T-33 operator.

▲ Hellenic target
Still wearing its USAF 'buzz-number', this Greek T-33A provides target facilities using a Dornier target system. The 'T-bird' is brightly painted to make it highly visible.

▲ Electronic stars
Most of Canada's remaining Silver Stars are used for electronic warfare training. Canadian aircraft are designated CT-133s.

FACTS AND FIGURES

▼ On 11 June 1948 the TP-80C was redesignated TF-80C and finally became the T-33A on 5 May 1949.

▼ Although the T-33A had no USAF name, it was universally known as the 'T-bird'.

▼ Several aircraft were used for test flying under the NT-33A-LO designation.

▼ A radical conversion of the T-33A, known as the Skyfox, was proposed by the Skyfox Corporation in the early 1980s.

▼ Until 1981 the armed AT-33A was Brazil's only jet combat aircraft.

▼ Canada uses one of its Silver Stars for ejection seat trials.

PROFILE

'T-birds' and SeaStars

Early in the P-80 programme, Lockheed ignored suggestions that a training variant of the new jet should be developed. By 1947, however, it was clear that pilots changing from piston- to jet-powered fighters found it was not as easy as expected, and the P-80 was suffering an alarmingly high accident rate.

A jet transition trainer was clearly required, and so Lockheed gained permission from the USAF to act as the prototype of the TP-80C. Fuselage

plugs fore and aft of the wing gave the extra length required to accommodate a second cockpit, but this was at the expense of internal fuel. Drop-tanks beneath the wingtips were to be a standard feature of the trainer, but these were later replaced by centrally-mounted tip-tanks.

An attack variant, which supplemented the standard twin 12.7-mm machine-gun armament of the T-33A with underwing hardpoints for 907 kg of ordnance, was developed for export to smaller air forces.

With the build-up of NATO forces in the 1950s Canada became a centre for aircrew training and 20 T-33A Silver Star Mk 1s from the US were joined by 656 licence-built, Nene-engined T-33AN Silver Star Mk 3s. Japan also built T-33As, and several examples remain in service around the world.

Left: Capable of carrier operations, the hook-equipped T2V-1 SeaStar joined TV-2s (standard T-33As) in US Navy service from late 1957.

Below: Four T-33As of the USAF fly in a tight formation. Unusually, the aircraft's tip-tanks have been removed.

T-33A

Type: tandem two-seat primary jet trainer

Powerplant: one 24.02-kN (5400-lb-thrust) Allison J33-A-35 turbojet

Maximum speed: 966 km/h (599 mph) at sea level

Cruising speed: 732 km/h (454 mph) at optimum altitude

Initial climb rate: 1484 m/min (4870 fpm) at sea level

Range: 1650 km (1025 miles) on internal fuel; ferry range 2050 km (1270 miles) with tip tanks

Service ceiling: 14,630 m (48,000 ft)

Weights: empty equipped 3794 kg (8347 lb); maximum take-off 6832 kg (15,030 lb)

Armament: two 12.7-mm (.50-cal.) machine guns

Dimensions:
span	11.85 m	(38 ft 10 in)
length	11.51 m	(37 ft 9 in)
height	3.55 m	(11 ft 8 in)
wing area	21.81 m²	(235 sq ft)

COMBAT DATA

MAXIMUM SPEED

All three of these early jet trainers were based on fighter designs, but the T-33A emerged with the best performance. It has also outlived the other two in regular service.

T-33A	**966 km/h (599 mph)**
METEOR T.Mk 7	**941 km/h (583 mph)**
VAMPIRE T.Mk 11	**884 km/h (548 mph)**

INITIAL CLIMB RATE

With two comparatively powerful engines, the Meteor T.Mk 7 had a good rate of climb. The de Havilland Vampire T.Mk 11 was not a great performer but was cheap to operate, and mainly replaced the Meteor. The T-33A continues to offer cost-effective training.

VAMPIRE T.Mk 11
1372 m/min
(4500 fpm)

METEOR T.Mk 7
2316 m/min
(7600 fpm)

T-33A
1494 m/min
(4870 fpm)

THRUST

The Meteor T.Mk 7's twin engines gave it greater thrust and a higher probability of survival in the event of an engine failure. It was more costly to operate, however, and was not as versatile as the T-33A.

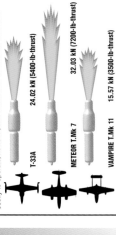

T-33A	24.02 kN (5400-lb-thrust)
METEOR T.Mk 7	32.03 kN (7200-lb-thrust)
VAMPIRE T.Mk 11	15.57 kN (3500-lb-thrust)

T-33A

This unusually marked T-33A wears a Bolivian camouflage scheme and a French ferry registration. This suggests that, like many 'T-birds', the aircraft has been sold on by its original owner.

Bolivia is typical of South American operators of the T-33A/AT-33A. Some countries have used their aircraft in combat, including Nicaragua, whose AT-33As were used to strafe Sandinista positions during 1979.

Lockheed invested $1 million of its own funds in the TP-80C project. After equipping a USAF P-80C with an extended fuselage and twin ejection seats as the TP-80C prototype, Lockheed was to see its faith in the project handsomely rewarded.

Early T-33s were delivered with the 20.05-kN (4500-lb-thrust) Allison J33-A-23 engine. Later production aircraft were powered by the 23.13-kN (5200-lb-thrust) J33-A-25, and most were eventually retrofitted with the 24.02-kN (5400-lb-thrust) J33-A-35.

Compared to the P-80C, the nose of the T-33A was considerably longer. This was due to a 0.98-m (3-ft) plug inserted forward of the wing. Even with the extended fuselage, some fuel capacity was lost, and the self-sealing wing tanks of the P-80C were replaced by higher-capacity nylon tanks to partially compensate.

F-WEQM

Each tip-tank had a capacity of 871 litres (230 gallons). These tanks were a standard feature and T-33As were rarely seen without them.

Simple intakes were used, since the Allison engine was non-afterburning and the T-33A was not expected to perform the extreme manoeuvres which are necessary in combat.

From fighter to trainer

■ **FOLLAND GNAT T.Mk 1:** Having decided not to procure the excellent Gnat fighter, the RAF ordered a two-seat training version which served with distinction.

■ **GLOSTER METEOR T.Mk 7:** Gloster developed the Meteor T.Mk 7 in much the same way that Lockheed had developed the T-33A from the P-80C.

■ **MIKOYAN-GUREVICH MiG-15UTI 'MIDGET':** MiG's trainer version of the MiG-15 was sold in thousands to several countries, but very few are likely to remain in service.

■ **NORTHROP T-38A TALON:** In the mid-1950s Northrop proposed the N-156 design, which was to become the F-5 series, and the derived N-156T, which became the Talon.

LOCKHEED

C-69/C-121 CONSTELLATION

● US and foreign transport ● Airliner derivative ● More than 35 years' use

O
ne of the most aesthetically pleasing aircraft of the immediate post-war years, the Lockheed Constellation took to the skies as a military transport in 1943, as the C-69. In World War II, it was the world's most advanced transport, billed as being faster than a Japanese 'Zero' fighter and quicker than contemporary bombers. In the 1950s and 1960s, as the C-121, the type served as a transport and as Presidential conveyance for Dwight D. Eisenhower.

▲ USAF and Navy logistics personnel were quick to see a military application for the long-range Lockheed Constellation, which represented the peak of piston-engined transport design.

LOCKHEED C-69/C-121 CONSTELLATION

▲ First flight, January 1943
Sharing the apron at Lockheed's Burbank plant with P-38 Lightnings, the first Model 049 (C-69) is seen on, or about, the date of its first flight. Though bearing its civil registration, NX25600, it carries a USAAF star and grey/green colour scheme.

Military 'Super Connie' ▼
Based on the US Navy's R7V-1, 34 C-121Cs delivered in 1955 boosted the USAF's long-range airlift capability.

Prototype Warning Star ▼
The first Constellation, 'stretched' to become the first Super Constellation, also served as the aerodynamic prototype for the WV-2.

▲ Limited C-69 production
Although 120 were ordered, only 22 C-69s were completed before VJ-Day. On its delivery flight to the USAAF, the prototype, flown by Howard Hughes, set a transcontinental speed record.

▲ USAF veterans in Vietnam
Former WV-2s became EC-121R relay aircraft for ground sensors detecting Viet Cong movements.

FACTS AND FIGURES

▼ VC-121As formerly used by US President Eisenhower and General Douglas MacArthur have been preserved.

▼ C-121A 48-616 was given to Ethiopia's Emperor Haile Selassie in 1957.

▼ The very first 'Connie' made its maiden flight in California on 9 January 1943.

▼ The first transatlantic crossing by a C-69 was made in August 1945, in 14 hours 12 minutes, between New York and Paris.

▼ Six ex-USAF C-121As were later modified for civilian agricultural spraying work.

▼ Model 1049G 'Super Connies' in the Indian Navy were the last military 'Connies'.

PROFILE

Long-range 'Connies' for the forces

M ilitary Lockheed Constellations gracefully brought together a mixture of beauty, brute power, and functional utility to provide top-notch air transport service for US military forces. This four-engined, low-wing, tricycle-gear aircraft with its uniquely contoured fuselage was a tribute to the design genius of Lockheed's Hal Hibbard and Kelly Johnson.

The 'Connie' was conceived as an airliner – a capacity in which it eventually served with distinction. The prototype of 1943 was the first of hundreds to serve airlines and equip US military transport units after World War II. C-69s entered service with Air Transport Command in 1945. This small group of 22 aircraft established records for speed and transport work, and were highly regarded, but were largely eclipsed in military service by the more workaday and more numerous Douglas C-54 Skymaster.

Post-war C-121 models, based on successive versions of the Constellation and 'Super Connie' were used for many duties with the USAF and Navy, though their main role remained that of

long-range transport, a role in which they served worldwide.

Included among later variants were the PO/WV/EC-121 Warning Star family of airborne early warning aircraft and a number of turboprop testbeds. Most Constellation transports were retired by the mid-1960s, though a few remained in service as late as the 1980s with foreign air forces.

Left: As well as 50 R7V-1 transports, the US Navy took delivery of four R7V-2s fitted with experimental Pratt & Whitney YT34 turboprops; two later went to the USAF as YC-121Fs. Another became a VC-121E presidential transport with the USAF.

Above: First post-war military Constellation variant was the C-121A. Ten were built for the USAF, two being converted later to VC-121A VIP transports. One of these, 48-613, was used by General Douglas MacArthur as Bataan.

C-121C Constellation

Type: long-range military transport

Powerplant: four 2423-kW (3250-hp) Wright R-3350-93 Cyclone 18 radial engines

Maximum speed: 593 km/h (368 mph) at 6100 m (20,000 ft)

Initial climb rate: 658 m/min (2160 fpm) at combat weight

Combat radius: 1853 km (1150 miles) at 390 km/h (242 mph) with maximum load

Combat range: 3354 km (2080 miles) at 417 km/h (259 mph) with maximum load weight

Service ceiling: 8320 m (27,300 ft) at combat weight

Weights: empty 33,028 kg (72,660 lb); combat 40,188 kg (88,415 lb); maximum take-off 62,368 kg (137,210 lb)

Dimensions: span 37.49 m (122 ft 11 in)
length 35.41 m (116 ft 2 in)
height 7.54 m (24 ft 9 in)
wing area 153.29 m² (122 ft 11 in)

COMBAT DATA

TROOPS

During World War II, the USAAF adopted the Douglas C-54 as its standard four-engined transport, despite its shorter range and inferior troop-carrying capacity. The Handley Page Hastings entered RAF service just after the end of World War II.

C-69 CONSTELLATION	60 troops
HASTINGS C.Mk 2	50 troops
C-54A SKYMASTER	50 troops

MAXIMUM SPEED

The post-war Hastings was a slightly faster aircraft than the C-69, but lacked the capacity and range of the latter. The Constellation, a much larger aircraft, was billed at the time of its first flight as being faster than contemporary bombers and some fighters.

C-69 CONSTELLATION	531 km/h (329 mph)
HASTINGS C.Mk 2	560 km/h (347 mph)
C-54A SKYMASTER	426 km/h (264 mph)

RANGE

Range was a C-69 strong point. The type had a 600-km (373 mile) advantage over the C-54, which in turn could fly further than the Hastings. In 1945 a USAAF C-69 made the type's first transatlantic flight, from New York to Paris. TWA crews flew the aircraft.

C-69 CONSTELLATION	3862 km (2400 miles)
HASTINGS C.Mk 2	2720 km (1685 miles)
C-54A SKYMASTER	3220 km (2000 miles)

C-121A Constellation

Ordered in 1948, 10 C-121As (of which 48-616 was an example) were delivered to the USAF's Military Air Transport Service as cargo- and personnel transports. The type was phased out by the USAF as late as 1968.

One C-121A was completed on the production line as a VC-121B VIP transport with suitable interior fittings and extra fuel capacity. A nose-mounted weather radar was later added.

C-121As were able to accommodate up to 44 passengers in the personnel transport role, or 20 stretchers and medical attendants in the medical evacuation duties. Nine aircraft were delivered with reinforced flooring and a 2.84 m (9 ft) by 1.83 m (6 ft) cargo loading door on the aft port side.

In cargo/passenger transport service C-121As generally carried a crew of five, with a relief crew of four on long-range flights.

Like the C-69 before it, the C-121A 'Connie' was powered by four Wright R-3500 Cyclone 18-cylinder radials. The -75 variant in the C-121A was rated at 1864 kW (2500 hp) and drove a three-bladed propeller. Later versions were powered by Turbo-Compound Cyclones with greatly increased power.

A military version of Lockheed's Model 749 airliner design intended for overseas use, the C-121A shared the former type's long-range performance, carrying extra fuel tanks in the outer wing panels. Total fuel capacity was 22,030 litres (5820 gallons).

The USAAF's wartime Air Transport Command became the USAF's Military Air Transport Service (MATS) after the creation of the air force in 1947. Later known as Military Airlift Command (MAC), it became Air Mobility Command (AMC) in 1992.

'Connies' in uniform

■ **C-69 CONSTELLATION:** The small C-69 fleet was made up of nine Model 049 airliners ordered by Pan American and TWA and impressed by the USAAF, plus 13 aircraft built to USAAF order. Most were disposed of after World War II.

■ **WV-2 WARNING STAR:** First ordered as PO-2Ws, 142 of these airborne early-warning aircraft based on the Model 1049A Super Constellation were delivered to the US Navy; another 72 were transferred to the USAF as RC-121Ds.

■ **SUPER CONSTELLATION:** India, along with France, Israel and Indonesia, employed ex-airline 'Connies' into the transport role as late as the 1980s. India's aircraft were former Air India aircraft and had a secondary maritime reconnaissance role.

LOCKHEED

F-94 STARFIRE

● All-weather interceptor ● Cold War defender ● T-33 development

I n the 1950s the Lockheed F-94 Starfire was the first jet aircraft to combine weaponry with an air-to-air radar set. The F-94 was the USAF's first jet-powered, all-weather interceptor. This fighter, with its crew of pilot and radar operator, saw useful service in the Korean conflict (1950-53), but its reputation was made in guarding the North American continent from the threat of bomber attack during the volatile Cold War.

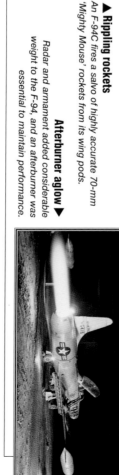

▲ For more than three years, from late-1949 until 1953, the F-94 was the USAF's only all-weather jet fighter. As such, it played a vital part in the Cold War, protecting the US from a perceived Soviet threat.

LOCKHEED **F-94 STARFIRE**

▲ **Swept tailplane**
The modified tailplane of the F-94C is obvious here. Starfires devoid of rocket pods but carrying wingtip tanks were introduced from the 100th aircraft.

▲ **First prototype**
Modified from a TF-80C Shooting Star (later known as the T-33A), the first two YF-94s lacked some operational equipment and were used as test aircraft.

▲ **Rippling rockets**
An F-94C fires a salvo of highly accurate 70-mm 'Mighty Mouse' rockets from its wing pods.

Afterburner aglow ▶
Radar and armament added considerable weight to the F-94, and an afterburner was essential to maintain performance.

▲ **From F-97A to F-94C**
Initially designated F-97A due to an extensive redesign, 387 examples of the improved variant were delivered as F-94Cs between 1951 and 1954. The last examples were retired in 1959.

FACTS AND FIGURES

➤ The F-94 was the world's first two-seat combat aircraft to exceed the speed of sound in a dive.

➤ The YF-94 prototype, piloted by Tony LeVier, first flew on 16 April 1949.

➤ The first 17 production F-94As were modified from T-33 airframes.

➤ The shootdown of an La-9 on 30 January 1953 was the first air victory achieved solely on cockpit instruments.

➤ In all, 854 Lockheed F-94 interceptors were built between 1948 and 1952.

➤ The F-94C became the first production fighter to use a braking parachute.

F-94B Starfire

Type: two-seat all-weather interceptor

Powerplant: one 26.69-kN (6000-lb-thrust) Allison J33-A-33 afterburning turbojet

Maximum speed: 975 km/h (605 mph) at sea level

Cruising speed: 727 km/h (450 mph) at sea level

Initial climb rate: 2088 m/min (6850 fpm)

Maximum range: 1455 km (900 miles)

Service ceiling: 14,630 m (48,000 ft)

Weights: empty 4565 kg (10,043 lb); maximum take-off 7640 kg (16,808 lb)

Armament: four 12.7-mm (.50-cal) machine guns

Dimensions: span 11.86 m (38 ft 11 in)
length 12.22 m (40 ft 11 in)
height 3.86 m (12 ft 8 in)
wing area 21.81 m² (235 sq ft)

ACTION DATA

MAXIMUM SPEED

All three of these jet designs were capable of speeds around 950 km/h (600 mph) – about the maximum speed of straight-winged aircraft. All subsequent designs had swept wings.

F-94C STARFIRE	1030 km/h (639 mph)
METEOR NF.Mk 11	960 km/h (595 mph)
F3D-2 SKYKNIGHT	965 km/h (598 mph)

RANGE

By the time the Meteor night-fighters were produced, their airframes were reaching the outer limits of development. Consequently, the aircraft was limited in its fuel capacity and its engines were outdated. Both of these factors affected its range performance.

METEOR NF.Mk 11 1480 km (920 miles)

F-94C STARFIRE 1930 km (1200 miles)

F3D-2 SKYKNIGHT 1930 km (1200 miles)

ARMAMENT

Once teething problems with the F-94C's rocket armament were solved, the system proved highly accurate and was a major improvement over the earlier F-94B's machine guns.

F-94C STARFIRE 48 x 70-mm rockets

METEOR NF.Mk 11 4 x 20-mm cannon

F3D-2 SKYKNIGHT 4 x 20-mm cannon

America's Cold War defender

When the Lockheed F-94 Starfire began to reach Air Defense Command squadrons in the early 1950s, many thought that it looked familiar. This was because the F-94 was a development of the Lockheed F-80 Shooting Star, the first operational US jet fighter. The F-80 also gave its design features to the famous T-33 trainer, the 'T-bird', from which the F-94 was derived.

The F-94 Starfire all-weather interceptor was created by adding radar, fitting a rear-seat observer and equipping the aircraft to

detect and intercept approaching bombers.

The F-94 was rushed to Japan for action when it became clear that the enemy was employing both prop and jet warplanes in an effort to control the night sky. At the time, the F-94's radar was considered so secret that aircraft were not allowed to fly beyond enemy lines – but they still managed to down several warplanes. F-94s also served with more than two dozen air defence squadrons in the USA and Alaska. When sent aloft to

intercept a bomber, the F-94 was given directions by a ground control intercept (GCI) operator using ground-based radar, as the aircraft's air-to-air radar was useful only over a distance of about 32 km (20 miles). Replaced by supersonic interceptors, the F-94 was retired less than a decade after it entered service.

The earlier-production F-94B bore a stronger resemblance to the TF-80C (later redesignated T-33) from which it was developed. The F-94C introduced a swept tailplane, a broader rear fuselage and wing-mounted rocket pods.

Introduced on the 100th aircraft and retrofitted to earlier machines, wing-mounted rocket pods held 12 rockets each and doubled the F-94C's armament.

The F-94C's long-range wingtip fuel tanks added 1893 litres to the Starfire's fuel load. Wing and fuselage tanks held 1385 litres, with the total capacity being much improved over the F-94A and B.

The afterburner-equipped F-94 had a much fatter tailpipe than the T-33. This was enlarged further on the F-94C to accommodate the bigger J48 engine.

'Buzz numbers' were introduced after 1945 to quickly identify low-flying aircraft. Each aircraft type had a two-letter code, the first of which identified its role. 'FA' was the F-94's code. This was followed by the last three digits of the aircraft's serial number.

The rear seat, which was occupied by a flying instructor in the T-33, was used by the radar operator. Both cockpits were fitted with ejection seats; F-94As and Bs had their cockpits widened after a number of pilots were injured during ejection.

The initial production versions of the F-94 were powered by an afterburning version of the T-33's Allison J33 turbojet. The F-94C was fitted with a Pratt & Whitney J48, a licence-built version of the afterburning Rolls-Royce Tay turbojet.

US AIR FORCE 15641

FA-641

F-94C STARFIRE

51-5641 carries the markings of the 84th Fighter Interceptor Squadron, Air Defense Command (ADC), as seen at the 1954 Yuma, Arizona, gunnery meet.

Six 'Mighty Mouse' 70-mm folding-fin aerial rockets (FFARs) were fitted behind four snap-action doors surrounding the radome. The weight of the nose radar and armament offset that of the afterburner, thus preventing a major change in the aircraft's centre of gravity.

An APG-32 radar and Hughes E-1 fire control system (in the F-94A and B) or an APG-40 and E-5 in the F-94C provided the F-94's all-weather capability.

The USAF's first all-weather jets

■ **CURTISS XP-87 BLACKHAWK:** Cancelled in 1948, the XP-87 was one of two all-weather aircraft (along with the XP-89) ordered in 1945/46.

■ **NORTH AMERICAN F-86D SABRE:** While the F-94 was an interim solution, the radar-equipped 'Sabre Dog' served from 1951 to 1965.

■ **NORTHROP F-89 SCORPION:** As a result of teething problems, the F-89 did not enter service until 1952.

■ **DOUGLAS F3D SKYKNIGHT:** The US Navy's F3D was inconclusively evaluated to fill the gap created by problems with the XP-87 and F-89.

LOCKHEED

F-104 STARFIGHTER

● Interceptor ● Lightweight fighter ● Record holder

T he Lockheed F-104A Starfighter was known as the 'Zipper' to pilots who flew the aircraft during its brief, unsuccessful US military career. But the sleek, futuristic fighter was not a failure. Designed with speed as its primary feature, the F-104A was a fast performer. It extended the boundaries of fighter performance in the 1950s, and brought Mach 2 capability to more than two dozen air forces around the world.

▲ An F-104A pilot stands next to the powerful 20-mm Vulcan cannon fitted to the USAF Starfighters and one of its ancestors, the 19th-century Gatling gun.

238

▲ Record breaker
The USAF set many performance records with its F-104As, especially for speed and altitude. But the operational success of the aircraft was less spectacular.

▲ Two-seat trainer
Conversion training was made easier by the introduction of the F-104B tandem-seat trainer.

▼ NASA test
The F-104's high speed made it useful for NASA, both in high-speed test flights and as a chase aircraft.

Wing-tip ▶ missiles
Originally designed for US Navy aircraft, the early versions of the Sidewinder missile were brought into USAF service with the F-104. They initially proved only marginally more reliable than the Starfighter.

▲ Single engine
The Starfighter was powered by a single J79 engine, the same one that powered the later F-4 Phantom in twin-engine configuration.

FACTS AND FIGURES

▶ The first Starfighters were transferred from the US Air Defense Command to the Air National Guard.

▶ The Lockheed XF-104 Starfighter made its first flight on 4 March 1954.

▶ At its deepest point the F-104A wing was only 10.16 cm (4 in) thick.

▶ In history's first encounter between Mach 2 fighters in 1965, a Pakistani F-104A outran pursuing Indian MiG-21s.

▶ Improved F-104Cs were operated by Tactical Air Command into the mid-1960s.

▶ The F-104A was the first aircraft to hold simultaneous speed and altitude records.

PROFILE

First of the Starfighters

The Lockheed F-104 Starfighter was just what the public of the 1950s expected a supersonic fighter to look like. Long, sleek and with a rocket-like fuselage and tiny, impossibly sharp-edged wings, it looked as though it was itching to break the sound barrier even when sitting motionless on the ground.

Designed by the great 'Kelly' Johnson to be as small as possible, the F-104's wings were optimised for Mach 2 performance. However, at subsonic speeds where most combat takes place the F-104

was at a disadvantage. Its small size meant that there was very little room for extra equipment, and it fell out of favour with the US Air Force. Its speed, however, made it popular with air forces around the world.

The F-104 has seen relatively little combat. USAF fighters flew uneventful patrols in Vietnam, while Pakistan's F-104As were involved in actions against India, and Taiwanese aircraft tussled with Chinese MiGs. But to most who flew it the F-104 was simply the incredibly fast fighter that was never needed during the Cold War.

Left: The USAF never really liked the concept of light fighters, preferring heavy, fast, expensive all-weather types like the F-4 Phantom. The F-104 had more success in the new role as a tactical nuclear bomber in Europe.

Right: Designers went to great lengths to turn out very fast missile-armed interceptors in the mid 1950s. Pilots then discovered that agile, slower aircraft with reliable cannon were often more effective in real battles.

F-104A Starfighter

Type: single-seat supersonic fighter

Powerplant: one 65.83-kN (14,770-lb-thrust) afterburning General Electric J79-GE-11A turbojet engine

Maximum speed: 2100 km/h (1302 mph) at 12,190 m (39,000 ft)

Combat radius: 800 km (496 miles)

Service ceiling: 16764 m (55,000 ft)

Weights: 9880 kg (21,736 lb) loaded

Armament: one 20-mm General Electric M61A1 Vulcan six-barrel rotary cannon with 725 rounds; two AIM-9 Sidewinder missiles and up to 1814 kg (3390 lb) of bombs

Dimensions:
span	6.68 m (21 ft 11 in)
length	16.69 m (54 ft 9 in)
height	4.11 m (13 ft 6 in)
wing area	18.22 m² (196 sq ft)

COMBAT DATA

MAXIMUM SPEED

The F-104, like the Lightning, had staggering speed and climb rate gained at the expense of versatility, range and weapon load.

F-104A STARFIGHTER	2100 km/h (1302 mph)
MIG-21F 'FISHBED'	2000 km/h (1240 mph)
LIGHTNING F.Mk 1	2414 km/h (1497 mph)

AGILITY

Short wings with high wing loading meant that both the F-104 and the Lightning could be out-turned by the more agile MiG-21 with its delta wing.

The T-tail configuration was used to retain pitch control authority at transonic speed. This had been a problem in earlier designs flying close to the sound barrier.

USAF F-104s were originally left in bare metal finish. However, deployment to Southeast Asia led to the adoption of a three-tone tactical camouflage.

The tiny 6-m (22-ft) wing was optimized for Mach 2 performance. The wing had large anhedral, or downward angle, which gave a very high rate of roll. The leading edge had to be covered with a guard when the aircraft was on the ground to prevent injuries to the ground crews.

F-104C STARFIGHTER

The 479th TFW operated the F-104C from Da Nang in 1965 to provide cover for tactical operations. The Starfighter did not see extensive service in Vietnam, being too short on range to be a useful escort fighter.

The F-104C Starfighter was powered by an afterburning J79-GE-7. Later versions of the F-104 used even more powerful variants of this engine which went on to power the F-4.

Designers of the F-104 regarded the missile as its main armament, but did not dispense with the gun, retaining a Vulcan 20-mm rotary cannon.

Original F-104s had a downward-firing ejector seat, a feature more usually found in Soviet jets. The reason for this was that designers feared an upward-firing seat might hit the tailplane, which turned out not to be the case.

Visibility from the F-104 was surprisingly good for a fighter of the time. The area in front of the canopy was painted black to reduce glare for the pilot.

The Starfighter was not originally designed to have radar, a decision that was soon changed. A simple range-only set was fitted, and later versions built abroad had greatly improved radars.

Early century series fighters

■ **F-100 SUPER SABRE:** The F-100 was the first American fighter to exceed Mach 1 in level flight. It saw extensive service in the Vietnam War as a tactical fighter-bomber.

■ **F-101 VOODOO:** Big, heavy and very complicated, the Voodoo was the antithesis of the F-104. It was a potent aircraft, with advanced fire-control and nuclear rocket armament.

■ **F-102 DELTA DAGGER:** Another heavy and costly fighter, the F-102 was a problematic design at first, but like the F-104 it eventually matured into a more successful aircraft.

LOCKHEED

P-2 NEPTUNE

- Anti-submarine patrol aircraft ● Long service ● Export success

One of the greats of naval aviation, the Lockheed P2V (P-2 from 1962) Neptune was the West's answer to the Soviet Union's awesome submarine threat during the first half of the Cold War. This superb land-based maritime patrol aircraft not only searched for submarines, but also filled an anti-surface vessel role. Neptunes performed various specialised duties for the US and other nations, and some saw war service as late as 1982.

▲ A veteran of wars in Southeast Asia and the South Atlantic, the P-2 was built in large numbers. More than 1000 served with US and foreign forces.

LOCKHEED P-2 NEPTUNE

Neptune and its quarry ▶
The Neptune's anti-submarine weapons included rockets, bombs, mines, depth charges and torpedoes. It was never called upon to sink a submarine during the volatile years of the Cold War.

▲ Turbine engines on the P-2J
Between 1969 and 1979 Kawasaki built 82 Neptunes with General Electric T64 turboprop engines and improved avionics.

▼ Popular P2V-5
Built in larger numbers than any other version, P2V-5 production totalled 372. Most later had a MAD boom and jet boosters fitted.

▼ Later colours
This VP-31 SP-2H wears the grey and white colours carried during the last years of US Navy service.

'Midnight blue' P2V-2 ▶
This 'midnight blue' Neptune is typical of the earliest Neptune variants, before the addition of a raised cockpit, jet engines, tip-tanks and a MAD boom.

FACTS AND FIGURES

- During the 1950-53 Korean War P2Vs dropped secret agents behind enemy lines, even into Manchuria.

- In all, 1181 of these great planes were built; the prototype flew on 17 May 1945.

- Twelve modified P2Vs served briefly as carrier-based atomic bombers.

- In 1982 an Argentine Neptune guided the Super Etendard which sank the destroyer HMS *Sheffield* with an Exocet missile.

- The largest foreign P-2 fleet was Japan's, and included Japanese-built P-2Js.

- In Vietnam the US Army used AP-2Es to relay communications from secret agents.

PROFILE

Patrolling 'king of the sea'

With a crew of between seven and 12 men, depending on the model and mission, the Lockheed P2V Neptune spent most of its career stalking Russian submarines, but it also served in other capacities, including electronic intelligence, drone launching and electronic countermeasures training.

Perhaps the most famous achievement of this maritime patrol aircraft was a distance record that has stood the test of time. Piloted by Commander Thomas

P. Davies, a P2V-1 named *The Truculent Turtle* flew 18,227 km (11,300 miles) from Perth, Australia, to Columbus, Ohio, in 55 hours and 17 minutes, demonstrating the Neptune's superb range and endurance.

The Neptune's ease of handling and manoeuvrability, with its unusually large rudder, and its spacious accommodation made it popular with Navy crews. Best remembered are the blue-painted Neptunes that prowled the world's oceans. With its maritime patrol capabilities

and potential for other military duties, the Neptune was also widely exported, with customers including Australia, Argentina, Brazil, Britain and Canada.

Below: In 1952 P2V-5s entered service with four squadrons of RAF Coastal Command as the Neptune MR.Mk 1. The majority were later fitted with MAD (magnetic anomaly detector) 'stings' and a Plexiglass nose.

Above: The Royal Canadian Air Force took delivery of 25 P2V-7s in the mid 1950s. When they were replaced in the early 1970s by the CP-107 Argus, many were converted for civilian fire-fighting.

SP-2H Neptune

Type: long-range anti-submarine and maritime patrol aircraft

Powerplant: two 2610-kW (3500-hp) Wright R-3350-32W Turbo-Compound radial piston engines and two 15.1-kN (3400-lb-thrust) Westinghouse J34-WE-36 turbojets

Maximum speed: 648 km/h (402 mph) at 4265 m (14,000 ft)

Maximum range: 5930 km (3667 miles)

Service ceiling: 6800 m (38,550 ft)

Weights: empty 22,650 kg (49,830 lb); maximum take-off 36,240 kg (79,728 lb)

Armament: two 12.7-mm (.50-cal.) machine guns in dorsal turret, plus provision for underwing rockets and up to 3628 kg (7982 lb) of weapons

Dimensions:
span	31.65 m (103 ft 10 in)
length	27.94 m (91 ft 7 in)
height	8.94 m (29 ft 4 in)
wing area	92.90 m² (1000 sq ft)

COMBAT DATA

MAXIMUM SPEED

With its Turbo-Compound engines, which used the piston engines' exhausts as a source of extra thrust, and jet boosters, the P2V-7 (P-2H) had a good speed advantage over the RAF Shackleton and Soviet Be-6.

P2V-7 NEPTUNE 648 km/h (402 mph)

SHACKLETON MR.Mk 3 486 km/h (301 mph)

Be-6 'MADGE' 415 km/h (257 mph)

ARMAMENT

Although the later Neptune variants could carry a large weapons load, this was bettered by almost a tonne in the final maritime version of the Shackleton. Outdated gun armament was modest.

P2V-7 NEPTUNE 2 x 12.7-mm (.50-cal.) machine guns 3628-kg (7982-lb) weapon load

SHACKLETON MR.Mk 3 2 x 20-mm cannon 4536-kg (9979-lb) weapon load

Be-6 'MADGE' 5 x 23-mm cannon 4400-kg (9680-lb) weapon load

RANGE

Both the Neptune and Shackleton were capable of impressive range, which also allowed longer loiter times while on patrol. The Beriev Be-6's range was 1000 km (600 miles) less than that of the Western machines, but it was not reliant upon land bases.

SHACKLETON MR.Mk 3 5890 km (3652 miles)

Be-6 'MADGE' 4800 km (2976 miles)

P2V-7 NEPTUNE 5930 km (3667 miles)

SP-2H NEPTUNE

Originally designated P2V-7S, the SP-2H was a conversion of the last Neptune production variant, the P2V-7. Aircraft 140967 carries the 'YP' tailcodes of Patrol Squadron 1 (VP-1) in the early 1960s.

A clear, bulged canopy, a smaller radome and wingtip tanks characterized the P-2H and its variants. Popular with US Navy ASW crews, a P-2 would often stay on patrol for up to 15 hours.

Neptunes from the P2V-5 onwards had mixed powerplants, consisting of two Wright R-3350 Cyclone 18 Turbo-Compound engines and two Westinghouse J34 turbojets. The J34s were carried in underwing pods.

The colour scheme worn by this aircraft was an intermediate livery between the early all-over 'midnight blue' and the white and grey used in later years.

Neptunes had a reputation for easy handling and manoeuvrability, the latter due to its unusually large rudder. In its heyday, the P-2 served with 35 patrol (VP) squadrons.

The P-2's tail was dominated by the MAD 'sting' and antennas associated with the aircraft's other detection systems.

A 'tail bumper' was positioned directly below the tailplane to prevent damage if the tail touched the ground on take-off.

The SP-2H had new submarine detection gear, codenamed 'Julie' and 'Jezebel', installed. Avionics and navigation equipment in the SP-2H weighed almost four times that of the original P2V-1. The dorsal turret was often removed on this variant.

A large radome, forwards of the weapons bay, contained an APS-20B radar scanner for the detection of surface targets. A searchlight was also installed in the nose of the starboard wingtip fuel tank.

Neptunes in service worldwide

■ **BRITISH STOP-GAP:** This Neptune MR.Mk 1 wears the markings of No. 217 Squadron, one of four Coastal Command units equipped with Neptunes under the Mutual Defense Assistance Program. They were replaced by Avro Shackletons.

■ **OVER THE HO CHI MINH TRAIL:** US Navy unit VAH-21 operated the AP-2H as a 'gunship' from Cam Ranh Bay, South Vietnam. Armed with guns and grenade launchers, these aircraft attacked truck convoys resupplying the Viet Cong.

■ **FALKLANDS VETERANS:** Argentina acquired a number of P2V-5s from Great Britain and later operated SP-2Hs. A number of SP-2Hs were flown on support missions during the Falklands War. Argentina was one of the last P-2 operators.

LOCKHEED

P-3 ORION

● Maritime patrol ● Anti-submarine warfare ● Electronic listener

A dapting airliner designs to the maritime reconnaissance role has long been an inexpensive solution adopted by nations requiring an airborne sea-search capability. The Lockheed Orion, based on the civil Electra, offered four-engined reliability and the necessary range and 'loiter' time for hours of patrol duty. Capable of considerable modification and updating, the Orion has served the US Navy and other air arms for nearly four decades.

▶ The four-turboprop Lockheed Orion maritime patrol aircraft has remained virtually unchanged in appearance from the initial P-3 to the US Navy's latest P-3C Update IV.

▲ Overseas equipment
P-3s have been supplied to 13 air arms around the world, including Australia, Canada, the Netherlands (P-3C-II above) and Spain, in addition to the US Navy.

▲ Anti-submarine
When a submarine or ship is identified on the surface, it is visually identified and photographed using the fixed KA-74 camera and hand-held equipment.

▲ Attack
Various offensive weapons can be carried on underwing pylons, including mines, rocket projectiles or Harpoon medium-range anti-ship missiles. In addition, the P-3 can carry torpedoes, mines and depth bombs internally.

▲ Updates
Older P-3s are being updated to incorporate the latest equipment. Australian P-3s, for example, are having new data processors and weapons fitted.

▲ Maritime patrol
The Lockheed P-3 Orion's primary task is to detect, identify and track submarines. For this role it is equipped with a variety of sensors, including a sting-tail mounted MAD and electronics equipment.

FACTS AND FIGURES

▶ The first flight of the P-3 derivative of the Lockheed Electra airliner took place on 19 August 1958.

▶ P-3Cs delivered to Norway and South Korea are named Update IIIs.

▶ Orions have been in production for nearly 40 years, the most recent going to Korea.

▶ To keep its crew alert on long missions, the P-3 has two rest bunks and a dinette to serve food around the clock.

▶ EP-3 is an electronic intelligence-gathering (ELINT) version of the P-3C.

▶ US Coast Guard Orions are used for anti-smuggling patrols.

PROFILE

Lockheed's sub-hunter

One of the most enduring maritime reconnaissance aircraft in service today, the Lockheed P-3 Orion is a powerful submarine hunter. Equipped with an array of advanced sonics equipment including DIFAR (Directional Acoustics-Frequency Analysis and Recording) sonobuoy processing gear and APS-115 search radar, the P-3 can find a periscope in a choppy sea or listen to the noise of a propeller in deep water. The first P-3 flew in the summer of 1962.

The upgraded P-3B with better engines but similar mission avionics flew in 1965. The P-3C which first flew in 1968, and remains in service today, has achieved great export success with countries as far apart as New Zealand and Norway.

To undertake its new military role, the P-3 inherited good shortfield performance and handling as well as ample fuselage space from its civil forebear. A flight crew of four flies the Orion, while a team of six operates the sonics,

electronic surveillance and radar equipment in the centre fuselage section. Update programmes have kept the P-3 abreast of advances in military technology, and a new version has been offered to the RAF to replace its current Nimrod patrol aircraft.

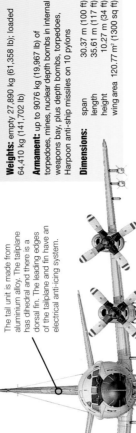

The US Navy received large numbers of all three main production models: the P-3A/B from 1961 and P-3C from 1968. The latter version remains in service to this day, also equipping the forces of Australia, Canada, Japan, Norway, the Netherlands and Pakistan.

P-3C Orion

Type: long-range anti-submarine patrol and early-warning aircraft

Powerplant: four 3661-kW (4900-hp) Allison T56-14 turboprop engines

Maximum speed: 761 km/h (472 mph)

Mission radius: 2494 km (1546 miles)

Service ceiling: 8625 m (29,290 ft)

Weights: empty 27,890 kg (61,358 lb); loaded 64,410 kg (141,702 lb)

Armament: up to 9076 kg (19,967 lb) of torpedoes, mines, nuclear depth bombs in internal weapons bay, plus depth bombs, torpedoes, Harpoon anti-ship missiles on 10 pylons

Dimensions:
span	30.37 m (100 ft)
length	35.61 m (117 ft)
height	10.27 m (34 ft)
wing area	120.77 m² (1300 sq ft)

P-3C ORION

The land-based Lockheed P-3 Orion has been the premier maritime patrol and anti-submarine warfare aircraft with the US Navy and many other nations since its introduction in 1962.

The crew consists of 10 – four on the flight-deck, plus the tactical co-ordinator who has a team of five in the main cabin.

The tail unit is made from aluminium alloy. The tailplane has dihedral and there is a dorsal fin. The leading edges of the tailplane and fin have an electrical anti-icing system.

Conventional aluminium-alloy construction fin and rudder are fitted, the latter being hydraulically-boosted.

The tailcone has been adapted to house electronic equipment, namely the AN/ASQ-81 magnetic anomaly detector (MAD) for detecting and tracking submerged submarines.

Launch tubes for sonobuoys and sound signals carried internally run along the rear, lower fuselage.

The pylons between the fuselage and inboard engines usually carry a Loral AN/ALQ-78A ESM pod.

The main cabin is the tactical centre and contains advanced electronic, magnetic and sonar detection systems. Computers and data processing equipment analyse inputs from the sensors.

There are two weapons pylons permanently fitted outboard of the engines.

Four Allison T56A turboprops power the Orion, each driving four-bladed Hamilton Standard constant-speed propellers.

A tricycle-type undercarriage has hydraulically, forwards-retracting twin-, main- and nosewheels.

COMBAT DATA

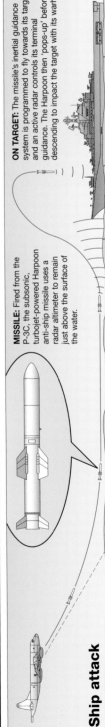

ENDURANCE

The twin-engined Atlantic has a staggering 18 hours' endurance on its maximum fuel load, although this is at the expense of speed (315 km/h/195 mph). With a normal endurance of 13 hours at a patrol speed of 381 km/h (236 mph) the P-3C can increase this to over 17 hours by flying on two engines. The Russian Ilyushin Il-38 derivative of the Il-18 airliner has an endurance of 12 hours at a patrol speed of 400 km/h (248 mph).

P-3C ORION   13 hours
Il-38 'MAY'   12 hours
ATLANTIC   18 hours

Ship attack

ON TARGET: The missile's inertial guidance system is programmed to fly towards its target and an active radar controls its terminal guidance. The Harpoon then 'pops-up' before descending to impact the target with its warhead.

MISSILE: Fired from the P-3C, the subsonic, turbojet-powered Harpoon anti-ship missile uses a radar altimeter to remain just above the surface of the water.

COMBINED OPERATIONS: The enemy warship is tracked by the Orion's search radar, infra-red detector and electronic support measures. In addition, a submarine uses its sonar devices to help the P-3C to fire its sea-skimming missile towards its target.

LOCKHEED
P-3 ORION (SPECIAL)

- Naval spy plane ● Intelligence gathering ● Ocean watching

Much more than a patrol aircraft, the amazing P-3 Orion has been used for many other purposes. The EP-3 is the electronic intelligence-gathering version, prowling the world's oceans using radar to spy on the enemy. But the practical Orion has enough other uses to fill a small encyclopedia. Orions serve as training, VIP transport, sensor research, Antarctic research, weather observation and fire-fighting aircraft.

▲ A radar specialist prepares to send a classified message from within the fuselage of a P-3. Numerous variants of the P-3 have been adapted to perform special missions.

PHOTO FILE

LOCKHEED P-3 ORION (SPECIAL)

▼ **Fin extension**
Classified as an RP-3A, this variant is fitted with phased array antennas in its tail. Duties include monitoring missile tests over the Western USA.

▲ **Unexpected guest**
Specialised variants of the Orion often operate from overseas bases, employing their sophisticated sensors to monitor the world's navies.

▼ **Weather watcher**
Taking over from where the Lockheed Constellation left off, the US Navy operates this WP-3A on weather reconnaissance patrols.

Orange Orions ▶
Painted in a bright red/orange and white colour scheme, five Orions operate as oceanographic research aircraft, monitoring the ocean's currents by performing acoustic and thermal tests.

▲ **Command and control**
With a large dish-mounted radar on its fuselage, this P-3 AEW acts as a control centre for aircraft during missions.

FACTS AND FIGURES

▶ Crew strength on the P-3 variants can be as high as 15 with the addition of electronics operators.

▶ One Orion is used as an electronic aggressor aircraft during air exercises.

▶ EP-3Es were active during Desert Storm, operating against Iraqi shipping.

▶ The first use of specialized Orions was in Vietnam where the aircraft monitored Vietnamese and Soviet supply ships.

▶ Orions operating with the US Customs are fitted with a radar from the F-15.

▶ One squadron of EP-3Es is based at Rota in Spain.

PROFILE

Anti-Soviet ship snooper

The EP-3E-II Aries reconnaissance aircraft is evidence of the versatility of more than a dozen models of the famous Lockheed P-3 Orion. The EP-3E Aries uses electronic snooping devices to 'fingerprint' foreign vessels, enabling intelligence experts to keep track of naval and commercial ship movements. Other EP-3 reconnaissance ships jam enemy communications, monitor them, or spy from the sky with radar or cameras. Sheer beauty lies beneath the pragmatic design of

this four-engined turboprop, which is best known for its maritime anti-submarine work but which performs so many other tasks so well. One P-3 has been modified as a non-acoustic sensor research aircraft. Two optical windows installed in the floor house a laser generator and receiver for a tactical laser device. Another has four optical windows on its floor for sensors or cameras and is nicknamed the 'Glass Bottom Orion'. A few Orions serve as pilot trainers for the US Navy.

Whether spying or (in the civilian world) fighting forest fires, the Orion is the world champion of diverse aerial achievements.

Despite these numerous roles, the US Navy is now looking for a replacement for the Orion as the fatigue threshold of some of the airframes is rapidly approaching.

Left: Stripped of operational equipment, six Orions are used as VP-3As, or 'Admiral's Barges'. These are used as transports for high-ranking naval commanders.

Above: Fitted with extra windows on the fuselage and a nose-mounted pitot boom, this Orion is used for weather research and hurricane hunting.

EP-3E ORION

As the US Navy's principal intelligence-gathering platform, the EP-3E Orion's mission is to locate and record foreign vessels. For this mission the aircraft is fitted with highly sophisticated electronics.

A specialised mission requires highly trained operators. These are seated within the large fuselage of the Orion to operating the sensors and antennas. The number of specialists can be as high as 15. Though the design is spacious, the room available within the aircraft is reduced by the bulky electronic equipment.

A comprehensive set of antennas is positioned along the top of the fuselage; these vary for each individual aircraft and the requirements of the mission.

Positioned behind the rear of the cockpit is a large flattened retractable radome. This offers 360-degree coverage to search for shipping.

The long dorsal fairing houses additional electronic equipment to relay information to other friendly aircraft or ships. Data can also be sent directly back to a home base for further analysis. A replacement for the Orion is desperately needed because of the threat of airframe fatigue.

Because of their different missions the extended rear tail, and associated magnetic-anomaly detection (MAD) equipment, of the standard anti-submarine Orions have been removed from the EP-3 variants.

A large 'canoe' fairing is located on the underside of the fuselage. This allows the sensors to look directly down onto the ocean's surface.

Four Allison turboprops offer the Orion exceptional range with the ability to loiter over a target area for an extended period.

Ocean watchers

■ **EC-121 CONSTELLATION:** Developed from the cargo version, the Lockheed Constellation was the first long-range patrol aircraft in US Navy service. The P-3 is its successor.

■ **P-2 NEPTUNE:** Equipped with a MAD 'sting' in its tail the Neptune saw considerable action the skies of Vietnam where specialised variants were used to intercept arms-carrying Vietnamese 'junks'.

■ **S-3 VIKING:** Operating directly from carrier decks, the Viking has been continually upgraded with the latest avionics to offer a formidable naval reconnaissance platform.

EP-3E Orion

Type: long-range, intelligence-gathering aircraft

Powerplant: four 3661-kW (4910-hp) Allison T56-A-14 turboprops

Maximum speed: 703 km/h (437 mph) at 4575 m (15,010 ft); patrol speed 333 km/h (207 mph)

Initial climb rate: 633 m/min (2077 fpm)

Range: 8143 km (5060 miles)

Service ceiling: 8535 m (28,000 ft)

Weights: empty 27,890 kg (61,487 lb); maximum take-off 64,410 kg (142,000 lb)

Accommodation: 15 electronic mission specialists; three flight crew

Dimensions:
span	30.37 m (99 ft 8 in)
length	35.61 m (116 ft 10 in)
height	10.27 m (33 ft 8 in)
wing area	120.77 m² (1300 sq ft)

COMBAT DATA

MAXIMUM SPEED

Because of its jet engines the Tu-16 was capable of operating at high speed in comparison to other turboprop aircraft. Powered by four turboprops, the Orion is one of the slowest patrol aircraft.

EP-3E ORION — 703 km/h (437 mph)
An-12 'CUB-B' — 777 km/h (483 mph)
Tu-16 'BADGER-F' — 991 km/h (616 mph)

RANGE

Long range is of vital importance for maritime patrol aircraft. Without the ability to refuel in flight the Orion is restricted in its ability to search for hostile ships at great distances. Compared to the Russian naval reconnaissance assets the Orion is superior, however.

An-12 'CUB-B' 5697 km (3540 miles)
EP-3E ORION 8143 km (5060 miles)
Tu-16 'BADGER-F' 6292 km (3910 miles)

OPERATIONAL CEILING

Even when carrying all the equipment for its special mission, the Orion's ceiling compares well with that of the less sophisticated An-12. Higher altitude operations do increase the search area and detection rate of the radar, however.

Tu-16 'BADGER-F' 12,298 m (40,348 ft)
An-12 'CUB-B' 10,200 m (33,465 ft)
EP-3E ORION 8535 m (28,000 ft)

LOCKHEED

U-2

● Spy aircraft ● 'Skunk Works' design ● Gary Powers shoot-down

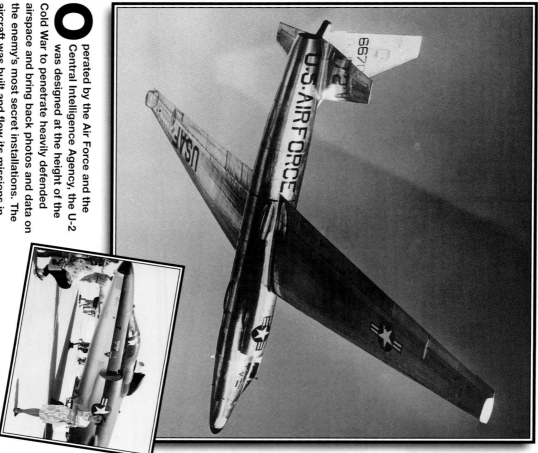

O perated by the Air Force and the Central Intelligence Agency, the U-2 was designed at the height of the Cold War to penetrate heavily defended airspace and bring back photos and data on the enemy's most secret installations. The aircraft was built and flew its missions in great secrecy. When one was shot down over Russia, the U-2 became a household name. The type was used over Iraq in the 1990s and remains in service with NASA.

▲ The U-2 program was kept a secret from the public for many years, but after the Gary Powers incident the veil was lifted – a little. This U-2 at an airshow has missile-tracking cameras on the spine.

LOCKHEED U-2

▲ **First production model**
About 40 of the U-2A model were built, along with seven U-2Bs, which had a more powerful engine and greater fuel capacity.

Blacked out ▼
Not to be confused with the later U-2R and TR-1 variants, this all-black U-2D was one of only five of this model to be made.

▲ **Safety problems**
Until a U-2A was rebuilt as a two-seat U-2CT conversion trainer in 1973, accidents were not infrequent. This aircraft crashed in Germany in 1975.

Cuban crisis ▼
U-2s were involved in the Cuban Missile Crisis in 1962 and flew over Cuba looking for Russian nuclear missiles. This U-2D was based in Florida in the early 1960s.

▲ **Spies in the sky**
Most of the earliest U-2s were operated by the CIA before being passed to the Air Force.

U-2 in the U.K. ▼
This U-2C was used in trials of a radar-locating system from UK bases in the mid 1970s.

FACTS AND FIGURES

▼ U-2Gs undertook trials to see if the type could operate from aircraft carriers.

▼ The only other country to use U-2s was Taiwan, a number of which were lost over mainland China.

▼ The U-2's wing worked well at high altitude, but made landings tricky.

▼ The U-2 was put back into production twice, and improved U-2R models have seen service over Bosnia and Iraq.

▼ NASA uses a version of the U-2 called the ER-2 for earth resources mapping.

▼ The U-2 pilot used an external mirror to check if he was leaving a contrail.

Cold War spies

The Experimental Department of Lockheed Aircraft Corporation was known as the 'Skunk Works'. The first, and arguably the most famous, of their secret projects was the U-2. Designed in record time under the direction of the Works' director, Clarence 'Kelly' Johnson, it met a joint Central Intelligence Agency (CIA)/USAF requirement for an espionage reconnaissance aircraft.

Work began in 1954, on what was essentially a powered glider. The 'Dragon Lady', as it became known, first

flew in 1955 and entered service in the late 1950s, crewed by CIA personnel. The U, for Utility, designation was used by the Department of Defense to hide the true role of the aircraft. Flights over the Soviet Union were made until 1 May 1960, when one was shot down over Sverdlovsk. From then on flights were

restricted to spy sorties over non-Soviet territory and secondary tasks like high-altitude sampling, the USAF eventually taking over their operation.

Up to 1960 around 54 had been built in all. In 1967, a second-generation aircraft, the U-2R, flew for the first time and remains in service today.

The traditional matt-black finish became synonymous with the U-2. Few markings or national insignia were carried, other than a serial number, though this was often bogus.

U-2B

Type: single-seat high-altitude reconnaissance aircraft

Powerplant: one non-afterburning 75.65-kN (17,000-lb-thrust) J75-P-13B turbojet

Maximum speed: more than 853 km/h (530 mph) at 42,000 ft

Initial climb rate: 1524 m/min (5000 fpm)

Range: more than 6840 km (4520 miles)

Service ceiling: 24,080 m (79,000 ft)

Weapons: none

Weights: empty 5888 kg (12,980 lb); loaded 10,478 kg (23,100 lb)

Dimensions:
span   24.38 m (80 ft)
length   15.14 m (49 ft 8 in)
height   4.62 m (15 ft 2 in)
wing area   447.42 m² (600 sq ft)

Two 'slipper' fuel tanks with a capacity of 477 litres (105 gallons) each were fitted to U-2Bs and Cs to improve range performance. Total fuel capacity was 6956 litres (1530 gallons). Range was over 7275 km (4520 miles).

A rearward-facing radar warning receiver (RWR) was fitted inside a fairing on the trailing edge of the starboard wing. This warns the pilot of the presence of hostile radar associated with a surface-to-air missile site or fighter aircraft.

This camouflage scheme was worn by aircraft used on the 1975 ALSS trials flown from RAF Wethersfield, codenamed 'Constant Treat'.

66700
U.S. AIR FORCE

The U-2A used a Pratt & Whitney J57 turbojet, however all subsequent variants were fitted with a larger J75, of the type fitted, with an afterburner, to the F-105 Thunderchief.

To shield the exhaust from infrared sensors or missile seeker heads, a 'sugar scoop' was fitted to the lower portion of the jetpipe.

Jettisonable wheels, known as 'pogos', were mounted under the wings to support them during taxi and take-off.

The key to the U-2's altitude and range performance was its long-span wings. It was effectively a powered glider, with its high aspect ratio wing and lightweight structure.

Communications, navigation and mission equipment was housed in the long dorsal spine of the U-2C. U-2Fs were similar but had a refueling receptacle at the front.

The Q-bay behind the pilot housed the principal sensors and/or cameras. A smaller bay was built into the nose of the aircraft.

56-6700 was built in the late 1950s as a U-2A. Converted to a U-2C, it was involved in the Pave Onyx Advanced Location and Strike System trials in 1975, with ALSS orbiting aircraft precisely located hostile radar sites.

To save weight the first U-2s were not fitted with an ejection seat, though they were added later. The type has a reputation for being difficult to handle on landing.

For the Pave Onyx program, the Q-bay had a bulged dielectric lower hatch for the 18 ALSS electronic intelligence antennas.

The U-2 incident

SECRET MISSION: On 1 May 1960, CIA U-2 pilot Francis Gary Powers took off from a secret base in Pakistan to fly over and photograph several strategic bases in the Soviet Union. He would fly at 22,860 m (75,000 ft), out of the range of surface-to-air missiles.

TARGET SVERDLOVSK: For the photo run, Powers had to concentrate on flying straight and level over the target. MiG-15 fighters climbed to intercept the U-2, but could not reach its height.

SHOT DOWN: Possibly because of a technical problem, the U-2 came within range of SA-2 missiles and was hit. Powers ejected and was captured. A missile also destroyed a MiG-15.

SPY FLIGHT PLAN: Gary Powers's U-2 took off from Peshawar, Pakistan, to fly over the Soviet missile test base at Sverdlovsk. His route avoided known SA-2 missile sites and the plan was to carry on to Bodø in Norway rather than return over a predictable flight path.

INTERCEPTED: The Soviets were aware of the spy flights and did all they could to destroy a U-2. They were lucky to hit Powers's aircraft with an SA-2. Much propaganda was made of Powers's capture and arms talks were disrupted. He was tried as a spy, and later returned to the United States in a swap with a Russian agent.

BODØ
SVERDLOVSK
USSR
PESHAWAR

LOCKHEED

SR-71A

● Mach 3+ performance ● Dangerous missions ● Operational use

F lying the SR-71 has much in common with a Space Shuttle mission. The crew of pilot and reconnaissance systems officer (RSO) will have passed the same rigorous medical and physical examination as astronauts, and completed at least 100 simulator hours before they fly the aircraft for real. Some 100 hours of training missions follow before they are qualified to fly operationally, and, whether in training or on a real mission, there is never a moment's rest.

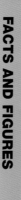

▲ Always expensive to operate, the SR-71A was retired from service for a time because of its intensive maintenance requirements and its need for specially equipped support facilities. In 1996, three aircraft were briefly returned to service.

LOCKHEED SR-71A

Evening mission ▶
Reaching altitude against a dark sky, this SR-71A demonstrates the distinctive shock diamonds produced when afterburner is selected on the J58 turbo-ramjets. The Blackbird represents a breathtaking combination of technologies.

▼ Recovery
Missions in excess of 24,000 km (14,190 miles) have been recorded by SR-71As using in-flight refuelling. At the end of such a mission crew fatigue can be a major problem, and both members must cooperate to land the tricky Blackbird safely.

▲ Futuristic veteran
Decades after initial service entry, the Blackbird's chines, sinister paint scheme, and huge, complex intakes give it a futuristic air.

National identity
During the later stages of the SR-71A's 'first career', the aircraft flew with a minimum of markings, apparently contravening international law by displaying only a serial number with no national insignia.

SR-71A in the nest ▶
Each SR-71A base operated a dedicated support facility. Bases were permanently available in the US, UK and Japan. However the SR-71A has now been retired by the USAF.

FACTS AND FIGURES

▶ Restoration of the first two SR-71s to flying condition cost only US$100 million, half the expected amount.

▶ Spare parts for refurbishing the aircraft were found in several scrapyards!

▶ A new generation of unmanned aircraft will replace the SR-71.

▶ During 1996, one SR-71A was used to test a reusable launch vehicle, as a potential Space Shuttle replacement.

▶ Unconfirmed reports suggest that SR-71As may have flown over Bosnia.

▶ Blackbirds took part in the 1996 Red Flag and Green Flag exercises.

Return of Lockheed's Mach 3 Blackbird

Before their mission the Blackbird's crew don custom-made pressure suits. Portable air-conditioning units keep them cool on the ride to the aircraft. Once in the cockpit, they breathe pure oxygen for at least 30 minutes, eliminating any nitrogen in their bloodstreams that could cause decompression sickness at their cruise altitude.

A take-off roll of about 1350 m (4430 ft) is needed to reach the lift-off speed of around 380 km/h (236 mph). The landing gear must be retracted before airspeed reaches 555 km/h (345 mph), then the aircraft climbs at 740 km/h (460 mph) to a tanker rendezvous at about 8000 m (26,240 ft). Next comes the acceleration to the cruising altitude and speed.

To maintain the required altitude in Mach 3 flight, the Blackbird's stability augmentation system compensates for the aircraft's inherent instability. The pilot still must monitor the instruments throughout the flight, checking continuously that he is on the correct course. Deceleration and descent are rigidly controlled by the autopilot down to a speed of Mach 1.3, after which the pilot takes over to land manually, with a brake parachute helping to bring the aircraft to a halt.

Left: No currently declassified aircraft is able to outperform the SR-71A. Blackbird pilots tell of accelerating away from MiG-25s at Mach 3.

Right: In-flight refuelling is an integral part of every mission. Fuel leakage on the ground is severe and the SR-71A would require an impractical length of runway to take-off with a full fuel load. A tanker rendezvous is therefore made soon after take-off.

SR-71A

Type: strategic reconnaissance aircraft

Powerplant: two 144.57-kN (32,528-lb-thrust) Pratt & Whitney J58-1 afterburning turbo-ramjets

Maximum speed: in excess of 3700 km/h (2300 mph) in level flight at 24,000 m (78,740 ft) or in excess of 2125 km/h (1320 mph) at 9145 m (30,000 ft)

Range: 4000 km (2485 mph) unrefuelled at 24,000 m (78,740 ft) and 3190 km/h (1982 mph) without refuelling

Endurance: 1 hour 30 min at 3220 km/h (2000 mph) at 24,000 m (78,740 ft) without refueling

Service ceiling: 25,900 m (84,974 ft)

Weights: empty 27,215 kg (60,000 lb); maximum take-off 77,110 kg (170,000 lb)

Accommodation: pilot and reconnaissance systems officer

Dimensions:
span	16.95 m (55 ft 7 in)
length	32.74 m (107 ft 5 in)
height	5.64 m (18 ft 6 in)
wing area	167.23 m² (1800 sq ft)

SR-71A

Although some SR-71A missions have probably been CIA-sponsored, the US Air Force's 9th Strategic Reconnaissance Wing at Beale Air Force Base, California, has always been the Blackbird's home.

On the SR-71A's return to service the aircraft carried the ASARS (Advanced Synthetic Aperture Radar System)-1 with a datalink which allowed near real-time transmission of information.

Extensive use was made of blended wing/fuselage technology in the SR-71. This gives good supersonic cruise capabilities and minimum radar cross-section.

Each of the crew members wears a full pressure suit. Ejection seats are provided but they are realistically only for escape at lower altitudes and speeds. Most SR-71 accidents have occurred in the difficult landing and take-off phases.

A complex system of adjustable inlet spikes, auxiliary inlets and bleed-air doors ensures that the right volume of subsonic air throughout the flight. The bypass nature of the engines dictates that a large proportion of the air entering the inlet does not pass through the hot core of the engine and is expelled by the special ejector nozzles.

Most of the fuselage and wing internal volume is consumed by fuel tanks. The special JP7 fuel of the Blackbird may cause a problem when the aircraft are redeployed abroad, since special tankers and handling techniques are required. Stockpiles of JP7 are held at RAF Fairford and a recent USAF evaluation of the base suggests that this might be a likely European base.

Most of the SR-71's airframe is made of titanium alloy in order to withstand the kinetic heating of prolonged Mach 3 cruise. Groundcrew use special tool kits, since conventional steel tools would damage the aircraft.

In order to reduce radar cross-section, the SR-71A is painted overall in a radar absorbent paint, containing microscopic ferrous balls. Markings are kept to a minimum.

Massive nozzles are a feature of the J58. In cruising flight they are comparatively cool because of the large volume of bypassed air being ejected. No SR-71A has ever been lost to a heat-seeking or radar-guided missile.

COMBAT DATA

CEILING

Both the MiG-25RB 'Foxbat-B' and Dassault Mirage IVP are flown as high-speed, high-altitude reconnaissance platforms. Here the figures for both represent service ceiling, while that for the SR-71A is operational ceiling. Much Blackbird data remains classified; true ceiling and maximum speed are probably greater than published.

SR-71A 24,000 m (78,740 ft)

MiG-25RB 'FOXBAT-B' 21,000 m (68,900 ft)

MIRAGE IVP 20,000 m (65,618 ft)

Mach 3 yaw

1 NORMAL FLIGHT: In normal flight the computer-controlled engine inlet spikes form a supersonic shockwave at the inlet mouth, and are positioned to allow the correct volume of air to reach the engines.

2 UNSTART: It is a common occurrence for the shockwave to move out of the inlet, causing a loss of air to the affected engine and a dramatic loss of thrust on one side of the aircraft. The pilot takes over spike control manually.

3 VICIOUS YAW AND OVER-CORRECTION: Unstarts are most severe in the acceleration phase, where both engines are delivering huge power. Asymmetric thrust causes severe yaw, often at Mach 3 speeds. Moving the inlet spike forwards recaptures the shockwave and restores thrust, but an overcorrection in the opposite direction to the initial yaw can cause a temporary weave to set in.

249

LOCKHEED

U-2R

- High-altitude reconnaissance ● Earth resources survey

▲ Clarence L. 'Kelly' Johnson was one of the best-known aircraft designers. He was responsible for the U-2 series, the F-104 Starfighter and the SR-71 'Blackbird'. Here he is seen in front of a NASA ER-2, a special version of the U-2R.

Today's high-flying Lockheed U-2R is an improvement on the Cold War's most famous reconnaissance plane, updated with microchip technology for the 1990s. The U-2R is easy to spot with its huge, sailplane-like wing. Painted black and flown by a pilot in an astronaut-style pressure suit, this remarkable craft can loiter for hours higher than most planes can fly, gathering intelligence with its cameras and electronic sensors.

PHOTO FILE

LOCKHEED U-2R

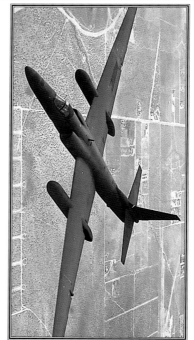

▲ Dragon Lady
The sinister black paint and elegant manoeuvres of the U-2 earned it this nickname. Its huge wings carry it to extreme altitude, from where its sensors can peer sideways many miles into denied territory. With radars, cameras or electronic receivers onboard, little escapes the watchful eye of the U-2R.

The first ▶
generation
Today's U-2R is based on the original U-2, which was developed by Lockheed's famous 'Skunk Works' under the direction of Clarence L. Johnson.

▼ Delicate wings
The wings are very fragile, and the pilot has to take great care not to overstress them.

▼ Motor glider
The U-2 has often been likened to a giant glider with a jet engine. Like gliders, the Dragon Lady is very efficient in the air, but is also very tricky to land. A second pilot drives behind the U-2 and gives a running commentary of the approach to aid the pilot.

▼ Black paint
The U-2 is coated with a special paint containing iron. This makes the aircraft difficult to see on radar.

FACTS AND FIGURES

▶ The original U-2 prototype, for the series that preceded today's U-2R, first flew on 4 August 1955.

▶ The prototype of the enlarged U-2R initially flew on 28 August 1967.

▶ A total of 49 U-2Rs and TR-1s were built in two batches.

▶ Lockheed's production line was reopened in November 1979 for the TR-1 (now also known as the U-2R).

▶ The U-2R and TR-1 employ ASARS-2 battlefield surveillance radar.

▶ Some U-2Rs have a satellite communication system.

Lockheed's black dragon

First introduced in the Vietnam era, the U-2R is similar to but bigger and more powerful than the U-2 in which Francis Gary Powers was shot down over Russia on 1 May 1960. A few identical aircraft used for battlefield surveillance in the 1980s were known by the designation TR-1. The 'Dragon Lady', as this unique aircraft is sometimes

called, is designed to monitor potential enemy forces or to police arms agreements. It carries photographic, radar and electronic sensors in a long, detachable nose cone, in the fuselage and in wingpods. The sensor fit is changed depending on the mission.

Although the basic design is nearly 50 years old, the U-2R still flies higher than all but a

handful of aircraft. It is difficult to fly, with a cramped cockpit and challenging handling properties. It lands and takes off using an odd bicycle-style landing gear with outrigger wheels at the wingtips which detach and fall away after take-off. Recent missions have involved flights over Bosnia, which helped locate mass graves.

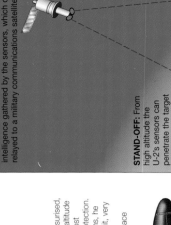

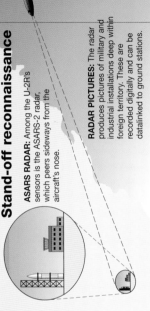

U-2R

Type: single-seat high-altitude reconnaissance aircraft

Powerplant: one 75.61-kN (16,950-lb-thrust) Pratt & Whitney J75-P-13B turbojet engine

Maximum speed: Mach 0.8 or 960 km/h (595 mph) at sea level

Cruising speed: 692 km/h (429 mph) at 10,000 m (33,000 ft)

Range: 10,060 km (6237 miles)

Service ceiling: 24,835 m (81,459 ft)

Weights: empty 7031 kg (15,468 lb); maximum take-off 18,733 kg (41,213 lb)

Equipment: a variety of sensors and recorders, imaging radars, radar locators and high-resolution cameras for high-altitude reconnaissance missions

Dimensions:	span	31.39 m (103 ft)
	length	19.13 m (63 ft)
	height	4.88 m (16 ft)
	wing area	92.90 m² (1000 sq ft)

NASA uses two ER-2s, which are based on the U-2R airframe. They are employed for high-altitude research into the ozone layer and for monitoring the earth's crust.

U-2R

The U-2R's altitude performance and incredible endurance make it the perfect vehicle for maintaining a long watch on hostile territory. The small hand-built fleet is very important to the US Air Force, which has re-engined the aircraft. Radar reconnaissance and communications intelligence gathering are the U-2's main tasks, although the type still carries traditional cameras on some missions.

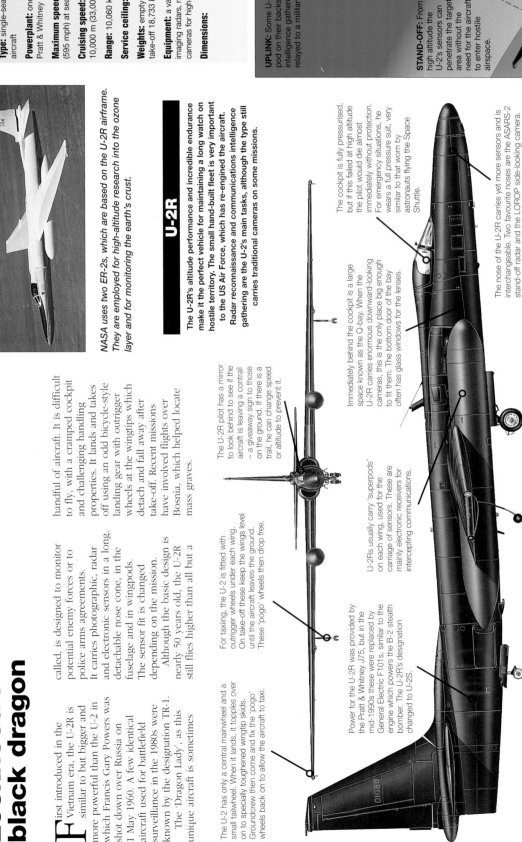

The U-2 has only a central mainwheel and a small tailwheel. When it lands, it topples over on to specially toughened wingtip skids. Groundcrew then come and fix the 'pogo' wheels back on to allow the aircraft to taxi.

Power for the U-2R was provided by the Pratt & Whitney J75, but in the mid-1990s these were replaced by General Electric F101s, similar to the engine which powers the B-2 stealth bomber. The U-2R's designation changed to U-2S.

For taxiing, the U-2 is fitted with outrigger wheels under each wing. On take-off these keep the wings level until the aircraft leaves the ground. These 'pogo' wheels then drop free.

The U-2R pilot has a mirror to look behind to see if the aircraft is leaving a contrail – a giveaway sign to those on the ground. If there is a trail, he can change speed or altitude to prevent it.

Immediately behind the cockpit is a large space known as the Q-bay. When the U-2R carries enormous downward-looking cameras, this is the only place big enough to fit them. The bottom door of the bay often has glass windows for the lenses.

U-2Rs usually carry 'superpods' on each wing, used for the carriage of sensors. These are mainly electronic receivers for intercepting communications.

The cockpit is fully pressurised, but if this failed at high altitude the pilot would die almost immediately without protection. For emergency situations, he wears a full pressure suit, very similar to that worn by astronauts flying the Space Shuttle.

The nose of the U-2R carries yet more sensors and is interchangeable. Two favourite noses are the ASARS-2 stand-off radar and the LOROP side-looking camera.

UPLINK: Some U-2s are fitted with the Senior Span pod on their backs. This digitally processes the intelligence gathered by the sensors, which can be relayed to a military communications satellite.

STAND-OFF: From high altitude the U-2's sensors can penetrate the target area without the need for the aircraft to enter hostile airspace.

DOWNLINK: The images are relayed down from the satellite straight into a command post anywhere in the world. This allows battle staff to view the U-2's intelligence the moment it is gathered.

Stand-off reconnaissance

ASARS RADAR: Among the U-2R's sensors is the ASARS-2 radar, which peers sideways from the aircraft's nose.

RADAR PICTURES: The radar produces pictures of military and industrial installations deep within foreign territory. These are recorded digitally and can be datalinked to ground stations.

SERVICE CEILING

The U-2 is renowned for its altitude capability and is only bettered by the Lockheed SR-71. However, the U-2's main advantage is its ability to remain in the same area at this incredible altitude for hours at a time, whereas the SR-71 has been and gone in a matter of seconds. The Russian M-55 'Mystic' has some of the U-2's capabilities, but cannot achieve the operational altitude of the 'Dragon Lady'. It is slightly faster, but the U-2R has a much greater endurance and can carry a far heavier load of sensors.

SR-71 BLACKBIRD
25,000 m
(82,000 ft)

U-2R
24,385 m
(81,459 ft)

M-55 'MYSTIC'
20,000 m
(65,600 ft)

252

LOCKHEED
QT-2/Q-STAR/YO-3

- Advanced technology ● Quiet covert ● Observation aircraft

Many years before the word 'stealth' earned its place in the vocabulary of aviation, Lockheed's QT-2, Q-Star and YO-3 were pioneering deception. This family of fine aircraft was developed to fly in almost total silence over the enemy, carrying reconnaissance sensors on an efficient airframe and powered by a silencer-equipped engine driving a slow propeller. These 'quiet flyers' had an important role in Vietnam.

▲ The QT-2 'Quiet Thrust', the Q-Star (above) and the more developed YO-3 light observation aircraft (main picture), were produced for the US Army by the Lockheed Missiles and Space division.

LOCKHEED QT-2/Q-STAR/YO-3

▲ Sailplane origins
Although the Lockheed QT-2 differs quite markedly in appearance from the YO-3, both aircraft were based on the Schweizer SGS 2-32 sailplane. The main differences on the YO-3 are a nose-mounted engine, two-seat cockpit, low wings and fully retractable undercarriage.

▼ Service tests
The YO-3A underwent extensive pre-service testing for the US Army in May and June 1970, during which time the tenth pre-production aircraft was destroyed in a crash.

▲ Glider wings
With high aspect ratio wings and low wing loading, the YO-3A could climb at 187 m/min (615 fpm) to an altitude of 4265 m (13,993 ft).

▼ Powered X-26A
The two Lockheed QT-2s were 75-kW (100-hp) Continental-powered conversions of X-26A gliders.

▲ Q-Star
A third glider was converted in 1969 as the Q-Star. It subsequently had a de-rated Wankel rotary engine, cooled by an automobile radiator, fitted in the nose.

FACTS AND FIGURES

➤ The QT-2 was first tested in great secrecy at a remote civil airstrip in the Mojave Desert from July 1967.

➤ The YO-3A had a nose-mounted engine and fully retractable landing gear.

➤ The Q-Star was a 'one-off' testbed that was flown with two types of engines.

➤ These stealthy observation aircraft carried sensors, listening devices, cameras and infra-red detectors.

➤ Lockheed's Missiles and Space division produced only these aircraft.

➤ Nine YO-3As flew 1,116 missions in Vietnam without the loss of any aircraft.

Silent spies over the battlefield

The Lockheed QT-2, Q-Star and YO-3 combined a Schweizer sailplane fuselage with the quietest engines that had ever been developed for a military aircraft. These were almost totally silent reconnaissance aircraft that flew directly over the enemy without being detected.

After the first two QT-2s were evaluated in Vietnam, Lockheed proceeded with the YO-3A version of these stealthy powered gliders for the US Army. Thirteen YO-3As went to Vietnam in 1970 for operational evaluation.

Proven in war, they were retired in 1972 and used for military research though some went to civil operators. One was used by fisheries authorities to track an enemy convoy. It then transmitted details to a patrolling Hercules gunship. Another was used by NASA as a microphone-carrying vehicle to measure rotor blade noise in a helicopter test programme.

The small, versatile, virtually silent observation aircraft has great value in both peacetime and war. These planes showed the way for a new kind of practical flying, but no modern-day equivalent of them has been developed.

Above: Various types and sizes of propellers were fitted to the YO-3A's Continental engine, including this six-bladed unit.

Above: The civil-registered Q-Star was re-engined in 1969 with a Wright RC2-60 liquid-cooled rotary engine. This was the first time that a Wankel-type powerplant was used in an aircraft.

LOCKHEED YO-3A

This quiet, single-engined observation aircraft was converted from Schweizer's SGS 2-32 sailplane. A specially silenced Continental IO-360D engine was fitted with a variety of airborne sensors.

Sensors, including an infra-red illuminator and infra-red designator were fitted beneath the nose and rear fuselage. A night viewing aerial periscope was fitted in the front cockpit.

Production YO-3As were fitted with a nose-mounted Teledyne Continental IO-360D six-cylinder, air-cooled piston engine. Early aircraft had a six-bladed fixed-pitch propeller, but later a three-bladed variable-pitch unit was fitted.

The modified tandem, two-seat cockpit was covered by a large, single-piece, upward-hinged bubble canopy with a separate front windscreen.

The long-span, all-metal wings had a trailing-edge extension to the inner section from mid-span, giving a total wing area of 19.05 m² (205 sq ft).

The basic Schweizer SGS2-32 all-metal structure was retained for the wings and fuselage. A normal tailwheel undercarriage had the main legs retracting inwards into the wings.

U.S. ARMY 18001

Vietnam spy in the sky

1 ENEMY OBSERVATION: Flying quietly at low level, using the lie of the land to remain covert, the YO-3A used its onboard sensors to track an enemy convoy. It then transmitted details to a patrolling Hercules gunship.

2 TARGET PINPOINTED: Using information radioed from the spyplane, the heavily armed AC-130 swooped down to make its attack.

YO-3A

Type: two-seat single-engined 'quiet' observation aircraft

Powerplant: one 158-kW (212-hp) Continental IO-360D six-cylinder air-cooled piston engine

Maximum speed: 222 km/h (138 mph) at sea level

Cruising speed: 177 km/h (110 mph) at sea level

Initial climb rate: 187 m/min (614 fpm)

Service ceiling: 4265 m (13,993 ft)

Endurance: 4 hours 25 min at sea level

Weights: empty 1419 kg (3128 lb); loaded 1596 kg (3519 lb); maximum 1724 kg; wing loading 83.30 kg/m² (56 lb/ft)

Dimensions:
span	17.37 m (57 ft)
length	8.94 m (29 ft 4 in)
height	2.77 m (9 ft 1 in)
wing area	19.05 m² (205 sq ft)

ACTION DATA

CRUISING SPEED

Although they represent designs separated by several years, the YO-3A and Optica were intended to fulfil similar roles and offered very similar performance. Cruising at low speeds over the operational area, these aircraft offered long endurance and low noise for tasks normally undertaken by helicopters.

YO-3A	177 km/h (110 mph)
OPTICA	174 km/h (108 mph)
MH-6H	246 km/h (153 mph)

INITIAL CLIMB RATE

McDonnell Douglas' specially modified MH-6H for use by US Special Forces offers the low noise of the other types in addition to impressive climb performance. The helicopter cannot compete in terms of range, endurance or cost-effectiveness, however.

YO-3A	187 m/min (614 fpm)
OPTICA	219 m/min (719 fpm)
MH-6H	631 m/min (2070 fpm)

SERVICE CEILING

Both the YO-3A and Optica were built with prolonged flight at very low altitudes as their main area of operation. Vulnerability to small-arms fire and the modern generation of high-performance attack/escort helicopters mean that pilots seek the safety of higher altitudes in combat.

YO-3A	4265 m (13,993 ft)
OPTICA	4270 m (14,009 ft)
MH-6H	4875 m (15,994 ft)

LOCKHEED

EC-130

- Electronic warfare Hercules variants ● Highly classified equipment

▲ The USAF operates an EC-130E version as an airborne battlefield command and control centre. Internal consoles can display digitised maps covering any area of the world.

Under the designation EC-130, the USAF operates four special mission variants of the ubiquitous Hercules transport.

One is an airborne control centre, while the other three have a much more sensitive role: electronic warfare. Although routinely seen on the outside, the inside is a secret world. To gain access to the interior of the aircraft a top-secret codeword is required, as the task of the EC-130E and EC-130H is to listen to and disrupt enemy communications.

LOCKHEED EC-130

EC-130H Compass Call ▶

The EC-130H is used for communications intrusion and jamming duties. Previously operated from Sembach in Germany, the 10 operational aircraft are now based at Davis-Monthan in Arizona.

▲ Jamming equipment

An array of wire antennas is suspended on a gantry under the tail. Blisters on the rear fuselage contain two further antennas.

▲ EC-130(RR) Rivet Rider

Working in conjunction with the EC-130H is the EC-130(RR) Rivet Rider, which is also tasked with jamming enemy communications. It can tap into and rebroadcast radio and TV transmissions for propaganda and psychological warfare missions.

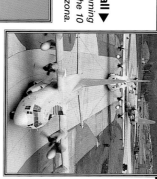

▲ Rivet Rider antennas

The Rivet Rider is easily identified by a single, large axehead antenna under each wing.

TACAMO – TAke Charge And Move Out ▶

A US Navy C-130Q relays communications to its ballistic nuclear missile submarines.

FACTS AND FIGURES

➤ EC-130 crew often exceed the USAF's recommended maximum of 155 days away from home each year.

➤ Incredibly, the original C-130 airframe made its first flight on 23 August 1954.

➤ US Navy EC-130Q aircraft were replaced in 1989 with the Boeing E-6 Mercury.

➤ Comfy Levi, Rivet Rider and ABCCC EC-130Es and EC-130Hs were operational during Operation Desert Storm.

➤ The US Coast Guard operates an EC-130E as an electronic calibration aircraft.

➤ A major role during the Cold War was eavesdropping in the Berlin Corridor.

PROFILE

USAF electronic warriors

The EC-130 may look like a transport aircraft but it is a saboteur with wings, using the marvel of electronics to break up an enemy's military radio and television broadcasting.

The USAF operates several intelligence-gathering versions of the Hercules transport under the designation EC-130E. A Hercules version, unofficially designated EC-130E and now retired, operated from Frankfurt and gathered signals, electronic and communications intelligence.

Another EC-130E version, the ABCCC, is an airborne battlefield control aircraft.

There are two types of intelligence-gathering EC-130Es, both operated by the 193rd Special Operations Squadron,

based at Harrisburg in Philadelphia.

The EC-130E(CL) Comfy Levi undertakes Elint (electronic intelligence) and probably jamming missions under the codename 'Senior Scout'.

Special mission equipment uses antennas that are fitted to removable undercarriage doors and fairings. Five of these aircraft carry sensor operators in the cargo hold, who use black boxes to intrude into an enemy's communications and extract information.

The most heavily-modified version, the EC-130E(RR) Rivet Rider, intrudes into enemy radio and television broadcasts and flies under the name 'Commando Solo'.

The Rivet Rider's mission is to disrupt enemy communications. It can broadcast on any frequency, including AM/FM radio, black and white and now colour TV, as well as short-wave (HF) and other communication bands.

EC-130H Hercules

Type: electronic warfare aircraft

Powerplant: four 3020-kW (4046-hp) Allison T56-A-15 turboprop engines

Maximum speed: 611 km/h (379 mph)

Range: 4100 km (2546 miles)

Service ceiling: 13225 m (43,400 ft)

Weights: empty 34105 kg (75,200 lb); maximum take-off 74202 kg (163,615 lb)

Accommodation: two pilots, navigator, electronic warfare officer, flight engineer, loadmaster and five electronic equipment operators

Dimensions: span   40.41 m (132 ft 7 in)
length   29.79 m (97 ft 8 in)
height   11.66 m (38.25 in)
wing area   162.11 m (1745 sq ft)

Above: The huge blade antenna on the fin leading edge and the Vietnam-style camouflage distinguishes early Rivet Riders. The latest upgraded version wears a smart two-tone grey scheme.

Above: For anti-drug trafficking duties, the US Coast Guard bought an early-warning EC-130V fitted with an APS-145 search radar. High costs, however, forced it out of service and the role was taken over by Customs Service P-3s. The EC-130 was reported to have gone to the USAF for an undisclosed 'black' programme.

EC-130E(RR) HERCULES

All EC-130E(RR)s are operated by the 193rd Special Operations Squadron, Pennsylvania Air National Guard. They are based at Harrisburg International Airport.

The Rivet Rider has recently been extensively upgraded. The latest model differs considerably from the one shown here. Current versions have worldwide colour television broadcast capabilities. Externally, these aircraft have four bullet fairings on the fin and two large pods under the outer wings.

There are two retractable trailing antennas: a high-frequency one reeled horizontally behind the aircraft and a 304-metre (1000 ft) AM-band antenna held in a near-vertical position by a weight.

The dark 'European One' colour scheme, as shown here, replaced the earlier Vietnam 'Southeast Asia' camouflage.

The most prominent feature of the early Rivet Riders was the blade aerial ahead of the tailfin. This was believed to be related to TV broadcasting.

Underwing stores include long-range fuel tanks, as on standard Hercules, a pod containing a trailing aerial and an 'axe-head' antenna.

USAF 637793

An in-flight refuelling receptacle is fitted above the cockpit. Refuelling capability means that crew fatigue is the limiting factor during a mission.

EC-130Es are powered by four Allison T56-A-15 turboprops, as fitted to the standard C-130H transport variant.

77B3

EC-130 Hercules missions

The C-130, with the minimum of modification to the basic airframe, has proved ideal for the various EC-130 roles.

1 COMMAND MODULE: The ABCCC is a regular Hercules transport fitted with a removable battle command module. This houses equipment for 16 mission specialists.

2 COMMUNICATIONS JAMMER: The EC-130E(RR) Rivet Rider is fitted with comprehensive jamming equipment in the tail, fuselage and wings to disrupt enemy communications.

3 RADAR CALIBRATION: Air traffic search and control radars need to be constantly checked. The US Coast Guard uses the Hercules to calibrate these.

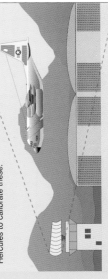

COMBAT DATA

MAXIMUM SPEED

All manner of different aircraft have been used as ELINT platforms. The Soviet An-12 is broadly similar to the C-130 in size and configuration, whereas the C-47 is a cheap and reliable alternative.

EC-130E HERCULES	612 km/h (380 mph)
An-12 'CUB-C'	777 km/h (483 mph)
C-47	346 km/h (215 mph)

RANGE

A useful feature of the Hercules is its range. Long range allows long-distance ELINT missions to be carried out or, alternatively, shorter range flights can be made with longer 'loiter' times in the air over the 'target'.

An-12 'CUB-C'
5700 km
(3540 miles)

C-47
2430 km
(1509 miles)

EC-130E HERCULES
7560 km
(4695 miles)

LOCKHEED
C-141 StarLifter

- Strategic freighter ● Troop carrier ● Long-range heavy lifter

▲ The USAF's first purpose-built, long-range jet cargo and troop transport, the C-141 StarLifter was designed with its own ground-based handling system.

Lockheed's C-141 StarLifter is the heavy muscle of the American military air transport fleet. Although growing old and being replaced, slowly, by the McDonnell Douglas C-17 Globemaster III, the C-141 has logged millions of miles since entering service in the mid 1960s. As the principal long-range airlifter for US forces (helped by smaller numbers of the outsized C-5 Galaxy), the C-141 has carried equipment and freight to and from every crisis in recent history.

PHOTO FILE
LOCKHEED C-141 StarLifter

▲ Short-field performance
A large wing area and full deflection, 60 per cent span Fowler-type flaps allows a fully laden C-141 to clear a 15-m (50-ft) obstacle with a roll of just 1731 m (5675 ft). It has an equally impressive very short landing run.

▲ Clamshell doors
The C-141's large rear cargo doors allow vehicles and equipment to be loaded via a ramp that lowers to ground level.

▲ Inflight refuelling
The C-141B introduced air-to-air refuelling to the StarLifter, increasing it to a potential global range. It has a prominent fairing on the top of the forward fuselage to receive the boom from the refueller.

▲ First paradrop jet
The first paradrop from a jet transport aircraft was made from a C-141 in August 1965. It made its first heavy cargo drops from the ramp later in the year.

▲ Long range
At just under 800 km/h (500 mph), a fully laden C-141B StarLifter can fly nearly 5000 km (3100 miles) on internal fuel, and much further with inflight refuelling.

FACTS AND FIGURES

▼ The StarLifter first flew on 17 December 1963, 60 years after the Wright Brothers.

▼ The first operational C-141A was delivered to Tinker AFB, Oklahoma, in October 1964.

▼ The C-141B has a 7.11-m (23-ft) longer fuselage and inflight refuelling capability.

▼ The C-141B can carry 205 passengers or 168 fully equipped paratroopers.

▼ In 1984, C-141Bs carried tents, water, blankets and 118,000 kg (259,00 lb) of foodstuffs to famine victims in Sudan.

▼ The last of 270 rebuilt C-141Bs was delivered to Military Air Command in 1982.

C-141B StarLifter

Type: strategic airlifter (troop/cargo transport)

Powerplant: four 93.42-kN (20,950-lb-thrust) Pratt & Whitney TF33-P-7 turbofan engines

Maximum speed: 933 km/h (578 mph)

Maximum cruising speed: 911 km/h (565 mph) with maximum payload

Range: 4773 km (2960 miles) with maximum payload

Service ceiling: 12,879 m (42,250 ft)

Weights: empty weight (C-141A) 60,678 kg (133,491 lb); (C-141B) 67,187 kg (147,811 lb); maximum take-off 155,585 kg (342,287 lb)

Accommodation: has carried every cargo from vehicles to a whale; normal payload is 32,135 kg (70,697 lb); maximum payload 41,223 kg (90,690 lb)

Dimensions:
span	48.74 m	(159 ft 10 in)
length	51.29 m	(168 ft 3 in)
height	12.15 m	(39 ft 10 in)
wing area	299.90 m²	(3227 sq ft)

The USAF's strategic lifter

Famous for finally bringing home the Prisoners of War from Vietnam in 1973 and for dramatic paratroop drops in Panama in 1989, the C-141's main task is far less glamorous but equally as important. For over 30 years the C-141 StarLifter has supplied US military and sometimes civilian installations around the world with vital supplies and reinforcements. In times of crisis the C-141 can, in partnership with the massive C-5, fully equip an entire army in a matter of days anywhere in the world.

StarLifters began hauling supplies to Vietnam in the 1960s. A decade later, Lockheed won an ambitious contract to 'stretch' the 263-plane C-141A fleet by 7.11 m (23 ft) and to add an air refuelling receptacle. The lengthened StarLifter, known as the C-141B, flew for the first time on 24 March 1977 and was put into service soon after. The improvements have given the StarLifter global reach and made it a familiar sight almost everywhere. Except for a couple of test aircraft, all of today's StarLifters are lengthened C-141B variants.

Wearing the original Military Airlift Command colour scheme, this is the first C-141B StarLifter. The scheme was later changed to the drab green and grey 'lizard' European camouflage. They have now been repainted in overall medium-grey.

The StarLifter is powered by four Pratt & Whitney TF33-P-7 turbofan engines, each rated at 93.42 kN (20,950 lb thrust), mounted in underwing pods and fitted with clamshell-door thrust reversers.

A conventional two-spar, box-beam, cantilever high-wing is mounted on top of the fuselage with 25° sweepback. It has Fowler-type trailing-edge flaps and hinged spoilers on the upper and lower wing surfaces.

An all-metal, variable-incidence tailplane is mounted at the top of the fin. Elevators are controlled by dual hydraulic units with manual reverse.

The swept vertical fin and rudder has a prominent bullet fairing where it meets the horizontal tailplane. The rudder is hydraulically controlled by electric trim tabs.

The stretched C-141B can house three extra pallets, although the weight capacity is no greater. Volumetric limitations of the C-141 have therefore been overcome.

The large rear ramp doors can be opened fully in flight for aerial load dropping, while a built-in loading ramp can be extended and lowered for vehicle access when on the ground.

C-141B STARLIFTER

The StarLifter was the USAF's first pure-jet transport designed to meet a Specific Operational Requirement for a strategic transport.

The raised area above the forward fuselage houses the inflight-refuelling receptacle, into which the tanker's boom is connected to pass fuel to the StarLifter.

The spacious cockpit accommodates a flight crew comprising two pilots, flight engineer and navigator. It contains modern instrumentation for all-weather operations around the world.

The nosewheel retracts rearwards into the fuselage and is enclosed by two doors.

Modification of the C-141A to the C-141B involved the insertion of newly-fabricated fuselage sections ahead of and behind the wing, resulting in a stretch of 7.11 m (23 ft). This gave an increase in the volume of cargo that could be carried. The C-141B also had a new, more streamlined wingroot fairing and inflight-refuelling capability.

The four-wheel bogie main undercarriage units retract forwards into fairings on the sides of the lower fuselage. To assist with short-field landings the aircraft has hydraulic, multiple-disc, anti-skid brakes.

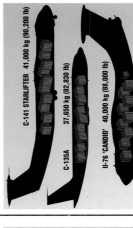

COMBAT DATA

PAYLOAD

The USAF had a small number of Boeing 707s adapted as C-135s for interim cargo transport before the C-141 came into service. With no ramp or rear loading doors, the volume of freight was limited. The Russian Il-76 has a similar weight-lifting capacity to the C-141, but its smaller fuselage limits the size and volume that can be accommodated.

C-141 STARLIFTER 41,000 kg (90,200 lb)

C-135A 37,650 kg (82,830 lb)

Il-76 'CANDID' 40,000 kg (88,000 lb)

Lockheed's 'Star' lifter

BULK CARRIER: The C-141's hold is of almost constant cross-section along its entire length. This gives a usable cargo volume of 322.79 m³ (3474 sq ft). To assist with the insertion of newly-fabricated in the C-141B, enabling it to transport up to four military vehicles.

CONVERTIBLE: An extensive array of internal equipment, including fold-away floor rollers, tie-down points and seat tracks, enables the passenger/cargo mix to be changed rapidly.

HEAVY LIFTER: In terms of tonne/miles per flying hour, one C-141 could equal four C-124 Globemasters. Just 18 StarLifters could have accomplished the same as 142 C-54 Skymasters in the Berlin Airlift of 1948/49.

FAST FREIGHTER: In Vietnam, under combat conditions, the C-141 could offload in 17 minutes using its special handling equipment. A full palletised load could be installed in only 30 minutes and flown to its destination in half the time of the C-124 it replaced.

LOCKHEED
C-5 GALAXY

● Strategic transport ● Heavylift heavyweight

▲ Slowly disappearing into the opened 'mouth' of a C-5 Galaxy, a mothballed F-5 fighter demonstrates the huge Lockheed transport's unrivalled ability to handle large loads.

This monster aircraft, the world's biggest transport for two decades, hauled cargoes in American military actions from Vietnam onwards. Although not as large as the Antonov aircraft of today, the C-5 Galaxy has an unmatched service record for transporting the weaponry of war. To pilots, perched 10 metres (30 feet) off the ground before starting engines, the Galaxy is rated as the biggest and the best.

LOCKHEED C-5 GALAXY

▼ Global reach
Inflight refuelling means that the C-5 can deliver its outsize loads anywhere in the world.

▲ Flight deck
The C-5 is flown by a pilot and co-pilot, with flight engineer and navigator facing outwards at the rear of the flight deck.

▲ Rear loader
The C-5's tail is upswept, enabling a huge rear-loading door and ramp to be fitted.

▲ 'Fat Albert'
Nicknamed with back-handed affection by its crews, the C-5 was for two decades the biggest and heaviest aircraft in the world.

▲ Easy to fly
The Galaxy's four-man flight crew sit high in the upper decking of the forward fuselage. In spite of its size, the C-5 is reasonably easy, if a little sluggish, to fly.

FACTS AND FIGURES

➤ The C-5 was chosen by the Air Force over transports proposed by Boeing and Douglas.

➤ Eighty-one C-5A transports were built in 1967-71; 50 similar C-5Bs were built when production resumed between 1984 and 1989.

➤ Many C-5 loadmasters have logged 20,000 flight hours, more than most airline pilots.

➤ The crash of a C-5A at Ramstein, Germany, on 29 August 1990 was the only loss of a transport plane during the massive Desert Shield airlift preparing for the Gulf War.

➤ Lockheed claims that the C-5's four engines have the same power as 48 railroad locomotives.

C-5B Galaxy

Type: heavy, long-range logistic freighter

Powerplant: four 191.24-kN (41,000-lb-thrust) General Electric TF39-GE-1C turbofans

Maximum speed: 760 km/h (570 mph) at 10,000 m (32,800 ft)

Range: 6033 km (3700 miles) with maximum payload

Service ceiling: 10,900 m (34,000 ft) with typical payload

Weights: empty 170,000 kg (375,000 lb); loaded 380,000 kg (838,000 lb)

Payload: vehicles and outsize loads up to 120,200 kg (264,440 lb) in main freight compartment plus 73 passengers or fully equipped combat troops in upper rear personnel compartment

Dimensions:
span 67.88 m (222 ft 8 in)
length 75.54 m (247 ft 10 in)
height 19.85 m (63 ft 2 in)
wing area 576.00 m² (6200 sq ft)

The tip of the C-5's nose houses a Bendix APS-133 digital colour weather radar. The entire nose hinges upwards for access to the hold.

The bullet fairing at the top of the huge T-tail houses an air data recorder as well as a flight data and crash recorder – the so-called 'Black Box'.

There are three inboard and three outboard sets of slotted flaps on the trailing edge of the wing, with slotted slats on the outboard leading edge.

The original C-5A had considerable problems with wing fatigue, which was corrected in the C-5B. In the 1980s the entire fleet was given new, stronger wings at a cost of more than one billion dollars.

The T-tail is fitted with hydraulically-actuated four-section elevators and a twin-section rudder. There are no trim tabs; the whole of the horizontal tail can be adjusted.

The massive hold can accommodate a wide variety of outsize loads, from helicopters and tanks to trucks and cargo containers. It can also carry over 360 fully equipped troops.

Aircraft of the Galaxy's size became possible only with the development of large, powerful jet engines. The C-5 is powered by four General Electric TF39-GE-1C twin-shaft high bypass turbofans, each delivering 191.24 kN (41,000 lb thrust).

The main landing gear of the Galaxy consists of four bogies each with six wheels, two forwards and four aft.

PROFILE

Giant from Georgia

The revolutionary thing about the Lockheed C-5 Galaxy is its sheer size. Many big aircraft have won fleeting cameo roles in history's cast of aviation characters, but few of the real giants actually register a full working day, all day, every day, doing a real job in the real world. The C-5 combines greatness with unromantic achievement.

At over 300 tonnes, the C-5 was the biggest and heaviest aeroplane in its class when test pilots thundered aloft in the first example on 30 June 1968. Since then, even larger Antonov

transports have appeared in the former Soviet Union, but for its first two decades of operation the Galaxy was without rival.

The C-5 can carry almost any item in the US military inventory, from Abrams main battle tanks to over 360 fully equipped paratroops. It was the backbone of the 1991 Desert Shield airlift, the entire force of 85 Galaxies being used to carry 42 per cent of all air-delivered cargo – nearly a quarter of a million tonnes.

The C-5 was vital to the success of the Gulf War. Its record-breaking effort saw the Galaxy lifting a heavier tonnage in the first 21 days of Desert Shield than was carried in the entire Berlin airlift.

C-5B GALAXY

First built in the 1960s, the C-5 went back into production as the improved C-5B in the 1980s. There are more than 120 C-5s in service with the US Air Force, 50 of which are 'B' models.

COMBAT DATA

RANGE

The arrival of the Galaxy in the late 1960s meant that for the first time the US military had the capacity to deliver outsize loads anywhere in the world at jet speeds. The Galaxy can fly intercontinental distances even when carrying a payload of 118 tonnes; the huge Antonov An-124 is its only rival. The An-124, known as 'Condor' to NATO but called 'Ruslan' after a fairytale giant by its makers, can carry even heavier loads, but not over such great distances.

An-124 RUSLAN	4400 km (2700 miles)
C-5B GALAXY	6033 km (3200 miles)
C-17 GLOBEMASTER III	5200 km (3200 miles)

Heavylift specialist

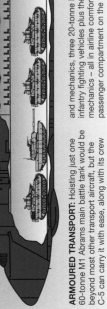

ARMOURED TRANSPORT: Hoisting just one 60-tonne M1 Abrams main battle tank would be beyond most other transport aircraft, but the C-5 can carry it with ease, along with its crew and mechanics, three 20-tonne M2 Bradley infantry fighting vehicles plus their crews and mechanics – all in airline comfort in the passenger compartment on the top deck.

HELICOPTER MOVER: Galaxies were vital during Operation Desert Shield, especially when they were used to fly Apache gunship helicopters out to Saudi Arabia. The AH-64s were packed two by two, six at a time, and three C-5 trips could move a whole battalion. Once in the Gulf, the helicopters were reassembled and operational within 24 hours.

LOCKHEED

S/ES-3 VIKING

● Twin-jet anti-submarine ● Elint version ● Gulf War veteran

A
lthough it may not be as glamorous as the F-14 and F/A-18 'fast jets' which also serve aboard the United States' super-carriers, the S-3 Viking has, arguably, a more crucial role. One of the biggest enemies of a carrier battle group is the submarine. The Viking's task is to find these undersea machines and stop them in their tracks. For this role Lockheed packed sophisticated electronics and potent weapons into a surprisingly compact airframe.

▶ The S-3's main task is outer-zone anti-submarine warfare (ASW). Inner-zone ASW is tackled by carrier-borne helicopters, such as the SH-3 Sea King and SH-60 Seahawk.

260

PHOTO FILE

LOCKHEED S/ES-3 VIKING

▲ Improved Viking
Most surviving S-3As were converted to S-3B standard in the late-1980s, with the addition of Harpoon anti-ship missiles and new avionics. Number 159742 was the first conversion.

▲ Carrier-borne transport
Six US-3A COD aircraft deliver vital replenishment supplies to the Pacific Fleet.

▼ 'Bombed-up' Viking
Vikings were active in the Gulf War, undertaking bombing missions against land targets and small vessels in the Persian Gulf.

▲ ES-3A eavesdropper
Packed with extra sensors and a third systems operator, the ES-3A is an electronic intelligence (Elint) variant of the Viking. Sixteen conversions are deployed in pairs aboard US carriers.

'Stinger' deployed ▶
With its MAD boom extended, this Viking drops a torpedo. The weapons bay can hold up to 1814 kg (4000 lb) of ordnance, which, until recently, included nuclear depth charges.

FACTS AND FIGURES

▶ In partnership with Lockheed, Vought designed and built the wings, tail, landing gear and engine pods for the Viking.

▶ The US-3A COD transport aircraft have been stripped of their ASW gear.

▶ ES-3A Elint Vikings have replaced the last carrier-based EA-3B Skywarriors.

▶ Modified, so-called 'Brown Boy', Vikings were used to drop ground movement sensors in Bosnia.

▶ At one time the S-3A equipped 14 squadrons.

▶ In February 1974 the S-3 made its first carrier landing, on USS Forrestal.

PROFILE

US Fleet's Nordic sub-hunter

In 1964 the US Navy began its search for a replacement for the proven Grumman S-2 Tracker. Lockheed, a company with comparatively little experience in building carrier-borne aircraft, teamed with Vought to build the S-3 Viking. After a January 1972 first flight, a further seven development airframes and

179 production aircraft were built. Operations began in 1974 and the last S-3As were delivered in 1978. A number have been modified for the carrier onboard delivery (COD) role as US-3As, and a dedicated in-flight refuelling version, the KS-3A, was trialled but did not go into production. There are also 16 ES-3A electronic intelligence variants operating in pairs from US Navy carriers.

The current ASW version is the S-3B, introduced in 1987. This aircraft features greatly improved avionics and a Harpoon air-to-surface missile capability.

This Viking is in its natural environment, in search of submarines. All S-3s are operated by the US Navy and represent the most capable carrier-borne anti-submarine force in the world.

Two General Electric TF34 turbofans provide the power for the S-3 family. Both main wings fold inwards and the vertical tail to the left on the Viking, to make it relatively compact and easy to manoeuvre on a crowded aircraft-carrier deck.

S-3B VIKING

Air Antisubmarine Squadron 30 flew from the USS Saratoga during the Gulf War. Facing an enemy without submarines, VS-30 undertook bombing raids against Iraqi land targets.

The chief sensors aboard the S-3 include a large APS-137(V)1 search radar in the nose, for the detection of surface vessels and submarine periscopes, and a retractable forward-looking infra-red (FLIR) turret under the forward fuselage.

Vikings have a crew of four. Two pilots sit side-by-side and handle flight control and navigation. Behind them are the mission crew of Tactical Co-ordinator ('Tacco') and Sensor Operator ('Senso'). All sit in ejection seats.

As well as carrying 60 sonobuoys in the aft fuselage, the two internal weapons bays can hold bombs, torpedoes or depth charges. Harpoon missiles are carried on the wing pylons.

Two 1136-litre (250-gallon) auxiliary fuel tanks are often carried to improve range. An in-flight refuelling probe is also fitted. In the 'buddy' refuelling role a D-704 'probe-and-drogue' refuelling pod is carried on the port wing pylon.

The S-3B is virtually indistinguishable from the S-3A. However, the later version has a small chaff dispenser fitted to the rear fuselage.

Apart from the FLIR turret and radar, the Viking's most important sensor is the magnetic anomaly detector (MAD) 'sting' deployed from the rear of the aircraft. This detects changes in the earth's magnetic field caused by a large metallic mass like a submarine.

S-3B Viking

Type: carrier-borne anti-submarine aircraft

Powerplant: two 41.2-kN (9270-lb-thrust) General Electric TF34-GE-2 turbofans

Maximum speed: 814 km/h (505 mph) at sea level

Endurance: 7 hours 30 min

Ferry range: more than 5558 km (3445 miles)

Service ceiling: over 10,670 m (35,000 ft)

Weights: empty 12,088 kg (26,594 lb); maximum take-off 23,832 kg (52,430 lb)

Armament: up to 3175 kg (6985 lb) of ordnance (up to 1814 kg/4000 lb in internal weapons bays), including bombs, depth charges, torpedoes and AGM-84 Harpoon air-to-surface missiles

Dimensions:
span	20.93 m (68 ft 8 in)
length	16.26 m (53 ft 4 in)
height	6.93 m (22 ft 9 in)
wing area	55.56 m² (554 sq ft)

COMBAT DATA

MAXIMUM SPEED

Powered by turbofan engines, the Viking has an impressive top speed compared to propeller-driven aircraft – almost twice that of the S-2E. When the Viking is loaded this speed is appreciably reduced, but it can still reach its given patrol area faster than other carrier-borne, fixed-wing ASW machines.

S-3B VIKING	814 km/h (505 mph)
S-2E TRACKER	426 km/h (264 mph)
Br.1150 ALIZÉ	323 km/h (200 mph)

ENDURANCE

The Viking has a shorter patrol endurance than the propeller-driven aircraft, but has the ability to be refuelled in the air, which greatly increases its flexibility. Vikings have a secondary in-flight refuelling role, for which they can be fitted with 'buddy' refuelling tanks. A tanker version of the Viking was also used until recently.

S-3B VIKING	7 hours 30 min
S-2E TRACKER	9 hours
Br.1150 ALIZÉ	7 hours 40 min

ELECTRONIC INTELLIGENCE: Elint is the role assigned to the small ES-3A fleet. A large collection of new sensors (and their associated antennas) was installed in the aircraft modified and these are used in pairs from carriers.

CARRIER ONBOARD DELIVERY: A small number of S-3As were modified as COD aircraft to supplement the Pacific Fleet's C-2 Greyhounds. Avionics equipment was removed to make space for passengers and cargo.

IN-FLIGHT REFUELLING: Development of a specialised KS-3A tanker variant of the Viking was abandoned and ASW Vikings were modified to carry 'buddy' IFR equipment. The 'probe-and-drogue' gear is carried in a pod attached to the port underwing pylon.

Multi-role Viking at work

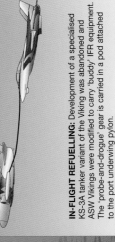

ANTI-SUBMARINE WARFARE: ASW remains the S-3's most important task. The S-3B is found aboard all of the US Navy's super-carriers, providing protection from the ever-present underwater threat. During the Gulf conflict the S-3 displayed its versatility, and was deployed as a bomber.

LOCKHEED
F-117 NIGHTHAWK

● 'Stealth' fighter-bomber ● Fly-by-wire control ● First Gulf War veteran

▲ Two weapons bays in the F-117 are equipped with a trapeze to carry bombs of up to 907 kg (2000 lb). The usual weapon for raids on Iraq was the laser-guided GBU-27. AGM-65 Maverick or AGM-88 HARM missiles can also be carried.

Developed in great secrecy, the F-117A Nighthawk quickly became one of the world's best known aircraft after its success in the First Gulf War. Making use of the stealth technology that renders the aircraft virtually invisible to radar, the USAF's F-117s attacked important targets in Iraq from the opening moments of Desert Storm. Not only did they reach Baghdad unseen, but they could hit their assigned targets with pinpoint accuracy using laser bombs.

PHOTO FILE

LOCKHEED **F-117 NIGHTHAWK**

▼ **Baghdad bombers**
Striking unexpectedly at night, the F-117s were the only warplanes to fly missions against the heavily defended targets of central Baghdad.

▲ **Under cover of darkness**
As during the first seven years of its existence, the F-117 flew almost exclusively at night to maintain the secrecy of its missions and capability.

▲ **Rarely seen**
There was little evidence at their bases at home or overseas that the Nighthawks were operating, other than the standard joke signs.

First major deployment ▼
Apart from the invasion of Panama in 1989, the Gulf War was the first major use of the F-117A. Nighthawks were assigned nearly one-third of the Baghdad targets during the first 24 hours.

▲ **Protective shelter**
This Nighthawk is seen inside its hardened shelter, in which the F-117s spent much of their daylight hours between night attack missions.

FACTS AND FIGURES

▶ Laser-guided bombs used by the F-117 are specially modified with 'clipped' fins so that they will fit in the weapons bay.

▶ The most missions flown by an F-117 pilot during Desert Storm was 23.

▶ Successive missions were flown over different routes to confuse the Iraqis.

▶ Khamis Mushait airfield was at an altitude of 2073 m (6800 ft), which affected take-off and necessitated in-flight refuelling.

▶ On rare occasions F-117 missions were supported by EF-111s and F-4Gs.

▶ The 1271 sorties undertaken totalled around 7000 flight hours.

PROFILE

Unseen bomber of Baghdad

High-tech 'stealth' capabilities allowed the F-117A to operate undetected at night in Iraqi airspace until it reached Baghdad. Transferred in great secrecy from its home base in Nevada to Khamis Mushait in the south of Saudi Arabia, the F-117A spearheaded the opening of the air war by coalition forces in January 1991. The dual infra-red weapons delivery system and laser-guided bombs gave it the means to attack targets with the utmost precision. In addition to attacking important military areas in central Baghdad, the

Nighthawks hit strategic targets such as communications facilities, bridges, airfields and command centres. In all, 1,271 combat missions were flown by the F-117s, with each pilot averaging 21 sorties. Despite an estimated 3000 Iraqi anti-aircraft artillery (AAA) pieces and 60 surface-to-air missile (SAM) sites in the areas attacked, no F-117 was hit while dropping around 2000 laser-guided bombs (LGBs) onto targets deep inside Iraq. The normal flight-time for a Gulf War mission which included air-to-air refuelling was just over five hours.

In-flight refuelling played a vital part in most raids during the war, not least those flown by F-117s.

F-117A NIGHTHAWK

The 37th Tactical Fighter Wing, based at Tonopah Air Force Base, Nevada, is the sole F-117A operator, and sent 44 aircraft to the Gulf.

All air data for the F-117's instruments are collected by four faceted plastic and metal sensor probes in the aircraft's nose.

The pyramid-shaped cockpit canopy restricts the area around the pilot's shoulders and head. The cockpit itself is a modern 'all-glass' environment dominated by large video displays.

Weapons are carried internally, to avoid the radar reflections associated with external stores. In the Gulf, F-117s were normally armed with 907-kg (2000-lb) laser-guided bombs.

Two imaging infra-red (IR) turrets (FLIR and DLIR) are recessed into the aircraft's nose. They are fully integrated with, and provide data for, the weapons release system.

A receptacle incorporated in the spine running along the top of the Nighthawk's fuselage is used for in-flight refuelling, via the USAF's standard 'flying boom' system.

The F-117 is manufactured from aluminium and composites with radar-absorbing material (RAM) sprayed onto the surface and key points, such as the joints between each facet of the fuselage and the wing leading edges.

Tailfins are carefully positioned to keep radar reflections to a minimum and to help shield the engine exhausts from infra-red sensors of a pursuing fighter or missile.

The F-117's wings are swept at 67°. This is again intended to reduce radar reflections as well as being for high-speed performance.

The Nighthawk's sharply swept twin butterfly tailplanes act both as rudders and elevators. The 'ruddervators' work in opposition for yaw control and together for pitch control.

The two General Electric turbofans are buried in the fuselage. The unique 'platypus' exhaust system mixes hot gasses with cold air, reducing the aircraft's infra-red signature.

Black jets over Iraq

DESERT SHIELD: The Iraqi invasion of Kuwait and the decision by the coalition powers to come to Kuwait's aid gave the USAF its first opportunity to test the F-117 on a large scale.

TANKER SUPPORT: As the F-117s' Saudi base was situated at high altitude, the aircraft were required to take off with a reduced fuel load and 'top up' their tanks from a KC-135 once airborne.

STRATEGIC TARGETS: Among the F-117s' targets on the first night of Desert Storm were Iraqi Tu-16/H-6 bombers believed to be preparing for a chemical weapon raid.

GBU-27A/B PAVEWAY III: (below) Seen here with wings stowed, this LGB variant has a 907-kg (2000-lb) BLU-109 'I-2000' penetrator warhead for use against hardened targets. The F-117's weapons bay is limited to two LGBs.

GBU-27/B PAVEWAY III: (above) This laser-guided bomb, seen here with tail wings deployed, was one of the F-117s' primary offensive weapons. It has a standard 907-kg (2000-lb) Mk 84 general-purpose warhead.

F-117A Nighthawk

Type: single-seat strike fighter

Powerplant: two 48.04-kN (10,809-lb-thrust) non-afterburning General Electric F404-GE F1D2 turbofans

Maximum speed: Mach 1 (estimated) or 1100 km/h (684 mph)

Combat radius: 1200 km (746 miles) unrefuelled, with a 2250-kg (4960-lb) weapon load

Armament: range of tactical fighter ordnance up to 2268 kg (5000 lb) carried internally; principal weapons were GBU-10/GBU-12 Paveway II or GBU-27 Paveway III laser-guided bombs

Weights: empty 13,600 kg (29,983 lb); maximum take-off 23,814 kg (52,500 lb)

Dimensions: span 13.2 m (43 ft 4 in)
length 20.08 m (65 ft 11 in)
height 3.78 m (12 ft 5 in)
wing area about 105.9 m² (1140 sq ft)

COMBAT DATA

MAXIMUM SPEED

Maximum speed and other performance parameters do not have the same relevance in an aircraft like the F-117. Its shape is optimized for stealth rather than speed.

F-117A NIGHTHAWK	1100 km/h (684 mph)
F-15E EAGLE	2655 km/h (1650 mph)
F-111F	2655 km/h (1650 mph)

BOMBLOAD

The F-111F has been unequalled for its range and load-carrying capabilities for many years, and performed well in the Gulf. However, like other conventional aircraft, it was heavily reliant on its low-level speed and electronic countermeasures support.

F-117A NIGHTHAWK	2268-kg (5000-lb) bombload
F-15E EAGLE	11,113-kg (25,000-lb) bombload
F-111F	14,228-kg (25,550-lb) bombload

LOCKHEED MARTIN

F-16C FIGHTING FALCON

- Second-generation fighter ● Multi-role ● Export success

ockheed Martin's best-selling F-16 Fighting Falcon is the most important and widely used fighter aircraft in the West, and it seems set to maintain this position well into the next century. The F-16C is the second-generation development of this versatile 'fly-by-wire' fighter-bomber and reconnaissance aircraft. Earlier production F-16As are now sought after by smaller air arms, often after they have been upgraded with advanced systems.

▶ By far the most numerous aircraft in the USAF inventory, the earlier F-16A and F-16B have been supplanted by the F-16C and F-16D, respectively. The new aircraft feature a host of improvements, including new engines and night-attack systems.

264

LOCKHEED MARTIN F-16C FIGHTING FALCON

▲ New radar
The APG-66 radar was replaced by an APG-68 set in the F-16C. This is compatible with the AGM-65 air-to-surface missile.

▲ Improved cockpit
The F-16C introduced an updated cockpit with a wide-angle HUD and advanced computers.

▲ Performance boost
A General Electric F110-GE-100 or Pratt & Whitney F100-P-220 turbofan powers the F-16C.

Public performance ▶
This development F-16C, owned by Lockheed Martin, is regularly displayed with wingtip 'Smokewinders'.

▲ Weapons for the 21st century
This F-16C is carrying the latest AIM-120 active-radar guided missiles on the wingtips, in addition to a heavy underwing load.

FACTS AND FIGURES

▶ The F-16C was part of a USAF two-ship hunter-killer 'Wild Weasel' team with the F-4G Phantom II.

▶ In the Gulf War an F-16D scored the first ever AIM-120 victory over an Iraqi MiG-25.

▶ The F-16D is a two-seater development of the 'C' and replaces the earlier F-16B.

▶ The F-16N was an ultra-agile stripped-down F-16C used by the US Navy for air-combat training of pilots.

▶ Block 25 series F-16Cs are the lightest members of the Fighting Falcon family.

▶ The ultimate F-16C Block 50D can fire the AGM-88 HARM anti-radar missile.

PROFILE

Next-generation Fighting Falcon

Unrivalled as the world's most successful warplane of recent times, the Lockheed Martin (formerly General Dynamics) F-16 Fighting Falcon replaced large numbers of F-104 Starfighters, F-4 Phantoms and F-5 Freedom Fighters serving with air arms across Europe, Southeast Asia and, in particular, the USA. More than 3500 F-16s of all variants have been delivered since the USAF received its first aircraft on 6 January 1979, and it has seen service with 20 air arms.

The current production single-seat F-16C and the two-seat F-16D introduced progressive high-tech changes to give added

capabilities for night flying and new operational roles. These included the Hughes APG-68 multi-mode radar, provision for the AGM-65D Maverick missile and a variety of avionics upgrades. The General Electric F110 afterburning turbofan produces 22.24 kN more thrust than the Pratt & Whitney engine in the F-16A/B.

In August 1994 the F-16 was selected by the USAF for the SEAD (Suppression of Enemy

Above: The prototype F-16C first flew in 1984, and could be identified from the F-16A by its lengthened dorsal fairing, dorsal blade antenna and a new gold-tinted cockpit canopy.

Air Defences) role, while a continuing development programme may see a tactical reconnaissance RF-16 built.

Above: After reduction of the USAF A-10 Thunderbolt II force, the F-16C, armed with the AGM-65 Maverick ASM, has become a useful anti-tank and close-support aircraft.

F-16C FIGHTING FALCON

This early production F-16C carries the markings of the 50th Fighter Wing stationed at Hahn Air Base, Germany. This unit received LANTIRN-equipped examples in 1990.

A graphite/epoxy cover protects the VHF/FM antenna, which has extended operating range and is incorporated into the fin leading edge.

This aircraft wears the standard two-tone grey air-defence colour scheme with low-visibility national markings. It has a 'fighting falcon' insignia on the tail fin plus the 'HR' Hahn Air Base code in black.

F-16C/D models have an enlarged base at the rear of the fin to incorporate a Dalmo Victor AN/ALR-69 radar-warning receiver.

A large head-up display (HUD) dominates the cockpit, with the throttle control on the left and sidestick flying control on the right. The pilot sits on a McDonnell Douglas ACES II zero-zero ejection seat which is reclined at 30° to help withstand high g forces.

There are up to nine weapon pylons – six under the wings, one under the fuselage and two wingtip missile rails.

A radome covers the nose-mounted Westinghouse AN/APG-68(V) pulse-Doppler multi-mode, digital fire-control radar. This incorporates the Westinghouse Advanced Programmable Signal Processor on the latest aircraft.

During a mid-life upgrade, some USAF F-16C/Ds are being fitted with a new modular mission computer and the Lockheed Martin Enhanced Envelope Gunsight in the cockpit.

The air-conditioned cockpit is covered by a one-piece bubble canopy. Gold film on the inside dissipates radar energy, which reduces the radar cross-section.

A large engine intake, with a special splitter plate designed to reduce radar signature, is positioned under the fuselage.

F-16C Fighting Falcon

Type: single-seat multi-role fighter

Powerplant: one 122.77-kN (27,263-lb-thrust) General Electric F110-GE-100 or Pratt & Whitney F100-P-220 afterburning turbofan

Maximum speed: 2124 km/h (1320 mph) clean at 12,190 m (40,000 ft)

Initial climb rate: 15,240 m/min (50,000 fpm)

Combat radius: 547 km (340 miles) on a hi-lo-hi mission with six 454-kg (1000-lb) bombs

Service ceiling: 15,240 m (50,000 ft)

Weights: maximum take-off 19,187 kg (42,300 lb)

Armament: one internal six-barrel 20-mm cannon and up to 9276 kg (20,450 lb) of ordnance

Dimensions:
span	9.45 m	(31 ft)
length	15.03 m	(16 ft 6 in)
height	5.09 m	(16 ft 8 in)
wing area	28.87 m²	(311 sq ft)

COMBAT DATA

MAXIMUM SPEED

Although the F-16 is slightly slower in 'clean' configuration at altitude than its competitors, this represents little disadvantage in combat when carrying a large fuel and weapons load.

F-16C FIGHTING FALCON 2124 km/h	(1320 mph)
MiG-29 'FULCRUM-A' 2445 km/h	(1519 mph)
MIRAGE 2000C 2338 km/h	(1453 mph)

INITIAL CLIMB RATE

Although the F-16C has a lower climb rate, it has similar manoeuvrability to the MiG-29. Unlike the MiG and Mirage, the F-16C performs equally well in air defence and attack roles.

MiG-29 'FULCRUM-A' 19,800 m/min	(64,960 fpm)
MIRAGE 2000C 17,060 m/min	(55,971 fpm)
F-16C FIGHTING FALCON 15,240 m/min	(50,000 fpm)

WEAPONS LOAD

The MiG-29 and Mirage 2000C are optimised for the interceptor/fighter role and specialised versions must be bought for ground attack. With its heavy weapon load the F-16C is not as restricted.

9276 kg	(20,450 lb) F-16C FIGHTING FALCON
3000 kg	(6614 lb) MiG-29 'FULCRUM-A'
6300 kg	(13,889 lb) MIRAGE 2000C

Colours of the Fighting Falcon

■ **BAHRAIN:** Four F-16D two-seat trainers are used to convert pilots onto the eight F-16C fighters purchased by Bahrain.

■ **GREECE:** At least 80 F-16C/Ds are operated by Greece. Together with Turkish machines they are the only C/Ds with braking parachutes.

■ **TURKEY:** Turkey has purchased a total of 160 C and D model F-16s. Greece and Turkey strive to match each other's forces.

■ **UNITED STATES:** Most USAF F-16s are painted in two-tone grey camouflage, but some have special markings.

LOCKHEED MARTIN
F-16N AGGRESSOR

● Threat simulation ● Adversary training ● Navy dogfighter

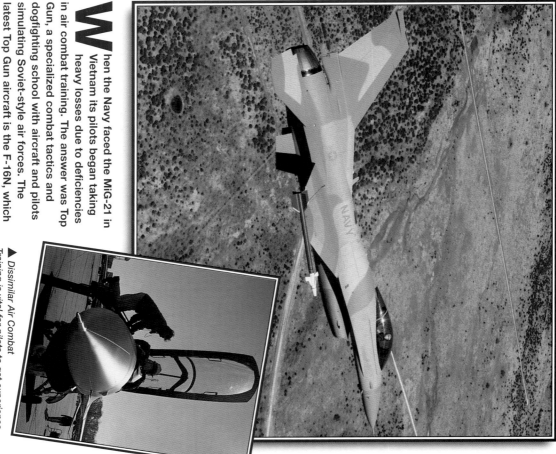

W hen the Navy faced the MiG-21 in Vietnam its pilots began taking heavy losses due to deficiencies in air combat training. The answer was Top Gun, a specialized combat tactics and dogfighting school with aircraft and pilots simulating Soviet-style air forces. The latest Top Gun aircraft is the F-16N, which replicates the latest Soviet superfighters, such as the MiG-29, in high-g dogfights over California.

▲ Dissimilar Air Combat Training is vital for pilots to get experience flying against a realistic adversary. The F-16N provides one of the most challenging opponents in the air today.

LOCKHEED MARTIN F-16N AGGRESSOR

▲ Red driver
The pilots at Top Gun brief their opponents on the strengths and weaknesses of the F-16N.

▲ Stunning performance
Comparable in most respects to the MiG-29, the F-16N is slightly smaller. It also lacks a helmet-mounted sight, infrared tracking and a fifth-generation missile like the R-73.

▲ Warsaw Pact paint scheme
Top Gun aircraft are painted in Soviet-style camouflage with individual aircraft numbers.

▲ Flight line
Ready to fly, the F-16N is armed only with an acquisition Sidewinder missile for simulating missile lock-on.

▲ Smoking approach
The primary opponent for the F-16N is the F-14 Tomcat, a large fighter with smoky engines that make it highly visible. The F-16N is extremely hard to spot in combat, since it is small and its engine is smokeless. The MiG-21 was similar in this respect.

FACTS AND FIGURES

➤ The F-16N is one of the best performing F-16 variants since it is slightly lighter than the other types.

➤ Navy pilots had a lower loss rate in Vietnam after Top Gun training.

➤ Top Gun formerly operated the Israeli Kfir as a MiG-23 simulator.

➤ In a dogfight, the F-16N can pull 9g turns, and is probably one of the finest dogfighting aircraft in the world.

➤ The Air Force Aggressor squadrons formerly operated the F-16, too.

➤ The Air Force has recently disbanded its Aggressor squadrons.

PROFILE

Top Gun war games

C onsidered the ultimate version in terms of agility in the whole F-16 series, the F-16N was the the Navy's prime Aggressor fighter. Previous aircraft for the role were the A-4, simulating the MiG-21, and the F-21 (Kfir C-2), simulating the MiG-23. Wearing Soviet-style codes and colour schemes, the F-16Ns of VF-126, VF-45 and VF-43 trained the fast-jet pilots of the Navy.

The highly agile, stripped-down Fighting Falcons took the role of MiG-29 adversaries, as they flew realistic combat dogfights against the Navy's

frontline F-14 and F/A-18 fighter jets. In order to replicate Soviet flying tactics, the Aggressor pilots studied the combat techniques of the former Eastern Bloc. Plus, to bring the F-16N on par with new Soviet fighters like the MiG-29 and Su-27, the aircraft was stripped of all excess weight, internal gun and radar. The F-16 has superior dogfight performance to the F-14 and F/A-18, so instructors could give student pilots an increasingly high workload. Pilots loved flying these practice missions in the great F-16N.

Above: With the perceived threat from the former Soviet Union no longer existent, U.S. forces have disbanded their Aggressor style units. This may well turn out to be a false comfort, since a large number of nations are now using MiG-29s with R-73 missiles, and several nations are updating MiG-21s to a very high standard.

Above: There are still few fighters that can match the staggering performance of an F-16N, especially in a turning fight at medium levels.

F-16N Fighting Falcon

Type: single-seat lightweight adversary and threat simulation aircraft

Powerplant: one General Electric F110-GE-100 turbofan rated at 122.78 kN (27,625 lb thrust)

Maximum speed: 2448 km/h (1521 mph)

Initial climb rate: more than 15,235 m/min (49,990 fpm)

Ferry range: 3862 km (2400 miles)

Combat radius: 924 km (574 miles)

Service ceiling: 15,240 m (50,000 ft)

Weapons: two AIM-9 Sidewinder missiles.

Weight: maximum take-off 11,348 kg (25,018 lb)

Dimensions: span 9.45 m (31 ft)
length 15.04 m (49 ft 4 in)
height 5.08 m (16 ft 8 in)
wing area 27.87 m² (300 sq ft)

ACTION DATA

SPEED

There is little to choose between the F-16N and its main adversaries in terms of speed. In a real air combat situation all-out maximum speed is of little consequence. Performance is more likely to vary according to the amount of fuel a pilot has left, his weapon load and the distance from his home base.

F-16N FIGHTING FALCON	2448 km/h (1521 mph)
MiG-29 'FULCRUM'	2440 km/h (1516 mph)
KFIR C-2	2433 km/h (1512 mph)

g-LIMITS

In a turning fight the F-16N is lethal, simulating the excellent MiG-29 very well. In fact, the MiG-29 is limited to 9g's (below Mach 0.85) only for service use; display pilots are cleared to 11g's in the aircraft. The Kfir simulated the MiG-23 well, since it also had a g limit of about 7.5 depending on speed.

MiG-29 'FULCRUM' +9
F-16N FIGHTING FALCON +9
KFIR C-2 +7.5

CLIMB RATE

The performance of the F-16N is superb in the climb, even better than standard F-16s. The MiG-29 is better still, thanks to the power of the superb RD-33 engine. This has a much lower interval between major servicing than the F110 in the F-16N. The Kfir has a reasonable rate of climb considering that its engine and airframe technology are a generation behind.

MiG-29 'FULCRUM' 19,795 m/min (64,945 fpm)
F-16N FIGHTING FALCON 15,235 m/min (49,990 fpm)
KFIR C-2 13,990 m/min (45,900 fpm)

Like its Air Force counterpart, the F-16N has a tail-mounted radar warning receiver antenna. This gives pilots an aural and visual warning (through the head-up display) of a hostile radar acquiring the aircraft.

Long periods of high-g manoeuvring caused many fatigue problems, and the F-16N fleet was grounded in 1991 due to wing fatigue cracking.

The F-16N is powered by a single F110 turbofan, giving an outstanding thrust-to-weight ratio.

This F-16N is carrying a live AIM-9L model Sidewinder missile. Usually, the aircraft carries an acquisition round with no fins fitted, which gives the pilot an aural warning tone of missile lock-on when he acquires a target.

When practicing dogfighting, the pilot will look for aircraft using a guidance marker on his head-up display, provided by the radar. The missile seeker head is guided to the target by the radar.

One piece of equipment frequently carried by the F-16N on its missile pylon is the ACMI (Air Combat Maneuvering Instrumentation) pod, which sends performance data from the aircraft to ground monitoring stations.

F-16N FIGHTING FALCON

Used by VF-43, VF-45 and VF-126 of the Navy, the F-16N was numerically the most important Aggressor type in service, having replaced the F-21 and most TA-4s.

Unlike most late model F-16s, the F-16N has the APG-66 radar, which was originally fitted to the F-16A. This is less capable than the F-16C's APG-68.

The gun is left off of the F-16N to save weight. In a real dogfight, other F-16s can engage targets at close range with the Vulcan M-61 20-mm cannon.

Aggressor trainers

TA-4J SKYHAWK: Stripped of much of their earlier equipment and fitted with an increased-thrust version of the J52 turbojet, the TA-4J was a highly effective dogfighter.

F-5E TIGER II: With its excellent subsonic acceleration, small size and good sustained turn rate at medium speeds, the F-5E was a formidable Aggressor in the class of the MiG-21.

F-21 KFIR C-2: This Israeli-built fighter was fast and accelerated rapidly, but it did not have high performance in sustained turns, making it a good simulator for the MiG-23.

LOCKHEED MARTIN (ROCKWELL)

AC-130U SPECTRE

- Airborne gunship ● Special Forces ● Improved model

After its successful combat debut in Vietnam, the AC-130 Spectre became the standard USAF night attack gunship. The early 'Herc' gunships were subsequently upgraded, up-gunned and, more recently, replaced by newer airframes. The ultimate model is the AC-130U, which carries fewer guns than its predecessor but, with its computer-controlled 105-mm howitzer, can bring down devastating firepower on the enemy.

▲ *Ungainly in looks, the AC-130U is extremely simple in concept. The airborne gunship looks set to remain in the front line for the future, providing fire support for ground troops.*

▲ State of the art
The AC-130 was used to develop the gunship role in Vietnam. The AC-130U is equipped with the most advanced avionics available.

Old colours ▲
Early AC-130Us wore the old-style European One colour scheme. Later models wear an overall Gunship Gray camouflage.

▲ Test flights
Equipped with a nose-mounted probe, the prototype AC-130U undertook a long series of developmental flights. Crews found the aircraft was ideal for the role.

▲ Special crews
Because of the unique requirements of AC-130U operations, only the very best Hercules crews are selected to fly the specialised aircraft.

▲ Broadside attack
Retained on the latest Hercules gunship variant is the positioning of the cannon and guns along the port side of the fuselage. During combat missions the AC-130U maintains a circular orbit to maximise fire accuracy.

FACTS AND FIGURES

▶ Thirteen aircraft were delivered to the 16th Special Operations Squadron at Hurlburt Field, Florida, in 1995.

▶ Rockwell was awarded a $155 million contract to develop the new C-130 gunship for the USAF.

▶ The radar of the AC-130U is derived from that of the F-15E Strike Eagle.

▶ The first AC-130U was rolled out on 20 December 1990.

▶ Flight trials were conducted at Edwards AFB during 1992–93.

▶ The calibre of the guns aboard the aircraft ranges from 25 mm to 105 mm.

PROFILE

Prowler of the battlefield

In the Vietnam air war, one of the more important developments was that of the aerial gunship. This involved heavily-armed converted transport aircraft orbiting a point and delivering deadly firepower with great precision.

From its origins in the crude 'Spooky' AC-47s left over from an earlier war, 'hosing' the target with multiple Miniguns, the gunship concept has developed into a highly sophisticated combination of sensors and weapons able to bring each round to the target. The AC-130A of the Vietnam era had up to eight machine guns. The AC-130U developed by Rockwell International has only three guns – one 25-mm multi-barrelled cannon, a 40-mm Bofors and a 105-mm howitzer. However, the guns can be brought to bear with greater precision – even engaging two targets at once – by the four mission computers and the extremely accurate GPS-based navigation system. For self-defence, the AC-130U is equipped with powerful jammers, together with a number of radar-warning antennas. On the underside are three combined chaff/flare launchers.

Although the AC-130U has yet to prove itself in combat, the other post-Vietnam version, the AC-130H, saw action in Grenada in 1983, Panama in 1989 and over Iraq during the Gulf War. It has gained a reputation as an efficient destroyer of enemy vehicles, and troops.

Left: Retained on the new model is the 'Spectre' nose art. This dates back to the earliest days of gunship operations over Vietnam.

Above: The AC-130U can be distinguished from earlier models by the lack of the distinctive nose-mounted radome.

AC-130U HERCULES

The gunship has proved itself in Vietnam and the Gulf War. The latest development of the Hercules gunship is the AC-130U, equipped with state-of-the-art avionics.

Dramatic improvements in the survivability for the crew have been made since the first AC-130A was developed. Crews are now surrounded by Spectra ceramic armour and the fuel is carried in explosion-suppressing fuel tanks.

AC-130Us are unique among the gunship Hercules variants in that they are based on the C-130H. They thus feature the strengthened wing box and derated 3363-kW (4500-hp) Allison T56-15 engines.

Required to operate over hostile territory, the AC-130U is equipped with an extensive array of electronic countermeasures equipment. This includes wing-mounted ALQ-172 jammers and less sophisticated chaff/flare dispensers.

The heavy punch of the AC-130U is provided by the 105-mm howitzer and the 40-mm Bofors cannon. They are positioned in the rear of the fuselage. Situated opposite these guns are racks for the vast amount of ammunition required.

The observer's station is on the rear loading ramp. This crewman is equipped with a small clear dome from which to observe firing by the aircraft. Firing corrections can then be reported to the pilot.

AC-130U Spectre

Type: aerial gunship

Powerplant: four 3363-kW (4500-hp) Allison T56-A-15 turboprops

Cruising speed: 602 km/h (373 mph)

Initial climb rate: 597 m/min (1960 fpm)

Range: 7876 km (4883 miles) with maximum fuel

Service ceiling: 10,060 m (33,000 ft)

Weights: operating weight 34,356 kg (75,583 lb); maximum take-off 79,380 kg (174,636 lb)

Armament: GAU-12/U 25-mm cannon with 3000 rounds; 40-mm Bofors cannon; 105-mm howitzer

Dimensions:
span	40.41 m (132 ft 7 in)
length	29.79 m (97 ft 9 in)
height	11.66 m (38 ft 3 in)
wing area	162.12 m² (1744 sq ft)

GUNSHIP HISTORY

'STINGER': Having developed the concept of airborne artillery with the AC-47, the USAF looked round for a more suitable aircraft to lift the necessary equipment into the air. The result was the conversion of the large twin-boom C-119 Flying Boxcar. Emerging as the AC-119K 'Stinger' (pictured below), the aircraft was soon pressed into combat against the North Vietnamese. The 'Stinger' was highly successful in this role, although limitations of the design soon became apparent. The aircraft was extremely vulnerable to ground fire, and soon operations switched to night-time to offer some degree of protection.

'SPECTRE': Already a well proven transport aircraft, the Lockheed C-130 was soon adapted to the gunship role. Known as the AC-130A 'Spectre' (below), the design was one of the most valued aircraft in Vietnam for supporting ground forces. Equipped with Miniguns, the 'Spectre' proved to be the ideal platform for 'truck-busting' along the network of trails that the North Vietnamese used for transporting troops and materials. The 'Spectre' took part in some of the final missions of the war, and after returning to the United States remained in front-line service with the USAF Special Operations Squadrons.

Legendary Lockheed C-130s

■ **AUSTRALIA:** Providing the heavy lift element of Australia's air force are C-130Hs, which continue in front-line service.

■ **FRANCE:** Operated alongside France's C.160 Transalls, the Hercules has been used on countless French combat operations in Africa.

■ **NEW ZEALAND:** The C-130H has been in production for over 30 years. The first C-130H built was sold to New Zealand in 1965.

■ **SAUDI ARABIA:** Resplendent in an overall desert camouflage, Saudi Arabian C-130s are often used as VIP transports.

LOCKHEED MARTIN

C-130H HERCULES

- Four-engine turboprop transport ● Used worldwide

There have been so many versions of the 'Charlie One-Thirty' during its 40 years of service that it is hard to imagine it ever being grounded because of old age. Over the years it has undertaken dozens of useful tasks ranging from maritime patrol to secret agent support. Its main task, however, remains in the STOL transport role for which it was designed. The prototype first flew in August 1954, and the C-130H version was the biggest seller.

▲ The 'Herc' was designed to meet a US Air Force requirement for a tactical transport able to use rough airstrips and carry 11,317 kg (24,950 lb) of cargo, 92 ground troops or 64 paratroops.

LOCKHEED MARTIN **C-130H HERCULES**

▼ Desert airlift
The Gulf War of 1990-91 brought together numerous C-130s from several nations as part of the Coalition force.

First exports ▶
The first export customer was Australia, which received 12 C-130As in 1958 and later batches of both the E and H models.

▲ Providing relief
Worldwide, the C-130's airlift tasks today often involve mercy flights and supply drops.

▲ Stretched 'Dash-30s'
Originally known as the C-130H(S), C-130H-30s have been delivered to several air forces including those of Algeria, France, Indonesia and Saudi Arabia.

▼ Swedish 'Hercs' over Bosnia
Due to the country's neutrality, few units of Sweden's air force deploy overseas. An exception has been its C-130 unit, F7, which deployed to the former Yugoslavia.

FACTS AND FIGURES

▶ There is also a civilian version of the C-130, which is known as the L-100.

▶ US Air Force C-130s have seen combat in Vietnam, Grenada, Panama and the Persian Gulf.

▶ The US Navy tested a scale model of an amphibious version of the C-130.

▶ New Zealand's air force regularly uses its C-130Hs in Antarctica; the USAF also deploys ski-equipped 'Hs' to the Arctic.

▶ The first USAF C-130Hs were search-and-rescue HC-130Hs built in 1964.

▶ RAF Hercules are based on the C-130H with British radar and other equipment.

PROFILE

H-model Herky-bird

The C-130H was fitted with a redesigned and strengthened wing box, additional power (provided by uprated engines), and better brakes to distinguish it from the earlier main production variant of the Hercules. The first H model aircraft flew on November 19, 1964. Two years later, examples were delivered to the Royal New Zealand Air Force, the initial customer for the new model in Lockheed-Martin's already impressive catalog of aircraft.

The C-130H has since entered service with over 50 air forces around the world and although originally intended for export only, has also been ordered by the United States Air Force.

An important version of the C-130H was the Dash-30 which has a 4.57-m (15-ft) fuselage extension to significantly increase payloads without any detrimental effect on performance. The first examples of this model were delivered to Indonesia in September 1980 and this stretched version has

Above: The basic soundness of the original 1950s design is reflected in the fact that the C-130H and earlier versions have been adapted for roles as diverse as gunships and mobile hospitals.

since found wide appeal.

Built-in adaptability has also enabled a number of other major modifications to be made to the basic C-130H for a variety of extra roles.

C-130H HERCULES

The Algerian air force operates 12 C-130Hs that were delivered between 1981 and 1990, replacing Antonov An-12s, on the understanding that the aircraft would not be used on operations against Polisario guerillas.

C-130 Hercules in the transport role generally fly with a crew of five: aircraft commander, co-pilot, flight engineer, navigator and loadmaster.

The bulbous 'Pinocchio' nose of the C-130H contains a navigational radar set.

The new Allison T56-A-15 engines introduced on the C-130H removed the need for rocket-assisted take-off equipment as fitted to some earlier models. Four-blade propellers are standard.

External fuel tanks, each holding 5150 litres (1360 gallons), are fitted between the engines of each wing and are standard on all C-130Hs.

Algerian air force C-130s carry quasi-civilian registrations that are used when the aircraft fly overseas. The camouflage is a USAF-style, Vietnam-era scheme.

The rear loading ramp gives access to a hold capable of accommodating over 19 tonnes of cargo. A Low-Altitude Parachute Extraction System (LAPES) is used to make drops in combat zones.

Above: Cameroon, another operator of the C-130H-30, has its aircraft painted in a sand camouflage scheme. These aircraft often carry civilians during the Haj pilgrimage season.

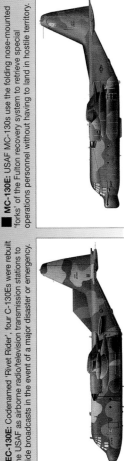

The many labours of Hercules

■ **HERCULES W. MK 2 'SNOOPY':** Modified in 1973 from a standard Hercules C Mk.1, XV208 replaced a Vickers Varsity operated by the RAF Meteorological Flight for weather research.

■ **EC-130E:** Codenamed 'Rivet Rider', four C-130Es were rebuilt by the USAF as airborne radio/television transmission stations to provide broadcasts in the event of a major disaster or emergency.

■ **MC-130E:** USAF MC-130s use the folding nose-mounted 'forks' of the Fulton recovery system to retrieve special operations personnel without having to land in hostile territory.

C-130H

Type: medium-range STOL transport

Powerplant: four 3362-kW (4500-hp) Allison T56-A-15 turboprop engines

Maximum speed: 618 km/h (383 mph)

Service ceiling: 10,058 m (33,000 ft)

Range: 3791 km (2350 miles) with maximum payload

Maximum payload: 19,350 kg (42,570 lb)

Weights: empty 34,357 kg (75,585 lb); loaded 79,380 kg (174,636 lb)

Dimensions:
span	40.41 m (132 ft 6 in)
length	29.70 m (97 ft 9 in)
height	11.66 m (34 ft 3 in)
wing area	162.12 m² (1744 sq ft)

ACTION DATA

SPEED

The jet-powered Kawasaki C-1 has a higher top speed than the An-12 and C-130, both of which are powered by turboprop engines. While the C-130 has a considerably lower top speed than the An-12, it has a better range, especially with a maximum fuel load on board.

C-130H	618 km/h (383 mph)
An-12	777 km/h (482 mph)
KAWASAKI C-1	806 km/h (500 mph)

PAYLOAD

The C-130 and C-1 have a rear loading ramp, while the An-12 has a pair of clamshell doors. The C-130 and C-1 are able to lower their ramps in flight so that troops and equipment can be deployed, usually with the aid of parachutes. The C-130 and An-12 are large enough to carry a medium-sized armoured vehicle.

C-130H	**An-12**	**KAWASAKI C-1**
19,350 kg (42,570 lb)	20,000 kg (44,000 lb)	11,900 kg (26,180 lb)

TAKE-OFF RUN

The engines on the jet-powered C-1 are positioned so that the exhaust is directed over the lower surface of the aircraft's flaps to provide more lift. Take-off distance is therefore shortened. Short take-off runs are particularly important for a tactical transport that needs to land in confined spaces near the battlefield.

KAWASAKI C-1	**An-12**	**C-130H**
640 m (2100 ft)	700 m (2300 ft)	1000 m (3300 ft)

LOCKHEED MARTIN/BOEING

F-22 RAPTOR

● Stealthy superjet ● World's most expensive fighter ● Highly agile

The Lockheed Martin/Boeing F-22 represents a quantum leap in fighter design. Incorporating the latest radar-evading stealth technology, computer-controlled manoeuvrability at extreme angles of attack, thrust-vectoring and a futuristic 'glass' cockpit, it can 'guarantee' shooting down any current enemy fighter every time. Each F-22 costs $150 million, but will be the ace of aces in 21st-century warfare.

▲ Lockheed test pilot Dave Ferguson conducted much of the extended flight test programme. Right from the start, the aircraft showed blistering performance and amazing agility for its size.

LOCKHEED MARTIN/BOEING F-22 RAPTOR

PHOTO FILE

LOCKHEED MARTIN/BOEING F-22 RAPTOR

▼ Super agility
The F-22 has a large number of flight control surfaces, which are controlled by a computer.

▲ Internal weapons
Unlike current fighters, the F-22 carries its weapons in internal bays along the sides and bottom of the fuselage. For a missile shot the doors snap open and the missile is ejected clear of the aircraft into the airflow before its rocket motor fires.

▲ Thrust vectoring
First seen on the Harrier V/STOL fighter, thrust vectoring has been applied to the F-22 for improved manoeuvrability.

▲ Stealth design
Many of the surfaces on the YF-22 have a sawtooth edge, such as that at the front of the cockpit. This helps stop radar from detecting the aircraft.

▲ Technology demonstrator
Two YF-22s were built to demonstrate the technology intended for the production F-22 fighter, which will look more sleek.

FACTS AND FIGURES

➤ The F119 engine's two-dimensional nozzles can be vectored 20 per cent up or down to increase agility.

➤ The YF-22 prototype made its first flight on 29 September 1990.

➤ Lockheed's proposal for the F-22 was 20,000 pages long and weighed 2041 kg (4500 lb).

➤ The F-22's 'glass' cockpit took 17,500 hours of engineering work to design.

➤ Northrop's YF-23 fighter lost out to the F-22 in a fly-off competition.

➤ Lockheed people refer to the F-22 as 'Alien' because, like the science-fiction monster, it strikes quickly and silently.

PROFILE

21st century superfighter

The F-22 pilot will have the world's best fighter in his hands. This remarkable jet will blaze across the sky pushed by F119 engines, staying at supersonic speed all the way to the objective.

The engines are 100 per cent new and are the most advanced science can make. The F-22's Westinghouse AN/APG-77 fire-control radar is also new, and pushes back the boundaries. Speed and marksmanship mean real trouble for any enemy stalked by the potent F-22 with its deadly missiles.

Most amazingly, the F-22 can turn and snap like a pit-bull terrier. The 'final frontier' in combat aviation is the realm of close-quarters agility. The jet jock who can turn in the least amount of space, or shoot in one direction while flying in another, will win the fight.

Advances in stealth technology have been incorporated into the F-22 making it almost invisible to ground radar, or enemy aircraft, whilst it's fly-by-wire control system and colour head-up display give the pilot all the electronic help currently available.

YF-22 PAV No.1

Lockheed Martin/Boeing built two prototype air vehicles (PAVs) for the US Air Forces Advanced Tactical Fighter programme. The YF-22 was eventually selected in preference to the even more radical Northrop/McDonnell Douglas YF-23.

The F-22's advanced cockpit is the manned end of the most advanced fighter avionics system ever built. Flight control, engines, radar, weapons and countermeasures will all be fully integrated and computer-controlled.

The YF-22 is equipped with a Westinghouse LPI – Low Probability of Intercept – unit, which has very long range but is difficult for an enemy to detect.

No matter how high the technology, there will be occasions when air combat depends on seeing the enemy. The F-22's clear canopy gives the pilot marvellous all-round visibility.

The key edges and surfaces of the YF-22 are not only angled to deflect radar beams but are also coated in radar-absorbent material to increase stealthiness.

The F-22's striking front view is dominated by diamond shapes. The front fuselage, intakes and tails share the same 48° angle, deflecting and absorbing enemy radar and making the aircraft very difficult to detect.

The F-22 is the very best, and needs to be. Its stunning price tag of $150 million is proof of its value.

The diamond-shaped intakes follow the alignment of other surfaces, while the 'S'-shaped trunk shields the highly reflective engine compressor blades from prying enemy radar.

The F-22's amazing agility is achieved by computer-controlled flaperons, ailerons, tailplanes and rudders which combine with thrust-vectoring nozzles.

The F-22's control surfaces are supplemented by thrust-vectoring jet nozzles, which can be vectored up and down by just under 20°.

Power is provided by a pair of Pratt & Whitney F119 low-bypass turbofans. They are immensely powerful and also very efficient, allowing the F-22 to cruise supersonically without afterburning.

The F-22 is an air superiority fighter. For maximum stealth it will carry its missiles in bays in the side of and under the fuselage.

COMBAT DATA

CRUISE SPEED

The F-22 does not have as high a maximum speed as its contemporaries or even earlier fighters like the F-15. But it is notable for the extremely high speed at which it can cruise economically, and it can easily sustain supersonic speeds without afterburning.

F-22 RAPTOR
1900 km/h (1181 mph)

EF 2000
1350 km/h (839 mph)

RAFALE
1350 km/h (839 mph)

COMBAT RADIUS

The F-22 is a big aircraft, larger even than the F-15 which it has been designed to replace. It carries a lot of fuel, and with its advanced, extremely efficient engines it can make an interception a very long way from its base.

F-22 RAPTOR
more than 2500 km (1553 miles)

RAFALE
1800 km (1118 miles)
with external tanks

EF 2000
more than 1000 km (620 miles) with external tanks

AIR-TO-AIR WEAPONS

All three fighters will be equipped with advanced radars and the latest fire-and-forget missiles. The F-22's LPI radar has exceptional range even when operating at very low power to avoid detection by the enemy.

RAFALE
1 x 30-mm cannon
2 x short-range and
8 x medium-range missiles

F-22 RAPTOR
1 x 20-mm cannon
4-6 x short-range and
4 x medium-/long-range missiles

EF 2000
1 x 27-mm cannon
2-4 short-range and
8 x medium-/long-range missiles

F-22A Raptor

Type: advanced-technology fighter

Powerplant: two 155.69-kN (35,030-lb-thrust) Pratt & Whitney F119-PW-100 turbofans with afterburners

Maximum speed: over 2000 km/h (1243 mph)

Range: more than 5700 km (3542 miles) with maximum fuel

Service ceiling: over 15,000 m (49,200 ft)

Weights: empty 14,061 kg (31,000 lb); loaded 26,308 kg (58,000 lb)

Armament: one Martin Marietta M61A1 Vulcan 20-mm cannon with 500 rounds; four AIM-120A AMRAAM missiles in belly weapons bay; four AIM-9M Sidewinder missiles in side bays

Dimensions:
span   13.56 m (44 ft 6 in)
length   19.05 m (62 ft 6 in)
height   5.39 m (17 ft 8 in)
wing area   78.00 m² (840 sq ft)

First look, first launch, first kill

1 LONG-RANGE RADAR: The F-22 has stealthy radar with long range. It locks onto the Su-27 long before the enemy knows it is there, and fires off an AIM-120 AMRAAM missile when locked on.

2 STEALTH MEANS SAFETY: The F-22's stealthy design makes it very difficult to detect, even by the powerful radar carried by fighters such as the Sukhoi Su-27 'Flanker'.

3 NO ESCAPE: The first time an enemy knows it is under attack is when it detects the incoming missile, by which time it is too late.

4 FIRE AND FORGET: With modern missiles such as AMRAAM an aircraft can simply fire and turn away, never getting within the enemy's missile or even detection range.

LOCKHEED MARTIN

X-35/F-35 JSF

● Single-seat strike fighter ● Multi-service ● Service entry 2008

he X-35, Lockheed Martin's winning contender in the Joint Strike Fighter contest, is the product of the biggest military aircraft procurement programme in history. The aircraft embodies a wide range of capabilities that will fulfil the requirements of the US Air Force, US Navy, US Marine Corps and the British armed forces well into the twenty-first century. Twenty-two development aircraft are currently in production.

▶ US Congressional pressure produced the JSF: an amalgamation of the CALF (Common Affordable Lightweight Fighter) and JAST (Joint Advanced Strike Technology) programmes. The USN, USAF and USMC require 2852 examples.

LOCKHEED MARTIN X-35/F-35 JSF

▶ Conventional demonstrator
The first version of the X-35 to fly was the conventional X-35A, which validated the basic handling characteristics.

Colour cockpit ▶
The F-35C cockpit will have full-colour displays and a sidestick.

▶ Lift fan and vectoring nozzle
To provide vertical lift (required in the naval JSF variant), the X-35 has a lift fan shaft-driven from the main engine – behind the cockpit – which means a separate lift engine is not required.

▶ Ultra-manoeuvrable
A vectored engine nozzle and computer-controlled power-by-wire flight controls make the JSF virtually spin-proof.

▶ Flexible refuelling options
The X-35 prototypes had a USAF-style boom and receptacle refuelling system, but British, US Navy and Marine Corps F-35s will have a retractable probe.

FACTS AND FIGURES

▶ Lockheed Martin's proposal used design data purchased from the Russian builder of V/STOL aircraft, Yakovlev.

▶ Boeing's unsuccessful design for the JSF was designated X-32.

▶ Export potential for the JSF has been identified in several countries, including Australia, Canada, Germany and Spain.

▶ General Electric/Rolls-Royce and Pratt & Whitney are both developing interchangeable engines for the JSF under a unique arrangement.

▶ By 2011 the JSF production rate is expected to reach 122 per year, with manufacturers in the UK producing various elements.

21st century strike-fighter

The Joint Strike Fighter (JSF) will replace Harriers and Hornets, F-16s and A-10s within the US services and will likely equal the F-16 for export sales. More than 3000 are to be built for the US and UK alone, but this may eventually reach more than 6000 examples, with many nations almost certain to select it as their next fighter.

The JSF programme began in 1994, and by 1997 two manufacturers had been selected to produce two demonstrators each to prove their designs. Boeing's X-32

used a similar propulsion system to the Harrier, in a tailless delta configuration with a huge air intake under the nose. Lockheed Martin's X-35 looked more conventional, but the X-35B variant featured a 'lift fan' arrangement, a thrust-vectoring jet pipe and roll-control ducts. The winning X-35 design was the first ever aircraft to perform a short take-off, level supersonic dash, and vertical landing, all in a single flight.

The details of the actual F-35 will differ considerably from the

X-35s, as will the performance specifications. An estimate of the relative costs puts the USAF's conventional F-35A at $40 million, while the lift-fan and roll-control X-35B and C will be $50 million apiece. So far costs have been kept in check, but the most complicated, risky part of the programme has yet to be undertaken.

Left: One of the specific features of the X-35C is a stronger undercarriage able to take the added stresses of catapult take-offs and arrested landings.

The pilot's full-colour helmet-mounted display (HMD) will give him a 'through-the-floor' simulated display provided by three focal plane array sensors arranged to give a spherical field of view. This information is particularly useful during a vertical landing.

F-35B JSF

This is an artist's impression of the carrier version (CV) of the F-35. It will have larger wings and tail surfaces, strengthened undercarriage, arrester hook and other naval features for deck operations.

The use of a vectoring exhaust and a shaft-driven lift fan rather than a direct lift system avoids many of the problems associated with jet engines reingesting hot exhaust gases. Operations from carrier decks are also less hazardous for deck crew when using the lift fan system.

The F-35 has a noticeable bulge in its fuselage just in front of the air intakes. This works in conjunction with the swept-forward inlet lip to provide stealth.

The variant produced for the US Navy will have a larger wing area, 57.6 m² (620 sq ft) rather than 42.7 m² (460 sq ft), to allow greater range and better low-speed handling around the carrier.

Unlike other STOVL aircraft like the Harrier, the entire powered lift and propulsion system is controlled by computers, making the F-35 much easier to fly. As the aircraft transitions from wing-borne to jet-borne flight, the throttle and stick functions change automatically.

Replaced by the Joint Strike Fighter?

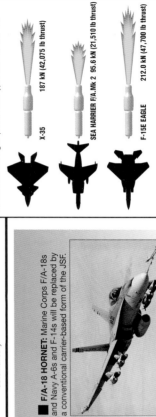

■ **HARRIER II:** The US Marine Corps will use the JSF to replace the AV-8B Harrier II. The RAF is also a potential customer.

■ **SEA HARRIER:** The Royal Navy is hoping to purchase up to 60 JSFs to operate from its aircraft-carriers.

■ **F-16 FIGHTING FALCON:** The largest single order for JSFs will come from the USAF, which requires 2036 to replace its large F-16 fleet.

■ **F/A-18 HORNET:** Marine Corps F/A-18s and Navy A-6s and F-14s will be replaced by a conventional carrier-based form of the JSF.

F-35 JSF (STOVL)

Type: advanced STOVL strike-fighter

Powerplant: one approx 187 kN (42,075 lb) thrust Pratt & Whitney F135 or General Electric/Rolls-Royce F136 turbofan engine

Maximum speed: Mach 1.5

Combat radius: 1112 km (691 miles)

Service ceiling: over 15,240 m (50,000 ft)

Weights: 13,921 kg (30,697 lb) empty; 22,680 kg (50,000 lb) loaded

Armament: Six AIM-120C AMRAAM or two AIM-120C AMRAAM and two 907-kg (2000 lb) JDAM in internal fuselage bay; provision for one 20-mm M61A2 rotary cannon; four underwing pylons with 2268 kg (5000 lb) capacity each

Dimensions: span   10.66 m (35 ft)
length   15.39 m (50 ft 6 in)
height   4.07 m (13 ft 4 in)
wing area 42.73 m² (460 sq ft)

ACTION DATA

JSF REQUIREMENTS

The USAF currently has the largest initial requirement for JSF aircraft, as the type will replace the large fleet of F-16s amassed by Air Combat Command during the 1980s. The JSF also represents the US Navy's long-awaited A-6 replacement, while the STOVL version will take over from Harriers in both the USMC and Royal Navy.

US NAVY 480

US AIR FORCE 1763

RAF/RN 150

US MARINE CORPS 609

MAXIMUM THRUST

Few figures have been released regarding the JSF's final specification. The X-35 prototype had an engine which developed around 187-kN (42,075-lb-thrust); production aircraft are likely to be a little more powerful. The X-35 falls between the thrust figures of the Harrier and higher performance types such as the F-15.

X-35   187 kN (42,075 lb thrust)

SEA HARRIER F/A.Mk 2   95.6 kN (21,510 lb thrust)

F-15E EAGLE   212.0 kN (47,700 lb thrust)

MARTIN

B-10

- Medium bomber ● Pioneering construction ● Pacific warrior

W hen the Martin B-10 joined the US Army in 1934, it was a revolution in every way. Suddenly, fabric-covered biplane bombers were replaced by a silvery, all-metal monoplane. And the bomber, once easy pickings for any enterprising fighter pilot, was now faster than any fighter. The B-10's moment of glory was brief, as other manufacturers followed its lead, but it stayed in service until the first days of the war in the Pacific.

▲ Martin was determined to break back into the bomber market after years of domination by other manufacturers. It built medium bombers for many years, based on the success of the B-10 family.

▼ America's finest
The B-10 was seen as America's first line of defence by the bomber strategists of the mid-1930s. B-10s remained in service until the introduction of B-17s and B-18s in the late 1930s.

▲ First of a new breed
The prototype XB-10 had an open cockpit but no nose turret. It first flew in the summer of 1933, with the first production B-10s seen a year later.

▼ World's finest
The USAAC was the envy of the world in 1934 when it first took delivery of the B-10. Between mid 1936 and 1939, 189 were exported.

▲ Finished product
In service the B-10 looked very modern with its aggressive gun turrets and clean fuselage design.

▼ Floatplane version
Martin produced the YB-12 floatplane for the Army for coastal defence, a responsibility previously held by the US Navy.

FACTS AND FIGURES

➤ In July/August 1934, 10 B-10s set a round-trip record from Washington to Alaska, flying a total of 13,341 km (8720 miles).

➤ The US Army's first order was for 48 B-10s costing a total of $2,440,000.

➤ The B-10 was not the first US all-metal bomber; this was the Boeing B-9.

➤ A total of 152 B-10 and B-12 bombers were delivered to the US Army, plus 190 to foreign allies.

➤ China flew its B-10 bombers on raids against Japan in 1938.

➤ Dutch pilots used their B-10 variant in action in the Dutch East Indies.

PROFILE

Martin's metal wonder-bomber

Martin's B-10 (and similar B-12) were the forerunners of advanced World War II bombers. The B-10 was an all-metal, twin-engine, mid-wing monoplane with retractable landing gear.

The pilot sat in the cockpit, the radio operator and one gunner in the dorsal turret, and one other gunner positioned in the rotating nose turret. Winner of the 1932 Collier Trophy for achievement, the B-10 featured such refinements as internal

bomb racks, Norden bombsight, enclosed crew stations and controllable pitch props.

A prototype had a turbo-supercharger fitted which gave a maximum speed of 343 km/h (212 mph), faster than any fighter aircraft in the US arsenal. Some B-12s were fitted with twin floats and used on coastal patrols. A Martin B-12 floatplane bomber was flown from Langley Field, Virginia, on 24 August 1935 to set three world payload-speed records. The aircraft also achieved

considerable export success, with sales to Argentina, China, The Netherlands, Thailand, Turkey and the USSR.

By the time the war began the B-10 was obsolete, but a handful of the Dutch East Indies aircraft were among the first aircraft to see action in the Pacific in December 1941.

Below: Despite the high performance of the standard B-10, the Army wanted more. It ordered the YB-10A, with turbosupercharged engines, and the YB-14, with powerful Twin Wasp engines.

Above: Aircraft design was moving at a tremendous pace in the 1930s. The B-10 looked far more modern than any aircraft in service in 1934, but was soon obsolete.

MODEL 139WH-1

The Martin 139WH was the export model of the B-10 bomber developed for The Netherlands. In all, 118 were produced in two versions and were among the very first aircraft to fight in the Pacific theatre against invading Japanese forces in December 1941.

The nose turret mounted a single machine gun. It was manually traversed, unlike the powered turrets in later bombers.

The rear cockpit was modified to accommodate a radio operator and a gunner operating a 7.62-mm (.30-cal.) machine gun. The bomb-bay was in the bottom of the fuselage under the front cockpit, with a second gun firing through the floor of the rear cockpit.

In the late 1930s, when fighters seemed like a remote threat to high-flying fast bombers and the Dutch forces in the Pacific faced little threat of attack, high-visibility paint schemes were common.

Among the many innovative features was a retractable tailwheel. A ski-wheel undercarriage was also tested.

The bomb-bay could accommodate an extra fuel tank to extend the impressive range even further. This was especially useful for operations in the Pacific. Total offensive armament was four 227-kg (500-lb) bombs, all of which were carried internally.

Martin B-10s were powered by a variety of Wright Cyclone engines, the prototype having the 503-kW (675-hp) R-1820-25. The YB-13 used the Pratt & Whitney R-1820-33 engine.

B-10B

Type: three-seat medium bomber

Powerplant: (B-10) two 578-kW (775-hp) Wright R-1820-33 Cyclone radial piston engines; (B-12) two 578-kW Pratt & Whitney R-1690-11 radial piston engines

Maximum speed: 343 km/h (212 mph)

Range: 1996 km (1240 miles)

Service ceiling: 7375 m (24,200 ft)

Weights: empty 4391 kg (9660 lb); maximum take-off 7439 kg (16,366 lb)

Armament: three 7.62-mm (.30-cal.) machine guns in nose and rear turrets and a ventral position, plus up to 1025 kg (2255 lb) of bombs in fuselage bomb-bay

Dimensions:
span	21.49 m (70 ft)
length	13.64 m (45 ft)
height	4.70 m (15 ft)
wing area	62.99 m² (678 sq ft)

COMBAT DATA

MAXIMUM SPEED

Although the B-10 was obsolete by the outbreak of war, it was still faster than some bombers in service, such as the SM.81, and when introduced it could outrun any fighter in the world.

B-10B	343 km/h (212 mph)
WELLINGTON Mk III	411 km/h (255 mph)
SM.81 SERIES 5	336 km/h (208 mph)

RANGE

For the long-range bombing missions to attack an invasion fleet heading for America, the B-10 needed good range. This was one of the reasons the design was so popular with the Dutch East Indies air force, which had to fly long missions over the sea. The B-10 could carry extra fuel if required in the bomb-bay.

WELLINGTON Mk III 2478 km (1536 miles)

SM.81 SERIES 5 2000 km (1240 miles)

B-10B 1996 km (1238 miles)

ARMAMENT

For its time the B-10 had respectable armament, especially considering that most fighters only had a pair of machine guns. By 1940 most bombers carried at least twice the B-10's payload.

B-10B	**WELLINGTON Mk III**	**SM.81 SERIES 5**
3 x 7.62-mm (.30-cal.) machine guns 1025 kg (2255 lb) of bombs	8 x 7.7-mm (.303-cal.) machine guns 2041 kg (4490 lb) of bombs	4 x 7.7-mm (.30-cal.) machine guns 2000 kg (4400 lb) of bombs

---

Bombers from the Martin Company

■ **MARYLAND:** Rejected by the USAAC in its original form, the Martin 167 was ordered by France and ended up in the hands of the RAF following the French surrender. It was used as a light bomber and reconnaissance aircraft, and performed the pre-strike missions over Taranto harbour in November 1940.

■ **BALTIMORE:** Developed to a British specification, the Baltimore was used by the RAF in the Middle East, gaining a good record as a day and night medium-bomber and reconnaissance aircraft. Like the B-10, it had a narrow, deep fuselage that made it difficult for the crew to change positions.

■ **MARAUDER:** One of the fastest medium bombers of World War II, the B-26 suffered from a reputation as a dangerous aircraft when it was first introduced. However, when crews had gained experience with it, the Marauder went on to record the lowest loss rate of any bomber aircraft used in Europe.

MARTIN

B-26 MARAUDER

● Very fast ● Difficult to fly ● USAF's most potent medium bomber

▲ Designed in 1939 for the US Army Air Corps, the sleek, fast, twin-engined Martin Model 179 Marauder was ordered straight into production without a prototype or trials.

During World War II the Martin B-26 Marauder was considered a 'hot' ship – high-powered, unforgiving and risky to fly. But in spite of unflattering nicknames like 'Widowmaker' and 'Flying Coffin', the Marauder was not as dangerous as was widely believed. In fact, it was a potent warplane – a silvery sleek bullet of a medium bomber which could carry a respectable bombload and outrun the opposition.

278

PHOTO FILE

MARTIN B-26 MARAUDER

▲ **Streamlined for speed**
The B-26 was designed with a very sleek, circular section fuselage, curving to the nose and tail cones. The cockpit windscreen was streamlined, and the wing was designed for speed rather than lift.

▲ **Medium bombload**
A stick of 250-lb (114-kg) bombs falls from the internal bomb-bay of a raiding B-26. The aircraft could carry a rather modest total weight of 2359 kg (5200 lb).

▲ **Fast targets**
Some Marauders were stripped of their armour and used as high-speed target tugs and trainers by the US Air Force and Navy.

▼ **Tactical bomber**
Flying with the US 9th Air Force from May 1943, the B-26 quickly became the hardest-worked Allied daylight medium bomber over Europe.

▲ **Shot down**
As crews got used to the B-26's performance it became less vulnerable. By VE Day it had the lowest loss rate of any US bomber in Europe.

FACTS AND FIGURES

➤ The first flight of the B-26 took place at the Martin factory in November 1940.

➤ B-26s began service with the 22nd Bomb Group in Australia just after Pearl Harbor.

➤ Future American president Lyndon B. Johnson received a Silver Star for a Marauder mission in New Guinea.

➤ During an attack on Ijmuiden, Holland, in May 1943, an entire group of 10 B-26s was shot down by fighters, flak and collisions.

➤ The price of a B-26 was $261,000 in 1940, which had reduced to $192,000 by 1944.

➤ Of the 5157 Marauders built, 522 were supplied to the Royal Air Force.

The flying torpedo

The Martin Marauder went straight into production, the first aircraft to fly being a service model and not a prototype. It made an immediate impact, rumour giving the new medium bomber an (exaggerated) top speed of almost 600 km/h (370 mph), faster than most fighters then in service. Its engines were in streamlined nacelles underslung from a shoulder-mounted wing, enhancing the image of the Marauder as a silvery 'Flying Torpedo'.

As a medium bomber the B-26 crew varied from five to seven. One gunner manually operated the nose machine guns and others the electrically operated dorsal turret, tail turret and the manually aimed waist guns.

The B-26C had a heavier armament and more powerful engines than the major production version, the B-26B, that preceded it.

Although employed to good effect for conventional and torpedo bombing, the Marauder never made its mark in the Pacific theatre where the more conventional, less challenging B-25 Mitchell was preferred.

In Europe the story was very different, with B-26s joining US squadrons in 1942. The initial deployment by the 319th Bomb Group was trouble-plagued. The Marauder landed at 210 km/h (130 mph) and could betray an unskilled pilot. But the B-26 soon made its mark over the continent, proving to be a rugged, accurate and extremely hard-hitting tactical weapon. Following their success in covering the invasion of Normandy, Marauders again proved successful in attacking the heavily defended German V-1 flying bomb launch sites during 1944.

The 525 Marauders that flew with the RAF and the South African air force replaced Blenheims in the Mediterranean theatre.

When it entered service the B-26 had the highest wing loading of any aircraft in the USAAF. The high-set, short-span wing and two large, powerful engines optimized it for high speed rather than bombload or handling.

B-26B Marauder

Type: seven-seat medium day-bomber

Powerplant: two 1432-kW (1920-hp) Pratt & Whitney R-2800-43 Double Wasp radial piston engines

Maximum speed: 454 km/h (317 mph) at 4570 m (15,000 ft)

Climb rate: to 4600 m (15,000 ft) in 13 minutes

Range: 1851 km (1148 miles) with 1361 kg (2994 lb) of bombs

Service ceiling: 6400 m (23,500 ft)

Weights: empty 10,886 kg (23,950 lb); normal take-off 16,783 kg (36,923 lb)

Armament: up to eight 12.7-mm (.50-cal) machine guns with 3950 rounds of ammunition, plus a maximum internal bombload of 2359 kg (5170 lb)

Dimensions: span late models 21.64 m (71 ft)
early models 19.12 m (63 ft)
length 17.75 m (58 ft)
height 6.55 m (21 ft)
wing area 61.13 m² (679 sq ft)

In order to save weight, the Marauder's flying control surfaces (rudder, elevators and ailerons) were wooden ribbed and covered with doped fabric.

In order to improve handling performance on take-off and landing, the B-26's fin and rudder was extended and the wing span was increased.

This B-26 carries the black and white invasion stripes applied at the time of the Normandy landings of June 1944. It is in standard USAAF colours with the KS code letters of the 557th Squadron.

When it entered service the Marauder had the highest wing loading of any USAAF aircraft. This gave it high take-off and landing speeds, which caused problems for inexperienced pilots.

The engine nacelles housed the large, single wheels of the tricycle undercarriage. All three units had single strut legs, the nosewheel retracting rearwards into the lower fuselage below the cockpit.

B-26C MARAUDER

This B-26C, nicknamed 'Baby Bumps II', was flown by the 557th Squadron of the 98th Wing based at Chipping Ongar.

The B-26 was powered by two 1432-kW (1920-hp) Pratt & Whitney R-2800-43 piston engines, which drove large four-blade propellers.

Baby Bumps II

COMBAT DATA

ARMAMENT

The B-26's defensive armament was better than its German or Japanese contemporaries. Having both fixed and mobile guns in the nose, dorsal and tail turrets, together with rear side-window guns, it had an all-round arc of fire.

Ki-49-IIA 'Helen'
1000 kg (2200 lb) of bombs
5 x 7.7-mm
(.30-cal) machine guns
1 x 20-mm cannon

Ju 88A-4
3000 kg (6614 lb) of bombs
4 x 7.92-mm machine guns

B-26B MARAUDER
2359 kg (5200 lb) of bombs
8 x 12.7-mm (.50-cal.) machine guns

Medium bombers: the rivals

■ **JUNKERS Ju 88:** One of the Luftwaffe's main bombers, the Ju 88 was designed as a medium-range tactical aircraft that was also used as a dive-bomber and night-fighter. It was nearly 100 km/h (60 mph) slower than the B-26 but could carry nearly double the weight of bombs. Total production of the Ju 88 was about 15,000.

■ **MITSUBISHI KI-67 HIRYU 'PEGGY':** This Japanese army Type 4 was Japan's fastest medium-range bomber of the war, with a top speed of 537 km/h (334 mph), nearly 100 km/h (60 mph) greater than the B-26. The penalty for this was a small bombload of just 800 kg (1760 lb). Only 698 Ki-67s were built before the war ended.

■ **NORTH AMERICAN B-25 MITCHELL:** The USAAF's 'gull-wing' B-25 was developed at the same time as the Marauder. It carried a smaller bombload, was a good deal slower, but was more rugged and relatively easy to fly. Nearly twice as many B-25s were built (9816) than B-26s (5157).

MARTIN
PBM MARINER

● Flying boat ● Amphibian ● Anti-submarine and SAR aircraft

O ne of the truly great flying boats of all time, the Martin PBM Mariner was produced in seaplane and amphibian versions. It was the most important naval aircraft in its class during World War II. Largely used as a replacement for the Consolidated PBY Catalina, which was perhaps the only better-known flying boat, the big, sturdy PBM Mariner served in every combat theatre. Many other countries used the Mariner well into the 1950s.

▲ The amphibious capabilities of the later Mariner versions made them versatile aircraft. The high-mounted engines, search radar and gull wing were distinctive features.

MARTIN PBM MARINER

▲ Search and rescue
Used in the search and rescue role after World War II, the Mariner served on into the 1950s with the US Coast Guard and US Navy.

▼ Onto the ocean
Launched from a slipway at NAS Norfolk, Virginia, this Mariner is being prepared for a mission in late 1942. The aircraft is armed with eight machine guns.

▲ Rocket assistance
Rockets fixed to the fuselage sides helped heavily loaded aircraft get airborne. Drag from the water was a serious problem.

▼ Full power
The two huge Wright Cyclone engines haul the Mariner into the air on another long-range patrol mission.

Search radar ▶
Radar allowed the Mariner to hunt for submarines and ships. Later it was useful in the search and rescue role, operating far out to sea.

FACTS AND FIGURES

➤ The prototype for the Mariner series completed its maiden flight on 18 February 1939.

➤ British Mariners were returned to the US without seeing operational service.

➤ Seven PBMs sank the submarine U-615 near Aruba on August 6, 1943.

➤ The Navy first used RATO (rocket-assisted take-off) boosters to fly a stranded PBM off the Colorado river.

➤ A 3/8 scale model of the Mariner was flown before the prototype PBM flew.

➤ The Martin 162-A scale model was manned and had Chevrolet engines.

PBM-3D Mariner

Type: seven- or eight-seat patrol flying boat

Powerplant: two 1417-kW (1900-hp) Wright R-2600-22 Cyclone radial piston engines

Maximum speed: 338 km/h (210 mph) at 520 m (1700 ft)

Cruising speed: 303 km/h (188 mph) at 520 m (1700 ft)

Ceiling: 6095 m (20,000 ft)

Combat radius: 1162 km (722 miles)

Range: 3597 km (2235 miles)

Weights: empty 15,017 kg (33,106 lb); maximum take-off 26,253 kg (57,878 lb)

Weapons: eight 12.7-mm (.50-cal.) machine guns in nose, dorsal turrets, waist and tail; plus up to 747 kg (1646 lb) of bombs, torpedoes or depth charges

Dimensions:
span	35.97 m (118 ft)
length	24.38 m (80 ft)
height	8.23 m (27 ft)
wing area	130.71 m² (1407 sq ft)

ACTION DATA

WEAPONS

Carrying a heavier bomb load, the Mariner was designed to replace the smaller Catalina. Although it carried fewer bombs, the Sunderland had more defensive guns.

SUNDERLAND GR.Mk 5   463-kg (1021-lb) bombload
10 x 7.62-mm (.303-cal.) machine guns

PBM-5A MARINER   1654-kg (3646-lb) bombload
8 x 12.7-mm (.50-cal.) machine guns

PBY-5A CATALINA   374-kg (824-lb) bombload
1 x 12.7-mm (.50-cal.) machine gun
3 x 7.7-mm (.303-cal.) machine guns

RANGE

The Catalina was renowned for its excellent range. The Mariner comes a close second and both aircraft beat the Sunderland by almost 1000 km (620 miles).

PBY-5A CATALINA   3774 km (2345 miles)

PBM-5A MARINER   3597 km (2235 miles)

SUNDERLAND GR.Mk 5   2482 km (1766 miles)

MAXIMUM TAKE-OFF WEIGHT

The Sunderland and Mariner are closely matched in weight. In the Mariner, however, far more of this weight consists of fuel and weapons. The lighter Catalina, although very successful, would have been more difficult to handle on open sea.

SUNDERLAND GR.Mk 5   26,253 kg (57,878 lb)

PBM-5A MARINER   26,218 kg (57,800 lb)

PBY-5A CATALINA   16,033 kg (35,347 lb)

U.S. Navy patrol flying boat

The Mariner was designed in 1937 when the U.S. Navy wanted a new patrol flying boat. The big, gull-wing Mariner was sturdy and tough, and featured weapons bays in its engine nacelles.

The pilots and crew of the Mariner had tremendous confidence in a ship that had been optimized to give them the strongest chance of surviving combat and getting home safely.

There were numerous combat actions in which the PBM Mariner excelled, beginning on

30 June 1942, when a crew headed by Lieutenant Richard E. Schreder sank the German submarine *U-158* near Bermuda. Exactly a dozen U-boats had been sent to the bottom of the sea by Mariners by the time the war ended.

In the Pacific, Mariners fought just about everywhere, but were particularly active at Saipan and in the liberation of the Philippines. In the postwar era, Mariners took part in atomic weapons tests in the Pacific and fought in the 1950–53 Korean

War. Production of the Mariner ceased in 1949, but the aircraft remained a mainstay of the US Coast Guard for many years.

Below: The Royal Air Force received 27 Mariners. Fitted with British equipment, they were never used operationally and were returned to the United States.

Above: The Mariner could reach an altitude of 6095 m (20,000 ft), but patrols were normally flown at low level. Attacks on submarines were made at wave-top height using bombs and depth charges.

PBM-5 MARINER

The PBM-5 variant was used post-war by the US Navy and Coast Guard, mainly in the search and rescue role. This aircraft carries a Pacific theatre colour scheme.

The large search radar was enclosed by a streamlined fairing, mounted above and behind the cockpit.

The two Wright R-2600 engines were mounted high on the gull wings to keep the propellers clear of corrosive saltwater spray.

A fixed float under each wing kept the wingtips clear of the water and allowed a stable take-off and landing in rough seas.

The prototype mounted its twin fins and rudders on horizontal tailplanes. Those on production aircraft were angled upward, keeping them in line with the inboard section of the wings.

The large engine nacelles were each able to carry up to 1811 kg (3993 lb) of bombs, depth charges or air-dropped rescue equipment.

Nose, dorsal and tail turrets contained a total of six 12.7-mm (.50-cal.) machine guns. These were supplemented by two more guns in the waist positions.

The boat-shaped underside was the key to easy operations from any large area of water. Early aircraft had retractable wing floats, while the PBM-5 was amphibious, with retractable wheeled landing gear.

U.S. Navy patrol aircraft

■ **CONSOLIDATED PB2Y CORONADO:** Similar in size to the PBM, the PB2Y carried a heavier bomb load and had more power.

■ **CONSOLIDATED PB4Y-2 PRIVATEER:** This was a long-range patrol version of the B-24 Liberator developed for the US Navy.

■ **CONSOLIDATED PBY CATALINA:** Hugely successful, the Catalina served throughout World War II in the long-range patrol mission.

■ **LOCKHEED PV-2 HARPOON:** Developed from the Lodestar airliner, the PV-2 was a well-armed coastal patrol aircraft.

MARTIN

167 MARYLAND/187 BALTIMORE

- Desert operations ● Export only ● Reconnaissance

▲ All 400 Baltimores initially ordered by the RAF were sent to Egypt to help the Allied effort against Rommel's 1942 offensive. Escorted by Curtiss Kittyhawks, they excelled in the Battle of El Alamein.

I n the late 1930s the Glenn L. Martin Company created the Maryland for the US Army (later selling it to France) and the Baltimore for Britain's RAF. Both were twin-engined light bombers with a modest bombload, defensive armament and performance that compared poorly with modern fighters like the Supermarine Spitfire and the Messerschmitt Bf 109. Although they were solidly designed aircraft, they were not advanced enough for World War II.

▲ Maryland prototype
The prototype first flew on 13 March 1939 and was given the designation XA-22. It lost out to the Douglas A-20 in the US Army competition.

▲ Narrow fuselage
The Baltimore's narrow fuselage prevented the crew from moving about and stretching on long trips.

British Marylands ▼
Both the RAF and Royal Navy operated Marylands in the long-range reconnaissance role.

Turkish delight ▶
A number of Baltimores were supplied to Turkey during the later stages of World War II under the Lend-Lease arrangement. This is an ex-RAF aircraft.

▲ Advancing through Italy
An RAF Baltimore Mk III drops its load over the railway station and sidings at Sulmona in northern Italy. British and South African Baltimores fought throughout the Italian campaign.

FACTS AND FIGURES

▼ Martin built 496 Maryland bombers, all but one for France; many of these were transferred to the RAF and Royal Navy.

▼ The Maryland was produced at what was the USA's largest aircraft factory in 1939.

▼ More than 20 Baltimores were lost during delivery by sea to Great Britain.

▶ In all, 1575 Baltimores were built – more than any Martin aircraft except for the B-26 Marauder (5266).

▶ The Baltimore cost $120,000, compared with $78,000 for a B-26 Marauder.

▶ After the war a Baltimore was used by the US Navy to test experimental airfoils.

Distinguished desert bomber

The Maryland was designed by Martin engineer James S. McDonnell, who later gave his name to the McDonnell Douglas Corporation. It was tested by the US Army as the XA-22 and performed better than other manufacturers. The Army withheld a production contract, however, and the Maryland was exported instead to France. The first Marylands left the factory on 2 September 1939, the day before France and Britain declared war on Germany. They had little impact on the conflict, however.

The Maryland led to the Baltimore, which was known by the US Army as the A-30. Built to satisfy British requirements, the Baltimore was a somewhat more formidable attack bomber that was used extensively in North African fighting at El Alamein in June 1942. The Baltimore also achieved moderate success in Italy later in the war.

The last Baltimores served with the RAF in Kenya, performing aerial mapping and locust control duties until 1948.

Above: Ordered before the prototype had even flown, France received 140 Marylands. A number of them served with the Free French forces until 1943.

Right: No. 13 Squadron re-equipped with the Baltimore in December 1943, and spent the next 10 months on day and night operations in northern Italy.

BALTIMORE MK V

This example flew with No. 232 Wing, comprising Nos 55 and 223 Squadrons, of the North-West African Tactical Air Force in the Italian campaign during 1944.

With the narrow fuselage, communication between crewmembers was difficult. If the pilot was injured it was almost impossible for anyone else to reach the controls.

Originally powered by two Wright R-2600-19 engines, the more powerful Mk V was fitted with two 1268-kW (1700-hp) R-2600-29 radials. These improved speed and climb performance.

With a distinctive curved rudder and a low-mounted tailplane, the Baltimore had responsive controls which were necessary for a single pilot on long-range operations.

The rear fuselage was virtually a boom carrying the tail unit. The Baltimore featured a much deeper front fuselage than the Maryland.

All Baltimores delivered to the RAF served in the Mediterranean theatre and were painted in a brown/sand desert camouflage scheme.

Early versions of the Baltimore had only poor protection from the mid-upper gun position. This made the aircraft extremely vulnerable to attacks from above and behind. The problem was solved in the Mk III with the introduction of a Boulton-Paul hydraulically operated turret containing four Browning 7.7-mm (.303-cal.) machine guns.

Much of the Baltimore's design was based on its predecessor, the Maryland. Its all-metal wing was practically identical and was similarly mounted in the low-mid position.

Up to 907 kg (2000 lb) of bombs could be carried in the Baltimore's bomb-bay. The aircraft could bomb very accurately and on some occasions dropped bombs from more than 3500 m (12,000 ft) on targets situated only 700 m (2300 ft) from Allied troops.

RAF Lend-Lease bombers

■ **BOEING FORTRESS:** Of 125 Lend-Lease Fortresses delivered to the RAF, 19 were Mk IIs (equivalent to the B-17F). Most were used by Coastal Command for maritime reconnaissance.

■ **CONSOLIDATED LIBERATOR:** Famous for helping to close the U-boat 'gap' in the middle of the Atlantic, Liberators also served with Bomber Command and in the Middle and Far East.

■ **MARTIN MARAUDER:** Around 525 Marauders were delivered to the RAF and SAAF under the Lend-Lease arrangement. They were used exclusively in the Mediterranean theatre.

■ **NORTH AMERICAN MITCHELL:** The Mitchell proved to be a capable close-support bomber for the RAF when operating with the 2nd Tactical Air Force during the Allied advances of 1944/45.

Baltimore Mk IV

Type: four-seat light bomber (Martin 187 Baltimore)

Powerplant: two 1238-kW (1660-hp) Wright R-2600-19 Cyclone 14 radial piston engines

Maximum speed: 491 km/h (304 mph) at 3505 m (11,500 ft)

Range: 1741 km (1080 miles)

Service ceiling: 7100 m (23,300 ft)

Weights: empty 7013 kg (15,429 lb); maximum take-off 10,251 kg (22,550 lb)

Armament: four 7.7-mm (.303-cal.) wing-mounted machine guns, two or four similar guns in ventral position and provision for four 7.62-mm (.30-cal.) machine guns in fixed, rear-firing position, plus a bombload of up to 907 kg (2000 lb)

Dimensions:
span	18.69 m	(61 ft 4 in)
length	14.78 m	(48 ft 6 in)
height	5.41 m	(17 ft 9 in)
wing area	50.03 m²	(528 sq ft)

COMBAT DATA

CRUISING SPEED

Although the Baltimore had more powerful engines than the Maryland, they had similar top speeds. The Maryland actually cruised faster than the Baltimore, thanks to its more aerodynamically streamlined shape. Both were slower than the Boston, however.

BALTIMORE Mk IV 362 km/h (224 mph)
MARYLAND Mk I 399 km/h (247 mph)
BOSTON Mk III 402 km/h (249 mph)

POWER

The Boston and Baltimore had a distinct power advantage over the Maryland. This allowed them to carry more defensive armament and gave them a better rate of climb.

BALTIMORE Mk IV 2476 kW (3320 hp)
MARYLAND Mk I 1566 kW (2100 hp)
BOSTON Mk III 2386 kW (3200 hp)

ARMAMENT

Later marks of the Baltimore had heavy defensive armament and could put up a stubborn defence against enemy fighters. The Maryland had poor defence against attack from behind. All three types carried a similar bombload.

BALTIMORE Mk IV
8 x 7.7-mm (.303-cal.) machine guns
4 x 7.62-mm (.303-cal.) machine guns, 907-kg (2000-lb) bombload

MARYLAND Mk I
4 x 7.62-mm (.303-cal.) machine guns
2 x 7.7-mm (.30-cal.) machine guns, 907-kg (2000-lb) bombload

BOSTON Mk III
7 x 7.7-mm (.30-cal.) machine guns
4 x 20-mm cannon, 907-kg (2000-lb) bombload

MARTIN

PB2M MARS

● Maritime patrol ● Water-bomber ● Four-engine flying-boat

F ew modern sights in aviation can equal that of a huge scarlet Martin Mars coming straight at you over a Canadian lake. These 50-year-old Navy veterans of World War II are among the biggest flying-boats ever built and hold the record as the largest aircraft used for fighting forest fires. Capable of dumping thousands of litres of water and foam to extinguish forest fires, the two remaining Mars 'boats' are survivors of six that were originally built.

▲ Like so many large flying-boat projects in the late 1940s, the Mars was an excellent aircraft that became irrelevant when the war ended. The fact that two are still flying is testament to the aircraft's usefulness.

PHOTO FILE

MARTIN PB2M MARS

▲ Mightier Mars
The JRM-2 Mars, named 'Caroline Mars' by the Navy, was even heavier and more powerful than the first JRM-1s. It was fitted with Pratt & Whitney R-4360s, which were the most powerful engines in existence at the time.

▲ Mars formation
A rare sight even in the 1950s, this formation of four JRM-3s was headed by 'Philippine Mars' and 'Marianas Mars'. The JRM-1s were eventually upgraded to the same standard as the JRM-2, and were then known as JRM-3s.

▼ 'Hawaii Mars'
Flying cargo between the mainland and Honolulu, the Mars could operate in worse conditions than land-based aircraft and carried its larger load more economically.

▲ Pearl Harbor patrol
The first Mars was berthed at the Naval Air Station at Alameda, California. It made the round trip to Pearl Harbor in Hawaii in just five days, including all servicing and cargo loading. The massive wing contained large fuel tanks.

FACTS AND FIGURES

▼ Designer Glenn Martin saw the Mars as a flying battleship, carrying enough bombs and troops to storm an enemy island.

▼ All six Mars flying-boats were named after islands, the first being 'Hawaii'.

▼ Until the B-36 bomber, the Mars was the largest aircraft used by the US military.

▼ The Mars might have had a future after World War II if airlines had not opted to use landplanes rather than flying-boats.

▼ The US Navy retired its last Mars in August 1956 despite its success.

▼ Mars flew three sorties a week between San Francisco and Honolulu.

PROFILE

Patrol aircraft turned water-bomber

Designed to meet a US Navy requirement for a patrol bomber, the Mars started life as the Martin Model 170 or XPB2M-1. The flying-boat was so large that inside it was fitted out like a ship with separate mess rooms for troops, officers' quarters, staterooms and berths.

Flying for the first time on 5 November 1941, the twin-tailed Mars prototype did not become the forerunner of a huge wartime fleet of combat aircraft as designer Glenn Martin

had hoped. Instead, the Navy asked for a transport and the XPB2M was stripped of its turrets and bombing equipment. In this role the Mars was impressive and the Navy began regular runs across the Pacific, packing thousands of kilograms of freight into the huge interior.

After the war the Navy ordered 20 examples of an XPB2M derivative designated JRM-1 and fitted with a single fin and rudder, but in the event only five were completed. The original 'Hawaii Mars' and

'Marshall Mars' were destroyed in crashes, and the other four, joined by a single example of the heavier JRM-2, served until 1956. When no post-war boom in civil flying-boat operations materialized, the five aircraft were sold to Forest Industries Flying Tankers of Canada for use as water-bombers.

Post-war flying-boats were killed off by the introduction of larger jet-powered and turboprop-powered landplanes. Those that survived, however, were found extremely useful for everything from rescue to fire bombing.

JRM-1 Mars

Type: long-range flying-boat

Powerplant: four 1715-kW (2300-hp) Wright Duplex Cyclone R-3350 radial piston engines

Maximum speed: 360 km/h (225 mph)

Range: 7039 km (4360 miles)

Service ceiling: 4450 m (14,600 ft)

Weights: empty 34279 kg (75,414 lb); loaded 74,844 kg (164,657 lb)

Dimensions: span 60.96 m (200 ft)
length 35.76 m (117 ft)
height 11.73 m (38 ft)
wing area 342.15 m² (3681 sq ft)

Dihedral tailplanes help give the Mars stable and slow handling in pitch and roll. The rudder has a large trim tab to assist in control movement.

A small access walkway was retained in the JRM-2 even though the rear fuselage had been extensively modified. Doorways to the rear fuselage are located ahead of the tailfin.

The original twin-tail was replaced by a taller, single-fin unit with a large rudder. This was essential for good handling on the water in windy conditions.

High-wing designs were almost universal for flying-boats to ensure that the propellers and flying surfaces were as far above the water as possible. The long-span wing gives the Mars very long range.

The bulk of a flying-boat fuselage could accommodate very large loads. In 1949, 'Marshall Mars' carried no fewer than 315 passengers as well as its crew of seven.

The main cargo-bay door is located in the fuselage side. It was the size of this door rather than payload weight limitations that dictated what a Mars could carry.

The Mars has a very spacious cockpit, entered via doors in the port and starboard side of the nose and stairs up to the flight deck.

JRM-1s were powered by Wright Cyclone engines, replaced by Pratt & Whitney R-4360s in JRM-2 'Caroline Mars'.

The Mars' planing hull is an excellent design, giving the aircraft very good handling on the water and making take-off and landing surprisingly easy for such a massive aircraft.

For the water-bomber role, the Mars contains enormous water tanks fitted in the fuselage. These can be filled in as little as 15 seconds as the aircraft taxies across the surface of a lake.

JRM-3 MARS

Still flying after more than 50 years of continuous operation, the last two Martin Mars flying-boats are 'Hawaii Mars' and 'Philippine Mars'.

ACTION DATA

MAXIMUM SPEED

Flying-boats require range, capacious fuselages and a boat hull, all factors which mitigate against a fast design. With streamlining and powerful engines, the flying-boats of the 1940s were reaching almost 400 km/h (250 mph), an impressive achievement.

JRM-1 MARS 360 km/h (225 mph)	
SHETLAND	424 km/h (263 mph)
BV 222 VIKING	382 km/h (237 mph)

RANGE

American aircraft were often built with impressive range, which was essential as long trans-oceanic flights were needed to reach other countries. The Shetland was designed with British Empire sea routes in mind and the availability of frequent fuel stops. The BV 222 was almost as long-ranged as the Mars.

SHETLAND 4000 km (2480 miles)

BV 222 VIKING 5988 km (3713 miles)

JRM-1 MARS 7039 km (4360 miles)

Flying firemen in North America

■ **GRUMMAN TURBO FIRECAT:** The Firecat is used extensively in North America as an effective fire-fighter even though it is a small land-based design. It has also been sold to France. The airframe is a turboprop variant of the naval S-2 Tracker anti-submarine warfare aircraft.

■ **DOUGLAS DC-6:** Fitted with a large canoe-shaped external fuel tank under the belly, this DC-6 named 'Spirit of '76' is another early post-war design which was pressed into service for fire bombing. Its tanks contain chemical fire-suppressant rather than water.

■ **CANADAIR CL-215:** Operated in Canada and across Europe, the CL-215 is one of the most common sights above a forest fire today. It was used by the French Securité Civile to fight the large fires near the Riviera region in 1985. It is also operated in Venezuela as a transport and in Thailand as a surveillance aircraft.

MARTIN

P4M MERCATOR

● Dual piston/jet power ● Patrol bomber design ● 'Ferret' aircraft

O ne of the secrets of the Cold War would be a good way to describe the little-known Martin P4M Mercator. From outside, the Mercator resembled the better-known Lockheed Neptune patrol aircraft. Inside, it was very different. This twin-engine aircraft was actually designed from the beginning for four engines. Also, although designed for maritime patrol work, the Mercator spent most of its career as a spy in the sky.

▲ The U.S. Navy tried to find an aircraft that could combine the range of a propeller-driven machine with the speed of a jet. The results were often an unsatisfactory compromise.

286

MARTIN P4M MERCATOR

▲ **First production Mercator**
The first production P4M-1 early on in its career; the main undercarriage did not retract fully into the Mercator's wing and was surrounded by a fairing on the lower wing surface.

▲ **Last of 19**
P4M-1 124373 was the last example off the production line. All became P4M-1Q 'ferrets'.

▲ **Designed for speed and range**
Like the Consolidated PB4Y before it, the P4M used a long, thin wing to provide fuel capacity and long range. The jet engines, while providing more speed, actually compromised range performance.

▲ **Second XP4M-1**
Aircraft 02790 was the second Mercator prototype. The J33 jet engine air intake is below the propeller, in the open position.

Three-blade propellers ▶
One of the two P4M prototypes is seen on an early flight. Note the three-blade propellers and lack of armament.

FACTS AND FIGURES

▶ The first XP4M flew on September 20, 1946, with three-blade propellers, not the four-blade type on later aircraft.

▶ In its brief service as a patrol aircraft, the P4M replaced the PB4Y Privateer.

▶ Chinese MiG fighters shot down a P4M near Shanghai on August 22, 1956.

▶ Production totaled 21 Mercators; two prototypes and 19 maritime patrol/radar reconnaissance conversions.

▶ Another P4M-1Q was damaged by North Korean MiG-17s on June 16, 1959.

▶ J33 engines also powered the USAF's first operational jet fighter, the P-80.

Naval bomber turned 'ferret'

Naval patrol missions were originally envisioned when the fabulous Glenn L. Martin Company designed the P4M Mercator.

Power provision in the P4M was unique. It had one piston and one jet engine on each side, each buried in the same engine nacelle, hanging from the wing. This gave the Mercator tremendous power and speed, as well as excellent range – exactly the qualities the US Navy needed in a patrol bomber.

The Mercator was a muscular aircraft. It was the only patrol ship in which a crew member could stand fully erect inside the fuselage. It was strong and heavy, and was extremely stable. For a brief period in the early 1950s, a few Mercators served with a single navy patrol squadron and these qualities produced excellent performance.

However, intelligence needs led the Navy to quickly decide to modify its small fleet of Mercators to spy on Soviet and Chinese radar transmitters. As a 'ferret', or radar reconnaissance aircraft, the Mercator was usually present when the Cold War heated up. One was shot down and another fired upon before the Mercator was retired from service in 1961.

P4M-1 MERCATOR

Only 19 production P4Ms were built, and the only squadron equipped with the basic Dash-1 variant was Patrol Squadron VP-21. The first examples reached the squadron in June 1950.

In the 'ferret' signals intelligence role, the P4M-1Q had a crew of 14: pilot, co-pilot, navigator, electronics officer, six system operators, plane captain and three gunners.

The combination of two R-4360 radial piston engines and two Allison J33 turbojets gave the P4M a 660 km/h (409 mph) top speed and 4500-km (2790-mile) range. The J33 was positioned in the bottom half of the nacelle, breathing air from an intake below the propeller and exhausting to the rear of the nacelle, near the trailing edge of the wing.

External antennas, other than the two ventral radomes, indicate a SIGINT role.

Mercator was a cantilever high-wing monoplane with tricycle undercarriage. In the maritime reconnaissance role, the P4M lost out to the similarly configured Lockheed P2V Neptune, which went on to be built in large numbers.

The dorsal turret was equipped with two 12.7-mm (.50-cal.) machine guns; two more could be fuselage mounted, one on either side in the observer's position. The latter were not always carried.

The standard US Navy color scheme for its aircraft in the 1950s was this dark shade known as 'midnight blue'. Other than national and Navy markings, this P4M carries VP-21's 'HC' tail code and a number (below the cockpit) for identity within the unit.

As built, P4M tail and nose turrets each carried twin 20-mm cannon for self-defence. These, plus the dorsal turret position, were manned during 'ferret' flights that took the craft close to Chinese, Soviet and North Korean territory.

Above: Martin's Model 219 was ordered on 6 July 1944 to fill a US Navy requirement for a patrol bomber. All Martin's previous naval bombers had been flying boats like the PBM Mariner.

Right: Only three units were ever equipped with the Mercator. The two SIGINT units were VQ-1 in the Pacific and VQ-2 in the Atlantic. From 1958, carrier-borne EA-3 Skywarriors performed a similar role.

P4M-1 Mercator

Type: maritime patrol aircraft

Powerplant: two 2423-kW (3250-hp) Pratt & Whitney R-4360-20A Wasp Major radial piston engines and two 20.5-kN (24,610-lb-thrust) Allison J33-A-10A turbojet engines

Maximum speed: 660 km/h (409 mph) at 6125 m (20,090 ft)

Range: 4570 km (2833 miles)

Service ceiling: 7666 m (25,145 ft)

Weights: maximum take-off 40,088 kg (88,194 lb); gross (approx.) 37,421 kg (82,326 lb)

Weapons: four 20-mm cannon; four 12.7-mm (.50-cal.) machine guns; plus up to 2722 kg (5988 lb) of bombs

Dimensions:
span	34.75 m (114 ft)
length	25.60 m (198 ft)
height	7.95 m (26 ft)
wing area	121.79 m² (1310 sq ft)

ACTION DATA

RANGE

The P4M's piston engines gave it a range marginally better than the Privateer, but less than was possible if all-piston power had been used, as in the P2V Neptune. For a maritime patrol aircraft, good range means long endurance.

P4M-1 MERCATOR — 4570 km (2833 miles)
P2V-1 NEPTUNE — 6613 km (4100 miles)
PB4Y-2 PRIVATEER — 4506 km (2794 miles)

DAMAGE SUSTAINED: Unlike the Chinese incident of 1956, this attack left the Mercator damaged, but able to limp back to its base. The P4M continued in this role until 1960, in both the Atlantic and Pacific theaters.

NORTH KOREA REACTS: North Korea reacted by sending two MiG-17 fighters to intercept the 'snooping' American aircraft. This was the second major incident in which a Mercator had been attacked while on a spy flight.

'Ferret' missions by VQ-1

Though it lost out to the P2V in the maritime patrol role, the P4M received a new lease on life as a spy aircraft.

JUNE 16, 1959: From a base in Japan, a P4M-1Q of electronics squadron VQ-1 took off on a signals intelligence 'ferret' flight, following a route that passed Vladivostok and then headed south along the coast of North Korea.

MARTIN

B-57

● Bomber ● High-altitude reconnaissance ● Vietnam service

Britain's English Electric Canberra was so successful that the US Air Force immediately selected the aircraft after the failure of the Martin XB-51. Used as a bomber-interdictor and a high-altitude reconnaissance aircraft, the American-built B-57 saw service in Vietnam, attacking the Ho Chi Minh Trail. It went on to operate into the 1980s as a target tug, weather research and electronic warfare machine.

▲ Derived from one of the most successful jet light bombers ever built, the Martin B-57 became a world-class night intruder over Vietnam and a high-altitude reconnaissance platform.

MARTIN **B-57**

▼ Cartridge start
Like a number of turbojet aircraft of the period, the B-57's engines were started by cartridge and produced a spectacular belch of black smoke from the intakes.

▲ High-altitude recce
The RB-57F, 21 of which were built, superceded the RB-57D high-altitude reconnaissance platforms. It had two performance-enhancing auxiliary turbojets slung under the long-span wings.

▼ Night intruders
Operational in Vietnam, the B-57B dedicated night intruder was very similar to the Canberra B.Mk 2 and the pre-production B-57A. The RB-57A operated vital night reconnaissance missions over North Vietnam.

▲ B model derivations
The B-57D trainer (above) and B-57E target-tug were developed from the B-57B night intruder.

Test platform ▶
Later in its career the B-57 series became a useful platform for USAF and NASA experiments and trials.

FACTS AND FIGURES

➤ Pakistani B-57s took part in counter-air bombing raids against Indian airfields during the 1971 war.

➤ A B-57 was involved in a 'friendly fire' attack on a Coast Guard ship in Vietnam.

➤ American B-57s were constructed at Martin's plant in Baltimore, Maryland.

➤ The first B-57A prototype flew on 20 July 1953; 67 production RB-57As entered service in April 1954.

➤ The B-57B night intruder first flew on 5 January 1955.

➤ NASA used an RB-57F for weather reconnaissance and trials until 1994.

A British bomber for the USAF

When US Air Force officers saw a Canberra demonstrated in 1949, their approval was immediate. The aircraft had great flexibility, good range, superb performance at height (in excess of most fighters of the day) and a potent bombload.

Martin built the aircraft in lieu of its failed XB-51, but the first example delivered was a British B.Mk 2. The original B-57As were manufactured almost exactly to this standard by

Martin. A reconnaissance version, the RB-57A, was very similar to the 'A' model. Other versions produced were the B-57B 'night-raider' bomber, which had a tandem cockpit, and the B-57C trainer and B-57E target tug.

The B-57 went to war in the mid 1960s in Vietnam, chiefly flying interdiction missions over the delta and border areas and the Ho Chi Minh Trail. Finally, the RB-57D, with a long-span wing, was built.

Below: The RB-57D's long wing produced excellent high-altitude performance. Unfortunately, the aircraft suffered from wing fatigue cracks.

Above: B-57s often went into combat in South Vietnam alongside British-built Australian Canberras.

B-57B

Type: two-seat multi-role attack and reconnaissance bomber

Powerplant: two 32.01-kN (7200-lb-thrust) Wright J65 turbojets

Maximum speed: 937 km/h (581 mph) at altitude

Initial climb rate: 1066 m/min (3500 fpm)

Range: 3700 km (2300 miles)

Service ceiling: 18,288 m (60,000 ft)

Weights: empty 11,793 kg (25,945 lb); loaded 24948 kg (50,000 lb)

Armament: eight 12.7-mm (.50-cal.) Colt-Browning machine guns or four 20-mm cannon, plus up to 2268 kg (5000 lb) of bombs in weapons bay

Dimensions:
span	19.50 m (64 ft)
length	19.90 m (65 ft 3 in)
height	4.75 m (15 ft 7 in)
wing area	89.18 m² (960 sq ft)

COMBAT DATA

CEILING

British Canberras had already demonstrated superb high-altitude performance, flying over the southern Soviet Union with impunity for a number of years. The large-wing RB-57s flew even higher, reaching 25,000 m (82,000 ft).

B-57B 18,288 m (60,000 ft)
Il-28 'BEAGLE' 12,300 m (40,300 ft)
VAUTOUR 15,000 m (49,000 ft)

RANGE

The B-57's engines and high internal fuel capacity gave it very long range. This allowed Pakistani aircraft to bomb airfields deep in Indian territory from bases near Peshawar in 1971. The Il-28 was fast, but its engines consumed much more fuel than the Wright J65.

B-57B 3700 km (2300 miles)
VAUTOUR 2575 km (1600 miles)
Il-28 'BEAGLE' 1135 km (700 miles)

WEAPONS LOAD

B-57s could carry 2268 kg of bombs internally and more under the wings. The versatility of the weapon load was even more impressive; the aircraft could carry almost any weapon in the US arsenal in the 1950s, including napalm, cluster bombs and nuclear bombs.

B-57B 3175 kg (7000 lb)
Il-28 'BEAGLE' 3000 kg (6600 lb)
VAUTOUR 2400 kg (5300 lb)

B-57B

First deployed to Europe in 1956 with the units of Tactical Air Command, including the 38th and 345th Bomb Groups, the B-57B later served in Vietnam.

The B-57 used the Wright J65 engine, a licence-built derivative of the British Armstrong-Siddeley Sapphire engine. This was roughly equivalent in performance to the British Rolls-Royce Avon.

Wingtip fuel tanks were fitted to the B-57B and D, but other variants like the B-57E dispensed with them.

Unlike the British Canberras, most B-57's had tandem cockpits. Equipment varied widely, with target towing controls, ECM displays and extra radios for forward air control fitted.

The success of the B-57 was mainly due to its large wing, which gave superb handling at high altitude.

The ultimate strike B-57 variant was the 'G' model, with nose-mounted, low-light television and radar.

Although the B-57 could carry a heavy load in its bomb-bay, additional armament could be carried under its large wings.

For high-altitude reconnaissance and night-intruder work, the B-57 was painted semi-gloss black, but some units had bright tail codes and unit emblems.

Reconnaissance RB-57As had a camera pack fitted in a bay just aft of the weapons bay.

Like its British equivalent, the B-57 had a large internal bomb-bay with the capacity for 2268 kg (5000 lb) of bombs, including tactical nuclear weapons. Rocket packs could be mounted on the inside of the bomb-bay door.

B-57 variants

■ **PAKISTANI B-57B NIGHT INTRUDER:** This night-camouflaged Martin B-57B, based at Masroor with No. 7 Squadron, was heavily involved in the 1971 bombings of Indian airfields. Pakistan received surplus USAF aircraft after the end of their night intrusion role over Vietnam.

■ **USAF B-57B:** The USAF's B-57 fleet saw much service over Vietnam and Southeast Asia, often in partnership with forward air control Cessna O-2s and AC-130A night-attack gunships. The B-57 was also a useful EW platform and the basis of the B-57G multi-sensor aircraft, which was never put into production.

■ **NASA WB-57F:** NASA's B-57s were ex-USAF strategic reconnaissance RB-57s used by the service for a variety of tasks, including weather reconnaissance, atmospheric sampling and high-altitude trials work. The long-wing WB-57 variants were capable of altitudes approaching 25,000 m (82,000 ft).

MARTIN

P5M MARLIN

- The last American flying-boat ● Anti-submarine/rescue

T he USSR's 600-strong submarine force was considered a huge threat to the West in the 1950s. The threat may have been exaggerated, but it spurred the development of anti-submarine planes. The Martin P5M Marlin was the US Navy's last operational flying-boat, designed to stalk and kill submarines as they hid in the ocean's depths.

▲ Military flying-boats are a rare breed today. The Martin Marlin was retired in 1966, after 14 years with the US Navy and Coast Guard. Of its contemporaries, only the Japanese ShinMaywa and the Russian Beriev Be-12 remain in service.

MARTIN P5M MARLIN

▼ Sub-chaser

The Marlin was designed to hunt enemy submarines, but could also be used to resupply friendly ones when needed.

▲ Gull wing

The gull-shaped profile of the Marlin's wing was retained from its predecessor, the Martin Mariner. It was designed to keep the propellers clear of the water's surface on landing.

Vietnam missions ▼

Designed for deep-water submarine hunting, the Marlin's only real combat use was in Vietnam. It monitored coastal shipping and performed search-and-rescue missions.

▲ In the dock

Amphibious dock landing ships were trialled with some success as Marlin bases. The US Navy tried to operate the seaplanes as strike aircraft, independent of land bases.

▲ Stranded at sea

Although Marlins usually operated from sheltered waters, sometimes they had to brave the open ocean. This one lost an engine, and had to taxi home to its base in Japan. The voyage took more than nine hours.

FACTS AND FIGURES

- ▼ The prototype Marlin flew on 30 May 1948. It entered service in April 1952.

- ▼ The only overseas operator of the Marlin was France, which acquired 10 P5M-2s under the Military Assistance Program.

- ▼ Although designed to carry two 20-mm cannon in the tail, most Marlins did not carry guns operationally.

- ▼ The P5M-2 (SP-5B) differed from the P5M-1 (P-5A) in having a T-shaped tail and more sophisticated equipment.

- ▼ One Marlin was evaluated with an auxiliary jet engine in its tail, as a possible retrofit to the entire fleet.

- ▼ US Coast Guard Marlins did not carry anti-submarine sensors or weapons.

Submarine hunter

The Glenn L. Martin Company was one of the great builders of flying-boats, those large aircraft with ship-like hulls which operate from water, free of dependency on fixed airfields. The P5M Marlin followed upon the great success of the company's PBM Mariner of World War II. The Marlin was a creature for the 1950s, intended to fly and fight on the world's great oceans. This aircraft was packed with detection gear to find submarines and with weapons to destroy them.

Marlins achieved a fine record with a dozen patrol squadrons while in service from 1952 to 1965. The familiar deep-blue paint on the Marlin became a combination of grey and white when the Navy shifted colours in 1955. In its final years (the P5M was re-named the P-5 in 1962) this reliable aircraft went to Vietnam, where it flew offshore patrols to choke off seaborne infiltration. In US

submarines and with weapons to destroy them.

The original Marlin had a conventional tail. The P5M-2 of 1953 featured a T-tail and more powerful engines.

Coast Guard Service Marlins were used for rescuing downed pilots, using the aircraft's superb endurance to conduct long search missions, helping to save many lives. It was the US Navy's last operational flying-boat.

P5M-2 MARLIN

The French Aéronavale received 10 Marlin P5M-2s. Like many other nations, France replaced the seaplane with search-and-rescue helicopters and large land-based maritime patrol aircraft.

Marlins operated from a variety of land bases and ships. This P5M has run up onto an inflatable platform alongside the assault ship USS Ashland. This allowed the aircraft to be serviced without needing to be winched aboard.

Early Marlins were armed with a pair of 20-mm cannon in the tail, but these were deleted in the improved P5M-2.

The tail 'stinger' housed a magnetic anomaly detector (MAD). This tracked submarines by the distortions they caused in the Earth's magnetic field.

Marlins carried both active and passive sonobuoys, deployed through hatches by the ASW technicians. Jezebel was a long-range low-frequency buoy which could detect a snorkelling diesel submarine at 150 km (93 miles).

The cockpit of the Marlin housed the two pilots. The rest of the crew consisted of navigator, mission co-ordinator, electrician and six ASW specialists, who were housed in the capacious fuselage.

Weapons and sensors were carried in bays in the engine nacelles, and on eight underwing hardpoints. Weapon options included bombs, mines, depth charges or Mk 46 air-launched ASW torpedoes.

Power was provided by a pair of Wright R-3350 radial piston engines, each delivering 2573 kW (3450 hp).

The APS-80 radar was the most powerful surface search unit of its day, capable of detecting a periscope at up to 90 km (56 miles).

Taking off from water

The speed of flying-boats ploughing through the water is limited by water resistance. To take off they have to be skimming across the surface, which offers less resistance and allows much higher speeds to be attained. The hull of the flying-boat is designed with a sharply defined 'step'. At high enough speeds, the hull and aquaplanes on the step and accelerates away to flying speed.

At rest, the Marlin floats low in the water.

Accelerating forward, hydrodynamic forces lift the hull higher, but speed is limited to about 65 km/h (40 knots).

Once 'on the step' the Marlin hydroplanes across the surface of the water, and when flying speed is reached it takes off.

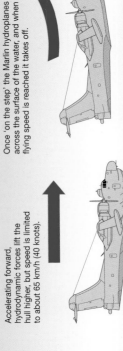

P5M Marlin

Type: patrol flying-boat with 11-man crew

Powerplant: two 2573-kW (3450-hp) Wright R-3350-32WA Turbo-Compound radial piston engines

Maximum speed: 404 km/h (251 mph) at sea level

Combat radius: 3300 km (2046 miles)

Service ceiling: 7315 m (24,000 ft)

Weights: empty 22,900 kg (50,380 lb); loaded 38,555 kg (84,821 lb)

Armament: four torpedoes, four 907-kg (2000-lb) bombs or mines, or smaller weapons up to 3629 kg (8000 lb) total carried internally, and up to eight 454-kg (1000-lb) bombs, mines or rocket projectiles carried externally

Dimensions:
span	36.02 m (118 ft 2 in)
length	30.66 m (100 ft 7 in)
height	9.97 m (32 ft 8 in)
wing area	130.62 m (1405 sq ft)

COMBAT DATA

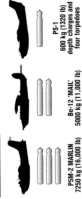

MAXIMUM SPEED

The Marlin was designed before the advent of turboprops. The new engines were lighter and more powerful, which is reflected in the faster performance of the two more modern boats. The Beriev dates from the late 1950s and the ShinMaywa from the late 1960s and both will remain in service for many years to come.

P5M-2 MARLIN	404 km/h (251 mph)
Be-12 'MAIL'	600 km/h (372 mph)
PS-1	522 km/h (324 mph)

RANGE

Hunting submarines can be a time-consuming process. As a result, maritime patrol aircraft should have the ability to loiter economically on station for very long periods, which means they need equally long range enabling patrols to reach far out into the oceans.

- PS-1 3800 km (2356 miles)
- Be-12 'MAIL' 7500 km (4650 miles)
- P5M-2 MARLIN 6600 km (2050 miles)

COMBAT LOAD

PS-1	600 kg (1320 lb) depth charges and four torpedoes
Be-12 'MAIL'	5000 kg (11,000 lb)
P5M-2 MARLIN	7250 kg (16,000 lb)

The size that enables maritime aircraft to carry large crews on long patrols means that the aircraft usually have the capacity to carry large amounts of anti-submarine weaponry. Both the Beriev and the Marlin could carry as much as contemporary bombers. The more modern Japanese boat had a much smaller warload.

McDONNELL

FH-1 PHANTOM

● Twin-engined fighter ● US Navy's first jet ● Late-1940s design

▲ Three units operated the small FH-1 fleet: one naval and two US Marine Corps fighter units. The last examples were replaced in 1950 by Grumman F9F-2s.

First to carry the famous Phantom name, the FH-1 was a robust, twin-engined fighter – the first all-jet aircraft ordered into production by the US Navy and the first jet aircraft to operate from the deck of a US carrier. The FH-1 Phantom (originally designated FD) enjoyed a brief, but pioneering, career in the late-1940s before McDonnell moved on to the larger and more successful Banshee – the start of the McDonnell naval fighter dynasty.

McDONNELL FH-1 PHANTOM

▲ Outside the factory
These brand-new Phantoms are seen outside McDonnell Aircraft Corporation's St Louis factory.

▼ Buried engines
As with a number of early jet fighters the FH-1's engines were buried in the wingroots, which made access for maintenance difficult.

▼ Rapidly designed
In the early days of jet aircraft, designs developed so rapidly that types like the FH-1 were soon superseded.

▼ Aboard Saipan
Fighter Squadron VF-17A was the first operational FH-1 unit and flew from USS Saipan in 1948.

▲ Cramped carriers
Conditions for jet operations aboard US carriers designed during World War II were often cramped. New, bigger jets required larger ships to be built.

FACTS AND FIGURES

➤ The first Phantom completed its maiden flight on 26 January 1945, with only one of its two engines installed.

➤ The FH-1 was the first US Navy aircraft to reach a speed of 804.67 km/h (500 mph).

➤ One Phantom took off successfully from a beach after landing there by mistake.

➤ Three FH-1s have survived in museums in Washington D.C. Quantico, Virginia, and Pensacola, Florida.

➤ The FH was known as the FD before 1946; the production aircraft were all FH-1s.

➤ Plans for 100 Phantoms were changed and just 60 production aircraft were built.

First jet fighter for US carriers

Although McDonnell was a new and unproven company when it was first contacted by the US Navy in 1942, the manufacturer did a superb job of designing and building the FD-1 Phantom (renamed the FH-1 in 1946), the Navy's first carrier-based jet fighter aircraft.

The Phantom completed successful trials and became the first US jet aircraft to be flown to and from an aircraft-carrier, the USS *Franklin D. Roosevelt*.

Production versions of this jet fighter (slightly longer and more

powerful than the prototypes) began flying with the Navy in the immediate post-war years. When a Navy squadron set sail aboard the USS *Saipan* in 1948, it was the first time a jet aircraft had performed regular operational duties on board an aircraft-carrier.

Most Phantom operations were land-based, however, with the McDonnell twin-jet assigned to two US Marine Corps squadrons. The Marines briefly operated one of the world's first jet aerobatic teams, the 'Flying Leathernecks', with the

Above: In all, 62 Phantoms were built: two XFD-1 prototypes and 60 production FH-1s.

Left: On 21 July 1946, the XFD-1 (as it was then known) landed for the first time aboard the Franklin D. Roosevelt; the first occasion on which a US pure-jet aircraft had operated from an aircraft-carrier.

Phantom. As a fighter designed to exploit the new jet engine in the closing stages of the war, the FH's career was brief; it had been replaced by 1950. However, McDonnell was now an established builder of naval 'fast jets'.

FH-1 PHANTOM

Wearing the US Navy's midnight-blue colour scheme of the period, this FH-1 was typical of the VF-171 aircraft based aboard the USS *Franklin D. Roosevelt*.

The relatively light main armament of the FH consisted of four 12.7-mm (.50-cal.) machine guns mounted on top of the nose and fed with 325 rounds per gun. They had a blinding effect on pilots during night firing.

The Phantom's pilot sat in a relatively conventional cockpit. The aircraft did not have an ejection seat, which was not introduced on naval fighters until the F2H Banshee entered service.

Production FH-1s differed from the two XFD-1s in having a marginally longer fuselage, a square-tipped vertical tail of increased area and greater fuel capacity. While the XFD-1s carried 984 litres/260 gallons (or 1514 litres/400 gallons with drop-tanks), the FHs had room for 1420 litres (375 gallons); 2536 litres (670 gallons) with drop-tanks.

To speed up production in the closing stages of the war and allow easy maintenance, the Phantom's designers were required to produce an aircraft of a conservative design, the only exception being made to accommodate the jet powerplant.

A feature of the Phantom's conventional construction was the tailplane, which had a marked dihedral to keep it out of the jet efflux. The tricycle undercarriage layout was followed on most subsequent designs.

During the design stage several engine proposals were examined before the two relatively lightweight, 48.3-cm (19-in) Westinghouse J30s were selected. The initial design called for six even smaller engines.

Early carrier-borne jet fighters

■ **DE HAVILLAND SEA VAMPIRE:** Developed from the RAF's second jet fighter, the Royal Navy's Sea Vampire was the first pure jet in the world to operate from a carrier deck.

■ **NORTH AMERICAN FJ-1 FURY:** The next step in the evaluation of jet aircraft by the US Navy was the FJ, which was developed into the swept-wing Fury and F-86 Sabre for the USAF.

■ **SUPERMARINE ATTACKER:** The Fleet Air Arm's first jet fighter to become standardised in squadron service, the Attacker first flew in 1946 and was in service from 1951 to 1957.

■ **SNCASE AQUILON:** France's first carrier-borne jets included 109 licence-built de Havilland Sea Venoms, which served from 1954 until 1961. Nineteen were dual-control trainers.

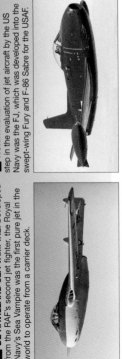

FH-1 Phantom

Type: single-seat carrier-based jet fighter

Powerplant: two 7.12-kN (1600-lb-thrust) Westinghouse J30-WE-20 turbojet engines

Maximum speed: 771 km/h (478 mph) at sea level; 780 km/h (484 mph) at 4570 m (15,000 ft)

Range: 1241 km (770 miles) at 502 km/h (312 mph) at 6100 m (20,000 ft) with ventral drop-tank; maximum 1575 km (975 miles)

Service ceiling: 12,525 m (41,000 ft)

Weights: empty 3031 kg (6688 lb); maximum take-off 5459 kg (12,000 lb)

Armament: four 12.7-mm (.50-cal.) Colt-Browning M2/M3 machine guns, with 325 rounds per gun, mounted in the nose

Dimensions:
span	12.42 m (40 ft 9 in)
length	11.35 m (37 ft 3 in)
height	4.32 m (14 ft 2 in)
wing area	25.64 m² (276 sq ft)

COMBAT DATA

MAXIMUM SPEED

The FH was slower than contemporary jet types. Because it was intended to operate against piston-engined Japanese opposition, however, this was not a major problem – it had a comfortable margin over these aircraft.

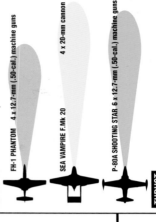

FH-1 PHANTOM	780 km/h (484 mph)
SEA VAMPIRE F.Mk 20	847 km/h (525 mph)
P-80A SHOOTING STAR	898 km/h (557 mph)

ARMAMENT

The USAAF and Navy were slow to adopt cannon armament for their fighters and relied on machine guns. The British, however, had used cannon since the war years.

FH-1 PHANTOM	4 x 12.7-mm (.50-cal.) machine guns
SEA VAMPIRE F.Mk 20	4 x 20-mm cannon
P-80A SHOOTING STAR	6 x 12.7-mm (.50-cal.) machine guns

THRUST

Naval jets tend to have two engines to provide a safety margin if one fails. The P-80 was a USAF design and the Vampire was also developed from a land-based aircraft.

FH-1 PHANTOM	2 x 7.12 kN (1600 lb thrust)
SEA VAMPIRE F.Mk 20	1 x 13.35 kN (3000 lb thrust)
P-80A SHOOTING STAR	1 x 17.80 kN (4000 lb thrust)

McDonnell
F2H BANSHEE

● Single-seat jet fighter ● Phantom development ● Korean War

W hile McDonnell's first naval jet, the FH-1 Phantom, had proven the viability of operating jet fighters from carriers, the FH was slower than contemporary USAAF jets. To address this problem the US Navy asked the St Louis, Missouri, company to develop a successor to the Phantom. The result was essentially an enlarged derivative of the earlier design with bigger guns and, eventually, radar. The Korean War was its testing ground.

▶ Known affectionately as the 'Old Banjo', the F2H Banshee served with the US Navy and Marine Corps as their first carrier-borne, single-seat jet night-fighter.

McDonnell F2H BANSHEE

PHOTO FILE

▲ Blue and grey Banshees
This factory-fresh McDonnell F2H-3 has yet to be painted in its top coat of bright pearly grey, as applied to most of the Dash-3s and Dash-4s. Earlier aircraft carried the standard glossy 'midnight blue' which was applied to other US Navy aircraft.

▲ Versions compared
The marked differences between the F2H-2 and F2H-3 can be compared above, including the longer fuselage and tail.

▶ Last US operator
Marine Corps fighter unit VM(AW)-11 retired its last Banshees at the end of September 1959. This F2H-4 carries the markings of VMF-214.

▼ Wing folding and 'kneeling leg'
To aid storage aboard aircraft-carriers, the F2H featured folding wings, an unusual nose dolly and a 'kneeling' front leg to tilt the tail upwards.

▼ Banshees over CVA-43
USS Coral Sea, with Banshees arranged on its deck, provides the backdrop for a quartet of F2H-2s. The type flew its first combat mission in Korea from USS Essex on 23 August 1951 and equipped fighter squadrons VF-11, -22, -62 and -171 during two years in the war zone.

FACTS AND FIGURES

▶ On 9 August 1949 Lieutenant J.L. Fruin, flying an F2H-1, made the first emergency ejection by a US pilot.

▶ An F2H-1 set an unofficial altitude record for a jet, of 15,850 m (52,000 ft), in August 1949.

▶ Late-build F2H-2s and -3s were retrofitted with an in-flight refuelling probe.

▶ Banshees were among the first aircraft to use the first US steam catapult aboard USS Hancock in June 1954.

▶ In 1952 two F2H-2Ps were used to radio-guide a Regulus missile to its target.

▶ The film The Bridges of Toko-Ri, based on Michener's novel, featured the F2H-2.

PROFILE

Shrieking son of the Phantom

First flown in January 1947, three Banshee prototypes were followed by 56 production F2H-1s. The most numerous variant was the F2H-2, which appeared at the beginning of the Korean War. More than 400 were built, including a number of F2H-2Ps (the Navy's standard carrier-based reconnaissance aircraft for many years) and radar-equipped F2H-2Ns, which had limited all-weather capability.

The Banshee's high-altitude capability made it ideal for escorting USAF B-29s on bombing missions over North

Korea. Five squadrons with Task Force 77 and a land-based Marine reconnaissance unit were active with the type for two years.

A true all-weather jet fighter entered Navy service in 1952 when the F2H-3 left the St Louis factory. During its production life the Banshee was produced with fuselages of three different lengths; few other fighters were 'stretched' 25 per cent during their lives. The F2H-3 had a 2.44-metre longer fuselage, which could accommodate more fuel, and a much improved radar. In all, 250 were delivered, the last

in 1953, together with 150 F2H-4s with bigger engines and yet another radar set.

The only other nation to fly the Banshee was Canada, whose navy operated 39. In 1962, the few surviving F2H-3s and -4s were redesignated F-2C and D.

The photo-reconnaissance version of the F2H-2 was the F2H-2P, which had space for up to six cameras in its lengthened nose. No more than two were usually fitted, however.

Pronounced tailplane dihedral was a feature of the three Banshee prototypes and the F2H-3, although on the latter the tailplane was set lower on the tail fin.

Four 20-mm cannon were fitted in the F2H. These were positioned under the nose in the F2H-1 and -2, but were set further back, beneath the cockpit, in the F2H-3 and -4.

F2H-3 BANSHEE

This was one of the 39 F2H-3s transferred to the Royal Canadian Navy from November 1955. It carries the markings of VF-870 which operated the type until September 1962.

An APQ-41 radar set, with a large 71-cm (28-in) dish, was fitted in the F2H-3's nose, and provided a true night/all-weather capability. It was much improved over that of the F2H-2N.

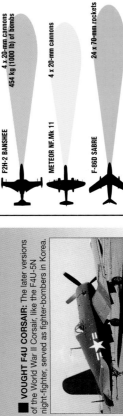

The Banshee was the Canadian navy's first operational jet and equipped two squadrons, VF-870 and VF-871. Both units were deployed aboard HMCS *Bonaventure*. They were Canada's last carrier fighters.

Underwing racks were fitted to carry two 227-kg (500-lb) or eight 113-kg (250-lb) bombs. Royal Canadian Navy Banshees were modified to carry two Sidewinder air-to-air missiles – a capability that US Navy Banshees did not have.

By the time the final US Navy Banshee was retired in the mid 1960s, it was the last machine in the service that was fitted with Westinghouse turbojet engines. The most powerful J34s fitted were those of the F2H-4, which produced 16 kN (3600-lb-thrust).

COMBAT DATA

F2H-2 Banshee

Type: single-seat all-weather carrier-borne fighter

Powerplant: two 14.46-kN (3250-lb-thrust) Westinghouse J34-WE-34 turbojets

Maximum speed: 856 km/h (530 mph) at 3050 m (10,000 ft)

Initial climb rate: 1192 m/min (3900 fpm)

Range: 2374 km (1470 miles)

Service ceiling: 13,655 m (44,800 ft)

Weights: empty 5055 kg (11,121 lb); maximum take-off 10,120 kg (22,264 lb)

Armament: four 20-mm cannon and up to 454 kg (1000 lb) of bombs

Dimensions:	span	13.67 m (10 ft 5 in)
	length	12.24 m (40 ft 2 in)
	height	4.42 m (14 ft 6 in)
	wing area	27.31 m² (294 sq ft)

MAXIMUM SPEED

The lead taken by the USAF in all-weather fighter development could be seen in the F-86D, a considerably faster swept-wing design. The Meteor was a development of a wartime design.

F2H-2 BANSHEE 856 km/h (530 mph)	
METEOR NF.Mk 11 931 km/h (577 mph)	
F-86D SABRE 1138 km/h (706 mph)	

RANGE

Although the Sabre had a speed advantage over the straight-winged designs, it was deficient in range. It had even shorter 'legs' than the RAF's Meteor, a two-seat design.

METEOR NF.Mk 11 1480 km (920 miles)	
F-86D SABRE 1344 km (830 miles)	
F2H-2 BANSHEE 2374 km (1470 miles)	

ARMAMENT

Different approaches to air-to-air armament can be seen here. The USAF fitted a number of fighter designs with rockets in place of cannon. The Banshee also had a secondary air-to-ground capability.

F2H-2 BANSHEE	4 x 20-mm cannons 454 kg (1000 lb) of bombs
METEOR NF.Mk 11	4 x 20-mm cannons
F-86D SABRE	24 x 70-mm rockets

Aircraft of Task Force 77 over Korea

■ **DOUGLAS AD SKYRAIDER:** In the close support role the Skyraider carried rockets, bombs and napalm as well as 20-mm cannon.

■ **GRUMMAN F9F-2 PANTHER:** The principal USN fighter of the Korean War, a Panther downed the Navy's first jet opponent, a MiG-15, in 1950.

■ **SIKORSKY HO3S:** Derived from the Army's R-5, the HO3S gave good service with squadron HU-1 in Korea, especially in the rescue role.

■ **VOUGHT F4U CORSAIR:** The later versions of the World War II Corsair, like the F4U-5N night-fighter, served as fighter-bombers in Korea.

296

McDONNELL
F3H DEMON

● Fleet defence ● Carrier fighter ● Sparrow armed

▲ Like many of the fighters of the early-1950s, the F3H was marred by the combination of weak engines and swept-wing aerodynamics. The result was an aircraft which pilots did not like.

With its needle nose and swept-back contours, the McDonnell F3H Demon looked supersonic while on the ground. But the Demon (which perhaps should have been named the Gremlin) did not fly supersonically, in fact, it barely flew at all. After years of development work, an operational Demon served briefly with the fleet, but the aircraft never overcame its lack of thrust and pilots regarded it as a dangerous killer.

McDONNELL F3H DEMON

Intercept training ▶
Demon pilots found that despite lacking thrust the aircraft was in fact a good dogfighter – if the engine worked.

▲ Four Sparrows
Armed with four of the then-revolutionary Sparrow missiles, the F3H was formidable as an interceptor. These first-generation Sparrows had to be launched in steady flight and guided to the target by the pilot.

▲ Doomed Demon
Such were the Demon's failings that a Senate committee, headed by future President Lyndon B. Johnson, investigated the aircraft.

Comfortable cockpit ▶
For all its faults, the F3H had a large and well laid-out cockpit with excellent visibility. The pilot sat on a Martin-Baker ejection seat.

▲ Pilot killer
The total lack of thrust meant that a botched take-off often became fatal. Many Demon pilots took off with the canopy open to allow a quick escape.

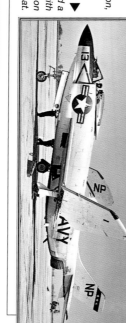

FACTS AND FIGURES

▶ The Allison J71 engine was widely regarded as a successful 'fix' for the Demon's powerplant troubles.

▶ The Demon's 7 August 1951 maiden flight was uneventful.

▶ F3H fighters cruised the Atlantic and Pacific but never saw actual combat.

▶ In a poll of 94 historians in Washington DC in 1996, 36 chose the Demon as 'the worst airplane in history'.

▶ Some 519 Demons had been built when production was halted suddenly in 1959.

▶ A Demon with a General Electric J73 engine was designed but never built.

McDonnell F3H Demon

F3H-2 Demon

Type: single-seat carrier-based fighter

Powerplant: one 42.15-kN (9660-lb-thrust) Allison J71-A-2E turbojet engine with an afterburning rating of 62.27 kN (13,970 lb thrust)

Maximum speed: 1041 km (649 mph) at 9145 m (30,000 ft)

Range: 2205 km (1367 miles)

Service ceiling: 13,000 m (42,640 ft)

Weights: empty 10,039 kg (22,085 lb); maximum take-off 15,377 kg (33,928 lb)

Armament: four 20-mm cannon plus up to 2722 kg (5988 lb) of bombs or rockets; F3H-2M version has up to four AAM-N-6 Sparrow III missiles

Dimensions:
span	10.77 m (35 ft)
length	17.96 m (59 ft)
height	4.44 m (15 ft)
wing area	48.22 m² (158 sq ft)

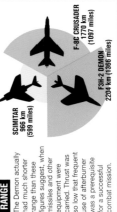

COMBAT DATA

MAXIMUM SPEED

The feeble engines made the Demon very slow, at a time when land-based fighters such as the J79-engined F-104 were already pushing Mach 2. The Crusader, which appeared soon after, had a huge speed advantage over the Demon and Scimitar.

F3H-2 DEMON 1041 km/h (645 mph)
SCIMITAR 1143 km/h (709 mph)
F-8C CRUSADER 1802 km/h (1117 mph)

MISSILE RANGE

Sparrow missiles gave the Demon huge reach in combat. The 40-km range, however, was a purely theoretical advantage as the pilot had to point his aircraft at the target until impact, bringing him very close to his adversary's weapons by the time the missile hit.

F3H-2 DEMON 40 km (25 miles) (SPARROW)
F-8 CRUSADER 17.7 km (11 miles) (AIM-9C)
SCIMITAR 3.2 km (2 miles) (AIM-9B)

RANGE

The Demon actually had much shorter range than these figures suggest, when missiles and other equipment were carried. Thrust was so low that frequent use of afterburner was a prerequisite for a successful combat mission.

SCIMITAR 966 km (599 miles)
F-8C CRUSADER 1770 km (1097 miles)
F3H-2 DEMON 2204 km (1366 miles)

McDonnell's ugly duckling

McDonnell F3H Demons were first delivered to the US Navy by barges trundling down the Mississippi River. Early Demons (with Westinghouse XJ40 engines) never entered service and were conscripted as ground trainers in Memphis, Tennessee, after being transported from the factory in St Louis, Missouri. Many of the first aircraft were simply scrapped.

With a J71 engine, radar and other changes, the improved F3H-2 Demon appeared more hopeful. In fact, one of them flew around Missouri and Kentucky for three hours after a test pilot ejected during an inflight emergency. The pilotless Demon crashed harmlessly. That pilot was lucky. When Demons reached aircraft carrier decks, aviators who had to eject did not always escape with their lives.

The Demon's shortcomings were so serious that after 11 accidents in which two pilots were killed, production was brought to an abrupt halt. Eleven squadrons flew the Demon over an eight-year period, but it was never loved and is little missed. Despite its enormous shortcomings, the F3H was the first swept-wing McDonnell design, and introduced new weapons like the Sparrow III and AIM-9C Sidewinder.

Demons gained a fearsome reputation among US politicians as well as pilots. Two aircraft crashed, killing one pilot, in a demonstration of firepower for President Eisenhower in 1957.

F3H-2 DEMON

VF-31 first flew the Demon in late 1956 aboard USS *Enterprise*. The unit's commander, Jack Tefft, became one of the first of many pilots to survive an ejection in a Demon in June 1957.

For an aircraft of its day the F3H had very good visibility.

The APG-51 was a formidable radar, and the F3H pilots could detect RB-66s in practice intercepts from over 300 km (185 mph).

'Felix the Cat' is the logo of VF-31, a fighter squadron that is still in existence flying the F-14 Tomcat.

The APG-51 had variable frequency settings, allowing the pilot to avoid enemy jamming by resetting the frequency.

The stabilator was so powerful that if a Demon was on the deck and stationary, with a strong wind blowing the pilot could dip the nose by pushing the control column.

One notable feature of the Demon was the very thin intakes, an indication of just how feeble the original engines were to require such a small mass of air flow.

Four Sparrow or Sidewinder missiles could be carried on underwing pylons. Sparrows needed to be fired from a level altitude without manoeuvring.

F3Hs were built with four 20-mm cannon, but two were often removed to save weight.

If the F3H had been re-engined with a J79 it might have been remembered as an all-time great, but instead it had the indifferent Allison J71 in place of the failed Westinghouse J40.

McDonnell Douglas naval fighters

■ **FH1 PHANTOM:** The first purely jet-powered fighter in the US Navy and Marine Corps, the FH1 was a straight-winged design armed with machine guns, and could reach 770 km/h (477 mph).

■ **F2H BANSHEE:** Seeing extensive service in Korea as a fighter-bomber, the F2H was produced in very large numbers. Following their withdrawal, some were sold to Canada.

■ **F4H PHANTOM II:** Sharing no more than the name of its predecessor, the F-4 was a powerful and very versatile machine and was one of the most successful post-war fighters.

McDonnell Douglas
A-4 Skyhawk

● Smallest nuclear bomber ● Export orders ● Vietnam veteran

T he Douglas A-4 Skyhawk (originally called the A4D) was intended to carry an atomic weapon under its belly on a one-way suicide mission if a third world war came. Instead, the Skyhawk became the most impressive conventional bomber of its era – a lightweight 'hot rod' that pilots loved. It flew like a fighter but bombed with great accuracy, as was shown during the Vietnam War and once again in Operation Desert Storm.

▲ An incredible aircraft by every measure, the diminutive Skyhawk met the performance specification at half the maximum weight allowed and remained in production for over 20 years.

McDonnell Douglas A-4 Skyhawk

▲ Carrier trainer
TA-4Js have been used to train budding naval aviators for more than two decades.

▲ Latin attackers
This battered example is a re-manufactured A4D-2 (A-4P) in the markings of the Fuerza Aerea Argentina (Argentine air force).

▲ Black Vultures over the Middle East
Outside the USA, Israel was the largest operator of A-4s. These were fitted with an extended jet tailpipe to reduce heat signature.

▲ Aerobatic performer
For several years Skyhawks were the favoured mounts for the US Navy display team, the Blue Angels. They have since been replaced by F/A-18s.

Rocket tests ▶
Intended primarily to operate from aircraft carriers, the A-4 was also tested with jet-assisted take-off (JATO) rockets for rapid departure from land bases.

FACTS AND FIGURES

▼ A feature of the A-4 was the fact that it was one of a very few carrier-based aircraft not to have folding wings.

▼ Only two years elapsed from conception to first flight of the XA4D-1 prototype.

▼ The very last Skyhawk built was an A-4M delivered to the US Marine Corps in 1979.

▶ On one occasion a Skyhawk was struck by several 30-mm shells but still managed to return to base 300 km (190 miles) away.

▶ Argentinian examples sank three British vessels in the 1982 Falklands War.

▶ The Skyhawk is known as the Ahit (Black Vulture) in Israeli service.

PROFILE

Douglas' bantam bomber

A classic of US naval aviation, the A-4 Skyhawk was an extraordinary aircraft. Douglas' famous designer Edward Heinemann created the Skyhawk at half the weight allowed. When the 'Bantam Bomber' was ordered in 1952, it was remarkably light, but nothing had been stripped from the design, or left out. So small it did not require folding wings aboard carriers, the Skyhawk was easy to fly, but in war it was a deadly foe.

The pilot of the Skyhawk sat in one of the narrowest, most cramped cockpits in aviation, but comfort was more than adequate, visibility was superb, and flying the A-4 was a little like being at the controls of a bullet in flight. In Vietnam, Skyhawks performed traditional bombing and other duties, like 'Iron Hand' missions against North Vietnamese missile sites.

Left: For a bantamweight aeroplane, the Skyhawk could carry an impressive array of ordnance. Here, a US Marine Corps TA-4F fires an unguided rocket while on a training sortie.

Right: Powered by a single Wright J65 turbojet, the XA4D-1 took to the air for the first time on 22 June 1954.

Intended for production from 1954 until 1957, the Skyhawk came out of the factory for 26 years. Built in 23 variants, the Skyhawk is one of the great success stories of all time.

A-4F Skyhawk

Type: single-seat light-attack aircraft

Powerplant: one 41.4-kN (9310-lb-thrust) Pratt & Whitney J52-P-8A turbojet

Maximum speed: 1054 km/h (653 mph)

Initial climb rate: 2440 m/min (8000 fpm)

Combat radius: 612 km (379 miles)

Range: 1127 km (700 miles)

Service ceiling: 12,878 m (42,200 ft)

Weights: empty 4581 kg (10,078 lb); maximum take-off 12,437 kg (27,361 lb)

Armament: two 20-mm Mk 12 cannon plus 3719 kg (8182 lb) of various external stores

Dimensions:
span	8.38 m (27 ft 6 in)
length	12.29 m (40 ft 4 in)
height	4.57 m (15 ft)
wing area	24.16 m² (260 sq ft)

COMBAT DATA

MAXIMUM SPEED

Being so small and light, the Skyhawk was a fast aeroplane and was later chosen for the adversary role because of its good performance. Its successor, the Vought A-7, was much slower. The ground-attack Hunter FGA.Mk 9 was even quicker than the A-4.

A-4E SKYHAWK	1100 km/h (682 mph)
A-7A CORSAIR II	930 km/h (578 mph)
HUNTER FGA.Mk 9	1143 km/h (709 mph)

RANGE

If there was one drawback to the Skyhawk it was its poor range. In Vietnam, A-4s often required multiple air-to-air refuellings while on sorties. Ground-attack Hunters were similarly affected by poor endurance. The under-powered A-7 Corsair had exceptional range for a light-attack aircraft.

A-7A CORSAIR II	2300 km (1426 miles)
A-4E SKYHAWK	1127 km (700 miles)
HUNTER FGA.Mk 9	708 km (439 miles)

MAXIMUM TAKE-OFF WEIGHT

One of the Skyhawk's most endearing features was its ability to carry an incredible amount of ordnance, relative to its size. A-7s could carry more external stores but were bigger and heavier.

A-4E SKYHAWK	11,113 kg (24,449 lb)
A-7A CORSAIR II	14,750 kg (32,450 lb)
HUNTER FGA.Mk 9	10,880 kg (23,936 lb)

A-4G SKYHAWK

The Royal Australian Navy purchased Skyhawks to operate from its small carrier HMAS *Melbourne*. These were designated A-4Gs in service and the survivors were transferred to New Zealand in 1984.

A-4G pilots sat on an Escapac 1C-3 ejection seat, first introduced on the A-4F model.

Mounted just below the windscreen was a small jet which kept the screen clear by blasting engine-bled air onto the surface.

A feature of all production Skyhawks from the A-4B model onwards, was the 'inside-out' rudder with external spars. This was fitted to counter tail buzzing at high speed. Designer Ed Heinemann saw it as an interim solution, though no time was ever found for a long-term fix and thus the distinctive rudder stayed.

A-4Gs were basically similar to the standard US Navy A-4F, though they lacked the distinctive avionics dorsal 'hump'. They were tailored for the air-defence role and could carry AIM-9 Sidewinder heat-seeking missiles on all four wing pylons. In addition, the Australian examples also retained ground-attack capability though they were seldom used in this role.

Second-generation Skyhawks, including the Australian A-4G, were fitted with a Pratt & Whitney J52 turbojet. This engine was more powerful and fuel efficient, plus it had greater development potential than the old Wright J65.

Concerned with the possibility of swept wing aircraft dragging their tails, the US Navy required the landing gear oleos be lengthened. On the ground, the Skyhawk had a very distinctive 'nose up' attitude.

Skyhawks around the world

■ **ARGENTINA:** This South American nation acquired a number of old, refurbished A-4Bs which were given the designation A-4P in air force and A-4Q in naval service. This is a navy example.

■ **MALAYSIA:** The Royal Malaysian Air Force received approximately 40 Skyhawks. All of them are ex-US Navy machines and serve with two units, Nos 6 and 9 Squadrons.

■ **US NAVY:** Two-seat A-4s have been an integral part of the USN training programme for many years. TA-4Js are being replaced by T-45 Goshawks but still serve in large numbers.

300

McDonnell Douglas

A-4 SKYHAWK II

- Light attack ● 1950s design ● Upgraded for the 21st century

▲ While no two-seat Skyhawk IIs were built, a number of early-model two-seaters have been included in the upgrade programmes carried out by the Malaysian and New Zealand air forces. The US Marine Corps also rebuilt a number of TA-4Fs to OA-4M standard for forward air control duties.

O riginally called the A4D, the Douglas A-4 Skyhawk was conceived in the 1950s to carry an atomic weapon on a one-way mission if a third world war was declared. In practice, the Skyhawk provided the US Navy and Marines with an impressive, conventional light-attack aircraft for the next 20 years. The improved A-4M Skyhawk II flew in 1970 and more recently several nations have updated their early-model A-4s with new engines, avionics and weapons.

McDonnell Douglas A-4 SKYHAWK II

▲ Singaporean two-seater
The Royal Singaporean Air Force TA-4S is a rebuilt A-4B and is unique in having two cockpits each with a separate canopy.

▲ From 'dumb bombs' to LGBs
The refurbished A-4s are able to deliver laser-guided bombs and missiles and later versions of heat-seeking air-to-air missiles like the Sidewinder.

▲ Skyhawk II for the Marines
Entering service in the mid 1970s, the A-4M operated until about 1994 mainly in the close air support role. This example is firing an unguided Zuni rocket during exercises.

▼ AGM-12 Bullpup
The main air-to-surface missile carried by Skyhawks before recent upgrades was the Bullpup.

Combat in the Gulf ▼
Twenty Kuwaiti A-4KUs escaped to Bahrain during the 1991 Iraqi invasion and later flew daylight attack missions from Dhahran, Saudi Arabia. Kuwait also has one two-seat TA-4KU remaining in service.

FACTS AND FIGURES

- ▼ New Zealand has now retired all of its A-4Ks and now has no fighter aircraft.

- ▼ Designed by Ed Heinemann, the A-4 has been nicknamed 'Heinemann's Hot Rod'.

- ▼ On their first Gulf War mission, Kuwaiti A-4s mistakenly bombed Saudi Arabia.

- ▼ F404 turbofans fitted to Singapore's A-4s are heavier than the J52 but are more fuel efficient and cheaper to maintain.

- ▼ Pave Penny laser designators, used on USAF A-10s, may be fitted to RSAF A-4s.

- ▼ American companies Lockheed and Grumman have updated foreign A-4s.

PROFILE

Bantam bomber reborn

The A-4 Skyhawk became a classic of US naval aviation, but it began as an extraordinary design. Douglas' famous designer Ed Heinemann created the Skyhawk at half of the specified weight. When the aircraft was ordered in 1952 it was remarkably light, but nothing had been stripped from the design or omitted. The Skyhawk was easy to fly and an effective attack aircraft, and because of its small size it did not require folding wings for use aboard carriers.

In Vietnam, Skyhawks performed traditional bombing raids and 'Iron Hand' missions against North Vietnamese surface-to-air missile sites.

Intended for production from 1954 until 1957, the Skyhawk was produced for a further 26 years in many variants. Significant numbers were exported, some operating from land bases. More recently, retired ex-Navy aircraft have been refurbished and sold overseas. Malaysia and Singapore operate updated

Below: With the GE F404 fitted to Singapore's A-4S aircraft, Skyhawks have used three types of engine, including the Wright J65 fitted in very early marks and the Pratt &Whitney J52 in versions after the A-4E.

Above: Malaysia bought 88 ex-US Navy A-4s in 1979, but abandoned a major upgrade. Grumman refurbished 40 examples which now carry Maverick and Sidewinder missiles.

former US Navy machines; while New Zealand has recently retired its A-4s.

A-4M SKYHAWK II

US Marine Corps Attack Squadron 324 operated the first production A-4M Skyhawk IIs from 1971. By 1976 five USMC squadrons used the variant.

Skyhawk IIs introduced a more bulged cockpit canopy giving improved visibility.

Upgraded A-4s often carry an attack radar, equipment which was not fitted on the production line.

Two 20-mm Mk 12 cannon were fitted to the A-4M. Singaporean A-4S aircraft have been equipped with two 30-mm ADEN cannon, as carried by the SEPECAT Jaguar and the BAe Sea Harrier.

Intended to hold avionics, 'humps' were fitted to early versions of the Skyhawk, starting with the A-4F of 1966. Some upgraded A-4s have had these removed.

This A-4M carries the high-visibility markings common to US Navy and Marine aircraft in the 1970s. Today 'low-viz' colour schemes are more usual.

Skyhawk IIs have a later version of the Pratt & Whitney J52 turbojet engine. Singapore's 'Super Skyhawks' use a non-afterburning variant of the F-18's General Electric F404 turbofan.

Marine Corps aircraft generally carry a two-letter unit tailcode and the last four digits of the aircraft's 'BuNo', or serial number.

In its day the Skyhawk could carry a substantial weapons load. While this is modest by modern standards, upgraded A-4s can deliver much more up-to-date and effective weapons than before.

A-4S-1 Super Skyhawk

Type: single-seat attack aircraft

Powerplant: one 48.04-kN (10,779-lb-thrust) General Electric F404-GE-100D non-afterburning turbofan

Maximum speed: 1128 km/h (700 mph) at sea level

Initial climb rate: 3326 m/min (10,910 fpm)

Range: 1158 km (718 miles) with maximum ordnance

Service ceiling: 12,190 m (39,983 ft)

Weights: empty 4649 kg (10,228 lb); maximum take-off 10,206 kg (22,453 lb)

Armament: two Mk 12 20-mm cannon, plus ordnance including bombs, rockets, air-to-surface missiles and AIM-9 air-to-air missiles

Dimensions:
span	8.38 m (28 ft)
length	12.72 m (42 ft)
height	4.57 m (15 ft)
wing area	24.14 m² (260 sq ft)

COMBAT DATA

MAXIMUM SPEED
The twin-engined A-5 is a relatively fast aircraft compared to the Skyhawk. The straight-winged A-10 was designed for low-speed close air support missions over a battlefield.

A-4M SKYHAWK II	1006 km/h (624 mph)
A-5 'FANTAN'	1190 km/h (738 mph)
A-10A THUNDERBOLT II	682 km/h (438 mph)

COMBAT RADIUS
The A-10's longer range is used to give it extended loiter time over a battlefield. The range of both the A-4 and A-10 can be extended by using air-to-air refuelling, unlike the A-5.

A-4M SKYHAWK II 547 km (339 miles)

A-5 'FANTAN' 600 km (372 miles)

A-10A THUNDERBOLT II 1000 km (620 miles)

BOMBLOAD
The design of the A-5 was based on that of a lightweight fighter, and therefore could not carry as much ordnance as the A-4 and A-10 which were designed from the outset as attack aircraft.

A-4M SKYHAWK II 4153 kg (9137 lb)

A-5 'FANTAN' 2000 kg (4400 lb)

A-10A THUNDERBOLT II 7258 kg (15,968 lb)

Fighter upgrade projects

■ **F-5E TIGER IV:** With the equipment installed in the Tiger IV, Northrop hopes to capture some of the market for updated F-5s.

■ **MIRAGE 50CN PANTERA:** Chile's Mirage 50Cs are being rebuilt with canards and new avionics with help from Israel Aircraft Industries.

■ **F-4E KURNASS 2000:** Originally intended to include new engines, this Israeli project is now restricted to an avionics and airframe upgrade.

■ **MIG-21-2000:** First flown in May 1995, the Israel Aircraft Industries MiG-21-2000 has a comprehensive Western avionics fit.

302

McDonnell
F-101A/C Voodoo

- Long-range interceptor ● Reconnaissance ● Tactical nuclear strike

▲ Voodoo crews lived exciting lives, flying a tricky aircraft with startling performance in roles such as one-way nuclear strike sorties and high-speed reconnaissance flights at treetop height.

To pilots, the McDonnell Douglas F-101 Voodoo was a friendly monster. It was not a forgiving mount; in fact, it was one of the hardest-to-fly aircraft ever to serve in the US Air Force. But once a pilot learned its quirks, the Voodoo was an extravagant performer. Designed as a bomber escort, it became a tactical nuclear striker and an interceptor defending North America. But its greatest moments came in Southeast Asia, when reconnaissance versions flew history's fastest combat missions over North Vietnam.

McDonnell F-101A/C Voodoo

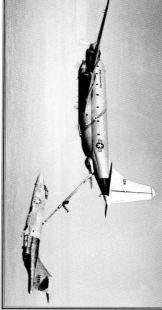

▲ **Racing speed**
When MiGs chased Voodoos in Vietnam, pilots usually selected afterburner and made a high-speed escape.

▲ **More fuel**
The original Voodoos used the standard USAF refuelling boom, but were unusual in having a probe for a drogue system as well.

▲ **All stop**
The Voodoo needed its brake chute, being fast and heavy. A field arrester hook was also fitted for emergency landings at high speed.

Flaps down ▶
The Voodoo was built to fly very fast, but its large split flaps and leading-edge flaps gave it good handling at low airspeed, even when fitted with large external fuel tanks.

▲ **Escort fighter**
The Voodoo was originally designed to fly long-range missions alongside nuclear bombers like the B-47.

FACTS AND FIGURES

▶ F-101A and F-101C models were designed to carry a nuclear weapon to the USSR from air bases in Britain.

▶ A Korean War ace, Major Lonnie R. Moore, was killed in an F-101A crash.

▶ The RF-101C reconnaissance version was the only Voodoo to fight in Vietnam.

▶ The only export user of the Voodoo was Canada, which operated two batches of around 60 F-101B interceptors.

▶ In all, 480 two-seaters, known as TF-101B and F-101F, served as interceptors.

▶ Two-seat Voodoos in USAF service could carry the Genie nuclear air-to-air missile.

PROFILE

McDonnell's monster fighter

The Voodoo was possibly the first warplane to exceed supersonic speed on its first flight (on 29 September 1954), but it never became easy to fly. Tucking in the Voodoo's nosewheel was a challenge and the aircraft had a tendency to 'pitch up', for which various cures were attempted, never with success. It killed test pilots, and challenged service pilots. Throughout its career it remained totally unforgiving – but when used properly, it was a world-beater. Development of the F-101

Voodoo was drawn out because of its teething troubles, but its service career was also surprisingly long (1956–1987).

Daylight reconnaissance missions over Hanoi by the RF-101C routinely exceeded Mach 1.8, faster than any other aircraft has ever flown under fire. The two-seat F-101B interceptor, in both American and Canadian hands, was one of the most complex warplanes ever fielded, and was deemed a nightmare by mechanics – but it could intercept bombers thousands of kilometres from their targets.

The sleek shape of the F-101 was very close to the shape of the original XF-88 fighter design on which it was based. Like many designs of the 1950s, gains in performance were made at the cost of difficult handling.

F-101A VOODOO

Designed as escort fighters, Voodoos were quickly adapted to a new role as tactical nuclear bombers. This example served with the 81st Tactical Fighter Wing based in Suffolk in the late 1950s.

F-101As and Cs were equipped with a Hughes fire-control system, which linked a primitive computer to the radar system.

The Voodoo housed most of its fuel internally, in nine tanks running along the spine of the aircraft from behind the cockpit to the fin. Total capacity was 8123 litres (2000 gallons).

F-101 fighter variants carried three M39 20-mm cannon, two on the port side and one on the starboard side of the fuselage.

The plan view is of a reconnaissance Voodoo, which differs from the fighter primarily in having a camera nose rather than radar.

The wing was fitted with 'fences'. These reduced induced drag by limiting the outward flow of air over the upper surface.

The airbrakes were mounted on the upper rear fuselage sides, just above the tailpipes. Single-seat Voodoos were powered by the J57-P-55 engine, and the afterburner nozzles were much shorter.

Voodoos were usually either all-metal in colour or finished in grey, but the reconnaissance machines in Vietnam received a brown and green jungle paint scheme.

Due to the wing-mounted intakes and the unusual fuselage shape, the Voodoo's main wing spar was not continuous; it divided around the intake ducts.

The high-set tail was the main cause of the Voodoo's unpleasant tendency to pitch up unexpectedly. The tailplane was an all-moving unit, with a VHF antenna on top of the fin.

The J57 engine was a very powerful one for its day. It was not without its problems initially, being prone to compressor stalls.

USAF

41455

U.S. AIR FORCE

F-101A Voodoo

Type: single-seat tactical fighter bomber

Powerplant: two Pratt & Whitney J57-P-13 turbojets each rated at 66.20 kN (14,850 lb thrust) with maximum afterburner

Maximum speed: Mach 1.9 or 1982 km/h (1229 mph) at 10,000 m (33,000 ft)

Range: 3040 km (1885 miles)

Service ceiling: 15,850 m (51,988 ft)

Weights: empty 11,617 kg (25,557 lb); loaded 23,135 kg (50,897 lb)

Armament: four 20-mm cannon, 3050 kg (6710 lb) of bombs, including tactical nuclear weapons

Dimensions:
span	12.09 m (40 ft)
length	20.54 m (67 ft)
height	5.48 m (18 ft)
wing area	34.19 m² (368 sq ft)

COMBAT DATA

MAXIMUM SPEED

F-101A VOODOO	1982 km/h (1229 mph)
HUNTER	1144 km/h (709 mph)
MiG-21 'FISHBED'	2125 km/h (1317 mph)

The Voodoo was one of the fastest fighters of its time, and considerably quicker than the contemporary British Hunter. The MiG-21 appeared several years later, and although faster at altitude it still could not match the sheer brute power of the Voodoo at low level.

RANGE

F-101A VOODOO	3040 km (1885 miles)
HUNTER	2900 km (1798 miles)
MiG-21 'FISHBED'	1200 km (744 miles)

The Voodoo was a very big fighter, and could carry a large amount of fuel. This meant that it had a very long range, and it was therefore ideally suited to long-range missions;

Voodoos based in Britain during the Cold War were tasked with low-level nuclear strike, and were expected to destroy targets deep into Eastern Europe.

WARLOAD

F-101A VOODOO	3050 kg (6710 lb)
HUNTER	1000 kg (2210 lb)
MiG-21 'FISHBED'	1500 kg (3300 lb)

The Voodoo carried a considerable bombload for a single-seat fighter of the 1950s. Its primary ground-attack mission called for the accurate delivery of large tactical nuclear weapons, but it could also deliver a wide variety of conventional weapons.

Voodoo 'over the shoulder' nuclear strike

1 HIGH-SPEED APPROACH: Armed with a Mk 7 nuclear bomb, the Voodoo's attack profile called for the approach to the target to be made at high speed and low level.

2 WEAPONS RELEASE: Approaching the target, the fighter pulls up into the first half of a loop, releasing the weapon in a climb of about 45° for maximum range.

3 BOMB FLIGHT: The bomb follows a high ballistic arc. It is not a very accurate delivery method, but is precise enough to hit a large target like a railway junction or airfield, especially when using a nuclear weapon.

4 ESCAPE: At the top of the loop, the fighter rolls and dives away at full speed to get clear of the titanic blast effects when the nuclear weapon detonates.

McDonnell
RF-101A/C Voodoo

- Photo-reconnaissance ● Unarmed ● Superior speed

Used for tactical reconnaissance, the version of the Voodoo fighter of the 1950s to be used in combat. The RF-101 did an outstanding job of spying on the enemy with its aerial cameras, even though it was a difficult aircraft to fly and could easily pitch up when handled by an inexperienced pilot. A big, powerful aircraft which set many flying records, the RF-101 was always a challenge but earned the affection of pilots.

McDonnell RF-101 was the only an outstanding job of spying on the enemy

▶ At the start of the Vietnam War, the RF-101C was the only US aircraft capable of recording certain kinds of enemy activity. This example is preparing to leave for the war zone.

McDonnell RF-101A/C Voodoo

▼ Extending the range
Despite the long range of the Voodoo, a refuelling probe was located in the nose to allow 'hook-ups' with tankers.

▼ Voodoos abroad
In Europe, operations were flown at heights as low as 150 m (500 ft) along the edge of the Iron Curtain.

▲ Camouflaged bird
At the start of hostilities in Vietnam, the bare metal finish of the Voodoo was covered with a pattern of green and tan in order to reduce the conspicuity of the aircraft.

▲ Outrun everything
Devoid of both weapons and external fuel tanks, the sleek Voodoo earned much praise from its pilots for its high speed.

Post-war service ▶
After seeing considerable action in Vietnam, surviving RF-101s were returned to the United States to be assigned to Air National Guard units. Still in wartime colours, an RF-101C is prepared for a practice recce flight.

FACTS AND FIGURES

▶ Reconnaissance Voodoos were the only variant of the aircraft to see combat, over Vietnam and Cuba.

▶ The first flight of the RF-101C Voodoo took place on 12 July 1957.

▶ RF-101s were deployed to bases in Europe and the Pacific Ocean.

▶ In their early service, RF-101s suffered many landing accidents because of undercarriage collapse.

▶ Thirty-nine RF-101s were shot down over Vietnam by AAA and SAM missiles.

▶ During the Vietnam War, 12 Voodoo pilots were killed in action.

PROFILE

McDonnell's Voodoo magic

When the RF-101 Voodoo entered service in the mid 1950s, it was the culmination of years of work by the McDonnell Aircraft Company on combat jets with evocative 'spirit' names such as Phantom, Banshee and Demon. The Voodoo also existed in fighter-bomber and interceptor versions, but the reconnaissance RF-101 became the best-known member of this McDonnell family, serving the US Air Force well into the 1970s.

The RF-101 combined high speed, long range and the ability to carry a variety of heavy cameras. It performed a critical role during the Cuban missile crisis of 1962, bringing back photos of the Soviet build-

up in Cuba. In Vietnam, the RF-101 Voodoo performed like a champion. Pilots who took the RF-101C to Hanoi flew higher and faster than anything around them, often leaving their escorting fighter aircraft behind. But the challenging and formidable air defences over North Vietnam meant that these missions were not without risk.

The RF-101 later became the backbone of Air National Guard reconnaissance squadrons, often participating in NATO exercises in Germany where missions along the Iron Curtain were routinely undertaken. The Voodoo was eventually replaced by the twin-engined, twin-seat RF-4C Phantom which, although a more capable design overall,

was found to be far slower at low level than the older type. The Voodoo has been retired from USAF service, but only after making a permanent mark on aviation history, having brought back images at crucial periods in America's history.

Cruising at high altitude, the Voodoo was able to provide American commanders with excellent images of the enemy's activities. This example displays the standard natural metal finish employed before the Voodoo went to war.

The all-moving stabilators were positioned high on the tail and made the aircraft particularly stable at high supersonic speeds, which was vital while taking pictures.

McDonnell Douglas maintained the reliability of the twin-engine layout on the Voodoo, which offered the pilot a greater chance of survival if an engine was lost during a mission. The swept rear fuselage appeared later on the F-4 Phantom.

Primarily a reconnaissance aircraft, the Voodoo was also capable of delivering a nuclear bomb, which could be mounted on a single centre-line fuselage station. During such missions no external tanks could be fitted.

The Voodoo was regarded as a 'hot' aircraft because of its high landing speed, but its wide-track undercarriage significantly reduced the accident rate.

RF-101C Voodoo

This RF-101C was initially based in France, but after that country's eviction of US forces it moved to Upper Heyford, England. On the nose is the emblem relating to the NATO exercise Royal Flush.

The instrument panel of the RF-101C was dominated by a large circular scope for the VF-31 viewfinder. It revealed a vertical view as seen from the tri-camera station. The cockpit layout was praised by pilots.

The original nose of the Voodoo was extended to allow installation of the necessary camera equipment. This gave the aircraft a sharper nose profile, while still allowing the high speed performance to be maintained.

RF-101Cs were equipped with a 30-cm camera facing forward, three 15-cm cameras in a tri-sensor station behind, and two 91-cm cameras facing downward.

Two additional fuel tanks could be attached to the centre fuselage if extra range was required for missions, but because of the good endurance of the Voodoo they were rarely carried on combat missions; they also restricted the 'dash' speed of the aircraft. The range of the Voodoo helped the aircraft remain in service until replaced by the RF-4 Phantom.

RF-101C Voodoo

Type: single-seat tactical reconnaissance aircraft

Powerplant: two 45.4-kN (10,213-lb-thrust Pratt & Whitney J57-P-13 turbojets with afterburner

Maximum speed: 1629 km/h (1010 mph); cruising speed 886 km/h (549 mph)

Initial climb rate: 13,855 m/min (45,445 fpm)

Range: 3290 km (2040 miles)

Ferry range: 3453 km (2146 miles)

Service ceiling: 16,855 m (55,280 ft)

Weights: empty 11,855 kg (26,080 lb); loaded 21,832 kg (48,030 lb)

Dimensions:
span	12.09 m (39 ft 8 in)
length	21.13 m (69 ft 4 in)
height	5.49 m (18 ft)
wing area	34.19 m² (368 sq ft)

ACTION DATA

MAXIMUM SPEED

Some USAF pilots claimed that the Voodoo could not be intercepted at low level, and, even if it was, it would simply outrun its pursuer. This technique was often used during operations. Lockheed's SR-71 was immune to all intercepting aircraft.

RF-101C VOODOO	1629 km/h (1010 mph)
RA-5C VIGILANTE	2230 km/h (1383 mph)
SR-71A BLACKBIRD	3220 km/h (1996 mph)

RANGE

The Voodoo had an adequate range on internal fuel and was also equipped with an IFR probe. During the Vietnam War operations were often accomplished without tanker support. The large size of the Vigilante allowed an increased internal fuel load to be carried in the no-longer-utilised weapons bay.

RF-101C VOODOO 3290 km (2040 miles)

RA-5C VIGILANTE 4800 km (2976 miles)

SERVICE CEILING

By operating at high altitude, reconnaissance aircraft are able to photograph a wider area for intelligence operators. Leader in this field was the SR-71. Despite this the Voodoo was also required to fly at tree-top height on some missions over Vietnam.

SR-71A BLACKBIRD	25,900 m (84,950 ft)
RA-5C VIGILANTE	19,500 m (63,960 ft)
RF-101C VOODOO	16,855 m (55,280 ft)

Photographing the battlefield

■ **RF-4B PHANTOM:** Operated by both the US Navy and Marines, the Phantom flew from carriers in the South China Sea during the Vietnam War.

■ **RF-4C PHANTOM:** Replacing the Voodoo in USAF service, the Phantom was an extremely capable design but was not as fast, and had to rely on escorting fighters during missions.

■ **RA-5C VIGILANTE:** Developed from the bomber, the aircraft had exceptional performance for its size. The RA-5C was the US Navy's primary reconnaissance aircraft during the Vietnam War.

McDonnell Douglas

F-4 Phantom II (US Navy)

● Classic carrier fighter ● MiG-killer ● Ground-attack capability

McDonnell's F-4 Phantom II was developed to meet a US Navy need for an interceptor to meet a US Navy need for an interceptor to defend its aircraft-carriers from attack. After the Phantom became operational, it grew into a multi-role warplane with many capabilities – all of them superior. The Phantom could fight MiGs and drop bombs. It was bigger, heavier, more powerful, faster and further-reaching than any other contemporary combat aircraft.

► McDonnell's incredible warplane began life as a shipboard interceptor with the US Navy, and it is perhaps these examples which are the true classic Phantom variants.

McDonnell Douglas F-4 Phantom II

▲ More capable variant
By the early 1970s, most Navy units had re-equipped with the more capable F-4J, which boasted a number of improvements, including more powerful engines and a datalink system.

▼ Launch the Phantom
A trio of F-4Bs from VF-102 'Diamondbacks' prepares for launch from one of the bow catapults on the USS Enterprise. Both the carrier and this squadron later saw combat in Southeast Asia.

▲ Armament
Operating primarily as fleet defence fighters, USN F-4s were seen most often carrying Sparrow and Sidewinder AAMs. The wing fuel tanks were seldom fitted.

► Smoky engines
This flypast fully illustrates the characteristic smoke trails which were a Phantom trademark.

▲ Trapping aboard 'Connie'
After a routine combat air patrol, a VF-92 F-4J lands aboard USS Constellation in 1974.

FACTS AND FIGURES

► Only the larger US Navy carriers could operate Phantoms. The aircraft were too heavy for 'Essex'-class carriers.

► Unlike their USAF counterparts, Navy F-4s were never fitted with guns.

► Lieutenant Randy Cunningham was the USN's only Phantom ace in Vietnam.

► In 1967 a Zuni rocket was accidentally fired on the deck of USS Forrestal; the resulting fire claimed a number of F-4s.

► Some USN F-4Js were later refurbished and delivered to the RAF.

► Grumman F-14 Tomcats began to supplant Phantoms in the mid 1970s.

PROFILE

Elite of the US Navy

In the early 1960s, the Phantom was the hottest thing in the sky. To show off its new fighter, the US Navy flew the new craft faster and higher than any operational warplane had gone before. Typical was a world altitude record of 30,218 m (99,140 ft). In 1961 a specially prepared Phantom reached a speed of 258.15 km/h (1603 mph). Not surprisingly, the Phantom was already becoming vital to US naval aviation when the American role in Vietnam expanded during the mid 1960s.

Phantoms participated in the first US air strikes against North Vietnam and were still around at the end of the war a dozen years later. For the pilot and radar intercept officer of a Phantom, part of the challenge consisted of taking off from and landing on an aircraft-carrier deck, sometimes at night, sometimes in bad weather. High over Hanoi, Phantoms faced North Vietnamese MiG-17 and MiG-21 fighters and fought well. The US Navy's only ace pilot of the war flew a Phantom. Other

Phantoms were operated from land bases in South Vietnam by US Marine crews. Long after Vietnam, the Phantom retained a key position in US naval aviation until its eventual retirement in the 1980s.

F-4B PHANTOM II

Carrying a full load of Mk 82 bombs, this F-4B is depicted as it would have appeared during its first Vietnam cruise with VF-84 'Jolly Rogers' on board the USS Independence in late 1965. During this cruise, the squadron lost three aircraft in combat.

As the first major production Phantom variant, the F-4B featured a Westinghouse APQ-72 radar, which was state of the art in 1965. A small under-nose pod housed an infra-red seeker, though this was removed from the F-4J.

The medium-range AIM-7 Sparrow air-to-air missile was designed as part of the F-4's weapons system. When it was working, the Sparrow was an excellent missile, although in Vietnam it was prone to malfunctioning.

Unlike USAF Phantoms, the F-4B could not be flown from the rear cockpit. In Navy parlance, the backseater was the RIO (Radar Intercept Officer), whose job it was to operate the weapons system.

Sufficient clearance for the twin J79 engines resulted in the distinctive bulky profile, which gave rise to the type's nickname 'Double Ugly'. Above the engines were the fuselage fuel cells.

Although used by the Navy primarily as an interceptor, the F-4B was wired to carry air-to-ground weapons. As the war in Southeast Asia intensified, USN Phantoms were often seen flying bombing missions over North Vietnam, especially when there were not sufficient attack aircraft available. Most F-4 crews despised bombing sorties.

Early in their service careers, F-4Bs featured slick fin-tips, although later most aircraft were retro-fitted with radar homing and warning receiver (RHAW) antennas housed in distinctive bullet fairings facing both fore and aft.

Below: This quartet of F-4Bs, belonging to VF-21 'Freelancers', is shown posing for the camera. The wing fuel tanks are unusual.

Above: With afterburners blazing, a VF-41 Phantom hurtles skyward. This unit was one of several Atlantic Fleet squadrons deployed on combat cruises to the Gulf of Tonkin.

F-4B Phantom II

Type: two-seat carrier-borne interceptor

Powerplant: two 79.65-kN (17,920-lb-thrust) General Electric J79-8A afterburning turbojets

Maximum speed: 2390 km/h (1482 mph)

Combat radius: 1450 km (900 miles)

Range: 3700 km (2294 miles)

Service ceiling: 21,640 m (71,000 ft)

Weights: empty 12,701 kg (27,942 lb); maximum take-off 24,766 kg (54,485 lb)

Armament: four AIM-7 Sparrow medium-range and four AIM-9 Sidewinder short-range air-to-air missiles, plus various air-to-ground stores

Dimensions:
span	11.71 m (38 ft 5 in)
length	17.75 m (58 ft 3 in)
height	4.95 m (16 ft 3 in)
wing area	49.24 m² (530 sq ft)

COMBAT DATA

During the 1960s the F-4's main rival in the naval fighter stakes was the Vought F-8 Crusader. The Crusader was often overrated because it was a single-seat fighter with guns. The Phantom was considerably faster thanks to its powerful twin J79 turbojets.

MAXIMUM SPEED

F-4B PHANTOM II — 2390 km/h (1482 mph)
F-8J CRUSADER — 1802 km/h (1117 mph)
A-4E SKYHAWK — 1083 km/h (671 mph)

COMBAT RADIUS

Operational radius was where the Phantom came up short. It was a thirsty beast and needed regular air-to-air refuelling. By contrast, the smaller Crusader and even smaller Skyhawk were longer-legged, an important factor when flying sorties deep into the heart of North Vietnam.

F-4B PHANTOM II — 1450 km (900 miles)
A-4E SKYHAWK — 1865 km (1156 miles)
F-8J CRUSADER — 1930 km (1197 miles)

MAXIMUM WEIGHT

Among its many records, the Phantom had the distinction of being the heaviest fighter to have served aboard a carrier up to that time. This weight factor prolonged the career of the F-8, which continued to operate from the smaller wooden-deck carriers.

F-4B PHANTOM II — 24,766 kg (54,585 lb)
F-8J CRUSADER — 12,474 kg (27,443 lb)
A-4E SKYHAWK — 7355 kg (16,818 lb)

US Navy Phantom MiG-killers in Vietnam

■ **VF-161:** During Operation Linebacker in May 1972, two F-4Bs from VF-161 'Chargers' tangled with two MiG-19s, downing both. The victorious crews, Lts Brown, Bartholomy, Arwood and Bell, are seen back in the squadron ready room.

■ **VF-92:** 10 May 1972 saw a number of MiG-kills for US Navy Phantoms. Lt Curt Dose of VF-92 'Silver Kings' successfully despatched an NVAF MiG-17 with an AIM-9 Sidewinder, and is seen here describing his tangle.

■ **VF-114:** Seen in high spirits after his return to the USS Kitty Hawk, Lt Robert Hughes, and his RIO Lt (jg) Adolph Cruz, managed to shoot down a MiG-21 on 6 May 1972. Hughes' wingman also scored a kill during the same successful sortie.

McDONNELL DOUGLAS
RF-4 PHANTOM II

- Tactical reconnaissance ● Vietnam service ● Upgraded aircraft

First flying in 1963, the RF-4 multi-sensor day reconnaissance variants of the tried and tested F-4B/C fighter found fame in USAF and Marine operations over Vietnam, and later in the First Gulf War. Widely exported, the capable RF-4C remained in front-line USAF service until 1994. Already blessed with phenomenal performance and load-carrying ability, the McDonnell Douglas F-4 was an ideal basis for this progressively modernized 'photo-Phantom'.

▲ One of the most successful jet combat aircraft, the original F-4 interceptor has spawned many derivatives filling strike, defence-suppression and reconnaissance roles.

McDONNELL DOUGLAS RF-4 PHANTOM II

▲ Shipboard reconnaissance
VMFP-3 'The Eyes of the Corps', the most famous US Marine Corps RF-4 operator, flew the RF-4B from its establishment in 1975 until 1990. The unit often deployed aboard USS Midway.

▲ Large USAF fleet
The USAF was by far the largest RF-4 user, taking delivery of most of the the 503 RF-4Cs built. Spain and Korea have also operated small C-model fleets.

▲ Long-range navigation aid
AN/ARN-92 LORAN was fitted to a number of RF-4Cs, its aerial mounted along the aircraft's spine.

▼ Japanese service
Japan's Air Self Defence Force took delivery of 14 RF-4EJ Phantoms in 1974-75 as replacements for its RF-86F Sabres. Unlike the JASDF's locally assembled F-4EJs, these RF-4s were built in St Louis.

▼ Nose-mounted cameras
A Marine Corps RF-4B of VMCJ-1, based at Da Nang, South Vietnam, in 1970, shows off its KS-56 and KS-87 cameras. The US Navy, with a large fleet of RF-8 Crusaders, did not order the 'recce Phantom' for its fleet.

FACTS AND FIGURES

➤ Israel's RF-4Es are fitted with indigenous reconnaissance equipment and also carry air-to-air missiles for self-defence.

➤ Compared with other versions, the RF-4 models have an 84-cm (33-in) nose stretch.

➤ Japanese RF-4Es, known as RF-4EJs, have been upgraded by Mitsubishi.

➤ The RF-4C was in production longer than any other F-4 Phantom variant, the last being delivered in December 1973.

➤ European-based USAF RF-4Cs were equipped to deliver a single nuclear bomb.

➤ Luftwaffe RF-4Es carried side-looking radar and uprated J79-GE-17 turbofans.

PROFILE

McDonnell's 'photo-Phantom'

By the time production ended, McDonnell Douglas had completed 713 RF-4 Phantoms. More than 500 of these were RF-4Cs, primarily for the USAF, with whom it served as the service's last dedicated fast-jet tactical reconnaissance aircraft. The RF-4E was the main export version.

Over Vietnam, the rugged RF-4 was used extensively by the USAF and, to a lesser extent, by the US Marine Corps which had a small fleet of 46 RF-4Bs. Flying generally unarmed, USAF RF-4Cs used speed as their only protection. Cruising at medium altitude, the primary tool

employed by the RF-4C was the KS-127 LOROP (LOng-Range Oblique Photography) camera, used to sweep the ground target from up to 90-kms' distance.

In addition to an AN/APQ-99 mapping and terrain-following radar, 24 USAF examples received the AN/ALQ-125 'TEREC' (Tactical Electronic REConnaissance) pod, which provided a still unmatched capability for the detection of electronic emitters. For nighttime operations the aircraft were fitted with photo-flash ejectors.

After the RF-4C's success in Vietnam, air forces accepting the RF-4C included South Korea and

Spain, both these taking ex-USAF examples. The main export version was the RF-4E operated by Germany, Greece, Iran, Israel, Turkey and Japan. While the US and Germany have retired their aircraft, most other operators continue to fly them.

Below: Operating from the USS Midway in May 1980, this VMFP-3 RF-4B clearly shows the aircraft's nose design incorporating the camera suite.

Above: The first YRF-4C was unveiled by McDonnell Douglas in August 1962. It was first flown by test pilots Krings and McIntyre; 713 others followed.

RF-4B Phantom II

The US Marine Corps' VMFP-3, based at El Toro, California, and aboard the USS Midway, was known as 'The Eyes of the Corps' and operated only RF-4s. In 1987 the unit was renamed the 'Rhinos'.

The RF-4B introduced a revised fin panel with a built-in high-frequency antenna. In addition it contained photoflash cartridge dispensers.

The RF-4B was powered by two General Electric J79 turbojets. These were later upgraded in the RF-4B SLEP (Service Life Extension Program). This also brought a new side-looking airborne radar, different ejection seats, a more rounded nose and heavier-duty undercarriage.

Unarmed, the RF-4B stretched its range with underwing fuel tanks. Its wings used to F-4B standard, rather than being the later 'thicker' F-4J type. Hinged inboard flaps were a feature.

Seated in tandem Martin-Baker Mk H5 ejection seats, the RF-4's crew comprised pilot and a navigator/systems operator. Flying from the rear cockpit was possible, though tricky.

The front fuselage of the RF-4B was equipped with the ASW-25B one-way digital data link and ALQ-126 radar jammer, eliminating the need for an external jamming pod.

As well as the standard AN/APQ-99 radar set in the nose, the RF-4B carried the ASN-48 navigation and deck-landing system, ARC-105 communications transceiver and an ASN-48 or ASN-58 navaid, as well as a side-looking airborne radar and other systems.

The LS-58A camera mounting station in the lower nose of the RF-4B could lift KS-56 and KS-87 cameras for typical missions, or the larger KS-91 or KS-127A units.

RF-4E Phantom operators

■ **GERMANY:** The Luftwaffe has flown two wings of 'recce Phantoms': AKG 51 'Immelmann' and AKG 52. AKG 51 is since taken on the Tornado, whilst AKG 52 was disbanded in 1994.

■ **GREECE:** The Hellenic air force procured eight RF-4Es under the 'Peace Icarus' programme. The six remaining aircraft serve with 348 Mira Taktikis Anagnoriseos 'Matia'.

■ **JAPAN:** All the JASDF's RF-4EJs are flown by the 501st Hikotai. After wearing various colours, the fleet has not adopted a standard low-level camouflage and a woodpecker badge.

RF-4C Phantom II

Type: two-seat tactical reconnaissance aircraft

Powerplant: two 75.62-kN (17,101-lb-thrust) General Electric J79-GE-15 afterburning turbofans

Maximum speed: 2348 km/h (1455 mph) 'clean' at 12,190 m (40,000 ft)

Maximum climb rate: 14,630 m/min (48,000 fpm)

Combat radius: 1353 km (840 miles)

Service ceiling: 18,105 m (59,400 ft)

Weights: empty 12,826 kg (28,217 lb); maximum take-off 26,308 kg (57,880 lb)

Dimensions:
span	11.71 m (38 ft 5 in)
length	19.17 m (62 ft 10 in)
height	5.03 m (16 ft 6 in)
wing area	49.24 m² (530 sq ft)

COMBAT DATA

MAXIMUM SPEED

Both the RF-4C and the single-seat Dassault Mirage F1CR are dedicated tactical reconnaissance types derived from interceptor fighters. This accounts for their impressive performance. The RF-4C Phantom with its fixed reconnaissance package is marginally slower than a 'clean' F-4E fighter-bomber variant.

RF-4C PHANTOM II	2348 km/h (1455 mph)
F-4E PHANTOM II	2390 km/h (1482 mph)
MIRAGE F.1CR	1915 km/h (1187 mph)

SERVICE CEILING

Although single-engined, the more modern Mirage F1CR has a slightly superior ceiling to both Phantoms. The RF-4C is actually optimised for low-level daylight work, for example in the Gulf, where it hunted 'Scud' missiles with the LOROP system.

MIRAGE F.1CR	20,000 m (65,600 ft)
F-4E PHANTOM II	18,975 m (62,200 ft)
RF-4C PHANTOM II	18,105 m (59,400 ft)

MAXIMUM TAKE-OFF WEIGHT

The RF-4C, without internal cannon and armament systems, is somewhat lighter than the USAF's F-4E aircraft. Lighter than both is the Mirage, which also has the capacity to carry an offensive and defensive weapons load.

RF-4C PHANTOM II	26,308 kg (57,880 lb)
MIRAGE F1CR	16,200 kg (35,540 lb)
F-4E PHANTOM II	28,030 kg (61,670 lb)

McDonnell Douglas

F-4G Phantom II

● Defence suppression ● Converted F-4E ● Gulf War veteran

When the McDonnell Douglas F-4G 'Advanced Wild Weasel' was retired from service in 1995, the USAF lost its only warplane designed specifically for the task of finding, fighting and defeating the air defence radars guiding an enemy's surface-to-air missile batteries.

The F-4G was a converted F-4E Phantom II fighter, with all the superb performance characteristics of the Phantom, but armed with radar-hunting missiles.

▶ The 'Advanced Wild Weasel' proved the worth of its unique capabilities in the First Gulf War in the twilight years of its career. This added to the controversy surrounding its retirement.

McDonnell Douglas **F-4G Phantom II**

▲ **Heart of the 'Weasel'**
The undernose fairing that housed a 20-mm cannon in the F-4E contained receivers for the APR-38 radar homing and warning system.

▼ **Standard-armed**
The F-4G in the foreground carries an AGM-78 Standard anti-radiation missile, a design based on the Standard naval surface-to-air missile.

▶ **HARM-toting Gs**
In its later years of service the principal weapon of the F-4G was the AGM-88 HARM. These aircraft are carrying four each.

Versatile airframe ▶
The F-4G was the last USAF Phantom variant. Its retirement ended more than 30 years of USAF service.

▶ **'Hunter-killer' teams**
Prior to the F-4G's retirement, 'hunter-killer' teams employing Phantoms and F-16C Fighting Falcons were introduced. The F-4Gs passed targeting information to the F-16s, which were equipped with HARM targeting pods and missiles.

FACTS AND FIGURES

▶ F-4Gs accounted for 74 per cent of the Iraqi air defence radars destroyed during Operation Desert Storm.

▶ The maiden flight of the prototype F-4G took place on 6 December 1975.

▶ Only one F-4G was lost in action during the First Gulf conflict.

▶ The last F-4Gs in operational service were operated by the Air National Guard from Boise, Idaho.

▶ F-4Gs have been replaced with HARM-equipped F-16C Block 50 aircraft.

▶ The F-4G designation was first used for a modified datalink-fitted US Navy F-4B.

PROFILE

'Weasels' to ferret out enemy radars

As a replacement for the 'Wild Weasel' version of the F-105G, the Pentagon ordered development of the F-4G 'Advanced Wild Weasel'. It benefited from experience in Vietnam, where Soviet-built, radar-guided SA-2 'Guideline' surface-to-air missiles were a constant threat to American combat aircraft.

The F-4G was created by modifying the F-4E Phantom II fighter, removing its 20-mm cannon and adding electronic 'black boxes' aimed at detecting, and firing on, enemy missile sites. The system, known as AN/APR-38, provides

comprehensive radar warning and homing with the help of 52 special antennas. The F-4G's crew had an array of weapons at their disposal, including specialised anti-radiation missiles (ARMs) like Shrike, Standard and HARM (High-speed Anti-Radiation Missile).

The first F-4G reached the USAF's 35th Wing in California in 1978. When Operation Desert Storm exploded in 1991, more than 100 F-4G 'Wild Weasels' were still in service; this aircraft became the backbone of the

'suppression of enemy air defences' (SEAD) effort against Iraq during coalition air raids. Defence cuts spelled the end of the dedicated SEAD platform in the USAF, and the last F-4Gs were retired in 1995.

Below: The F-4G's General Electric J79-GE-17A turbojet engines were modified to reduce smoke emission.

Above: The 52nd Tactical Fighter Wing provided NATO's principal anti-radiation capability for more than 10 years.

F-4G PHANTOM II

69-0247 is shown in the markings of the 52nd Tactical Fighter Wing, based at Spangdahlem Air Base, Germany. The 52nd received its first F-4Gs in 1979, one of three wings equipped with the 'Weasel'.

As a two-seater the Phantom was ideally suited to the SEAD task, with the Electronic Warfare Officer (EWO), or 'Bear', positioned in the rear seat monitoring threats.

USAF F-4Gs carried three different colour schemes. The first examples wore Vietnam-era 'Southeast Asia' two-tone green and tan, and later examples carried so-called 'lizard' or European One colours like this aircraft.

The F-4G was easily distinguished from the F-4E by the fin top 'torpedo' fairing that contained the high band antenna for the APR-38 radar homing and warning system (RHAWS). The low band receiver was located in the leading edge of the tail fin.

In all, 116 late-production F-4Es were converted to 'G' standard between 1975 and 1981. A further 18 attrition replacements followed. Some of the airframes used had seen service in Vietnam.

'Wild Weasel' Phantoms carried an F-15-type centreline fuel tank on re-stressed mounts. The tank was stressed to 5g when full, compared to 3g for a standard F-4 tank.

The F-4G could be armed with AIM-9 Sidewinder missiles for self-defence, together with an AN/ALQ-119 jamming pod. AGM-65 Maverick surface-to-air missiles were also useful against ground targets.

'Wild Weasel' operations

IN THE GULF: One of the first and most important tasks for the USAF was to destroy Iraq's air defence radar network. F-4Gs attacked these sites with HARM missiles.

AIRFIELD ATTACK: F-4Gs targeted the powerful radars situated on Iraqi air bases. This allowed aircraft such as the Tornado to attack the runways with much less danger.

HUNTER-KILLER TEAMS: In addition to effectively eliminating enemy radar, the F-4G could also act in a team with HARM-equipped F-16s. Targets were found by the F-4G and fired on by the F-16.

F-4G Phantom II

Type: two-seat SEAD aircraft

Powerplant: two 79.62-kN (17,910-lb-thrust) General Electric J79-GE-17A afterburning turbojet engines

Maximum speed: 2300 km/h (1429 mph) at 12,190 m (40,000 ft)

Cruising speed: 919 km/h

Combat radius: 964 km (600 miles)

Range: 3184 km (1978 miles)

Service ceiling: 18,975 m (62,000 ft)

Weights: empty equipped 13,300 kg (29,260 lb); maximum take-off 28,300 kg (62,260 lb)

Armament: (typical) AGM-88 HARM anti-radar missiles, AGM-65 Maverick electro-optical air-to-ground missiles, plus AIM-9 Sidewinder air-to-air missiles for self-defence

Dimensions:
span	11.71 m	(38 ft 5 in)
length	19.20 m	(62 ft 11 in)
height	5.02 m	(16 ft 6 in)
wing area	49.24 m²	(530 sq ft)

COMBAT DATA

MAXIMUM SPEED

The Phantom and Tornado both have impressive top speeds at high altitude. However, at low level, where most of the missions are carried out, all three types operate at around 1100 km/h (700 mph).

F-4G PHANTOM II	2300 km/h (1429 mph)
TORNADO GR.Mk 1	2338 km/h (1450 mph)
Su-24 'FENCER-D'	1435 km/h (890 mph)

COMBAT RADIUS

The Tornado has the best unrefuelled combat radius, allowing it to penetrate deep into enemy territory. The Phantom had a good radius for a 1960s design, however. Intended for the European theatre the Su-24 has a much shorter range.

Su-24 'FENCER-D'
560 km
(350 miles)

F-4G
PHANTOM II
964 km
(600 miles)

TORNADO GR.Mk 1
1390 km
(860 miles)

LOW-LEVEL MISSILE RANGE

The HARM missile fitted to the F-4G had a reasonable low-level range and was regarded as highly accurate. The ALARM and AS-12 'Kegler' are both second-generation anti-radar missiles.

F-4G PHANTOM II   25 km (16 miles)

TORNADO GR.Mk 1   30 km (19 miles)

Su-24 'FENCER-D'   25 km (16 miles)

McDonnell Douglas
C-9 Nightingale

- VIP carrier ● Airborne ambulance ● Civilian design

After its successful introduction into the civil airline market during the mid-1960s, the McDonnell Douglas DC-9 was selected by the USAF in 1967 as its dedicated aeromedical evacuation aircraft. Experience in Vietnam showed just how vital such an aircraft was in modern war theatres. Ordering such an aircraft 'off-the-shelf' kept costs low, and the enduring nature of the type has ensured that it remains in service more than 30 years later.

▲ Essentially based on the commercial DC-9 Series 30, the C-9A Nightingale has given sterling service to the USAF, yet it is often overshadowed by more glamorous aircraft.

McDonnell Douglas C-9 Nightingale

▼ **Cargo carrier**
When operated by the US Navy, the type is known as the C-9B Skytrain II. For this role it is equipped with a large cargo door.

▲ **International rescue**
With a large Red Cross on its tail, a C-9 Nightingale lands at the scene of another disaster.

Naval reserve ▶
After a review of its transport assets, the US Navy turned over its fleet of Skytrain IIs to the naval reserve. In time of war, however, the aircraft would be deployed to front-line naval bases.

Great white bird ▼
Throughout their entire service life the aircraft have retained a smart white and grey colour scheme. This has proved to be very appropriate for missions involving high-ranking personnel or government figures.

▲ **Angel in the air**
The US Navy has operated the C-9B Skytrain II since the early seventies. The aircraft required minor modifications for military service but retained the grace of its civilian counterparts.

FACTS AND FIGURES

▶ C-9A Nightingales flew home the American hostages released from Iran in 1981.

▶ One C-9A Nightingale is configured as a VIP transport within Europe.

▶ Flight crew consists of two pilots with a crew chief or loadmaster.

▶ On aeromedical missions, the C-9A Nightingale can accommodate 40 stretcher patients or 40 seated patients.

▶ One C-9A was lost in a mishap at Scott Field on 16 September 1971.

▶ In March 1981 C-9Bs replaced the long-serving C-118B Liftmaster in the USN.

PROFILE

America's airborne saviour

From Vietnam to the Gulf War, the C-9A Nightingale has become indispensable in support of front-line US troops. Up to 40 stretcher cases or 40 walking wounded can be accommodated along with trained medical staff on these vital evacuation flights.

Based on the DC-9 Series 30, the Nightingale entered service in June 1968. Modifications to the standard airliner included a new access door with an in-built hydraulic ramp for the loading of stretchers, and a specialist medical care compartment.

The USAF also received three C-9C VIP transport versions.

The success of the DC-9 in military service was soon appreciated by the US Navy which ordered the C-9B Skytrain II in an effort to modernise its small but important logistics support service. First entering service in 1972, a dozen aircraft were acquired along with two for the US Marine Corps. Also based on the Series 30, the C-9B features additional fuel capacity for extended range and can operate in all-cargo, all-passenger or mixed configuration. The

aircraft were deployed to Saudi Arabia during the Gulf War.

Other military users include Kuwait and Italy which operate two examples on light transport and VIP duties.

Above: Operated on behalf of the special air missions airlift wing, this particular Nightingale is used as a personal VIP transport. The aircraft is especially configured for the role.

Above: Taxiing to the main runway, this C-9B Skytrain II operates with the US Navy on support duties. This example is capable of airlifting 107 naval personnel.

C-9B SKYTRAIN II

Though not as glamorous as the fighters operated by the US Navy, the C-9B Skytrain II has proved to be the ideal aircraft for transporting personnel and cargo to various naval bases throughout the world.

A flight deck crew of three is used for standard operations. Positioned on the port side of the nose is a set of hydraulically-operated self-contained airstairs. Often flown by reserve crews, who are full-time commercial airline pilots, the aircraft has proved itself to be a highly versatile transport asset for the USN.

To allow the C-9B to undertake cargo operations the aircraft is equipped with a large cargo door. This is hydraulically raised to ease loading and is operated from within the cockpit.

With room for 107 passengers, sufficient safety equipment is of vital importance. For ditching at sea, the aircraft is equipped with four 25-man life rafts located at various positions along the fuselage.

Despite being in military service, the C-9B Skytrain II retains a smart civil-looking colour scheme. Although it rarely enters a combat zone, the aircraft is equipped with an infra-red jammer on the tail. This reduces the risk of attack by missiles.

The fuselage area of the C-9B Skytrain II can contain up to eight standard military freight pallets when in all-cargo configuration. For these operations the aircraft is fitted with a specially-adapted cargo roller floor to reduce the loading and unloading times.

Airliners in military service

■ **BOEING E-4B:** Adapted from the Boeing 747 Jumbo, the military E-4B is used as an Advanced Airborne Command Post. The aircraft is equipped with highly sophisticated communications equipment. Four aircraft are currently in service.

■ **BOEING KC-135A:** Operated both as an airborne tanker and transport aircraft, the KC-135 has served with the USAF since the 1960s. Current upgrades of the aircraft involve the adoption of more fuel-efficient engines.

■ **DOUGLAS EC-24A:** Serving with the US Navy as an Electronic Warfare Support aircraft, the EC-24A is used against naval vessels to assess their ability to defend themselves against attack during military exercises.

C-9A Nightingale

Type: transport/medical evacuation aircraft

Powerplant: two 64.5-kN (14,500-lb-thrust) Pratt & Whitney JT8D-9 turbofan engines

Maximum cruising speed: 907 km/h (562 mph) at 7620 m (25,000 ft)

Initial climb rate: 885 m/min (2900 fpm)

Range: ferry range 3327 km (2060 miles); range with full accommodation 2388 km (1480 miles)

Weights: empty 25,940 kg (57,068 lb); maximum take-off 54,885 kg (120,747 lb)

Accommodation: four crew; 30 to 40 stretcher patients with medical attendants

Dimensions:
span — 28.47 m (93 ft 5 in)
length — 36.37 m (119 ft 3 in)
height — 8.38 m (27 ft 6 in)
wing area — 92.97 m² (1000 sq ft)

ACTION DATA

MAXIMUM SPEED

With the need to reach an emergency situation in the shortest period of time, the speed of the C-9A Nightingale is high compared to that of its contemporaries. Fastest of all the current military airliners is the CT-43A.

C-9A NIGHTINGALE	907 km/h (562 mph)
Tu-134 'CRUSTY'	900 km/h (558 mph)
CT-43A	927 km/h (575 mph)

RANGE

Although equipped with additional fuel tanks to extend its range, the C-9 Nightingale still has a relatively short endurance. The Russian Tu-134 'Crusty' offers only a slightly increased range. Although its lack of range is a problem, the C-9 operates in concert with longer-range C-141s.

C-9A NIGHTINGALE 3327 km (2060 miles)

CT-43A 4818 km (2987 miles)

Tu-134 'CRUSTY' 3500 km (2170 miles)

SERVICE CEILING

Designed originally for the civil airliner market, the C-9 Nightingale has retained its ability to operate at high altitudes. When operating with a full load of casualties its performance is significantly reduced, however. The highest performer is the Tu-134 'Crusty'.

C-9A NIGHTINGALE	Tu-134 'CRUSTY'	CT-43A
11,280 m (37,000 ft)	11,900 m (39,000 ft)	10,668 m (35,000 ft)

McDonnell Douglas
F-15C Eagle

- Air superiority fighter ● Advanced weapons ● Unbeaten in combat

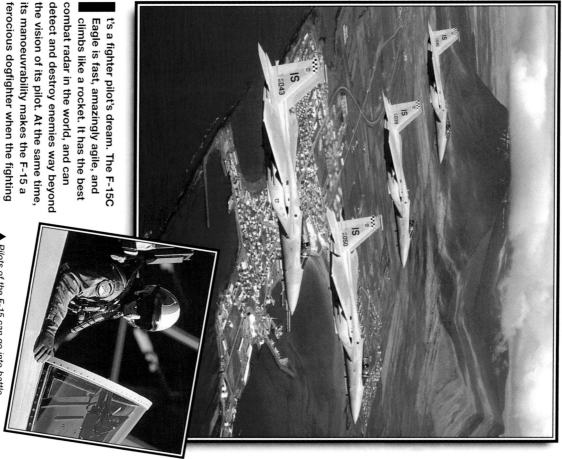

It's a fighter pilot's dream. The F-15C Eagle is fast, amazingly agile, and climbs like a rocket. It has the best combat radar in the world, and can detect and destroy enemies way beyond the vision of its pilot. At the same time, its manoeuvrability makes the F-15 a ferocious dogfighter when the fighting gets close and dirty. Even today, 20 years after its first flight, few aircraft can match the Eagle in combat.

▲ Pilots of the F-15 can go into battle confident that they can take on any opponent and win. Its combat record is impressive, especially in Israeli hands.

McDonnell Douglas F-15C EAGLE

▲ Dressed to kill
The Eagle's powerful armament has always been a great strength, and has only been surpassed by the Russian Su-27 family. The very capable avionics and radar systems remain among the best in the world, and the aircraft is also a superb dogfighter, thanks to its large wing and high thrust-to-weight ratio. With a new generation of missiles, it remains a lethal foe.

Big bird ▶
The huge size of the Eagle makes its blistering performance even more remarkable. It earned the name 'flying tennis court' from pilots because of its dimensions.

▼ Intercept
Eagles routinely intercepted Soviet aircraft, but occasionally met ships like this 'Kiev'-class carrier. The infra-red seeker head of the underwing Sidewinder can be seen on the left of the picture.

▲ Loading up
For short-range engagements, the Sidewinder missile remains the Eagle's main weapon, but it now needs replacing.

▼ Sparrow launch
The Sparrow medium-range radar-guided missile has now been replaced by the far more capable AMRAAM, which can operate autonomously.

FACTS AND FIGURES

- ▶ The Eagle flew in July 1972, with the first of the improved F-15Cs taking to the air in February 1979.

- ▶ In the Gulf War, Eagles shot down 32 Iraqi aircraft without loss.

- ▶ Overseas operators of the Eagle include Israel, Japan and Saudi Arabia.

- ▶ FAST – Fuel And Sensor, Tactical – packs allow the Eagle to make unrefuelled transatlantic flights.

- ▶ Production of F-15 fighters has now ended after more than 1000 aircraft.

- ▶ The F-15 can 'zoom-climb' to an astonishing altitude of 30,000 m (98,400 ft).

PROFILE

The unbeaten king of the skies

As a fighter, the F-15 is hard to beat. Two powerful Pratt & Whitney turbofans push the big fighter skywards at two-and-a-half times the speed of sound, and it can reach its normal operating ceiling of 18,000 m (59,000 ft) in only two minutes. In a fight, the Eagle's primary weapons are its four AMRAAM Advanced Medium Range Air-to-Air Missiles, which can destroy targets at up to 70 km (45 miles). The F-15 also carries four AIM-9 Sidewinder heat-seeking missiles

and a superfast-firing M61 Vulcan 20-mm cannon for close-quarter combat.

The Eagle can turn tightly and make abrupt manoeuvres that would never have been remotely possible in its predecessors. All-round pilot view from the high-set cockpit is superb, thanks to the large bubble canopy.

In spite of rivals to its position the F-15 remains the most successful air superiority fighter in service. Nearly 100 enemy aircraft have fallen to F-15s, including over 30 Iraqi

Like the Russian MiG-25, the F-15 gets its high speed from a pair of enormously powerful engines, fed by huge intakes, which are adjustable for high-speed flight.

warplanes during the Gulf War of 1991. However, no Eagle has ever been lost in aerial combat. It is an amazing record, which the big McDonnell Douglas fighter will carry on the front line well into the 21st century.

The F-15 has a very large speed brake mounted on the top of the centre fuselage. This design feature also appeared on the Su-27 after early trials with other layouts.

The M61 Vulcan cannon is mounted in the starboard wingroot. The port wingroot houses the refuelling receptacle for the USAF's 'flying boom' refuelling system.

Twin tailfins were used in the F-15 to give good control in slow-speed dogfights. The tailplane was built with a dogtooth to cure flutter problems.

The twin Pratt & Whitney F100 engines were initially troublesome, especially when afterburner was selected. Their tremendous power-to-weight ratio was unmatched for many years.

The fuselage of the F-15 is immensely strong, with a large number of composite, titanium and steel components. The airframe is stressed to withstand nine times the force of gravity.

The F-15 design brief called for good dogfight performance, so the view from the canopy was given priority. It is better than the more recent MiG-29 'Fulcrum'.

The F-15C's cockpit has multi-function display screens in place of conventional instruments.

The large APG-63 radar has been replaced in the F-15C by the improved APG-70. This radar has very long-range, good lookdown/shootdown performance and improved reliability.

The Tracor AN/ALE-45 chaff and flare dispenser system, also fitted to the F-15E, is located just behind the nosewheel doors.

F-15C EAGLE 'GULF SPIRIT'

The F-15Cs of the 58th Fighter Squadron claimed 16 victories over the Iraqi air force during the Gulf War. This aircraft shot down a MiG-23 and two Sukhoi Su-22s during Operation Desert Storm.

Eagle combat air patrol

EAGLE FLIGHT: F-15s generally operate in flights of two or four aircraft. One of their key functions is the Combat Air Patrol. This is used to deny enemy access to friendly air space, or to 'sanitise' the space over a target to allow an attack force to raid without fear of enemy fighters.

MAXIMUM COVERAGE: The F-15 flight will usually break into two pairs in combat formations, taking up positions on opposite sides of an imaginary 'racetrack' in the sky. This can be anything from 10 to 25 km (6 to 15 miles) long. Sometimes the Eagles fly 'figure of eight' patterns to give pilots some variety.

RADAR COVERAGE: The flight splits into two pairs primarily to make sure that at least some of the Eagles are heading towards a possible enemy advance at all times. This ensures continuous radar coverage, since the Eagle's sophisticated radar only works in the forward arc.

F-15C Eagle

Type: single-seat air-superiority fighter

Powerplant: two 105.92-kN (23,760-lb-thrust) Pratt & Whitney F100-PW-220 afterburning turbofans

Maximum speed: Mach 2.5 or 2655 km/h (1650 mph)

Range: more than 5750 km (3656 miles) with external conformal fuel tanks

Service ceiling: 18,300 m (60,000 ft)

Weights: empty 12,800 kg (28,160 lb); maximum 30,850 kg (67,870 lb)

Armament: one 20-mm M61A1 Vulcan cannon; up to four AIM-9 Sidewinder missiles; up to four AIM-120 AMRAAM missiles; provision for up to 4852 kg (10,700 lb) of bombs and missiles

Dimensions:
span	13.05 m	(43 ft)
length	19.43 m	(64 ft)
height	5.63 m	(18 ft)
wing area	56.48 m²	(608 sq ft)

COMBAT DATA

MAXIMUM SPEED

The Eagle was designed to intercept high-flying 'Foxbat' reconnaissance aircraft, and while not as quick as the powerful MiG design it was faster than any other fighter in service today. The Sukhoi Su-27, the F-15's only current rival, is slightly slower.

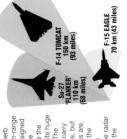

F-15 EAGLE	**2655 km/h (1650 mph)**
Su-27 'FLANKER'	**2280 km/h (1414 mph)**
F-14 TOMCAT	**2000km/h (1210 mph)**

CLIMB RATE

The Eagle climbs like a rocket, thanks to the immense power of its two Pratt & Whitney F100 engines. However, it cannot match the even more powerful 'Flanker', which first flew 10 years after the American jet, and which in some respects is an even better performer.

Su-27 'FLANKER' more than 15,250 m/min (50,020 fpm)

F-14 TOMCAT 10,000 m/min (32,800 fpm)

F-15 EAGLE 19,800 m/min (64,944 fpm)

WEAPONS RANGE

The Eagle is a superb short- and medium-range fighter. It is not designed for ultra-long-range interception, unlike the F-14 Tomcat with its huge Phoenix missiles. The 'Flanker' can also carry long-range missiles, but its normal weapons are similar to those of the Eagle. However, in modern fighters the radar is as important as the weapons.

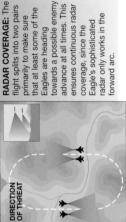

F-14 TOMCAT 150 km (93 miles)

Su-27 'FLANKER' 110 km (68 miles)

F-15 EAGLE 70 km (43 miles)

McDonnell Douglas

F-15E EAGLE

- Two-seat fighter-bomber
- F-111 replacement
- Gulf War service

S trike Eagle – the McDonnell Douglas F-15E – is one of the fastest and deadliest warplanes. Developed from the F-15 air-superiority fighter, this 'smart' two-seat aircraft uses advanced radar and avionics to deliver a vast array of weapons at night and in all weathers to targets many kilometres away. One of the stars of the Gulf War, the F-15E has at the same time retained the single-seat Eagle's excellent air-to-air capability.

▲ Without doubt the most advanced tactical bomber in the West, the F-15E provides the USAF with a unique night/all-weather capability and replaces the capable but ageing F-111.

McDonnell Douglas F-15E EAGLE

▲ 'Buckets of instant sunshine'
An early production 57th Fighter Wing 'Strike Eagle' carries two Dayglo-painted dummy B61 nuclear weapons. The B61 can be fitted with a warhead up to 25 times more powerful than the Hiroshima bomb.

▼ Range enhancement
F-15Es refuel from a KC-10A Extender. One criticism of the F-15E has been its lack of range compared to aircraft it has replaced, like the F-111F.

▲ Anti-radar missiles
This aircraft is armed with AGM-88 HARMs, one of a number of weapons options for the F-15E.

▲ LANTIRN pods
The AAQ-14 targeting pod is fixed to the right intake, with the AAQ-13 navigation pod on the left.

▼ Wing tanks
To increase range, up to three 2309-litre (580-gallon) drop-tanks are often carried on operations.

FACTS AND FIGURES

▼ Although the last of 209 'Strike Eagles' was delivered in 1994, the USAF has ordered further attrition replacements.

▼ The first production F-15E made its initial flight on 11 December 1986.

▼ F-15Es are known by the nicknames 'Beagle' (Bomber Eagle) and 'Mud Hen'.

▶ Fighter-bomber F-15s similar to the F-15E are currently being produced for Saudi Arabia (F-15S) and Israel (F-15I).

▶ Two F-15Es were lost in combat during Operation Desert Storm.

▶ USAF orders for the F-15E were cut to protect funding for the Lockheed F-22.

PROFILE

'Strike Eagle' tactical bomber

McDonnell Douglas' F-15E 'Strike Eagle' – the fast and far-reaching fighter-bomber version of the famous F-15 – has replaced Genral Dynamics' F-111 as the US Air Force's long-range tactical strike aircraft and equips eight squadrons.

The original plans for a ground-attack Eagle were abandoned in 1975, but revived in 1982 when trials began using a two-seat TF-15A. The first production aircraft flew in 1986 after competition from the F-16XL had been seen off.

Although budget cuts reduced deliveries to just over 200, the F-15E performed with distinction in the 1991 Gulf War, attacking a variety of targets on missions that included hunting for 'Scud' missile sites during sorties lasting up to six hours.

The F-15E has acquired its bomb-carrying capacity without giving up any of its air-to-air ability. This is where it differs from the F-111, which used sheer speed to escape from hostile fighters. The 'Strike Eagle' can fight back and win.

The broad wing of the F-15E has a reputation for subjecting crews to a rougher ride in low-level, high-speed flight than the F-111.

F-15E EAGLE

Veterans of action against Libya and in the Gulf, USAFE's 48th Fighter Wing, based at RAF Lakenheath, traded its venerable F-111Fs for F-15Es in 1992. 90-0248 was their first example.

At the heart of the F-15E's capability is the APG-70 radar. As well as air-to-air modes it offers high-resolution ground mapping for accurate weapons aiming.

The cockpit is state-of-the-art. The pilot has a wide-angle head-up display (HUD) and three multi-function displays (MFDs). The Weapons Systems Officer (WSO) has four MFDs.

Complementing the radar is the LANTIRN (Low-Altitude Navigation and Targeting Infra-Red for Night) system, consisting of two pods under the engine intakes; one with terrain-following radar and a forward-looking infra-red sensor, the other with FLIR and a laser designator.

Late-production F-15Es have two Pratt & Whitney F100-PW-229 Improved Performance Engine (IPE) afterburning turbojets giving Mach 2 capability.

As on fighter versions of the F-15, an M61 20-mm rotary cannon is mounted in the starboard wingroot.

For self-defence AIM-9 Sidewinder, AIM-7 Sparrow and/or AIM-120 AMRAAM air-to-air missiles may also be carried. This example carries two Sidewinders.

This aircraft is loaded with 14 SUU-30H cluster bombs for a close air support/battlefield air interdiction mission. A vast array of 'smart' and unguided weapons can be carried.

To improve range performance Conformal Fuel Tanks (CFTs) are fitted to either side of the fuselage. These each hold 2737 litres (700 gallons) of fuel and have pylons attached for the carriage of weapons.

F-15E Eagle

Type: two-seat strike fighter-bomber

Powerplant: two 129.45-kN (29,000-lb-thrust) Pratt & Whitney F100-P-229 afterburning turbofan engines

Maximum speed: 2655 km/h (1646 mph)

Range: 4445 km (2756 miles)

Service ceiling: 18,290 m (60,000 ft)

Weights: empty 14,379 kg (31,634 lb); maximum take-off (36,741 kg (80,830 lb)

Armament: one 20-mm M61 Vulcan rotary cannon and up to 11,000 kg (24,000 lb) of weapons, including AIM-7, AIM-120 or AIM-9 air-to-air missiles, AGM-65 or AGM-88 HARM air-to-ground missiles, laser-guided or 'iron' bombs and cluster and nuclear munitions

Dimensions:
span	13.05 m (43 ft)	
length	19.43 m (64 ft)	
height	5.63 m (18 ft)	
wing area	56.48 m² (608 sq ft)	

COMBAT DATA

GBU-28
The GBU-28 is one of a family of 'laser-guided' bombs used in the Gulf. The seeker head and moving fins are fitted to a standard 'dumb' bomb and provide precision guidance.

CBU-87
For use against 'soft-skinned' targets the CBU-87 cluster bomb contains a variety of sub-munitions, including armour-piercing and anti-personnel devices.

AGM-88 HARM
HARM, or the High-speed Anti-Radiation Missile, is a specialised weapon for use against radar installations, especially those used to guide surface-to-air missiles, homing in on their radar emissions.

'Strike Eagles' strike Iraq

KEY WEAPON: The F-15E was one of the key aircraft of the Gulf conflict, able to make precision attacks in all weathers and at night.

STRATEGIC TARGETS: One mission of the F-15Es was to hit strategic targets, including bridges, using laser-guided bombs.

'SCUD' HUNTING: 'Scud'-busting missions were guided by AWACS aircraft and involved the use of cluster munitions against the launchers.

'TURN AND BURN': When chased by a SAM during a bombing run, a quick escape could be attempted by the pilot by jettisoning fuel tanks and firing 'chaff' and flares to confuse the missile.

SAM THREAT: Heat-seeking surface-to-air missiles (SAMs) were a threat to F-15Es on daytime missions.

318

McDonnell Douglas

F/A-18 HORNET

● Carrier fighter ● Multi-role strike ● Anti-ship/radar bomber

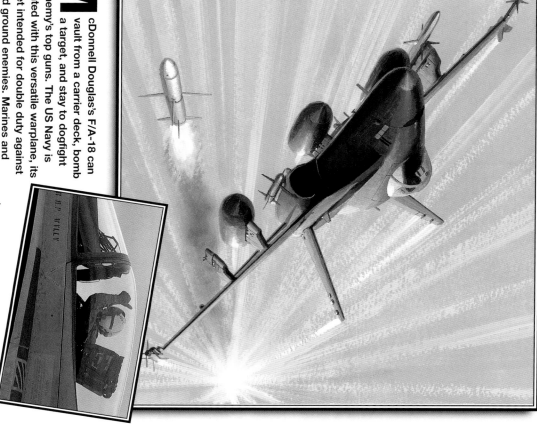

McDonnell Douglas's F/A-18 can vault from a carrier deck, bomb a target, and stay to dogfight the enemy's top guns. The US Navy is delighted with this versatile warplane, its first jet intended for double duty against air and ground enemies. Marines and overseas operators also love the Hornet. The F/A-18E/F is a bigger, more robust version of this superb fighter for carrier squadrons in the 21st century.

▲ Being an F/A-18 Hornet pilot is perhaps the ultimate aviation job – flying a single-seat high-performance jet from a carrier, tasked with both air-to-air combat and dropping bombs.

McDonnell Douglas F/A-18 HORNET

▲ **Angels of thunder**
The US Navy's elite 'Blue Angels' formation team flies the Hornet. It offers outstanding agility while thrilling air show crowds with explosively noisy power displays.

▲ **Export success**
Nations which have chosen to operate the Hornet include Australia, Canada and Spain.

▲ **Fighting office**
The Hornet had the first truly modern cockpit aboard a carrier jet, designed around large TV-style screens and a head-up display.

▲ **Carrier-borne versatility**
The Hornet is one of the world's most capable and versatile warplanes, and yet it still finds room to combine its talents with the demanding requirements of operating from the carrier deck.

▼ **Marine mud-mover**
The Marine Corps uses the two-seat F/A-18D Hornet on night attack missions, armed with laser bombs and other 'smart' weapons.

▼ **Killer on the prowl**
Armed with AMRAAM and Sidewinder missiles, and with an internal cannon, the F/A-18 can fight and win against the world's best air-to-air combatants.

FACTS AND FIGURES

➤ Land-based F/A-18 Hornets make up the front line of defence in Australia, Canada, Finland, Kuwait and Spain.

➤ About 65 crack pilots apply for three or four annual vacancies with the US Navy's Hornet-equipped 'Blue Angels'.

➤ An RF-18 Hornet photo ship was tested but not adopted.

➤ NASA uses a much modified F/A-18 to explore manoeuvring at extremely high angles of attack.

➤ The digital cockpit of the sophisticated Hornet has been described as a cross between 'Star Wars' and a video game.

➤ First flight of an F/A-18 Hornet took place on 18 November 1978.

PROFILE

Multi-mission master

This magnificent fighting jet from McDonnell Douglas has established a place as the backbone of US Navy and Marine aviation; sailors and marines wanted the F/A-18 Hornet so badly they relinquished other aircraft to get it. Their faith is justified: the F/A-18 performed superbly in raids on Libya and in Operation Desert Storm.

To keep the F/A-18 on top in the crucible of air combat, they are improving the Hornet

constantly. Better flight instruments and avionics have been added to new aircraft along with the capability to use far-reaching missiles, including the air-to-air AMRAAM and the air-to-ground HARM. None of these changes detract from the manoeuvrability of the Hornet, an exceedingly agile adversary.

The future F/A-18E (single-seat) and F/A-18F (two-seat) will be 86 cm (2 ft 10 in) longer and carry 1360 kg (2998 lb) more fuel. Navy

Defender of the frozen North – Canada has Hornets standing by to deter any attack across the vast areas that straddle the north of the country. The Hornet can react quickly to any intruder.

carrier air wings will soon boast as many as four Hornet squadrons, giving a formidable strike and fighter capability. With the F/A-18 on board the US Navy can project power globally knowing it has the world's best aircraft.

The ends of the Hornet's wings fold up so that the aircraft does not take up much room in the confines of the aircraft-carrier deck or hangar.

Long strakes ahead of the wing give the Hornet pilot outstanding control of his aircraft when flying very slowly.

F/A-18C HORNET

Popularly called the 'Swing Fighter' because it can swing between air-to-air fighting and ground attack with great ease, the Hornet can perform a wide range of missions, including radar-killing and 'Fast FAC' – guiding other attack aircraft to their targets.

This Hornet carries a mixed load of weapons – Sidewinders and Sparrows for enemy fighters, and Mk 82 bombs for ground targets.

Above the radar is the trusty M61 20-mm Vulcan cannon which is used for close-range air-to-air combat. A drum containing 570 rounds of ammunition is mounted below the gun and aft of the radar.

In the nose of the Hornet is the APG-73 radar, which is at the heart of the aircraft's versatility. It can see and track other aircraft at great distances, while also mapping the ground to make precision bombing easy.

→ VFA-87

Under the rear fuselage of the Hornet is an arrester hook for carrier landings. When lowered, this hook catches wires which are strung across the deck of the carrier.

The Hornet's undercarriage is immensely strong, since it has to withstand the repeated 'controlled crashes' of carrier landings.

Killing radars with the Hornet

PRE-EMPTIVE SHOT: As the main attack force approaches the target, an F/A-18 lobs a HARM anti-radar missile over the top of the attack force. If any enemy radars are up and running, they will be destroyed immediately before the attackers enter the lethal zone.

ANTI-RADAR ESCORT: After the pre-emptive HARM missile has been fired, other HARM-carrying Hornets lead the attack force into the lethal zone. Any enemy radars that attempt to turn on are fired at by these strike escort aircraft.

ENEMY MISSILES AND RADAR BATTERY

LETHAL ZONE

ATTACK FORCE

DETECTION ZONE

F/A-18C Hornet

Type: carrier-based naval strike fighter

Powerplant: two 71.2-kN (16,020-lb-thrust) afterburning General Electric F404-GE-400 turbofans

Maximum speed: Mach 1.8 or 1915 km/h (1190 mph) at 12,190 m (40,000 ft)

Combat radius: 1060 km (659 miles)

Initial climb rate: 305 m/sec (1000 fps)

Service ceiling: 15,240 m (50,000 ft)

Weights: empty 10,455 kg (23,049 lb); loaded 22,328 kg (49,225 lb)

Armament: one Martin Marietta M61A1 Vulcan 20-mm cannon; two AIM-9L Sidewinder missiles; 7000 kg of ordnance

Dimensions:
span		11.43 m (37 ft 6 in)
length		17.07 m (56 ft)
height		4.66 m (15 ft 3 in)
wing area		37.16 m² (400 sq ft)

COMBAT DATA

SPEED

F/A-18C HORNET	1915 km/h (1190 mph)
MIRAGE 2000	2330 km/h (1448 mph)
TORNADO GR.Mk 1	2300 km/h (1429 mph)

The Hornet is optimized for subsonic combat and weapons delivery, so while it is comfortably supersonic its simple intake design limits it to about 1.8 times the speed of sound.

LOW-LEVEL COMBAT RADIUS

TORNADO GR.Mk 1
1400 km (870 miles)

F/A-18C HORNET
600 km (383 miles)

MIRAGE 2000
750 km (466 miles)

Hornets have always had the reputation of being 'short-legged', even though they have longer range than the preceding F-4 Phantom. However, this is no real handicap in these days of aerial refuelling, and the F/A-18's superb fighting ability more than makes up for any minor defect, as shown in Operation Desert Storm.

WEAPONS LOAD

TORNADO GR.Mk 1	9000 kg (19,842 lb)
F/A-18C HORNET	7000 kg (15,432 lb)
MIRAGE 2000	6300 kg (13,889 lb)

Although the Hornet is one of the most manoeuvrable fighters in the world, it carries almost as large a weapons load as a specialized bomber like the Tornado. And with its sophisticated targeting and laser designation system it is one of the most accurate bombers currently in service.

320

McDONNELL DOUGLAS
KC-10 EXTENDER

● USAF tanker ● Strategic transport role ● Gulf War veteran

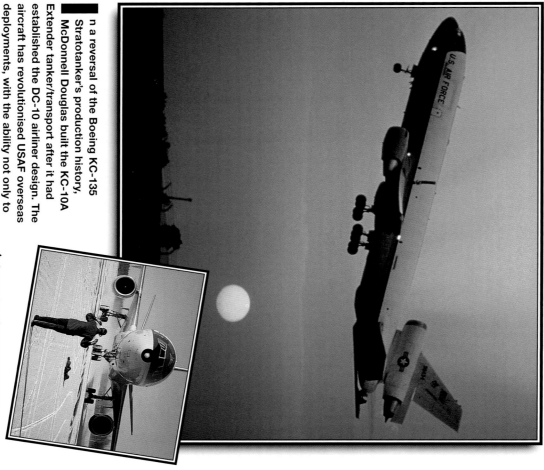

n a reversal of the Boeing KC-135
Stratotanker's production history,
McDonnell Douglas built the KC-10A
Extender tanker/transport after it had
established the DC-10 airliner design. The
aircraft has revolutionised USAF overseas
deployments, with the ability not only to
refuel formations of tactical jets, but also to
carry their support equipment and
personnel. The Extender is now a key
element in USAF operations.

▲ Supporting USAF aircraft deploying
to bases all over the world, the Extender has
become a symbol of US power projection. Forty-
six KC-10As flew 25 per cent of the tanker
missions over the Persian Gulf.

McDONNELL DOUGLAS KC-10 EXTENDER

▼ Gulf-bound Extender
During Desert Storm, 46 of the
USAF's 59 surviving KC-10As
were used to support coalition air
power. The KC-10A enabled the
deployment of US-based fighters.

▲ Refuelling options
The principal Extender tool is the 'flying boom', but for refuelling
US Navy and other NATO aircraft a hose drum unit is also carried.

▲ KC-10A achievements
In September 1982, seven
KC-10As met 20 C-141Bs over
Goose Bay, Labrador, delivering
an incredible 29484 kg of fuel to
each. The C-141Bs went on to
drop troops over West Germany.

▼ Premier tanker
The Extender can transfer
90,720 kg (200,000 lb) of fuel to one
or more receivers.

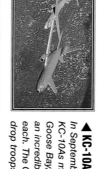

▲ Changing colours
Originally operated in a blue and white colour
scheme the KC-10 fleet has appeared in number of
different colours including lizard green, dark grey
and the current light grey scheme.

FACTS AND FIGURES

➤ During its initial operational assessment,
the KC-10A supported eight A-7Ds on a
deployment to the UK.

➤ McDonnell Douglas based its KC-10A on
the DC-10-30CF airframe.

➤ Royal Netherlands Air Force KDC-10
tankers are conversions of DC-10s.

➤ A typical KC-10A mission might involve
accompanying and refuelling eight
fighters, while carrying 25 cargo pallets.

➤ A digital fly-by-wire control system is
fitted to the air-refuelling boom.

➤ A six-month evaluation was carried out
on the KC-10A before it entered service.

PROFILE

USAF's tactical Extender

Ordered off-the-shelf as a version of the DC-10 airliner to satisfy a USAF requirement for a dual-role Advanced Tanker/Cargo Aircraft, KC-10A deliveries began in 1981. Unlike the KC-135, the Extender has a permanent probe-and-drogue refuelling system in addition to its flying boom, allowing the support of USAF and USN aircraft on the same mission.

Officially credited with the best USAF aircraft safety record (only one aircraft has been lost, in a ground fire), the KC-10A was involved in the 1986 raids on Libya, operations in Panama in 1989, and in the Gulf War.

While the KC-135 force is mostly tasked with the support of strategic bombers, the KC-10A mission is almost wholly tactical. The KC-10A currently forms part of the USAF's primary tactical force, which is capable of rapid deployment to foreign airfields.

The Extender offers an unrivalled combination when it comes to transport and refuelling. A full payload of 76,843 kg (169,055 lb) can be carried over a 7033-km (4360-mile) range.

Just prior to Desert Storm, an experiment to fit additional, British-built hose refuelling pods beneath each wingtip was completed, providing a three-point refuelling capability.

KC-10A EXTENDER

During the Libyan Crisis of 1986, Extenders were based at RAF Mildenhall, tasked with the support of the USAF strike force of F-111s.

This 2nd Wing KC-10A, seen on take-off from Barksdale AFB in Louisiana, has its crew provided by the Air National Guard.

KC-10A Extender

Type: in-flight-refuelling tanker/strategic airlifter

Powerplant: three 233.53-kN (52,535-lb-thrust) General Electric CF6-50C2 turbofans

Maximum speed: 982 km/h (609 mph) at 7620 m (25,000 ft)

Range: 18,507 km (11,475 miles) in ferry configuration

Service ceiling: 10,180 m (33,400 ft)

Weights: operating empty 108,891 kg (240,064 lb) as a tanker; maximum take-off 267,620 kg (588,764 lb)

Max payload: 76,843 kg (169,055 lb) cargo, plus maximum internal fuel 161,508 kg (355,310 lb)

Dimensions: span 47.34 m (115 ft 3 in)
length 55.35 m (181 ft 7 in)
height 17.70 m (58 ft)
wing area 358.70 m² (3860 sq ft)

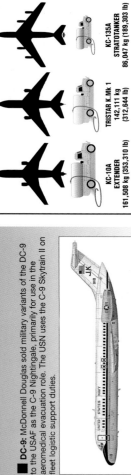

COMBAT DATA

INTERNAL FUEL CAPACITY

A huge amount of internal fuel allows the KC-10A to refuel fighters several times on long missions, while retaining enough fuel for its own needs. The KC-135A does not fly such support-type missions, although the RAF's Tristar does.

KC-10A EXTENDER 161,508 kg (353,310 lb)

TRISTAR K.Mk 1 142,111 kg (312,644 lb)

KC-135A STRATOTANKER 86,047 kg (189,303 lb)

No navigator is needed, thanks to the KC-10A's comprehensive navigation systems. On long-range missions, the flight deck accommodates a pilot, co-pilot and a flight engineer. The flight engineer has a secondary role as loadmaster when cargo is being carried.

The last KC-10A to be built carries a single Flight Refuelling Limited Mk 32B probe-and-drogue refuelling pod beneath each wing. The remainder of the fleet may be similarly equipped.

Manufactured by McDonnell Douglas, the Advanced Aerial Refuelling Boom (AARB) is located opposite an additional refuelling hose reel unit for probed aircraft.

Additional or emergency power is provided by a Garrett TSCP-700-4 auxiliary power unit.

The KC-10A is favoured over the KC-135 by boom operators at least, for its comfortable aft-facing seating position in the rear fuselage.

Power for the Extender's long-range activities is provided by three General Electric turbofans, fitted with thrust reversers for shortening landing distances. For improving its own endurance, the KC-10A has a refuelling receptacle fitted.

The KC-10A fuselage can accommodate up to 25 freight pallets, or mixed loads. A typical mixed load might be 75 seated troops and 17 pallets.

The KC-10A has a 2.59-m (8-ft 5-in) by 3.56-m (11-ft 8-in) upward-hinged cargo door on the fuselage side. Rollers and winches are fitted within the freight compartment.

For tanker missions, the lower fuselage carries fuel bladder cells, taking maximum usable capacity to a total of 206,134 litres (45,343 gallons).

Lacking the nuclear flash curtain and electro-magnetic pulse shielding of the KC-135, the KC-10A is unable to support strategic nuclear strikes.

Douglas airliners in military form

■ **DC-3:** From its world-beating DC-3, Douglas developed the C-47 Skytrain for military operations. A mainstay of the Allied transport fleet during World War II, the aircraft also served as a gunship in Vietnam. Several remain in service.

■ **DC-6:** While the USAF and US Navy both operated military versions of the DC-6, several other air forces flew DC-7 airliner conversions. A number of nations, mostly in South America, still had DC-7s on strength in the mid-1990s.

■ **DC-9:** McDonnell Douglas sold military variants of the DC-9 to the USAF as the C-9 Nightingale, primarily for use in the aeromedical evacuation role. The USN uses the C-9 Skytrain II on fleet logistic support duties.

McDD HELICOPTERS

AH-64 APACHE

● Combat proven ● All-weather capability ● Advanced weapons systems

Hughes developed the AH-64 Apache in response to the Warsaw Pact's massive armoured strength.

Produced by McDonnell Douglas, the AH-64 can engage tanks, often at a safe distance, even at night and in bad weather. The Apache uses advanced sensors to detect enemy vehicles. It then stalks them, using natural cover as a shield, before rising above the treeline to launch laser-guided Hellfire missiles.

▲ Apache crews go into battle confident that they have one of the world's most capable anti-armour weapons, especially when it is flown alongside the Bell OH-58D Kiowa Warrior scout and target designation helicopter.

McDD HELICOPTERS **AH-64 APACHE**

Although the AH-64 often attacks from cover, high speed and manoeuvrability are important factors for survival.

Apache agility ▶

▲ Hellfire launch
An AGM-114 Hellfire missile is fired by an Apache during tests. The missile homes in on a laser-designated target, which has been marked by another aircraft, ground forces or the AH-64 itself.

▲ Purposeful appearance
Hughes designed the AH-64 for maximum survivability and effectiveness – not good looks.

▼ Hidden danger
In a classic example of terrain masking, this Apache demonstrates the aircraft's ability to use natural cover while preparing to attack.

▶ Rocket fire
Rocket pods are an important back-up to the Apache's Hellfire armament. Unguided rockets are extremely effective against soft targets and are essential in the fire support role.

FACTS AND FIGURES

▶ An Apache battalion consists of 18 AH-64s and 13 OH-58 scout helicopters for target spotting and designation.

▶ AH-64s escorted MH-53J helicopters in the first mission of Desert Storm.

▶ More than 500 Iraqi tanks were destroyed by US Army Apaches.

▶ Apaches of the 101st Aviation Regiment fired the first Allied shots of the Gulf War against Iraqi radar installations.

▶ Leased US Army AH-64As were delivered to the Netherlands army in 1996.

▶ New developments have led to the advanced AH-64D Longbow Apache.

At war with the Apache

To defend against an armoured thrust into Western Europe, especially Germany, where 40,000 Warsaw Pact tanks once threatened NATO, the US Army developed an anti-tank strategy which hinged on the McDonnell Douglas AH-64 Apache.

One of the leading battlefield helicopters in the world, the tandem-seat AH-64, which has the gunner forward and pilot aft, uses high-tech sensors, a Chain Gun cannon and far-reaching Hellfire missiles to destroy tanks and other key targets. At night or in bad weather – even in dust storms as during Operation Desert Storm – the Apache crew can monitor enemy tank movements, using the PNVS (Pilot's Night-Vision System) and TADS (Target Acquisition and Designation System) to pinpoint and fire at targets. In the Gulf, these sensors and weapons also enabled Apaches to attack Iraqi air defence radar sites.

During war, the Apache crew is constantly challenged by the cat-and-mouse contest waged against enemy tank commanders. Flying low over the modern battlefield is extremely dangerous, but the Apache has all of the qualities needed for its tank-destroying mission.

AH-64A Apache

Type: two-seat all-weather attack helicopter

Powerplant: two 1265-kW (1696-hp) General Electric T700-GE-701 turboshaft engines

Maximum speed: 293 km/h (182 mph)

Range: 428 km (266 miles)

Service ceiling: 6400 m (21,000 ft)

Weights: empty 5165 kg (11,387 lb); maximum take-off 9525 kg (21,000 lb)

Armament: one 30-mm M230 Chain Gun cannon with 1200 rounds of US, ADEN or DEFA ammunition; up to 16 AGM-114 Hellfire laser-guided missiles or up to 76 folding-fin rockets; various other combinations of rocket projectiles, guns and missiles

Dimensions: main rotor diameter 14.63 m (50 ft)
fuselage length 14.97 m
height 4.66 m
main rotor 168.11 m² (1810 sq ft)
disc area

Apaches performed with devastating effect during the first Gulf War, with crews finding and destroying targets even in thick smoke when visibility was often down to 200 m (656 ft).

Armour protects key engine components, and the upper parts of each engine cowling fold down to form maintenance platforms. Engines were uprated to 1409 kW from the 604th aircraft.

Hellfire has been steadily improved and can home automatically on to a ground target. Video footage taken during the Gulf War demonstrated the missile's deadly accuracy.

Should the powered flight control system fail, a Honeywell secondary fly-by-wire system is activated, allowing full control of both rotors and the tailplane.

Unusually, the AH-64's tailrotor consists of two twin-bladed units mounted at 55° to each other. This arrangement keeps noise to a minimum.

A maximum load of 76 folding-fin rockets may be carried, although the configuration shown is almost standard.

A centre fuselage ammunition drum holds a maximum of 1200 rounds of 30-mm ammunition. The McDonnell Douglas M230 Chain Gun fires at a maximum of 625 rounds per minute.

Constructed of glass-fibre, stainless steel and composites, the main rotor blades are proof against hits by 23-mm cannon shells. They have swept tips for increased performance.

Apache crewmembers sit on lightweight Kevlar seats and are protected by boron cockpit armour.

Lockheed Martin builds the AN/AAQ-11 TADS/PNVS system which is turret mounted in the extreme nose.

AH-64A APACHE

This early production aircraft carries standard US Army markings and paint scheme. In service the aircraft rarely sports any form of individual or unit marking.

The tailplane incidence is controlled automatically by a Hamilton Standard flight control system. This allows it to hold the aircraft in an optimum position in all flight phases.

The energy absorbing main landing gear combines with crash-resistant seat and airframe design to give the crew a 95 per cent chance of surviving a 12.8 m (42 ft) per second ground impact.

KIOWA WARRIOR: Other aircraft, primarily the OH-58D with its more powerful laser, can also designate targets for the Apache.

KIOWA IN THE TREES: Small and agile, the OH-58D can often get closer to the enemy, and provides a 'cone' of reflected laser energy for the AH-64's missiles.

APACHE STAND-OFF: As it is a high-value target itself, the Apache often stands off at a safe distance and launches Hellfires at targets that are not visible.

Apache attack profiles

LASER GUIDANCE: The Apache is capable of designating its own targets, which means the Hellfire missile can be used in autonomous mode.

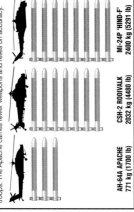

COMBAT DATA

MAXIMUM CRUISING SPEED

The Apache is the fastest of the helicopters shown here. This was a great asset on the long-range, covert missions into enemy-held territory during the Gulf War.

AH-64A APACHE	293 km/h (182 mph)
CSH-2 ROOIVALK	278 km/h (173 mph)
Mi-24P 'HIND-F'	270 km/h (168 mph)

WEAPON LOAD

The 'Hind-F' is a developed version of the earlier 'Hind' gunships. The armed assault role has been largely abandoned, with the aircraft carrying spare ammunition and a heavy weapon load instead of troops. The Apache carries fewer weapons and relies on accuracy.

AH-64A APACHE 771 kg (1700 lb)	**CSH-2 ROOIVALK** 2032 kg (4480 lb)	**Mi-24P 'HIND-F'** 2400 kg (5291 lb)

McDonnell Douglas
T-45 Goshawk

- US Navy trainer ● Navalized BAe Hawk ● Latest technology

When it wanted a new trainer, the Navy looked at several aircraft before deciding on Britain's well-established Hawk. Given the designation T-45 and named Goshawk, the aircraft is manufactured in the US. This well-known British jet is becoming the standard flying schoolhouse for all who earn the wings of gold worn by US Naval aviators. The T-45 replaces the Rockwell T-2 Buckeye and the Douglas TA-4J Skyhawk.

▶ *Many modifications to the basic Hawk produced the T-45. The nose undercarriage unit is a completely new, stronger unit and features twin wheels and a catapult launch bar.*

McDonnell Douglas T-45 Goshawk

▲ **Trainer supreme**
Sitting on a raised ejection seat, the instructor has an excellent view forward over the student's head. Carrier landings demand optimum visibility.

▶ **Carrier launch**
Steam rises from the catapult as a Goshawk crew prepare to leave the carrier. The T-45 launches at 224 km/h (139 mph).

▲▼ **Flying 'dirty' and flying 'clean'**
The robust undercarriage, flaps, slats, airbrakes and arrestor hook are all deployed (above) in the landing configuration above while the aircraft is seen below in 'clean' cruising configuration.

▲ **Complex wing design**
Full-span hydraulically operated leading-edge slats were developed by McDonnell Douglas and are not found on the simpler wing of the BAe Hawk.

FACTS AND FIGURES

▶ Compared to previous U.S. Navy training, the cost saving T-45 system uses 42 per cent fewer aircraft.

▶ First squadron to with the T-45A is VT-21 Fighting Redhawks at Kingsville, Texas.

▶ French Navy Rafale pilots will be trained in the US using the Goshawk.

▶ Compared with the British Hawk, the T-45 has an extra ventral fin and a tailfin heightened by about 15 cm (6 in).

▶ The T-45A will train about 600 new naval pilots each year.

▶ Each Navy T-45 is expected to make 16,000 carrier deck landings.

Navy trainer for the next generation

Development of the T-45 Goshawk was criticized for taking a long time and costing plenty, but the result gives the US Navy an advanced trainer second to none in the world. Looking very much like a fighter and performing in many ways like one, the T-45 Goshawk is an extensively altered version of the British Hawk, strengthened to permit operation on aircraft carriers.

The T-45 Goshawk is operated as a land-based trainer replacing both the intermediate

and advanced trainers of the past and it also operates from aircraft carriers as part of the student pilot programme.

Since the Goshawk began carrier trials in 1991, the Navy has been generally pleased with its performance and has moved – too slowly, according to critics – to place the Goshawk in service with training squadrons.

Initially flying from Kingsville, Texas, and soon to be operating at four locations, the T-45 will be the first jet flown by Navy, Marine and

Coast Guard aviators (after they fly the Beech T-34 Turbo Mentor) and student pilots will fly it until they graduate with their wings.

T-45A Goshawk

Type: two-seat intermediate and advanced flight trainer

Powerplant: one 26.00-kN (5850-lb-thrust) Rolls-Royce/Turboméca F405-RR-401 turbofan

Maximum speed: 997 km/h (618 mph)

Rate of climb: 2128 m/min (7000 fpm) at sea level

Ferry range: 1854 km (1147 miles)

Service ceiling: 12875 m (42,250 ft)

Weights: empty 4252 kg (9374 lb); maximum take-off 5775 kg (12,731 lb)

Dimensions: span 9.39 m (30 ft 9 in)
length 11.97 m (39 ft 3 in)
height 4.24 m (13 ft 11 in)
wing area 16.69 m² (180 sq ft)

ACTION DATA

SPEED

High speed is important for a jet trainer, both to give the student pilot a taste of fast-jet speeds and to shorten any time spent flying between home base and the training area. In the case of the Goshawk, for example, this might allow extra carrier training.

T-45A GOSHAWK	997 km/h (618 mph)
ALPHA JET E	1000 km/h (620 mph)
MB-339C	902 km/h (559 mph)

CLIMB RATE

Rate of climb is important in a similar way to maximum speed. Much training takes place at high altitude in order to give the student room for mistakes. The T-45 loses out here due to the extra weight of its unique naval systems.

ALPHA JET E	3660 m/min (12,000 fpm)
MB-339C	2225 m/min (7300 fpm)
T-45A GOSHAWK	2128 m/min (7000 fpm)

THRUST

Although some critics have suggested that the Goshawk is underpowered, its upgraded F405-RR-401 engine provides adequate thrust for carrier operations and is extremely fuel efficient. The MB-339C is unusual amongst modern trainers in having a turbojet engine that is much less fuel efficient.

ALPHA JET E	26.48 kN (5960 lb thrust)
MB-339C	19.57 kN (4400 lb thrust)
T-45A GOSHAWK	26.00 kN (5850 lb thrust)

SMURFS (Side-Mounted Unit horizontal Root tail Fins) help to limit aerodynamic interference between the deployed flaps and the tailplane.

All Hawk variants are fitted with a gas turbine starter unit for starting the engines and onboard systems. The unit exhausts through this distinctive aperture on the spine.

A HUD in the front cockpit can show navigation, flight instrument and weapon aiming data. Two underwing pylons may carry practice bombs.

T-45A GOSHAWK

This aircraft belongs to VT-21 Red Hawks, Training Wing Two and was based at NAS Kingsville, Texas, in 1995 in standard high-visibility markings.

All Goshawks will eventually be fitted with Cockpit 21. This development replaces the original instruments with two multi-function display screens in each cockpit.

Student and instructor each sit on a Martin-Baker Mk 14 NACES (Naval Aircraft Common Ejection-Seat). The seat allows safe escape at zero height and zero air-speed.

Power comes from a single F405-RR-401 engine. With this engine the T-45 burns 55 percent less fuel than its T-2 Buckeye predecessor.

With a launch weight of 5787 kg (13,675 lb), the T-45's catapult launch bar withstands huge stress. The catapult launches the aircraft at flying speed even with the brakes on.

In order to accommodate the new nose undercarriage unit, a deeper nose section was designed. The nosewheel doors close once the leg is locked down.

The strengthened rear fuselage has two side-mounted airbrakes and a modified F/A-18 arrestor hook, which is capable of holding the T-45 in the event of an accidental snagging of the arrestor cable while the aircraft is still airborne.

Carrier-capable trainers

■ **NORTH AMERICAN T-28B TROJAN:** From 1952 the T-28 was the US Navy's standard on-and-off-ship basic trainer.

■ **ROCKWELL T-2 BUCKEYE:** Entering service in 1959, the T-2 is now being replaced in service by the T-45A Goshawk.

■ **GRUMMAN TF-9J COUGAR:** Developed from the 1950s fighter, the trainer variant continued in service into the 1970s.

■ **McDonnell Douglas TA-4 SKYHAWK:** A two-seat version of the highly successful attack jet. A few trainers continue in service.

McDonnell Douglas/BAE
AV-8B HARRIER II

● Vertical take-off ground-attack fighter ● Tactical air support

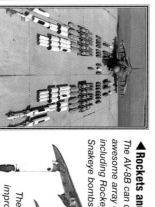

▲ Flying the AV-8 is not easy, and only the best are chosen by the US Marine Corps to fly the revolutionary combat 'Jump Jet'.

When US Marines go to war in the AV-8B, they have at their command an aircraft of incredible versatility and striking-power. The AV-8B Harrier II is a red-hot, modern-day version of the famous British 'Jump Jet'. Marines depend on immediately-available air power to protect their troops, and the AV-8B, flying from assault-carriers or makeshift airstrips, is the perfect means of supplying it.

McDonnell Douglas/BAE **AV-8B HARRIER II**

▼ **Harrier carrier**
The US Marine Corps is the largest user of the AV-8B, operating from 'Tarawa-'class amphibious assault ships or US Navy carriers. Four squadrons were deployed during Operation Desert Storm.

▲ **On the floor**
Streaking over the desert at very low level, the AV-8B is in its element. Harrier pilots like to operate as low and fast as possible.

▲ **Missile away!**
The Harrier can carry two Sidewinder missiles, and is capable of giving enemy fighters a hard time in a dogfight.

▲ **Rockets and bombs**
The AV-8B can deliver an awesome array of weapons, including Rockeye and Snakeye bombs.

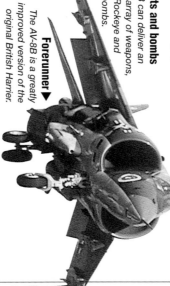

Forerunner ▲
The AV-8B is a greatly improved version of the original British Harrier.

FACTS AND FIGURES

▶ The GAU-12/A cannon can fire at a rate of 4200 rounds per minute with a muzzle velocity of 1097 m/s (4000 fps).

▶ The first service-test AV-8B made its maiden flight on 9 November 1978.

▶ Spain and Italy operate Harrier II warplanes based upon the AV-8B design.

▶ The AV-8B's cannon system is made up of two detachable pods, one for the gun and one for the ammunition.

▶ Much of the Harrier II's fuselage is made from graphite composite materials.

▶ The two-seat TAV-8B is used to train Harrier pilots.

PROFILE

The meanest Harrier yet

The US Marine Corps became interested in the British-designed Harrier during the Vietnam era. Decades later, the McDonnell Douglas AV-8B Harrier II combines the STOVL (short take-off/vertical landing) capability of this special warplane with the hi-tech prowess of today's 'smart' bombs. Not surprisingly, this advanced craft was known for a time as the Super Harrier.

During Operation Desert Storm, AV-8B Harrier IIs fought in a 'down and dirty' environment with the Marines at the front. One weakness is that its advanced aircraft are near the

centre of the airframe, meaning that a hit by a heat-seeking missile is almost certain to be fatal. Harriers flew more than 2000 combat missions and did a great job, but suffered five aircraft lost in combat.

For tomorrow's Marines, the Harrier II is available in day, night and radar-equipped versions, and as the TAV-8B two-seat trainer. Its unique V/STOL capability makes the Harrier perfect for shipborne operations, and it has been chosen to equip the Spanish and Italian navies.

Italy realised the potential of the Harrier and ordered 18 AV-8Bs for operation from the carrier Giuseppe Garibaldi.

Television- or infra-red-guided Maverick missiles are key Harrier anti-tank weapons. They were used in large numbers against Iraqi armour during the Gulf War.

The AV-8B incorporates a new, larger composite wing, which allowed far greater fuel and stores carriage than in the original Harrier.

The nose of the AV-8B contains an advanced FLIR (forward-looking infra-red) system.

The cockpit of the AV-8B is a considerable improvement on the original Harrier. It features a larger, raised canopy, giving a much clearer view, and has far better instruments, including an advanced head-up display.

Captain Andrew Hall of the US Marine Corps carried out 54 bombing sorties in his AV-8B in the Gulf War.

AV-8B HARRIER II

AV-8B of VMA 124 'Black Sheep', based at Yuma, USA. This aircraft is one of the 'night-attack' capable machines with a night-vision-compatible cockpit and wide-angle head-up display.

The rugged undercarriage allows the AV-8B to operate from unprepared sites close to the battlefield. A short length of road makes an ideal Harrier base.

For self-defence, the Harrier II can carry a pair of AIM-9 Sidewinder heat-seeking missiles.

The tail pod contains a 'puff port', which uses engine air to control the aircraft during hover and low-speed manoeuvres.

AV-8B Harrier II

Type: single-seat attack aircraft

Powerplant: one 105.87-kN (23,820-lb-thrust) Rolls-Royce F402-RR-408 (Pegasus 11-61) turbofan

Maximum speed: 1065 km/h (662 mph) at sea level

Combat radius: 1100 km (684 miles) hi-lo-hi

Service ceiling: 15,240 m (50,000 ft)

Weights: empty 6336 kg (13,968 lb); loaded 14,061 kg (31,000 lb)

Armament: one 25-mm GAU-12/A Equalizer five-barrel cannon with 300 rounds; two AIM-9 Sidewinder missiles; provision for up to 6000 kg (13,228 lb) of bombs, rockets or missiles

Dimensions:
span	9.25 m (30 ft 4 in)
length	14.12 m (46 ft 4 in)
height	3.55 m (11 ft 8 in)
wing area	22.18 m² (239 sq ft)

COMBAT DATA

MAXIMUM SPEED

YAK-38 'FORGER'	1110 km/h (690 mph)
F/A-18 HORNET	1900 km/h (1181 mph)
AV-8B HARRIER II	1065 km/h (662 mph)

Harriers are subsonic aircraft. On paper, they are much slower than high-performance jets like the McDonnell Douglas Hornet, but in practice few aircraft can sustain supersonic speeds for long, and at combat speeds the Harrier is fast enough for most purposes. Thanks to its powerful engine it has extremely good subsonic acceleration.

COMBAT RADIUS

AV-8B HARRIER II	1100 km (684 miles)
F/A-18 HORNET	750 km (466 miles)
YAK-38 'FORGER'	370 km (230 miles)

One weakness of the original Harrier was lack of range. The Harrier II carries much more fuel than its predecessor, and with a full warload can strike targets at distances of up to 1000 km (620 miles). It outranges the notoriously short-legged Hornet, and leaves the Russian STOVL Yak-38 'Forger' a long way behind.

ARMAMENT

F/A-18 HORNET	7000 kg (15,432 lb)
AV-8B HARRIER II	6000 kg (13,228 lb)
YAK-38 'FORGER'	2000 kg (4409 lb)

The original Harrier was a light-strike aircraft with a smallish weapons load. Increased power and the far more efficient wing on the AV-8B means that it now hoists a respectable warload, taking it into the range of the Hornet and other high-agility superfighters currently setting combat aircraft standards.

Marine Corps close support

RAPID RESPONSE: The ability of the Harrier to operate from forward bases means that it can get into action in a third of the time of more conventional fighters.

FORWARD DEPLOYMENT: In the field, Marine Corps Harriers operate from rough or temporary airfields close to the forward edge of the battle area.

ON CALL FOR ACTION: Harriers are designed for quick-reaction close support of Marine ground units. As such, they are on call at all times, ready to go into action at a few minutes' notice.

CLOSE SUPPORT: Harriers are equipped with a precision angle-rate bombing system which allows them to deliver ordnance accurately only metres ahead of advancing Marine troops and armour.

McDonnell Douglas/BAE
AV-8B HARRIER II PLUS

● Latest Harrier variant ● Air-to-air capability ● Export orders

Internationally recognized as one of the most potent and versatile warplanes in service, the original second-generation Harrier II was penalized by its lack of radar. In the UK, British Aerospace (BAe) had produced the Sea Harrier by adding radar to the basic Harrier, a trend that has been repeated with the Harrier II Plus. With the APG-65 radar from the F/A-18A Hornet, the Harrier II Plus has gained a formidable beyond-visual-range (BVR) capability.

▲ Outwardly almost indistinguishable from the standard AV-8B, the Harrier II Plus embodies many improvements, including a new radar, new weapons and an upgraded engine.

McDonnell Douglas/BAE AV-8B HARRIER II PLUS

▼ European operators
Italy and Spain have procured the latest AV-8B. Both countries employ the aircraft primarily in the air defence role.

▲ First rebuild
Unpainted and showing the various different structural materials, the first rebuilt Harrier II Plus performs a hover.

'Flying Tigers' ▼
The first unit of the US Marine Corps to receive the Harrier II Plus was VMA-542, which took delivery of its first example in 1993. One of its aircraft is seen here dropping Mk 82 Snakeye bombs during a training sortie.

▲ Variation in colours
Different paint schemes can be seen on the Harrier II Plus. Most sport two-tone Ghost Grey, though these two examples have much darker upper surfaces.

Reduction in orders ▶
Originally it was hoped that the entire USMC fleet would be upgraded to Harrier II Plus standard, but defence cutbacks during the 1990s have reduced the total to 99 aircraft.

FACTS AND FIGURES

▶ Since the first Harrier II Plus took to the air in 1992, engine failure has resulted in one of the prototypes crashing.

▶ A primary motivation for the programme was experience from the Gulf War.

▶ All of the improved AV-8Bs have now been delivered and saw action in Iraq.

▶ All the Harrier II Plus variants are to receive entirely new fuselages. This is cheaper than modifying the old ones.

▶ The introduction of the new aircraft has resulted in a true multi-role Harrier.

▶ Italy has been the first country to acquire trainers before single-seat variants.

PROFILE

Harrier II receives an update

Already a proven dogfighter with the short-range AIM-9 Sidewinder air-to-air missile (AAM), the Harrier II has now matured into an all-weather fighter, with the capability to engage BVR targets using AIM-7 Sparrow and AIM-120 AMRAAM radar-guided AAMs. The Harrier II Plus retains the close-support capability of its predecessor, but adds an important air defence role.

In June 1987 McDonnell Douglas and BAe announced

their intention to develop a radar-equipped Harrier as a private venture. By late 1990, Italy, Spain and the US had signed a joint agreement for Harrier II Plus funding. The first prototype flew on 22 September 1992.

Since then, the USMC has received 27 new aircraft, with at least another 72 to be converted from AV-8Bs. Spain has received eight machines, and Italy has ordered 16, with options on a further eight.

Above: Another feature has been to increase the number of wing pylons from six to eight, in line with the RAF's aircraft. The new APG-65 radar and AIM-120 AMRAAM can be carried.

Left: Pilots have welcomed the introduction of the new aircraft and one, serving with VMA-542 'Flying Tigers', went so far as to describe it as a 'quantum leap for the Marines'.

AV-8B Harrier II Plus

Type: single-seat air-defence/close-support V/STOL aircraft

Powerplant: one 105.9-kN (23,825-lb-thrust) Rolls-Royce Pegasus vectored-thrust turbofan

Maximum speed: 1065 km/h (660 mph)

Endurance: 3 hours

Combat radius: 1101 km (683 miles)

Range: 3035 km (1886 miles)

Weights: empty 6336 kg (13,939 lb); loaded 14,061 kg (31,000 lb)

Armament: one 25-mm GAU-12/A cannon plus 11 hardpoints for various external stores

Dimensions:
span	9.25 m	(30 ft 4 in)
length	14.55 m	(47 ft 9 in)
height	3.55 m	(11 ft 8 in)
wing area	21.37 m²	(230 sq ft)

COMBAT DATA

MAXIMUM SPEED

As the only truly effective V/STOL combat aircraft in service, the Harrier II has an impressive turn of speed. It is quicker than the Russian Sukhoi Su-25, which was also designed for battlefield support, but the Jaguar A is quicker still.

AV-8B HARRIER PLUS II	1065 km/h (660 mph)
Su-25K 'FROGFOOT'	950 km/h (589 mph)
JAGUAR A	1350 km/h (837 mph)

COMBAT RADIUS

Today's attack aircraft are designed to reach their targets at low level, in order to avoid tracking by enemy radar. Compared to the Jaguar and Su-25, the Harrier II Plus has a greater radius of action which is also a great improvement over the original Harrier.

Su-25K 'FROGFOOT-A' 495 km (307 miles)

JAGUAR A 852 km (528 miles)

AV-8B HARRIER II PLUS 1101 km (683 miles)

CLIMB RATE

With its twin afterburning Adour turbofans, the SEPECAT Jaguar A (for Attack) has a phenomenal climb rate. The Su-25K 'Frogfoot' is not far behind, nor is the Harrier II, both of which can carry a greater amount of external stores.

JAGUAR A 6076 m/min (19,930 fpm)

Su-25K 'FROGFOOT-A' 5099 m/min (16,725 fpm)

AV-8B HARRIER II PLUS 4485 m/min (14,710 fpm)

Compared to the original Hawker design, the AV-8B series makes greater use of composite materials and graphite epoxy. The fuselage is somewhat longer and also stronger, with a much longer fatigue life than that of the early variants.

For self-defence, the latest AV-8B is fitted with a forward- and aft-looking RWR (radar warning receiver), a Goodyear AN/ALE-39 chaff dispenser and a Doppler MAW (missile approach warning) radar. This last item is fitted to the protruding tail boom unit.

AV-8B Harrier II Plus

BuNo.164553 was one of the first Harrier II Plus variants to be delivered, being taken on charge by VMA-542 'Flying Tigers' at NAS Cherry Point in North Carolina, which has been a centre of US Marine Corps Harrier operations since the early 1970s.

The lack of an adequate radar remained a handicap of the Harrier force for many years. Fitting the APG-65 into the AV-8B has resulted in a vastly superior machine, and has turned it into an effective sea defence fighter, offering better capability than the British Sea Harrier.

Unlike early Harriers, the second-generation aircraft have retractable refuelling probes, which can be fitted to the port side of the fuselage above the intake. They are not always fitted, as is shown on this particular example.

One improvement of the Harrier II Plus has been to increase the number of underwing hardpoints from six to eight. The latest AV-8B is also capable of carrying the AIM-120 AMRAAM (Advanced Medium-Range Air-to-Air Missile).

Evolution of the Harrier

■ **HAWKER P.1127:** Forerunner of what became known as the Harrier, the P.1127 performed its first hover in October 1960.

■ **HAWKER KESTREL FGA.Mk 1:** With the success of the P.1127, nine development aircraft, known as Kestrels, were procured.

■ **HAWKER SIDDELEY AV-8A HARRIER:** First-generation Harriers were acquired by the USMC. They have been replaced by AV-8Bs.

■ **HAWKER SIDDELEY HARRIER GR.Mk 3:** Representing the pinnacle of early Harrier development, the GR.Mk 3 served until 1993.

McDonnell Douglas

C-17 GLOBEMASTER III

● Modern airlifter ● Next-generation technology ● Service proven

▲ Providing relief to crisis-hit regions and delivering military supplies around the world, the C-17 is said by pilots to handle more like a fighter than an airlifter in spite of its large size.

A t first glance the C-17 could be mistaken as a run-of-the-mill transport, but those who have been inside the Globemaster III never forget it. This four-turbofan, hi-tech aircraft's interior is like a giant cavern. The C-17 can carry huge cargoes and can be 'turned around' quickly thanks to its 'roll-on, roll-off' capability. This is achieved by locating the ramp near ground level and using a palletized system with floor-mounted rollers for rapid loading.

McDonnell Douglas C-17 GLOBEMASTER III

▲ Squadron service
Lockheed C-141B Starlifters began to make way for the Globemaster III at Charleston AFB in June 1993. The 17th Airlift Squadron was the first unit to receive production aircraft.

▼ Fighter or freighter?
For the first time on a transport aircraft, the C-17 introduced twin, fighter-style, head-up display units for the two flight crew.

▼ Always ready
The C-17, carrying heavy and bulky loads, can be rapidly deployed to unprepared airstrips, by night and day, and in all weathers.

▼ Armoured mobility
One of the C-17's load requirements was the ability to accommodate large armoured vehicles, such as this 28,349-kg (62,368-lb) payload of an M110A2 self-propelled Howitzer and support vehicles.

▲ Global reach
Air-to-air refuelling, which allows worldwide transport missions, is vital for any airlifter.

FACTS AND FIGURES

▶ In honour of the Douglas C-74 and C-124, the Globemaster III name was given to the C-17 in February 1993.

▶ The USAF is aiming for 140 C-17s, 70 of which have currently received funding.

▶ The C-17 is the world's third most expensive aircraft, after the B-2 and E-3.

▶ The C-17's fin contains a tunnel which enables a crewmember to climb up inside for stabilizer maintenance.

▶ In 1993 C-17s flew their first operational mission from the US to Kenya.

▶ The C-17 prototype completed its first flight on 15 September 1991.

Transport for the next century

Combining long range, a capacity to carry heavy cargoes and the capability to land near the front line, the C-17 Globemaster III is the world's newest military transport. The high-wing aircraft is able to carry almost any cargo and it bears a slight resemblance to the airlifter it is replacing, the C-141 Starlifter. The C-17 boasts an ergonomic

flightdeck (that is, one optimised for pilot comfort) with digital displays. The C-17's two pilots sit side-by-side and the plane is flown with a control stick instead of the yoke which is traditionally used on transport aircraft. The wing is swept at 25° and has winglets for fuel

efficiency. The wing accounts for almost one-third of the aircraft's structural weight.

This fine aircraft is only just beginning to prove its global airlifting abilities. It is the hi-tech hauler of the future, and the USAF expects to establish a fleet of more than a hundred aircraft.

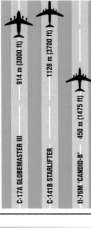

Left: A parachute fixed to a freight pallet drags cargo from the C-17's cabin as the Low-Altitude Parachute Extraction System (LAPES) is used.

Above: All aircraft likely to be deployed anywhere in the world must be able to operate in extreme conditions. This C-17 is undergoing cold weather trials.

C-17A Globemaster III

Type: long-range transport

Powerplant: four 185.49-kN (41,73-lb-thrust) Pratt & Whitney F117-PW-100 turbofan engines

Maximum cruising speed: 648 km/h (402 mph) at low altitude

Ferry range: 8710 km (5400 miles)

Service ceiling: 13,715 m (45,000 ft)

Weights: empty 122,016 kg (268,435 lb); maximum take-off 263,083 kg (578,783 lb)

Accommodation: two pilots, one loadmaster and up to 102 troops/paratroops in stowable seats or 48 stretchers with attendants, or up to 78,108 kg (172,199 lb) of cargo including an M1 Abrams main battle tank

Dimensions:
span	50.29 m (164 ft 11 in)
length	53.04 m (174 ft)
height	16.79 m (55 ft 1 in)
wing area	353.02 m² (3798 sq ft)

ACTION DATA

MAXIMUM PAYLOAD

Compared to other similarly sized four-jet transports, and particularly the C-141B which the C-17A is partly replacing, the Globemaster III offers exceptional payload capabilities.

C-17A GLOBEMASTER III 78,108 kg (172,199 lb)

C-141B STARLIFTER 41,222 kg (90,688 lb)

Il-76M 'CANDID-B' 40,000 kg (88,000 lb)

RANGE

McDonnell Douglas' C-17A has only slightly better range than that of the Il-76M, but the American aircraft achieves this figure with almost twice the payload. Air-to-air refuelling is an important part of the C-17A capability and is also available to extend the range of the C-141B.

C-17A GLOBEMASTER III 5190 km (3220 miles)

C-141B STARLIFTER 4725 km (2930 miles)

Il-76M 'CANDID-B' 5000 km (3100 miles)

LANDING DISTANCE

Ilyushin used advanced systems to give the Il-76M excellent field performance, with a maximum payload only slightly below that of the C-17A. The C-17A is equally impressive, requiring twice the distance of the Il-76M for landing but with twice the payload.

C-17A GLOBEMASTER III 914 m (3000 ft)

C-141B STARLIFTER 1128 m (3700 ft)

Il-76M 'CANDID-B' 450 m (1475 ft)

C-17A GLOBEMASTER III

This C-17A is the first production aircraft and was used for tests at Edwards AFB. It was successfully tested at 100 per cent loading before its first flight and was subsequently used for in-flight load tests.

A flight crew of two fly the C-17A. Two extra seats are provided at the rear of the flightdeck to accommodate a relief aircrew on long flights.

The C-17 carries a large amount of internal fuel. Six wing tanks are positioned between the main spars and fill almost the entire wing span, giving a capacity of 102,614 litres (27,110 gallons).

A front view of the C-17A shows how close to the wing the engines are positioned. This is a result of the complex propulsive-lift technology used to give the aircraft its short take-off and landing (STOL) capability.

Four F117-PW-100 turbofan engines give outstanding fuel economy and a combined maximum thrust of 742 kN (166,920 lb thrust). The engine is based on the PW2040 turbofan, which powers many Boeing 757s and has already achieved in excess of six-million flying hours in regular service.

Only one loadmaster is required to supervise and handle the C-17A's large payload, using an internal cargo handling system to load up to 18 standard 463L cargo pallets.

Each main undercarriage unit has six wheels and, when retracted, is accommodated in a fairing against the lower fuselage.

In common with many long-range airliners, the C-17A is fitted with winglets. These provide greater range and improved cruising characteristics.

When retracted, the rear loading ramp is able to carry heavy cargo, including two 463L pallets for air-dropping.

A quadruple-redundant fly-by-wire system operates the C-17A's 29 control surfaces. As well as the complex wing systems, these include the twin rudders, tailplanes and four elevators.

USAF's Douglas airlifter dynasty

■ **C-54 SKYMASTER:** Douglas flew the first C-54 in 1942 and more than 1,000 were delivered to the US Army Air Force and Navy.

■ **C-74 GLOBEMASTER I:** Having flown for the first time in September 1945, many C-74s were cancelled at the end of the war.

■ **C-124 GLOBEMASTER II:** Developed from the C-74, the C-124 gained 2610-kW (3450-hp) engines, a deeper fuselage and nose loading doors.

■ **C-133 CARGOMASTER:** Only 35 of these advanced turboprop transports were built. They were retired in 1971 after fatigue problems.

McDonnell Douglas
F/A-18E/F Hornet

- Naval attack fighter ● Second-generation Hornet ● New weapons

Sleek and powerful, the F/A-18E/F Super Hornet is the Navy's hope for the future. The Super Hornet is more than an improved version of today's superb F/A-18 Hornet: the Super Hornet is 86 cm (34 in) longer and is bigger, heavier and packed with new equipment. With new radar and weapons it should prove to be a winning formula in both air-to-air and air-to-ground action; flying from land-based airstrips or carrier decks with equal ease.

▲ Since its transformation into the new F/A-18E/F 'Super Hornet' guise, the previously underrated Hornet has become the West's most versatile and advanced air defense and all-weather strike aircraft.

McDonnell Douglas F/A-18E/F Hornet

▲ Aerodynamic refinement
The new Hornet is quickly distinguished from its predecessor by long wing leading-edge extensions and modern intakes for better agility.

Next ▼ generation

The E/F is 25 percent bigger than previous Hornets. It features a new larger-area wing, longer fuselage, new engines for increased range and consistent performance, RAM, and new electronics.

▲ Stealthy construction
The new Hornet has been designed with reduced RCS in mind: weapons pylons and key areas are RAM coated, intakes baffled, and it has provision for an ALQ-165 self-protection jammer and three ALE-50 towed decoys.

▲ 21st century defense
The F/A-18E/F will replace existing F/A-18s and A-6 Intruder all-weather strike aircraft with the Navy. The two-seat Super Hornet will be the principal attack variant.

Heavy metal ▼
Weapons for the Hornet include the AIM-9, AGM-88, AGM-84D, AGM-84H, AIM-120, AAS-46 FLIR, BLU-109, AGM-154 and AGM-65s.

FACTS AND FIGURES

▼ Plans call for 660 US Navy Super Hornets, plus 340 for the Marines, whose participation is now being debated.

▼ The F/A-18E/F is about 4525 kg (9977 lb) heavier than the earlier F/A-18 Hornets.

▼ The prototype made its first flight in St. Louis, Missouri, on 29 November 1995.

▼ The development of the F/A-18E/F Super Hornet is currently among the costliest of military aircraft programmes.

▼ The Super Hornet uses composite materials and protective coatings to make it stealthy.

▼ The F/A-18E/F uses the advanced Hughes APG-73 radar.

PROFILE

The Hornet's new sting

The F/A-18E/F Super Hornet will be able to out-fly and out-fight just about any other combat aircraft in the world, and it will need to – the stakes are high. The Pentagon and the Navy have invested $81 billion into the program to develop the single-seat F/A-18E and two-seat F/A-18F Super Hornet and make them operational on aircraft carriers early in the next century.

The Super Hornet brings together power, speed and high-tech weapons systems to give the Navy a carrier-based warplane that can compete with the world's

best. The Navy has retired the ageing Grumman A-6 Intruder attack jets as one of the measures that will pay for the planned purchase of 1000 Super Hornets. In its time, the Intruder was unequalled in flying long distance, in bad weather, to drop bombs with precision accuracy. With improved radar and navigation systems, the Super Hornet will far exceed the Intruder's capabilities, but will also be able to win in a dogfight – something the Intruder was never intended for.

F/A-18E Hornet

Type: tactical fighter and strike aircraft.

Powerplant: two afterburning 97.34-kN (21,901-lb-thrust) General Electric F414-GE-400 turbofan engines

Max speed: 1910 km/h (1187 mph) at 6096 m (20,000 ft)

Range: 2036 km (1265 miles)

Combat radius: 912 km (567 miles)

Ceiling: 15,240 m (50,000 ft)

Weight: maximum take-off 29,874 kg (65,861 lb)

Weapons: One 20-mm M61A1 cannon and typically 8165 kg (18,000 lb) of other weapons including AIM-9 Sidewinder, AIM-120 AMRAAM, AGM-88 HARM, AGM-154 JSOW, BLU-109 JDAM, AGM-65E Maverick, AGM-84H SLAM-ER and AGM-84D Harpoon or various free-fall bombs

Dimensions:
span 14.02 m (46 ft)
length 18.59 m (61 ft)
height 4.88 m (16 ft)
wing area 46.45 m² (500 sq ft)

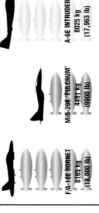

Left: This computer-generated impression of the F/A-18E illustrates a typical combat load of wingtip AIM-9s, two AIM-120 AMRAAMs, two AGM-88 HARM anti-radar missiles, four Mk 82 454-kg (1000-lb) Snakeye free-fall bombs and a belly drop-tank.

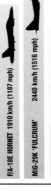

Right: Before the first flight of the new-generation Hornet, exhaustive and vitally important trials were undertaken with McDonnell's own F/A-18, as well as with Navy and Naval Weapons Center test aircraft. The F/A-18 shown here went under went weapons trials and integration with the all-new Hughes radar.

ACTION DATA

WEAPONS LOAD

The F/A-18E is truly outstanding for the amount and variety of weapons it can carry. Compared to other designs such as the MiG-29K, the Hornet can pack almost twice the punch.

F/A-18E HORNET	8165 kg (18,000 lb)
MIG-29K 'FULCRUM'	4491 kg (9900 lb)
A-6E INTRUDER	8025 kg (17,963 lb)

SPEED

The F/A-18E is outperformed by the MiG-29K at high level, however, it is manoeuvrability and speed without afterburner at low-level that are important to the modern fighter-bomber.

F/A-18E HORNET	1910 km/h (1187 mph)
MIG-29K 'FULCRUM'	2440 km/h (1516 mph)
A-6E INTRUDER	1102 km/h (685 mph)

SERVICE CEILING

Most air-to-ground sorties would be flown at low-level. If the F/A-18 took part in high-level air-to-air combat, it could be outperformed by the MiG-29K, but it is superior to the older A-6E.

MIG-29K 'FULCRUM'	16,995 m (55,760 ft)
F/A-18E HORNET	15,240 m (50,000 ft)
A-6E INTRUDER	12,924 m (42,400 ft)

F/A-18E HORNET

The F/A-18E/F otherwise known as the Super Hornet is the next generation of the outstanding Hornet. First flown in November 1995, entered service in the year 2001.

To help prevent detection by enemy radar the aircraft is designed with aligned edges in the wings and fuselage, which are treated with radar-absorbent material.

The radar is the same highly advanced system fitted to current Hornets. The APG-73 is effective in air-to-air combat, where it can engage multiple targets, and air-to-ground, where its accuracy has already been proved.

Defensive systems will include a radar-warning receiver, the ALQ-165 Advanced Self-Protection Jammer (ASPJ) along with three Raytheon ALE-50 towed monopulse decoys to confuse hostile missiles.

The General Electric F414-GE-400 engine is almost entirely new. It gives the aircraft a much better thrust-to-weight ratio and has lower infrared and radar signatures.

New 'stealthy' weapons, such as the AGM-154, will be carried along with almost any air-to-ground or air-to-air weapon in the US inventory.

The F/A-18E is one-third larger than the original Hornet allowing the fuselage to carry more fuel and armament, as well as incorporating more powerful engines.

The F/A-18E's cockpit is based largely on existing systems. The only major changes are a new flat-panel multi-colour head-down display and an imagery-compatible, touch-screen LCD control.

Compared to the F/A-18C, the F/A-18E has 25 per cent more wing area, with much larger control surfaces. It also incorporated a new leading-edge dogtooth.

The US Navy in the 21st century

■ **GRUMMAN F-14D:** This improved multi-role versions of the venerable Tomcat will continue to serve the Navy, but numbers will be reduced.

■ **LOCKHEED S-3B:** The Viking is a more important asset than ever, serving in ASW, anti-shipping, ELINT, tanking and transport roles.

■ **McD D/GD A-12:** The Avenger II stealth was the cancelled replacement for the A-6 Intruder and F-111. Thus, the F/A-18E/F.

■ **BOEING E-X:** A projected design, based on the Lockheed S-3, the E-X is intended to replace the veteran E-2 Hawkeye AWACS platform.

NORTH AMERICAN

B-25 MITCHELL

● Surplus World War II bomber ● Movie star ● Camera-equipped

T he B-25 Mitchell has been the star of a number of Hollywood films, most famously Catch 22 in which 16 B-25s flew together for the cameras. The B-25 not only shone in front of the cameras, but also served as the camera platform for many of the best-known aviation films of the 1960s, 1970s and 1980s. Film-makers appreciated the Mitchell's reliability, spaciousness and has supplied numerous images for the turret positions that gave the cameras a clear view of the action in all directions.

▲ Seen preparing for another filming sortie, the B-25 Mitchell has proved itself to be a dependable and highly versatile aircraft. This example has supplied numerous images for various film and television companies across the United States and Europe.

NORTH AMERICAN B-25 MITCHELL

▲ Cameras away
A special wide-angle camera was installed in this example, and could be raised and lowered from within the bomb bay.

▲ Take five
A common image during World War II was a Mitchell parked on the tarmac awaiting its next mission; it is still repeated today.

▲ Room with a view
Replacing the bombardier's compartment with a clear Perspex nose lets the camera operator obtain air-to-air images.

▼ Painted lady
Following the tradition established during the war years, the 'modern' Mitchells still carry a female figure on their noses.

▼ Weekend flight
With its engines set at full power, this Mitchell belonging to Aces High prepares to take off for a display in front of an air show audience.

FACTS AND FIGURES

➤ After World War II, surplus Mitchell bombers could be purchased for a few thousand dollars, including delivery.

➤ One converted example operates from Duxford in Cambridgeshire.

➤ No suitable modern replacement has yet been found for the B-25 Mitchell.

➤ Before each filming session, the nose of the aircraft is covered in paper for protection; this is blown off in flight.

➤ The few examples that are converted are in constant demand in America.

➤ As long as spares are available, the camera-equipped Mitchells will remain.

PROFILE

Mitchell, 'the movie maker'

N orth American Aviation's famous B-25 Mitchell medium bomber found more uses in post-war civilian life than most of its contemporaries. While thousands of Martin Marauders and Douglas Havocs were being turned into scrap metal, the Mitchell soldiered on with the armed forces of a number of nations well into the 1950s. Many B-25s were converted to executive transports, freighters, firebombers and crop-sprayers. During the 1950s, Paul Mantz, a

Californian businessmen who had bought many surplus warplanes for use in the World War II films that he knew would be made, put a B-25 to use as an aerial camera platform. Mantz first used the modified B-25 in *This is Cinerama*, a showcase film for the new projection technique. Other films made included *Seven Wonders of the World* and *America the Beautiful*. In 1967 Mantz's company, Tallmantz Aviation, filmed *Catch 22* in Mexico with two camera B-25s

Below: The most common type of camera installation is seen on this example operated privately in the United States.

Above: This B-25 camera ship was based at Shoreham for a number of years.

and 14 more 'actors'. Other companies adapted B-25s for airborne cinematography and films made with their help included *633 Squadron*, *The Battle of Britain*, *Memphis Belle* and *Cliffhanger*, in addition to numerous TV commercials.

B-25J MITCHELL

Operated as part of the Aces High company, this converted Mitchell has been a regular air show performer and has earned its keep by acting as a camera ship for film work.

Positioned on top of fuselage is a large clear dome which allows the director in charge of filming to observe the proceedings during flights. An additional camera can be installed here so that more filming angles can be obtained, if required by the film company.

Positioned on the nose is a rather provocative painting of a woman, along with the name of the operator. The clear, sectioned nose is evident when viewing the Mitchell from side on.

Resplendent in its high-gloss brown colour scheme, used to protect the airframe against corrosion, this Mitchell is based at the Imperial War Museum at Duxford in England. Flying throughout the summer months, the aircraft has proved to be an excellent camera platform.

In wartime a tail gunner was stationed in the rear of the fuselage. For peacetime operations, the guns have been removed and the tail of the aircraft has been faired over. On this particular model, the gunner's seat is retained.

The aircraft retains the standard tricycle undercarriage; its high setting means additional equipment associated with filming can be carried in the redundant bomb bay. Operations can be flown from grass runways.

Multi-purpose Mitchells

■ **EXECUTIVE TRANSPORT:** Converted from surplus wartime bombers, these B-25s saw extensive service immediately after the ending of World War II.

■ **MOVIE STAR:** This Mitchell appeared on the other side of the camera in the film *Hanover Street*, in which it was used to recreate an American wartime bomber group.

■ **WARBIRD:** Restored to full military specifications, these Mitchells are treasured flying museum pieces and are displayed at air shows across Europe and America.

B-25J Mitchell

Type: converted medium/light bomber

Powerplant: two 1268-kW (1700hp) Wright R-2600-92 radial piston engines

Maximum speed: 438 km/h (272 mph) at 3960 m (12992 ft)

Initial climb rate: 261 m (856 ft) per minute

Range: 2173 km (1350 miles)

Service ceiling: 7375 m (24,196 ft)

Weights: empty 8836 kg (19,480 lb); maximum take-off 15876 kg (35,000 lb)

Accommodation: two pilots and up to four camera operators

Dimensions:		
span	20.60 m (67ft 7in)	
length	16.13 m (52ft 11in)	
height	4.98 m (16ft)	
wing area	56.67 m² (610 sq ft)	

CAMERAS IN THE AIR

SKY WATCHERS: Utilising aircraft as camera platforms is nothing new; this was one of the first roles undertaken by the flimsy biplanes of WWI. Since that time, the commercial market has been quick to see the potential of operating cameras in the sky to obtain the desired film images.

HEADLINE MAKER: Operated throughout the United States on behalf of the various news network stations, the Bell JetRanger has been brought to the world's attention such images as forest fires and the Los Angeles riots. The helicopter is also used in limited numbers across Europe in a similar role.

MILITARY APPLICATIONS: Despite the passing years, the T-6 Harvard continues to be flown by many air forces as a photographic platform for recording weapons drops and providing pictures for public relations work. This example served with the Royal Canadian Air Force at Cold Lake. T-6s are also operated by the Royal Air Force at Boscombe Down to take pictures of new test aircraft.

NORTH AMERICAN

TEXAN/SNJ/HARVARD

- Allied aircrew trainer ● Thousands built ● Licence-production

▲ Derived from the privately financed NA-16 prototype, the Texan was adopted by a USAAC which was looking for an aircraft with performance close to that of combat types.

More than 300,000 American and Allied student pilots earned their wings in this renowned aircraft. So important was it to the Allied effort during World War II that it was dubbed 'the pilot maker'. A conventional low-wing 'tail-dragger', the aircraft was a forgiving 'classroom' for trainee pilots, providing a bridge between initial flight training and operational duties. Texans served widely in wartime; some air forces continue to train pilots in them to this day.

▲ Pre-war US Navy SNJ
In 1936 the US Navy ordered four NJ-1s, derived from the USAAC's BT-9. The SNJs that followed, from 1938, became the Navy's standard trainer.

▼ Captured French NA-57
France took delivery of 230 NA-57s pre-war. After the German invasion these AT-6 forerunners, with fixed landing gear, were used by the Luftwaffe.

▼ Wartime camouflage
In wartime camouflage, this AT-6 shows off the squarer wingtips that characterised this and subsequent members of the Texan family. Wartime demand led to the establishment of a second production line in Dallas to assist the California factory.

▲ Non-strategic materials
Low-alloy steel and plywood were used in the AT-6C variant to save 565 kg (1246 lb) of aluminium alloy.

RAF's first American type ▶
Harvard Mk Is, the first of which were delivered in late 1938, were the RAF's first US-built aircraft. Total deliveries to Commonwealth air forces exceeded 5000.

FACTS AND FIGURES

▶ More than 17,000 trainers in this series were manufactured before, during and after World War II.

▶ The prototype NA-16 that led to the AT-6 Texan made its initial flight in April 1935.

▶ One AT-6D was fitted with a Ranger V-770 inline engine, as the XAT-6E.

▶ Australia's Commonwealth Aircraft Corporation built NA-33s as Wirraway armed multi-role combat aircraft.

▶ Some air forces maintained ex-wartime Texan/Harvard fleets into the 1970s.

▶ A few US Navy SNJs were equipped with arrester hooks for deck landing training.

AT-6A Texan

Type: two-seat advanced pilot trainer

Powerplant: one 447-kW (600-hp) Pratt & Whitney R-1340-47 radial piston engine

Maximum speed: 330 km/h (205 mph) at 1525 m (5000 ft)

Initial climb rate: 7.4 minutes to 3048 m (10,000 ft)

Range: 1207 km (750 miles)

Service ceiling: 7376 m (24,200 ft)

Weights: empty 1769 kg (3900 lb); maximum take-off 2338 kg (5154 lb)

Armament: one fixed forward-firing 7.62-mm (.30-cal.) machine gun and one flexible rear-mounted 7.62-mm machine gun

Dimensions: span 12.80 m (42 ft)
height 8.84 m (29 ft)
length 3.58 m (11 ft 9 in)
wing area 23.60 m² (254 sq ft)

Above: The AT-6 Texan advanced trainer started life as the BC-1A 'basic combat' trainer with the equipment and attributes of operational aircraft. This AT-6A has a rear-mounted 7.62-mm (.30-cal.) machine gun fitted for gunnery training.

Above: Although the early examples were built by North American, most of Canada's Harvards were constructed by Noorduyn. The RAF received 900, designated Harvard Mk IIB.

ACTION DATA

POWER

Compared to contemporary trainer types, the Texan was moderately powered. The RAF's Miles Master, in Wasp radial-engined form, was more powerful than the Texan/Harvard and equipped advanced flying schools in the same way as the Harvard. The Luftwaffe equivalent was the Arado Ar 96.

MAXIMUM SPEED

The USAAF's Texan was faster than the biplane trainers of the late 1930s, having been produced to simulate more closely the flying characteristics of combat aircraft. The Miles Master, with its larger engine, was faster, while the less powerful Ar 96 was able to maintain a top speed similar to that of the Texan.

RANGE

An area in which the AT-6 Texan performed well was range. Good range (around 1200 km/746 miles) meant that the aircraft was able to stay aloft on a training sortie for a longer time. The more powerful Miles Master had only half the range ability, and the Arado Ar 96 fell between the two in endurance.

Aircrew trainer extraordinaire

North American's AT-6 Texan was known by many other designations and names, perhaps the most well-known of which were Harvard (in the RAF and Commonwealth air forces) and SNJ (in the US Navy). One of the most famous of all time, the AT-6 family trained the majority of Allied pilots and other aircrew during World War II.

Developed from the original NA-16 of 1935, the design was first ordered as the BT-9 basic trainer, with fixed undercarriage, a fabric-covered fuselage and a 298-kW Wright R-975 radial engine. With the aim of

producing a trainer to reproduce the characteristics of operational aircraft, various airframe changes were made and a new engine with 50 per cent more power installed. The result was the BC-1 basic combat trainer, the BC-1A variant of which was later redesignated the AT-6.

With the onset of World War II, thousands of AT-6s were built for the Allies' flying training schools, a significant number under licence in Canada. Small numbers train pilots to this day.

Pratt & Whitney's reliable nine-cylinder R-1340-49 Wasp radial powered the Harvard family. A two-bladed propeller was fitted, the high-speed tips of which produced the well-known 'rasping' note familiar to pilots.

HARVARD MK I

Equivalent to the USAAC's BC-1 of 1937, the Harvard Mk I entered RAF service in December 1938. This aircraft flew with No. 2 Flying Training School at RAF Brize Norton during the early years of World War II.

For 17 years the Harvard was the RAF's standard advanced training aircraft. The last pilots to gain their 'wings' on the Harvard graduated from No. 3 Flying Training School, RAF Feltwell, in March 1955.

A curved rudder was fitted to the BC-1 and Harvard Mk I. On later versions this had a straight trailing edge.

As a dual-control trainer, the Harvard was equipped to accommodate the student in the front cockpit and the instructor in the rear seat. USAAF gunnery trainers had a rear-mounted machine gun.

Harvard Mk Is, in common with the BC-1, had a steel tube rear fuselage structure with fabric covering. Most later marks had a light alloy monocoque with metal skinning, apart from the Mk IIB, which had a plywood rear fuselage.

RAF Harvards carried this semi-camouflaged colour scheme during the early war years. Later, camouflage was extended to cover all the upper surfaces. The undersides remained yellow for safety reasons.

Texan evolution from NA-16 to P-64

■ **NA-16:** The privately funded NA-16 prototype had a 298-kW (400-hp) engine, open cockpits, fixed gear and a fabric-skinned fuselage.

■ **BT-9:** This 'basic trainer' was the first NA-16 variant to enter US service in 1935. Changes were few, but included enclosed cockpits.

■ **BC-1/BC-1A/YALE:** A short step from the AT-6 was the basic combat BC-1 trainer, still with a 298-kW (400-hp) engine and fixed undercarriage.

■ **P-64:** In 1939, NAA developed this fighter version of the AT-6. A few were sold to Peru and Siam, but the Siamese ones were not delivered.

NORTH AMERICAN
P-51 EARLY VERSIONS

● Initially Allison-engined ● RAF service ● High speed at low level

T hough designed to a World War II RAF requirement, the Mustang was destined to become the finest of the USAAF's fighters and, arguably, the finest such machine of the war. With an Allison V-1710 liquid-cooled engine, the Mustang's performance at altitude was limited, the P-51 thus being initially employed as a ground-attack and reconnaissance aircraft (as the A-36 in the former role). The British Merlin engine was to transform the type.

▲ P-51A, B and C aircraft served in large numbers until the end of World War II. All performed exceptionally well, flying close-support, reconnaissance and escort missions.

NORTH AMERICAN P-51 EARLY VERSIONS

▲ US Army Air Force service
Although it received its Mustangs some time after the RAF, the USAAF was to operate the type in huge numbers. This trio of P-51As carries tanks to disperse smoke screens and tear gas, the latter only for training.

▼ Asian combat service
These P-51As were operated by the 1st Air Commando Group in Burma during 1944.

▲ British Malcolm hood
This rocket-armed Mustang Mk III demonstrates the blown 'Malcolm' hood, for improved visibility.

'Ski Fifty-One' ▼
Two P-51As were tested with retractable skis in Alaska. Although few problems were found, no further use was made of this special undercarriage.

▲ First of the thoroughbreds
AG345 was the first production Mustang Mk I for the RAF and made its first flight on 23 April 1941. The aircraft features the early, short carburettor air intake above the nose.

FACTS AND FIGURES

➤ The USAAF's first P-51s differed from RAF Mustangs in having wing-mounted cannon armament.

➤ The first USAAF Mustangs in action were A-36As in the invasion of Sicily and Italy.

➤ Mustangs were built by North American at plants in California and Texas.

➤ It reportedly took the personal intervention of General 'Hap' Arnold for the USAAF to accept the P-51.

➤ A-36A ground-attack aircraft sported wing-mounted dive brakes.

➤ Camera-equipped USAAF Mustangs were designated F-6s.

PROFILE

Flying thoroughbred for the RAF

After the end of World War II, Reichsmarschall Hermann Goering, supreme commander of the mighty Luftwaffe, declared, 'When I saw Mustangs over Berlin, I knew the war was lost.' The aircraft he was describing was conceived with haste in 1940 and proved to be arguably the finest piston-engined fighter of World War II.

Starting life with an Allison engine, the Mustang was designed in early 1940 in response to an RAF requirement for a new fighter which would benefit from

experience gained in Europe the previous year.

Flown in 1941, the Mustang Mk I entered RAF service in 1942 in the armed tactical reconnaissance role, because of the Allison engine's poor performance at altitude. After some convincing the USAAF ordered Mustangs in 1942, initially as the A-36 ground-attack aircraft (sometimes referred to as the Apache).

In an attempt to address the altitude performance problem, the RAF proposed the installation of the Rolls-Royce

Merlin engine, the result being the P-51B and C fighters. Delivery of the first B models in 1943 immediately gave the USAAF the ability to escort its bombers over Germany.

P-51B Mustang

Type: single-seat long-range escort fighter

Powerplant: one 1029-kW (1380-hp) Packard (Rolls-Royce) V-1650 Merlin piston engine

Maximum speed: 708 km/h (440 mph) at 9144 m (30,000 ft)

Cruising speed: 583 km/h (362 mph)

Initial climb rate: 12.5 minutes to 9144 m (30,000 ft)

Range: 3347 km (2080 miles)

Service ceiling: 12,741 m (41,800 ft)

Weights: empty 3168 kg (6984 lb); gross 5352 kg (11,799 lb)

Armament: four 12.7-mm (.50-cal.) machine guns plus up to 907 kg (2000 lb) of bombs

Dimensions:
span	11.28 m (37 ft)
length	9.83 m (32 ft 3 in)
height	3.70 m (12 ft 2 in)
wing area	21.90 m² (236 sq ft)

Carrying serial number 43-6013, this aircraft was one of the first P-51As of an order for 310. The RAF received 50 of these aircraft, designated Mustang Mk II, while a further 35 were converted to F-6B standard for photo-reconnaissance duties.

No fewer than eight machine guns armed the Mustang Mk I. A pair of 12.7-mm (.50-cal.) M2 Brownings was mounted in the nose. Synchronised to fire through the propeller blades, they were canted over so that they could be fed from magazines fitting neatly into the bottom of the nose.

COMBAT DATA

MAXIMUM SPEED

Initially the Allison-engined P-51 was employed in the ground-attack role. It compared favourably with other ground-attack types of the period, like the marginally faster Focke-Wulf Fw 190A-8 and Supermarine Spitfire Mk V.

P-51A MUSTANG	628 km/h (390 mph)
Fw 190A-8/U3	657 km/h (408 mph)
SPITFIRE LF.Mk VB	575 km/h (357 mph)

MAXIMUM RANGE

A strength of the Mustang was always its range performance, that of the P-51A being well over twice that of both the Spitfire Mk V and Fw 190A-8. Merlin-engined P-51Bs carried out long-range escort.

P-51A MUSTANG	4104 km (2550 miles)
Fw 190A-8/U3	1516 km (942 miles)
SPITFIRE LF.Mk VB	1827 km (1135 miles)

ARMAMENT

Early Mustang variants were comparatively lightly armed, with just four machine guns. However, they were able to lift greater bombloads than their contemporaries.

P-51A MUSTANG	4 x 12.7-mm (.50-cal.) machine guns 454-kg (1000-lb) bombload
Fw 190A-8/U3	2 x 13-mm machine guns 4 x 20-mm cannon 250-kg (550-lb) bombload
SPITFIRE LF.Mk VB	4 x 7.7-mm (.303-cal.) machine guns 2 x 20-mm cannon 227-kg (500-lb) bombload

---

A heavily framed canopy gave the pilot poor visibility, even when compared with other contemporary fighters. Later versions had bulged clear-vision hoods and the P-51D had a bubble canopy.

The Mustang Mk I was powered by a single Allison V-1710-39 in-line liquid-cooled piston engine, rated at 857.6 kW (1150 hp). This gave the aircraft excellent performance at low altitude, but at higher level the early Mustangs were disappointing.

MUSTANG Mk I

AM101 served with No. 26 Squadron, based at Gatwick in East Sussex, from early 1942. The unit's main tasks were flying 'Rhubarbs' (fighter sweeps over German-occupied northern France) and reconnaissance sorties.

A single F24 oblique camera was fitted behind the pilot's seat, facing to port. No. 26 Squadron also flew photo-recce missions, dubbed 'Poplars', over the French coast.

The Mustang was fitted with a laminar flow wing to reduce drag and improve performance. This was a major innovation at the time.

RM·D. AM101
THE BLACK CAT

From NA-73X prototype to Mustang

■ **NA-73X:** Registered NX19998, this was the first member of the Mustang family. The prototype flew on 26 October 1940. The RAF had already ordered 320 examples the previous May.

■ **MUSTANG Mk I:** Depicted in the markings of No. 613 Squadron, RAF Mustang Mk I AG522 was delivered in mid-1942 and employed on 'Poplar' reconnaissance missions over France.

■ **F-6B:** Malcolm hood-equipped 43-6163 began life as a P-51A but was converted to F-6B standard for service with the Ninth Air Force's 107th Tactical Reconnaissance Squadron.

NORTH AMERICAN

P-51 MUSTANG

● Bomber escort ● Long-range fighter ● Best fighter of the war

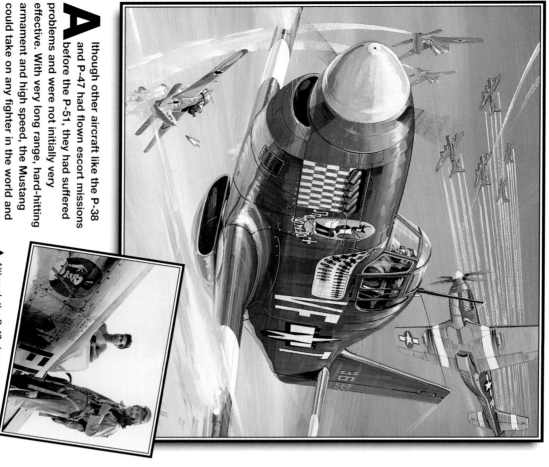

▲ Although the P-47 always outnumbered the P-51 in escort missions, it was the more successful Mustang that spelt the end for Germany's air forces, causing huge casualties to the defenders.

Although other aircraft like the P-38 and P-47 had flown escort missions before the P-51, they had suffered problems and were not initially very effective. With very long range, hard-hitting armament and high speed, the Mustang could take on any fighter in the world and win easily. The P-51 allowed the Eighth Air Force to bomb any target at will over Germany, spelling the end for the Luftwaffe's fighter force.

NORTH AMERICAN P-51 MUSTANG

▼ **Belly landing**
Damage to the hydraulics of 'Danny Boy 2nd' meant a belly landing for its pilot from 353rd Fighter Group in December 1944. This aircraft was probably repaired and flown again.

▲ **Mass formation**
By the end of the war Mustangs had huge numerical superiority. Over 400 took part in a massive attack on an Me 262 base in 1945.

▼ **To Japan**
By 1945 B-29s were being escorted to Japan by Mustangs based on the island of Iwo Jima.

▲ **Wing tanks**
With extra fuel under the wings, the Mustang had the range required to reach Berlin. The fuel in the tanks was used first, and then they were dropped before combat began.

◀ **Little friend**
If a bomber was crippled on its way home, a Mustang pilot would shepherd the aircraft, protecting the crew from fighter attacks.

FACTS AND FIGURES

➤ P-51s flown from Italy by pilots of the 332nd Fighter Group never lost a single bomber that they escorted.

➤ Just one Mustang pilot, Major James Howard, won the Medal of Honor.

➤ In December 1943 Eighth Air Force P-51s first went to Germany for a raid on Kiel.

➤ On 6 March 1944, 644 fighters flew with 814 B-17s on a mission to Berlin, opposed by 400 Luftwaffe fighters.

➤ Over 15,586 Mustangs were built, but fewer than 2000 were in Europe at any one time.

➤ Bell X-1 pilot Chuck Yeager shot down an Me 262 in a P-51 Mustang.

P-51B Mustang

Type: single-seat escort fighter and fighter-bomber

Powerplant: one 1029-kW (1380-hp) Packard V-1650-3 Merlin in-line piston engine

Maximum speed: 708 km/h (440 mph)

Initial climb rate: 1000 m/min (3280 fpm)

Combat radius: 400 km (249 miles)

Range: 820 km (510 miles)

Service ceiling: 12,700 m (41,667 ft)

Weights: empty 3168 kg (6984 lb); loaded 5352 kg (11,799 lb)

Armament: four 12.7-mm (.50-cal.) Browning M3 machine guns; provision for two 454-kg (1000-lb) bombs, or underwing stores in place of drop-tanks

Dimensions:
span	11.29 m (37 ft)
length	9.84 m (32 ft 3 in)
height	4.10 m (13 ft 5 in)
wing area	21.83 m² (235 sq ft)

COMBAT DATA

MAXIMUM SPEED

Nothing could catch the Mustang except the Me 262 jet, and even this aircraft was not a great threat. Specially lightened P-51s were reaching 850 km/h (528 mph) in trials at the end of the war.

P-51D MUSTANG 704 km/h (437 mph)

Fw 190D-9 685 km/h (426 mph)

Ki-84 'FRANK' 631 km/h (392 mph)

RANGE

The Mustang's range was incomparable to any other single-engined fighter. The defending Fw 190 traded fuel for additional armament and armour, so it had a much shorter range.

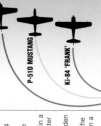

Fw 190D-9 837 km (520 miles)

Ki-84 'FRANK' 1695 km (1053 miles)

P-51D MUSTANG 3347 km (2080 miles)

TURN RADIUS

Agility was another strong point of the Mustang, although the superb Ki-84 was probably the most manoeuvrable monoplane fighter of the war. The Fw 190 was not as good in a dogfight, especially the later versions that took on the bombers, as they were laden with extra rockets and cannon. Pilot ability was the real test in a fight between a P-51 and an Fw 190.

Fw 190-9
P-51D MUSTANG
Ki-84 'FRANK'

Berlin and back in the P-51

Sending bombers over Europe without fighter protection was a mistake. P-51 Mustangs first went to Berlin on 4 March 1944 and proved that only with fighter escort could bombers survive. Luftwaffe Messerschmitts and Focke-Wulfs were aggressive and even against P-51s they remained deadly.

At first, fighters stayed too close to the bombers. They were ineffective and suffered heavy losses. It became obvious that

the fighters needed tactics of their own, and so they began to weave above and below bomber formations, and to range ahead of the bombers.

The pilot of a P-51 Mustang on a round trip to Berlin was zipped inside heavy clothing for protection from cold, and wore oxygen mask, leather helmet and goggles. His US-made Merlin engine suffered from teething trouble, his guns often jammed and his heater was unreliable. One-third of Mustangs on the

first big Berlin mission turned back, but reliability soon improved. The remainder fought hard – and proved the value of the escort fighter. Hermann Goering reportedly said: 'When I saw fighter escorts arriving with the bombers, I knew we had lost the war.'

Unusually, the Mustang had been built in response to a British specification, and used an American-built version of a British engine, the Rolls-Royce Merlin.

Power was supplied to a four-bladed Hamilton-Standard Hydromatic constant speed airscrew.

Many escort Mustangs were finished in bare metal, with an anti-glare strip in front of the canopy.

The front of the cockpit was optically flat five-ply laminated bulletproof glass with safety glass side panels.

The only part of the airframe that was not aluminium, or Alclad, was the pilot's sheet of armour.

The fuselage consisted of a front section with engine bearing struts, a middle section containing the fuselage fuel tank and oil radiators, and the detachable tail section. Rudder and elevators were alloy-framed with fabric covering.

Much of the P-51's vast petrol supply was stored in a large fuel tank in the lower fuselage. All the tanks in the P-51 were of the self-sealing type. The rear fuselage of the Mustang was completely redesigned in the P-51D.

Escort missions were flown predominately by later model Mustangs with a bubble-type canopy replacing the earlier 'Malcolm' hood.

The underwing pylons of the P-51D were strengthened to enable the fighter to carry the new 416-litre (92-gallon) and 625-litre (137-gallon) drop-tanks. They could also carry 454-kg (1000-lb) bombs or 127-mm (5-in) rockets on the pylons.

P-51D MUSTANG

'Alabama Rammer Jammer' belonged to the 352nd Fighter Squadron, 353rd Fighter Group. It was named after the Alabama University student newspaper. The pilot, Lieutenant Arthur Cundy, destroyed six enemy aircraft while flying this P-51.

Armament for the P-51D consisted of six 12.7-mm (.50-cal.) Browning machine guns. Ammunition load was 400 rounds for each inboard gun and 275 rounds for each of the remaining four guns.

Mustang massacre

1 RADAR ERROR: During an air raid in 1944, a German fighter controller plotted a formation of slow-flying aircraft heading in from the direction of the UK.

2 FIGHTER ATTACK: He thought they were bombers, and sent in a flight of Me 410 fighters. They encountered a B-17 on the way and shot it down, expecting the target formation to consist of more of them.

3 NASTY SURPRISE: The 'slow movers' were cruising Mustangs hiding behind a flight of B-17s. The Messerschmitts fell into the well-laid trap and were quickly engaged by the far superior P-51s. The battle was over quickly as the Mustangs shot down the entire formation within minutes.

NORTH AMERICAN
P-51D MUSTANG

- Long-range escort fighter ● Most Allied kills ● 281 Mustang aces

As the bombers of the Eighth Air Force fought their way deep into Hitler's German heartland, it was the Mustang that cleared the skies of Luftwaffe fighters. No other combat airplane of the war could fly as high, go as far and fight as hard as the mighty Mustang. In the skilled hands of young USAAF pilots, it took on all comers and accounted for more kills than any other

▲ One of the great Mustang heroes, Major Don Gentile, with his favourite machine 'Shangri-La' during 1943. He made 15 kills in Mustangs – half of them in one month!

NORTH AMERICAN P-51D MUSTANG

▲ All the way!
With underwing tanks, Mustangs had enough range to be able to escort their charges more than 1200 km (746 miles) to the target, and were agile enough to beat all comers when they got there.

▼ High flyer
The Mustang's phenomenal range and performance made it ideal for escorting high-flying B-29s across the vast Pacific.

▲ Mud movers
The Mustang's hard-hitting and accurate guns made it an excellent ground-attack aircraft, which could also deliver air-to-ground rockets or bombs.

Powerpack ▼
The early Mustang was transformed into a superb high-level fighter by the British-designed, Packard-built Rolls-Royce Merlin engine, which could deliver 1186 kW (1590 hp).

▼ Flying veterans
The Mustang's impeccable handling characteristics, bubble canopy and performance make it a popular rich man's toy; many of them are still flying. This example even carries a passenger!

FACTS AND FIGURES

▶ Ordered by the British, the prototype Mustang was proposed, designed, built and flown in an incredible 117 days.

▶ That initial aircraft was the first of 15,586 examples of the P-51 produced.

▶ The Mustang was flown by 11 Allied air forces in addition to the USAAF.

▶ A total of 281 Allied Mustang pilots were to qualify as 'Aces', with five or more kills.

▶ The late-model P-51H was, at 760 km/h (472 mph), one of the fastest piston-engined fighters.

▶ In October 1944, Mustang pilot Lieutenant Urban L. Drew managed the astonishing feat of shooting down two Me 262 jets.

P-51D Mustang

Type: single-seat long-range escort fighter, fighter-bomber

Powerplant: one 1186-kW (1590-hp) Packard V-1650-7 (US-built Rolls-Royce Merlin 61) inverted-vee 12-cylinder inline water-cooled piston engine

Maximum speed: 716 km/h (445 mph) at 7620 m (25,000 ft)

Combat radius: 525 km (326 miles) on internal fuel; 1210 km (752 miles) with two 491-litre (108-gallon) tanks

Service ceiling: 12770 m

Weights: empty 3232 kg (7125 lb); loaded 5265 kg (11,607 lb)

Armament: six 12.7-mm (.50-cal.) Browning machine guns in wings; two 227-kg (500-lb) bombs or eight 75-mm rockets in place of long-range drop-tanks

Dimensions:
span	11.29 m (37 ft)
length	9.83 m (32 ft 3 in)
height	3.71 m (12 ft 2 in)
wing area	21.83 m² (235 sq ft)

COMBAT DATA

RANGE

The Mustang's combat radius was better than that of any other Allied fighter, and could stretch to Berlin.

- 400 km (249 miles) SPITFIRE Mk IX
- 580 km (360 miles) P-47D THUNDERBOLT
- 1207 km (750 miles) P-51D MUSTANG

MAXIMUM SPEED

Bf 109G	623 km/h (387 mph)
P-47D THUNDERBOLT	708 km/h (440 mph)
P-51D MUSTANG	716 km/h (445 mph)

The P-51D's clean, low-drag airframe and powerful Merlin engine endowed it with superb performance.

ARMAMENT

The P-51D packed a powerful punch, with its fast-firing 12.7-mm (.50-cal.) machine guns proving deadly against enemy fighter targets, although they lacked the stopping power of a 20- or 30-mm cannon.

- **P-51D MUSTANG** 6 x 12.7-mm (.50-cal.) machine guns
- **Bf 109G** 1 x 30-mm cannon in the spinner 2 x 13-mm machine guns in the nose 2 x 20/30-mm cannon underwing
- **SPITFIRE Mk IX** 4 x 7.7-mm (.303-cal.) machine guns 2 x 20-mm Hispano cannon

Top Gun to the bomber force

Faced with imminent invasion in 1939 and desperately short of fighters, the Royal Air Force asked North American Aviation to produce urgently the existing but obsolete P-40 Warhawk. But instead the company designed, built and flew a new airplane in just 117 days – the Mustang.

Using an existing Allison engine and the latest laminar-flow wing, the new fighter immediately went into service with the RAF. In December 1941 America joined the war, and it too needed good fighters fast. So the USAAF took the basic RAF Mustang, re-armed it with four machine guns, and added an uprated engine. It was a good performer, but couldn't operate well alongside the high-flying long-range bomber.

By 1944 the aircraft used the Rolls-Royce Merlin engine, had a new bubble cockpit and

increased firepower to six 12.7-mm (.50-cal.) machine guns. It was now the best fighter in the war and fought superbly in all theatres, as fighter, fighter-bomber and reconnaissance platform. It was loved by its aircrews, and no fewer than 281 Mustang pilots became aces by scoring five kills apiece.

Mustangs were flown by more aces than any other Allied fighter. Their prey even included the Me 262 jet.

The P-51 was transformed by the adoption of the Merlin engine. The original Allison engine delivered plenty of power at low altitude, but was disappointing at higher altitude.

P-51K MUSTANG 'NOOKY BOOKY IV'

This shortened propeller version of the P-51D was flown by Major Leonard 'Kit' Carson (left) of the 362nd Fighter Squadron, based at Leiston, Suffolk, during 1944. Carson was one of the top-scoring Mustang aces, with 18½ air-to-air victories.

The bubble canopy and cut-down rear fuselage of the P-51D gave the pilot an unsurpassed all-round view.

Initially painted with olive drab camouflaged top surfaces, paint was soon stripped off to save weight, and the bare skin was highly polished to reduce drag.

The low-drag laminar-flow wing was largely responsible for the Mustang's combination of agility and long-range capability, and accommodated six 12.7-mm (.50-cal.) machine guns.

Despite having an inline, liquid-cooled engine and a prominent and vulnerable ventral (underfuselage) radiator, the P-51D was remarkably tolerant of battle damage.

Even without optional underwing fuel tanks, the Mustang had a good radius of action: with tanks fitted it could escort bombers all the way to Berlin. These tanks could be jettisoned if the Mustang had to engage in manoeuvring combat.

Mustang: the all-the-way escort fighter

■ **THE BOMBERS:** Eighth Air Force bombers left their British bases an hour ahead of the Mustangs, escorted in the first part of the mission by shorter-ranged P-38s and P-47s.

■ **HAND OVER:** The faster Mustangs would catch the formation over the Dutch/German border, where they would relieve the P-47 and Thunderbolts high above the B-17s.

■ **ESCORT:** Some fighters flew close escort. Their nearness boosted the morale of the bomber crews, who had been so severely mauled over Germany the year before.

■ **DOGFIGHTER:** The Mustang had more than long range. It was fast and it was a ferocious dogfighter, as the pilot of this Messerschmitt Bf 109G shot down by a P-51 discovered to his cost.

■ **CONTROL OF THE SKIES:** It was the appearance of swarms of these graceful fighters in the skies over Germany that was to signal the death knell of the Luftwaffe.

NORTH AMERICAN
P-82 TWIN MUSTANG

- Compound design ● Night-fighter ● Long-range fighter

▲ Unlike many coupled aircraft, the F-82 was very useful and lived up to the reputation of its predecessor. It made the night skies over Korea dangerous for Communist pilots.

North American's F-82 Twin Mustang (originally P-82) was conceived in 1943 for the Pacific War where pilots spent six to eight hours in their cockpits on long-distance missions. During the Korean fighting, where the F-82 scored the war's first aerial victory, the long reach of this large, twin-boomed, twin-engined fighter enabled it to operate from bases in Japan. Fitted with radar under the wing, it was a highly lethal night-fighter.

PHOTO FILE

NORTH AMERICAN P-82 TWIN MUSTANG

▼ States guardian
Wearing a tail pattern of stars, these F-82s served with the 52nd All-Weather Fighter Squadron at Mitchell AFB, New York.

▲ Well-armed hunter
As well as the six 12.7-mm (.50-cal.) machine guns, a gun pack could be carried on the centreline. Note the high-velocity aircraft rockets (HVARs) and bombs fitted for the ground-attack mission.

▲ Allison engines
Unlike many twin-engined American aircraft, such as the P-38 Lightning, the F-82 had non-handed engines with the propellers turning in the same direction.

▼ All-round success
The Twin Mustang retained all the positive features of the single-seater, being both fast and manoeuvrable.

▲ Long distance flight
In February 1947 a Twin Mustang flew non-stop from Hawaii to New York in just over 14½ hours, demonstrating the aircraft's great endurance.

FACTS AND FIGURES

▼ The K-18 gunsight of the F-82 was equipped to compensate for the pilot not being at the centre of the aircraft.

▼ A total of 275 Twin Mustangs were produced by North American.

▼ The F-82 was difficult to service and was referred to as a 'mechanic's nightmare'.

▼ Night-fighter versions of the F-82 carried SCR-720C radar in a pod between the two fuselage structures.

▼ The first Twin Mustang prototype made its initial flight on 15 April 1945.

▼ Several non-flying F-82s are on display in the US, including one at Lackland, Texas.

PROFILE

Twice the power of the Mustang

Radical in appearance, the Twin Mustang was not, as it seemed, two P-51 Mustang aircraft joined to a single wing. It was actually a totally new aircraft which used existing fuselage shapes but with a new wing structure. The two-man crew consisted of a pilot (on the left side) and a navigator sufficiently trained to fly the pilot for short periods during long-distance flights.

Although the primary US Air Force fighter at the time was the

F-80 Shooting Star, the F-82 fought in the Korean War, as a night-fighter, from the very beginning. The first kill of the war was scored on 27 June 1950 when an F-82 shot down a North Korean Yak-7U.

The Twin Mustang's combat service in Korea lasted only a few months, but this big, trustworthy fighter made a valuable contribution. Setting off from bases in Japan, the F-82 could reach Korea, flying ground-attack and reconnaissance as well as night-fighter missions.

Below: The reign of the F-82 was very brief. The US Air Force replaced it with the jet F3D Skyknight in the night-fighter role.

Above: In late 1948 Air Defence Command was equipped with 225 Twin Mustangs. Two years later, most of them were based in Japan.

The Twin Mustang was an adventure to fly and demanded great skill and concentration. It was a tough and enduring aircraft, however, and had a good combat record, gaining several notable kills in Korea.

F-82 Powerplant note

Like the wartime P-51, the prototype P-82 was powered by the Packard Merlin V-12 liquid-cooled engine, but production aircraft used Allison V-1710s.

F-82G TWIN MUSTANG

'Dottie Mae', an F-82G, was a Korean War night-fighter. F-82Gs were operated by the 68th and 339th Fighter Squadrons from Johnson AB, Japan.

The large SCR 720C or APS-4 radar was carried in an under-fuselage pod. The operator sat in the starboard cockpit.

The crew sat on adjustable seats, designed to alleviate the discomfort of long patrols. Both cockpits had complete controls, but only the pilot's cockpit to port had full instruments.

The Twin Mustang had a long dorsal fillet to improve stability. The pilot could uncouple the rudder pedals if required in order to stretch his legs safely without moving the rudder.

Almost all Twin Mustangs were painted midnight blue for night operations. Unit and aircraft serials were red, with the national insignia in white.

The fuselage for the F-82 was a lengthened P-51H design. Centre of gravity problems meant that ammunition storage was limited to less than the capacity of 1800 rounds.

The F-82 could carry underwing fuel to extend its already impressive range. Offensive armament of four 454-kg (1000-lb) bombs or 25 rockets could also be carried. The six machine guns were wing mounted.

Korean War night-fighters

■ **F7F TIGERCAT:** The US Marine Corps flew F7F night-fighters from bases in South Korea. Although too late for World War II, Tigercats achieved considerable air-to-air success in Korea.

■ **F-94 STARFIRE:** F-94s were used to escort B-29 bombers flying night missions. However, their radar were not good enough and they were replaced by the F3D.

■ **F3D SKYKNIGHT:** The marauding MiG-15s, which claimed a large number of B-29s at night, were in for a shock when the F3D appeared. Its excellent radar allowed it to achieve many kills.

F-82G Twin Mustang

Type: twin-engine long-range fighter

Powerplant: two 1193-kW (1600-hp) Allison V-1710-143/145 V-12 piston engines

Maximum speed: 742 km/h (460 mph) at 6400 m (21,000 ft)

Range: 3605 km (2450 miles)

Service ceiling: 11,855 m (39,000 ft)

Weights: empty 7256 kg (15,963 lb); maximum take-off 11,608 kg (25,538 lb)

Armament: six wing-mounted 12.7-mm (50-cal.) Browning MG-53-2 air-cooled machine guns with 400 rounds each plus up to four 454-kg (1000-lb) bombs, 25 HVARs, or four auxiliary fuel tanks on underwing racks

Dimensions:
span	15.62 m (51 ft 3 in)
length	12.93 m (42 ft 5 in)
height	4.22 m (13 ft 10 in)
wing area	37.90 m² (408 sq ft)

COMBAT DATA

MAXIMUM SPEED

Twin-engined fighter development had reached its zenith by the end of World War II, with very high speeds being attained. Aircraft like the Twin Mustang and Hornet were almost as fast as early jets.

F-82G TWIN MUSTANG	742 km/h (460 mph)
F7F-3N TIGERCAT	700 km/h (434 mph)
HORNET F.Mk 3	750 km/h (465 mph)

RANGE

Piston-engined aircraft were much more economical than the early jets, and with their large wings they had very good fuel capacity. Designed for long-range fighter missions over the Pacific, all of these aircraft were capable of flying very long combat patrols.

F-82G TWIN MUSTANG	3605 km (2450 miles)
F7F-3N TIGERCAT	1930 km (1200 miles)
HORNET F.MK 3	4022 km (2500 miles)

ARMAMENT

Like its single-engined counterpart, the F-82 retained 12.7-mm (.50-cal.) machine guns. While these were powerful, they did not have the impact of the 20-mm cannon fitted to the Hornet and Tigercat.

F7F-3N TIGERCAT	4 x 20-mm cannon
F-82G TWIN MUSTANG	6 x 12.7-mm (.50-cal.) machine guns
HORNET F.MK 3	4 x 20-mm cannon

NORTH AMERICAN
F-86 SABRE

● Jet vs jet combat ● US vs Soviet pilots ● Multiple kills

T ogether, the F-86 Sabre and MiG-15 brought swept wings and the sonic bang to modern warfare. Developed at the same time, both aircraft were just supersonic in a dive. In 1950 the Sabre was rushed to Korea to confront the MiG in a new kind of combat with closing speeds and performance never before experienced. High over the Yalu River, Sabres and MiGs tested each other in the biggest jet-versus-jet battles in history.

▲ Even in its initial form the F-86 was a match for the Soviet-flown MiG-15s. However, improved Sabres, such as the F-86E, soon dominated when the MiGs were flown by less experienced pilots.

▲ **Dixon's tail**
Lieutenant Colonel Dixon was about to fire at a MiG-15, when his F-86F was hit by anti-aircraft artillery fire.

▲ **MiG testing**
Senior Lieutenant Kum Suk No took his MiG-15 to the Americans when he landed at Kimpo airfield as a defector. The MiG was first tested at Kadena in Japan by Chuck Yeager and later at Wright-Patterson in the USA, where it survives at the USAF museum.

▲ **Victorious Sabre**
This rare photograph was taken by the gun camera of an F-86 which had just peppered the MiG with 12.7-mm (.50-cal) machine-gun fire. The pilot ejected seconds later, leaving the MiG-15 to its fiery fate.

▲ **Improved interceptor**
As the F-86A was entering combat in Korea, North American was putting the F-86E into production. This improved model was superior to the MiG-15.

US air power for the United Nations ▶
Large numbers of US aircraft were committed to the United Nations' effort in Korea. This photograph shows several combat-ready F-86 Sabres.

FACTS AND FIGURES

▶ Design of both the Sabre and the MiG-15 was made possible by German swept-wing research.

▶ The first Sabres arrived at Kimpo airfield, near Seoul, Korea, in December 1950.

▶ Captain Joseph P. McConnell, a top Sabre ace, scored 16 victories in Korea.

▶ Late-model Sabres had a redesigned wing, known as the 6-3 wing, which improved manoeuvrability in combat.

▶ One downed F-86 was test-flown by the Soviets near Moscow.

▶ Total production of all versions of the Sabre exceeded 9000 aircraft.

PROFILE

Swept wings over Korea

America's Sabre pilots were well trained, confident and ready to face the MiG-15. Many of the pilots had flown combat in World War II, just five years earlier, and in 1950 they introduced the first US swept-wing jet into battle.

Mikoyan-Gurevich had produced an aircraft more than worthy of the Sabre's challenge, however, and the MiG-15 was capable of flying higher than

the F-86 and was armed with cannon rather than the Sabre's six machine guns. Both fighters were fast and manoeuvrable. Ultimately, the result of each aerial battle was largely determined by the pilots.

Unknown to the Americans at the time, the first MiGs were flown by experienced Soviet pilots. It was only later, when Chinese and North Korean pilots took over, that the better training of the US pilots won through. As the Sabre gained the upper hand, the Americans claimed that 15 MiGs were shot down for every F-86 lost. After

the war research revealed that the correct figure was seven to one, but this was still a remarkable statistic in the history of air-to-air combat.

North American, in common with Mikoyan-Gurevich, relied on the work of German aeronautical engineers to produce the swept wings for its aircraft.

F-86E SABRE

Elenore 'E' was flown by Major William T. Whisner of the 25th Fighter Interceptor Squadron, 51st Fighter Interceptor Wing.

North American developed and built the ejection seat used in the F-86. Such escape systems were vital at the high speeds reached by the new jets.

All Sabres flying over Korea had followed the instructions of the Far East Air Force (FEAF) by the summer of 1952, with the adoption of yellow theatre markings.

Sabres always flew with drop-tanks. The extra fuel allowed a transit to North Korea and increased loiter time in the combat zone. The tanks were jettisoned as soon as MiGs were sighted.

Both the F-86A and E models were powered by the General Electric J47-GE-13 turbojet. The F-86F used the J47-GE-27, which improved time taken to reach 9144 m (30,000 ft) by almost one minute and added an extra 244 m (800 ft) to its maximum altitude.

F-86E Sabre

Type: single-seat fighter and fighter-bomber

Powerplant: one 23.13-kN (5204-lb-thrust) General Electric J47-GE-13 turbojet engine

Maximum speed: 1086 km/h (675 mph) at 762 m (2500 ft)

Initial climb rate: 2326 m/min (7631 fpm)

Range: 1263 km (785 miles)

Service ceiling: 14,722 m (48,300 ft)

Weights: empty 4760 kg (10,494 lb); maximum take-off 4987 kg (10,994 lb)

Armament: six 12.7-mm (.50-cal.) machine guns with 267 rounds per gun; provision for two 454-kg (1000-lb) bombs or 16 127-mm (5-in) rocket projectiles

Dimensions:
span	11.31 m (37 ft 1 in)	
length	11.43 m (37 ft 6 in)	
height	4.47 m (15 ft 5 in)	
wing area	26.76 m² (288 sq ft)	

COMBAT DATA

ARMAMENT

With its cannon armament the MiG-15 had much greater firepower than the Sabre. Improvements in power and controllability, together with superior training, allowed the US pilots to overcome this, but immediately after the war a cannon-armed F-86 was developed.

F-86A SABRE — 6 x 12.7-mm (.50-cal.) machine guns

F-86H SABRE — 4 x 20-mm cannon

MiG-15 'FAGOT' — 1 x 37-mm cannon / 2 x 23-mm cannon

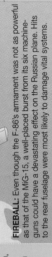

COMBAT ZONE: Only Sabres were allowed into the area known as 'MiG Alley'; other United Nations aircraft, even the jets, were considered to be too vulnerable. In response to this decision, the Soviets moved more MiGs into North Korea, making 'MiG Alley' a hotbed of air combat.

'MiG Alley' · PYONGYANG · KIMPO · SUWON · 38th Parallel

Low-level manoeuvrability was improved on the F-86A and E, with the use of leading-edge slats. These were a disadvantage at altitude, however, and they were deleted on the F-86F.

On the F-86E, the tailplane of the F-86A was replaced by an all-moving surface, which included larger, power-boosted elevators. The entire control system was given improved 'feel'.

Guided missile development was some way behind the technology of the jet aircraft and both the F-86 and MiG-15s were gun-armed in Korea.

FIREBALL: Even though the F-86's armament was not as powerful as that of the MiG-15, a well-placed burst from its six machine-guns could have a devastating effect on the Russian plane. Hits to the rear fuselage were most likely to damage vital systems.

TARGET MiG: With its good manoeuvrability, altitude advantage and heavy weaponry, the MiG-15 in Russian hands was a difficult opponent. The advantage was never clear-cut between the MiG and Sabre.

MiG IN SIGHT: This MiG is in a desperate situation, with the 'pipper' of an F-86's gunsight closing in on its tail. A simple radar allowed gun-ranging.

A pair of Sabres takes off in search of MiGs. Many missions involved flying top cover for US fighter-bombers.

MiG-killing over Korea

LAUNCH: United Nation bases were scattered around the coast of Korea, but the base closest to the action was Kimpo, just south of the 38th Parallel.

USAF

U.S. AIR FORCE 127.35

FU-735

NORTH AMERICAN

F-86D/H/K SABRE DOG

● All-weather operations ● Interceptor ● Ground attack

To defend North America, the USAF worked frantically in the 1950s to develop fighter-interceptors which were able to fly and fight in any weather. As an interim measure, experts took the F-86 Sabre design from the Korean War and added radar and air-to-air rockets. This produced the F-86D Sabre Dog – an all-weather interceptor with a one-man crew. The Sabre Dog was developed into the F-86K/L by the addition of cannon armament.

▲ Distinguished by its nose-mounted radome, the F-86D/H/K series turned the basic F-86 into a specialised and highly competent all-weather interceptor and attack aircraft.

NORTH AMERICAN F-86D/H/K SABRE DOG

PHOTO FILE

German Sabre Dog ▶
The F-86K, which was supplied to European air forces, was produced by replacing the rockets of the F-86D with four 20-mm cannon.

NATO fighter ▶
Analogous to the F-16 programme, the F-86K became the standard fighter of several NATO air arms in Europe. It was paid for by the USAF.

▲ Defending Southeast Asia
A number of F-86Ds were delivered to the air force of the then newly-established Philippine republic, bolstering regional air defence.

European Sidewinders ▶
As new systems became available these were combined with the already advanced, complex avionics of the F-86D and K. New weapons included the AIM-9 Sidewinder, seen here on an F-86K, which was later licence-built in Europe.

▲ Rocket pack
A retractable rocket-launching pack was fitted to the belly of the F-86D for air-to-air work.

FACTS AND FIGURES

▼ Production of Sabre Dog interceptors totalled 2,626, including 120 export versions armed with cannon.

▼ An additional 121 aircraft were built for NATO use by Fiat in Italy.

▼ The Sabre Dog prototype first flew on 22 December 1949.

▼ In July 1952 mechanical faults were resolved in a modification programme called Project Pull Out.

▼ The F-86D's main flaw was a tendency for a sudden violent pitch downwards.

▼ A few Sabre Dogs were exported to Japan, South Korea and Thailand.

Developing the Sabre

The Sabre Dog interceptor version of the immortal North American F-86 Sabre was equipped with a distinctive nose radar unit and was flown by a pilot who was also tasked with the duties usually performed by a radar operator.

When approaching bombers were spotted on radar, an F-86D pilot was expected to rush to his aircraft and to get aloft within three minutes. He then followed instructions from a ground-control operator, who directed him to the bomber. In the later

F-86L version, this process of scrambling and engaging enemy bombers was largely automated. Once within a short distance of the bombers, the pilot was expected to 'paint' them on his own radar and to attack them at a 90° angle with rocket projectiles.

The export version of this interceptor was a much-simplified warplane and was armed with cannon, but it had

the same task of tracking down and destroying enemy bombers.

In service, the Sabre Dog was initially plagued by technical problems, mainly with its radar, but it evolved into a mature combat aircraft.

Above: Seen high over Mount Fuji, Japan, this F-86D typifies the Sabre Dogs belonging to the USAF.

Above: Some countries, including Greece, received second-hand USAF F-86Ds. This one is fitted with Sidewinder launch rails.

No guns were fitted to the F-86D, but 24 70-mm 'Mighty Mouse' rockets, each with a 3.4-kg (7.5-lb) warhead, could be fired from this retractable rocket pack.

F-86D Sabre Dog

Type: single-seat all-weather interceptor

Powerplant: one 33.4-kN (7515-lb-thrust) General Electric J47-GE-17B or J47-GE-33 turbojet with afterburning

Maximum speed: 1138 km/h (706 mph) at sea level

Range: 1344 km (835 miles)

Service ceiling: 16,640 m (54,600 ft)

Weights: empty 5656 kg (12,443 lb); maximum take-off 7756 kg (17,063 lb)

Armament: 24 70-mm 'Mighty Mouse' folding fin aircraft rockets (FFAR) or (F-86K only) four 20-mm cannon

Dimensions: span   11.30 m (37 ft 1 in)
length   12.29 m (40 ft 4 in)
height   4.57 m (15 ft)
wing area 27.76 m² (299 sq ft)

COMBAT DATA

RANGE

A comparison of contemporary American all-weather interceptors reveals their complementary nature. The F-94C Starfire covers the middle ground between the large, heavily-armed F-89D, providing long-range defence, and the shorter ranged, but much higher performing, F-86D.

F-89D SCORPION
4184 km
(2595 miles)

F-86D SABRE DOG
1344 km (835 miles)

F-94C STARFIRE
1930 km (1200 miles)

SERVICE CEILING

All three aircraft provided air defence of the US, and any aircraft making an attack would have done so from high altitude. Armed only with rockets, an interceptor would be forced to get very close to the target so altitude performance was of great importance.

F-89D SCORPION
14,995 m
(49,200 ft)

F-94C STARFIRE
15,665 m
(51,400 ft)

F-86D SABRE DOG
16,640 m
(54,600 ft)

ARMAMENT

The primary armament was the unguided rocket, fired either from retractable launchers, batteries in the aircraft nose or wing pods. As the first guided air-to-air missiles, such as the AIM-9 and Hughes Falcon, became available, these were also employed.

F-86D SABRE DOG   24 x 70-mm rockets

F-94C STARFIRE   48 x 70-mm rockets

F-89D SCORPION   104 x 70-mm rockets

F-86D SABRE DOG

This aircraft wears the colourful markings typical of its era and belongs to the 94th Fighter Interceptor Squadron of the 1st Fighter Group. The squadron flew F-86Ds from 1953 to 1956.

Once the AN/APG-37 radar detected a target within its 48-km (30-mile) range, the AN/APA-84 computer calculated an interception course.

D model Sabres retained the standard slatted Sabre wing, but the fuselage was redesigned and was both longer and wider to accommodate the new engine and avionics.

Drop-tanks of 454-litre (120-gallon) capacity were a near-permanent fixture of the F-86D. Fuel was also carried in internal tanks below the intake trunking and in the inboard wing sections between the spars.

A single strut braced the drop-tank outboard of the pylon in an installation similar to that on the MiG-15.

A retractable airbrake was positioned on either side of the rear fuselage. When closing head-on with a target, the pilot must be certain of the aircraft's ability to slow down quickly.

All Sabres had this distinctive fuel dump pipe, which allowed fuel to be jettisoned in an emergency. The pipe on the F-86D was longer, however, to keep fuel away from the afterburner section.

A very basic afterburner was fitted to the J47-GE-17 turbojet. In early aircraft this provided 23.14 kN (5200 lb thrust), but later variants produced up to 34.04 kN (7600 lb thrust).

Rocket-armed interceptors

■ **DE HAVILLAND SEA VIXEN:** Retractable launching batteries were built into the forward fuselage of the Sea Vixen, but were rarely used.

■ **ENGLISH ELECTRIC (BAC) LIGHTNING:** Provision was made for two retractable launchers, which were sealed shut when in service.

■ **LOCKHEED F-94C STARFIRE:** Each wingtip pod held 12 rockets and a further 24 were carried in a ring of launchers around the nose.

■ **NORTHROP F-89D SCORPION:** Permanently attached wingtip pods held the Scorpion's powerful 104-rocket armament.

NORTH AMERICAN

FJ FURY

- 1950s carrier-borne jet fighter ● F-86 design derivative

Beginning life as the straight-winged FJ-1, the North American Fury became the first jet fighter to go to sea under operational conditions. After the US Navy belatedly followed the USAF in using German research data to produce swept-wing fighters, the FJ Fury was reborn as a carrier-based equivalent of the F-86 Sabre. The swept-wing Fury was one of the Navy's first fighters to carry missiles and served widely in the 1950s.

▲ Although there were initial concerns about the suitability of swept-wing designs for carrier operations, the performance of the USAF's F-86 Sabre persuaded the US Navy to adopt the FJ-2.

350

NORTH AMERICAN **FJ FURY**

▲ 'Navalised' Sabre
The first swept-wing variant, the FJ-2, was effectively a navalised F-86F Sabre with folding wings and 20-mm cannon armament.

▲ Rocket motor boost
To test a rocket installation, two FJ-4s were fitted with an AR-1 motor and nose instrumentation.

▲ Air-to-air refuelling FJ-4s
Like the FJ-3, the FJ-4B had an in-flight refuelling receptacle on the port wing and could carry 'buddy' refuelling gear.

▲ VMF-232 'Red Devils'
Marine Fighter Squadron 232's FJ-2s set a Navy-Marine flight record, flying 2558 hours in one month. Twenty-one aircraft and 52 pilots participated. The FJ-2 shared its 'slatted wing' with the F-86F Sabre.

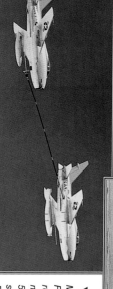

▲ FJ-4B attack-fighter
This final Fury variant had six underwing pylons, for stores like Bullpup air-to-surface missiles.

FACTS AND FIGURES

➤ After its first flight on 27 November 1946, the FJ-1 became the US Navy's first operational carrier jet.

➤ FJ-3Ms and FJ-4s were able to carry AAM-N-7 Sidewinder air-to-air missiles.

➤ Starting in January 1954, all 200 FJ-2s were delivered to Marine Corps fighter units.

➤ The final Fury variant, the FJ-4B, was equipped with the LABS low-altitude nuclear weapon delivery system.

➤ Furies remained in Naval Reserve service into the 1960s.

➤ In all, North American's Columbus, Ohio, plant delivered 1115 swept-wing Furies.

PROFILE

First operational jet carrier fighters

From the fat, straight-winged, dark blue FJ-1 to the sleek, swept-winged, grey and white FJ-4, the North American FJ Fury fighters of the US Navy and Marine Corps marked a decade of progress that began at the start of the jet age and continued to the brink of the supersonic era. Although the Fury never went to war, from the late 1940s to the Beirut crisis of 1958, the aircraft was armed and ready to fight if the need arose.

Thirty straight-winged FJ-1 Fury fighters were briefly the newest and fastest machines in

the sky when they went aboard the carrier USS *Boxer* in 1948. Quickly overtaken by other jets (the Navy focusing on the straight-wing F9F Panther which became its standard fighter in the Korean War), the FJ-1 Fury was relegated to Reserve duty and then retired, in less than two years.

North American, meanwhile, had developed a faster, swept-wing aircraft, based on the FJ-1 and called the F-86 Sabre, for the USAF. The swept-wing FJ-2, FJ-3 and FJ-4 Fury fighters resulted from an effort to produce a

navalised F-86. While the first FJ-2 was little more than a Sabre in blue paint, the FJ-3 and much improved FJ-4 missile-armed attack fighter introduced new engines and major airframe and equipment changes.

Above: The first Fury, XFJ-1 39053, took to the air on 27 November 1946. The 30 FJ-1s were destined to be 'fighter familiarization' aircraft, rather than combat types.

Above: FJ-3s of VF-21 Squadron fly over the USS Forrestal. The last FJ-3s were delivered in 1956, a year after this new carrier was commissioned.

FJ-1 FURY

Carrying the markings of the only unit equipped with the FJ-1, Fighter Squadron VF-5A (later VF-51), this aircraft is one of 30 FJ-1s delivered. They were transferred to the Reserve after just 14 months of service.

Fitted with six 12.7-mm (.50-cal.) machine guns in the nose, the FJ-1 was the last US Navy aircraft to have 'half-inch' guns.

Like the McDonnell FH-1 Phantom which followed it, the FJ-1 was able to 'kneel' on the carrier deck by retracting its nose gear and resting on a tiny wheel. This facilitated stowage without wing folding.

To increase its somewhat limited range, the FJ-1 was soon fitted with 625-litre (165-gallon) wingtip fuel tanks. Airbrakes were a feature of all FJ variants, especially the FJ-4B attack version.

Designed around the General Electric J35 axial-flow turbojet, the production Fury used an Allison-built variant of this engine, producing 17.8 kN (4000 lb thrust). This was fed by an intake in the aircraft's nose.

FJ-4 Fury

Type: single-seat carrier-based fighter

Powerplant: one 34.25-kN (7700-lb-thrust) Wright J65-W-16A turbojet engine

Maximum speed: 1094 km/h (678 mph) at sea level

Endurance: 859 km/h (534 mph)

Initial climb rate: 2334 m/min (7655 fpm)

Range: 3250 km (2015 miles)

Combat ceiling: 14,265 m (46,800 ft)

Weights: empty 5991 kg (13,180 lb); loaded 10,750 kg (23,650 lb)

Armament: four 20-mm cannon, plus up to 1360 kg (3000 lb) of weapons (including bombs, rockets or four AAM-N-7 Sidewinder air-to-air missiles) on four wing pylons

Dimensions:
span	11.91 m	(39 ft 1 in)
length	11.07 m	(36 ft 4 in)
height	4.24 m	(13 ft 11 in)
wing area	31.49 m²	(339 sq ft)

ACTION DATA

THRUST

Although the afterburner had been introduced, naval jet fighter design in the 1950s was hampered by the lack of powerful engines. Supermarine overcame this by installing twin engines in the Scimitar.

FJ-4 FURY	34.25 kN (7700 lb thrust)
SCIMITAR F.Mk 1	100.0 kN (22,500 lb thrust)
F3H-2 DEMON	43.1 kN (9700 lb thrust)

MAXIMUM SPEED

Even though it had twin engines, the Scimitar was a heavy aircraft which limited its top speed. The McDonnell F3H Demon was a bigger machine than the Fury, but early examples were underpowered.

FJ-4 FURY	1094 km/h (678 mph)
SCIMITAR F.Mk 1	1143 km/h (709 mph)
F3H-2 DEMON	1041 km/h (645 mph)

CLIMB RATE

Advances in wing and engine design and improved power-to-weight ratios were reflected in better climb rates of aircraft like the Scimitar and the Demon.

F3H-2 DEMON	3900 m/min (12,800 fpm)
SCIMITAR F.Mk 1	3658 m/min (12,000 fpm)
FJ-4 FURY	2334 m/min (7655 fpm)

US Navy aircraft from North American

■ **SNJ TEXAN:** Like the USAAF and Allied air forces, the US Navy took delivery of hundreds of Texans for pilot training from the late 1930s.

■ **AJ SAVAGE:** Ordered as a carrier-borne nuclear strike aircraft in 1946, the AJ had two piston engines and a small turbojet in the tail.

■ **T2J BUCKEYE:** The T2J entered service as the US Navy's all-purpose trainer, in single- and twin-engined forms, from 1959.

■ **A3J VIGILANTE:** Known as the A-5 from 1962, the A3J entered service as an all-weather attack aircraft in 1961 aboard USS *Enterprise*.

NORTH AMERICAN

T-28 TROJAN

- Basic trainer ● Counter-insurgency aircraft ● International service

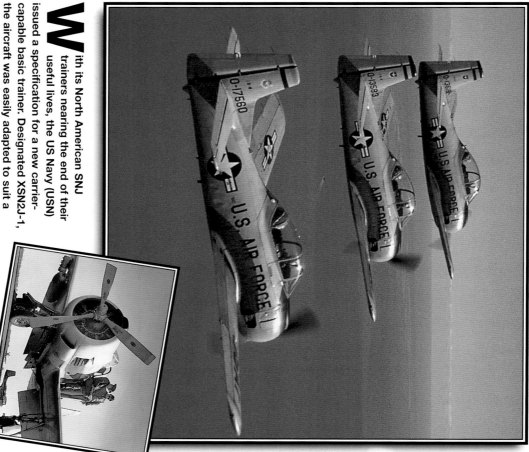

W ith its North American SNJ trainers nearing the end of their useful lives, the US Navy (USN) issued a specification for a new carrier-capable basic trainer. Designated XSN2J-1, the aircraft was easily adapted to suit a similar US Air Force (USAF) requirement as the XBT-28 and went on to train many thousands of US pilots. However, it was with combat missions over Vietnam that the aircraft gained lasting fame.

▲ For a generation of US airmen, the T-28 was the aircraft in which they earned their wings. In Vietnam the aircraft proved useful in the counter-insurgency role against the Viet Cong.

Navy birds▶
Possibly the most colourful of all T-28s were those operated in high visibility markings by the US Navy. These flew for more than 20 years, before finally being retired in 1984.

▼ Turbo Trojan
In an attempt to cure some of the T-28's shortcomings, three YAT-28Es were built with turboprop engines. Although the trials were fairly successful, this variant did not enter production.

▲ Regeneration
Surplus T-28As, fitted with engines and equipment from later versions were sold on the civilian market.

◀ Counter-insurgency
The T-28D fighter-bomber was developed primarily for use by small air arms against guerrilla forces.

Blind-flying hood ▶
For instrument flying or night flying training, a blind-flying hood was fitted over the student's position.

FACTS AND FIGURES

- ▶ T-28s played a prominent part in 'Air Commando' operations over Vietnam, before being replaced by A-1 Skyraiders.

- ▶ All three of the US armed services operated North American's big trainer.

- ▶ French versions, known as Fennecs, were used in Algeria against terrorists.

- ▶ Fairchild Aircraft Services was tasked with the conversion of early examples into T-28D light-attack aircraft.

- ▶ T-28s are popular display aircraft on the international 'Warbird' circuit.

- ▶ One T-28 was fitted with a strengthened canopy for poor weather trials.

Trojan goes to war

Having flown for the first time on 26 September 1949, the XT-28 evolved into the T-28 Trojan with a minimum number of changes. Capable of flying in the basic and weapons training roles, some 1,194 Trojans were eventually ordered.

In service, the T-28 proved something of a disappointment, with the USAF eventually introducing a 30-hour pre-T-28 course on the T-34 Mentor, in an effort to overcome the shortcomings of the Trojan. Having

been the original instigator of the design, the USN received navalised T-28B and C models. The USN was more satisfied with its T-28s than the USAF, largely because of their increased power.

With the experience of the Navy in mind, the USAF decided to fit more powerful engines into its T-28As, which were thus modified to T-28D standard during the 1960s. The new version was a dedicated Counter-Insurgency (COIN) aircraft and saw extensive service in Vietnam. Several

examples were also exported. A French requirement for a COIN machine to operate in Algeria led to an in-country modification scheme which produced the T-28S Fennec.

Above: Some 148 T-28As were converted to T-28S Fennec standard by France's Sud Aviation.

Below: As well as a smaller nosewheel and arrester hook, the T-28B differed from the T-28A by the installation of an under-fuselage speed brake. A number of T-28Bs were converted to T-28BD drone-controller aircraft.

T-28D Trojan

Type: two-seat counter-insurgency aircraft

Powerplant: one 1063-kW (1425-hp) Wright R-1820-86 Cyclone 14-cylinder radial piston engine

Maximum speed: 552 km/h (342 mph) 'clean' at 3050 m (10,000 ft)

Maximum climb rate: 1079 m/min (3540 fpm) at sea level

Ferry range: 1706 km (1060 miles)

Service ceiling: 10,820 m (35,500 ft)

Weights: empty equipped 2914 kg (6410 lb); loaded 3856 kg (8483 lb)

Armament: up to 1814 kg (4000 lb) of bombs, gun-pods, rockets and napalm tanks on six underwing hardpoints

Dimensions:
span	12.22 m (40 ft 1 in)
length	10.06 m (33 ft)
height	3.86 m (12 ft 8 in)
wing area	24.90 m² (268 sq ft)

COMBAT DATA

MAXIMUM SPEED

North American successfully replaced its own T-6 Texan in USAF service with the T-28A. The new machine was much faster than the late 1930s vintage T-6, and was a better platform from which to progress on to the new generation of jet warplanes.

T-28A TROJAN	552 km/h (342 mph)
T-6 TEXAN	330 km/h (205 mph)
T-34A MENTOR	455 km/h (282 mph)

(speeds shown: T-28A TROJAN — 552 km/h (342 mph); T-6 TEXAN — 330 km/h (205 mph); T-34A MENTOR — 455 km/h (282 mph))

RANGE

With its usefully long range, the T-28A was an excellent airframe for conversion to the light-attack role. External tanks were never fitted to the T-28A, but the T-28D could carry two tanks, giving an extended loiter in the combat zone.

- **T-6 TEXAN** 1207 km (750 miles)
- **T-34A MENTOR** 1186 km (735 miles)
- **T-28A TROJAN** 1609 km (1000 miles)

RATE OF CLIMB

With its powerful Cyclone engine, the T-28A could easily out-climb the T-6 and the T-34A which was purchased to supplement the T-28A in service. The performance of the T-28A allowed for an easy transition to the T-33 advanced jet trainer.

- **T-28A TROJAN** 570 m/min (3500 fpm)
- **T-6 TEXAN** 411 m/min (1350 fpm)
- **T-34A MENTOR** 375 m/min (1230 fpm)

T-28A TROJAN

The Chinese Nationalist air force received a number of T-28As. The aircraft were subject to a local modification programme in which they were re-engined with 1080-kW (1450-hp) Lycoming T53 turboprops.

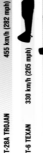

A large, powerful radial engine gave the T-28 the distinctive 'drooped' cowling profile shown here. US experiments with turboprop power came to nothing, despite the success later enjoyed by Taiwan's Aero Industry Development Centre (AIDC)-modified aircraft.

North American abandoned the traditional tail-wheel undercarriage arrangement of basic trainers when it made the T-28 the first tricycle-undercarriaged US trainer.

For the basic training role the T-28A was equipped with tandem seats with full dual controls and blind-flying equipment. T-28Ds featured armoured seat-backs and headrests, while many AT-28Ds (T-28Ds converted by Fairchild) were fitted with ejection seats.

Fatigue problems caused the premature withdrawal of T-28Ds from Vietnam. These were detected after the constant stresses of combat operations caused two aircraft to shed wings.

North American service aircraft of the 1950s

■ **AJ-1 SAVAGE:** Designed as a mixed-powerplant, carrier-based nuclear bomber, the AJ-1 served throughout the early 1950s.

■ **B-45 TORNADO:** Though designed as a bomber, the B-45 was to see more use as a reconnaissance platform in its RB-45C version.

■ **F-86 SABRE:** America's first swept-wing jet fighter was hugely successful in the skies over Korea, where it downed many MiG-15s.

■ **FJ-2 FURY:** As a successor to its straight-winged FJ-1, the US Navy adopted this navalised version of the Sabre.

354

NORTH AMERICAN

B-45 TORNADO

● Early jet bomber ● Reconnaissance aircraft ● Secret missions

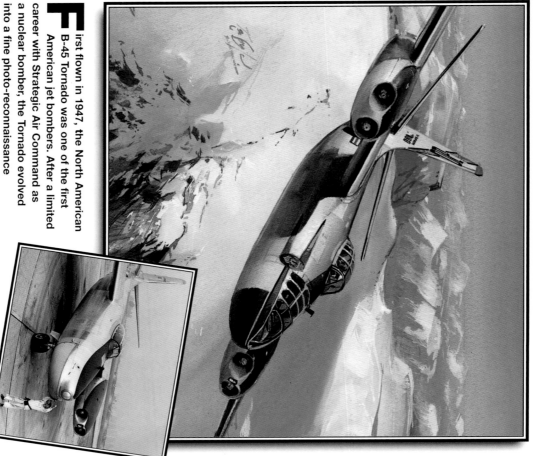

▲ Although it represented little new in terms of technology, the Tornado provided an important stop-gap bomber for the USAF and a useful photographic reconnaissance platform.

First flown in 1947, the North American B-45 Tornado was one of the first American jet bombers. After a limited career with Strategic Air Command as a nuclear bomber, the Tornado evolved into a fine photo-reconnaissance aircraft, known as the RB-45C. In the reconnaissance role the Tornado carried out some of the most secret spy missions of the Cold War, and a handful of the aircraft fought in Korea.

NORTH AMERICAN B-45 TORNADO

▲ Tornado features
North American fitted two jet engines beneath each wing. Otherwise, the only innovative features in the airframe were the canopy design and a refuelling receptacle above the fuselage.

▲ RB-45C tip-tanks
Additional fuel was carried by the B-45C by way of two wingtip tanks, each of 4542-litre (1200-gallon) capacity. These tanks were retained on the RB-45C.

▲ In-flight refuelling
RB-45Cs, especially those flying long-range spy missions from the UK, were supported by Boeing KB-29P tankers.

New-build B-45C ▼
Most B-45Cs were converted from B-45As, although 10, of which this is the second, were built new. This machine appears to be flying test duties.

▲ Conventional bomber
Although its main mission was tactical nuclear strike, the B-45A could also deliver conventional bombs. The frameless canopy was a distinctive feature of the B-45A.

FACTS AND FIGURES

➤ The reconnaissance RB-45C Tornado carried 25 M122 photo-flash bombs in its internal bay.

➤ A small number of Tornados were used as TB-45As for target towing.

➤ The first B-45 took to the air at Muroc Dry Lake, California, on 17 March 1947.

➤ RB-45Cs were secretly flown by RAF pilots on intelligence missions over the Soviet Union.

➤ An RB-45C was shot down by a MiG-15 over Korea on 4 December 1950.

➤ A 9979-kg (22,000lb) bombload could be carried by the improved B-45C.

PROFILE

Cold War 'ferreting' bomber

America's first four-jet bomber to reach the flight-test stage, the North American B-45 Tornado was the result of early scientific advances in jet design which dated back to 1944. Combining the then-new turbojet propulsion system with existing heavy bomber practice and techniques, the B-45 was very much an outdated, propeller-era airframe with up-to-the-minute jet engines.

Originally designed for a crew of four (two pilots, bombardier and tail gunner), the B-45 served briefly with the Strategic Air Command at Barksdale Air Force Base, Louisiana, from 1948 to 1952, and in Britain for a short time after this.

However, this was a period of rapid change and the B-45 lacked the capacity to carry the huge Mk III nuclear bombs. The Tornado was also too slow to survive against Soviet fighters and anti-aircraft defences, so its role as a bomber was cut short.

As the RB-45C reconnaissance aircraft, the Tornado (minus its tail gun) had improved performance and was in service longer. These machines tested the limits in 'ferret' missions along – and sometimes across – Soviet borders and a number were engaged by Soviet fighters. A small contingent of RB-45Cs was deployed to Japan for combat in Korea.

Above: The frameless, fighter-style canopy of the early aircraft can clearly be seen on this B-45A. Tip-tanks were not fitted to the B-45A, but all bombers had nose glazing.

Above: A heavily framed canopy was introduced on the B-45C. Unusually, this Tornado is not fitted with the wing tip-tanks and is flying as an engine testbed.

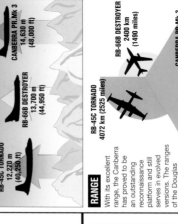

B-45C TORNADO

In 1952 the US based B-45C tactical nuclear bombers at RAF Sculthorpe, Norfolk. The 47th Bomb Group was established with three squadrons, including the 86th, one of whose aircraft is shown here.

All the bomber variants featured this glazed nose area which accommodated the bomb-aimer. A solid nose was introduced in reconnaissance aircraft.

To prevent turbulence around the falling bombs, the bomb doors partially retracted into the fuselage.

Visibility through the raised canopy was excellent. Two pilots flew the Tornado, seated in tandem in a pressurized cockpit.

Up to 9979 kg (21,950 lb) of conventional or nuclear bombs could be carried in the bomb-bay. Additional fuel tanks and photo-flash bombs were carried by the RB-45C.

During conversion to B-45C standard the 17.8-kN (4000-lb-thrust) General Electric J47 turbojets of the B-45A were replaced by 23.1-kN (5200-lb-thrust) J47-GE-13/15 engines. With water injection these engines gave 26.7 kN (6000 lb thrust). The water was contained in jettisonable tanks beneath the engine nacelles.

Twin 7.62-mm (.30-cal.) Browning M7 machine guns were fitted for rear defence.

A tail gunner was accommodated in the pressurised tail turret. The bulbous radome covered a ranging radar for gun aiming.

Pronounced dihedral was a feature of the tailplanes. They were angled upwards to avoid blast damage the structure and made the tailplanes less aerodynamically efficient. The hot gases could from the jet exhausts.

USAF 'snooper' aircraft

■ **DOUGLAS RB-66B DESTROYER:** This specialised reconnaissance development of the B-66B bomber flew dangerous missions over Vietnam, probing into neighbouring countries.

■ **LOCKHEED SR-71A 'BLACKBIRD':** Reports suggest that while probing Soviet air space, SR-71As out-accelerated MiG-25 'Foxbats' that were sent to intercept them.

■ **LOCKHEED U-2:** Several variants of the U-2 have been used in some of the world's most infamous spy flights. At least two aircraft were shot down during the Cold War.

■ **MARTIN (GENERAL DYNAMICS) RB-57F:** General Dynamics added new wings, tail, engines and sensors to the B-57 Canberra to produce the high-altitude reconnaissance aircraft.

B-45C Tornado

Type: four-engined medium-range tactical nuclear bomber

Powerplant: four 26.7-kN (6000-lb-thrust) (with water injection for take-off or emergency power) General Electric J47-GE-13/5 turbojet engines

Maximum speed: 917 km/h (570 mph)

Range: 4072 km (2525 miles)

Service ceiling: 12,270 m (40,250 ft)

Weights: empty 22,672 kg (90,125 lb); maximum take-off 50,222 kg (110,488 lb)

Armament: two 12.7-mm (.50-cal.) Browning M7 machine guns with 400 rounds in tail gunner's position and up to 9979 kg (21,950 lb) of nuclear or conventional bombs

Dimensions:
span	29.26 m (96 ft)
length	23.14 m (76 ft)
height	7.67 m (25 ft)
wing area	109.16 m² (1200 sq ft)

COMBAT DATA

MAXIMUM SPEED

These three types represent typical early jet reconnaissance assets. The RB-66C, with its swept wings, is the fastest, while the English Electric Canberra PR.Mk 3 and the RB-45C are closely matched. The Tornado was rapidly overtaken by more modern technology.

RB-45C TORNADO	917 km/h
RB-66B DESTROYER	1125 km/h (700 mph)
CANBERRA PR. 3	871 km/h (540 mph)

(570 mph)

SERVICE CEILING

During early jet missions, before the advent of effective surface-to-air missile systems, flying at high altitude offered some degree of immunity from interception by enemy fighters. Using high-altitude cameras these aircraft could photograph large areas from great heights.

RB-45C TORNADO 12,270 m (40,250 ft)
RB-66B DESTROYER 13,700 m (44,950 ft)
CANBERRA PR.Mk 3 14,630 m (48,000 ft)

RANGE

With its excellent range, the Canberra has proved to be an outstanding reconnaissance platform and still serves in evolved versions. The ranges of the Douglas RB-66C and the RB-45C were more limited, but both types benefited from the ability to refuel in flight.

RB-66B DESTROYER 2400 km (1490 miles)
CANBERRA PR.Mk 3 7080 km (4390 miles)
RB-45C TORNADO 4072 km (2525 miles)

NORTH AMERICAN

F-100 SUPER SABRE

- ● USAF's first supersonic jet ● Zero-length launches ● War service

▲ *In its heyday, the F-100 equipped 16 full USAF wings, assuming a fighter-bomber role as faster interceptor types became available. It was the USAF's first fighter to reach Mach 1 in level flight.*

Sabre 45 was the name given to North American's private efforts to produce a supersonic development of its highly successful F-86 Sabre. The name referred to the wing's 45° of sweep. This programme proved not to be as easy as envisaged, but after early problems the final product was to prove its worth, especially in Vietnam. Though it always had an accident rate higher than other types, the Super Sabre had plenty of fans among aviators.

NORTH AMERICAN F-100 SUPER SABRE

▲ **Zero-length launches**
The final F-100Ds were able to be 'zero-length launched' from atom bomb-proof shelters using a 667-kN (150,075 lb thrust) rocket booster.

▼ **Two-seat combat trainer**
An F-100C was modified as a two-seat TF-100C, the prototype for the F-100F; 339 were built.

▼ **'Thunderbirds'**
The first F-100C fighter-bomber flew in September 1955. In all, 476 were built, some equipping the USAF's display team.

▲ **Short-tail F-100A**
The first 70 production F-100As had shorter fins, which caused roll control problems.

▲ **Armée de l'Air 'Hun'**
Super Sabres were exported to France, Taiwan, Denmark and Turkey, the last named being the final operator until the late 1980s. Ex-USAF examples are used as QF-100 target drones.

FACTS AND FIGURES

▶ Test pilot George Welch likened the effect of the first YF-100's afterburner to 'a kick from a well-fed mule'.

▶ More than 200 surplus F-100s were converted into QF-100 target drones.

▶ Between mid 1956 and mid 1970, more than 500 F-100Ds were lost in accidents.

▶ On 20 August 1955 a USAF colonel in an F-100C set the first world speed record over Mach 1 – 1323.03 km/h (820.27 mph).

▶ The first F-100 model flown overseas was the F-100C, using in-flight refuelling.

▶ USAF F-100s were deployed overseas to Germany and Japan in 1956.

PROFILE

First of the 'Century' fighters

Considering it suffered from so many inherent problems, including landing characteristics described by a pilot with 2000 hours on the type as 'a controlled crash', the F-100 is remembered with respect and some affection by a generation of aviators.

Its good features were v: iceless handling, a robust airframe and reliable systems. The Super Sabre was the latest product from the North American team that produced P-51 Mustangs and F-86 Sabres.

Attempts to build a supersonic Sabre had been killed by the limitations of its wing and engine. The latter problem was solved by Pratt & Whitney's JT3 (J57) turbojet, so, with USAF agreement, an new aircraft was designed.

After the 24 April 1953 first flight, the Super Sabre went into production for the USAF as the F-100A day-fighter. However, a fatal crash caused by handling problems brought groundings and delays. A taller tail fin and longer wings were the solution.

A key feature of the F-100D was the redesigned wing. This had a kinked trailing edge incorporated broad, slotted landing flaps. These were much needed and appreciated by pilots used to the high-speed landing run of the F-100C. Extra internal tankage was provided. D-models were built at North American's Inglewood, California and Columbus, Ohio factories.

F-100D SUPER SABRE

In the markings of the 481st TFS, this 'Hun' (as it was nicknamed – short for 'Hundred') was the personal aircraft of World War II P-47 ace Lieutenant Colonel Hal Comstock. It carries the skull insignia that adorned his P-47, and seven German kill markings.

This aircraft represents an F-100 in the early years of USAF involvement in the Vietnam War. Camouflage was later applied to all tactical aircraft in Southeast Asia. Note the bomb mission symbols painted on the nose.

For ground-strafing and self-protection, four M39 20-mm cannon were fitted in the nose of the F-100D. Two AIM-9 Sidewinder air-to-air missiles were also fitted on occasions. Air-to-ground ordnance totalling over three tonnes could be carried, including napalm, bombs, rockets and Bullpup missiles.

U.S. AIR FORCE
FW-604
481TFS
53604

The most obvious identification feature of the D-model was its taller vertical tail, introduced to improve handling. This incorporated a deeper fairing for the fuel dump pipe (later used to mount the radar warning receiver antenna).

An afterburning version of Pratt & Whitney's J57 turbojet was fitted to the 'Hun'. This engine had already been flown in such types as the B-52 bomber and the Navy's A-3 Skywarrior and F-8 Crusader, the latter also using an afterburning variant.

External fuel tanks, like the 1268-litre (300-gallon) examples fitted to this aircraft, were necessary to give the Super Sabre an acceptable range figure. An in-flight refuelling probe could also be fitted under the right wing.

Above: Demonstrating the afterburner fitted to its Pratt & Whitney J57 engine, this F-100 starts its take-off run. Poor fuel economy resulted in the aircraft carrying underwing fuel tanks.

Above: Bullpup air-to-surface missiles could be fired from a number of modified F-100Ds. Some D-model 'Huns' were also wired to carry Sidewinder air-to-air missiles.

From 1954, the F-100C fighter-bomber was built, and it was this and the much-improved D-model that were built in the biggest numbers – 1750 in all.

Sabre/Super Sabre family

■ **FJ FURY:** NA's first jet fighter was the US Navy's straight-winged Fury, which served as the basis for a swept-wing version and the F-86.

■ **F-86 SABRE:** The USAF's first swept-wing jet fighter, the Sabre was to see extensive service in the Korean War and served until 1965.

■ **YF-93:** Initially designated F-86C, the F-93 had an afterburning engine, but was hampered by the limitations of the Sabre wing design.

■ **YF-107A:** An all-weather interceptor/fighter-bomber F-100 development, initially known as the F-100B, the F-107 lost out to the F-105.

F-100D Super Sabre

Type: single-seat fighter-bomber

Powerplant: one 75.4-kN (17,000-lb-thrust) Pratt & Whitney J57-P-21A afterburning turbojet

Maximum speed: 1436 km/h (890 mph) at altitude

Initial climb rate: 5045 m/min (16,548 fpm) (clean)

Range: 2494 km (1546 miles) with two drop tanks

Service ceiling: 14,020 m (45,986 ft)

Weights: empty 9526 kg (20,957 lb); maximum take-off 15,800 kg (34,760 lb)

Armament: four M-39E 20-mm cannon plus up to 3402 kg (7484 lb) of external stores including bombs, napalm, rockets and missiles

Dimensions:
span	11.82 m (39 ft)
length	14.36 m (47 ft)
height	4.94 m (15 ft)
wing area	35.77 m² (385 sq ft)

COMBAT DATA

MAXIMUM SPEED

The F-100 and MIG-19 faced each other across the Iron Curtain as the first supersonic types produced by the chief Cold War adversaries. The RAF's main fighter type was the subsonic Hunter.

F-100D SUPER SABRE	1436 km/h (890 mph)
MiG-19SF 'FARMER'	1454 km/h (901 mph)
HUNTER F.Mk 6	1004 km/h (622 mph)

ARMAMENT

Cannon armament was the primary means of air-to-air defence as these types were introduced. Missiles were still in their infancy. The F-100 had a prodigious bomb load capacity.

F-100D SUPER SABRE	4 x 20-mm cannons	3193-kg (7484-lb) bombload
MiG-19SF 'FARMER'	3 x 30-mm cannons	500-kg (1100-lb) bombload
HUNTER F.Mk 6	4 x 30-mm cannons	907-kg (2000-lb) bombload

RANGE

The Hunter had a good range performance compared to the other, faster types. All three needed to carry external fuel tanks for anything but the shortest sorties.

F-100D SUPER SABRE	2494 km (1546 miles)
MiG-19SF 'FARMER'	2200 km (1346 miles)
HUNTER F.Mk 6	2961 km (1836 miles)

358

NORTH AMERICAN

F-100F SUPER SABRE

● First supersonic two-seater ● Vietnam warrior ● First 'Wild Weasel'

T wo-seat F-100F Super Sabres earned battle stars in Vietnam as 'Wild Weasels', by stalking and attacking missile sites. In this role it was a true pioneer. It was also a forward air controller, guiding other warplanes to their targets. Elsewhere in the world, this popular version of America's first supersonic fighter flew valiantly as a fighter-bomber and fulfilled the secondary, but no less important, task of providing valuable training.

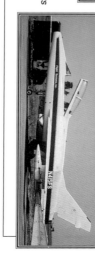

► Despite the popularity of the F-100, very few two-seaters were built and only a handful found their way to air forces overseas. The Royal Danish Air Force was one such customer.

NORTH AMERICAN F-100F SUPER SABRE

PHOTO FILE

► 'Thunderbirds'
The famous USAF display team flew the 'Hun', as it was known, between 1965 and 1968.

► Valuable in Vietnam
Two-seat 'Huns' served alongside single-seaters in Vietnam and made a valuable contribution.

► Fastest two-seater
A very advanced aircraft for its day, the F-100F was the first supersonic two-seat aircraft to enter service.

► Export orders
Denmark acquired six two-seat Super Sabres. Others were delivered to France and Turkey, with Turkish examples serving until the mid-1980s.

► New roles
Once retired from front-line service, many F-100s went on to become pilotless drones and test aircraft. This one served with Flight Systems Inc.

FACTS AND FIGURES

▼ A total of 2294 Super Sabres was built. Out of this number, 339 were two-seat F-100F models.

▼ First flown in August 1956, the prototype (TF-100C) crashed the following year.

▼ The last production aircraft was delivered to the USAF in 1959.

▼ The F-100F was the first aircraft configured for defence suppression missions against missile sites in Vietnam.

▼ The last F-100F left Vietnam in 1971 after almost six years of operations.

▼ All the F-100Fs were produced at North American's Inglewood, California, plant.

PROFILE

First of the 'Wild Weasels'

When North American introduced a two-seat version of the fabulous F-100 Super Sabre supersonic fighter, the idea seemed revolutionary. Yet from the 1956 debut of the prototype (TF-100C), the two-seater filled training and operational roles with the same spectacular performance that characterised the single-seat versions. The very first production F-100F, based on the F-100D, performed so well that it was used for research in the US space exploration programme.

In Vietnam, a two-seater was needed for the 'Wild Weasel' mission: finding and neutralising Hanoi's lethal surface-to-air missile batteries. The F-100F was fitted with Shrike anti-radar missiles and became the pace-setter in this new kind of warfare until bigger F-105F Thunderchiefs became available. The first of these missions was flown in December 1965, under the codename Iron Hand.

Other F-100Fs handled the dangerous, low-level forward air control (FAC) duty, spotting Viet Cong targets, often while flying through a hail of hostile gunfire. F-100F Super Sabres pioneered the use of two-seat aircraft in combat and in the 'Wild Weasel' defence suppression role, paving the way for the two-seat Republic F-105F and G Thunderchiefs and later F-4 Phantom IIs.

Left: F-100s amassed many combat sorties over Vietnam. Air-to-air refuelling was an important capability.

Below: This F-100F 'Misty' FAC flew with the 352nd Tactical Fighter Squadron based at Phan Rang Air Base during the Vietnam War.

F-100F Super Sabre

Type: two-seat tactical fighter

Powerplant: one Pratt & Whitney J57-P-21A 75.39-kN (16,960-lb-thrust) afterburning turbojet

Maximum speed: 1239 km/h (781 mph) clean at low level; Mach 1.3 at high altitude

Range: 760 km (470 miles)

Service ceiling: 14,020 m (46,000 ft)

Weights: empty 9256 kg (20,363 lb); loaded 15,800 kg (34,760 lb)

Armament: two 20-mm M39E cannon, plus up to 2722 kg (5600 lb) of external bombs, missiles or rockets; four AGM-45A Shrike ARMs for 'Wild Weasel' duties; various bombs and marker devices in 'Misty' FAC role

Dimensions:
span	11.82 m (38 ft 9 in)
length	15.27 m (50 ft 1 in)
height	4.94 m (16 ft 3 in)
wing area	35.77 m² (385 sq ft)

COMBAT DATA

THRUST

The two-seat F-100 Super Sabre was a powerful aircraft for its day, though it was considerably heavier than other contemporary tandem-seat training/close support aircraft such as the Northrop F-5B and Douglas TA-4F. Compared to their modern equivalents, all three aircraft were flown in the Vietnam War.

F-100F SUPER SABRE 75.4 kN (16,960 lb thrust)
F-5B FREEDOM FIGHTER 36.4 kN (8188 lb thrust)
TA-4F SKYHAWK 41.3 kN (9290 lb thrust)

MAXIMUM SPEED

These aircraft were designed in an era when it was thought that speed was more important than range or manoeuvrability; indeed, the F-100 was one of the first production aircraft to break the sound barrier. All three aircraft were flown in the Vietnam War, which ultimately proved that manoeuvrability and combat radius were still vital for success.

F-100F SUPER SABRE 1390 km/h (862 mph)
F-5B FREEDOM FIGHTER 1434 km/h (889 mph)
TA-4F SKYHAWK 1085 km/h (673 mph)

CLIMB RATE

At the time the F-100F entered service the F-100F had an exceptional climb rate compared to its contemporaries such as the TA-4F. Later aircraft such as the F-5B Freedom Fighter could climb faster, but could not carry as much ordnance.

F-100F SUPER SABRE 5791 m/min (19,000 fpm)
F-5B FREEDOM FIGHTER 9266 m/min (30,400 fpm)
TA-4F SKYHAWK 1753 m/min (5750 fpm)

F-100F SUPER SABRE

F-100 58-1226 was the first 'Wild Weasel' to destroy a surface-to-air missile site in Vietnam, in 1965. It operated as part of the 6234th Tactical Fighter Wing flying from Korat Air Base.

Originally delivered as a two-seat trainer, the F-100F proved highly suitable for conversion to the 'Misty' FAC and 'Wild Weasel' roles which required a two-man crew.

Antennas mounted under the nose were the main distinguishing feature of the 'Wild Weasel' variant. They formed part of the radar homing and warning system (RHAWS).

Unlike some other USAF aircraft of the period, F-100Fs were equipped with an air-to-air refuelling probe.

F-100Fs could carry a variety of external weapons. For defence suppression work against surface-to-air missiles, the AGM-45 Shrike proved highly effective.

Although blessed with great performance, like many jets of its era the F-100 had inadequate range. This was partly rectified by the carriage of external fuel tanks.

This early 'Wild Weasel' sports the three-tone camouflage but not the two-letter tailcodes. These signified the squadron to which a particular aircraft was assigned, and were in widespread use by mid 1967.

Powered by a single Pratt & Whitney J57 turbojet, the F-100 had tremendous power for its day, though it was noisy and thirsty.

Two-seater variants of combat jets

■ **MCDONNELL DOUGLAS F-15E EAGLE:** A dual-role variant of the single-seat F-15C interceptor, this aircraft is one of the most advanced fighter-bombers currently in service.

■ **DASSAULT RAFALE B:** This aircraft is France's newest combat jet. The two-seater is designed to replace SEPECAT Jaguars and Dassault Mirage III/5s in the strike role.

■ **MCDONNELL F-101B VOODOO:** A two-seat derivative of the F-101A fighter/bomber, these aircraft served as interceptors with the USAF and RCAF for many years.

■ **GLOSTER METEOR NF.Mk 14** First flown in the early 1950s, the NF.Mk 14 was a dedicated two-seat night-fighter variant and represented the pinnacle of Meteor development.

NORTH AMERICAN

A-5 VIGILANTE

● Vietnam reconnaissance ● Converted nuclear bomber ● Mach 2

During the Vietnam war, Vigilante reconnaissance planes flew from aircraft-carriers in the Gulf of Tonkin on intelligence-gathering missions to identify the most heavily guarded areas of North Vietnam. This information was incorporated into a computerised data bank on board the carrier. The aircraft's automatic flight controls and radar guidance system kept it precisely on course whether at high altitude or skimming the surface of the earth.

▲ Designed as a strategic nuclear bomber, the A-5 Vigilante's success in the Vietnam campaign lay in its role as a long-range reconnaissance aircraft.

NORTH AMERICAN A-5 VIGILANTE

▼ Carrier launch

The Vigilante was a particularly long aircraft – an important feature when it came to being launched from the deck of a ship where space was at a premium.

▲ Advanced reconnaissance systems

This formation of RA-5C Vigilantes was attached to reconnaissance squadron RVAH-7. Beneath their fuselages are the long central pods which carry the side-looking radar and photographic equipment.

▲ Speed and grace

With its long fuselage and swept wings, the Vigilante was perfect for long-distance missions. Its Mach 2 capability meant that its Phantom escorts often struggled to keep up.

▼ Ready for combat

Only a few Vigilantes were painted in camouflage colours for service over the North Vietnamese jungle.

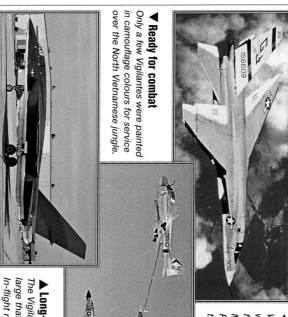

▲ Long-range capacity

The Vigilante's internal fuel tanks were so large that it never flew with drop-tanks. In-flight refuelling, here from a KA-6 Intruder, considerably extended its range.

FACTS AND FIGURES

▶ The Navy was initially reluctant to let the Vigilante fly over North Vietnam because of its expensive equipment.

▶ The word 'vigilante' means one who is watchful and ever-alert to danger.

▶ Eighteen Vigilantes were lost in the war, all but one over North Vietnam.

▶ More than 90 RA-5C reconnaissance versions were built and more were converted from A-5As.

▶ The first squadron equipped with the RA-5C was RVAH-5.

▶ The first A-5A became operational on board USS Enterprise in February 1962.

RA-5C Vigilante

Type: two seat reconnaissance plane

Powerplant: two 79.45-kN (17,876-lb-thrust) afterburning General Electric J79-GE-10 turbojets

Maximum speed: Mach 2.1 (2230 km/h / 1356 mph) at 12,000 m (39,370 ft)

Range: 4800 km (2983 miles)

Service ceiling: 19,500 m (63,976 ft)

Weights: empty 17,009 kg (37,498 lb); loaded 29,937 kg (98,219 lb)

Payload: AN/ALQ-31 electronic countermeasures pod, two panoramic cameras with rotating prisms, side-looking radar, infra-red system

Dimensions:
span	16.15 m (53 ft)
length	23.32 m (76 ft 6 in)
height	5.91 m (19 ft 5 in)
wing area	70.05 m² (754 sq ft)

COMBAT DATA

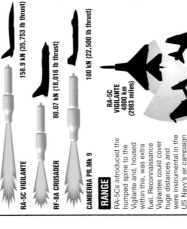

THRUST

Powered by twin General Electric J-79 engines, the Vigilante was one of the most powerful attack bombers ever built and far more powerful than other reconnaissance aircraft of the era such as the RF-8A Crusader and English Electric Canberra PR.Mk 9.

RA-5C VIGILANTE 158.9 kN (35,753 lb thrust)
RF-8A CRUSADER 80.07 kN (18,016 lb thrust)
CANBERRA PR.Mk 9 100 kN (22,500 lb thrust)

RANGE

RA-5Cs introduced the humped spine to the Vigilante and, housed within this, was extra fuel. Reconnaissance Vigilantes could cover huge distances and were instrumental in the US Navy's air campaign against North Vietnam. The Canberra had even greater range and could operate from carriers, but was heavier.

RA-5C VIGILANTE 4800 km (2983 miles)
RF-8A CRUSADER 1660 km (1031 miles)
CANBERRA PR.Mk 9 8160 km (5070 miles)

CEILING

As it did not have any defensive armament, the Vigilante had to fly as fast and as high as possible to avoid contact with any North Vietnamese MiG-21 interceptors. The Vigilante could reach altitudes of nearly 20,000 m (65,600 ft).

RA-5C VIGILANTE 19,500 m (63,976 ft)
RF-8A CRUSADER 17,983 m (59,000 ft)
CANBERRA PR.Mk 9 18,300 m (60,039 ft)

Fast flying photo bird

Originally designed as a nuclear bomber, the Vigilante saw combat in Vietnam solely as a reconnaissance aircraft, where its only defence was its supersonic capability.

Initially restricted to flying in the safer South Vietnamese skies because of its extremely expensive equipment, the RA-5C did eventually go north. The Vigilantes and their crews provided invaluable information on troop concentrations and movements during missions over North Vietnam. The RA-5Cs

were so important to the Navy that, despite their tremendous speed, they were often escorted by F-4 Phantoms in order to keep enemy MiGs at bay.

Most missions were flown at speeds of between Mach 1.1 and Mach 1.3. The Vigilante carried plenty of internal fuel, and flew in maximum afterburner throughout the mission. The RA-5Cs were always the last aircraft to be launched since they had the speed to catch up with their Phantom escorts. Indeed, the Phantom pilots often requested that the Vigilantes

slow down as their aircraft, loaded with missiles, rapidly ran out of fuel.

Despite its failure as a bomber, during the Vietnam conflict the RA-5C was unparalleled in its provision of intelligence material.

Above: This RA-5C, part of RCAH-11 squadron, is pictured on board the USS Constellation in 1972. Despite the prototype first being tested in 1958, operational Vigilantes were still being flown as late as 1979.

Above: With its combination of speed and range and its highly advanced electronic counter-measures and radar, the Vigilante was unparalleled in its role, and remains so to this day.

RA-5C VIGILANTE

This RA-5C (BuNo 150834) was part of RVAH-12 squadron, carrying an experimental camouflage scheme of green, olive drab and tan uppersurfaces over gloss white undersurfaces.

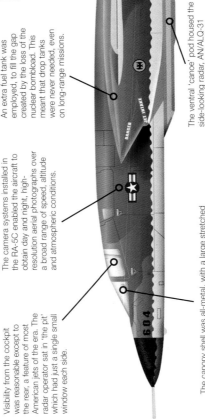

The swept wing of the Vigilante emerged from the earlier North American design theories that gave birth to the F-100. It was made with an aluminium-lithium alloy skin that gave it great strength, elasticity and a very low weight.

Directional control was provided by single-piece horizontal stabilisers and a single-piece vertical tail surface. The vertical tail could be folded about a hinge located at mid-height. This was a valuable asset when it came to stowage onboard a carrier.

An extra fuel tank was employed, to fill the gap created by the loss of the nuclear bombload. This meant that drop tanks were never needed, even on long-range missions.

The ventral 'canoe' pod housed the side-looking radar, AN/ALQ-31 electronic countermeasures, two panoramic cameras with rotating prisms, and infra-red system.

The camera systems installed in the RA-5C enabled the aircraft to obtain day and night, high-resolution aerial photographs over a broad range of speed, altitude and atmospheric conditions.

Visibility from the cockpit was reasonable except to the rear, a feature of most American jets of the era. The radar operator sat in 'the pit' which had just a single small window each side.

The canopy shell was all-metal, with a large stretched acrylic transparency. This permitted excellent vision to either side and above for the pilot. Hinge points were located towards the rear of each shell.

Inside the 'eyes of the fleet'

1. Pitot static probe
2. Air refuelling probe
3. Air refuelling probe light
4. Top cap fuel tank
5. Forward fuselage fuel tank
6. Sump tank
7. Integral wing fuel tank
8. Tacan-comm duplex antenna
9. Tail position light
10. Expendable tailcone
11. Fuel dump pipe
12. Arrestor hook
13. Anti-collision beacon
14. Catapult strop hooks
15. Reconnaissance fairing
16. Bombing computer
17. Television optical sight

NORTHROP

P-61 BLACK WIDOW

- Enormous but agile ● Powerful ● Complex fighter

Northrop's P-61 Black Widow was a creature of the night. This large, powerful, twin-engined craft was the first American combat plane designed from the beginning as a night-fighter and optimised for air-to-air combat during the nocturnal hours. Beneath its slick coat of black paint, the P-61 proved itself a deadly foe in the dark, invisibly approaching Japanese aircraft and blasting them from the sky.

▲ Long in development, the P-61 only saw service in the last year of the war. It was the biggest, heaviest and most powerful night-fighter of the war, but was also agile and fast.

NORTHROP P-61 BLACK WIDOW

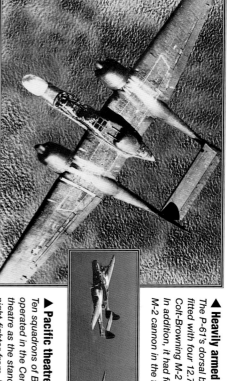

▲ Heavily armed
The P-61's dorsal barbette was fitted with four 12.7-mm (.50-cal.) Colt-Browning M-2 machine guns. In addition, it had four 20-mm M-2 cannon in the fuselage.

Slow development ▶
The original XP-61 prototype was flown on 26 May 1942 with most of its features mocked-up while awaiting the real parts.

▲ Pacific theatre
Ten squadrons of Black Widows operated in the Central Pacific theatre as the standard USAAF night-fighter from June 1944.

▲ Good night-fighter
Once the strict initial flight limitations were lifted, P-61s became highly regarded.

Long range ▶
This P-61B carries four drop-tanks, which increased fuel capacity by 4692 litres (1110 gallons) and provided for an impressive range.

FACTS AND FIGURES

▶ On 26 May 1942 famous test pilot Vance Breese flew the P-61 on its first flight.

▶ On 6 July 1944, the P-61 racked up its first air-to-air victory, a Japanese Mitsubishi G4M 'Betty' bomber.

▶ Production of the Black Widow totalled 706 aircraft of all variants.

▶ P-61 Black Widows shot down nine German V-1 'buzz' bombs.

▶ Design and development of the P-61's SCR-720 search radar involved 172,000 man-hours of work.

▶ Three P-61 pilots became aces, with two of them including kills flying other types.

PROFILE

Killer of the night

The P-61 Black Widow was the largest, heaviest and most powerful fighter of World War II. It resulted from efforts by designer Jack Northrop to create a night-fighter able to use air-to-air radar to destroy enemy warplanes after dark.

The Black Widow was deceptively agile, and challenged and defeated smaller fighters. More than a twin-engine, twin-boomed aircraft of great size and

strength, the Black Widow was truly a fighter, and it produced an impressive number of air-to-air kills.

The Black Widow looked like a strange, menacing machine. In fact, it was easy to fly and responsive to the touch. The unusual cockpit layout placed the radarman/forward gunner above and behind the pilot (the third crewman was behind both), and pilots disliked having the propellers in line with their cockpit position. But

once P-61s reached night-fighter squadrons in Europe and the Pacific in 1944, they achieved an impressive combat record.

P-61B BLACK WIDOW

The Northrop P-61 Black Widow was the first USAAF night-fighter designed for this role. This aircraft was called 'Time's a'Wastin' and was one of the most famous Black Widows of the Pacific theatre.

The nose-mounted SCR-720 radar scanner was covered by a painted dielectric nose cone.

P-61s were powered by two Pratt & Whitney R-2800-65 Double Wasp radial engines, powering Curtiss Electric propellers.

Additional firepower was provided by a General Electric dorsal barbette with four 12.7-mm (.50-cal.) Colt-Browning machine guns, each with 560 rounds.

The unique twin-boom configuration housed a crew of three in a large pod mounted onto a sturdy centre section. The fuselage nacelle also housed the radar and most of the armament.

Built as an early P-61B, 'Time's a'Wastin' was one of only two of the first 200 P-61Bs that retained the dorsal barbette. This was not revived until buffeting problems from the guns were solved.

Underwing drop-tanks extended the P-61's range to 2172 km.

Twin tailbooms extended aft from the engine nacelles. The fins were built integral with the tailbooms and the tailplane was located between the fins. The crew of three was housed in the large central pod.

The all-metal, shoulder-mounted wing had a broad chord and straight leading edge. It had a span of 20.11 m (66 ft) and a wing area of 61.53 m² (662 sq ft), giving a low wing loading and agile performance.

This XF-15A conversion of a P-61C was the second Black Widow adapted for the photographic reconnaissance role, fitted with six cameras in the lengthened nose.
It had a long, clear-view canopy over the tandem cockpits. Only 36 F-15As were built, although 175 were ordered.

P-61B Black Widow

Type: three-seat night-fighter

Powerplant: two 1491-kW (2000-hp) Pratt & Whitney R-2800-65 Double Wasp 18-cylinder radial engines

Maximum speed: 589 km/h (365 mph) at 6096 m (20,000 ft)

Range: 1513 km (940 miles) (2172 km/ 1350 miles with drop tanks)

Service ceiling: 12,445 m (40,800 ft)

Weights: empty 9654 kg (21,239 lb); loaded 13,471 kg (29,636 lb); maximum overload 16,420 kg (36,124 lb)

Armament: four 20-mm M-2 cannon each with 200 rounds; dorsal barbette with four 12.7-mm (.50-cal.) machine guns each with 560 rounds; four external pylons each rated at 726 kg (1600 lb) for bombs, rockets or other weapons

Dimensions:
span	20.11 m (66 ft)
length	15.11 m (50 ft)
height	4.47 m (15 ft)
wing area	61.53 m² (662 sq ft)

COMBAT DATA

MAXIMUM SPEED

The bigger and much heavier Black Widow was only slightly slower than the nimble Rolls-Royce Merlin-engined Mosquito night-fighter variant. The Ki-45 was appreciably slower.

P-61B BLACK WIDOW	589 km/h (365 mph)
MOSQUITO NF.Mk II	595 km/h (370 mph)
Ki-45 'NICK'	547 km/h (340 mph)

ARMAMENT

After development problems had been cured, the P-61B was equipped with four cannon and four powerful machine guns, giving it superb firepower. The Ki-45 had a 37-mm fixed forward-firing cannon which was a very powerful weapon but had a slow rate of fire.

P-61B BLACK WIDOW	4 x 20-mm cannon 4 x 12.7-mm (.50-cal.) MGs
MOSQUITO NF.Mk II	4 x 20-mm cannon 4 x 7.7-mm (.303-cal.) MGs
Ki-45 'NICK'	2 x 20-mm cannon 1 x 37-mm cannon 1 x 7.92-mm MGs

RANGE

The maximum range achieved by the Mosquito when fitted with two underwing drop-tanks was 2993 km (1860 miles), some 25 per cent greater than the P-61B with its four additional tanks. The ranges were similar on internal tanks only. The Ki-45 had the shortest range of the three night-fighters.

P-61B BLACK WIDOW	2172 km (1350 miles)
MOSQUITO NF.Mk II	2993 km (1860 miles)
Ki-45 'NICK'	2000 km (1240 miles)

Twin-engined night-fighters

■ **DE HAVILLAND MOSQUITO NF.Mk II:** The Mosquito night-fighter was developed throughout the war, the first NFMk IIs entering service in March 1942. Later versions had the same SCR-720 radar as the P-61, but were less heavily armed.

■ **JUNKERS Ju 88G-7B:** The Luftwaffe's definitive night-fighter, the Ju 88G entered service in the summer of 1944, becoming Germany's night fighter by the end of the war. It was used effectively for home defence in the final months.

■ **KAWASAKI Ki-45 'NICK':** The Japanese contemporary of the P-61, the Ki-45 Model C had good speed and performance but failed to receive its centimetric nose radar during the last year of the war. It was successful against B-29s for home defence.

NORTHROP

F-89 SCORPION

● Interim interceptor ● Changes in armament ● Lengthy service

P ossibly the most capable of the first-generation all-weather jet interceptors, the Northrop F-89 was created in response to a USAF proposal for a successor to the P-61 Black Widow. Entering service in 1950, the clumsy-looking Scorpion actually outlasted its contemporaries, the F-86D Sabre and F-94 Starfire, in service. During the course of its career, the F-89's armament changed from cannons to rockets and nuclear missiles.

▲ Conceived in 1945, the F-89, was among the first-generation all-weather jet interceptors. Intended as an interim type, the Scorpion enjoyed a lengthy career, serving until 1969.

PHOTO FILE

NORTHROP F-89 SCORPION

Biggest production run ▶
Most numerous of all Scorpion variants, with 682 built, was the F-89D. It could carry AIM-4 Falcon missiles on the wing pods.

New weapons for a new era ▶
In the 1950s, among the most popular weapons with which to attack the perceived Soviet bomber threat were unguided, nuclear-tipped rockets like the Genie.

◀ Wing design
A straight laminar flow wing made the Scorpion a rock-steady weapons platform, perfect for the interception role.

▲ Service in numbers
At peak strength, F-89 Scorpions equipped 36 front-line Air Defense Squadrons of the USAF.

▼ Change of armament
Designed around a four-gun nose armament, the XF-89 prototype was later reworked to feature a six-gun layout in the nose.

FACTS AND FIGURES

▶ In 1952 an F-89C crashed at the International Aviation Exposition in Detroit. The entire Scorpion fleet was grounded.

▶ Serviceability problems resulted in the F-89 fleet never achieving full strength.

▶ A Scorpion of the 74th FIS in Greenland was the first jet to land on a frozen sea.

▶ After their interception days were over, surviving Scorpions were used for drone launching and as chase aircraft.

▶ A swept-wing variant of the F-89 was proposed but was never built.

▶ The first variant of the Scorpion actually to enter service was the F-89B.

PROFILE

Cold War heavyweight

In the late 1940s, East-West relations cooled dramatically and the United States was caught in the grip of anti-communist hysteria. Believing that the USSR would soon have the ability to drop nuclear weapons by means of high-technology bombers, the newly formed USAF was in urgent need of interceptors to counter this very serious threat.

Among the three types which stood on guard over the continental US in the early 1950s was the Northrop F-89

Scorpion. This heavy two-seat interceptor was powered by twin Allison J35 turbojets slung underneath the fuselage.

The first prototype, XF-89, made its maiden flight on 16 August 1948 and was followed by 10 development aircraft, called F-89As. Service variants began with the F-89B and C models, though these proved barely adequate and were quickly succeeded by the definitive F-89D, of which 682 were built. This variant dispensed with the nose-

mounted cannon, instead carrying rockets in huge wingtip pods. Other production variants included the AIM-4 Falcon-armed F-89H and finally the F-89J, which could carry the Douglas MB-1 Genie nuclear rocket. F-89s were later passed on to the Air National Guard, where they served until 1969.

Above: Assigned to the 76th Fighter Intercept Squadron, based at Presque Isle Air Force Base, Maine, this F-89D carries extra underwing fuel tanks.

Throughout their careers, the F-89s remained primarily in natural metal finish. To reduce glare and prevent pilot distraction, the area just forward of the windscreen was painted black. This machine also had Day-Glo wings and tail surfaces to aid recognition in poor weather.

F-89D SCORPION

Wearing the 'buzz code' FV-959, this particular aircraft, a F-89D-45-NO, is seen in the colourful markings of the 59th Fighter Intercept Squadron at the time the unit was based at Goose Bay airport, Labrador, in north-eastern Canada.

Sitting under the sliding bubble canopy were a pilot and a radar operator. Unlike today, the crew of an F-89 were often current on several aircraft at the same time. Despite its drawbacks, the F-89 was rock-steady in the air.

F-89Ds introduced a longer and slightly slimmer nose profile. The six-cannon arrangement of earlier variants was dispensed with and extra fuel carried in the nose.

Mounting the engines under the fuselage resulted in a high rate of FOD (foreign object damage) and the F-89 was often referred to as the 'Hoover Model F-89' because of this trait.

A major factor in the stability of the Scorpion was its straight, laminar flow wing. It made take-offs and landings considerably easier.

Like the Canadian CF-100 Canuck, the Scorpion featured a mid-mounted tailplane with zero dihedral. The XF-89 had encountered severe turbulence and buffeting at high speeds and, from the 'A' model onwards, the rear fuselage was recontoured to solve the problem.

The 'D' model introduced new armament in the form of the FFAR (folding fin aircraft rockets). Crews were trained to fire these rockets in three salvoes.

An unusual feature of the F-89 was its large-diameter main wheels. They were deemed necessary because of the shape of the wing and the F-89's considerable weight.

F-89D Scorpion

Type: two-seat all-weather interceptor

Powerplant: two 32.03-kN (7200-lb-thrust) Allison J35 turbojets

Maximum speed: 1023 km/h (634 mph)

Initial climb rate: 2546 m/min (8350 fpm)

Range: 2200 km (1364 miles)

Service ceiling: 14,995 m (49,200 ft)

Weights: empty 11,428 kg (25,142 lb); loaded 19,160 kg (42,152 lb)

Armament: 104 70-mm folding fin unguided rockets, plus up to 16 127-mm (5-in) high velocity aircraft rockets

Dimensions:
span	18.19 m	(59 ft 8 in)
length	16.41 m	(53 ft 10 in)
height	5.36 m	(17 ft 7 in)
wing area	60.39 m²	(650 sq ft)

COMBAT DATA

MAXIMUM SPEED

None of these first generation all-weather interceptors was particularly fast and, indeed, they were often derided for their lack of speed. Despite this, both the Scorpion and CF-100 Canuck had lengthy, if somewhat uneventful, careers.

F-89D SCORPION	1023 km/h (634 mph)
F-94C STARFIRE	1030 km/h (639 mph)
CF-100 CANUCK Mk 5	1046 km/h (649 mph)

RANGE

Intended to intercept formations of Soviet bombers as far as possible from the US mainland, these aircraft needed considerable endurance. They were far more stable and long-legged than their successors.

F-89D SCORPION 2200 km (1364 miles)
F-94C STARFIRE 1455 km (902 miles)
CF-100 CANUCK Mk 5 3220 km (1996 miles)

SERVICE CEILING

Nicknamed the 'Clunk' because of its ungainly appearance, the CF-100 Canuck could operate at altitudes of up to 16,460 m (54,000 ft), considerably more than that of its ontemporares.
In order to catch the high-flying bombers, a high service ceiling was essential.

F-89D SCORPION 14,995 m (49,200 ft)
F-94C STARFIRE 14,630 m (48,000 ft)
CF-100 CANUCK Mk 5 16,460 m (54,000 ft)

Scorpion's prey

MYASISHCHYEV M-4 'BISON': During the 1950s this four-engined Soviet jet bomber was perceived as being one of the most serious threats to the United States.

TUPOLEV Tu-16 'BADGER': Smaller and more versatile than the M-4, the Tu-16 would become one of the longest serving warplanes, remaining in service during the mid 1990s.

TUPOLEV Tu-95 'BEAR': Initially dismissed because of its huge propellers, the massive Tu-95 would become a familiar sight to USAF interceptor crews for more than 30 years.

NORTHROP
F-5A FREEDOM FIGHTER

● Lightweight fighter ● Flown by 13 nations ● Vietnam veteran

D esigned in the late 1950s as a lightweight fighter for supply to friendly nations as part of the US Military Assistance Program, the F-5 remains a viable combat aircraft. Although the early examples are more than 30 years old, some late production aircraft are being upgraded with modern avionics. The type's advantages include supersonic performance and the ability to carry reasonable loads while maintaining economy of operation.

▲ Northrop's Freedom Fighter, as its name suggests, was a product of the Cold War. It was a means of providing an affordable yet capable aircraft for America's allies.

PHOTO FILE

NORTHROP F-5A FREEDOM FIGHTER

▼ Scandinavian Freedom Fighter
Norway operates seven F-5As and eight F-5Bs, upgraded under PAWS (Programme for Weapons and Systems Improvements), as lead-in trainers for its new F-16s.

▲ Canadian service
Known in RCAF service as the CF-116, the Freedom Fighter served in both A and D versions from Cold Lake CFB, Alberta.

Refuelled in the air ▼
From the outset, the F-5 incorporated air-to-air refuelling. These aircraft are seen being 'tanked' by a KC-135A prior to deployment in Vietnam.

Blooded in Vietnam
Skoshi Tiger F-5s were transferred to the Vietnamese air force (VNAF) in 1967. Here, an aircraft of the 522nd Fighter Squadron is seen in its revetment at Bien Hoa Air Base.

▲ In retirement
The Netherlands was a major F-5 operator, until it introduced the F-16.

FACTS AND FIGURES

▼ Canada operated a small number of aircraft, designated CF-116A(R), fitted with Vinten 70-mm nose cameras.

▼ Bristol Aerospace's upgrade for the CF-116 included HOTAS controls.

▼ A complete F-5A upgrade, as offered by Northrop, cost $4.5 million per airframe.

▼ The F-5A originated from the N-156 Fang aircraft, designated CF-116A(R), which also led to the USAF's T-38A trainer.

▼ F-5 development was funded under the Mutual Defense Aid Program.

▼ An F-5A has an eight-minute turnaround between missions, including refuelling.

PROFILE

Lightweight fighters for America's allies

Flown for the first time in May 1963, the F-5 entered service the following year with a USAF training squadron. A dozen of the first F-5As were sent to Vietnam in 1965, where they proved able to match the USAF's front-line fighters in some missions. They served with South Vietnam throughout the 10-year war with the North.

Air forces in Europe, the Middle East, South America and Southeast Asia acquired Freedom Fighters before production switched to the uprated Northrop F-5E Tiger II. The RF-5A was adapted as a camera-equipped photo-reconnaissance version.

F-5s were also built in Canada, where Canadair produced CF-5s for the RCAF (known as CF-116s in service) and the NF-5 for the Dutch. Many ex-Canadian F-5s went to Turkey, while Greece acquired some NF-5s.

By the mid 1980s, more than 400 of the 1100-plus Freedom Fighters built were still in service with a dozen air forces. The remaining Canadian CF-5s had been upgraded for sale, and Spain's fleet was refurbished to serve as weapons trainers.

For long-range missions, the Freedom Fighter's wingtip missile pylons can be replaced with fuel tanks.

F-5C FREEDOM FIGHTER

Serving with the 10th Fighter Commando Squadron, F-5C 64-13332 was based at Bien Hoa Air Base, South Vietnam. The 10th FCS, originally the 4503rd TFS (Provisional), was in combat for almost 18 months.

Mounted in the nose are two 20-mm M39A2 lightweight cannon, with 280 rounds of ammunition. A nose-mounted refuelling probe and night formation lights were also added to USAF Freedom Fighters. South Vietnamese RF-5As carried four KS-92 cameras in a modified nose.

Skoshi Tiger aircraft typically carried mission markings. Flying up to four times a day, the 10th FCS was kept busy on light attack duties.

The F-5's cockpit afforded good pilot visibility. Seated on a rocket-powered ejection seat, USAF Freedom Fighter pilots over Vietnam were fortunate that their aircraft had an additional 90 kg (200 lb) of cockpit and engine armour, upgraded avionics and an improved jungle camouflage scheme.

F-5Cs were powered by two afterburning General Electric J85 turbojets. For low-speed operations, air louvre doors on the rear fuselage provided improved air flow.

Serving over Vietnam between October 1965 and April 1967, the USAF Skoshi Tigers flew 9,985 missions, in which nine aircraft were lost. Around 17,000 general-purpose bombs had been dropped by the time these trials aircraft were handed over to South Vietnam.

Underwing, on jettisonable pylons specifically fitted for Vietnam service, the F-5C carried up to 2720 kg (6000 lb) of rockets, gun pods, bombs or, as shown here, four 340-kg (750 -lb) BLU-1 anti-personnel napalm tanks.

F-5A Freedom Fighter

Type: lightweight fighter and fighter-bomber

Powerplant: two 18.15-kN (4085-lb-thrust) General Electric J85-GE-13 afterburning turbojets

Maximum speed: 1487 km/h (922 mph) 'clean' at 10,975 m (36,000 ft)

Maximum climb rate: 8748 m/min at sea level

Combat radius: 989 km (615 miles) on hi-lo-hi mission with two 240-kg (525-lb) bombs and maximum fuel

Service ceiling: 15,390 m (50,500 ft)

Weights: empty equipped 3667 kg (8067 lb); maximum take-off 9379 kg (20,635 lb)

Armament: two 20-mm M39 cannon and up to 1996 kg of air-to-ground ordnance

Dimensions:
span (with tip tanks)	7.87 m (25 ft 10 in)
length	14.38 m (47 ft 2 in)
height	4.01 m (13 ft 2 in)
wing area	15.79 m² (170 sq ft)

COMBAT DATA

MAXIMUM SPEED

Northrop's F-5 family has been extensively developed from the Freedom Fighter to the Tiger II and ill-fated Tigershark. The F-5E Tiger II introduced more powerful J85 engines, and the F-20 (originally F-5G) had a single afterburning turbofan.

F-5A FREEDOM FIGHTER	1487 km/h (922 mph)
F-5E TIGER II	1700 km/h (1054 mph)
F-20 TIGERSHARK	2124 km/h (1317 mph)

MAXIMUM CLIMB RATE

Increased engine power and improved power-to-weight ratios contributed greatly to climb rates. A good climb rate allows a fighter aircraft to reach its patrol station quickly. The F-20 lost out to the F-16A ADF in the race to equip the US Air National Guard with a new air defence fighter.

F-20 TIGERSHARK	16,398 m/min (53,800 fpm)
F-5E TIGER II	10,455 m/min (34,300 fpm)
F-5A FREEDOM FIGHTER	8748 m/min (28,700 fpm)

ARMAMENT

Greater engine power also allowed higher loads to be carried. When the F-20 appeared, its maximum weapons load was double that of the original F-5As.

F-5A FREEDOM FIGHTER	1996-kg (4400-lb) bombload 2 x 20-mm cannon
F-5E TIGER II	3175-kg (7000-lb) bombload 2 x 20-mm cannon
F-20 TIGERSHARK	4080-kg (9000-lb) bombload 2 x 20-mm cannon

Freedom Fighter operators

■ **ROYAL CANADIAN AIR FORCE:** Canada recently retired its last CF-5s, which had been upgraded for use as CF-18 lead-in trainers with reworked wings and tail plus new avionics.

■ **ELLINIKI AEROPORIA:** Greece flies two Freedom Fighter squadrons, including ex-Dutch aircraft, from Thessaloniki, mainly for light ground attack and advanced weapons training duties.

■ **ROYAL THAI AIR FORCE:** Thailand operates the original F-5A/B and RF-5A in small numbers in the ground attack role, alongside the later F-5E/F Tiger II.

NORTHROP
F/RF-5E TIGER II/F-20 TIGERSHARK

- Upgraded 'Freedom Fighter'
- Lightweight, low cost
- Exports

As a result of the great success of Northrop's first F-5 – the 'Freedom Fighter' – the company won the contest to build its replacement as America's affordable, lightweight fighter for the world. The Tiger II, with more power and an emphasis on air-to-air capability, was a vast improvement over its predecessor. The Tiger II was a big seller, but the same could not be said of the Tigershark, which failed against F-16 opposition.

▲ The F-5 family answered a request from the US government for a relatively cheap fighter for export to smaller nations under the Mutual Assistance Plan (MAP).

PHOTO FILE

NORTHROP F/RF-5E TIGER II/F-20 TIGERSHARK

▼ Ill-fated Tigershark
Three F-20s were built, and a fourth was started but never finished. Two were lost in fatal accidents due to pilot incapacity, and the third went to a museum.

▲ RF-5E Tigereye
Malaysia, Saudi Arabia and Singapore have taken delivery of this camera-equipped variant. Cameras are fitted in the nose, in place of the radar, and can include night-reconnaissance sensors.

▲ Taiwanese Tiger IIs
The Republic of China operates a sizeable fleet of locally built F-5Es and Fs.

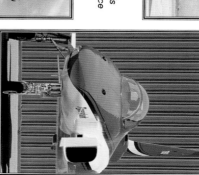

▲ Popular upgrades
Northrop Grumman is among several companies offering avionics upgrade packages for Tiger IIs.

▲ Increased capability
In addition to a top speed in excess of Mach 2, the F-20 had an avionics fit comparable to that of the F-16A and improved weapons capability.

FACTS AND FIGURES

► Total F-5 production, including 'Freedom Fighters', T-38 Talons and overseas production, totalled 3840.

► Overseas F-5E/F production has taken place in Korea, Switzerland and Taiwan.

► Israel's F-5 upgrade is known as Tiger III; Northrop Grumman's is the Tiger IV.

► The first F-5E flew on 11 August 1972, from Edwards Air Force Base, four months ahead of schedule.

► Taiwan considered re-engined F-5Es with new radar and AIM-120 missiles.

► Only 12 RF-5Es were built; Singapore converted six F-5Es to RF-5E standard.

PROFILE

Feline son of the 'Freedom Fighter'

Skoshi Tiger was the name given to the evaluation of the F-5E's predecessor, the F-5A 'Freedom Fighter', in combat in Vietnam in 1965. The F-5A (and two-seat F-5B) were lightweight, low-cost fighters intended for export to 'approved countries'.

When, in 1970, the USAF asked for proposals for a new international fighter aircraft, Northrop successfully suggested an updated F-5, the F-5E, which was dubbed Tiger II to perpetuate the name made

famous in Vietnam.

Export sales have been numerous, with aircraft going to both existing F-5 customers and to new converts to this capable, yet affordable, tactical fighter. While the F-5A sold well to NATO countries, the Tiger II has been popular with Middle Eastern, Asian and South American states.

The re-engined F-20 (at first designated F-5G) flew in 1982, but failed to sell. F-5 production has ended, but upgrades will ensure long-term service.

The principal modification made to the F-5 design to produce the F-20 Tigershark, was replacing the two J85 turbojets with an F404 turbofan, as fitted to early F/A-18 Hornets.

The standard radar of the F-5E was the Emerson Electric AN/APQ-159 search-and-track radar with a range of about 37 km.

The F-5E was developed with emphasis on the air-to-air role, although ground-attack capability was not ignored. Indeed, the earliest customers, Iran and Saudi Arabia, both acquired the type for this role.

Unlike earlier F-5s, the E model did not require wingtip fuel tanks but it did retain the rails for AIM-9 air-to-air missiles.

Because the F-5E was designed as a counter to the Soviet MiG-21, it was also an ideal threat simulator for the USAF and US Navy Dissimilar Air Combat Training (DACT) schemes. The Navy continues to operate a small number of F-5Es in this role.

The two 22.2-kN (5000-lb-thrust) General Electric J85 afterburning turbojets have separate, but cross-feedable, fuel supplies. The electrically operated louvre doors supply additional air to the engines during take-off and in flight below speeds of Mach 0.4–0.35.

Switzerland took delivery of 98 F-5Es and 12 two-seat F-5Fs, a number of which were assembled at FFA's Emmen factory. Originally tasked with air defence, some have been re-roled as ground-attack aircraft and replace Hunters.

The available upgrades concentrate on improving the aircraft's avionics and weapons capability. The leading suppliers are Northrop Grumman and Israel Aircraft Industries (IAI).

Two Pontiac (Colt-Browning) M39A2 20-mm cannon are fitted in the nose of a standard F-5E. The RF-5E Tigereye and two-seat F-5F use just one, fitted on the left hand side.

F-5E TIGER II

Once a renowned Hawker Hunter display team, Switzerland's Patrouille Suisse exchanged its elderly Hunters for Tiger IIs in 1994. J-3089 is one of the team's brightly-painted F-5Es based at Dubendorf Air Base.

The two-seat conversion trainer version of the F-5E was the F-5F, which has tandem cockpits in a 1.02-m (3-ft) longer fuselage (from the USAF's T-38 Talon). It retains the combat capabilities of the E model, but is fitted with just one 20-mm nose cannon.

Mutual Assistance Plan fighters

■ **REPUBLIC F-84F THUNDERSTREAK:** This French air force Thunderstreak was among a number of members of the F-84 family supplied, in particular, to NATO nations.

■ **NORTH AMERICAN F-100 SUPER SABRE:** Under the Mutual Assistance Plan, new-build F-100s were supplied by the USAF to Denmark, France and Taiwan.

■ **LOCKHEED F-104 STARFIGHTER:** The 'missile with a man in it' was built for the USAF under MAP contract in variants, like the F-104G, that did not actually serve with the USAF.

F-5E Tiger II

Type: light tactical fighter

Powerplant: two 22.2-kN (4000-lb-thrust) General Electric J85-GE-21B afterburning turbojets

Maximum speed: 1700 km/h (1054 mph) at 10,975 m (36,000 ft)

Ferry range: 3720 km (2300 miles) with empty tanks dropped; 3175 km (1970 miles) with tanks retained

Service ceiling: 15,590 m (51,100 ft)

Weights: empty 4349 kg (9568 lb); maximum take-off 11,187 kg (24,611 lb)

Armament: two M39A2 20-mm cannon in the nose, two AIM-9 Sidewinder air-to-air missiles on wing-tip launchers plus up to 3175 kg (6985 lb) of ordnance on fuselage and wing pylons

Dimensions: span   8.13 m (26 ft 8 in)
length   14.45 m (47 ft 5 in)
height   4.08 m (60 ft 9 in)
wing area 17.28 m² (186 sq ft)

COMBAT DATA

MAXIMUM SPEED

Among the world's most exported tactical fighters, the F-5E has an excellent speed performance which is only bettered by the MiG-21. Both the MiG and F-5E employ afterburning turbojet engines to achieve a high top speed. However, range tends to suffer as a result.

F-5E TIGER II	1700 km/h (1054 mph)
MiG-21bis 'FISHBED'	2175 km/h (1349 mph)
HAWK Mk 200	1065 km/h (660 mph)

ARMAMENT

The Tiger II represents a compromise between speed and range performance and lifting ability. Although limited to speeds of less than Mach 2 (unlike the MiG-21), the F-5 is able to lift more than 3 tonnes of ordnance. The smaller Hawk can also carry a good load.

F-5E TIGER II	2 x 20-mm cannon 3175 kg (6985 lb) of bombs
MiG-21bis 'FISHBED'	2000 kg (4400 lb) of bombs
HAWK Mk 200	2 x 25-mm cannon 3493 kg (7685 lb) of bombs

CLIMB RATE

The greater thrust of the MiG-21's powerful engine gives it the best climb rate. The Tiger II is not far behind, but the Hawk, powered by a non-afterburning engine, is significantly slower.

MiG-21bis 'FISHBED'	13,800 m/min (45,264 fpm)
F-5E TIGER II	10,455 m/min (34,292 fpm)
HAWK Mk 200	3508 m/min (11,506 fpm)

NORTHROP

B-2 SPIRIT

- Unique flying wing ● Advanced technology stealth bomber

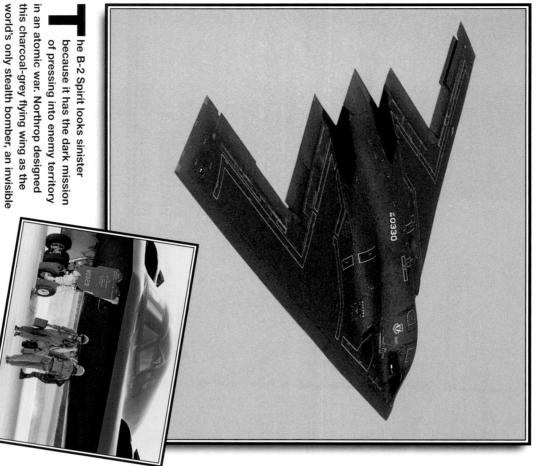

he B-2 Spirit looks sinister because it has the dark mission of pressing into enemy territory in an atomic war. Northrop designed this charcoal-grey flying wing as the world's only stealth bomber, an invisible ghost to enemy radar operators. Long kept under a cloak of secrecy, the B-2 is out in the open today and is soon to be fully operational, with both nuclear and conventional bombing duties.

▲ With its flowing, organic lines, the Northrop B-2 looks like no other aircraft in the world. But it offers power and combat capability unmatched by any other military aircraft.

NORTHROP B-2 SPIRIT

▲ First flight
Rolling out from the Northrop facility in Palmdale, the B-2 made its first flight, to Edwards Air Force Base, on 17 July 1989.

Stealth bomber revealed ▼
When the B-2 was first rolled out, photos were taken only from certain angles to keep its stealth features as secret as possible.

Compact power ▼
By doing away with the fuselage, the B-2's designers have produced a very powerful and capable aircraft with enormous range and payload, in a surprisingly small package.

▲ Long experience
Northrop has amassed a great deal of experience with flying wings; its first full-sized bombers, such as this XB-35, flew in the 1940s.

▲ Flying wing
The B-2 has no conventional fuselage; its entire structure is contained within a smoothly blended delta wing with 'W'-shaped trailing edges.

FACTS AND FIGURES

▶ Two B-2s can complete a bombing raid which previously required 32 F-16s, 16 F-15s and 27 support aircraft.

▶ Before the B-2 ever flew, wind tunnel models were tested for 24,000 hours – a record.

▶ The radar-absorbing body of the B-2 contains 900 materials and a million parts.

▶ Almost invisible to radar, the B-2 was also made difficult to hear or see.

▶ The B-2 Spirit's engines are concealed deep within the structure to hide them from radar and heat-seeking sensors.

▶ The USAF's first B-2 was delivered exactly 90 years after the Wright brothers' first flight.

Northrop's amazing Flying Wing

The boomerang-like Northrop B-2 Spirit began as one of the best-kept secrets in history. Its sleek shape and special materials foil radar detection. The stealthy B-2 also flies very well with no fuselage or tail, using the flying-wing concept pioneered by earlier Northrop aircraft.

The B-2 is a triumph of technology in many ways, able to leap halfway around the globe on a strategic mission with just two pilots, located side-by-side in the crew compartment bulge. If the Cold War had continued, the B-2's stealth qualities, four powerful turbofan engines and lethal bombload would have made it the spearhead of nuclear forces. In today's changing world, the B-2 is flexible enough to fly long-distance to a crisis zone with highly accurate conventional bombs.

The B-2 is also the most expensive warplane ever built, with a price tag of $2 billion, so only 20 of these remarkable bombers will be produced.

B-2A SPIRIT

Developed under great secrecy and at huge expense, the B-2 Spirit is the world's most advanced strategic bomber.

The B-2 has an advanced two-man cockpit with provision for a third crew member/observer. High technology has done away with the flight engineer and bombardier of earlier bombers.

The Hughes AN/APQ-181 attack radar has phased array transmitters buried in the fuselage, so there is no need for a dish aerial and its bulbous radome.

The B-2 is powered by four General Electric F118 non-afterburning turbofans. They are buried deep within the aircraft, keeping the highly radar-reflective fan blades away from enemy radar transmissions.

The engines exhaust through 'V'-shaped outlets set back and above the trailing edges to hide these heat sources from the ground.

Extensive use is made of graphite/epoxy materials in the aircraft's structure. These are not good reflectors of radar energy, and contribute to the bomber's stealthiness.

The B-2's undercarriage has been adapted from a commercial design, used on the Boeing 757 and 767 airliners.

Vapour trails are the enemy of any aircraft claiming to be stealthy. Chloro-fluorosulphonic acid is injected into the exhaust gases of the B-2 to inhibit the formation of contrails at high altitude.

The 33° sweep of the leading edge and the 'W' configuration of the trailing edge are designed to trap and deflect radar energy away from a hostile transmitter.

Above: In common with most stealth aircraft, the B-2 carries minimal markings: a serial number on the fuselage and a low-visibility star-and-bar on the wing.

Below: Control of an aircraft without a vertical stabiliser is difficult, and led to the downfall of earlier flying-wing projects. The B-2 gets around the problem by using the kind of modern computer control that was unavailable to the pioneers of tail-less flight.

Ancestry of the 'Flying Wing'

■ **PIONEERS OF WINGLESS FLIGHT:** Among the earliest pioneers were the German Horten brothers, whose radical Ho IX fighter evolved from pre-war gliders and which promised superb performance in 1945.

■ **SCALE MODELS:** American Jack Northrop had always been interested in flying wings, and his first designs for the US Air Force were scale designs exploring the potential of the configuration as a long-range bomber.

■ **AHEAD OF ITS TIME:** Northrop developed a full-size jet bomber to compete with the more conventional B-52, but control technology of the day meant that the resulting YB-49 of 1947 was not easy to handle in some conditions.

■ **LIFTING BODIES:** Between the demise of the XB-49 and the launch of the B-2, Northrop was involved in lifting bodies such as the X-24, shown here in 1969. These did away with wings, gaining lift from the shape of the fuselage.

B-2A Spirit

Type: two-seat long-range strategic bomber

Powerplant: four 84.52-kN (19,017-lb-thrust) General Electric F118-GE-100 turbofan engines

Maximum speed: approx. 960 km/h (597 mph) above 12,200 m (40,000 ft)

Range: 12,225 km (7596 miles)

Service ceiling: over 16,920 m (53,440 ft)

Weights: empty 79,380 kg (175,995 lb); loaded 181,437 kg (400,000 lb)

Armament: normal strategic load of eight B61 or B83 nuclear bombs, or 16 stand-off nuclear missiles on rotary launcher in bomb-bay; conventional load of 80 Mk 82 227-kg (500-lb) bombs or up to 22,600 kg (50,000 lb) of other conventional weapons

Dimensions: span 52.43 m (172 ft)
length 21.03 m (69 ft)
height 5.18 m (17 ft)
wing area 196.00 m² (2100 sq ft)

COMBAT DATA

RANGE

B-2A SPIRIT 12,225 km (7596 miles)

Tu-160 'BLACKJACK' 14,000 km (8700 miles)

B-1B LANCER 12,000 km (7500 miles)

Unrefuelled range

Thanks to its large fuel capacity and highly efficient turbofan engines, the Northrop B-2 has a truly global range. Others can fly as far, but not with such a heavy warload or such economy. Airborne refuelling allows the B-2 to strike anywhere in the world from its home base.

WEAPONS

B-2A SPIRIT 22,600-kg (50,000-lb) maximum weapons load

B-1B LANCER 60,000-kg (132,000-lb) maximum weapons load

Tu-160 'BLACKJACK' estimated 16,500-kg (36,000-lb) maximum weapons load

Although it is much smaller than the massive 'Blackjack', the B-2 can carry a much heavier load. The B-1B can carry far more, but a heavy warload strictly limits the Lancer's range.

SPEED

B-2A SPIRIT
Cruise: 750 km/h (466 mph)
Maximum: approx. 960 km/h (600 mph)

B-1B LANCER
Cruise: 960 km/h (600 mph)
Maximum: 1324 km/h (822 mph)

Tu-160 'BLACKJACK'
Cruise: 850 km/h (528 mph)
Maximum: 2000 km/h (1240 mph)

Both the B-1B and the Tu-160 are designed to make the last portion of an attack at supersonic speeds, to give the maximum chance of survival. The B-2's stealthiness means that it does not need this highly expensive and fuel-hungry capability.

PIASECKI

HUP RETRIEVER

- Single-engined, twin-rotor ● 'Planeguard' ● Utility helicopter

One of the first helicopters to serve aboard US Navy warships, the HUP Retriever was one of several tandem, twin-rotor helicopters designed by rotary-wing pioneer Frank Piasecki in the late 1940s and 1950s. Intended primarily for shore duty as a cargo hauler (in which role it also flew with the US Army), it is best remembered for its naval service and for rescuing many pilots who might otherwise have been lost at sea.

▲ Developed from the two XHJP-1 prototypes (Piasecki's Model PV-14), the HUP Retrievers earned their keep as 'planeguards' and rescue craft aboard the US Navy's carriers.

PIASECKI HUP RETRIEVER

▼ Winched aboard the Mule
In the rescue role the Retriever made use of a winch and an access hatch behind the cockpit.

▲ Army Mule for casualty evacuation
The H-25A Army Mule was derived from the HUP-2. It had hydraulically-boosted controls, a stronger floor and enlarged cargo doors for stretcher cases.

▲ Outrigger fins on the HUP-1
After trials with two XHJP-1s, the US Navy ordered 23 production HUP-1s, distinguished from later variants by their tail fins. Deliveries began in 1949.

▼ Army workhorse
The initial batch of 50 US Army H-25s also fulfilled a secondary utility transport role.

In Canadian colours with VH-21 ▶
The Royal Canadian Navy received three HUP-3s from the US Navy which were operated by squadron VH-21. These were among 50 ex-US Army H-25As transferred as surplus to the Navy.

FACTS AND FIGURES

▼ The Piasecki Aircraft Corp. of Morton, Pennsylvania, evolved into today's Boeing Helicopter Company.

▼ The first US Navy HUPs were delivered to squadron HU-2 in February 1951.

▼ A Retriever could hover at 15 m (50 ft) and hoist a downed airman weighing 75 kg (165 lb).

▼ After being transferred to reserve units, some HUPS were retained as rescue aircraft with an orange colour scheme.

▼ PV-18 production totalled 339, including 70 H-25s for the US Army.

▼ The Army's H-25s were procured by the USAF on the Army's behalf.

Twin-rotor US Navy rescuer

Designed to meet a US Navy need for a shipboard utility helicopter, the Piasecki Model PV-18, known in naval parlance as the HUP Retriever, first flew in 1948 and entered service three years later. Primitive by today's standards, the HUP was the finest helicopter in its class in the 1950s. It also served in the US Army as the H-25 Army Mule.

With a single engine driving twin rotors and with its functional but odd-looking tail-dragger' landing gear, the HUP

was the kind of helicopter for which the Navy had been looking. The Navy's HUP lacked the hydraulically boosted controls and strengthened cargo floor of the H-25, and was considered by some to be underpowered.

Though its primary mission was transport, the HUP also performed anti-submarine duties. Aboard aircraft-carriers, an important role was as 'planeguard', rescuing pilots if their aircraft was ditched on take-off or landing.

Above: Several US Navy HUP-2s had dunking sonar fitted for anti-submarine operations and were designated HUP-2S.

HUP-2 RETRIEVER

This HUP-2 carries the markings of Navy Utility Helicopter Squadron 1. This unit operated search-and-rescue HUPs from various aircraft-carriers during the Korean War.

Below: Retrievers also served with the Marine Corps in transport and rescue roles from shore bases. The HUP was redesignated UH-25 in 1962.

The twin rotor layout was a trademark of Frank N. Piasecki's helicopter designs. This layout was perpetuated in later Vertol and Boeing-Vertol designs like the CH-46 Sea Knight and CH-47 Chinook.

Two three-bladed rotors lifted the HUP into the air. On the HUP-2 an auto-pilot served as the primary controller. This improved hover performance and allowed the removal of the tail fins fitted to the HUP-1.

A large loading door (larger still in the H-25A Army variant) and ample cabin dimensions allowed the carriage of a variety of cargoes.

'Midnight blue' was the name given to this dark shade which adorned almost all US Navy aircraft in the 1950s.

Unlike later twin-rotor designs, the HUP was a single-engined machine. A 410-kW (550-hp) Continental R-975-46 radial mounted in the rear fuselage provided the power.

The HUP had capacity for a crew of two and either four passengers or three stretcher cases. An internally operated rescue hatch next to the pilot's seat was large enough to accommodate a loaded stretcher. A hydraulic hoist above the hatch was used to lift survivors aboard while hovering.

HUP-3 Retriever

Type: single-engined, twin-rotor utility, cargo and rescue helicopter

Powerplant: one 410-kW (550-hp) Continental R-975-46A radial engine

Maximum speed: 169 km/h (105 mph)

Maximum range: 547 km (340 miles)

Service ceiling: 3050 m (10,000 ft)

Weights: empty 1782 kg (3920 lb); maximum take-off 2767 kg (6087 lb)

Accommodation: pilot, co-pilot and up to five passengers or three hospital stretchers with attendant

Dimensions: main rotor diameter 10.67 m (35 ft)
fuselage length 17.35 m (56 ft 10 in)
height 3.81 m (12 ft 6 in)
rotor disc area 178.76 m² (1923 sq ft)

ACTION DATA

MAXIMUM SPEED

A maximum speed around 160 km/h (100 mph) was typical of these large helicopters. All were naval designs of American origin, the Dragonfly being a licence-built Westland version for the Royal Navy, fitted with a British engine.

HUP-2 RETRIEVER	169 km/h (105 mph)
DRAGONFLY HR.Mk 3	166 km/h (103 mph)
HRS-2	163 km/h (101 mph)

CLIMB RATE

The Retriever, with its twin rotors, had a superior climb rate to the other single-rotor designs, though horsepower ratings were broadly similar. The HRS had a bigger engine but was considerably heavier.

HUP-2 RETRIEVER	366 m/min (1200 fpm)
DRAGONFLY HR.Mk 3	296 m/min (970 fpm)
HRS-2	213 m/min (700 fpm)

ACCOMMODATION

The Retriever and Dragonfly both had limited load-carrying capacity. Even the larger HRS-2 was soon found to be too small for the US Navy's needs and was replaced by the HSS Seabat.

HUP-2 RETRIEVER
2 crew + 4 passengers

DRAGONFLY HR.Mk 3
2 crew + 2 passengers

HRS-2
1 crew + 8 passengers

US Navy carrier 'planeguards'

■ **SIKORSKY HO4S:** This naval version of the Sikorsky S-55 was primarily an anti-submarine and observation type, entering service in 1950.

■ **SIKORSKY HSS SEABAT:** Delivered in 1955, the first Seabats replaced the HO4S, which was short on range and load-capacity.

■ **SIKORSKY SH-3 SEA KING:** Purchased in large numbers by the Navy, the SH-3 has served for more than 30 years from 1961.

■ **SIKORSKY SH-60F SEAHAWK:** The carrier-borne version of the SH-60B, the F-model has a less comprehensive ASW suite.

PIASECKI/VERTOL

H-21

- Transport helicopter ● USAF's first twin rotor ● Vietnam action

▲ Frank Piasecki's H-21/HRP made use of the designer's well-known tandem rotor layout, perpetuated in the later Vertol H-25/HUP, H-46 and H-47 designs.

Developed for the USAF from the HRP tandem-rotor designs, the H-21 made its mark with the US Army, which named its the Shawnee. After missing the Korean War by just a year, the twin-rotor H-21 Workhorse (its USAF name) entered service with Army aviation units in the 1950s and went to war briefly in Vietnam in the 1960s, the swansong of its career. A few examples served with foreign forces, mainly under the Military Assistance Program.

PHOTO FILE

PIASECKI/VERTOL H-21

▲ Export Workhorse
Under Military Assistance Program Canada received six H-21As.

▲ Rescue colours
When operated by the USAF Military Air Transport Service, the aircrew rescue version was known as the HH-21B.

▼ Shawnee in Vietnam
Operated by the 8th and 57th Transportation Companies, and armed with Browning machine guns, the CH-21C served for just two years.

▲ Gallic 'flying banana'
Delivered in 1957, French army H-21Cs saw service during the conflict in Algeria.

Border-to-border flight ▶
An Army H-21 Shawnee became the first helicopter to fly non-stop from the US west coast to the east coast. On the way it was refuelled by a de Havilland Canada U-1A Otter via a rudimentary hose system.

FACTS AND FIGURES

- A few examples of the civil Piasecki PD-22 (Vertol 44) served with New York Airlines and other carriers.

- Two H-21Cs were re-engined with turboshafts, as XH-21Ds.

- Foreign H-21 operators included West Germany, France and Canada.

- Four US aviators killed in an H-21 in July 1962 are recognised by some sources as the first American fatalities in Vietnam.

- The YH-21 prototype for this series made its maiden flight on 11 April 1952.

- A total of 334 of these helicopters was produced for the United States Army.

H-21B Workhorse

Type: troop/cargo tandem rotor transport helicopter

Powerplant: one 1063-kW (1425-hp) Wright R-1820-103 Cyclone radial piston engine

Maximum speed: 204 km/h (126 mph) at sea level

Cruising speed: 158 km/h (98 mph) at sea level

Range: 644 km (400 miles)

Ceiling: 2360 m (7700 ft)

Weights: empty 4060 kg (8932 lb), maximum take-off 6895 kg (15,170 lb)

Accommodation: pilot, co-pilot, crew chief, and (in Vietnam) two gunners for door-mounted 12.7-mm (.50-cal.) M2 or 7.62-mm (.30-cal.) M60 machine guns, plus 20 troops or 12 stretchers

Dimensions: main rotor diameter 13.41 m (44 ft)
fuselage length 16.00 m (52 ft 6 in)
height 4.80 m (15 ft 9 in)
rotor disc area 282.52 m² (3040 sq ft)

COMBAT DATA

STRETCHERS

As a tandem rotor design, the H-21 was a large helicopter compared to other designs of the period. Its fuselage provided a sizeable troop and stretcher capacity, especially useful in Army use.

H-21A WORKHORSE | 12
H-34A CHOCTAW | 8
H-19B CHICKASAW | 6

POWER

All three of these types used single radial piston engines, the Wright Cyclone in the H-21 having to power two main rotors. The Sikorsky H-34 and H-19 were conventional single main rotor designs, the former having the most powerful engine. Ultimately, turboshaft engines replaced radials in most helicopters, as they are lighter and more powerful than a piston engine of similar weight.

H-21A WORKHORSE | 932 kW (1425 hp)
H-34A CHOCTAW | 1138 kW (1525 hp)
H-19B CHICKASAW | 597 kW (800 hp)

MAXIMUM SPEED

The twin main rotors of the H-21 gave it a superior top speed to the smaller designs. Large transport helicopter speeds later peaked at around 250 km/h (in aircraft like the turboshaft-powered CH-47) as design limits were reached.

H-21A WORKHORSE | 211 km/h (126 mph)
H-34A CHOCTAW | 198 km/h (123 mph)
H-19B CHICKASAW | 180 km/h (112 mph)

Frank Piasecki's 'flying banana'

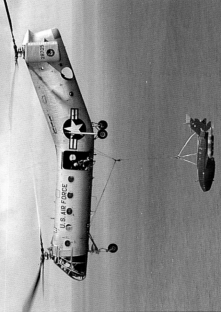

S eeing the H-21's potential, the US Army awarded Piasecki a production contract in 1952. H-21s had extensive armour and the ability to carry two external fuel tanks, and introduced a 2-tonne hook.

In 1955, by the time helicopter pioneer Frank Piasecki was forced out of the firm which bore his name (the company became Vertol, later Boeing-Vertol), the US Army was the biggest user of this tandem, twin-rotor helicopter. The H-21 was based on the US Navy's HRP-2, itself a

development of the fabric-covered HRP-1, Piasecki's first successful tandem rotor design. Over 400 H-21s were built for the Army, mostly of the H-21C variant. One of these made the first non-stop helicopter flight from one coast of the US to the other, refuelled aloft by a de Havilland U-1A Otter. H-21s arrived in Vietnam in December 1961, during the early days of the US build-up.

H-21s were exported under MAP, and a civil version, the Model 44, saw limited service with the Swedish navy.

Until replaced by the Sikorsky H-3, some USAF H-21Bs saw service as drone retrieval aircraft. Here a Ryan Firebee remotely piloted vehicle (RPV) has been picked up after a mission.

Model 44A

Vertol produced a small number of Model 44s, which originated as the Piasecki PD-22, a civil version of the Workhorse. Belgium's flag carrier SABENA operated a single leased example during the 1958 World Fair.

Customers for the primarily passenger-configured Model 44 civilian variant of the Workhorse included the French government (Model 44Bs) and the Swedish navy, which adapted its examples to perform the anti-submarine warfare role. The Model 44B had a 1.42-m³ (15 sq ft) mail and cargo compartment.

Each of the two three-bladed main rotors was driven from a single main engine mounted behind the main cabin: a 1063-kW (1425-hp) Wright Cyclone piston unit. Normal fuel capacity was 1136 litres (300 gallons).

Non-retractable tricycle landing gear was standard, but the Model 44/H-21 could also be equipped with inflatable pontoons, allowing operations from water.

Piasecki's Model 44 received its CAA Approved Type certificate in April 1957. It was intended for the Model 44 to be updated through the addition of two turboshaft engines instead of the single piston unit in order to increase performance.

A door was provided for the passengers at either end of the 6.10 x 1.73 x 1.68-m (20-ft 5-ft 6-in x 5-ft 6-in) cabin. The rear door had built-in passenger steps and a handrail. The Model 44B featured larger oval observation windows than the other civilian Vertol Workhorse models.

Model 44A utility versions could carry 19 civilians, 12 stretcher patients and two attendants, or a 2.5-tonne cargo sling. The 44B, shown here, was an airliner with 15 seats and a mail and cargo compartment. The Model 44C was an executive transport with a range of custom-built interiors.

Frank Piasecki's diverse designs

■ **MODEL PV-2:** Flown in April 1943, the single-seat, fabric-covered PV-2 was the second US-built helicopter flown publicly. In 1944 the Navy's HRP contract was awarded to Piasecki.

■ **MODEL 59/VZ-8:** Awarded a contract by the Army in 1957 to develop a 'flying jeep', Piasecki produced the Sky Car, powered by two piston or turbine engines driving ducted fans.

■ **MODEL 16H-1A PATHFINDER II:** A joint Army/Navy-funded programme to research compound helicopter designs led to the Pathfinder and Pathfinder II of the early-1960s.

■ **MODEL PV-15/H-16 TRANSPORTER:** At the time of its inception, the H-16 was the world's largest helicopter. Flown in 1953, it was judged unsuitable by the US Army.

PIPER
L-4 GRASSHOPPER

- Liaison role ● Artillery spotting and observation ● Military lightplane

T he Piper L-4 Grasshopper was an important aircraft for the infantryman. On the battlefield, the soldier wanted a quick, reliable way to guide artillery fire. The L-4 Grasshopper could take up position 100 to 200 m (328 to 656 ft) in front of troops, look down on the enemy and call in a devastating barrage of shellfire. Artillery spotting, however, was only one of the many military jobs assigned to the famous Grasshopper.

▲ Many Piper L-4 Grasshoppers and Cubs remain airworthy around the world as a testimony to the quality of Gilbert Taylor's original design.

PIPER L-4 GRASSHOPPER

▲ Still flying
An L-4 wearing the black and white stripes added for identification when the Allies invaded Europe.

▲ Rosie the Rocketeer
Aircraft which are admired by their crews often acquire 'nose-art'. This L-4 carries rocket tubes strapped to the wing struts.

▲ Cabin glazing
Compared with the basic civilian L-4 Cub, the Grasshopper provided its crew with brilliant all-round visibility.

▼ High-flying Grasshopper
Over the battlefield, Grasshopper pilots would keep low, using natural cover to hide the aircraft – especially from groundfire. L-4s operated in many theatres.

▲ Muddy tyres
With large 'balloon-type' tyres, the L-4 could operate from the roughest of muddy fields.

FACTS AND FIGURES

▶ General Douglas MacArthur was taken for several flights in an Australian military L-4 in the Philippines.

▶ Between 3 February 1942 and 22 August 1945, 5424 Piper L-4s were built.

▶ Grasshoppers were sometimes known by the nickname 'L-Birds'.

▶ A typical US Army combat division operated six to eight Piper L-4 Grasshoppers for spotting duties.

▶ The US Marine Corps operated L-4s in the New Britain campaign in the Pacific.

▶ After World War II many L-4s were used for primary training.

Piper's amazing Grasshopper

In 1930 C. Gilbert Taylor designed the E-2 Taylor Cub. William L. Piper took over production of the aircraft as the J-3C-65 Cub in 1935, and the civil J-3 Cub became a popular sporting aircraft in the years just before World War II.

Four machines were acquired by the US Army Air Corps in 1941 for evaluation in the role of artillery spotting and front-line liaison. Having more than satisfied the army, the Cub became the military Grasshopper by the expedient

of cutting away fabric and replacing it by transparent Pyralyn to give the back-seat observer the best possible visibility.

The Cub was a peppy, energetic aircraft which was propelled through the sky by ordinary automobile gasoline. Because it was small and lightweight, it could operate near the front lines where its spotting capabilities were most needed. And because it was so much slower than Luftwaffe fighters, the aircraft was also

relatively immune to fighter attack, although groundfire was a constant threat.

The L-4 Grasshopper was produced in greater numbers than any other liaison aircraft of World War II. More advanced models were used by the military for spotting and training duties in the post-war years and were not retired until the late 1950s.

Left: Many air forces used the Grasshopper after the war. With many restored aircraft flying, most enthusiasts recognise the classic high-wing design.

Above: Showing the elastic chord shock absorbers on the main undercarriage and wing-strut arrangement to advantage, this L-4 wears typical US Army Air Corps markings.

L-4 Grasshopper

Type: two-seat liaison and observation aircraft

Powerplant: one 48-kW (64-hp) Continental O-170-3 flat-four piston engine

Maximum speed: 148 km/h (92 mph); cruising speed 120 km/h (75 mph)

Range: 416 km (258 miles)

Service ceiling: 2835 m (9301 ft)

Accommodation: pilot and observer in tandem in two-seat cockpit; dual controls standard, observer on swivelling seat

Weights: empty 331 kg (730 lb); maximum take-off 533 kg (1175 lb)

Dimensions:
span 10.73 m (35 ft 2 in)
length 6.78 m (22 ft 1 in)
height 2.03 m (6 ft 8 in)
wing area 16.54 m² (178 sq ft)

COMBAT DATA

MAXIMUM CRUISING SPEED

Although speed is not an important factor for the artillery spotting role, it may be useful for liaison tasks and for some secondary duties such as casualty evacuation.

L-4 GRASSHOPPER	120 km/h (75 mph)
AUSTER Mk V	180 km/h (112 mph)
Fi 156C STORCH	130 km/h (81 mph)

ENGINE POWER

Small and lightweight, the Grasshopper had little need for extra power. More power would have required a heavier engine, and would have decreased range and only slightly improved performance.

L-4 GRASSHOPPER	**AUSTER Mk V**	**Fi 156C STORCH**
48 kW (64 hp)	97 kW (130 hp)	179 kW (240 hp)

RANGE

Being a much larger aircraft the Storch carried more fuel and therefore had a longer range. Large aircraft present large targets, however, and the L-4 boasted good range for its compact size.

L-4 GRASSHOPPER	**AUSTER Mk V**	**Fi 156C STORCH**
416 km (258 miles)	402 km (250 miles)	467 km (290 miles)

L-4 GRASSHOPPER

Finished in the olive-drab over neutral grey camouflage that was typical of many US Army Air Corps and Air Force types, this aircraft also carries D-Day invasion stripes.

Cables or struts braced the tailplanes and wings. These allowed the necessary strength to be built in without resorting to a heavy structure. Rough-field operations exert a lot of stress on airframes.

All Allied aircraft operating during and after D-Day were painted with distinctive stripes to avoid confusion with Luftwaffe aircraft. In the event, very few Luftwaffe machines operated over the beaches of Normandy.

For solo flights the pilot sat in the rear seat, which had a full set of controls but was normally used by the observer. The Grasshopper was also equipped with a map table and the radio fit varied between models.

Structurally, the L-4 was quite simple and had a fabric-covered wooden framework. The wing had no slats or flaps, but was equipped with large, long-span ailerons. Internally the wing was braced with wire.

Mounted semi-exposed, the Continental flat-four engine powered the majority of more than 5000 L-4s delivered to the Army. Several J-4 Cubs owned by civilians were pressed into service.

US Army Air Corps observation aircraft

■ **TAYLORCRAFT L-2 GRASSHOPPER:** Designed by the man who started the Piper L-4 line, 1866 Taylorcraft L-2s were built.

■ **AERONCA L-3 GRASSHOPPER:** Using more metal in its structure than the L-4, at least 1475 L-3s were manufactured.

■ **STINSON L-5 SENTINEL:** L-5s served mostly in the Pacific and later in Korea. A total of 3590 were built for the army.

■ **INTERSTATE L-6 GRASSHOPPER:** Outward angled windows on the 250 L-6s built allowed an excellent downwards view.

REPUBLIC
P-47 THUNDERBOLT (RAZORBACK)

● Fighter-bomber ● Heavy and powerful ● European service debut

Readily identified by their 'razorbacks' and framed canopies, the early versions of the immortal P-47 Thunderbolt laid the foundations for what was to become an unrivalled fast and immensely robust aircraft. 'Razorback' Thunderbolts were built by Republic and Curtiss-Wright and had a dominant role in the USAAF from 1943, firstly as a fighter, then as a fighter-bomber making sweeps over occupied Europe.

▶ If the 'razorback' early P-47s had a weakness it was the 20° blindspot behind the cockpit. This was rectified in the late-production P-47Ds and other 'bubble'-canopied variants.

▼ **RAF Thunderbolt Mk I**
In the RAF the P-47B (pictured below) and the P-47D were known as the Thunderbolt Mk I and Mk II, respectively. Most were deployed in the Far East.

▲ **First 'Juggernauts' in combat**
These P-47Bs were among the first delivered to a fighting unit, the 56th Fighter Group. They arrived in England in late 1942 to prove the type in combat.

▼ **Carrier-borne in the Pacific**
USAAF P-47s were delivered from Hawaii to the Marianas aboard USS Manila Bay in June 1944.

▲ **Built at three factories**
Thunderbolts were produced by Republic at factories in Evansville, Indiana, and Long Island, New York, and by Curtiss-Wright in Buffalo, New York.

Preserved 'warbird' example ▶
A number of 'razorback' P-47s, including this P-47G, have been restored to airworthy condition.

FACTS AND FIGURES

▶ Like the P-51 Mustang, the P-47 was conceived, tested and put into service entirely during the war years.

▶ The first P-47 was accepted by the USAAF on 21 December 1941.

▶ 'Razorback' P-47Ds were also supplied to the air forces of France and the USSR.

▶ The 56th Fighter Group, the first unit to take the P-47 into combat, was the top-scoring US fighter group with 674½ kills.

▶ A fully-loaded P-47D weighed more than 2.5 times as much as a Bf 109.

▶ The P-47's massive four-bladed propeller had a diameter of 3.76 m (12 ft 4 in).

Brute force of the 'Juggernaut'

Thunderbolts reached England just before Christmas 1942. The first operational sweep over Europe was made by the 4th Fighter Group on 10 March 1943 and was the beginning of an incredible success story.

The first known combat occurred on 15 April 1943 when the 4th Group came up against Focke-Wulf Fw 190s. P-47 pilot Major Donald Blakeslee intercepted a flight of three and was able to shoot one down over Ostend, Belgium, to claim the Thunderbolt's first aerial victory.

'Razorback' P-47s were flown by many of the best-known American air aces, including Francis Gabreski, Robert Johnson and 'Bud' Mahurin.

Unable to escort bombers far into Europe (until later versions were fitted with external fuel tanks), the P-47 gained a greater reputation as a fighter-bomber, sharing the role of train- and tank-buster with the British Typhoon. Like the Typhoon, P-47s were fitted with bombs and rockets.

The first version to enter service was the P-47B, of which 171 were built. This was followed

by the C model (602 built), with a lengthened fuselage and provision for a 227-kg (500-lb) bomb or drop-tank. The most widely produced version was the P-47D, which had increased power and bombload.

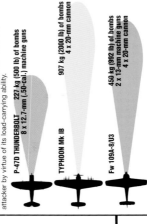

Below: This aircraft was one of two TP-47G trainers converted from Curtiss-Wright-built P-47Gs. The front seat displaced a fuel tank.

The 'razorback' of the early Thunderbolts was a feature of the earlier Kartveli designs, the Seversky P-35 and the Republic P-43 Lancer.

Above: On 4 August 1944, this XP-47J, powered by a 1566-kW (2100-hp) R-2800-57 engine, reached a record speed of 811 km/h (504 mph).

P-47D THUNDERBOLT

42-22490 'Beetle' was serving with the 358th Fighter Squadron, 355th Fighter Group on escort and attack missions when it force-landed at Caen, France, on 7 November 1943. It was soon flown by the Luftwaffe from their Rechlin test centre.

P-47Bs entered service in Europe in early-1943 in the bomber escort role. Early experience revealed an inadequate climb rate and poor manoeuvrability, but dive performance was good. Its ability to survive battle damage became legendary.

The R-2800 engine's turbocharger was positioned in the rear fuselage, fed by a duct from below the engine. Here it could be adequately cooled and allowed a more aerodynamic engine cowling arrangement. A waste gate either expelled the hot air to the atmosphere or diverted it to the turbo.

The P-47 was originally conceived as a lightweight fighter, but it was redesigned as the XP-47B to improve top speed. The prototype first flew on 6 May 1941. Weighing in at 6059 kg (13,358 lb), it was the heaviest single-seat fighter adopted by the USAAF.

Based on Alexander Kartveli's earlier P-44 design, the P-47 was built around one of the most powerful engines then available, the Pratt & Whitney R-2800 18-cylinder, two-row radial. The variant used in the P-47D employed water injection to boost performance at altitude.

Pre-war Seversky/Republic aircraft

■ **SEV-3:** This three-seat, twin-float aircraft first flew in June 1933. Seversky's first aircraft, the SEV-3M-WW version, was built for Colombia.

■ **BT-8:** This two-seat basic trainer for the US Army Air Corps was powered by a 335-kW Pratt & Whitney Twin Wasp. Thirty were built.

■ **P-35:** Flown in 1935, this fighter, with retractable landing gear, was built in limited numbers for the USAAC. Sweden received 60.

■ **P-43 LANCER:** By the time the P-43 appeared, Seversky had become Republic. This 580 km/h (360 mph) fighter was the basis for the P-47.

P-47B Thunderbolt

Type: single-seat fighter and fighter-bomber

Powerplant: one 1491-kW (2000-hp) Pratt & Whitney R-2800-21 Double Wasp 18-cylinder radial engine

Maximum speed: 690 km/h (429 mph) at 8473 m (27,800 ft)

Initial climb rate: 6.7 minutes to 4572 m (15,000 ft)

Range: 885 km (550 miles)

Service ceiling: 12,800 m (41,995 ft)

Weights: empty 4239 kg (9345 lb); loaded 6059 kg (13,358 lb)

Armament: eight 12.7-mm (.50-cal.) Browning M2 machine guns with 500 rounds per gun

Dimensions:
span	12.62 m (41 ft 5 in)
length	10.93 m (35 ft 10 in)
height	4.47 m (14 ft 8 in)
wing area	27.87 m² (300 sq ft)

COMBAT DATA

MAXIMUM SPEED

The P-47 proved to be one of the fastest fighters of the war, especially in its later versions. The early P-47D had an impressive dive speed. However, the marginally slower Fw 190 was smaller and nimbler than the other heavier types.

P-47D THUNDERBOLT	697 km/h (433 mph)
TYPHOON Mk IB	652 km/h (405 mph)
Fw 109A-8/U3	657 km/h (408 mph)

ARMAMENT

The earliest 'razorback' Thunderbolts were unable to carry a large bombload; this was rectified in later models. The Typhoon, like the P-47, had started life as a fighter and became a versatile ground-attacker by virtue of its load-carrying ability.

P-47D THUNDERBOLT 8 x 12.7-mm (.50-cal.) machine guns	227 kg (500 lb) of bombs
TYPHOON Mk IB 4 x 20-mm cannon	907 kg (2000 lb) of bombs
Fw 109A-8/U3 2 x 13-mm machine guns 4 x 20-mm cannon	450 kg (992 lb) of bombs

ENGINE POWER

Early 'razorback' P-47Ds were fitted with a 1491-kW R-2800 engine which left them short of power compared to similar types. The Typhoon's Sabre was an immensely powerful but unreliable engine, while the Fw 190's BMW 801 was a proven design.

P-47D THUNDERBOLT 1491 kW (2000 hp)	**TYPHOON Mk IB** 1626 kW (2180 hp)	**Fw 109A-8/U3** 1567 kW (2100 hp)

REPUBLIC

P-47D/M/N THUNDERBOLT

- Tactical fighter-bomber ● Long-range escort ● Train-buster

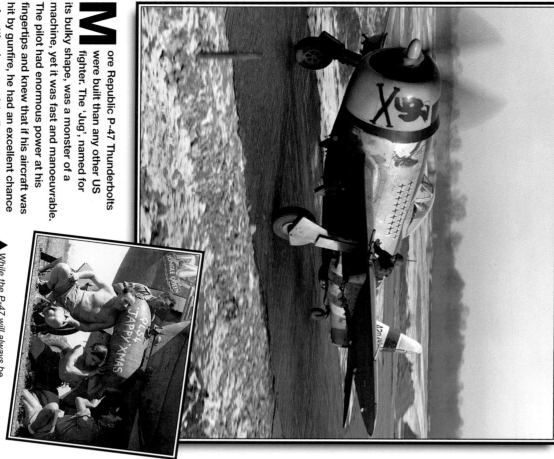

More Republic P-47 Thunderbolts were built than any other US fighter. The 'Jug', named for its bulky shape, was a monster of a machine, yet it was fast and manoeuvrable. The pilot had enormous power at his fingertips and knew that if his aircraft was hit by gunfire, he had an excellent chance of getting home safely. From the early XP-47B to the final P-47N, the 'T-bolt' was a real winner.

▶ While the P-47 will always be remembered as an escort fighter, the beefy warplane was perhaps even more effective as a fighter-bomber.

REPUBLIC P-47D/M/N THUNDERBOLT

▶ **Pacific island-hopper**
Two Thunderbolts power into the air from a temporary coral air strip on a Pacific island. P-47s were employed in every theatre of the war, flying air-to-air and air-to-ground missions.

Rocket launcher ▶
Tube-launched rockets were a fearsome addition to the Thunderbolt's armoury. The fighters decimated German armour in France in 1944 using this weapon, flying precision low-level attack missions.

▶ **Air superiority**
The P-47N was the ultimate Thunderbolt. It had an immensely powerful engine which made it the fastest piston-engined fighter in the world, and had increased fuel capacity to enable it to accompany B-29 bombers over the Pacific.

▼ **Crash and burn**
Thunderbolts were famed for their enormous strength and ability to survive damage, but this aircraft did not fly again after crash-landing.

▶ **French dive-bomber**
France was one of many countries that used the P-47 into the 1950s. The aircraft were used as dive-bombers in French Indochina, often dropping napalm tanks.

FACTS AND FIGURES

▶ The first Thunderbolt was the XP-47B, which flew on 6 May 1941.

▶ According to designer Alexander Kartveli, the layout of the P-47 was drawn on the back of an envelope at a meeting in 1940.

▶ 15,683 Thunderbolts were built between 1940 and 1945, with more 'D' models than any other aircraft sub-type in history.

▶ With a fully loaded weight of 9390 kg (20,701 lb), a late-model P-47N was heavier than a bombed-up Dornier Do 17 bomber.

▶ On 5 August 1944, a specially prepared Thunderbolt attained a speed of 811 km/h (504 mph), a record for World War II fighters.

▶ 'Jugs' flew over 500,000 combat sorties between March 1943 and August 1945.

PROFILE

Biggest, fastest and meanest

Never beautiful like the Spitfire, not as agile as the Bf 109, nor as long-legged as the P-51 Mustang, the big Republic P-47 Thunderbolt nevertheless was one of the most successful and best-loved fighters of all time. With its huge R-2800 engine driving a colossal 3.71-m (12-ft) propeller, the Thunderbolt was well suited to long-distance escort operations. With its ability to haul bombs and absorb punishment, it was equally well suited to ground attack.

The P-47 is remembered for ranging over European skies, where aces like those of Colonel Hubert 'Hub' Zemke's 56th Fighter Group valiantly fought the Luftwaffe. But the 'Jug' was widely used elsewhere. Among

Allied forces during World War II, Thunderbolts were flown by the Brazilian, British, French, Mexican and Russian pilots. The long-range P-47N fought in the Pacific, where it was a potent weapon against the Japanese. Another service variant was the 'hot-rod' P-47M, which was quickly produced in the summer of 1944 to counter the V-1 flying bombs.

P-47D THUNDERBOLT

This 'D' model P-47 was flown by the 527th Fighter Squadron, 86th Fighter Group, serving in North Africa, Sicily and Italy in the close-support role.

The P-47 was an excellent fighter, but gained its legendary reputation flying hard-hitting ground-attack missions.

Thunderbolts were fitted with eight '50-calibre machine guns. Although lightly-gunned by British or German standards, they proved highly effective.

The P-47's paddle-bladed propeller gave it an exceptional climb rate.

Drop-tanks greatly increased the P-47's already impressive range.

The huge fuselage of the P-47 was the cause of many jokes when the fighter entered service. A fully loaded 'Jug' was about three times heavier than an early Spitfire.

Early P-47s were known as 'Razorbacks' to pilots. Cutting down the rear fuselage and fitting a bubble canopy greatly improved rear views.

Tactical support missions were usually flown with an underwing armament of a pair of 500-kg (1100-lb) bombs or eight rockets.

The massive R-2800 engine was the most powerful fitted to a single-engine fighter in the war. With turbocharging, late variants delivered 2090 kW (2535 hp). An experimental P-47 touched 800 km/h (497 mph) in 1946, thanks to the power of this engine.

All-the-way bomber escort

The P-47 Thunderbolt and the P-51 Mustang changed the war in the air. American bombers could now attack anywhere in the Reich, secure in the knowledge that they were being escorted all the way.

TEAMWORK DEFENCE: The P-47 originally lacked the range to go all the way to Berlin with the bombers. It was used to protect the B-17s and B-24s on the outward and homeward legs of the flight, handing over responsibility to the long-range P-51 for the central portion of the mission.

1. 8th Air Force bombers form up over the English coast
2. P-47 Thunderbolts provide escort to the German border
3. P-47s are relieved by P-51 Mustangs
4. Mustangs escort the bombers all the way to the target and back
5. Fresh P-47s escort the bombers home

TARGET: BERLIN

P-47D Thunderbolt

Type: single-seat fighter and fighter-bomber

Powerplant: one 1715-kW (2535-hp) Pratt & Whitney R-2800-59 Double Wasp 18-cylinder radial engine

Maximum speed: 697 km/h (430 mph)

Range: 3000 km (1860 miles) with drop-tanks

Service ceiling: 13,000 m (42,000 ft)

Weight: empty 4853 kg (10,660 lb); loaded 7938 kg (17,500 lb); later versions: loaded 9390 kg (20,700 lb)

Armament: eight 12.7-mm (.50-cal.) Browning M2 machine guns with 267 to 500 rounds plus provision for maximum external load of 1134 kg (2500 lb) including bombs, napalm or eight rockets

Dimensions: span 12.42 m (40 ft 9 in)
length 11.02 m (36 ft 2 in)
height 4.30 m (14 ft 2 in)
wing area 27.87 m² (300 sq ft)

COMBAT DATA

MAXIMUM SPEED

Bf 109G	690 km/h (428 mph)
P-47D THUNDERBOLT	697 km/h (430 mph)
Ki-84 'FRANK'	624 km/h (388 mph)

The P-47D was introduced in 1943, and immediately proved itself at least as fast as anything else in the sky in Europe, until the advent of the powered Me 163 Komet rocket in 1944. It had considerably greater performance than the best of its Pacific opposition, although Japanese aircraft like the Nakajima Ki-84 'Frank' were much more agile.

RANGE

P-47D THUNDERBOLT	3000 km (1860 miles)
Bf 109G	700 km (435 miles)
Ki-84 'FRANK'	2900 km (1800 miles)

Nothing could be more striking than the difference between fighters intended for a close-range European war, such as the Bf 109, and those like the P-47 and the Ki-84, whose designers had the vast operational distances of the Pacific in mind. It was the Thunderbolt's range which made it such a capable escort fighter.

SERVICE CEILING

P-47D THUNDERBOLT	13,000 m (42,000 ft)
Bf 109G	11,600 m (38,000 ft)
Ki-84 'FRANK'	10,500 m (34,400 ft)

American bombers were designed to attack from high altitude, so American fighters had to be equally capable at great heights. The P-47's immensely powerful Double Wasp engine pulled the 'T-bolt' higher than most of its rivals. The Messerschmitt was also good near its slightly lower altitude limits, but Japanese fighters simply could not compete.

REPUBLIC

F-84 THUNDERJET

- Ground attack ● Straight wings ● Korean War veteran

W hen the first F-84 Thunderjets reached Korea in December 1950, the USAF found itself with a fighter not quite ideal for air-to-air action but unmatched as a bomber and ground-attack platform. In a sense, the F-84 Thunderjet always played second fiddle; it was developed as 'insurance' early in the jet age and it remained in widespread service across Europe long after newer, faster jets stole the headlines.

▲ Heading to the Korean war zone aboard a US Navy aircraft-carrier, Thunderjets and their pilots wait out the long cruise before their aircraft can be unloaded at the docks in Japan.

REPUBLIC F-84 THUNDERJET

▼ No runway required
Because runways are so vulnerable, some F-84s were fitted with a solid-fuel booster rocket, enabling them to be launched from the back of a lorry.

▲ The jet age
The XP-84 was rolled out in December 1945. Its clean lines were possible because the airframe was designed around an axial-flow engine.

▼ Rocket attack
This aircraft fires off a full load of ground-attack rockets on a practice range. The technique was used widely during the Korean War.

Star performers ▼
The 'Thunderbirds', the US Air Force's aerobatic team, flew F-84Gs from its inception in 1953 until the type was phased out in favour of swept-wing F-84Fs in 1955. Pilots praised the excellent handling of Republic's Thunderjet.

Tunnel vision ▶
The proposed XF-103 interceptor was fitted with a periscope, and the pilot flew the aircraft by looking through a sight.

FACTS AND FIGURES

▶ The F-84 was the first new American fighter to fly after the end of World War II in 1945.

▶ The first flight was made on 28 February 1946 at Edwards AFB in California.

▶ A record speed of 983 km/h (609 mph) was achieved on 6 September 1946.

▶ Thunderjets entered USAF service during the summer of 1947, and were initially known as P-84Bs; 'P' stood for pursuit.

▶ The F-84's first combat mission in the Korean War was on 6 December 1950.

▶ F-84s destroyed 105 MiG-15, mainly during ground-attack operations.

F-84E Thunderjet

Type: single-seat jet fighter-bomber

Powerplant: one 22.2-kN (5000-lb-thrust) Allison J35-A-17 turbojet

Maximum speed: 987 km/h (612 mph)

Initial climb rate: 1847 m/min (6060 fpm)

Range: 3138 km (1945 miles)

Service ceiling: 13,173 m (43,200 ft)

Weights: empty 4629 kg (10,183 lb); maximum take-off 10,189 kg (22,416 lb)

Armament: six 12.7-mm (.50-cal.) machine guns; plus up to 2041 kg (5000 lb) of bombs, or 32 HVAR rockets

Dimensions:
span	11.09 m (36 ft 4 in)
length	11.76 m (38 ft 7 in)
height	3.91 m (12 ft 9 in)
wing area	24.15 m² (260 sq ft)

COMBAT DATA

MAXIMUM SPEED

Though powered by an improved engine, the Thunderjet's maximum speed was limited by the type's straight-winged design. The Russians held the lead in fighter design with their MiG-15 'Fagot', aircraft which came as an unpleasant surprise to the USAF in Korea.

F-84E THUNDERJET	987 km/h (612 mph)
F-80C SHOOTING STAR	956 km/h (593 mph)
MiG-15 'FAGOT'	1073 km/h (665 mph)

CLIMB RATE

With its ability to out-climb the Thunderjet, the MiG-15 was able to out-fight the F-84 whenever a dogfight occurred. Because of this, the F-84 was restricted to ground attack duties for which an escort of fighters could be provided.

MiG-15 'FAGOT'	3500 m/min (11,480 fpm)
F-80C SHOOTING STAR	2094 m/min (6870 fpm)
F-84E THUNDERJET	1847 m/min (6060 fpm)

THRUST

Early jet engines were often limited in their power output, and the F-84E Thunderjet offered low performance compared to its contemporaries. The earlier F-80C Shooting Star had increased thrust but was unable to perform the many attack duties of the F-84E Thunderjet.

F-84E THUNDERJET	22.24 kN (5000 lb thrust)
F-80C SHOOTING STAR	23.13 kN (5200 lb thrust)
MiG-15 'FAGOT'	26.48 kN (5960 lb thrust)

PROFILE

Straight-winged warrior

The straight-winged Republic F-84 Thunderjet was a solid and versatile jet fighter that poured from the factory production line at a time when aviation was being revolutionised by other jets with swept-back wings. The F-84 was nevertheless a tough and reliable combat aircraft that blazed a trail of glory in Korea and equipped NATO nations for many years.

Straight-winged F-84D, F-84E and F-84G fighters flew thousands of fighter-bomber missions in Korea and shot down a few MiG-15s. Others served as escort fighters with Strategic Air Command. The 'ultimate' straight-winged Thunderjet, the F-84G, was more powerful than earlier models and was equipped for in-flight refuelling from the beginning. These fighters were the first to deploy in large numbers across oceans, and established several records for mass ferry flights across the Atlantic and Pacific.

The basic design of the F-84 was so good that it led to a swept-winged version, which also served with distinction.

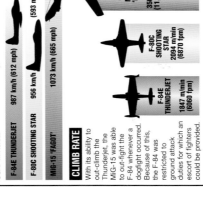

Faced with the need to bolster the defences of Europe, America supplied its NATO allies with 1936 examples of the Thunderjet. Here, an early Dutch model flies a low-level patrol.

Extensive modifications were incorporated into the Republic F-84 Thunderjet series. Most noticeable was the increase in the length of the fuselage.

The last of the straight-winged F-84s, the F-84G was the first single-seat fighter to have the capability of deploying nuclear weapons.

Later models of the F-84 Thunderjet were equipped with tip tanks that allowed the aircraft to operate at greater range with no loss in speed.

Being equipped with an Allison J35 engine increased the F-84G's top speed to 1000 km/h (620 mph). This allowed the aircraft to be used for fighter and attack missions.

The F-84 was the first fighter to be fitted with an in-flight refuelling receptacle, which was positioned within the starboard tip tank. Tanker aircraft were the KB-29Ps of SAC.

Having experienced developmental problems with the swept-winged F-84F, on the G model Republic re-introduced the straight wing to the USAF fighter fleet. Originally intended as purely an interim design, the F-84G was produced in the largest numbers and served with a number of NATO operators.

The cockpit was enclosed under a sliding canopy. Later models were fitted with bracing struts to increase the strength of the hood against bird strikes. This also considerably eased construction of the canopy.

F-84G THUNDERJET

Simple in design and layout, the Thunderjet offered the USAF an aircraft that could perform numerous operations during wartime. It earned the title of 'Champ of the Fighter-Bombers'.

Six M-3 machine guns were positioned above the intake in the nose. Loading of the guns was accomplished via an upward-hinging door.

Thunder over Europe

■ **DENMARK:** Denmark received its aircraft as part of the NATO build-up after World War II. The Thunderjet was the first Danish fighter to enter service after the war.

■ **PORTUGAL:** Operating well into the 1970s, the Thunderjet flew with numerous NATO allies including Belgium, Italy and Portugal. It was eventually replaced by the Mirage and F-104.

■ **TURKEY:** This brightly coloured example flew with the Turkish air force display team. Examples were operated in the ground-attack role and on fighter duties.

REPUBLIC

RF-84F THUNDERFLASH

- ● Tactical reconnaissance ● NATO stalwart ● Long service life

▶ A dedicated reconnaissance variant of the F-84F, the Thunderflash proved a popular and highly effective aircraft in service. Many enjoyed very long and active service careers.

E ntering service in 1953, the F-84F Thunderstreak soon proved itself to be highly suitable as a long-range fighter-bomber. A reconnaissance variant, the RF-84F Thunderflash, entered production at the same time. This variant differed in having a new nose containing cameras and intakes in the wing roots for the Wright J65 engine. It equipped several USAF units and became a mainstay of some other NATO air forces.

REPUBLIC

RF-84F THUNDERFLASH

PHOTO FILE

▶ **Extra fuel**
Thunderflashes were often seen carrying huge fuel tanks slung under the fuselage in an effort to extend endurance. This is a formation of Dutch aircraft.

▶ **Cold war reconnaissance**
Belgium was just one of many NATO countries to acquire RF-84Fs. These equipped the Bierset wing until the early 1970s when they were replaced by Mirage 5BRs.

▶ **External differences**
In company with a standard F-84F, a Thunderflash shows to good effect its redesigned nose and the small air intakes, located in the wing roots.

▶ **Last of the line**
During the 1970s the once numerous RF-84Fs began slowly to disappear from European skies. There were exceptions, however, the type soldiering on with Greece's Eliniki Aeroporia until retirement in 1991.

▶ **Stateside service**
USAF machines frequently displayed their capabilities during exercises such as 'Sagebrush'. This RF-84 is from the 18th TRW at Shaw AFB.

FACTS AND FIGURES

- ▶ Aircraft modified for parasite fighter experiments were known as RF-84Ks and featured special dorsal hooks.

- ▶ West Germany was the largest European operator, receiving 108 RF-84Fs.

- ▶ Wright J65 engines were built under licence in the US by General Motors.

- ▶ After service with regular USAF units, Thunderflashes were passed on to 11 Air National Guard Squadrons from 1956.

- ▶ A small number were handed over to Nationalist China during the mid-1950s.

- ▶ One aircraft was modified to become the XF-84H for high-speed propeller trials.

SPECIFICATION

RF-84F Thunderflash

Type: single-seat tactical reconnaissance aircraft

Powerplant: one 34.70-kN (7808 lb thrust) Wright J65 W-7 Sapphire turbojet

Maximum speed: 1093 km/h (679 mph)

Initial climb rate: 2438 m/min (133 fps)

Range: 1352 km (840 mph)

Service ceiling: 12006 m (39,389 ft)

Weights: loaded 6357 kg (14,017 lb)

Maximum fuel load: 6654 litres (1755 gallons)

Armament: four 12.7-mm machine guns

Dimensions:
span	10.23 m	(33 ft 6 in)
length	14.52 m	(47 ft 8 in)
height	4.57 m	(15 ft)
wing area	30.19 m²	(325 sq ft)

REPUBLIC'S FIRST JETS

RF-84B/C/D/E/G Thunderjet: The F-84 was the first Republic jet fighter and also the first USAF example to fly after World War II. It was built in five major variants and entered service in 1948. Most effective of all was the F-84G fighter bomber which equipped the USAF's Tactical and Strategic Air Commands until 1956. It saw extensive service during the Korean War of 1950-1953.

F-84F Thunderstreak: Success with the Thunderjet prompted Republic's design team to adopt several of its features for the succeeding aircraft. The first prototype took to the air in early 1951, powered by an imported Armstrong Siddeley Sapphire turbojet. It entered service with the USAF in large numbers and also equipped several NATO air arms, replacing straight-winged Thunderjets.

Streakin' reconnaissance

Despite being originally based on the straight-wing Thunderjet, the F-84F series had little in common with its predecessor. A dedicated photographic reconnaissance variant of the Thunderstreak was envisaged almost from the start.

Replacing the nose housing the a solid nose was expensive and specialised cameras. This resulted in a distinctive appearance and required the air intakes to be repositioned in the leading edge wing roots, which actually

improved performance (the new inlets being more efficient in directing air into the engine). More than 700 RF-84Fs were built and equipped five photographic reconnaissance squadrons and several other USAF units. In addition, 25 aircraft were modified for use in the FICON (Fighter Conveyor) project. This was basically a revival of the parasite fighter concept where the 'Flashes' were carried aloft by a Convair B-36 before being released at altitude. Many RF-84Fs equipped NATO countries

such as Belgium, Norway, the Netherlands and West Germany during the 1950s.

Surviving Thunderflashes were later passed down to Greece and Turkey.

Above: Although quicker than its straight-winged forebear, the Thunderflash was no lightweight and performance was adequate at best.

Right: Belgian aircraft later received a three-tone tactical camouflage, similar to the T.O. 1-14 adopted for USAF aircraft in Vietnam.

RF-84F THUNDERFLASH

This aircraft was one of 108 Thunderflashes delivered to West Germany. It served with Aufklarungsgeschwader 51 which re-equipped with the RF-104G Starfighter in 1964.

Long range made the F-84F an ideal candidate for the tactical reconnaissance role. Four cameras were fitted in the nose, two on each side. Access to the specialist equipment was made simple by a dorsal hatch located in front of the windscreen.

An extensive fuselage redesign, also resulted in a roomier cockpit. Considerable attention was paid to the ergonomic layout. The canopy was attached to twin hydraulic rams and hinged upwards.

Extensive use of duralumin was made on the airframe. The wings and tail surfaces incorporated a high proportion of pressed forgings, instead of the built-up components used on earlier F-84s.

A major asset of the swept-wing F-84 design, was the Wright J65 engine. This was little more than an American version of the Armstrong Siddeley Sapphire, used to power some marks of Hawker Hunter. The J65 found its way into many US types of the period, including the Douglas A4D Skyhawk and North American FJ-4 Fury.

Huge fuel tanks were often fitted below the wing roots in an effort to increase range, although these added considerable drag and weight.

Variations on a single theme

■ **F-84E:** This was the first of the redesigned Thunderjets and featured a longer fuselage and a more powerful J35 engine.

■ **F-84G:** Last of the straight-winged variants, the G model offered greater flexibility and was capable of in-flight refuelling.

■ **F-84F:** Although not quite in the same league as the F-86 and F-100, the 'Streak nevertheless excelled in the tactical fighter role.

■ **XF-84H:** Virtually a complete redesign, the two XF-84Hs were used to test propellers at supersonic speeds.

REPUBLIC

F-105 THUNDERCHIEF

● Fighter-bomber ● Heavy ordnance load ● MiG-killer

O
n a bombing mission to Hanoi, Republic F-105 Thunderchief pilots faced considerable danger. Surface-to-air missiles (SAMs), anti-aircraft guns and MiG fighters were all intent on downing the Thunderchief before it reached its target. Geography, however, gave the F-105 pilot one ally; a high ridge known as 'Thud Ridge' which extended from the Laotian border almost to Hanoi, along which targets could be approached in relative safety.

▲ During the arduous Rolling Thunder bombing campaign which lasted from 1965 to 1968, the US Air Force's F-105D Thunderchiefs bore the brunt of the missions. The aircraft were mainly employed in large strike packages, attacking strategic targets.

PHOTO FILE

REPUBLIC F-105 THUNDERCHIEF

▲ Early 'Thuds'
Some of the first F-105Ds to reach Vietnam retained their buzz-number below the cockpit. During 1965 a programme of camouflage application began.

▲ Into combat
All F-105D units were based in Thailand and undertook long transit flights to reach targets in North Vietnam.

▲ Air-to-air
Seen through the sight of a second F-105D, a Thunderchief is engaged by a MiG-17.

▲ Takhli Thunder
'RU'-tailcodes indicate that this aircraft was based at Takhli Royal Thai Air Force Base.

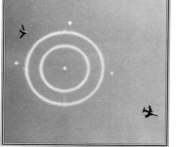

▲ Essential refuelling
Such was the length of F-105 missions that air-to-air refuelling was a feature of most sorties.

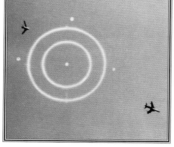

▲ Rolling Thunder
Seen at the height of Rolling Thunder operations during 1967, these fully camouflaged F-105s typify the many hundreds engaged in combat.

FACTS AND FIGURES

▼ During much of the Vietnam War, F-105 'fighters' bombed strategic targets while B-52 'bombers' flew tactical missions.

▼ Two F-105 pilots were awarded the Medal of Honor for their courage.

▼ F-105 pilots were required to complete 100 missions before leaving Vietnam.

▼ According to one analysis, an F-105 pilot would almost certainly be shot down by the time of his 68th sortie.

▼ F-105Ds shot down 25 MiGs, using cannon and AIM-9 Sidewinder missiles.

▼ The value of all aircraft lost in Vietnam was estimated at US$3,129,948,000.

PROFILE

Fighting 'Thuds' over Vietnam

Almost one-third of all Republic F-105 Thunderchiefs came to the end of their lives in the fiercely defended skies over North Vietnam, with a total of 397 being lost during the conflict. It was hostile terrain, except for the jagged, 100-km (62-mile) ridge line which aircrews called 'Thud Ridge' after the nickname of their F-105s.

An F-105, or 'Thud' heading north from Thailand with a typical load of eight 340-kg (750-lb) bombs would be able to attack its target successfully only by outwitting the enemy's missiles, MiGs, and anti-aircraft

fire. Typically, the F-105 pilot refuelled from a tanker, communicated with a command and control aircraft or a forward air controller (FAC), and then plunged into the hell of enemy airspace. Many aircraft fell and a host of pilots died fighting the most comprehensive anti-aircraft defences assembled up to that time.

Often, the pilot's approach to the target included hiding behind 'Thud Ridge' for a portion of the trip. This enabled the F-105 to attack targets like Kep airfield near Hanoi with a degree of surprise. It was some of the most dangerous flying in

the history of air warfare, but the F-105 was a fine aircraft and its well-trained pilots fought valiantly, attacking ground targets and destroying MiG-17s in air-to-air combat.

Decades after the conflict, the F-105 is still highly regarded by all who flew it.

Above: This 355th Tactical Fighter Wing (TFW) aircraft carries a load of M117 and Mk 82 bombs, some with extended fuses.

Below: Preparing for a 1962 weapons meet at Nellis Air Force Base, Nevada, this F-105 demonstrates the combat readiness of USAF aircrews and their aircraft.

F-105D THUNDERCHIEF

Two USAF tactical fighter wings flew the F-105 in combat over Vietnam. The aircraft arrived in-theatre, and began operations, wearing bright unit markings over their natural metal finish.

Several F-105D pilots put the faithful M61 20-mm, six-barrelled cannon to good use. The majority of F-105 MiG-17 kills were achieved with the cannon, although at least three involved AIM-9 Sidewinder shots.

An ejection seat was vital for combat operations. Almost 400 F-105s went down over Vietnam, with several pilots being the subject of successful and dramatic rescue attempts. Others were less fortunate.

A 1703-litre (375-gallon) drop tank was carried on the centreline pylon for most missions. In-flight refuelling was also necessary, but once topped up the F-105D could remain on station for long periods, with its large ordnance load giving good combat persistence.

This early configuration with single M117 bombs on the outboard pylons was soon replaced by the normal load of two tanks, six M117s on the centreline pylon, an electronic countermeasures pod on one outboard pylon and an AIM-9 on the other.

Even though it offered 117.92 kN (26,532 lb thrust), the J75 engine left the F-105D underpowered. Afterburner was needed to keep a heavily laden 'Thud' on the tanker at altitude.

The F-105 could absorb extensive combat damage. One aircraft returned with an accidentally fired AIM-9 embedded in the tailpipe!

'Thud' combat versatility

WEAPONS AND TACTICS: Having entered the war mainly as a 'dumb' bomber, the F-105 acquired new weapons and tactics.

BULLPUP OPERATIONS: F-105Ds employed the AGM-12A/B Bullpup missile against the Thanh Hoa Bridge, with little success.

PAUL DOUMER BRIDGE: Alternatively known as The Hanoi Railroad and Highway Bridge, the Doumer Bridge was an obvious and vital target against which many F-105s were committed. Although the 'Thuds' caused some damage, F-4Ds armed with laser-guided bombs were needed to complete the job.

CLOUD BOMBING: Bombing jungle targets through cloud cover was a common practice. The radar-equipped EB-66 acted as pathfinder.

F-105D Thunderchief

Type: single-seat tactical fighter

Powerplant: one 117.92-kN 26,532-lb-thrust) Pratt & Whitney J75-P-19W afterburning turbojet engine

Maximum speed: 2237 km/h (1390 mph) at 10,975 m (36,000 ft)

Initial climb rate: 10,515 m/min (34,498 fpm)

Combat range: 2975 km (1849 miles)

Service ceiling: 15,850 m (52,000 ft)

Weights: empty 12,474 kg (27,500 lb); maximum take-off 23,834 kg (52,545 lb)

Armament: one 20-mm M61A1 Vulcan cannon with 1028 rounds plus, typically, eight 340-kg (750-lb) bombs on a bombing mission to Hanoi or a maximum of 6350 kg (14,000 lb) of ordnance

Dimensions:
span	10.65 m (34 ft 11 in)
length	19.58 m (64 ft 3 in)
height	5.99 m (19 ft 8 in)
wing area	35.76 m² (385 sq ft)

COMBAT DATA

MAXIMUM SPEED

Until the McDonnell Douglas F-4 began to reach the Vietnamese theatre in numbers, the F-105D was one of the USAF's fastest combat aircraft. These figures are for speed 'clean' at altitude, but the F-105D was easily supersonic, bombed-up, at sea level.

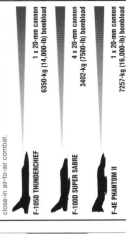

F-105D THUNDERCHIEF	**2237 km/h (1390 mph)**
F-100D SUPER SABRE	**1390 km/h (864 mph)**
F-4E PHANTOM II	**2390 km/h (1485 mph)**

CLIMB RATE

Even by today's standards the F-4E offered outstanding climb performance. The powerful Thunderchief was a better performer than the older North American F-100D and was able to use its performance in evading enemy defences.

F-4E PHANTOM II	18,714 m/min (61,398 fpm)
F-105D THUNDERCHIEF	10515 m/min (34,498 fpm)
F-100D SUPER SABRE	4875 m/min (15,994 fpm)

ARMAMENT

All three of these tactical aircraft featured gun armament. That on the F-4E was rushed into service in this model of Phantom after the all-missile-armed fighters had highlighted the need for guns during close-in air-to-air combat.

F-105D THUNDERCHIEF	1 x 20-mm cannon	6350-kg (14,000-lb) bombload
F-100D SUPER SABRE	4 x 20-mm cannon	3402-kg (7500-lb) bombload
F-4E PHANTOM II	1 x 20-mm cannon	7257-kg (16,000-lb) bombload

REPUBLIC
F-105F/G THUNDERCHIEF ('WILD WEASEL')

● Vietnam combat missions ● Air National Guard ● Two-seat 'Thud'

T he two-seat Republic F-105 Thunderchief was heavier and longer than the single-seat 'Thud', but it was an excellent combat aircraft and a key weapon in the Vietnam conflict. This big, powerful warplane began as a nuclear bomber which could also serve as a trainer for combat pilots. In Vietnam it became a night raider and a 'Wild Weasel' – an air-to-ground warrior with the specialized job of attacking SAM radar installations.

▲ F-105 'Wild Weasel' crews faced great danger during each anti-radar mission over Vietnam. Many aircraft served until the early 1980s with the US Air National Guard.

PHOTO FILE

REPUBLIC F-105F/G THUNDERCHIEF ('WILD WEASEL')

▲ **Anti-radiation role**
A range of special equipment allowed the F-105G to detect the radiation of hostile radar transmitters.

Drag chute ▶
An F-105F and a single-seat F-105D are slowed down by brake chutes as they land. Thunderchiefs required a long runway.

▶ **'Wild Weasel' sensors**
AN/ALQ-105 sensors, allowing the detection and location of enemy radars, were carried in long fairings along both sides of the lower fuselage of the F-105G.

▼ **Hunter-killer**
This Shrike-equipped F-105F is ready to destroy any emitting radar, while the bomb-carrying F-105D takes care of the rest of the radar site.

▲ **Shrike and ARM**
This aircraft carries examples of the two primary anti-radar missiles of the Vietnam era. The larger missile is an AGM-78 anti-radiation missile (ARM) and the smaller one is an AGM-45 Shrike.

FACTS AND FIGURES

▶ During its maiden flight on 11 June 1963 the first two-seat F-105F Thunderchief exceeded Mach 1.

▶ A total of 143 aircraft were built as two-seat proficiency trainers (F-105F).

▶ For anti-SAM duties, 61 two-seat F-105G 'Thuds' received improved electronics.

▶ A typical 'Wild Weasel' F-105 had 13 antennas, three computers and up to 100 km (60 miles) of internal wires.

▶ F-105G had AN/ALQ-105 countermeasures pods on the fuselage sides.

▶ An F-105 crew had a 60 per cent chance of surviving 100 missions in Vietnam.

PROFILE

Keeping enemy radars silent

With a two-man crew in tandem cockpits, the Republic F-105 Thunderchief had the same brute strength and combat capability as single-seat versions of the 'Thud'.

Early in the career of the huge, howling Thunderchief, Republic proposed two-seater models to serve both as transition trainers and as combat machines. The first two-seat designs (F-105C and F-105E) were not built, but when the F-105F finally appeared it had the same supersonic speed, bomb-hauling capacity and sturdiness as single-seat 'Thuds'.

In Vietnam, the two-seater became the only USAF warplane capable of attacking targets near Hanoi at night – spearheading 'Ryan's Raiders', a nocturnal attack force that performed duties similar to those of the US Navy's Grumman A-6 Intruder.

When North Vietnam's SAM batteries threatened friendly aircraft, the Thunderchief rose to immortality in the 'Wild Weasel' mission. Flying some of the most dangerous missions ever undertaken, the Thunderchief, carrying a pilot and electronic warfare officer (EWO, or 'Bear'), used radar-hunting missiles to engage surface-to-air missile sites, attack radar transmitters and shut down the enemy's defences. Many of these aircraft were modified with additional anti-SAM equipment (F-105G).

F-105G THUNDERCHIEF

Belonging to the 561st Tactical Fighter Squadron of the 23rd Tactical Fighter Wing, 63-8265 was based at McConnell Air Force Base. The 561st TFS was the first unit to receive 'Wild Weasel' F-105Gs.

Below: Originally, the F-105F was developed to fulfil the same tactical strike role as the F-105D, with training being secondary.

Above: With its distinctive sensor fairings, this F-105 is easily distinguished from other variants. All G models were converted from existing F airframes and, although the G is now the best known, it was an F-105F which flew the last service mission.

Additional firepower was provided by the internal M61 cannon, which was retained from the single-seat F-105D.

Fitting a second cockpit to the F-105 airframe entailed lengthening the fuselage by 0.79 m (3 ft). The resulting forwards shift in the centre of gravity meant that a taller vertical fin was required to maintain stability.

The F-105G had a far more comprehensive sensor fit than the F-105F, as shown by the fairings and antennas.

Auxiliary fuel tanks were fitted with a distinctively nose-down attitude on the middle wing pylons. This angle meant that the tanks generated minimum drag at high angles of attack.

A four-petal airbrake formed the tailcone of the F-105. The petals could be extended into the aircraft's slipstream either in flight or on landing to shorten the landing run.

An AIM-7 Sparrow missile body was adapted to form the basis of the AGM-45 Shrike. This primitive missile was not very reliable and lost its way if the emitting radar was closed down while the missile was in flight.

The J75 turbojet of the Thunderchief was powerful but not very fuel efficient. External fuel tanks were an almost permanent feature on combat missions.

F-105G Thunderchief

Type: two-seat tactical fighter and 'Wild Weasel' aircraft

Powerplant: one 109-kN (24,520-lb-thrust) Pratt & Whitney J75-P-19W turbojet engine with afterburning

Maximum speed: Mach 2.1 or 2237 km/h (1387 mph) at 10,970 m (36,000 ft)

Range: 1480 km (920 miles)

Service ceiling: 12,560 m (41,200 ft)

Weights: empty 12,775 kg (28,105 lb); loaded 25,100 kg (55,220 lb)

Armament: one 20-mm M61A1 Vulcan cannon, plus 6350-kg (14,000-lb) bombload; for the 'Wild Weasel' mission typically two to six AGM-45 Shrike or AGM-78 Standard Arm anti-radar missiles

Dimensions: span 10.59 m (34 ft 9 in)
length 20.42 m (67 ft)
height 6.12 m (20 ft 1 in)
wing area 35.77 m² (385 sq ft)

COMBAT DATA

MAXIMUM SPEED

Both the F-105G and McDonnell Douglas F-4D are appreciably faster than the Hawker Siddeley Buccaneer, although at low level the three are more closely matched.

F-105G THUNDERCHIEF	2237 km/h (1387 mph)
BUCCANEER S.Mk 2	1038 km/h (644 mph)
F-4D PHANTOM II	2390 km/h (1482 mph)

WEAPON LOAD

With its large weapons load, the Buccaneer was an exceptional strike aircraft. The F-4D carried a heavy load but, unlike the F-105G, was hindered in air-to-air combat by the lack of a gun.

F-105G THUNDERCHIEF	1 x 20-mm cannon, 6350-kg (14,000-lb) bombload
BUCCANEER S.Mk 2	7264-kg (16,000-lb) bombload
F-4D PHANTOM II	7257-kg (15,965-lb) bombload

THRUST

Some experts considered the F-105G to be underpowered, but pilots disagreed. It had poor take-off performance in the Vietnamese heat, however, and required long runways.

F-105G THUNDERCHIEF	109 kN (24,520 lb thrust)
BUCCANEER S.Mk 2	98.8 kN (22,225 lb thrust)
F-4D PHANTOM II	151 kN (33,970 lb thrust)

'Weaseling' over Vietnam

■ **McDONNELL DOUGLAS A-4 SKYHAWK:** A small number of Skyhawks also performed the defence-suppression mission using AGM-45s.

■ **McDONNELL DOUGLAS F-4G PHANTOM II:** The F-4G represented the most advanced 'Wild Weasel' aircraft available over Vietnam.

■ **NORTH AMERICAN F-100F SUPER SABRE:** Seven converted F-100Fs were the first true 'Wild Weasel' mission aircraft.

■ **VOUGHT A-7 CORSAIR II:** A number of US Navy A-7s were adapted for AGM-45 Shrike missiles, but carried no other special systems.

ROCKWELL

T-2 BUCKEYE

● Naval trainer ● Carrier capable ● Almost three decades of service

▶ Since 1959 the Buckeye has been taking students through their naval flight training syllabus, including the infamous carquals (carrier qualifications). Lectures and practice 'carrier' landings on an airfield are the only preparation the pilots receive for this hazardous activity.

For many years American naval aviators have earned their wings in the Rockwell International T-2 Buckeye, and navigators also train in it. Originally called the T2J, this sturdy aircraft began its career in 1959 as a single-engine design but evolved into a twin-jet trainer. Named after 'the Buckeye state', it was manufactured in Columbus, Ohio. The T-2 has now been replaced by the T-45 Goshawk.

390

ROCKWELL **T-2 BUCKEYE**

▶ **Deck landing configuration**
Large flaps, producing high lift at low approach speeds, and an arrestor hook are essential equipment on naval aircraft.

▲ **High-visibility colours**
Training aircraft must be easily seen 'in the circuit' and this is especially true around a carrier.

Tense moments ▶
On each landing the student pilot must catch one of four arrestor wires or 'go around again'.

▼ **South American Buckeye**
Venezuela acquired 12 T-2D trainers from Rockwell via the US Navy. Greece also operates the Buckeye and has 30 T-2Es.

▶ **On-deck servicing**
The T-2 used proven systems and was therefore ordered into service without a prototype. The carqual ship was USS Lexington, but the USS Forrestal has now taken over.

FACTS AND FIGURES

➤ The first T-2 Buckeye, a single-engined aircraft, took to the air for its maiden flight on 31 January 1958.

➤ The US Navy currently plans to have Buckeyes in service until 2002.

➤ More than 18,000 naval aviators have received training in the T-2C Buckeye.

➤ The Buckeye is fully carrier-capable and most naval aviators made their first carrier landing flying it.

➤ Production of 273 Buckeyes included 231 for the US Navy and 42 for export.

➤ The first twin-engined Buckeyes entered service in May 1966.

PROFILE

Introduction to the aircraft-carrier

When the US Navy wanted a versatile carrier-capable jet trainer, North American came up with the answer. The company's NA-241, known to the Navy as the T2J and later redesignated T-2, brought together proven components and equipment from earlier North American designs, including the wings from the FJ-1 Fury and the control systems of the T-28 Trojan. While T-2 Buckeyes were coming off the production line, North American changed its name to Rockwell International. Navy Air Training command received the first T-2 Buckeyes in the late 1950s. Typically, a pilot trained in the T-28 Trojan (later the T-34 Mentor) then went on to the Buckeye for intermediate training and carrier qualification, and finished flight training in the TA-4J Skyhawk. Only in the 1990s has the US Navy finally started to replace the Buckeye and the Skyhawk with the T-45 Goshawk, which will be used for both intermediate and advanced training.

T-2C BUCKEYE

Very few US Navy Buckeyes have been seen in camouflage. The fin of this aircraft carries a fist holding a 'broken MiG' emblem, identifying it as belonging to aggressor squadron VF-43.

Both crewmembers are seated on LS-1 ejection seats beneath a large clamshell-type canopy. The instructor is also equipped with a TV system allowing him to monitor the student's aim during gunnery practice.

Unlike other US carrier aircraft, the Buckeye does not have a nose leg catapult bar. It is launched by a detachable strop fixed to the underside.

Originally, the twin intakes of the Buckeye fed a single engine. Since 1962, however, each has supplied a separate engine.

The rear seat is raised by 0.25 m (9 in) to give the instructor a good view forwards over the student's head. The T-2 was one of the first trainers to have this facility.

A large speed brake is mounted on either side of the rear fuselage. Precise speed control is important during naval operations.

Wide-track gear gives the Buckeye stable landing characteristics. This is an important factor because carrier landings are difficult, especially for the student.

A 'sting-type' arrestor hook is anchored to the strong rear fuselage. The hook engages a cable stretched across the carrier deck. The cable reels out under tension, 'trapping' the Buckeye.

Wingtip fuel tanks, each of 390-litre (103-gallon) capacity, are not jettisonable and each carries a navigation light in its nose. The T-2 offers good range performance.

Although the T-2C Buckeye is now in the twilight of its career, it continues to provide an excellent training platform and introduction to the potentially dangerous world of carrier aviation.

T-2C Buckeye

Type: two-seat intermediate jet trainer

Powerplant: (early version) one 15.1-kN (3400-lb-thrust) Westinghouse J34-WE-6 turbojet engine; (later version) two 13.1-kN (2948-lb-thrust) General Electric J85-GE-4 turbojet engines

Maximum speed: 840 km/h (521 mph) at 7620 m (25,000 ft)

Maximum climb rate: 1890 m/min (6200 fpm)

Range: 1685 km (1045 miles)

Service ceiling: 12,320 m (40,400 ft)

Weights: empty 3680 kg (8113 lb); maximum take-off 5977 kg (13,149 lb)

Accommodation: student aviator in front seat and instructor in back; fuel load of 2616 litres (690 gallons); 290 kg (640 lb) of light ordnance or travel luggage

Dimensions:
span with tip tanks 11.62 m (38 ft 2 in)
length 11.67 m (38 ft 4 in)
height 4.51 m (14 ft 9 in)
wing area 23.69 m² (255 sq ft)

COMBAT DATA

MAXIMUM SPEED

Buckeyes often fly from land bases to the aircraft-carriers. Invariably, the carrier is in the Gulf of Mexico and the training value is increased if the student wastes as little time as possible in transit. A fast aircraft gives a good introduction to fast-jet carrier flying.

T-2C BUCKEYE	840 km/h (521 mph)
T-37B	685 km/h (425 mph)
L-29 DELFIN	655 km/h (406 mph)

MAXIMUM THRUST

Power is important for a carrier aircraft. If the 'wire' is missed the pilot must apply full power with the aircraft in 'dirty' configuration to enable it to clear the deck for another approach. Higher power allows for a heavier fuel load and greater range.

T-2C BUCKEYE	26.2 kN (5900 lb thrust)
T-37B	9.1 kN (2045 lb thrust)
L-29 DELFIN	8.7 kN (1960 lb thrust)

RANGE

At sea, range equates to long endurance. This means that when the student is operating from the ship he/she is able to fly several circuits and practise approaches before refuelling is required. The Delfin ranged but is able to carry underwing drop-tanks.

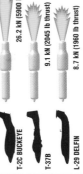

T-37B 1067 km (622 miles)

T-2C BUCKEYE 1685 km (1045 miles)

L-29 DELFIN 894 km (554 miles)

Other Rockwell International aircraft

■ **SABRELINER:** Known to the US military as the T-39, this jet has been used as a trainer and executive transport.

■ **SHUTTLE SPACECRAFT:** Rockwell is the prime contractor for NASA's re-usable space shuttle programme.

■ **B-1B LANCER:** The formidable, stealthy B-1B Lancer bomber is a devastating conventional and nuclear component of the USAF.

■ **ROCKWELL/DASA X-31:** Built in co-operation with MBB, the X-31 investigates 'post-stall' manoeuvring.

ROCKWELL
T-39 SABRELINER

- Communications ● Radar trainer ● VIP transport

In 1956 the United States Air Force announced a requirement for a utility jet trainer, to be designed and built to prototype stage under private finance. North American submitted its N.A. 246 Sabreliner as a contender in this UTX competition. It was the only one of eight entrants to fly and was subsequently ordered by the USAF, entering service in 1962. The aircraft has also been operated by the US Navy and a number of foreign air arms.

▲ Remaining in production for almost three decades, the T-39 Sabreliner provided both the US Air Force and Navy with an ideal VIP transport, liaison and radar training aircraft.

ROCKWELL T-39 SABRELINER

▼ Military executive jets ▶
Most of the USAF T-39As spent their lives as VIP transports, shuttling senior personnel between bases and major cities.

▼ Small beginnings
A month after the first prototype had flown, the USAF ordered seven aircraft.

▼ T-39 twilight
This sinister-looking example was one of the last Sabreliners in USAF service. Some aircraft received the three-tone wrap-round 'European One' camouflage before retirement.

Fleet induction ▶
Fitted with a Magnavox APQ-94 radar, housed in a distinctive elongated radome, the T-39D was procured to train US Navy F-4 Phantom and F-8 Crusader pilots.

▶ Fighter heritage
From above, the T-39 has a distinct wing profile, reminiscent of the North American F-100 Super Sabre interceptor.

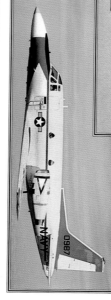

FACTS AND FIGURES

▼ Three USAF examples were converted for the Fighter Weapons School to train specialist F-105G 'Wild Weasel' crew.

▼ All military Sabreliners were certified to civil airworthiness standards.

▼ Sweden was the only nation to receive T-39s outside of the Americas.

▼ Some ex-military examples have been refurbished and snapped up by civilian operators as low-cost business jets.

▼ A possible order from the US Marine Corps failed to materialise.

▼ A dozen CT-39G aircraft were built for the USN as tactical transports.

PROFILE

An executive jet for the military

After winning the UTX competition, the Sabreliner entered production as the T-39A. As the first batch was delivered the USAF realized the aircraft would be ideal as a radar trainer for the Republic F-105D. The sixth aircraft was converted to this standard by enlarging the nose to house the R-14 radar and APN-131 Doppler. It was designated T-39B.

The US Navy recognized the Sabreliner's suitability in the radar training role and ordered a navalized version to train pilots and radar operators for its F-8 Crusaders and F-4 Phantoms. These 42 aircraft were initially designated T3J-1 and were

equipped with the Magnavox APQ-94 radar. The Navy also ordered the CT-39E for fleet support and communications.

The T-39F was a variant used by the USAF in training for the 'Wild Weasel' role, developed during the Vietnam War.

The aircraft also gained some success in the civil market as the Sabreliner 40, 60, 65, 75 and 80. These improved versions were ordered by several air arms including those of Argentina,

Ecuador, Mexico and Sweden. In the 1980s US Navy examples were upgraded to T-39N standard, and continue to serve in the radar training role. Most USAF T-39s have been retired, leaving the 453rd Test Squadron as the final operator.

Left: Only one USAF unit continues to operate the T-39. Most are held in long-term storage in Arizona, awaiting their ultimate fate.

T-39B Sabreliner

Type: utility transport and trainer

Powerplant: two 14.68-kN (3000-lb-thrust) Pratt & Whitney J60-P-3 turbojet engines

Maximum cruising speed: 808 km/h (501 mph)

Long-range cruising speed: 764 km/h (474 mph)

Initial climb rate: 1692 m/min (5550 fpm)

Range: 3138 km (1945 miles)

Service ceiling: 13,700 m (45,000 ft)

Weights: empty 4199 kg (9238 lb); loaded 8056 kg (17,723 lb)

Accommodation: two pilots and provision for up to 10 passengers

Dimensions:
span 13.54 m (44 ft 5 in)
length 13.34 m (43 ft 9 in)
height 4.88 m (16 ft)
wing area 31.82 m² (342 sq ft)

Above: CT-39Gs, which featured a lengthened fuselage, were used by several USN units, including VR-24 based at Sigonella, Italy. This example is seen at Gibraltar.

On top of the tail unit was a small anti-collision light which helped provide a visual fix on the T-39 while it was airborne.

Powering the Sabreliner were two small Pratt & Whitney turbojets. Known as J60s in US military parlance, these engines put out 14.68 kN of thrust each. They were reliable, though by modern standards they were noisy, thirsty and difficult to maintain.

A low-mounted tailplane was a distinguishing feature of the Sabreliner. It was an all-metal cantilever unit which incorporated full-span de-icer boots.

By 1950s' standards, when it was conceived, the wing of the T-39 had an incredibly raked angle for a subsonic utility transport. The trailing-edge flaps were electrically operated.

Tp 86

Given the local designation Tp 86, two Sabreliner 40s are operated by Sweden as test aircraft. Among many new systems which have been trialled was an airborne radar which can detect underground objects.

Two pilots could be accommodated in the cockpit, sitting side-by-side. Entry to the aircraft was provided by a built-in staircase, situated just aft of the flight deck on the port side.

From the T-39B variant onwards, Sabreliners were fitted with a Doppler navigational system and an all-weather search radar built in-house by North American's Autonetics division.

Other Rockwell projects

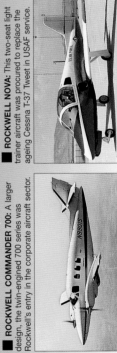

■ **ROCKWELL ALPINE COMMANDER:** Aimed at the burgeoning light aircraft market, the Alpine was not a commercial success.

■ **ROCKWELL COMMANDER 700:** A larger design, the twin-engined 700 series was Rockwell's entry in the corporate aircraft sector.

■ **ROCKWELL NOVA:** This two-seat light trainer aircraft was procured to replace the ageing Cessna T-37 Tweet in USAF service.

■ **ROCKWELL X-31:** This multinational venture was designed to produce a highly agile aircraft with post-stall manoeuvring ability.

ACTION DATA

MAXIMUM SPEED

Compared to its main rivals of the day, notably the Lockheed Jetstar and the early Gates Learjet, the Sabreliner offered better performance and was considerably faster. Interestingly, all three types were eventually acquired by the US military.

SABRELINER 75A	906 km/h (561 mph)
JETSTAR II	880 km/h (546 mph)
LEARJET 35A	872 km/h (540 mph)

MAXIMUM RANGE

Both the Learjet and Sabreliner had considerable range, far better than most combat jets of the era which were fitted with fuel-thirsty afterburning engines. The Jetstar had the greatest endurance of all, the result of the aircraft being somewhat larger, with greater fuel capacity.

JETSTAR II
5134 km
(3183 miles)

SABRELINER 75A
3170 km
(1945 miles)

LEARJET 35A
4168 km
(2584 miles)

PASSENGERS

Not designed as high-volume transports, the Sabreliner and Jetstar could still carry ten or twelve passengers in comfort. This factor made them extremely popular on the civil market, once their military careers were over. Their greater passenger capacity offered an advantage over the slightly smaller Learjet series.

SABRELINER 75A
10 passengers

JETSTAR II
12 passengers

LEARJET 35A
6 passengers

ROCKWELL
OV-10 BRONCO

- Forward air control ● Vietnam veteran ● Counter-insurgency

Rockwell's OV-10 Bronco was a product from early lessons learned in the Vietnam War.

Designed as a COIN (counter-insurgency) aircraft, it evolved into an armed, agile forward air control (FAC) machine directing fighter-bombers to their targets. The Bronco began as a US Air Force warplane, but performed its final service in the US Marine Corps, where the US Marine Corps used it over the battlefield to great effect.

▲ Forward air control is a demanding mission, in which pilots must call in strikes while they are exposed to gunfire. The excellent view from the Bronco is appreciated by FAC officers.

ROCKWELL OV-10 BRONCO

▲ Night striker
Marine Corps OV-10Ds have been updated for the night observation role. They are armed with the M197 20-mm cannon, which is aimed by an AAS-37 infra-red tracker and laser designator pod.

▲ Setting off
Despite its age, the Bronco was popular with crews, who enjoyed the excitement of low flying in a simple aircraft.

Rocket launcher ▶
Standard armament for the FAC mission in Vietnam was the rocket pod, usually containing phosphorus markers.

▲ USAF retirement
Repeatedly declared obsolete, the OV-10 was finally retired from the USAF's inventory. It has been replaced by the Fairchild OA-10.

▼ Strike pair
Armed with powerful fuel-air explosive bombs and machine guns, the Bronco has a potent tactical strike capability.

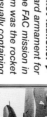

▲ Marine favourite
The Bronco was favoured by the Marines, who see close support as a key mission. They also used the type for clandestine special forces insertions.

FACTS AND FIGURES

▶ Eleven companies participated in the early 1960s FAC aircraft competition.

▶ The Bronco prototype first flew on 16 July 1965 at Columbus, Ohio.

▶ The Marine Corps and USAF took delivery of their first Broncos on the same day, 23 February 1968.

▶ In Vietnam, the US Navy briefly operated a light-attack squadron, the 'Black Ponies', equipped with 18 armed Broncos.

▶ Two OV-10s were shot down during Operation Desert Storm.

▶ A Bronco was shot down in Venezuela in November 1992 during a coup attempt.

PROFILE

Tree-top flying on the front line

The OV-10 was the subject of much debate, and the future of forward air control missions by fixed-wing aircraft is still contested.

After almost two decades of soldiering, seeing combat from Vietnam to the Persian Gulf, the familiar, twin-boomed shape of the OV-10 Bronco is no longer seen in military colours – except, possibly, in Venezuela, where a few may still be in service. Nowadays, you can see Broncos in Montana working with the US Forest Service, or in Virginia flying law enforcement missions.

The OV-10 was ordered in 1964 and reached Vietnam in 1969. Bronco variants served in Germany (which used a turbojet-boosted model for target towing), Indonesia, Morocco and Venezuela. The most advanced version was the Marine Corps OV-10D-Plus, which incorporated night observation capability and forward-looking infra-red sensors and was employed on covert special forces insertion missions.

as well as forward air control. By the 1990s, many in the Corps were arguing that the OV-10 was too slow to survive in modern combat, when it might fall victim to shoulder-mounted heat-seeking missiles, but there was strong protest within Marine ranks when in 1993 the decision was made to retire the Bronco.

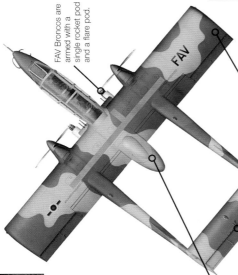

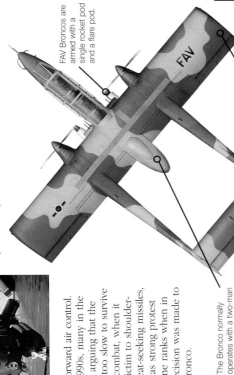

FAV Broncos are armed with a single rocket pod and a flare pod.

The broad high-lift wing gives the Bronco good low-speed handling and a short take-off capability. It can fly slowly enough to escort helicopters.

The long bulged canopy and short nose allows an excellent view of the target area. Both crew members have ejection seats.

The undercarriage is designed to permit operation from tactical airstrips just behind the front line.

The Bronco normally operates with a two-man crew, sitting in tandem.

The tailplane is a fixed-incidence unit with an inset elevator, providing excellent control at low speeds.

M60 machine guns are mounted in pairs in each sponson.

Uprated engines with infra-red suppressing exhaust ducts were fitted to the OV-10D in an attempt to reduce vulnerability to shoulder-launched heat-seeking missiles.

The central fuselage pod can accommodate two stretchers and a medical attendant, or five paratroopers.

A 568-litre (150-gallon) drop-tank can be carried, in addition to the 976 litres (250 gallons) of internal fuel.

OV-10A BRONCO

The OV-10s of the Fuerza Aerea Venezuela (FAV) serve with two squadrons, the 'Geronimos' of 151 Escuadron and 'Zorros' of 152 Escuadron.

Venezuelan Broncos are painted in a jungle colour scheme similar to US aircraft during the Vietnam War. The FAV operates in the surveillance role near the Colombian border.

Forward observation in action

■ **UNDER FIRE:** Ground troops are advancing on a suspected enemy position when they come under artillery fire. Taking cover, they look for the enemy.

■ **CALLING FOR HELP:** The ground troops call the Forward Air Controller. The only information they can give is the general direction of fire. However, modern infantry are often equipped with locating radar, which tracks the shells in flight and makes a fairly accurate estimate of the position of the enemy battery.

■ **LOCATING THE ENEMY:** High above, an observer in an OV-10 follows the vector of the incoming shells, eventually spotting the enemy guns about 10 km (6 miles) away.

■ **GROUND ATTACK:** The observer calls in patrolling F/A-18 Hornets, which destroy the enemy artillery battery with a salvo of high-explosive air-to-ground rockets.

OV-10D Bronco

Type: two-seat forward air control aircraft

Powerplant: two Garrett 533-kW (715-hp) T76-G-420/421 turboprops

Maximum speed: 452 km/h (280 mph) 'clean' at sea level

Range: 2300 km (1426 miles)

Service ceiling: 7315 m (24,000 ft)

Weights: empty 3161 kg (6954 lb); loaded 6552 kg (14,414 lb)

Armament: one or two GPU-2/A lightweight gun pods containing an M197 air-cooled, three-barrel Gatling gun coupled to a single-ended ammunition feed system with 300 rounds; high-explosive air-to-surface rocket pods

Dimensions:
span	12.67 m (40 ft)
length	13.41 m 42 ft)
height	4.62 m (15 ft)
wing area	27.03 m² (291 sq ft)

COMBAT DATA

MAXIMUM SPEED

The Bronco and the US Army Mohawk were designed as military aircraft. Both served extensively in Vietnam, where they had a considerable performance advantage over the Cessna O-2, a twin-engined 'push-pull' light plane that was minimally adapted from the commercial Cessna Model 337 Skymaster.

OV-10D BRONCO	452 km/h (280 mph)
OV-1 MOHAWK	496 km/h (308 mph)
O-2	320 km/h (200 mph)

RANGE

All three of the observation aircraft were used to support US and South Vietnamese ground troops. They were deployed to American bases all over Southeast Asia, and the excellent range each displayed meant that they could provide overhead observation wherever US troops were in action.

O-2	OV-1 MOHAWK	OV-10D BRONCO
1700 km (1054 miles)	2000 km (1240 miles)	2300 km (1426 miles)

ENDURANCE

The ability to stay in the air for long periods is a definite asset in a forward air control machine. Directing support missions for units cut off on mountain tops or in isolated fire bases, or co-ordinating the rescue of pilots shot down in enemy territory, could call for a FAC to stay in the air for several hours.

OV-10D BRONCO	OV-1 MOHAWK	O-2
7 hours 40 minutes	6 hours 30 minutes	6 hours

ROCKWELL
B-1B LANCER

- Strategic nuclear bomber ● Supersonic swing wing ● Cruise carrier

▲ The B-1B combines stealth features with highly sophisticated defensive avionics. It has the ability to carry more bombs than the old B-52, and can fly low-level attack missions at high speed.

t may lack the glamour of the stealthy B-2 flying wing or the reverence accorded to the 40-year-old B-52 Stratofortress, but the Rockwell B-1B Lancer is a highly advanced supersonic bomber. With its tremendous capacity to carry immense loads of nuclear and conventional weaponry, the Lancer has now become America's primary low-level, supersonic, nuclear strike asset.

396

ROCKWELL B-1B LANCER

Fast dash ▶
With its wings swept, the Lancer can exceed Mach 1 at height, and gives a comfortable low-level ride at near-sonic speeds.

▲ Sleek and deadly
The long nose of the B-1B houses the Westinghouse AN/APQ-164 attack radar, derived from the F-16's APG-66. Most of the other electronic gear is classified.

▲ Low and slow
The high-lift devices on the B-1B's wing and blended fuselage give the big bomber very smooth handling. The flight control system is a mix of traditional hydraulics, with fly-by-wire outboard spoilers.

▲ High tail
Like the Russian Tu-160, the B-1B has a high-set tail to avoid the engine efflux. The bulge under the tail houses the defensive tail warning components of the AN/ALQ-161 system.

▲ Loading the bomb
The main weapons for the B-1B are the SRAM nuclear missile and the B28, B61 and B83 free-fall nuclear bombs. Future weapons options include cruise missiles and advanced precision-guided conventional munitions.

▼ Sweeping wings
Fuel is moved automatically to counter the large changes in trim as the wings change position. The variable geometry allows the B-1 to operate from relatively short runways.

FACTS AND FIGURES

▶ The all-white B-1A flew at Palmdale, California, on 23 December 1974.

▶ On 4 September 1984, the first B-1B was rolled out at Rockwell's Palmdale plant.

▶ The B-1B made its first flight on 18 October 1984, 15 years after design work began.

▶ One B-1B crashed in trials when crew overrode the fuel transfer computer and unbalanced the aircraft.

▶ The first B-1Bs were assigned to the 96th Bomb Wing at Dyess AFB, Texas.

▶ The four crew sit in Weber-built ACES II (Advanced Concept Ejection Seats).

B-1B Lancer

Type: four-crew strategic bomber

Powerplant: four 133.57-kN (29,964-lb-thrust) General Electric F101-GE-102 turbofans

Maximum operational speed: Mach 0.99 or 1207 km/h (748 mph), although the aircraft can reach Mach 1.2

Range: 11,675 km (7239 miles)

Service ceiling: more than 15,000 m (49,200 ft)

Weights: empty 87,090 kg (191,598 lb); loaded 216,368 kg (476,010 lb)

Armament: eight cruise missiles or 12 B28 nuclear bombs, or 24 B61/B83 nuclear bombs; theoretical maximum conventional weapons load of 60,782 kg (133,720 lb)

Dimensions:
span (unswept) 41.66 m (137 ft)
span (swept) 23.84 m (78 ft)
length 47.80 m (157 ft)
height 10.24 m (34 ft)
wing area 181.10 m² (1949 sq ft)

Left: The evolution of the B-1B has not been easy. There have been many problems bringing into service such an advanced aircraft, especially involving the defensive ECM (electronic countermeasures) system and the engines.

Below: The B-1's origins date from the 1960s, when it was realized that Soviet air defences would imperil any high-flying aircraft, even the planned Mach 3-capable B-70 Valkyrie. But switching to low level presented designers with a whole new set of problems.

All USAF strategic aircraft now carry low-visibility markings, with black lettering and reduced-size coloured unit emblems.

COMBAT DATA

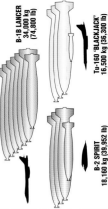

B-1B LANCER
34,000 kg
(74,800 lb)

Tu-160 'BLACKJACK'
16,500 kg (36,300 lb)

B-2 SPIRIT
18,160 kg (39,952 lb)

CONVENTIONAL WEAPONS LOAD

Although the B-1B can carry up to 60 tonnes of conventional weaponry in its three bomb-bays and on 12 underwing weapons stations, operationally it will probably be limited to 85 Mk 82 227-kg (500-lb) general-purpose bombs or 20 AGM-86C conventionally armed air-launched cruise missiles. As the B-52 force is retired, Lancers will acquire the ability to deliver a variety of precision-guided munitions as well as Harpoon anti-ship missiles.

Low-level strategic striker

Making a low-level penetration of enemy territory, the B-1B crew flies 'zipped up', shielded from thermonuclear flash-blindness by blast curtains equipped with PLZT (polarized lead zirconium titanate).

The B-1B incorporates a number of stealth features, and has a radar cross-section one-fourth that of a B-52. This gives the Lancer an excellent chance of penetrating enemy defences and dropping its bombs without being detected.

Pilot and co-pilot sit side-by-side in a cockpit with both digital and analogue instruments. The B-1B is flown like a fighter, using a stick and rudder pedals.

Crew members 3 and 4, known as the OSO and DSO (offensive and defensive systems operators), sit side-by-side behind the pilots. They have small windows but cannot see a great deal outside the aircraft.

The B-1 entered service primarily as a carrier of free-fall nuclear bombs, with a maximum load of 24 B61 devices. With minor modifications it can carry a heavy load of cruise missiles, and as the ageing B-52 fleet is retired the huge swing-wing bomber is now being used as a conventional bomber.

B-1B LANCER

The 95-strong B-1B force is operated by the US Air Force's Air Combat Command. This aircraft is assigned to the 28th Bomb Wing at Ellsworth AFB.

An advanced terrain-following radar system enables the huge bomber to make blind low-level attacks.

The wing has seven-segment leading-edge flaps and six-segment trailing-edge flaps. There are no ailerons, and roll control is effected by spoilers.

The engine intakes have been designed to shield the engine compressor fans from hostile radar beams. As the compressor would otherwise give a strong radar return, this feature automatically reduces the bomber's signature.

The original B-1A had an ejection capsule like the F-111, but the B-1B has separate crew compartments and individual ejection seats for the pilots and systems operators.

The fuselage structure is mainly aluminium and titanium alloy, with some composite glass fibre.

There are three internal weapon bays, two forward of the wing and one aft, covered by a large hydraulic-powered door. The bay can house the Common Strategic Rotary Launcher (CSRL) also used in the B-2 and B-52.

The B-1B has a pair of small composite vanes under the cockpit. These provide yaw and pitch damping, smoothing the ride at low level.

B-1 nuclear strike

STAND-OFF ATTACK: B-1s were designed to be armed with free-fall bombs, which could be 'tossed' several kilometres, or with SRAM nuclear missiles, with ranges of 50 km (30 miles) at low level or more than 200 km (125 miles) at altitude.

LOW-LEVEL PENETRATION: The B-1's swing wings meant that it was a superb performer at low level, and it entered service as a low-level penetration bomber.

HIGH-LEVEL STRIKE: The original attack profile envisaged for the B-1A called for the aircraft to attack at high speed and from high level. But surface-to-air missiles would have made this suicidal long before the first metal was cut on the prototype.

LAUNCH FROM SAFETY: The advent of the air-launched cruise missile meant that nuclear bombers could attack from ranges of 2000 km (1240 miles) or more and still hit targets with pinpoint accuracy.

SEVERSKY

P-35

- Single-seat fighter ● All-metal ● Retractable undercarriage

▲ After beating the Curtiss Hawk Model 75 in a US Army Air Corps (USAAC) fighter competition, the P-35 initially represented a great advance in US fighter design.

America's first modern all-metal fighter, the P-35 proved to be lacking in performance when delivered to the USAAC in 1938. It was underarmed and difficult to handle in comparison with more modern Allied fighters and was quickly obsolete. Consequently, it suffered badly during its brief operational career when pitted against the Mitsubishi and Nakajima fighters in the initial Japanese onslaught against the Philippines.

SEVERSKY P-35

▲ **Export version**
EP-106 was the designation given by Seversky to the 60 aircraft supplied to Sweden. Orders amounted to 120, but deliveries ceased in 1939.

▲ **Twin Wasp**
One very neat feature of the P-35 was its closely cowled Twin Wasp radial engine.

▼ **Thin wings**
The elegant elliptical wings of the P-35 were very thin and allowed only partial gear retraction.

Into combat ▶
When designed the P-35 was under-gunned, and in combat the aircraft suffered dreadfully. Of the 48 P-35As in the Philippines, 40 were lost during the first two days of the Japanese offensive.

▲ **Last of the line**
Seversky completed the last P-35 with an 895-kW R-1830-19 turbo-charged engine. Designated XP-41, this aircraft was further improved by Seversky and acted as the prototype for the Republic P-43 Lancer, which in turn led to the P-47.

FACTS AND FIGURES

▶ The P-35 introduced refinements such as an enclosed cockpit, a constant-speed propeller and a retractable undercarriage.

▶ The P-35 was America's first modern all-metal monoplane fighter.

▶ Three squadrons of the 1st Pursuit Group received P-35s in 1938.

▶ When Japan attacked Pearl Harbor, P-35As constituted the entire air defence of the Philippines.

▶ P-35As were supplied to the Ecuadorean air force and the Philippines.

▶ An export version was sold to the Royal Swedish Air Force.

PROFILE

Seversky's out-classed fighter

Although a robust aircraft, the P-35 lacked performance, and by the time that the last one was delivered in August 1938 it was already considered obsolete.

The initial P-35 was withdrawn from front-line service in 1941, but undelivered Swedish examples continued to serve with the US Army Air Force as the P-35A. They were severely mauled by the Japanese when deployed in the Philippines, and only eight of the 48 of the aircraft remained

airworthy after the first two days of enemy attack. This was the first and last time that the type was used operationally.

The P-35's armament was completely inadequate for a 'modern' fighter, especially when compared with the contemporary British Spitfire and Hurricane or the Luftwaffe's Messerschmitt Bf 109. Deliveries of the aircraft were extremely slow and in 1938 the USAAC was already beginning to have second thoughts about the P-35. Consequently, the USAAC

placed an order for 210 Curtiss P-36s, the aircraft that had been placed second in the competition won by the P-35.

EP-106

Sweden's aircraft, known as the J9 in service, were redesignated P-35A when diverted to the USAAF. This aircraft served with Flygflottilj 8 during 1942/43.

Two 7.62-mm (.30-cal.) synchronized machine guns were mounted within troughs in the upper section of the engine cowling.

Even though it was considerably modified, the P-35 still resembled the earlier SEV-2XP design. This was especially true of the cockpit glazing, which extended some way behind the cockpit.

The only non-metal components of the fighter were the control surfaces, all of which were fabric-covered. The fin and rudder shape was carried over to the P-43 and eventually to the P-47 Thunderbolt after Seversky became Republic.

Most of the P-35's airframe was constructed of metal. The elliptical wings were reminiscent of those of the Spitfire and were of the cantilever type.

The tailwheel of the P-35 was fully retractable and when stowed it was covered by a pair of doors. Seversky produced a hooked variant for the US Navy, but its appalling performance discouraged production.

As rival fighters had retractable undercarriages, Seversky designed a rather crude system for the P-35. The wheels remained semi-exposed when retracted.

Left: This pre-war photograph shows P-35s of the 27th Pursuit Squadron. The aircraft are wearing the flamboyant markings which were typical of the period.

Right: The two-seat Seversky 2PA-L, based on the P-35, was acquired by the Soviet Union in March 1938 and was powered by a 746-kW (1000-hp) Wright R-1820 engine.

Seversky developments

■ **SEV-3:** Seversky's first project was the three-seat SEV-3 amphibian. It set the world speed record for amphibians in 1935.

■ **SEV-3XAR:** A two-seat landplane was developed from the SEV-3. The USAAC took 30 of a developed version as the BT-8 trainer.

■ **SEV-2XP:** This aircraft was Seversky's original entrant in the USAAC competition. It was damaged in transit and repaired as the P-35.

■ **AT-12:** A number of SEV-2PAs were diverted from USSR and Swedish orders and used as AT-12 trainers with the USAAC.

P-35A

Type: single-seat fighter

Powerplant: one 783-kW (1050-hp) Pratt & Whitney R-1830-45 14-cylinder, air-cooled radial piston engine

Maximum speed: 499 km/h (310 mph) at 4359 m (14,300 ft)

Initial climb rate: 585 m/min (1919 fpm)

Maximum range: 1529 km (950 miles)

Service ceiling: 9571 m (31,400 ft)

Armament: two 12.7-mm (.50-cal.) and two 7.62-mm (.30-cal.) machine guns plus up to 159 kg (350 lb) of bombs

Weights: empty 2075 kg (4575 lb); maximum take-off 3050 kg (6724 lb)

Dimensions:
span	10.97 m (36 ft)
length	8.18 m (26 ft 10 in)
height	2.97 m (9 ft 9 in)
wing area	20.44 m² (220 sq ft)

COMBAT DATA

MAXIMUM SPEED

Although the P-35A was faster than the early Bf 109E, it would have been no match for the Bf 109E, which was fighting over Europe while the P-35A was being mauled by 'Zeros' over the Philippines.

P-35A	499 km/h (310 mph)
Bf 109B-2	465 km/h (289 mph)
A6M2 'ZERO'	533 km/h (331 mph)

RANGE

Long range is desirable in any fighter and here the P-35A performed admirably. In the event, the aircraft was only to see combat during last-ditch attempts at defence, where speed, manoeuvrability and firepower were more important.

P-35A	1529 km (950 miles)
Bf 109B-2	692 km (430 miles)
A6M2 'ZERO'	1897 km (1235 miles)

ARMAMENT

Compared to the early Bf 109B-2, the P-35A was well armed. Messerschmitt had the problem well in hand, however, unlike Seversky whose P-35A had no answer to the A6M2's cannon.

P-35A	2 x 12.7-mm (.50-cal.) machine guns 2 x 7.62-mm (.30-cal.) machine guns 159-kg (350-lb)bombload
Bf 109B-2	2 x 7.9-mm machine guns
A6M2 'ZERO'	2 x 7.7-mm (.303-cal.) machine guns 2 x 20-mm cannon

SIKORSKY
R-4/R-5

● First production helicopter ● Successful design ● Wartime service

Many people believe the role of the helicopter in World War II was restricted to experimental flights. The USAAC took it far beyond the test phase and Sikorsky's diminutive R-4 performed some of the most significant flights of the entire war. Pilots found themselves confronted with an entirely new era of flight, and the potential of the military helicopter was quickly seen. As a search and rescue platform, it was a life-saver.

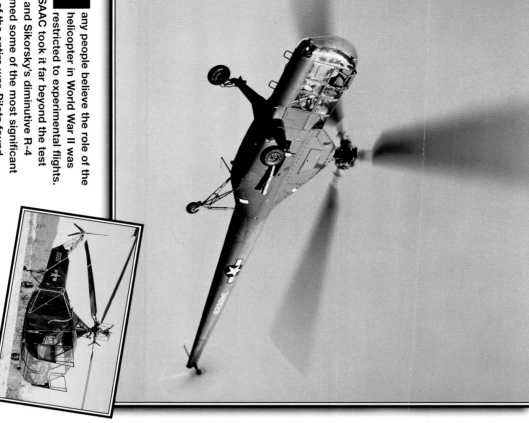

► Sikorsky's R-4 can rightly be considered as the world's first true production helicopter. First flying in 1939, it entered service with the USAAF, the USN, the RAF and the Royal Navy.

SIKORSKY R-4/R-5

Natural progression►
Following on from the R-4 was a slightly larger machine, the R-5. It is seen here in early configuration with a tailwheel undercarriage.

Workhorse forerunner►
Although the R-5 was successful, redesigning it resulted in the S-51, which did more to establish the concept of rotary-winged flight than any other helicopter.

▲ Production gets underway
With flight trials having been conducted successfully, the R-4 was put into production at Stratford, Connecticut in early 1942.

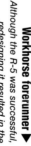

British helicopter evaluation ▼
After the R-4 had been ordered by the US armed services, a handful found their way overseas. The Royal Air Force and Fleet Air Arm evaluated the type during the closing months of World War II. In UK service, they were given the designation Hoverfly Mk I.

▲ Distinctive looks
Compared to later designs, the R-4 was an ungainly machine featuring a boxed spar fuselage covered in fabric.

FACTS AND FIGURES

➤ On 21 April 1945 a single Canadian R-4 became the first helicopter to rescue a downed crew in the Arctic.

➤ Thirty production machines (YR-4As and YR-4Bs) were ordered in total.

➤ US Army Air Force R-4s were used to rescue downed crews in the Pacific.

➤ By the time production switched to the improved R-5/S-51 series, a total of 130 Sikorsky R-4s had been built.

➤ A Sikorsky R-4 was the first true helicopter to make a landing at sea.

➤ On 17 May 1942, the XR-4 flew a distance of 1224 km (760 miles) from Stratford to Dayton.

PROFILE

Rotary-winged warriors

Igor Sikorsky finally managed to fly his first successful rotary-winged craft in 1939. Known as the VS-300, it was instrumental in the development of the world's first true production helicopter, the amazing Sikorsky R-4. With the VS-300 flying at speeds of up to 113 km/h (70 mph) by 1941, it was obvious that a more practical machine was viable.

The resulting XR-4 featured an enclosed cockpit with dual, side-by-side seating and a single Warner R500 piston engine. After successful trials, an order for 30 production aircraft (three YR-4As and 27 YR-4Bs) was placed by the United States Army Air Force. They were later

augmented by 100 more R-4Bs which featured more powerful engines. R-4s were pioneers in the development of the helicopter and, on 6 May 1943, an early production machine became the first helicopter to land successfully aboard a ship, touching down on the aircraft carrier, USS *Bunker Hill*.

Using the R-4 as a basis, Sikorsky developed the larger R-5, which featured an all-metal fuselage and other improvements. It first flew in 1943, but did not enter service until after World War II. Nevertheless, it proved tremendously successful and some 379 of these aircraft, later called S-51, were built.

Above: This photograph is unique, showing the Sikorsky R-4, R-5 and R-6 together. The evolution of the helicopter can already be seen.

Left: Col Frank Gregory, who helped to bring about the R-4, was the first person to land a helicopter on board ship.

GETTING IT RIGHT

MULTIPLE ROTORS: Igor Sikorsky's most successful testbed before the R-4 was the VS-300. This strange-looking machine made its maiden flight on 14 September 1939. Sikorsky had been experimenting with the idea of rotary-winged aircraft for many years, but until the late 1930s the technology was not sufficient to warrant a full working example. This tri-rotored layout was just one configuration tested on the VS-300.

FURTHER IDEAS: After experimenting with many configurations, Sikorsky discovered that stability and directional control problems could be solved by adopting an anti-torque rotor on the tail. This configuration has been adopted by the vast majority of helicopters since; the design is similar to that which ultimately emerged on the R-4 itself.

Tests were conducted in which the tail rotor was mounted horizontally, with the hub pointing skyward. Although the aircraft could get airborne with few problems, stability and directional control were still difficult. The XR-4 reverted to the more familiar layout.

Despite its appearance, the fuselage was extremely strong, with diagonally mounted spars increasing stiffness and strength. The rear section was uncovered.

R-4

During initial trials the Sikorsky R-4 wore an overall silver dope scheme with full colour insignia. Wartime operations saw the adoption of a drab green colour scheme to offer some form of camouflage to the vulnerable R-4.

The XR-4 was powered by a 123-kW (165-hp) Warner R-500 piston engine. From pre-production machines onward, this was substituted by a 138-kW (185-hp) R-550.

All R-4s were fitted with three-bladed main rotors. To reduce weight, they were constructed from spruce wood, which proved a problem during rescue operations in the Pacific theatre.

Because of the extreme upward tapering of the fuselage, a very long tail wheel was necessary to keep the R-4 level while on the ground.

At the time, the cockpit of the R-4 was quite unusual for many pilots. The aircraft commander sat in the right-hand seat. It was not a difficult machine to fly and pilots could go solo in just a few hours.

Another feature pioneered by the R-4 was the interchangeable undercarriage. R-4Bs in service with the US Navy aboard ships were often fitted with floats.

Early Sikorsky helicopters

■ **SIKORSKY R-6:** Installing the R-4's engine and gearbox in a new, much more streamlined fuselage resulted in the R-6. They were delivered to the RAF as Hoverfly Mk IIs.

■ **SIKORSKY S-52:** This little helicopter has the distinction of being the first of its type to feature all-metal rotor blades. It also established national helicopter records for speed and altitude.

■ **SIKORSKY S-55:** Entering service in 1952, the S-55 served with the US Army and Air Force in large numbers as the H-19. It was built under licence in France and the United Kingdom.

SIKORSKY
S-51/R-5

● Rescue helicopter ● Amphibious design ● Mail service

After its success with the R-4, the USAAF issued a requirement for a larger machine which was able to carry out tasks such as observation duties. Vought-Sikorsky's Model 327 was designed to meet the new specification and shared the R-4's basic layout. However, it was an entirely new design and seated two crew in tandem in a more streamlined fuselage. Sikorsky went on to develop the S-51 civil helicopter from the R-5.

▲ This S-51 is rescuing a member of the Canadian Armed Forces from a platform during a demonstration. The Sikorsky displayed excellent handling qualities, which are vital for rescue work.

SIKORSKY S-51/R-5

▼ Airborne angel
The Sikorsky S-51 saved lives by ensuring that casualties received medical attention quickly. This example carries two wounded men to a field hospital.

▲ Early days
With the fuselage panels removed for an engine test the small size of the R-5 is readily apparent.

Crop sprayer ▼
Seen displaying an unusual rig for spraying crops, the S-51 saw wide-spread civilian service as an air ambulance and work-horse.

▲ Cross-deck operations
Returning an admiral to his ship, an S-51 lands precariously on a gun turret.

Staying afloat ▼
A US Coast Guard H-5 sits on the water with emergency floatation bags inflated.

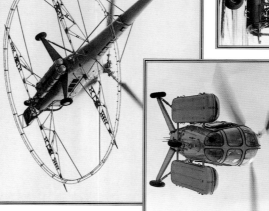

FACTS AND FIGURES

▼ Westland built the R-5 under licence in Britain as the WS.51 Dragonfly, for the RAF, Royal Navy and civil operators.

▼ Nine HO3S-1s were used by the US Coast Guard as HO3S-1Gs.

▼ HO3S-1s served with distinction in the Korean War with Squadron HU-1.

▼ In 1950 Sikorsky built and tested a single XHO3S-3 with a redesigned rotor head and blades.

▼ Two XR-5As were fitted with British instruments to an RAF requirement.

▼ The R-5B, R-5C and HO3S-2 were planned variants later cancelled.

PROFILE

The first rescue helicopter

Five prototypes were built under the designation XR-5, the first of which flew on 18 August 1943. Power was supplied by a fuselage-mounted 336-kW (450-hp) Pratt & Whitney R-985 radial engine. These were followed by 26 YR-5A evaluation aircraft and 34 R-5A service aircraft, which could be fitted with stretcher carriers for casualty evacuation.

These R-5As were the first helicopters employed by the Air Rescue Service (ARS). Of these, 21 were converted to R-5D standard with a rescue hoist and an external fuel tank.

On 16 February 1946, the first S-51 took to the air. This model had a larger four-seater cabin, a nosewheel (the first R-5s had a tailwheel behind the cabin) and a higher gross weight. More than 200 were built, including a batch for the Royal Canadian Air Force. The USAF bought 11 examples, as R-5Fs, in 1947.

From June 1948 the R-5 family was redesignated H-5 and, later that year, the ARS added H-5Gs (based on the H-5F with a hoist and other equipment) to its inventory. The last H-5s built (in 1949) were 16 H-5Hs, which were equipped with combined wheel/pontoon landing gear.

The US Navy took delivery of three R-5As, designated HO2S-1s, in late 1945, and later ordered 88 HO3S-1s, equivalent to the H-5F. Although officially designated as observation aircraft, they performed a number of tasks. Examples were also built under licence by Westland in Britain and served with the Fleet Air Arm and the RAF. In Royal Navy service the helicopters operated as 'plane-guards' flying from aircraft-carriers.

Left: The H-5, seen here returning after a rescue, was the primary SAR helicopter for the USAF throughout the 1950s and rescued both servicemen and civilians.

Above: The first amphibious helicopter for US service, the new wheel/float combination of the Sikorsky design greatly improved its capabilities.

Three main rotor blades were fitted to the R-5 producing enough lift for the helicopter to have a surprisingly good performance.

A simple tail rotor allowed for excellent low speed handling particularly when manoeuvring in the hover, a fact that many downed crew came to appreciate.

H-5

Displaying the title *Southern Comfort* on its nose, this example served with MAMs-33 in the Korean war. The helicopter patrolled the Sea of Japan retrieving downed pilots.

The fuselage was of an all metal design which offered a major improvement over the earlier fabric covered Sikorsky R-4. The design was far more resistant to the elements, which was vital as the helicopter was soon operating in a war zone.

To extend the capabilities of the design, a stretcher could be attached on each side of the helicopter to evacuate wounded personnel.

A standard tricycle undercarriage was installed on the helicopter to which floats could be attached for rescue work over water.

The cockpit provided accommodation for two crew seated in tandem. Excellent visibility was afforded to the pilot which was ideal for search and rescue work.

Sikorsky's rescue helicopters

SIKORSKY HO5S-1: Developed shortly after the S-51 the HO5S-1 offered a larger cabin area to accommodate more people. Used alongside the S-51 in the Korean War the type was used by both the US Navy and Marines. After Korea it was employed by the US Coast Guard.

SIKORSKY H-19: Continuous development of the helicopter fleet saw the H-19 become one of the most successful early designs. Constructed under licence by Westland in Britain the H-19 was often seen rescuing people from the sea, as illustrated here by this USAF example.

SIKORSKY HU5-1A: Operating over water, many helicopters were fitted with floats to allow landings on the sea. This proved invaluable during rescue work. Though highly effective, the use of floats resulted in a loss in performance and many operators did not use the extra capability.

R-5B

Type: two-/four-seat rescue and utility helicopter

Powerplant: one 336-kW (450-hp) Pratt & Whitney R-985-AN-5 radial piston engine

Maximum speed: 171 km/h (106 mph)

Cruising speed: 137 km/h (85 mph)

Initial climb rate: 3048 m (10,000 ft) in 15 minutes

Range: 579 km (360 miles)

Service ceiling: 4390 m (14,400 ft) with an operational load

Weights: empty 1715 kg (3773 lb); take-off 2189 kg (4815 lb)

Dimensions: main rotor diameter 14.63 m (48 ft)
length 17.40 m (57 ft 1 in)
height 3.96 m (13 ft)
rotor disc area 168.15 m² (1809 sq ft)

ACTION DATA

MAXIMUM SPEED

Constructed under licence by Westland as the Dragonfly, the Sikorsky R-5 showed the rapid improvements that helicopters were making by its speed advantage over the Sikorsky R-4B a design which was produced just a few years before. This was repeated again in the Whirlwind which offered a larger cabin area.

DRAGONFLY HR.Mk 3	165 km/h (102 mph)
WHIRLWIND HAS.Mk 7	176 km/h (109 mph)
R-4B	120 km/h (74 mph)

SERVICE CEILING

Though smaller than the Whirlwind the Dragonfly enjoyed one of the highest operational ceilings of the early helicopters. But this was reduced in the Air Rescue Service role when the fuselage was fitted with a hoist and an auxiliary fuel tank.

DRAGONFLY HR.Mk 3	4206 m (13,800 ft)
WHIRLWIND HAS.Mk 7	2865 m (9400 ft)
R-4B	2440 m (8000 ft)

WEIGHTS LOADED

The small fuselage of the Dragonfly restricted its capacity to lift any more than a minor load. The larger cabin area of the later Whirlwind proved to be far more practical, capable of carrying survivors, troops, and medical attendants.

R-4B	1153 kg (2537 lb)
WHIRLWIND HAS.Mk 7	2865 kg (6303 lb)
DRAGONFLY HR.Mk 3	2663 kg (5859 lb)

SIKORSKY

S-55/H-19

● Korea veteran ● Pioneering troop-lifter ● Air-sea rescue

The S-55 was the first in a long line of successful large Sikorsky helicopters. Starting life as a piston-powered machine with a limited load-carrying capacity, the S-55 later received a turbine engine and considerably more capability. It could perform a variety of roles, including airlifting troops, air-sea rescue work, air taxiing, cargo-hauling and anti-submarine patrol. The S-55 took part in the Korean War, but was still providing useful service to military and civil users in the 1980s.

▲ The S-55 was one of the first really practical large helicopters. Its career was an exciting one, with constant wartime use. With a turbine engine and more power, it shone as a versatile machine.

SIKORSKY S-55/H-19

▼ Piston power

The large, bulky radial was faired under twin clamshell doors. Engineers loved this as it meant easy access to the engine. But the marriage of helicopters and large piston engines was never really successful.

▲ At home on floats

From the start, the helicopter's unique ability made it ideal for maritime use, and the float-equipped S-55 served as a rescue machine for many years.

Troop carrier ▶

The S-55's ability to carry up to 10 fully-equipped troops was used in the development of an entirely new kind of warfare known as helicopter assault. Troop-carrying S-55s saw action around the world, from Malaya to Algeria.

Load-lifter ▶

Hauling logs in the Rockies was another task that earlier helicopters were not capable of. The need for a powerful turbine engine was demonstrated vividly when carrying loads at high altitudes.

Sling load supplies ▶

The ability to get supplies to troops miles from any airfield was especially useful in Korea, where UN units were frequently bypassed and surrounded. The narrow fuselage profile made underslung load-carrying preferable to using the tight cabin space.

FACTS AND FIGURES

▶ The US Army version of the H-19 was known as the Chickasaw.

▶ The US Navy HOS-4 version was used for anti-submarine warfare duties.

▶ Westland-built S-55s were sometimes powered by the Alvis Leonides Major piston engine or Gnome turboshaft.

▶ French S-55s in Algeria used rockets and machine guns in combat trials.

▶ The US Army was still using its last few H-19s in the early 1980s.

▶ In an air show stunt that went wrong, an RAF Whirlwind dragged a stuntman on a bicycle through trees.

First of the big Sikorskys

Helicopters really came of age after 1945, and the type owes much to the work of the great Igor Sikorsky. After building a utility machine for the US Air Force, designated H-19. The first of these, known to the manufacturer as the S-55, flew in November 1949. It was powered by a Pratt & Whitney radial piston engine, similar to those in wartime fighters. The drive shaft ran under the cockpit to the high-mounted rotor. With a rear cabin that could carry 10 passengers, the S-55 was an instant success, and its combat debut came in Korea. It was licence-built by Westland in Britain, and served with the Royal Navy's 'Jungly' squadrons in Malaya, dropping commandos into the forest. French S-55s, built by SNCA, served in Algeria, pursuing the FNLA into the Atlas mountains. In numerous wars from the African desert to the jungles of Vietnam, S-55s carried out thousands of troop lifts and medevac (medical evacuation) missions. Later, when re-engined with a turboprop instead of the heavy piston engine, it gained a new lease of life and soldiered on into the 1990s.

The S-55 was very similar to its Soviet counterpart, the Mi-4. Both types provided valuable new experience of operating helicopters in unusual roles and conditions.

H-19B

The US Air Force operated the S-55 as the H-19A and H-19B in the air-sea rescue role. The same version was known as the H-19C Chickasaw in US Army service.

The S-55 had an all-metal rotor, a great improvement on the wooden versions of early helicopters. The three-bladed rotor had conventional hinges.

Search-and-rescue S-55s had a starboard-mounted winch.

The wide, stable undercarriage was essential as the S-55 was tall, although the engine weight was low down. Early helicopters often suffered 'ground resonance' due to their shape, which on occasion caused bad accidents.

The main cabin accommodated up to 10 passengers, seated against the front and rear walls, and two on each side.

The two-man cockpit had full dual controls. It was extremely noisy, especially in the radial-powered versions.

The engines of the S-55 were consistently uprated. The first H-19 had a Pratt & Whitney R-1340 radial, but the Wright 1820 of the HRS-4 had twice the power.

The tail rotor was a simple two-bladed unit, driven by a long shaft from the main transmission under the main rotor.

The main fuselage was of conventional aluminium and magnesium semi-monocoque construction, except for the chrome-molybdenum steel rotor pylon.

In service around the world

■ **US MILITARY S-55s:** Known as the H-19 (Air Force), H-19 Chickasaw (Army), HO4S (Navy) and HRS-3 (Marine Corps), the S-55 was the first helicopter to serve in large numbers.

■ **EXPORT SUCCESS:** The S-55's capabilities were so far in advance of any other Western helicopter that it sold widely abroad, to more than a dozen countries, including Canada.

■ **ROYAL HELICOPTER:** The most luxurious of all S-55 variants, the turbine-powered Westland Whirlwinds of Britain's Queen's Flight flew until the late 1960s.

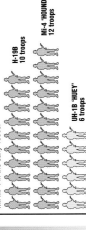

S-55 (H-19B)

Type: 10-passenger utility helicopter

Powerplant: one 522-kW (700-hp) Wright R-1300-3 radial piston engine

Maximum speed: 180 km/h (110 mph); cruising speed 146 km/h (90 mph)

Range: 580 km (370 miles)

Service ceiling: 3940 m (12,923 ft)

Weights: empty 2381 kg (5238 lb); take-off 3583 kg (7883 lb)

Armament: none designed, but machine guns and rockets were fitted in the field

Payload: 10 passengers or up to eight stretchers in ambulance role

Dimensions:
rotor diameter   16.16 m (53 ft)
length   12.85 m (42 ft)
height   4.07 m (13 ft)
rotor disc area 204.94 m² (2205 sq ft)

COMBAT DATA

MAXIMUM SPEED

The earliest helicopters were far from sprightly machines, and although capable of 180 km/h the original S-55 cruised at a stately 146 km/h. The Soviet Mil appeared after the S-55, but although it looked similar it was a much larger and more powerful machine, with slightly better performance. The turbine-powered 'Huey' flew in the late 1950s, and was to replace the S-55 in many of its roles.

H-19B	180 km/h (110 mph)
Mi-4 'HOUND'	210 km/h (130 mph)
UH-1B 'HUEY'	225 km/h (140 mph)

RANGE

No helicopter was economical, and the early generation of machines used fuel at a great rate. However, since they were designed for short-range tasks such as coastal rescue, amphibious assault or logistic support on the battlefield, their lack of range was seen as no real handicap.

Mi-4 'HOUND' 590 km (366 miles)

UH-1B 'HUEY' 600 km (370 miles)

H-19B 580 km (360 miles)

PAYLOAD

The helicopters which entered service at the end of World War II were pushed to carry two or three passengers as well as a pilot. So the S-55, which made its maiden flight in 1949, was a revelation. Capable of lifting 10 troops, it was easily the most capable helicopter of its time, only surpassed by the much bigger Mil Mi-4 in the early 1950s.

H-19B 10 troops

Mi-4 'HOUND' 12 troops

UH-1B 'HUEY' 6 troops

SIKORSKY

S-56/CH-37 MOJAVE

- US Army and Marines transport ● First twin-engined Sikorsky

▲ With experience gained in designing the S-56, Sikorsky went on to produce other large single-rotor designs, like the S-64 Skycrane (CH-54 Tarhe) and S-65 (CH-53 Sea Stallion).

F or 10 years after its first flight the S-56 was the largest helicopter flying outside the Soviet Union and, until the end of 1961, it was the largest helicopter operated by the US military. Designed to meet a US Navy and Marine Corps requirement for an assault transport, it was also the first twin-engined Sikorsky design. Designated HR2S by the Navy, the S-56 flew in 1953. It served in larger numbers with the US Army as the H-37 Mojave.

SIKORSKY **S-56/CH-37 MOJAVE**

▼ **Retractable landing gear**
Mojaves were not only novel in their engine arrangement; they also had a retractable undercarriage. The main gear assemblies retracted rearwards into the engine nacelle. Each leg was supported by twin wheels.

▲ **Valuable heavy-litter**
H-37s provided US Army logistics personnel with a heavy-lift capability that they had never had before.

▲ **On exercises in Puerto Rico**
HR2S-1s of HMR-461 touch down at a marked landing area during exercises.

▼ **YH-37 for the Army**
In 1954, the US Army tested a pre-production XHR2S-1 as a YH-37.

▲ **Early warning variant**
Two HR2S-1Ws, with APS-20E radar scanners fitted, were evaluated by the US Navy. However, airframe vibration badly degraded radar performance.

FACTS AND FIGURES

▶ Mojaves were replaced by the CH-54 Tarhe, which weighed less but could lift five times as much cargo as the CH-37.

▶ In all, 150 S-56s were built; a prototype, 55 for the USMC and 94 for the Army.

▶ The year 1959 saw the first overseas H-37 deployment, by the Army to Germany.

▶ Army H-37As entered service with the 4th Medium Helicopter Transportation Company in February 1958.

▶ With a fuselage capacity of 37.5 m³ (1324 cubic ft), the H-37A could hold three Army jeeps.

▶ The Army briefly evaluated one of the two HR2S-1Ws in 'Arctic' colours.

PROFILE

First heavy-lift chopper for the Corps

Despite being piston-engined at a time when most new helicopter designs were powered by lightweight and powerful turboshafts, the CH-37 (as it was known to the US Army and Navy after 1962) proved its worth as a heavy-lift helicopter.

This was illustrated by the type's brief deployment by the Army in the Vietnam conflict. Four CH-37Bs recovered $7.5 million worth of downed aircraft during June 1963, many of them

from otherwise inaccessible, enemy-dominated areas.

Sikorsky's S-56 was designed to meet a US Marine Corps requirement for an assault helicopter able to carry about 26 troops. The machine's unique configuration, with its engines in nacelles separate from the fuselage, left the latter clear for load-carrying. Large clam-shell doors in the nose allowed straight-in loading of up to 907 kg (2000 lb) of cargo into the winch-equipped hold.

Fifty-five HR2S-1s were delivered to the US Marines; two were later modified for early warning duties by the Navy as HR2S-1Ws with a large radar scanner installed in a radome fitted under the chin.

After evaluating an XHR2S-1 (YH-37), the Army took delivery of 94 H-37As, all of which were delivered by June 1960. Most were later converted to H-37B standard with improved systems. The last CH-37s were retired in the late 1960s.

Above: A Marine Corps CH-37C and UH-34D return to MCAS El Toro, California, from an exercise.

Right: Distinctive 'eyes' painted on the front of the engine nacelles were a common feature of both Marine Corps and Army CH-37s.

CH-37C

Originally designated HRS-1 by the USMC, the S-56 became the CH-37C when US military designation systems were unified in 1962.

Pratt & Whitney's ever-reliable R-2800 Double Wasp (that powered such types as the Northrop P-61 Black Widow night-fighter and Douglas A-26 Invader bomber) found yet another application in the S-56.

Industry practice at the time of the S-56's design was to employ fore- and aft-mounted tandem rotors. Sikorsky broke with convention, using a single large, five-bladed main rotor with a four-bladed anti-torque rotor at the rear.

Positioning the engines in separate nacelles allowed more payload room in the fuselage. A rail along the cabin ceiling and a 907-kg capacity winch aided loading.

A common feature of Army and Marine Corps CH-37s was a pair of auxiliary fuel tanks of 1136-litre (300-gallon) capacity, fixed to the fuselage inboard of the undercarriage. Fuel reached the engines direct via external pipes.

Clam-shell doors provided access to the CH-37's hold. A ramp was fitted for vehicles.

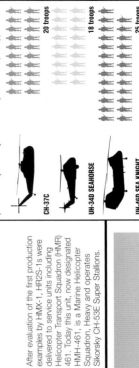

After evaluation of the first production examples by HMX-1, HR2S-1s were delivered to service units including Helicopter Transport Squadron (HMR) 461. Today this unit, now designated HMH-461, is a Marine Helicopter Squadron, Heavy and operates Sikorsky CH-53E Super Stallions.

HMR 461

COMBAT DATA

CRUISING SPEED

Marine Corps CH-37Cs (HR2S-1s) were marginally faster than the Sikorsky UH-34, which had been one of the Marines' larger helicopter types. The tandem-rotor Boeing-Vertol Sea Knight was a substantially faster aircraft.

CH-37C	185 km/h (115 mph)
UH-34D SEAHORSE	158 km/h (98 mph)
UH-46D SEA KNIGHT	248 km/h (154 mph)

TROOPS

US Navy and Marine Corps H-34s, H-37s and H-46s represent advances in helicopter design and a trend toward larger machines able to carry more troops and cargo. The UH-46 was specifically purchased by the Navy for vertical replenishment (vertrep) duties.

CH-37C — 20 troops
UH-34D SEAHORSE — 18 troops
UH-46D SEA KNIGHT — 25 troops

RANGE

Though able to lift heavy loads, the CH-37 was a little short on range compared to the Seahorse. In service with both the Marines and Army, the type was often fitted with extra external fuel tanks to boost range performance. Boeing-Vertol's Sea Knight took most performance standards to new heights on entering service in 1964.

CH-37C	233 km (145 miles)
UH-34D SEAHORSE	293 km (180 miles)
UH-46D SEA KNIGHT	370 km (230 miles)

Marine Corps helicopters at war

■ **BELL UH-1E IROQUOIS:** First employed by the US Army in Vietnam in 1962, the 'Huey' was adopted by the Marines in UH-1E form and quickly deployed to Southeast Asia.

■ **SIKORSKY HRS-2:** HRS-1s and HRS-2s equipped nine Marine transport (HMR) squadrons in Korea. Their main role was troop carrying, the type seating up to eight troops.

■ **SIKORSKY CH-53A SEA STALLION:** First deployed in Vietnam in January 1967, the CH-53 was specifically developed as a large assault type for the Marine Corps.

■ **SIKORSKY UH-34D (HUS-1) SEAHORSE:** The most widely used piston-engined helicopter of the war, the Seahorse was the USMC's main assault helicopter until the UH-1 entered service.

SIKORSKY
S-58/H-34 CHOCTAW

- ASW/utility helicopter ● US Army, Navy and Marines ● Piston engine

A new generation of helicopter design was ushered in by Sikorsky's S-58. Prior to its first flight in 1954, helicopters had been built for their unique capabilities, with little thought given to their role suitability. The S-58, operated by the US Navy, Marines and Army, was a highly versatile helicopter suited to a variety of roles. It went on to win many export orders in both military and commercial versions and a few still remain in service.

▲ The military S-58 series was so successful that examples soon started to appear all over the world. VH-34Ds were used to support President Eisenhower on a visit to Spain.

SIKORSKY S-58/H-34 CHOCTAW

▼ US Coast Guard rescue
Based on the Marines HUS-1A (CH-34E) version, six HUS-1G (HH-34F) helicopters, capable of operating on amphibious pontoons, were delivered to the Coast Guard.

▲ Japanese HSS-1
Japan obtained a large number of ex-US Navy HSS-1s (nicknamed the 'Hiss-1' in US service) and used them in the search-and-rescue role.

▲ Folded Choctaw
The US Army's CH-34A Choctaw retained the fuselage folding capabilities of its naval counterpart. Many Choctaws flew with US forces based in Germany.

▼ Back to Earth
HUS-1 helicopters belonging to the Marines had the honour of recovering several astronauts and their capsules from the sea.

▲ Bullpup shot
Several experiments were carried out with armed H-34s, but none entered service. This Marines HUS-1 makes an early test firing.

FACTS AND FIGURES

▶ When he checked in for a Sabena S-58 flight, Igor Sikorsky was asked if his name was spelt like the helicopter's.

▶ US military designation changes in 1962 led to the HSS-1 becoming the SH-34G.

▶ 'Doughnut' bags could be fixed to the S-58 undercarriage to make it amphibious.

▶ US Army CH-34s maintained a constant patrol along the border of West Germany with Czechoslovakia and East Germany.

▶ The US Army-Marines Executive Flight Detachment used VH-34D aircraft.

▶ A total of 603 S-58s were delivered to the US Marines.

PROFILE

Sikorsky's stunning S-58

When the Bell XHSL-1 anti-submarine warfare (ASW) helicopter proved disappointing, the US Navy was glad that it had ordered the Sikorsky XHSS-1 as a back-up. As the HSS-1 Seabat, the new helicopter entered US Navy service in August 1955, with aircraft often flying in hunter-killer pairs and later in close co-operation with ASW ships. The HSS-1N version pioneered the use of the auto-hover facility. Shipboard stowage was made easier by folding the rear fuselage and tail rotor forwards, and the main rotor could also be folded.

The US Marines used the 'stripped-out' HUS-1 Seahorse as a 12-seat utility transport. The US Army, in a similar position to the Navy, was disappointed with the Piasecki H-21 and ordered the H-34A Choctaw straight off the production line in 1955. The 359 ordered by the Army could

each carry 18 troops.

Civilian S-58B/Ds were used to carry cargo, while Sabena launched scheduled helicopter services with the 18-seat S-58C. Military S-58s were exported to many countries and a turbine engine conversion is available in the United States.

Left: Sabena, Belgium's national airline, was an early operator of passenger helicopters, flying S-55s. These were replaced by S-58s from 1956.

Above: The S-58T conversion is powered by a Pratt & Whitney Canada PT6T-3 Twin Pac coupled-turbine engine. Only a small number of customers have been found.

H-34G

Germany used its H-34s as utility transports supporting the army, and in the SAR role with a winch mounted above the cabin door. These SAR H-34s have now been replaced by Westland Sea King Mk 41s.

Pilots had an excellent view from the high-set cockpit and large cabin windows. These windows could be slid to the rear along rails, for cooling or a better view vertically downwards.

An R-1820 nine-cylinder diagonally-mounted engine drove the high-speed shaft to the main gearbox. Cooling air was drawn in through large grills around the upper nose. Complete engine access was provided by the clamshell doors which formed the nose.

The rugged, fixed undercarriage incorporated a rearwards-angled shock-absorber strut. Various flotation aids could be fitted.

The main rotors and tail rotors were driven by a large gearbox in the upper-rear fuselage which received drive from a high-speed shaft that ran upwards from the engine between the crew seats.

All S-58s had a small horizontal stabiliser. Within the tailfin structure immediately below this, was the gearbox which linked the tail rotor driveshaft to a long shaft that carried drive from the main gearbox to the tail.

Most S-58s retained the tail-folding of the original HSS-1. The tail folded along this hinge line to lie along the left fuselage side and was useful for transportation.

Two windows were fitted in the left-hand side of the cabin, with a large sliding door on the opposite side providing access. A slung load of 2268 kg (5000 lb) or 18 troops could be carried.

Sikorsky S-58 selection

H-34A CHOCTAW: H-34s became the standard US Army light transport helicopter. This helicopter has an unusual fin-mounted whip aerial and was later updated to H-34B standard.

H-34A: Sikorsky delivered 90 H-34s to the French army and Sud-Aviation built a further 166 under licence for army and navy use in the Algerian war.

S-58T: New York Helicopter received two of these turbine-engined conversions, which were fitted with a greater number of windows. S-58B/D models are the most popular for conversion.

COMBAT DATA

MAXIMUM SPEED

Westland in the UK developed the Wessex as a turbine-engined evolution of the S-58. Speed was increased by the new engine, but only slightly.

S-58	196 km/h (122 mph)
MI-4 'HOUND'	175 km/h (108 mph)
WESSEX HC.Mk 2	212 km/h (131 mph)

HOVERING CEILING

Improved altitude performance was the principal benefit of turbine power. The MI-4 'Hound' had poor performance compared to the S-58, with the Soviets trailing in helicopter technology in the 1950s.

S-58	730 m (2400 ft)
MI-4 'HOUND'	700 m (2300 ft)
WESSEX HC.Mk 2	1220 m (4000 ft)

MAXIMUM TAKE-OFF WEIGHT

In the transport role maximum take-off weight reflects the load that an aircraft can lift. For the ASW role cabin space for avionics is important, and the S-58 strikes a balance between the two.

S-58	6350 kg (13,970 lb)
MI-4 'HOUND'	7550 kg (16,610 lb)
WESSEX HC.Mk 2	6123 kg (13,470 lb)

410

SIKORSKY
S-61/SH-3 SEA KING

● Anti-submarine helicopter ● In service for 30 years

As a true rotorcraft pioneer, Sikorsky was quick to realise the potential of the helicopter for anti-submarine warfare (ASW) operations. With its HSS-1 Sea Bat already in service, Sikorsky designed the HSS-2 Sea King as its turbine-engined replacement. The company could not have realized that the Sea King would become one of the world's most important helicopters, in service with the US Navy (USN) and many export customers.

▲ One of the world's best known helicopters, the Sikorsky S-61 is also one of the longest-serving. Although now a rare sight in US Navy colours, the type continues to fly with other air arms.

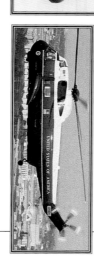

PHOTO FILE

SIKORSKY S-61/SH-3 SEA KING

▼ Topex
An SH-3H, belonging to HS-9 from Carrier Air Wing 8 aboard the USS Nimitz, flies in company with a Brazilian Navy machine during the annual 'Topex' anti-submarine warfare exercise in the Atlantic.

Dual-role helicopter ▶
In the early 1970s the USN needed a helicopter to perform both plane guard and ASW duties aboard its attack carriers and the SH-3 proved ideal.

▼ Enduring design
Despite being in service for nearly 40 years, the outward appearance of the S-61 has surprisingly changed very little, though the latest versions are considerably more capable than early variants.

▲ Space rescue
Sea Kings were used for recovering astronauts after the Apollo lunar landings.

▼ Helicopters for the White House
Possibly the most glamourous of all S-61s are the VH-3Ds in use as VIP transports for the US president and government officials.

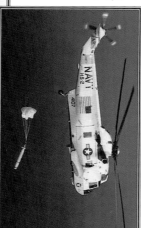

FACTS AND FIGURES

▶ Sea Kings were heavily involved in Vietnam, rescuing many downed USN pilots during the long conflict.

▶ A small number of RH-3A minesweeper variants entered service in 1964.

▶ The Royal Canadian Navy was the first export customer, ordering 41 of the type.

▶ Aeronautiche Giovanni Agusta acquired a licence to assemble Sea Kings for the Italian air force and navy.

▶ Argentina is unique in that it operates both Sikorsky and Agusta built examples.

▶ The SH-3 has been replaced aboard USN carriers by the SH-60F Sea Hawk.

PROFILE

Backbone of the world's navies

Known by Sikorsky as the S-61 and by the US Navy as the SH-3, the Sea King serves into the late 1990s in considerable numbers, having flown for the first time on 11 March 1959.

Combining the roles of submarine hunter and killer thanks to its Bendix AQS-10 dipping sonar, Ryan APN-130 radar, and torpedo or depth bomb weapon load, the SH-3A was an instant success. The few remaining USN Sea Kings have all been upgraded to SH-3H standard. The design has also formed the basis of the much-modified Westland Sea King.

In addition to its ASW machines, the USN also flew nine examples of the specialized RH-3A minesweeping version of the basic SH-3, while a number of combat search and rescue HH-3 aircraft, also based on the SH-3 airframe, were built for the US Air Force.

Export customers included Argentina, Brazil, Canada, Denmark, Iran, Italy, Japan, Malaysia, Peru, Spain, and the UK. Several of these deals have included production licences.

Below: In Italian naval service, the Agusta SH-3Ds wear this dark sea grey colour scheme with high visibility day-glo noses and tail bands.

Above: SH-3s can actually be refuelled in flight, though the usual method is somewhat different from that shown here!

SH-3H Sea King

Type: anti-submarine and plane guard shipboard helicopter

Powerplant: two 1044-kW (1400-hp) General Electric T58-GE-10 turboshafts

Maximum speed: 267 km/h (166 mph)

Cruising speed: 219 km/h (136 mph)

Initial climb rate: 670 m/min (2200 fpm)

Range: 1005 km (623 miles)

Service ceiling: 4480 m (14,700 ft)

Weights: empty 4428 kg (9742 lb); loaded 9525 kg (20,995 lb)

Accommodation: two pilots and two systems operators

Dimensions: rotor diameter 18.90 m (62 ft)
length 22.15 m (72 ft 8 in)
height 5.13 (16 ft 10 in)
rotor disc area 280.47 m² (3018 sq ft)

ACTION DATA

POWER

Even when it entered service, the Sikorsky Sea King was a powerful machine, able to lift substantial loads. In later years Westland built its own version with more powerful engines.

SH-3H SEA KING 2088 KW (2800 hp)

SEA KING HAS.MK5 2476kW (3320 hp)

SA 321G SUPER FRELON 3300kw (4425 hp)

RANGE

When employed for plane guard or search and rescue duties the Sea King does not operate far afield. In the ASW role Sea Kings work with longer-ranged fixed wing aircraft.The bigger Aerospatiale Super Frelon is primarily a tactical transport helicopter

SH-3H SEA KING 1005km (623 miles)

SEA KING HAS.MK5 1230km (763 miles)

SA 321G SUPER FRELON 1020 km (632 miles)

CLIMB RATE

Despite being fitted with more powerful engines, the Westland Sea King performs less well than its slightly older Sikorsky cousin. The lumbering Super Frelon is very slow by comparison .

SH-3H SEA KING 670 m/min (2200 fpm)

SEA KING HAS.MK5 616 m/min (2020 fpm)

SA 321G SUPER FRELON 300 m/min (980 fpm)

SH-3H SEA KING

This SH-3H of HS-7 'Shamrocks' served aboard the USS *John F. Kennedy* (CV-67) during the carrier's 1983-84 Atlantic cruise.

Powering the SH-3H variant are two General Electric T58-GE-10 turboshafts. These provide impressive performance for a relatively large helicopter and generate up to 1044 kW (1400 hp) each, allowing the aircraft to carry substantial underslung loads if so required.

All Sikorsky S-61s are amphibious and are capable of landing on water for brief periods if necessary. The underside of the fuselage is sculpted to act as a watertight hull.

All Sea Kings are fitted with five-blade main rotors. These can be folded aft and are interchangeable. They also feature the Sikorsky spar inspection system, which releases an inert gas if the blades are cracked, thus alerting maintenance staff to potential problems.

The anti-torque tail rotor is fitted on the port side and also features five blades. A single stabiliser is fitted on the opposite side. The entire tail section is moveable and can hinge to starboard for accessibility and stowage below carrier decks.

Equipment unique to the USN 'H' variant includes an AQS-13B sonar, a Canadian Marconi surveillance radar, and towed magnetic anomaly detector for hunting submarines.

NAVY HS-7
615
USS JOHN F KENNEDY
2112

Sea King goes foreign

■ **BRAZILIAN NAVY SH-3D:** A number of machines were delivered to the Brazilian Navy and operated by 1° Esquadro de Helicopteros Anti-submarinos from Sao Pedro de Aldeida.

MARINHA
N-3011

■ **JMSDF HSS-2B:** Mitsubishi of Japan acquired a licence to build Sea Kings and Japan's Maritime Self-Defence Force uses the type for anti-submarine warfare and rescue duties.

42

■ **SPANISH SH-3D:** This smart example is one of a batch of ex-USN machines transferred to Spain. These have been upgraded to SH-3H standard and serve with Escuadrilla 001.

005 012 MARINA

SIKORSKY

S-61R/CH-3

- USAF transport ● Combat search and rescue ● US Coast Guard

▲ Optimized for USAF use, the S-61R was built in four highly successful variants and under licence in Italy. Few aircraft can match the fame of the 'Jolly Green Giant'.

n 1962 the USAF borrowed three SH-3A helicopters from the US Navy. Used for transport as CH-3Bs, these aircraft from the Sikorsky S-61 series impressed the Air Force so much that it ordered a new version for its own use. Known as the S-61R, this transport helicopter went on to save many lives in the CSAR (combat search and rescue) role over Vietnam as the 'Jolly Green Giant' and, from 1968, with the US Coast Guard as the Pelican.

412

SIKORSKY S-61R/CH-3

▲ Italian navy SAR
Agusta built 20 HH-3Fs from 1973. These were similar to US Coast Guard aircraft.

▲ Inflight refuelling
In 1966 the USAF revealed a series of tests using a US Marine Corps KC-130F tanker. Ten contacts of up to five minutes duration were performed.

▼ Civilian model
Sikorsky's own S-61R hovers above the first USAF CH-3C. As the aircraft was designed around a USAF requirement, commercial buyers did not appear.

▲ Practice rescue
US Coast Guard machines used their search radar, hoist and amphibious capabilities to the full. The HH-3F was used to search coastlines and out at sea.

Test boom ▶
Carrying an air data boom for experimental and test purposes, the first CH-3C, in common with others of the model, was later upgraded to CH-3E standard.

FACTS AND FIGURES

▼ At least nine USAF surplus CH-3Es and HH-3Es were purchased by the US Coast Guard to supplement their 40 HH-3Fs.

▼ In 1975 CH/HH-3Es became the first helicopters in the US Air National Guard.

▼ Variants of Sikorsky's S-70 have replaced S-61Rs in US service.

▶ Two HH-3Es made the first non-stop transatlantic helicopter flights in 1967, making nine tanker contacts each.

▶ The first S-61R flew on 17 June 1963, almost one month ahead of schedule.

▶ The CH-3E could seat up to 30 troops or accommodate 2270 kg (5000 lb) of cargo.

PROFILE

USAF's 'Jolly Green Giant'

In order to satisfy the USAF's requirements, Sikorsky found that a major redesign of the SH-3 anti-submarine helicopter was necessary. The company designated the new helicopter S-61R and four versions of the basic amphibious transport design were built.

Principal amongst the design changes were a tricycle nose-wheel undercarriage and a large rear loading ramp door. Of the initial CH-3C model, 41 were built before production of the 1119-kW (1500-hp) T58-5 engined

CH-3E began in 1966. Meanwhile, the USAF had an urgent need for a helicopter capable of rescuing downed aircrew in a hostile environment – Vietnam.

Optimized for CSAR, the HH-3E had armour, defensive machine guns, jettisonable long-range fuel tanks and an in-flight refuelling (IFR) probe. Such was the ability of the HH-3E that it often rescued downed aircraft as well as aircrew and became known as the 'Jolly Green Giant'. The last development was the HH-3F Pelican for the US Coast

Guard. Basically an HH-3E with military equipment removed, the aircraft gave superb service into the 1990s, flying long-range rescue and anti-drug missions.

Below: The rear loading ramp had upper and lower parts, allowing vehicles up to 2.21 metres in height to be loaded. Large sponsons on either side of the fuselage kept the aircraft stable on water and accommodated the main landing gear.

Above: CH-3Es also carried a winch above the starboard forward door, adding extra flexibility and giving the helicopter a secondary SAR role.

HH-3E

This is an Air Force Reserve squadron HH-3E in standard 'European One' camouflage. In 1990 the HH-60G Pave Hawk began replacing HH-3Es. The new helicopter retains all the best features of its ancestor, including jettisonable external tanks and an IFR probe.

The main rotor did not retain the blade folding mechanisms of the naval SH-3. Vietnam pilots are rumoured to have used the rotor to trim branches from trees, allowing them to reach downed airmen.

A five-bladed aluminium tail rotor was adopted directly from the SH-3. A strut-braced tailplane was mounted opposite the rotor mounting. On the ground, the tail-low in-flight attitude was corrected by the length of the undercarriage.

Hydraulically operated doors formed the rear loading ramp. The open upper section retracted into the upper fuselage, while the lower part hinged downwards to form the ramp. In combat, the partially open ramp often held an extra machine gun.

The HH-3E provided its two-man flight crew with armour protection and a comprehensive radio and navigational avionics suite. Coast Guard HH-3Fs added search radar for maritime operations. Up to 15 stretcher patients could be accommodated in the square-section cabin.

Twin T58-GE-10 turboshafts gave the HH-3 good speed and climb performance. With the enemy closing in on a casualty, speed was essential for a successful rescue.

HH-3Es were the first helicopters to carry in-flight refuelling booms. The probe was telescopic, extending to twice its retracted length in order to keep the HC-130's drogue and refuelling hose well clear of the rotor blades.

Multi-mission S-61R

US COAST GUARD SAR: Having located the survivor using search radar, locater beacons and distress flares the HH-3F crew pluck casualties to safety using the rescue winch.

USAF VIETNAM CSAR: While a Douglas AD-1 Skyraider provided cover, the HH-3E winched shot-down aircrew from the jungle. The helicopter's own machine guns forced the enemy to remain undercover during the rescue.

USAF CH-3C DRONE RECOVERY: DC-130 Hercules released reconnaissance or target drones. After using up all their fuel these drones are recovered by the CH-3C and returned to base, where they may be prepared for re-use.

HH-3E

Type: long-range combat search-and-rescue helicopter

Powerplant: two 1044-kW (1400-hp) General Electric T58-GE-10 turboshafts

Maximum speed: 261 km/h (162 mph)

Climb rate: 6.7 m/sec (22 fps)

Range: 1005 km (625 miles)

Service ceiling: 3660 m (12,000 ft)

Weights: maximum take-off 10,002 kg (22,000 lb), usual gross 8165 kg (17,693 lb)

Armament: at least two 7.62-mm (.30-cal.) or 12.7-mm (.50-cal.) machine guns on flexible mounts, fired through the side doors

Dimensions: main rotor diameter 18.90 m (62 ft)
length 17.45 m (57 ft 3 in)
height 5.51 m (18 ft)
rotor disc area 280.5 m² (3013 sq ft)

COMBAT DATA

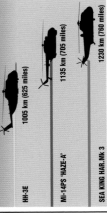

RANGE

All three of these helicopters offer good long-range performance, essential in the SAR role. Although the HH-3E's range is shortest, when equipped with in-flight refuelling capability its range is limited only by the endurance of the crew and the durability of the airframe.

HH-3E — 1005 km (625 miles)
MI-14PS 'HAZE-A' — 1135 km (705 miles)
SEA KING HAR.Mk 3 — 1230 km (760 miles)

SIKORSKY

S-62/HH-52 SEAGUARD

- Search and rescue helicopter ● Turbine-powered ● Overlooked

▲ Looking like a scaled-down version of the S-61 Sea King, the S-62 was not a great commercial success and only a handful were built. It served with the US Coast Guard and in Japan.

C onceived in the mid-1950s, the S-62 incorporated several new features. The US Coast Guard was sufficiently interested to purchase the type as the HH-52A Seaguard. A single T-58 turbine, a relatively spacious fuselage and amphibious capability made the S-62 an ideal search and rescue helicopter, particularly for coastal areas. It was capable of operating from almost any surface in just about any weather.

▲ On land and water
One of the prototypes performs a 'power-off' landing. As an amphibious helicopter, the HH-52 proved ideal in the coastal SAR role.

▼ Northern search and rescue
HH-52s operating from ice-breakers received a bright orange scheme with a white stripe for greater conspicuity over the frozen sea.

▲ Rig support
First order for the S-62 came from Petroleum Helicopters, which purchased a single example for serving large offshore oil rigs located in the Gulf of Mexico.

Sikorsky on the silver screen ▼
This strange-looking machine is actually a South African example, modified to represent an 'enemy' gunship, possibly an Mi-24, for film purposes.

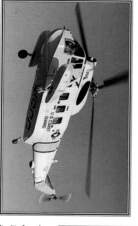

▲ Special equipment
As first delivered to the US Coast Guard, HH-52s featured automatic stabilisation, towing equipment and other features tailored for the rescue mission.

FACTS AND FIGURES

▼ HH-52s based at Houston, Texas, frequently practised recovery of the NASA Apollo astronauts.

▼ First flight of the Sikorsky S-62 took place on 22 May 1958.

▼ A small number of Seaguards were put on display in museums after retirement.

▼ Nine examples were built under licence for service with the Japanese Maritime Self-Defence Force (JMSDF).

▼ One US Coast Guard machine was used in the film Airport '77.

▼ A civilian S-62B model was built, but it was not popular on the civil market.

Unsung rescue helicopters

In commercial aviation, Sikorsky's S-62 was overshadowed by other helicopters. The US Coast Guard liked it enough to use the type from 1963 to 1989 for short- to medium-range rescue work. The ability to land on water, not found in any of today's Coast Guard helicopters, helped the HH-52A Seaguard in its rescue duties.

The HH-52A also joined the Coast Guard ice patrol operations aboard powerful ice-breakers. Typical was Operation Deep Freeze, the exploration of the

Antarctic in 1973. The aim of this project was to improve ice-breaking services, thus assisting the movement of maritime traffic through icy waterways.

Coast Guard pilots and crewmen were quite fond of the HH-52A – especially its ability to operate in all weathers. Although most flying was conducted from shore bases, Coast Guard crewmen also serviced the HH-52A onboard ship, which often proved to be a demanding task. By the time the last examples retired during 1989, HH-52s had

gained distinction for rescuing more people than any other helicopter. They were replaced by Aérospatiale HH-65 Dolphins.

In the late 1950s, the General Electric T-58 was one of the most advanced engines available for use in helicopters. It was light, powerful and efficient compared to piston engines of the period.

Below: This rare machine is one of a very small number of S-62s sold to non-US operators. It flew with the Canadian Department of Transport.

Above: Toward the end of their service lives, HH-52s were upgraded with Northrop forward-looking infra-red sensors, mounted in a small turret on the nose.

HH-52A Seaguard

Type: US Coast Guard all-weather amphibious rescue helicopter

Powerplant: one 932-kW (1250-hp) General Electric T58-GE-8 turboshaft engine

Maximum speed: 175 km/h (109 mph)

Cruising speed: 144 km/h (89 mph)

Range: 762 km (472 miles)

Service ceiling: 4785 m (15,700 ft)

Weights: empty 2224 kg (4693 lb); loaded 3765 kg (8283 lb)

Accommodation: two pilots sitting side-by-side and one loadmaster, plus seating for up to 11 fully equipped troops if required

Dimensions: rotor diameter 16.15 m (52 ft 11 in)
length 13.79 m (45 ft 3 in)
height 4.39 m (14 ft 5 in)

ACTION DATA

MAXIMUM SPEED

As one of the earliest turbine-powered helicopters, the HH-52 offered much better performance than several rival machines of the day. The 'Hormone' was twin-engined but was a relatively poor performer, unlike the single-engined Westland Wessex.

HH-52A	175 km/h (109 mph)
WESSEX Mk 1	212 km/h (131 mph)
Ka-25PS 'HORMONE-C'	209 km/h (128 mph)

SERVICE CEILING

Despite being single-engined, both the HH-52 Seaguard and the Wessex had impressive service ceilings, better than that of the twin-engined Ka-25 'Hormone'. The single-engined Wessex was essentially a licence-built, turbine-powered Sikorsky S-58.

HH-52A	3415 m (11,200 ft)
WESSEX Mk 1	4298 m (14,100 ft)
Ka-25PS 'HORMONE-C'	3350 m (10,990 ft)

MAXIMUM TAKE-OFF WEIGHT

A light but strong all-metal fuselage, combined with the low weight of the turbine engine, permitted the HH-52 to carry a substantial payload if required. At maximum take-off weight the aircraft was much lighter than either the Wessex or 'Hormone': the latter tipped the scales at almost 8000 kg (17,600 lb) fully laden.

HH-52A	3765 kg (8280 lb)
WESSEX Mk 1	5715 kg (12,570 lb)
Ka-25PS 'HORMONE-C'	7500 kg (16,500 lb)

HH-52A SEAGUARD

Some 99 examples of the Sikorsky S-62 were delivered to the US Coast Guard. They flew search and rescue (SAR) duties for nearly 30 years.

Although a considerable improvement over Sikorsky's S-55, the HH-52 did feature a sizeable number of components from the earlier machine, including the rotor blades, heads and gearbox.

The new all-metal fuselage was of aluminium construction. The aircraft was designed from the beginning to be able to operate from water, and the hull was fully watertight.

Like the main rotor, the tail rotor assembly was also from the S-55. Common components included the twin blades, the tail rotor head, auxiliary gearbox and shaft assembly. This permitted Sikorsky to save considerable time and reduce cost during manufacturing, and enabled the company to offer the S-62 at an attractive price.

Up to 11 troops or rescued personnel could be seated on fold-down seats in the spacious fuselage. Civilian S-62s had forward- and inward-facing seats for up to 10 passengers.

Sikorsky's amphibious family

■ **S-61 SEA KING:** Similar in appearance to the smaller S-62, the Sea King was one of the most successful helicopters built by Sikorsky. It was widely exported.

■ **S-61N:** Clearly resembling the military Sea King, the S-61N was developed as a civil passenger helicopter. It retained amphibious capability and entered service in 1964.

■ **S-61R:** Yet another derivative of the basic S-61 design, this variant had a completely redesigned fuselage with a rear loading ramp and a retractable tricycle undercarriage.

SIKORSKY
S-64 SKYCRANE

- Heavylift helicopter ● Flying crane ● Salvage and retrieval

▲ Groundcrew prepare the Tarhe to lift another massive load. A cargo net is used to gather lots of items together so that they can all be lifted at once.

T his bizarre-looking but superbly performing machine has got real muscle. Called the CH-54 Tarhe – an American Indian name meaning 'crane' – by soldiers and the S-64 by its makers and by civilians, the big Sikorsky SkyCrane lifts, hauls and delivers almost any cargo on a sling or in a van under its fuselage. Used in combat in Vietnam, this veteran went on to serve on construction projects, oilfields and logging sites, where the SkyCrane works today as a heavylift champion of the skies.

SIKORSKY S-64 SKYCRANE

▼ Flying crane
The S-64 was little more than a rotor system with a cockpit on the front. The giant legs could straddle just about anything the helicopter could lift.

▲ The office
The front end of the Tarhe looks like that of any large helicopter, but it incorporates a position in the back so that the crew can watch the load underneath.

◀ Rotor system
The upper part of the Tarhe consisted of a propulsion system with two engines, and a slender boom to hold the tail rotor.

▲ Troopship helicopter ▶
To turn the S-64 into a troop assault helicopter, Sikorsky designed a special pod which could be clipped underneath the aircraft. This could accommodate a large number of fully armed troops.

FACTS AND FIGURES

- CH-54 Tarhe helicopters in Vietnam retrieved 380 shot-down aircraft, saving $210 million.

- The S-64 made its first flight on 9 May 1962; about 20 are still flying today.

- The S-64's cargo pod is a box 8.36 m x 2.69 m x 1.98 m (27 x 9 x 6½ ft).

- When repairs were needed to the 11000 kg (24,255 lb) statue atop Washington's Capitol dome, it was lifted away and then returned by a hard-working SkyCrane.

- This colossal 'derrick of the air' was patterned after Sikorsky's earlier S-60 heavy lifter.

PROFILE

Sikorsky's heavy lifter

Sikorsky's pioneering efforts with heavylift helicopters reached a peak at the start of the Vietnam War. The US Army used the CH-54 Tarhe to sling-lift such weighty cargoes as artillery pieces, armoured vehicles and recovered aircraft. In the Southeast Asia conflict SkyCrane's cargo pod proved amazingly useful, for it could carry 87 troops, a mobile hospital or a command post. In a less typical mission, the SkyCrane carried a 4536-kg (10,000-lb) bomb used to blast away trees to create a landing zone.

The improved CH-54B model set international payload and climb records which stood for years before bigger, Russian-built craft exceeded them. The newer Chinook and Stallion have replaced the SkyCrane in the Army, releasing many of these sturdy ships for private use.

Today the ageing SkyCrane has been retired from military service and is much missed by the US Army. Some still soldier on in civil hands, however, hauling logs and outsize cargoes that no other helicopter can touch.

CH-54 TARHE

Now eclipsed by the CH-47 Chinook, the CH-54 was widely used by the US Army in a massive number of roles. If anything needed moving, then the Tarhe was called to move it. Those serving in Alaska became such a part of the local scenery that they made their way into traditional native art.

The CH-54 was one of the first modular aircraft. The cabin section, drive train and fuselage were interchangeable units which could be replaced with little effort in the field.

Designed S-64 by Sikorsky, the Tarhe used a modified version of the S-61 Sea King front end mated to a 'flying crane' type fuselage.

The Tarhe had two engines, which drove the main rotor through a central gearbox. The power from either engine could keep the CH-54 aloft in an emergency, but not while carrying a load.

As well as conventional forward-facing positions, the cockpit of the Tarhe also had a rearward-facing station with a large glazed area. This allowed the crew to make delicate manoeuvres when picking up loads.

As the CH-54's job was to lift heavy loads rather than fly fast or fight, much of the rotor system was left uncovered, which made maintenance easier. Running along the top of the tailboom from the engines to the tail was the drive-shaft for the tail rotor.

The Tarhe's tail rotor was a conventional four-bladed unit related to that of the Sea King from which it was derived.

The undercarriage legs were made very wide and tall so that the Tarhe could straddle most loads. Attachment points on the central fuselage could hold pods designed specially for the Tarhe or slung loads carried on strops and cables. In Vietnam the CH-54 even functioned as a bomber, dropping giant weapons to clear vegetation for landing sites or artillery emplacements.

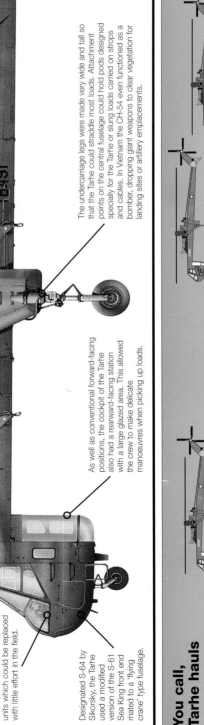

A huge variety of missions can be flown by the Tarhe, from airlifting field hospitals (left) through the recovery of crashed aircraft (below). The aircraft shown left is fitted with skis to operate from snow, and carries extra fuel tanks on the inside of the undercarriage legs.

CH-54A Tarhe

Type: heavylift helicopter

Powerplant: two 3400-kW (4500-hp) Pratt & Whitney T73-1 turboshafts

Cruising speed: 169 km/h (110 mph)

Range: 370 km (230 miles)

Hover ceiling out of ground effect: 2100 m (6900 ft)

Weights: empty 8724 kg (19,200 lb); loaded 19,050 kg (42,000 lb)

Armament: none, but has been used to carry 4536-kg (10,000-lb) bombs

Dimensions: main rotor diameter 21.95 m (72 ft)
length 26.97 m
height 5.67 m
main rotor disc area 378.10 m² (4070 sq ft)

COMBAT DATA

PAYLOAD

CH-54A	9070 kg (20,000 lb)
CH-53A	6000 kg (13,200 lb)
Mi-10	14,000 kg (31,000 lb)

Although the standard Tarhe could sling loads of up to nine tonnes, it was not so much its ability to hoist heavy weights but more its ability to deal with awkward or outsize loads which made the SkyCrane such a useful, and irreplaceable, workhorse.

RANGE

CH-54A	370 km (230 miles)
CH-53A	420 km (260 miles)
Mi-10	600 km (375 miles)

Heavylift helicopters are generally called on to move their loads over relatively short distances, to where they can be trans-shipped to more conventional means of transportation. As a result, they do not need a long operating range.

You call, Tarhe hauls

VEHICLE TRANSPORT: Many types of vehicle could be carried from the underfuselage attachment points.

AIRCRAFT RECOVERY: Tarhes regularly retrieved crashed or damaged aircraft.

MAKESHIFT BOMBER: In Vietnam CH-54s dropped the BLU-82 bomb to make clearings in the jungle.

OUTSIZE LOADS: A bewildering variety of loads has been carried by CH-54s, including boats.

PLACING ARTILLERY: The CH-54 was the principal means by which the US Army shifted its artillery around the battlefield.

SIKORSKY
S-65/HH-/MH-53

- Special forces helicopter ● Combat rescue ● Advanced sensors

O ne of the biggest and most versatile combat helicopters ever developed in the West, Sikorsky's S-65 serves with the USAF as the HH-/MH-53. In the hands of skilled pilots, the S-65 can lift heavy cargoes, carry special forces troops far behind enemy lines, or successfully rescue downed airmen, using the latest technology. From Vietnam as the HH-53C to the Persian Gulf as the MH-53J, the S-65 has been a great success story.

▲ Many airmen and civilians owe their lives to the gallant crews of the HH-/MH-53. Although primarily tasked with military operations, the aircraft have performed a number of highly publicized civilian rescues.

SIKORSKY S-65/HH-/MH-53

▼ Jolly Green doorman
An MH-53J crewman leans through the open escape hatch. A window may be fitted in this position, but is often omitted.

▲ First of the eight Bs
As the first of eight HH-53Bs, this aircraft introduced the S-65 into regular CSAR service with the USAF over Vietnam.

▼ Vietnam insertion
HH-53Bs were tasked with a number of covert missions in Vietnam. Troops were often dropped by rope to avoid the risk of landing in enemy territory.

▲ Evolving from the CH-53C
There was little difference between the pure transport CH-53C and the HH-53B, except for the latter's refuelling probe.

▲ Sensitive nose
All of the MH-53J's primary sensors are clustered around the nose. They include the AN/AAQ-10 FLIR below the in-flight refuelling probe on the starboard side.

▼ Pave Low III
Although short-lived, the six HH-53H helicopters introduced the Pave Low III sensor package.

FACTS AND FIGURES

- ► Having originally used the CH-53A in 1966/67, the USAF received a handful more in 1989 as TH-53A trainers.

- ► Sponson bracing struts allowed HH-53Bs to carry 2460-litre (650-gallon) drop-tanks.

- ► Two HH-53Cs flew 14,500 km (9000 miles) from the US to Vietnam with only seven stops.

- ► Some CH-53C and HH-53B helicopters remained unmodified until the late 1980s, when they became MH-53Js.

- ► MH-53H and MH-53J Pave Low IIs were involved in the US invasion of Panama.

- ► MH-53 pilots receive special operations training on the TH-53A.

PROFILE

Enhancing the 'Super Jolly'

Although more than three decades old, the S-65 remains at the front line with the USAF. Special forces rely on it for daring missions, such as the raid to destroy President Noriega's personal jet during the US invasion of Panama in 1989.

In November 1966 the US Marine Corps loaned two CH-53A helicopters to the USAF. This led to an order for eight specialized HH-53B combat search-and-rescue (CSAR) aircraft to replace the HH-3E

then flying with great distinction in Vietnam.

Having replaced the 'Jolly Green Giant', the HH-53B became the 'Super Jolly'. One modified aircraft unsuccessfully tested an all-weather sensor system known as Pave (Precision Avionics Vectoring Equipment) Low I.

From August 1968 the USAF Aerospace Rescue and Recovery Service began receiving the HH-53C. With improved armour and a comprehensive radio fit, allowing better communications

between the helicopter and HC-130 in-flight refuelling tankers, the HH-53C served into the late 1980s. The last machine was then converted to MH-53J Pave Low III Enhanced standard.

Developed via the unsuccessful HH-53H Pave Low II, the MH-53J is likely to serve for many more years.

MH-53J PAVE LOW III

This aircraft is shown in the markings worn while based at RAF Woodbridge, Suffolk, with the USAF's 67th Aerospace Rescue and Recovery Wing. The Wing has since withdrawn from Britain.

Most of the Pave Low III sensor package is clustered around the nose. The FLIR (forward looking infra-red) radome and the larger radome of the terrain-following radar have been removed from this aircraft.

Left: This MH-53J carries a gun mount on its loading ramp. It can be easily removed and stowed in flight.

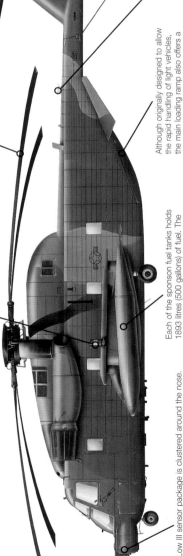

A number of systems are employed to protect the helicopter from the enemy. They include powerful infra-red countermeasures devices mounted above each sponson.

Each of the sponson fuel tanks holds 1893 litres (500 gallons) of fuel. The tanks are jettisonable in flight, but the MH-53J is rarely seen without them.

For versatility, the MH-53J can be operated from a variety of bases, including aircraft-carrier decks. The rotor blades fold to conserve space.

Although originally designed to allow the rapid handling of light vehicles, the main loading ramp also offers a quick method of entering or leaving the 'Super Jolly' in the heat of battle.

Secure communications facilities, a global positioning system and night-vision goggle compatibility enable the MH-53J to perform dangerous missions alone. The comprehensive avionics fit is indicated by the large number of antennas.

Above: With weapons fitted in all positions, this 'Super Jolly' shows a typical configuration for special forces operations. MH-53Js often fly alone on such missions.

'Super Jolly' in the Gulf

Few precise details of MH-53J operations in the Gulf have emerged, but it is known that the helicopter was used for anti-Scud missions as well as for its traditional roles.

STARTING THE WAR: Two forces of four AH-64A Apaches, each accompanied by an MH-53J pathfinder, eliminated two radar posts inside Iraq on the first day of the war.

AIR STRIKES BEGIN: With these two key installations removed, coalition warplanes entered Iraq undetected.

HIGH-RISK MISSIONS: Pave Low III helicopters used similar tactics when depositing special forces teams deep within Iraq. Many of these sorties were aimed at Scud missile launchers.

EGRESS: After leading the AH-64As to their target, the MH-53Js protected them from missile attack during egress using infra-red decoy flares.

MH-53J Pave Low III Enhanced

Type: twin-engined combat search and rescue and special operations helicopter

Powerplant: two 2935-kW (3935-hp) General Electric T64-GE-7A turboshaft engines

Maximum speed: 315 km/h (195 mph) at sea level

Cruising speed: 278 km/h (172 mph) at sea level

Initial climb rate: 631 m/min (2070 fpm) at sea level

Range: 868 km (540 miles) with maximum auxiliary fuel

Hover ceiling: 3565 m (11,700 ft) in ground effect; 1980 m (6200 ft) out of ground effect

Weights: empty 10,691 kg (23,520 lb); mission take-off 17,344 kg (38,157 lb); maximum take-off 19,051 kg (41,912 lb)

Armament: up to three 7.62-mm (.30-cal.) Miniguns or three 12.7-mm (.50-cal.) machine guns mounted in the side door, port side escape hatch and on the rear loading ramp

Dimensions: main rotor diameter 22.02 m (72 ft 3 in)
fuselage length 20.47m
height 5.22 m
main rotor 380.87 m² (4098 sq ft)
disc area

COMBAT DATA

PAYLOAD

Three powerful engines and an uprated rotor and transmission system allow the Sikorsky CH-53E to lift a heavier internal payload than the other types. External payload is even greater.

MH-53J PAVE LOW III ENHANCED	9072 kg (19,958 lb)
CH-53E SUPER STALLION	13,607 kg (29,935 lb)
CH-47D CHINOOK	10,341 kg (22,750 lb)

POWER

A third engine makes the CH-53E one of the most powerful and capable helicopters in the world. Among modern machines only the Russian-designed Mi-26 is more powerful.

CH-53E SUPER STALLION	8268 kW (11,087 hp)
MH-53J PAVE LOW III ENHANCED	5870 kW (7870 hp)
CH-47D CHINOOK	4474 kW (6000 hp)

MAXIMUM SPEED

The CH-53E and the MH-53J have identical maximum speeds at sea level. This high speed allows the MH-53J to spend as little time as possible over hostile territory.

MH-53J PAVE LOW III ENHANCED	315 km/h (195 mph)
CH-53E SUPER STALLION	315 km/h (195 mph)
CH-47D CHINOOK	298 km/h (185 mph)

SIKORSKY

S-80/CH-/MH-53E

● Heavy-lifter ● Minesweeper ● Three-engined variant of CH-53

W orldwide attention was focused on the US Marine CH-53E when helicopters from the assault ship *Kearsarge* landed a TRAP (Tactical Recovery of Aircrew Personnel) team to rescue an American pilot in Bosnia in 1995. Second-generation Sikorsky S-80s differ from the earlier S-65 in having three engines, expanded capacity and improved performance. They undertake heavy-lifting, rescue and minesweeping duties.

▲ The CH-53E is currently the West's most powerful helicopter. Like the world-beating Mi-26, it is a single-rotor type and can lift heavier loads than the twin-rotor Boeing-Vertol CH-47 Chinook.

SIKORSKY S-80/CH-/MH-53E

▼ **US Navy CH-53Es**
The Navy's interest in the Sea Stallion was as a supply helicopter for use between shore bases and naval vessels. Three Navy squadrons operate the CH-53E.

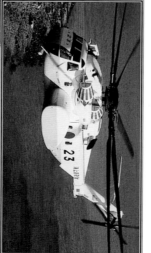

Export model ▶
Japan has been the only export customer for the three-engined CH-53: its S-80M-1 is similar to the MH-53E.

▲ **Marine Corps heavy-lifter**
The USMC has the largest CH-53E fleet, with six squadrons including a training unit. Their main role is in support of amphibious assaults.

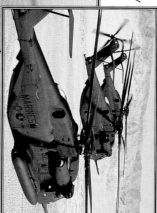

▼ **Refuelling in the air**
An important feature of many H-53Es is their ability to refuel in the air, greatly enhancing their flexibility. The US Marine Corps use KC-130 Hercules aircraft for the air-to-air tanker role.

▲ **Minehunter**
A cable with a tension of up to 13 tonnes is used to tow a hydrofoil sled, which skims through the water seeking out mines. This device is too large to be stowed aboard the helicopter.

FACTS AND FIGURES

▶ Overall production of the US Marine Corps and Navy Super Stallions is projected to reach 177 aircraft, MH-53Es about 50.

▶ The first S-80/CH-53E was a test aircraft and made its first flight on 1 March 1974.

▶ The H-53 family contains the most powerful helicopters used by US forces.

▶ The first MH-53E minesweeper, which flew in 1983, was not fitted with large sponsons; deliveries began in 1986.

▶ The first prototype of this series was tragically lost in a ground mishap.

▶ A CH-53E can lift 16 tonnes – 6 tonnes more than the twin-rotor CH-47 Chinook.

Super Stallion and Sea Dragon

Marine Corps' CH-53Es are well-known as the heavylift and rescue helicopters of the US fleet.

The MH-53E minesweeper, also known as the Sea Dragon, uses the airframe of the CH-53E but carries extra fuel and equipment, allowing it to sweep for mines for up to four hours while operating 30 minutes from its base.

The MH-53E has a new acoustic countermeasures system and the ALQ-166 mine countermeasures sled. The sled is towed by the helicopter to

neutralize mines, but as it is too bulky to be taken aboard, it is towed throughout the mission. In April 1987 the first MH-53Es joined MH-12 Squadron at Norfolk, Virginia. Japan has also purchased the minesweeper as the S-80M-1.

Both the CH-53E and MH-53E are developments of the proven twin-engined CH-53 Sea Stallion, itself a large helicopter. The Marines, however, wanted something even bigger. Sikorsky produced the S-80 model, which had an extra T64 engine fitted and a new main rotor.

CH-53E Super Stallion

Type: three-engined heavy-lift, assault and rescue helicopter

Powerplant: three 2756-kW (3700-hp) (continuous rating) General Electric T64-GE-416 engines

Maximum speed: 315 km/h (195 mph) 'clean'

Cruising speed: 278 km/h (172 mph) at sea level

Ferry range: 2075 km (1285 miles)

Service ceiling: 5640 m (18,500 ft)

Weights: empty 15,072 kg (33,158 lb); maximum take-off 31,640 kg (69,608 lb) with internal load or 33,340 kg (73,348 lb) with external load

Accommodation: two flight crew and up to 55 troops or 13,607 kg (29,935 lb) of cargo internally

Dimensions: main rotor diameter 24.08 m (79 ft)
length 30.19 m (99 ft)
height 8.97 m (29 ft 5 in)
rotor disc area 455.38 m² (4906 sq ft)

COMBAT DATA

MAXIMUM SPEED

The three-engined Super Stallion has a slight edge in straight-line speed, although 300 km/h (185 mph) is about the norm for this type. Speeds are drastically reduced when a helicopter is fully loaded.

CH-53E SUPER STALLION	315 km/h (195 mph)
Mi-26 'HALO'	295 km/h (183 mph)
CH-47D CHINOOK	298 km/h (185 mph)

FERRY RANGE

A ferry range of 2000 km (1250 miles) is average for this class of aircraft. In the case of the CH-53E and some versions of the Chinook, range can be increased by air-to-air refuelling.

CH-53E SUPER STALLION	2075 km (1285 miles)
Mi-26 'HALO'	2000 km (1240 miles)
CH-47D CHINOOK	2026 km (1255 miles)

PAYLOAD

The Mi-26 is currently the world's most powerful helicopter, with the capability to lift 20 tonnes. The three-engined CH-53E carries much more than the twin-rotor Chinook.

Mi-26 'HALO' 20,000 kg (44,100 lb)	CH-47D CHINOOK 10,341 kg (22,798 lb)
CH-53E SUPER STALLION 16,338 kg (35,944 lb)	

421

Rear-view mirrors are used by the crew to monitor the magnetic minesweeping sled towed behind the helicopter. An inflight-refuelling boom is also fitted to the nose. Japanese S-80M-1s lack this feature.

The main external features of the MH-53E are readily apparent: the seven-blade rotor, larger sponsons, a third engine and redesigned tail assembly.

To absorb the power of the third engine, the H-53E has an extra blade on its main rotor. Its diameter and blade chord are also increased.

The tail of the H-53E is unusually canted to port and has a large, four-blade rotor. To offset this the tailplane has a gull-wing configuration.

The key feature of the H-53E is the third General Electric T64 turboshaft engine which has been accommodated with comparatively little change to the basic H-53 airframe. Total power output is close to the equivalent of two twin-engined CH-53s.

Fitted with a 13,600-kg (29,920-lb) tension tow boom and a hydraulic winch with 140 m (460 ft) of cable, the MH-53E can tow various types of ALQ-166 minesweeping sled.

Moored mines are detached using an internal pod system. An ALQ-160 acoustic countermeasures system forms part of this equipment.

MH-53E SEA DRAGON

Helicopter Mine Countermeasures Squadron HM-14 operated this MH-53E from Naval Air Station Norfolk, Virginia, attached to the Atlantic Fleet. During the Gulf War HM-14 neutralized over 1000 Iraqi mines.

MH-53Es have a flight crew of three and three to five enlisted crew to operate the mine-hunting equipment and man the two 12.7-mm (.50-cal.) machine guns used to explode surfaced mines.

This aircraft carries a dark-grey low-visibility version of the standard US Navy helicopters.

Formerly equipped with the RH-53D, the HM-14 squadron is known as the 'Sea Stallions'; its aircraft carry a stallion's head on the sponson.

The enlarged sponsons of the MH-53E contain fuel, raising internal capacity from 3850 litres (1017 gallons) to 12,100 litres (3200 gallons).

USMC helicopters past and present

■ **BELL AH-1 SEACOBRA:** A twin-engined development of the HueyCobra, the SeaCobra serves aboard US Navy assault ships.

■ **BOEING-VERTOL CH-46 SEA KNIGHT:** Still in use after 30 years, the CH-46 remains the mainstay of USMC transport aviation.

■ **SIKORSKY HR2S:** Predecessor of the CH-53D, this troop-carrying assault helicopter was powered by two Pratt & Whitney radial engines.

■ **SIKORSKY HUS SEAHORSE:** Sikorsky's highly successful S-58 entered service with the USMC in the support role in 1957.

Sikorsky

UH-60 Black Hawk

- Tactical assault helicopter ● Gulf War transporter

S ikorsky's UH-60 Black Hawk is one of the most important combat helicopters in service today. Replacing the famous Bell Huey as the US Army's workhorse, the UH-60 was designed to haul a squad of 11 fully-equipped infantrymen into battle. The same basic airframe has also been developed for special forces, combat rescue, air-sea rescue and anti-submarine operations.

▶ Carrying troops into battle demands a tough, fast helicopter. The UH-60 entered service in this role at the end of 1979, and has been a great success.

Sikorsky UH-60 Black Hawk

▲ Squad carrier
The UH-60 can carry a larger squad of soldiers than the UH-1 it replaced, and in much greater comfort and protection.

Troops out ▶
The UH-60's doors are designed to allow an infantry squad to get into action in the minimum possible time.

▼ Weight lifter
Although designed as a troop carrier, the UH-60 can also carry a significant cargo load both internally and slung on hooks externally.

▶ Rope down
Special forces soldiers can abseil down from the UH-60 very quickly. This is useful in tight situations where the pilot cannot land safely.

▶ Air assault
One of the conditions for the bulk of the equipment supplied to the US Army is that it should be Black Hawk-portable.

▼ Medical evacuation
A flying ambulance comes in to land at a desert airstrip, the soldier on the ground guiding the pilot through the fog of rotor-blown sand.

FACTS AND FIGURES

➤ The original UH-60A prototype first flew on 17 October 1974.

➤ Black Hawks entered service with the 101st Airborne Division in 1979.

➤ Though the US Marine Corps has not adopted the UH-60, they fly nine VH-60N presidential transport helicopters.

➤ Black Hawks moved more than a million soldiers during the First Gulf War.

➤ In a tragic 'friendly fire' mishap, F-15 fighters shot down two US Army UH-60s in Iraq on 14 April 1994, killing 26.

➤ The Army is developing a UH-60Q medical evacuation model of the Black Hawk.

PROFILE

Sikorsky's flying troop-truck

Known to the manufacturer as the Sikorsky S-70, the remarkable UH-60 Black Hawk provides soldiers with speed and mobility in the middle of the action, freeing them from terrain obstacles.

While combat troops enter and leave the battle zone aboard the UH-60, versions of the helicopter carry out electronic warfare duties, fight with Special Operations forces, or perform ambulance or VIP transport duties.

Pilots in the UH-60 have excellent visibility and armour protection as they fly in and out of landing zones. An exhaust suppression system reduces their vulnerability to heat-seeking battlefield missiles.

The UH-60 fought in Grenada, Panama and Operation Desert Storm, and appears little changed after two decades of Army duty. In fact, the UH-60 has been continuously upgraded with more powerful engines and other improvements. The latest UH-60L has the power to lift a military Hum-Vee tactical vehicle loaded with TOW anti-tank missiles.

UH-60A BLACK HAWK

The UH-60A, the first of many versions of the Black Hawk family, saw action during the invasion of Grenada in 1981. The Black Hawk has since been in action in Lebanon, Somalia and the Gulf War.

The UH-60's rotor-head and blades were designed to withstand hits from large machine-gun rounds. The gearbox that drives it can run for half an hour after losing its entire oil supply.

The transparent panels in the nose are essential for safe landing in confined spaces.

In an assault landing, the UH-60 comes in fast. Its undercarriage is designed to absorb vertical impacts of up to 45 km/h (28 mph).

The UH-60 was designed with all the years of experience of battle in Vietnam in mind. The low profile of the airframe makes it a difficult target, and safer if it crashed.

As a precaution against battle damage, the UH-60's engines are as widely spaced as possible.

The UH-6's rotor system features swept tips, giving enhanced performance and allowing heavy loads to be lifted in 'hot and high' conditions.

The fuselage plan is noticeably broad and long, giving a generous internal capacity while allowing a very flat profile.

Sikorsky's designers intentionally built the tail rotor at an angle. This design feature means that lift is generated at the tail, allowing heavier loads at the rear of the cabin than would otherwise be possible.

The Black Hawk has an exhaust suppression system which dissipates hot engine gases. This makes the helicopter less of a target for heat-seeking infra-red missiles.

Although the Black Hawk can carry armament, it is essentially a troop carrier. Its cabin and hatches are designed to allow a squad of infantry to get into action fast.

UH-60A Black Hawk

Type: utility helicopter

Powerplant: two 1261-kW (1691-hp) General Electric T700-GE-700, -701 or -401 turboshafts

Maximum speed: 296 km/h (184 mph)

Range: 600 km (373 miles)

Weights: (Army UH-60) empty 4819 kg (10,624 lb); loaded 9185 kg (20,249 lb). (Navy SH-60) empty 6191 kg (13,649 lb); loaded 9926 kg (21,883 lb)

Armament: usually two 7.62-mm (.30-cal.) door guns

Dimensions: rotor diameter 16.36 m (53 ft 8 in)
length 19.76 m (64 ft 10 in)
height 5.13 m (16 ft 10 in)
rotor disc area 210.10 m² (2261 sq ft)

COMBAT DATA

RANGE

PUMA
570 km (354 miles)

Mi-8 'HIP'
900 km (560 miles)

UH-60A BLACK HAWK
600 km (373 miles)

The Mi-8's greater size and fuel-carrying capacity give it an advantage over the Black Hawk when operating on internal fuel only. But the UH-60 can be fitted with stub wings, onto which can be mounted weaponry or external fuel tanks. With four tanks fitted, the efficient Sikorsky helicopter has a ferry range of more than 2000 km (1240 miles).

MAXIMUM SPEED

Mi-8 'HIP' 250 km/h (155 mph)

UH-60A BLACK HAWK 296 km/h (184 mph)

PUMA 271 km/h (168 mph)

The Black Hawk's powerful engines and slender aerodynamic cross-section make it one of the fastest helicopters around. It is quicker than most of its rivals, and this, allied to its great agility, makes it a superb platform for mounting helicopter assaults.

PAYLOAD

Mi-8 'HIP' 28 troops or up to 4000 kg (8818 lb) of cargo

PUMA 15 troops or up to 3200 kg (7055 lb) of cargo

UH-60A BLACK HAWK 11 troops or up to 3700 kg (8157 lb) of cargo

Although the UH-60 is nominally an 11-seater, it can carry up to 20 troops in an emergency. The Black Hawk has enough power to lift the same kind of loads as its bigger Russian and European rivals, yet retains the agility of a much smaller machine.

Airborne helicopter assault in the Gulf

■ **FIRST GULF WAR DEPLOYMENT:** The Black Hawk was the most numerous helicopter in the Gulf, with over 350 serving.

■ **LOW-LEVEL FLIGHT:** The biggest users of UH-60s were the 1st Cavalry Division and the 82nd and 101st Airborne Divisions.

■ **COALITION SPEARHEAD:** Black Hawks were at the forefront of the Coalition offensive, taking spearhead troops deep into Iraqi-held territory.

■ **SADDAM DEFEATED:** By attacking in helicopters, elite US Army airborne troops were able to outflank Iraq's battlefield defences.

SIKORSKY
SH-60B/F SEAHAWK

● Anti-submarine warfare ● Air-sea rescue ● Helicopter delivery

▲ Sikorsky's SH-60B filled the US Navy's LAMPS (light airborne multi-purpose system) III requirement for a helicopter equipped with over-the-horizon search-and-strike capability.

A merica's navy would not be able to function without the SH-60 Seahawk, which flies from frigates, destroyers and aircraft-carriers. The Seahawk has to operate at night, in heavy seas, from the deck of a ship swaying and pitching and bombarded by salt water. When airborne it must fulfil its assigned role, searching for hostile submarines and surface vessels that may pose a threat to the battle fleet.

SIKORSKY SH-60B/F SEAHAWK

The mainstay of the US Navy ▼
The first SH-60B flew in 1983, with its initial shipboard deployment taking place in 1985. The first SH-60Fs were delivered in 1989.

▲ MAD bird
The red and yellow 'MAD bird', or towed Magnetic Anomaly Detector, helps to locate submarines by measuring changes in the earth's magnetic field.

▲ Frigate based
Some of the US Navy's FFG-7 'Oliver Hazard Perry'-class guided missile frigates operate with one SH-60B.

Australian Hawks ▼
Exported examples of the Seahawk use Sikorsky's S-70 model designation. In the foreground is an RAAF S-70A-9 Black Hawk; behind is a naval S-70B-2.

▲ Spanish Armada
The Spanish navy has operated SH-60Bs under the designation HS.23 since 1988. Twelve are based at Rota and regularly deploy aboard 'Santa Maria'-class guided missile frigates. They differ from US Navy SH-60Bs in having a dipping sonar.

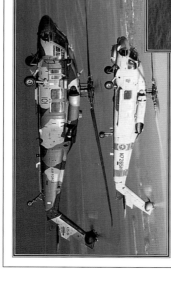

FACTS AND FIGURES

▼ Taiwan operates the S-70C(M)-1, equipped with new radar and torpedoes, from 'Kwang Hua I'-class frigates.

▼ During the Gulf War two downed pilots were rescued by US Navy SH-60s.

▼ Door-mounted machine-gun armament is often carried by US Navy SH/HH-60s.

▼ A third version operated by the US Navy is the HH-60H (unofficially called 'Rescue Hawk') for the rescue of downed aircrew.

▼ The US Coast Guard flies the HH-60J Jayhawk in the search-and-rescue role.

▼ The only US Marine Corps H-60s are nine VH-60N 'Presidential Hawks' for VIPs.

PROFILE

Ocean-going sub-hunter

With the proven airframe of the US Army's Black Hawk, the SH-60B Seahawk serves as the backbone of rotary aviation aboard the US Navy's surface vessels. The SH-60F (unofficially named 'Ocean Hawk') fulfills a similar role on aircraft-carrier decks.

The SH-60B operating from a frigate or destroyer and the SH-60F flying from a carrier both have a crew of three: pilot,

airborne tactical officer/co-pilot and sensor operator. These are primarily anti-submarine helicopters and their search for submarines is aided by the parent vessel's combat information centre. The final location of the submarine and its subsequent attack, however, are the responsibility of the SH-60B crew.

While the SH-60B is an over-the-horizon weapon system, the SH-60F, obtained to replace the elderly Sikorsky SH-3H Sea King, performs the Navy's 'inner zone' ASW mission for the Carrier

Battle Group, called 'CV-Helo'. The SH-60F also fills air-sea rescue 'plane guard' and utility transport roles.

Left: The main anti-submarine sensor carried by US Navy SH-60Fs is the Bendix AN/AQS-13F dipping sonar, used to 'listen' for submarines.

Below: The Greek navy has five S-70B-6 aircraft based aboard frigates. These are armed with the Norwegian Penguin anti-ship missile.

SH-60B Seahawk

Type: ship-based anti-submarine helicopter

Powerplant: two 1260-kW (1690-hp) General Electric T700-GE-401 or 1417-kW (1900-hp) -401C turboshaft engines

Maximum speed: 234 km/h (145 mph) at 1525 m (5000 ft)

Range: 966 km (600 miles)

Operational radius: 92.5 km (57 miles) with a 3-hour loiter; 278 km (172 miles) with a 1-hour loiter

Weights: empty 6191 kg (13,620 lb); maximum take-off 9182 kg (20,200 lb)

Armament: two Mk 46 or 50 torpedoes or one AGM-119B Penguin anti-ship missile; one door-mounted 12.7-mm (.50-cal.) machine gun

Dimensions:
main rotor diameter	16.36 m (53 ft 8 in)
length rotors turning	19.76 m (64 ft 9 in)
height	5.18 m (17 ft)
main rotor disc area	210.05 m² (2260 sq ft)

SH-60F SEAHAWK

This Seahawk carries the markings of Helicopter Anti-submarine Squadron 3 'Tridents', the first SH-60F unit in the US Navy's Atlantic Fleet, when it was deployed aboard *Theodore Roosevelt*.

The three crewmembers consist of pilot, air tactical officer and sensor operator.

The four main rotor blades feature swept-back tips known as 'tip caps'. These improve speed and reduce rotor noise.

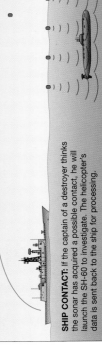

The General Electric T700 engines in the Seahawk have been modified for operation at sea. The SH-60 is able to hover on one engine if necessary.

Up to three torpedoes can be carried. Two may be fitted to the extended portside pylons, although the inboard of these usually carries a fuel tank.

To take up the minimum amount of space on the aircraft-carrier, the SH-60F has a folding tail, tailplane and rotors. The main blades fold back to lie above the rear fuselage.

The 'AJ' marking is that of the Carrier Air Group aboard the *Theodore Roosevelt* and is carried by all aircraft on the carrier.

Number 164099 carries the standard US Navy low-visibility grey colour scheme designed to make the helicopter difficult to spot for potential enemies to spot.

ACTION DATA

MAXIMUM SPEED

Anti-submarine warfare equipment is heavy, and so are the weapons, fuel, extra crewmembers, dipping sonar and processing gear. Naval helicopter therefore tend to be slower than their land-based equivalents: a land-based UH-60, for example, would easily outrun a Sea King Commando. Speed is largely irrelevant to naval helicopters, which mainly require range and endurance.

SH-3 SEA KING	267 km/h (166 mph)
SH-60B SEAHAWK	234 km/h (145 mph)
Ka-29 'HELIX'	250 km/h (155 mph)

Submarine hunting in the Seahawk

1 A line of passive sonobuoys, released from the helicopter, provides an approximate location of the submarine.

2 The SH-60's AN/ASQ-81 magnetic anomaly detector is then used to give the precise location.

3 Once located, the Seahawk launches a Mk 46 homing torpedo, which uses sonar to find its target.

SHIP CONTACT: If the captain of a destroyer thinks the sonar has acquired a possible contact, he will launch the SH-60 to investigate. The helicopter's data is sent back to the ship for processing.

SIKORSKY

HH-60H RESCUE HAWK

● Strike rescue ● Gulf War participants ● US Coast Guard service

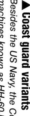

Based upon the SH-60B Seahawk, the HH-60H is a specialized combat rescue variant. Entering service in 1990 it has proved highly effective, giving the US Navy a much-needed dedicated rescue helicopter. Two detachments from HCS-4 and -5 took part in Operations Desert Shield and Desert Storm, where the HH-60s flew a total of more than 750 mission hours. The US Coast Guard also took delivery of a rescue Seahawk, known as the HH-60J.

▲ Based upon the ASW SH-60B, the Rescue Hawk is a dedicated strike rescue variant. It has the ability to recover a four-man crew, such as that from an EA-6B Prowler or S-3 Viking.

SIKORSKY HH-60H RESCUE HAWK

▲ Air force rescue
Like the Navy, the US Air Force also operates a fleet of rescue variants based on the UH-60 Black Hawk. These feature retractable refuelling probes.

▲ First 'Rescue Hawk'
Seen at the Stratford plant, the first HH-60H was rolled out in 1987. The aircraft is still known officially as a Seahawk.

▲ Coast guard variants
Besides the US Navy, the Coast Guard also operates a fleet of machines known as HH-60J Jayhawks. These have no armament.

▲ Unsung heroes
Although perhaps lacking the glamour of their naval counterparts, the Coast Guard Jayhawks have an important role and are often used on anti-drug smuggling missions off the south-eastern USA and around the Bahamas.

▲ Close co-operation
Since 1991 Rescue Hawks have been deployed aboard carriers, alongside SH-60F Ocean Hawks providing additional and useful rescue capability.

FACTS AND FIGURES

▶ During the Gulf War the two HH-60H detachments remained combat-ready 95 per cent of the time.

▶ Both the airframe and the engines are shared with the SH-60F Ocean Hawk.

▶ Surviving aircraft are being upgraded with defensive armament.

▶ First operational deployment of the HH-60H took place in 1990, when HS-2 took the type aboard USS Nimitz.

▶ US Coast Guard HH-60Js have greater endurance than their Navy counterparts.

▶ Forward looking infra-red turrets have been fitted to the HH-60s in recent years.

PROFILE

Combat rescue, Navy style

In the official terms used for American helicopters, an 'H' prefix tells us that the aircraft has a rescue mission. The US Navy's HH-60H and the Coast Guard's almost identical HH-60J fulfil the need for a dedicated rescue helicopter. Developed from the famous UH-60 Black Hawk, the naval variants – officially known as Seahawks – feature more powerful engines and specialist equipment.

HH-60s can operate from land, aircraft carriers and smaller

vessels such as frigates and destroyers. Coast Guard HH-60J Jayhawks are primarily land-based, but are sometimes deployed aboard cutters.

Experience with helicopter rescues in Vietnam confirmed the need for sturdier machines and the HH-60 features titanium rotors, capable of absorbing hits from large anti-aircraft shells, and considerable protection for both the pilots and cabin personnel. Coast Guard aircraft lack the comprehensive avionics fit and

Above: HH-60Js have somewhat larger sponson tanks because of their greater endurance requirements.

defensive armament of the naval machines, but do have a Bendix/King search radar. They are often deployed on drug traffic interdiction flights over the Bahamas.

Below: Purchased to replace ageing HH-3F Pelicans, the Jayhawks offered greater range, but the large cabin of the old helicopter is sorely missed.

HH-60H SEAHAWK

This HH-60H wears the markings of HS-3 'Tridents' which is shore-based at NAS Jacksonville in Florida. At present the unit operates a mixture of SH-60F and HH-60 variants and is assigned to Carrier Air Wing 3 and the USS *Theodore Roosevelt*.

Designed primarily for the combat rescue role, the HH-60F lacks the under-nose search radar and the data link equipment of the standard SH-60B Seahawk.

For combat operations, the HH-60H can be armed with twin 7.62-mm (.30-cal.) machine guns mounted on posts in the main cabin.

Propelling the Seahawk through the air is a four-bladed main rotor. Experience gained during the Vietnam War resulted in very strong titanium blades being fitted which were designed to absorb hits from 23-mm shells. The rotor head employs just six elastomeric bearings as opposed to 18 on many other designs, resulting in greater reliability and less maintenance time.

Unlike the SH-60F Ocean Hawks, recovery assist and traverse (RAST) gear can be fitted for operations from smaller vessels such as destroyers or frigates.

Like the main rotor, the tail rotor is four-bladed and incorporates titanium blades. For stowage in tight confines aboard ship, the tail unit can be hinged to port and the hub can even be canted 20 degrees if required. A long span, fully moveable tailplane is fitted for greater stability and control.

HH-60Hs feature the slightly more powerful 401C variant of the General Electric T700 turboshaft. These are immensely powerful and the aircraft is able to lift substantial loads if required.

Other features unique to the naval H-60 include a hovering in-flight refuelling capability, emergency floatation gear and extensive use of anti corrosion materials for extended use in a salt-water environment.

For naval operations, the Seahawk features a relocated tailwheel with twin tyres which are stressed for lower crash impact.

Combat rescue support aircraft

■ **BOEING E-3A SENTRY:** Amongst the most sophisticated military aircraft in service, the Sentry, with its sophisticated AEW system, is able to track and identify activity over great distances.

■ **FAIRCHILD OA-10A THUNDERBOLT II:** Currently A-10s are employed as rescue support aircraft, clearing a path for the rescue helicopters. Some are also used for observation work.

■ **LOCKHEED HC-130P HERCULES:** These specially equipped variants of the ubiquitous C-130 are used primarily to support helicopters during rescue operations.

HH-60H Seahawk

Type: strike rescue/covert operations helicopter

Powerplant: two 1417-kW (1900-hp) General Electric T700-GE-401C turboshafts

Maximum speed: 296 km/h (184 mph)

Initial climb rate: 213 m/min (699 fpm)

Combat radius: 463 km (288 miles)

Range: 966 km (600 miles)

Weights: empty 6114 kg (13,479 lb); loaded 8334 kg (18,373 lb)

Maximum payload: 3629 kg (8000 lb)

Dimensions:
main rotor diameter	16.36 m (53 ft 8 in)
tail rotor diameter	3.35 m (11 ft)
length	15.26 m (50 ft 1 in)
height	3.63 m (11 ft 11 in)
main rotor disc area	210.05 m² (2261 sq ft)
tail rotor disc area	8.83 m² (95 sq ft)

COMBAT DATA

MAXIMUM SPEED

Compared to its long-serving predecessor, the Sea King, the HH-60 is smaller, but faster and much easier to maintain. It has proved an ideal aircraft both with the US Navy and Coast Guard. The smaller Dolphin is one of the quickest helicopters in its class.

HH-60H RESCUE HAWK	296 km/h (184 mph)
SH-3 SEA KING	267 km/h (166 mph)
HH-65A DOLPHIN	257 km/h (160 mph)

RANGE

Theoretically not as far reaching as the Sea King, the HH-60s have still proved very suitable for long-range rescue and surveillance work, particularly with the US Coast Guard. The Dolphin has a reasonable radius for its size.

- **HH-60H RESCUE HAWK** 966 km (600 miles)
- **SH-3H SEA KING** 1005 km (624 miles)
- **HH-65A DOLPHIN** 760 km (472 miles)

POWER

Power is where the HH-60 really scores, the twin T700-410C engines putting out 2834 kW (3800 hp), a substantial amount more than those of its predecessor. The US Coast Guard has plans to re-engine its HH-65s with even more powerful engines.

- **HH-60H RESCUE HAWK** 2834 kW (3800 hp)
- **SH-3 SEA KING** 2088 kW (2800 hp)
- **HH-65A DOLPHIN** 1014 kW (1360 hp)

SIKORSKY

MH-60 PAVE HAWK

● Covert operations ● Combat search and rescue ● Combat-proven

Sikorsky's familiar 'Hawk' series is the basis for the MH-60 Pave Hawk, the USAF's special operations helicopter, intended to support secret missions behind enemy lines. Equipped with advanced navigation equipment, defensive machine guns and an in-flight refuelling probe, the MH-60 is establishing a fine reputation on long-range covert operations. The aircraft is designed to be easily transportable for worldwide deployment.

▲ USAF MH-60Gs and their similar US Army counterparts, MH-60Ks, fly hazardous missions with minimal support, and are an increasingly important asset.

SIKORSKY MH-60 PAVE HAWK

▲ Army special operations
At least 22 MH-60K helicopters serve with the US Army's 160th Special Operations Aviation Regiment (SOAR).

▼ Hawk over water
Rescues at sea are also possible with the MH-60G, although it lacks the amphibious capabilities of the HH-3E it replaced.

▲ Defence suppression
With its door-mounted guns, the MH-60G is able to keep enemy heads down in the drop zone.

▼ Special forces insertion
It is often too hazardous for the MH-60G to land in a hostile drop zone, so troops use ladders or ropes to leave the aircraft.

◄ MH-60K – enhanced army capability
The US Army has not suffered the budget constraints of the USAF and has been able to fit extra items, such as terrain-following radar.

FACTS AND FIGURES

▶ Slightly more basic aircraft assigned solely to combat search-and-rescue (CSAR) duties are designated HH-60Gs.

▶ Up to four combat-ready MH-60Gs may be stowed in the hold of a C-5 Galaxy.

▶ MH-60 Pave Hawks saw combat in Operation Desert Storm.

▶ MH-60Gs carry a Bendix-King 1400C colour weather radar in a port-side nose 'thimble' radome.

▶ The first MH-60Gs were delivered to the 55th SOS in December 1987.

▶ HC-130 Combat Shadow aircraft support MH-60Gs on long-range missions.

PROFILE

Special forces Sikorsky

USAF sources are reluctant to reveal much about how the Sikorsky MH-60G is used. Basically, the MH-60G is a UH-60A, or more powerful UH-60L helicopter, modified with radar, defensive weapons, an in-flight refuelling probe, options for external fuel-tank pylons, and additional cabin fuel tanks.

Pave Hawk helicopters are expected to go into combat deep behind enemy lines, operating at great distances from home, in support of special forces troops.

A primary requirement of the Pave Hawk programme was that the aircraft should be rapidly air transportable to any part of the world at a moment's notice. This capability was proven in 1989, when MH-60Gs were deployed to Ethiopia within 14 hours of the news of the loss of Congressman Mickey Lelands in an air crash.

Supported by warplanes such as the A-10, the MH-60G is also expected to insert itself into a 'hot' zone to rescue downed pilots. Several rescue missions were flown during the Gulf Wars and continuing upgrades will ensure that the MH-60 remains highly effective in the future.

Some criticism has been made of the lack of cabin space in the MH-60, compared to the HH-3E. The new helicopter is fully air transportable, however.

To enhance survivability at low level, most military S-70s, including the MH-60G, have sets of cable-cutters fitted above and below the fuselage.

All MH-60Gs are fitted with HIRSS (Hover Infra-Red Suppressor Subsystem). This reduces the aircraft's vulnerability to heat-seeking missiles.

A programme is currently underway to equip the MH-60G with an AA/AAQ-16 forward looking infra-red (FLIR) turret, which will be fitted in the lower nose. The HH-60G fleet will not receive the system.

Because it lacks terrain-following radar and some other advanced systems, the MH-60G has to use its colour weather radar to avoid the worst conditions. This is not ideal for a special forces aircraft.

Sikorsky used a one-piece forged titanium rotor head on the S-70. In addition to this advanced feature, the titanium and composite main rotor blades can withstand hits by 23-mm ammunition.

In its retracted state, the MH-60G's refuelling probe is almost long enough to clear the rotor disc. In operation it extends telescopically to keep the refuelling hose clear of the rotor.

MH-60G PAVE HAWK

Normally based at Hurlburt Field, the USAF's 55th Special Operations Squadron was deployed to Al Jouf in Saudi Arabia during the 1991 Gulf War.

From the outset, the S-70 series was developed for maximum survivability. The fin area is sufficient to allow a controlled crash-landing following loss of the tail rotor at low altitude.

Fuselage attitude is adjusted using the powerful, electrically operated tailplane. The surface is automatic and moves between +34° in the controlled hover and -6° during autorotation.

Several MH-53Js and MH-60Gs wore white identification stripes over rapidly applied desert camouflage during the Gulf War.

In addition to the normal door-mounted weapons, in this case 7.62-mm (30-cal.) miniguns, this aircraft also has a 12.7-mm (.50-cal.) machine gun mounted in the cabin.

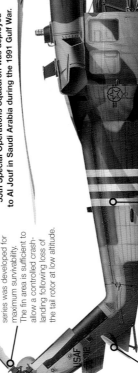

TERRAIN-FOLLOWING RADAR (TFR): Currently unique to US Army MH-60Ks is the nose-mounted Texas Instruments' AN/AFQ-174A TFR. This allows much safer low-level flight.

AIR-TO-AIR REFUELLING (AAR): US Forces pioneered helicopter AAR in order to extend the range of CSAR helicopters. Army and Air Force MH-60s regularly practise the technique.

Pave Hawk in action

COVERT INSERTION: With the MH-60G hovering just centimetres from the ground, troops are able to jump from the cabin as the door gunners lay down suppressive fire.

MH-60G Pave Hawk

Type: special operations warfare helicopter

Powerplant: two 1210-kW (1620-hp) General Electric T700-GE-700 turboshaft engines

Maximum speed: 296 km/h (184 mph)

Vertical climb rate: more than 137 m/min (450 fpm) at sea level

Operational radius: about 964 km (600 miles) with two 1703-litre (450-gallon) drop tanks

Service ceiling: 5790 m (19,000 ft)

Weights: empty 6114 kg (13,450 lb); maximum take-off 9979 kg (21,514 lb)

Armament: a range of external stores including Hellfire missiles and cannon or rocket pods may be carried, but usually two pintle-mounted 12.7-mm (.50-cal.) machine guns

Dimensions:
main rotor diameter 16.36 m (53 ft 8 in)
fuselage length 17.38 m (57 ft)
height 5.13 m (16 ft 10 in)
main rotor 210.05 m² (2260 sq ft)
disc area

COMBAT DATA

POWER

Although it has less power than the other principal US special forces helicopters, the MH-60G is much lighter. Pilots find that it has good reserves of power which make keeping in touch with Hercules tankers far easier than with some other helicopter types.

MH-60G PAVE HAWK 2420 kW (3240 hp)	MH-47E CHINOOK 6528 kW (9290 hp)	MH-53J PAVE LOW III 5870 kW (7870 hp)

PAYLOAD

Both the MH-47E and MH-53J are larger machines than the MH-60G, but they are not as easily deployable because of their size and the increased levels of support necessary. The MH-47E has the same systems as the MH-60K.

MH-60G PAVE HAWK 3629 kg (7985 lb)	MH-47E CHINOOK 10,341 kg (22,750 lb)	MH-53J PAVE LOW III 9072 kg (19,960 lb)

OPERATIONAL RADIUS

Both the Sikorsky MH-60G and MH-53J Pave Low III commonly employ two 1703-litre drop tanks as a means of increasing range. In the case of the MH-60G this gives an exceptional figure. The MH-47E carries no external fuel, but all three can be refuelled in flight.

MH-47E CHINOOK 560 km (350 miles)

MH-53J PAVE LOW III 290 km (180 miles)

MH-60G PAVE HAWK 964 km (600 miles)

VOUGHT

SB2U VINDICATOR

- US Navy scout-bomber ● Pacific 1942 ● Royal Navy trainer

▲ The Battle of Midway of 1942 was one of the few engagements in which the Vindicator saw combat in World War II. Its lack of performance against fighters such as the Japanese Zero meant it was replaced by the Douglas SBD Dauntless.

Built in 1935, while the service still favoured biplanes, Vought's SB2U Vindicator was the US Navy's first monoplane scout bomber. This two-seat, all-metal combat plane was a step forward in the 1930s, but by the time World War II began it was inferior to other fighting machines in its class. Vulnerable to fighter attack, the SB2U actually saw relatively little combat service, although it performed admirably in the training role.

VOUGHT SB2U VINDICATOR

PHOTO FILE

▲ **Improved variants**
Carrying bright pre-war markings, nine SB2Us formate. Later versions carried more fuel, armament and armour.

▲ **Prototype**
This is the first XSB2U-1 seen shortly after completion. The Vindicator was relatively lightly constructed compared to later dive-bomber types.

▲ **Fleet Air Arm Chesapeake**
The V-156 proved unsuitable for the Royal Navy's escort carriers due to its long take-off run, and was relegated to a land-based training role.

▲ **SB2U-3 of VS-1**
The US Navy did not officially adopt the name Vindicator until the SB2U-3 version was delivered.

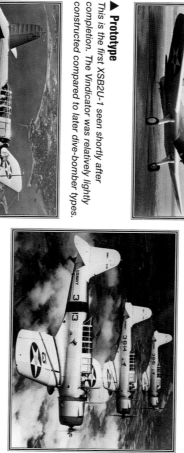

▲ **Based aboard USS Saratoga**
These three SB2U-1s are seen on 23 May 1939 in the full markings of bomber squadron VB-3.

FACTS AND FIGURES

▼ In 1936, tests at Anacostia Naval Station, Washington, showed the SB2U to be superior to its SB3U biplane competitor.

▼ The prototype for the SB2U series made its maiden flight on 4 January 1936.

▼ The first SB2Us went to US Navy unit VB-3 from 20 December 1937.

▼ Captured French V-156s are reputed to have been used to bomb Dover, although this was never confirmed.

▼ Two Marine Corps squadrons flew Vindicators in action in the Pacific.

▼ In 1939 a single SB2U-1 had floats added and flew as a seaplane XSB2U-3.

Diving pioneer monoplane

Configured much like other scout and torpedo-bombers of the 1930s, the Vought SB2U Vindicator was designed to fly from aircraft-carrier decks. However, once in the air it lacked the speed, manoeuvrability or defensive armament to survive against the nimble, single-seat fighters emerging in the late 1930s.

In the mid 1930s, it took the US Navy many months to choose the Vindicator in preference to a competing biplane design. Once production

Vindicators began to emerge from Vought Sikorsky's Stratford, Connecticut, factory in 1937, it was very clear that the monoplane was the wave of the future. Designers kept improving the Vindicator. Even so, it was at best only an equal for the Navy's other scout bomber of the era, the Douglas SBD Dauntless.

US Navy and Marine Corps SB2Us were active against the Japanese in the Pacific, including the Battle of Midway, during World War II, but were soon replaced by other types.

Vought built and delivered 24 of 40 planned aircraft to France under the designation V-156. Some of these fell into German hands after the French capitulated. Fifty more, called Chesapeakes, went to the British Fleet Air Arm, which used them in an operational training role serving with two squadrons.

Left: Bomber squadron VB-3 'Top Hatters' equipped with SB2U-1s in 1939. The squadron was still active in 1990, serving in the Gulf War as fighter squadron VF-14 with F-14 Tomcats.

Above: In 1938 France's naval air service ordered the SB2U under the Vought company designation V-156-F3.

SB2U-3 Vindicator

Type: carrier-based scout/bomber

Powerplant: one 615-kW (825-hp) Pratt & Whitney R-1535-02 Twin Wasp Junior radial piston engine

Maximum speed: 391 km/h (242 mph) at 2895 m (9500 ft)

Range: 1802 km (1117 miles)

Service ceiling: 7195 m (23,600 ft)

Weights: empty 2556 kg (5623 lb); loaded 4273 kg (9400 lb)

Armament: two 12.7-mm (.50-cal.) machine guns (one forward-firing and one on a trainable mount in the rear cockpit), plus up to 454 kg (1000 lb) of bombs

Dimensions:
span	12.80 m (42 ft)
length	10.36 m (34 ft)
height	3.12 m (10 ft 3 in)
wing area	28.33 m² (305 sq ft)

COMBAT DATA

BOMBLOAD

Even though it was an improvement over that of the SBU-1, the bombload carried by the Vindicator was still inferior to that of the Dauntless, the Navy's main wartime scout/bomber.

SB2U-3 VINDICATOR 454 kg (1000 lb)	
SBD-5 DAUNTLESS 1021 kg (2240 lb)	
SBU-1 227 kg (500 lb)	

MAXIMUM SPEED

Top speed performance of the Dauntless was only marginally better than that of the Vindicator. However, other more marked performance improvements made the SBD the superior aircraft.

SB2U-3 VINDICATOR	391 km/h (242 mph)
SBD-5 DAUNTLESS	406 km/h (251 mph)
SBU-1	330 km/h (198 mph)

ENGINE POWER

Power ratings climbed steadily to take advantage of better engines. SBDs introduced a significantly more powerful engine which improved flight performance and load-carrying capability.

SB2U-3 VINDICATOR 615 kW (825 hp)	
SBD-5 DAUNTLESS 895 kW (1200 hp)	
SBU-1 522 kW (700 hp)	

CHESAPEAKE MK I

In Royal Navy service the Vought V-156 was known as the Chesapeake. AL924 was one of 50 V-156-B1s ordered, and the first entered service in 1941 with No. 811 Squadron at Lee-on-Solent.

Pratt & Whitney's R-1535 Twin Wasp Junior engine powered the SB2U and V-156. This drove a two-bladed metal propeller.

A 'trapeze' below the cockpit was fitted to a bomb on the centreline pylon. This pulled the bomb downwards and clear of the aircraft.

A Fleet Air Arm three-tone grey colour scheme was applied to the Chesapeake. This aircraft also carries early-style national markings as displayed at the start of World War II.

The Chesapeake had provision for four forward-firing machine guns in the wings, with a further free-mounted gun in the rear cockpit. American SB2U-3s had one forward- and one aft-firing 12.7-mm (.50-cal.) machine gun.

Maximum ordnance load for Fleet Air Arm Chesapeakes was 680 kg (1500 lb) of bombs: either three 227-kg (500-lb) bombs or a dozen 53-kg (117-lb) bombs. US Navy Vindicators were restricted to 454 kg (1000 lb) of bombs.

The arrester hook can be seen in the retracted position on this aircraft. The arrester gear on British aircraft was of a different design to the American.

The undercarriage on the Vindicator retracted to the rear and rotated through 90°, with the wheels fitting into a recessed bay in each wing.

Naval dive-bombers of World War II

■ **AICHI D3A:** Known as 'Val' to the Allies, the D3A was a major participant in the Pearl Harbor attack of 1941. Over 1400 were built.

■ **DOUGLAS SBD DAUNTLESS:** Entering service in 1940, the SBD served with the Navy and Marine Corps, and replaced the SB2U.

■ **FAIREY BARRACUDA:** First flown in 1940, this aircraft was employed as a dive-bomber with the Royal Navy in the Atlantic and the Pacific.

■ **JUNKERS Ju 87:** The Ju 87C-1 variant of the 'Stuka' was intended for the German carrier *Graf Zeppelin* before construction was halted.

VOUGHT
F4U/AU-1 CORSAIR

- Long production run ● Service in Korea ● Powerful engine

▲ A major naval fighter of World War II, the Corsair became a stalwart of the US Marine Corps and French Aéronavale during the 1950s, fighting in both Korea and Indochina.

With the longest production run of any piston-engined fighter, the Corsair became a legend of US aviation. When the last F4U-7 was delivered to France's Aéronavale, production had reached 12,570, including Goodyear-built FGs and the Marine Corps' AU-1 attack variant. After 1945, the type served with the US and France in Korea, Indochina, Suez and Algeria. A few examples even survived into the late 1960s in Central America.

VOUGHT F4U/AU-1 CORSAIR

▼ **Post-war Production**
After World War II the Corsair remained an important element in US naval aviation. Such was the demand that production at the Dallas plant continued until 1952.

▲ Last of the gull wings
The final version of this incredible fighter was the F4U-7, which was essentially similar to the F4U-4C. None was supplied to the US armed forces, and all 94 aircraft were delivered to France.

Undercarriage retraction ▶
Because of the shape of the wings, the undercarriage had to retract backwards with the main oleos rotating through 90° to lie flat in the wing. The tail wheel retracted aft.

▲ **Navy night-fighters**
F4U-5Ns were the principal USN night intruders in Korea and played havoc with the Chinese supply lines during the nocturnal hours.

▲ **Marine stalwart**
Marine squadrons were the first units to operate the Corsair in World War II and became staunch post-war advocates of this capable and powerful fighter.

FACTS AND FIGURES

▼ During the 1956 Suez Crisis, Aéronavale F4U-7s were based aboard the aircraft carriers *Lafayette* and *Arromanches*.

▼ In Korea, US Navy and Marine Corps Corsairs were based on land and at sea.

▼ F4Us were active during a border dispute between Chile and Argentina in 1965.

▼ Shore bases were used by Aéronavale F4U-7s and AU-1s of 12, 14, 15 and 17 Flotilles in Algerian fighting during 1961.

▼ During the 1969 'Football War', Honduran Corsairs fought Salvadorean Mustangs.

▼ A Goodyear-built, R-4360-engined, 694-km/h (430 mph) F2G was cancelled in 1945.

PROFILE

More 'Whistling Death'

Despite the advent of the jet engine, the F4U Corsair remained the major US naval fighter in the Sixth and Seventh Fleets well into the 1950s.

Many F4U-4s and -5s (including night-fighter versions of the latter) saw service during the Korean War, often in the attack role. This Far Eastern 'police action' kept the type in production long after 1945.

For low-altitude close support duties, the Marine Corps ordered the F4U-6 in

1951. This had an R-2800 engine with a single-stage supercharger installed which produced maximum power at low altitude. Along with extra armour, four 20-mm cannon were fitted and the aircraft was stressed to carry 1814 kg (4000 lb) of ordnance. Vought built 110 production examples of this variant, which was soon redesignated the AU-1 to reflect its air-to-ground role.

The last Corsair variant of all was the F4U-7. This was essentially an AU-1 fitted with a two-stage R-2800 engine.

Ninety-four were built, all for French naval use in Korea, where they were bolstered by ex-US Navy aircraft. Aéronavale Dash-7s later served in the Suez theatre in 1956 and, in 1961, during the Algerian uprising.

Some of the last Corsairs in service were those flown by Honduras (F4U-4s) and El Salvador (FG-1Ds) during the 1969 'Football War'.

Left: F4U-7s had the same wing design as the AU-1 and could carry heavy weapon loads.

Below: During their later years of service with the US Navy and Marine Corps, F4Us were painted dark blue.

F4U-7 Corsair

Type: single-seat carrier-borne fighter/bomber

Powerplant: one 1715-kW (2300-hp) Pratt & Whitney R-2800-83W Double Wasp 18 cylinder radial piston engine

Maximum speed: 705 km/h (437 mph)

Initial climb rate: 890 m/min (2850 fpm)

Range: 485 km (300 miles)

Service ceiling: 12,040 m (39,500 ft)

Weights: empty 4461 kg (9814 lb); loaded 8800 kg (19,360 lb)

Armament: four 20 mm cannon and up to 1814 kg (4000 lb) of external stores

Dimensions:
span	12.50 m	(41 ft)
length	10.39 m	(34 ft 1 in)
height	6.15 m	(20 ft 2 in)
wing area	29.17 m²	(314 sq ft)

COMBAT DATA

MAXIMUM SPEED

All three of these aircraft were among the most powerful in their class in their day. Later Corsairs, such as the AU-1 were slightly faster than Grumman's pugnacious Bearcat. The Skyraider was larger and much heavier and thus not as quick.

AU-1 CORSAIR	705 km/h (437 mph)
F8F-1B BEARCAT	677 km/h (420 mph)
AD-6 SKYRAIDER	518 km/h (321 mph)

BOMBLOAD

AU-1s differed from other Corsairs in that they featured stronger wings. This enabled them to carry up to 1814 kg (4000 lb) of bombs, a considerable improvement over other fighter-bomber types such as the F8F-1B Bearcat. The Douglas Skyraider, was larger and heavier than both the others and could accommodate a huge 3630 kg (8000 lb).

AU-1 CORSAIR 1814 kg (4000 lb)	
F8F-1B BEARCAT 454 kg (1000 lb)	
AD-6 SKYRAIDER 3630 kg (8000 lb)	

CLIMB RATE

A light-weight airframe and powerful engine gave the Bearcat an impressive rate of climb, on a par with most jets of the day. Neither the Douglas Skyraider nor the Corsair could match it.

AD-6 SKYRAIDER 890 m/min (2920 fpm)

F8F-1B BEARCAT 1392 m/min (4570 fpm)

AU-1 CORSAIR 869 m/min (2850 fpm)

This particular machine was an F4U-5N night-fighter, flown by Lieutenant Guy Bordelon of VC-3. Bordelon was the only non Sabre ace of the Korean War and downed five aircraft, including four Yak-9s.

Visibility whilst taxiing was always a problem for tail draggers such as the Corsair. The F4U-5 model went some way towards improving this by adopting a lower profile cowl.

Inside, the F4U-5 featured a completely modernized cockpit. Automatic controls were introduced for the superchargers, cowl flaps, intercooler doors and oil cooler which considerably reduced pilot workload.

F4U-5s were also the first Corsairs to have a fully retractable tailwheel. Nevertheless, the long tail undercarriage leg remained and along with it, the tricky deck handling characteristics.

During World War II the Corsair had shown itself able to absorb tremendous punishment and this proved equally true in Korea. A thick fuselage skin and a spot welding process was the key to its rugged structure.

F4U-5s were powered by R2800-32 engines and were distinguished by a different engine cowling and exhausts located on each side as opposed to underneath as on earlier variants.

Armament comprised four 20-mm cannons, with two mounted in each wing. These provided effective firepower and one Corsair even downed a MiG-15.

Post-war piston-engined carrier fighters

■ **GRUMMAN F6F-5 HELLCAT:** Late model Hellcats continued in service after World War II with the US Navy and other air arms.

■ **GRUMMAN F7F-2N TIGERCAT:** A large twin-engined design, the superb Tigercat matured into a highly capable night-fighter.

■ **HAWKER SEA FURY FB. Mk 11:** Replacing the Seafire aboard Royal Navy carriers, the Sea Fury emerged as a surprising MiG killer in Korea.

■ **GRUMMAN F8F-1B BEARCAT:** Grumman's last single-seat piston engined carrier fighter, the Bearcat, only had a short career with the USN.

VOUGHT
F4U CORSAIR

- Carrier- and land-based ● MiG-killer ● New AU-1 attack version

A
fter their successes with the F4U Corsair in the Pacific during World War II, the US Navy and Marine Corps took Vought's 'Whispering Death' to war again in 1950. This time it was used in the night-fighter and close support roles during the 'police action' in Korea. The US was so reliant on the Corsair that it was put back into production for the Marines as the AU-1. In this age of the jet's ascendancy, the 'big props' still had a role.

▲ Marine Corps Corsair operations were flown from US Navy carriers and from shore bases. Together with the USAF's P-51 Mustang, the Corsair bore the brunt of the close support operations in the opening months of the war.

PHOTO FILE

VOUGHT F4U CORSAIR

▼ Night-fighter
F4U-5Ns were fitted with a wing-mounted radar and equipped USMC night-fighter units. Twin air intakes fed the supercharger on the R-2800 engine.

▲ Dedicated ground attack
Originally known as F4U-6, the AU-1 had a single-stage supercharger to improve low-level performance.

▲ F4U-4 with 'Tiny Tim' aboard
This Marine Corps machine carries a 227-kg (500-lb) bomb and a large 'Tiny Tim' unguided rocket. Other typical loads included a 1136-litre (250-gallon) drop-tank and 907 kg (2000 lb) of bombs.

▼ Korean winter at Yonpo
The 1st Marine Air Wing flew F4U-5s flew close support missions from Yonpo in the winter of 1950/51.

▲ Running into the target
Seen in a typical low-level close support pose, this F4U-4 carries a standard load of eight 12.7-mm (.50-cal.) rockets. The AU-1 variant carried the heaviest loads.

FACTS AND FIGURES

▶ During carrier landings and take-offs, Corsair pilots left the cockpit canopies open for a quick escape in an emergency.

▶ The famous 'Flying Nightmares', VMF(N)-513, flew F4U-5Ns on night missions.

▶ Land-based F4Us were often maintained outdoors in primitive conditions.

▶ During the war, AU-1s flew with all-up weights as high as 8799 kg (19,398 lb) including 2268 kg (5000 lb) of underwing ordnance and fuel.

▶ Corsairs were able to loiter over targets, unlike the early short-ranged jets.

▶ Including Korean War production, 12,571 Corsairs were built.

PROFILE

Gull-wing fighters return to war

Although it was a US Navy carrier-based F4U unit that opened the Korean campaign only eight days after the war began, it was the Marine Corps that flew the bulk of Corsair missions over Korea. Corsairs remained in intensive use for three years, from 1950 until the last day of the war on 27 June 1953.

With a radial engine that was far less vulnerable to small-arms fire, the Corsair was better suited than the USAF's P-51s to ground attack missions.

This was to be its main role in Korea – close support of USMC ground forces. Missions were flown from US Navy carriers 'on station' in the Yellow Sea and from shore bases, with units often alternating between the two.

Corsair variants in action over Korea included the F4U-4 (which had first appeared in 1945 and introduced four 20-mm cannon in the -4B), the F4U-5 (including the radar-equipped -5N and 'winterized'

-5NL) and the AU-1. First proposed by Vought in 1950 and boasting extra armour, a modified engine and greatly increased weapon load, the Corsair, as the AU-1, was put back into production 10 years after its first flight. By October 1952 111 AU-1s had been built.

The F4U-4 was powered by the proven Pratt & Whitney R-2800 Double Wasp 18-cylinder two-row radial engine, rated at 1566 kW (2100 hp). The F4U-5 and AU-1 used a 1715-kW (2300-hp) version, although the latter had only a single-stage supercharger as it was intended for low-altitude operations.

F4U-4B CORSAIR

BuNo. 97201 was flown by Captain Jesse Folmar, of VMA-312 aboard USS *Sicily*, when he claimed the only Corsair versus MiG kill. After successfully engaging the MiG he was himself shot down by four other MiGs. Folmar was rescued by an SA-16 amphibian.

The F4U-4 retained some fabric covering of the wing surfaces. This was replaced with an all-metal wing covering in the F4U-5 which reduced drag considerably.

Due to the conditions of the harsh Korean winter, the Dash-5NL variant had wing and tall de-icer boots and de-icer shoes fitted to the propeller. The windscreen had improved thermal de-icing.

Although earlier variants were armed with six 12.7-mm (.50-cal.) machine guns, the F4U-4B, -5 and AU-1 were fitted with four 20-mm cannon.

By the 1950s the standard naval colour scheme was an all-over coat of 'midnight blue'.

Late Corsair versions had increased load-carrying capability on underwing pylons. The AU-1 had six hardpoints under each wing for up to 2268 kg (5000 lb) of bombs, rockets and fuel tanks. The normal maximum load was 1815 kg (4000 lb).

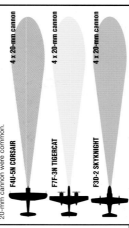

Left: Apart from detail improvements, the Corsair's airframe remained largely unchanged since World War II.

Below: An F4U-4 leaves the deck of a US Navy carrier. This major production version was intended to replace F4U-1s from 1945.

F4U-5N Corsair

Type: single-seat night-fighter and ground attack aircraft

Powerplant: one 1715-kW (2300-hp) Pratt & Whitney R-2800-32W radial engine

Maximum speed: 756 km/h (470 mph) at 8169 m (26,800 ft)

Cruising speed: 365 km/h (227 mph)

Climb rate: 1152 m/min (3780 fpm)

Service ceiling: 12,619 m (41,400 ft)

Weights: empty 4392 kg (9683 lb); maximum take-off 6398 kg (14,105 lb)

Armament: four 20-mm cannon, plus up to 907 kg (2000 lb) of bombs, rockets and external fuel

Dimensions: span 12.50 m (41 ft 1 in)
length 10.21 m (33 ft 6 in)
height 4.50 m (14 ft 9 in)
wing area 29.17 m² (314 sq ft)

ACTION DATA

MAXIMUM SPEED

The Dash-5 variant of the Corsair was one of the fastest propeller-driven fighters built – even faster than some versions of the twin-engined Tigercat. However, jets like the F3D were on the way.

F4U-5N CORSAIR 756 km/h (470 mph)	
F7F-3N TIGERCAT 700 km/h (435 mph)	
F3D-2 SKYKNIGHT 956 km/h (594 mph)	

ARMAMENT

The American forces were slow to adopt cannon armament during World War II, but by the late 1940s they had introduced it. Four 20-mm cannon were common.

F4U-5N CORSAIR — 4 x 20-mm cannon
F7F-3N TIGERCAT — 4 x 20-mm cannon
F3D-2 SKYKNIGHT — 4 x 20-mm cannon

KILLS

These kills by Marine pilots flying the three principal US night-fighter types of the war show that propeller-driven types like the Corsair were still useful, at least against slower targets like Po-2s.

F4U-5N CORSAIR
F7F-3N TIGERCAT
F3D-2 SKYKNIGHT

NIGHT ATTACK: Corsairs in Korea were perhaps at their most deadly in the night-time close-support role. Radar-equipped F4U-5Ns hit Chinese supply trucks.

SLOW SPEED ADVANTAGE: Corsairs were able to shoot down Po-2 and Yak-18 aircraft which were too slow targets for jet fighters.

Corsairs in action over Korea

MIG-KILLER: USMC pilot Jesse Folmar made the only MiG kill by a Corsair in Korea, shooting down a MiG-15 on 10 September 1952.

VOUGHT

F7U CUTLASS

● Tailless fighter ● Supersonic flyer ● 'Widow maker'

ought's highly unorthodox F7U Cutlass was really two different aircraft sharing a common configuration. Such were the weaknesses of the original F7U-1 that a production variant – the F7U-2 – was cancelled and the redesigned F7U-3 ordered instead. Though accident-prone and under-powered, the Cutlass nevertheless deserves a place among US Navy fighters, as it introduced systems now commonplace on today's Navy jets.

▲ To any Navy pilot flying in the 1950s, the allure of the Cutlass was irresistible, but there was a price to pay. The radical nature of the aircraft ensured that a high accident rate was inevitable.

VOUGHT F7U CUTLASS

▼ **Radical design**
Early design features of this F7U-1 were its small nosecone, lower canopy and deep-chord tail; all were modified later.

▲ **Photo-birds**
A developed model of the Cutlass was the unarmed F7U-3P which was a dedicated reconnaissance variant housing cameras in a lengthened nose. Although successful, only 12 aircraft were built, serving with a trials squadron.

Lack of power ▼
With afterburners alight, this late model Cutlass leaves Moffet Field in California for a night training sortie.

▲ **Missile testing**
A camera pod and a full load of Sparrow air-to-air missiles are evaluated on this F7U flying from the Navy's Point Mugu test facility in California.

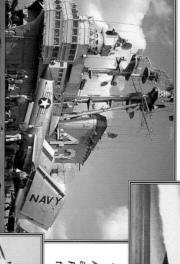

▲ **Carrier catastrophes**
Although the F7U was accepted for operational service, deck trials proved extremely hazardous; restrictions were imposed until it was modified.

FACTS AND FIGURES

▶ First flight of the Cutlass took place on 29 September 1948 at the Naval Air Test Center at Patuxent River, Maryland.

▶ The Cutlass helped establish techniques in the use of air-to-air missiles.

▶ Only 12 examples of the reconnaissance variant were produced.

▶ The last Cutlass in service was an F7U-3P which retired on 2 March 1959 from El Centro in California.

▶ Four of America's best test pilots were killed during development of this type.

▶ Astronauts John Glenn and Alan Shepard were former Cutlass pilots.

F7U-3 Cutlass

Type: single-seat carrier-based fighter

Powerplant: two 27.14-kN (6105-lb-thrust) Westinghouse J46-WE-8A afterburning turbojets

Maximum speed: 1094 km/h (678 mph) at 3048 m (10,000 ft)

Initial climb rate: 3399 m/min (11,150 fpm)

Landing speed: 220 km/h (136 mph)

Range: 1120 km (695 miles)

Service ceiling: 12,192 m (40,000 ft)

Weights: empty 8260 kg (18,172 lb); loaded 12,779 kg (22,114 lb)

Armament: four internal 20-mm cannon; four Sparrow AAMs

Dimensions:
span	12.09 m (39 ft 8 in)
length	13.13 m (43 ft 1 in)
height	4.36 m (14 ft 4 in)
wing area	46.07 m² (496 sq ft)

COMBAT DATA

POWER

Often criticized for its lack of power compared with similar types, the F7U was found to be extremely dangerous when operating aboard ships. This contrasted to the raw power of the F-8, whose less complex design offered better safety and reliability.

	F3H-2N DEMON (12,210 lb thrust)
F7U-3 CUTLASS 54.28 kN	
F3H-2N DEMON 63.39 kN (14,260 lb thrust)	
F-8A CRUSADER 72.06 kN (16,210 lb thrust)	

RANGE

Despite the complex design of the Cutlass, the fuselage left little room for fuel. Coupled with the poor performance of the engines, this meant that range was never going to be sufficient for shipboard operations. Although problems existed with the F3H, it proved to have longer range.

F3H-2N DEMON 2205 km (1367 miles)

F-8A CRUSADER 2474 km (1535 miles)

F7U-3 CUTLASS 1120 km (695 miles)

MAXIMUM SPEED

Fitted with twin afterburner engines, the maximum speed of the F7U proved to be high, although of short duration because of its low fuel capacity. During this period the F-8 Crusader was the dominant carrier fighter.

F7U-3 CUTLASS 1094 km/h (678 mph)	
F3H-2N DEMON 1041 km/h (645 mph)	
F-8A CRUSADER 1630 km/h (1010 mph)	

Vought's praying mantis

Large quantities of German aeronautical research data fell into Allied hands in 1945, among it the fruits of work carried out by Arado on tailless designs. Vought saw the benefits of this unorthodox layout and designed an aircraft to fill a US Navy requirement for a 966 km/h (600 mph) fighter.

The V-346A was chosen from 12 submissions in June 1946. Without a horizontal stabilizer, the Cutlass was controlled in pitch and roll by 'ailevators' (known today as elevons). Conventional landing flaps were replaced by leading-edge slats. The first of three XF7U-1s, fitted with J34 afterburning turbojets, flew on 29 September 1948.

Fourteen F7U-1s followed, but many problems, especially with the engines, prevented squadron service. These snags, combined with development delays with the improved J46 engine, led to the cancellation of 88 follow-on F7U-2s. By the time the first F7U-3 flew in late-1951, it had been radically redesigned with a new nose, deeper fuselage, revised fins and extra fuel, and thus more weight. An attack version, the

A2U-1, was cancelled in favour of the Sparrow missile-equipped F7U-3M, which soon replaced the F7U-3 in four carrier-based fighter units. Up to 1955, 290 F7U-3/3Ms were built.

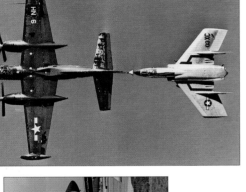

Above: Seen at Oceana in September 1955, this Cutlass displays the futuristic design of the aircraft.

Above: In-flight refuelling from this North American Savage required the Cutlass pilot to stand up in the cockpit.

F7U-1 CUTLASS

To improve the image of the Cutlass the 'Blue Angels' formation aerobatic team was allocated two aircraft for display work. It was an excellent performer, but technical reliability was less impressive.

A feature of early models was the small nose and low profile canopy, which reduced pilot visibility on carrier approaches. Although this was modified in later models, forward vision continued to be a problem.

The bold design of the Cutlass gave the US Navy a radical airframe that was to test and develop systems that are still in use today. It was the first US aircraft designed from the outset with afterburners. Separation of stores at supersonic speeds was pioneered on the airframe.

Because of the small wing span, the twin dorsal mounted fins were fitted with rudders that were one-third the span of the large ventral fins.

The two Westinghouse J34 engines proved to be the main flaw in use in the aircraft, often referred to as the 'Gutless' by pilots because of its poor performance.

Positioned between the engine exhausts was the arrester hook; later models featured an extended tailcone.

For the first time, nosewheel steering was fitted on the undercarriage. The main landing gear retracted backwards into pylons under the tail.

U.S. NAVY

124426

'Blue Angels' display mounts

■ **GRUMMAN F6F-5 HELLCAT:** The first aircraft allocated to the display team in 1946, this example was flown by the then-team leader Commander 'Butch' Voris.

■ **GRUMMAN F8F-1 BEARCAT:** Displaying the earliest markings used on the team's aircraft, the Bearcat was the display mount from late 1946 until 1952.

■ **GRUMMAN F9F-8 COUGAR:** Various models of the Cougar were operated from 1953 to 1968, and they proved to be fine display aircraft. A single TF-9J flew with the team for VIP flights.

438

VOUGHT
F-8 CRUSADER

● Fleet air defence ● Vietnam MiG killer ● Variable-incidence wing

▲ Just as the US Navy was looking forward to receiving the heavy, complex F-4B, the F-8 was proving that a simple cannon-armed aircraft was ideal for taking on MiG-21s in a dogfight.

C rusader jocks boasted that their manoeuvrable, cannon-armed jet was hotter than anything in the skies and scoffed when 'experts' said that missiles would make their fighters obsolete. In battle, the pilots were proved correct when their fighter was able to dogfight with Vietnamese MiGs on equal terms. The Crusader was the best-loved fighter in the post-war US Navy, and remained in French service into the 1990s.

VOUGHT F-8 CRUSADER

▲ Raised wing
The Crusader has a variable-incidence wing, which reduces speed when the aircraft lands.

▲ Two-seater
One XF8U was converted to a two-seater, with only two cannon but a second set of controls. It first flew in 1962, but did not see active service.

▲ Folded up
Wings folded and starboard flap down, an F-8 is prepared for combat. Crusaders shot down 18 MiGs with Sidewinders over Vietnam.

▲ French fighters
Armed with MATRA missiles, the Crusader provided the French navy with their only fighter asset.

Air to ground ▼
The F-8 was quite capable of bombing as well as air defence, but this capability was seldom used as the US Navy had plenty of A-4 and A-7 bombers.

▼ Philippine defender
The Philippine air force was the only other user, but their F-8Hs are now retired. Like the French Crusaders, the F-8H had boundary-layer control and improved avionics.

FACTS AND FIGURES

➤ Test pilot John Konrad flew the XF8U-1 prototype on its maiden flight on 25 March 1955.

➤ The Philippines air force acquired F-8H Crusaders in the 1980s.

➤ Vought's XF8U-3 Crusader III was not ordered into production.

➤ RF-8A photo Crusaders helped to spot new Soviet bases in Cuba during the Missile Crisis of 1962.

➤ Seventy-one US Navy and Marine Corps squadrons operated F-8 Crusaders.

➤ Crusaders could also carry the AGM-12 Bullpup missile for ground attack.

PROFILE

MiG killing with the US Navy

One of the first supersonic fighters, Vought's F-8 Crusader (originally F8U) pushed back the boundaries of naval aviation in the 1950s and battled with MiGs in Vietnam a decade later.

Pilots saw the F-8 as the ultimate dogfighter: light, manoeuvrable and packing heavy cannon armament. Unlike many of its contemporaries in Vietnam, notably the F-4 Phantom, the F-8 eschewed missiles, complex avionics and radar in favour of old-fashioned guns and thrust, and pilots loved it.

With its supersonic 'area rule' shape and powerful J57 engine, the Crusader set many speed records and was clearly the world's best carrier-based fighter when it went to war in Vietnam. In action near Hanoi, Crusaders shot down 18 MiG-17s and MiG-21s without a single air-to-air loss. It also took on an extra duty as a carrier-based reconnaissance platform.

With its variable-incidence wing raised for low-speed flight, an F-8 refuels from a Skyraider. French F-8(FN)s had even better low-speed handling than the US versions.

Some Crusaders acquired air-to-ground capability and served the US Marine Corps well during the Tet fighting of 1968. France used this superb jet on its light carriers *Foch* and *Clemenceau* until 1999, when the F-8 was replaced with the Rafale M.

F8U-1E CRUSADER

Known after 1962 as the F-8B, this Crusader variant had APS-67 radar providing a limited all-weather capability; 130 of this variant were built by Vought.

The F8U-2N version had an illuminating radar in the nose for the AIM-9C radar-guided Sidewinder missile. Earlier versions had a simple ranging radar. Crusader pilots sat on Martin-Baker Mk 5 ejector seats.

Another innovative feature of the F-8 was the dogtooth, which provided vortexes to improve control at high alpha. The wing also had large leading-edge flaps.

F-8E Crusader

Type: single-seat naval fighter (F-8E)

Powerplant: one 80.07-kN (17,963-lb-thrust) Pratt & Whitney J57-P-20A afterburning turbojet engine

Maximum speed: 1802 km/h (1117 mph) or Mach 1.7 at 12,192 m (40,000 ft)

Initial rate of climb: 8290 m/min (27,198 fpm)

Range: 1660 km (1029 miles)

Service ceiling: 17,983 m (59,000 ft)

Weights: empty 9038 kg (19,883 lb); maximum (with external stores) 15,422 kg (33,925 lb)

Armament: four 20-mm Mk 12 cannon with 144 rounds per gun; up to four AIM-9 Sidewinders AAMs; or 16 113-kg (250-lb) or eight 227-kg (500-lb) bombs; or eight Zuni rockets; or two AGM-12A or AGM-12B Bullpup attack missiles

Dimensions:
span	10.87 m (35 ft)
length	16.61 m (90 ft)
height	4.80 m (16 ft)
wing area	32.52 m² (350 sq ft)

The variable-incidence wing allowed a lower nose attitude for a given angle of attack, providing the pilot with a good view of the deck when landing. The wing was hinged at the back, and raised by hydraulic jacks.

Two AIM-9B Sidewinders were carried on rails on the fuselage sides. Zuni air-to-ground rockets could also be fitted.

The large main fuel tank was fitted in the rear fuselage, just ahead of the engine. Air was ducted to the engine through the nose, over the mainwheel bay and under the wing. Later F-8s fitted for Bullpup air-to-surface missiles had a distinct 'hump' over the mid-fuselage, which housed the electronics guidance system.

F-8E Crusaders had a small tail-warning radar system, located in the fintip. The top of the fin contained a VHF aerial covered by a fairing.

Power was provided by the same J57 engine used in the F-100 and F-102 land-based fighters. F-8Js received the more powerful 87.39-kN (19,600-lb-thrust) J57-P-420 engine.

Four 20-mm Mk 12 cannon were fitted in the lower fuselage, fed from ammunition tanks behind the pilot. These were replaced by cameras in the reconnaissance RF-8A.

COMBAT DATA

MAXIMUM SPEED

The Crusader was very fast for a naval fighter and could even outrun most land-based types. The MiG-21s which it faced in Vietnam were slightly faster, but only at high level.

F-8C CRUSADER	1802 km/h (1117 mph)
MiG-21F 'FISHBED'	2000 km/h (1240 mph)
SEA VIXEN FAW.Mk 1	1050 km/h (651 mph)

ARMAMENT

Gun armament was seen as obsolete when Crusaders first went to war, a view rapidly ignored by the pilots when the unreliability of early missiles became apparent. Despite this, the Crusader actually scored most of its kills with Sidewinders. The first MiG-21s were gun armed only, then missile armed. Like the F-8, it could also carry free-flight rockets for air-to-air use.

F-8C CRUSADER	4 x 20-mm cannon 2 missiles
MiG-21F 'FISHBED'	2 x 30-mm cannon 32 rockets
SEA VIXEN FAW.Mk 1	4 missiles

RANGE

Designed as a naval fighter from its inception, the F-8 had long range. The MiG-21 was designed as a short-range 'point-defence' interceptor, and was always dogged by a lack of fuel.

F-8C CRUSADER	1770 km (1029 miles)
MiG-21F 'FISHBED'	560 km (347 miles)
SEA VIXEN FAW.Mk 1	965 km (598 miles)

Death of a Crusader

HARD TOUCHDOWN: During a landing on the carrier USS *Franklin D. Roosevelt* in 1961, Lieutenant J. Kryway misjudged his approach and broke the starboard undercarriage of his F-8.

BLOWING UP: The crash ruptured the engine and fuel tank bays, causing the stricken aircraft to catch fire and then blow up. Lieutenant Kryway was already starting his ejection.

OVER THE SIDE: With all control lost, the doomed F-8 went over the side of the ship. Here, the canopy is just beginning to lift off the cockpit as part of the ejection sequence.

BLASTED TO SAFETY: With only milliseconds to spare, Kryway is blasted to safety by his Martin-Baker ejection seat. He was rescued shortly after and survived.

VOUGHT

F-8 CRUSADER

● Shot down 18 Vietnamese MiGs   ● Close-support and recce roles

▲ Commander Richard Bellinger, an F-8 squadron leader, shows typical fighter pilot bravado as he describes his aerial victory over a North Vietnamese MiG-21 in October 1966.

US Navy and Marine Corps pilots flying the Crusader in Vietnam had a powerful fighter with which to face the North Vietnamese MiGs near Hanoi. All US aircrews had fierce respect for the old, but manoeuvrable MiG-17 'Frescos' and the more modern, high-performance MiG-21 'Fishbeds' flown by the North Vietnamese Air Force (NVAF), but the F-8 was capable of meeting that challenge.

VOUGHT F-8 CRUSADER

▲Photo reconnaissance in Vietnam
RF-8s flew crucial recce missions. This one has photographed a burning Vietnamese patrol boat.

▼ Carrier fighter
Unlike the heavier F-4, the F-8 could be deployed on smaller USN carriers, such as the USS Bonne Homme Richard.

▼ Close support
Navy and Marine Corps F-8s also had an important role providing close air support for US troops.

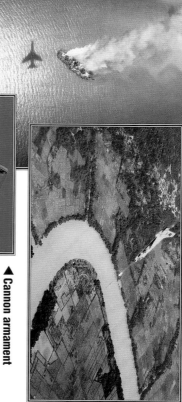

▲ Cannon armament
The Crusader's internal 20-mm cannon were valuable for both air combat and ground strafing.

▼ Missile armament
AIM-9 Sidewinders are loaded onto an F-8. This type of missile scored all but one of the Crusader's MiG kills in Vietnam.

FACTS AND FIGURES

▶ Pilots often considered landing on a carrier at sea to be almost as dangerous as going into combat near Hanoi.

▶ Crusaders shot down 18 MiGs in air-to-air combat over North Vietnam.

▶ Most of the USN's larger carriers had a detachment of reconnaissance RF-8s.

▶ Ten RF-8As and seven RF-8Gs were lost in combat over Vietnam, but none was downed by a MiG.

▶ An F-8 scored the final air-to-air victory of the Rolling Thunder campaign.

▶ Some F-8 pilots bombed targets as little as 90 m (295 ft) ahead of friendly troops.

PROFILE

Last of the 'gunfighters'

Vought's F-8 Crusader was one of the finest jet fighters of the Vietnam War. When the US Navy went to war in Southeast Asia, the Crusader had already been replaced on larger carriers by the F-4 Phantom II. However, the smaller carriers of the World War II 'Essex' class could not handle the heavy Phantom, and this fact ensured a continued role for the Crusader.

The F-8 proved exceptionally popular with its pilots, who found that the highly agile single-seater more closely fitted their requirement for a traditional dogfighter than the F-4 Phantom. The Crusader also

boasted one crucial advantage over the missile-armed F-4: it had built-in gun armament.

In Vietnam, the US Navy's carrier-based Crusaders were backed up by Marine Corps F-8s deployed to land bases in South Vietnam. The Crusader carried out three major roles: fighter, close-support and photo-reconnaissance. But it was as the US Navy's top scoring fighter that the Crusader found its forte. Between June 1966 and August 1968, Crusaders shot down 18 North Vietnamese MiGs, a tally which was not overtaken by Navy Phantoms until 1972. All but one of the F-8's kills were scored with the

AIM-9 Sidewinder heat-seeking air-to-air missile. The respect and affection in which the Vought F-8 was held by those who flew it is perhaps best summed up by the following quote, which was inspired by the arrival of the F-4: 'When you're out of Crusaders, you're out of fighters.'

Left: The prominent 'Shark's mouth' markings identify this F-8F as belonging to US Navy Squadron VF-111 'Sundowners', deployed aboard the USS Oriskany in 1966.

F-8E CRUSADER

This F-8E was flown during 1967/68 by Major Robin Ruthven of Marine squadron VMF(AW)-235 'Death Angels' (Motto: 'Laugh Now!'). The unit was the third Marine F-8 squadron in Vietnam.

The F-8 featured a variable-incidence wing which was raised during take-off and landing. This increased the angle of attack of the wing to the airflow, improving lift and therefore performance.

Fitted out for the close support mission, this F-8E is armed with eight 127-mm Zuni air-to-ground rockets, as well as eight 113-kg (250-lb) Mk 81 low-drag, unguided bombs.

An uprated engine was fitted to the F-8E compared to previous versions. It was powered by a single Pratt & Whitney J57-P20 turbojet which produced 48.93 kN (11,009-lb-thrust) in military rating, and 80.07 kN (18,016 lb thrust) with the afterburner engaged.

The F-8's offensive capability was increased dramatically by the addition of four wing hardpoints and by the development of 'Y-racks' for the fuselage pylons which allowed it to carry eight Zuni rockets or four Sidewinder missiles.

The Crusader's built-in armament comprised four Mk 12 20-mm cannon. Soot stains around the ports show that they have been heavily used.

VMF(AW)-235 decorated its F-8s with patches of red on the nose, tail and ventral fins, with white stars superimposed. The 'Death Angels' made two deployments to Vietnam and flew 9,140 operational missions in 1967-68.

F-8J Crusader

Type: single-seat, carrier-capable fighter and fighter-bomber

Powerplant: one 80.07-kN (18,016-lb-thrust) Pratt & Whitney J57-P-20A afterburning turbojet engine

Maximum speed: 1802 km/h (1120 mph) at 12,192 m (40,000 ft)

Climb rate: 6 min 30 sec to 17,375 m (57,000 ft)

Range: 1660 km (1031 miles)

Ceiling: 17,983 m (59,000 ft)

Weights: empty 9038 kg (19,925 lb); maximum take-off 12,474 kg (27,500 lb)

Armament: four 20-mm Mk 12 cannon with 144 rounds per gun; up to four AIM-9 Sidewinder AAMs; or eight 113-kg (250-lb) Mk 81 or 227-kg (500-lb) Mk 82 bombs; or eight Zuni rockets; or two AGM-12A or AGM-12B Bullpup attack missiles

Dimensions:
span	10.87 m (35 ft 8 in)
length	16.61 m (54 ft 6 in)
height	4.80 m (15 ft 9 in)
wing area	34.84 m² (375 sq ft)

COMBAT DATA

The F-8 was faced with two formidable opponents at both ends of the performance envelope. It was slower than the Mach 2-capable MiG-21 and less agile than the MiG-17. However, superior pilot training and tactics made the Crusader a winner in air combat.

MAXIMUM SPEED

F-8J CRUSADER	1802 km/h (1120 mph)
MiG-17F 'FRESCO-C'	1100 km/h (684 mph)
MiG-21PFS 'FISHBED-E'	2230 km/h (1386 mph)

MAXIMUM THRUST

F-8J CRUSADER	80.07 kN (18,016 lb thrust)
MiG-17F 'FRESCO-C'	33.14 kN (7457 lb thrust)
MiG-21PFS 'FISHBED-E'	60.80 kN (13,680 lb thrust)

Although its J57 engine was much more powerful than that of the MiG-21 or MiG-17, the F-8's heavier weight gave it a slightly inferior thrust-to-weight ratio than that of the MiG-21 (0.65 vs 0.68).

ARMAMENT

The Crusader was much more heavily armed than its rivals. Although armed with heavy cannon, the MiG-17 carried no missiles, while the MiG-21 carried only one cannon and two missiles.

F-8J CRUSADER	4 x 20-mm cannon / 4 x AIM-9 missiles
MiG-17F 'FRESCO-C'	1 x 37-mm cannon / 2 x 23-mm cannon
MiG-21PFS 'FISHBED-E'	1 x 23-mm cannon / 2 x K-13A 'Atoll' missiles

---

F-8 Vietnam missions

INTERCEPTOR: The F-8 was popular with its pilots because of its gun armament, but ironically all but one of the MiG kills scored by the Crusader were achieved with the AIM-9 air-to-air missile. Most were MiG-17s, but the Crusader also shot down MiG-21s.

ATTACK AND CLOSE SUPPORT: Marine Corps and Navy Crusaders were heavily committed in the air-to-ground role, mainly providing close air support for friendly troops under fire.

STRIKE RECONNAISSANCE: Photo Crusaders were among the most important US reconnaissance aircraft of the Vietnam War. The RF-8 variant carried out pre-strike reconnaissance to determine targets, as well as post-strike damage assessment.

VOUGHT

A-7 CORSAIR II

● Vietnam veteran ● Subsonic bomber ● Carrier deployments

T here is a saying in aviation, 'if something looks right, it flies right.' Taking into account the stubby appearance of the A-7 Corsair II, one may think the aircraft was therefore a poor performer. In fact the Corsair II proved to be one of the most capable attack aircraft in the US Navy. Replacing the diminutive Douglas A-4 Skyhawk, the Corsair II provided a quantum leap in technology that the US Navy was quick to exploit.

▲ A typical carrier-deck scene as a US Navy A-7 Corsair is re-armed and prepared for flight. The aircraft achieved an excellent maintenance record whenever operating on deployment.

442

VOUGHT A-7 CORSAIR II

▲ High visibility
Upon entering service, Navy Corsairs proudly displayed colourful squadron markings on their tails and wings.

▼ Leemoore line-up
Early A-7As are positioned prior to inspection by naval ground crews at Leemoore Naval Air Station. One aircraft already has its starboard avionics access panel open.

▲ Compact Corsair
Carrier operations have always been restricted by space. With its folding-wing, a 'Golden Dragons' A-7 Corsair II can taxi while aboard ship.

▼ On the approach
Trailing its tail hook, a Corsair II returns to the carrier from a combat sortie with empty bomb racks.

▲ Carrier attack
A true naval attack aircraft in every way, this Corsair II displays its folding wings and enormous warload. The Corsair II has been used around the world by the US Navy for attack duties and flew its last combat missions during the Gulf War of 1991.

FACTS AND FIGURES

▶ The A-7 Corsair II was designed as a replacement for the A-4 Skyhawk in the attack role.

▶ Vought named the Corsair II after the World War II F4U naval fighter.

▶ The first combat mission for the Corsair II took place in December 1967.

▶ In all, 395 A-7As, A-7Bs and A-7Es took part in the Vietnam War. They flew with a total of 27 US Navy squadrons.

▶ The improved A-7E entered service off the Vietnam coast in May 1970.

▶ Altogether, 54 US Navy A-7s were lost to enemy fire.

PROFILE

Vought's venerable warrior

Often overshadowed aboard the aircraft carrier by the sleek fighters nestled alongside it, Vought's A-7 Corsair II hid its enormous capabilities beneath a short bulky fuselage. Observers seeing the aircraft for the first time often mocked the design, but to naval pilots the A-7 presented them with an ideal attack platform from which to deliver a wide range of bombs and air-to-air missiles.

The A-7A flew its first combat mission in Vietnam in 1967 with VA-147, more commonly known

as the 'Argonauts.' Operating aboard USS *Ranger*, the first combat deployment included a cadre of Air Force officers assigned to test the A-7A's combat potential.

A few years later, the USAF would request Vought to develop a land-based equivalent for them.

Despite its success, the Corsair II encountered problems in service. Pilots found the aircraft had a tendency to suck up catapult steam during launches, which resulted in more than a few accidents.

Above: With its nose leg extended, a Corsair II from USS Coral Sea returns to its home port after a cruise.

Yet the Corsair II achieved the reputation of being one of the most able attack aircraft ever.

Improvements to the avionics allowed the A-7 Corsair II to remain in the front line with the US Navy for more than 20 years, before being retired in 1991.

Below: The striking capability of the naval carrier is depicted in this view of four Corsair IIs over-flying their home carrier.

Having built numerous attack aircraft for the US Navy, the Vought designers listened to advice and gave the pilot exceptional visibility with the Corsair II. An upward-hinging canopy was provided. The pilot was seated on an Escapac ejection seat.

Positioned on the lower port fuselage was a single six-barrelled cannon. This was provided with 500 rounds of ammunition housed behind the cockpit.

A-7B CORSAIR II

This early A-7B bears the 'AB' tail-code of carrier air wing CVW-1. The wing flew from the USS *John F. Kennedy* (CV-67), a *Kitty Hawk*-class carrier which was assigned to the Atlantic Fleet.

This particular aircraft was part of attack squadron VA-46 'Clansmen', whose home base was at Cecil Field, Florida. The unit's tartan trim can be seen on the fin of the Corsair II.

A moderately swept wing was adopted for the Corsair II and six pylons were installed under the wings roughly in line with the centre of gravity, to reduce pitching movements during weapons release.

The airframe configuration adopted was unusual but well suited to undertaking attack missions at high subsonic speeds, both at high and medium altitudes.

To allow stowage beneath aircraft carrier decks, the outer wings of the Corsair could be folded. The aircraft could taxi around the carrier deck like this. The wings would be unfolded prior to launch.

A-7E Corsair II

Type: single-seat carrier-based attack aircraft

Powerplant: one 66.6-kN (15,000-lb-thrust) Rolls-Royce Allison TF41-A-2 turbofan

Maximum speed: 1123 km/h (696 mph) at sea level

Initial climb rate: 4572 m/min (15,000 fpm)

Combat radius: 1151 km (714 miles)

Service ceiling: 12,800 m (42,000 ft)

Weights: empty 8988 kg (19,744 lb); maximum take-off 19,050 kg (41,910 lb)

Armament: one M61A1 Vulcan six-barrel 20-mm cannon, plus up to 6804 kg (14,970 lb) of ordnance

Dimensions: span 11.81 m (38 ft 9 in)
length 14.06 m (46 ft 2 in)
height 4.88 m (16 ft)
wing area 34.83 m² (375 sq ft)

US NAVY ATTACK JETS

GRUMMAN A-6 INTRUDER: Providing the United States Navy with heavy attack capability, the A-6 Intruder (pictured below) could undertake solo precision attack missions in all weathers. Constantly upgraded with new avionics, the A-6 Intruder saw heavy combat use in Vietnam. The aircraft was so complex that a dedicated weapons officer accompanied the pilot. One specialized variant – the KA-6D – was a dedicated tanker. This often supported A-7 Corsair IIs on their missions. Despite early problems with its complex radar, the A-6 Intruder proved itself to be a highly capable attack platform.

DOUGLAS A-4 SKYHAWK: Often called the 'Scooter' because of the way it flew off carrier decks, the A-4 Skyhawk (pictured below) was so small that folding wings were not required on the aircraft. Having entered service in October 1956, the Skyhawk was found to be limited in capability and, by the early 1960s, the Navy and Marine Corps were already planning a replacement for the aircraft. Although improvements in attack capability were introduced, the

small size of the design restricted the Skyhawk's use. The limited future potential of the Skyhawk having been established, a request for a more capable attack aircraft was developed. The winning design was ultimately Vought's A-7 Corsair II. Despite its removal from carrier operations, the Skyhawk remained in service with the USMC as a forward-air-control aircraft. For this role, two-seat trainers were specially adapted. The USN and USMC also used the Skyhawk extensively in Vietnam.

Colourful Corsairs

■ **'BLUE BLAZERS:** An early A-7A, as it appeared in the colours of VA-93. This particular example was based at Atsugi in Japan, but was assigned to the USS *Midway*.

■ **BICENTENNIAL BIRD:** Celebrating America's Independence this Corsair flew in a patriotic red, white and blue colour scheme. The aircraft remained in these colours during 1976.

■ **CAMOUFLAGE CORSAIR:** One of several A-7Es which adopted a low-visibility trial paint scheme for the US Navy. This particular example operated aboard USS *Enterprise*.

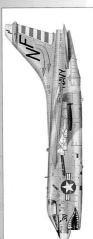

VULTEE

A-31/A-35 VENGEANCE

● Dive-bomber ● Gunnery trainer ● Unique wing structure

O ften vilified as an inferior warplane that should not have been produced in large numbers, the Vengeance was, in truth, a robust, fast aircraft with good flying characteristics. It was built for a military tactic – dive-bombing – that was rapidly falling out of favour. A true vertical dive-bomber, the Vengeance proved quite effective when used against targets that required its special capability, such as Japanese jungle positions in Burma and New Guinea.

▲ Despite harsh jungle operating conditions, the Vengeance had the best targets destroyed per loss of aircraft record of any RAF type in the Far East.

VULTEE A-31/A-35 VENGEANCE

▲ Training the French
This A-35B was one of 36 ex-USAAF examples delivered to the French during 1943.

▲ Official disapproval
Throughout World War II the British Air Ministry insisted that dive-bombers were out-moded despite their success in the Far East.

Wing structure ▶
The Vengeance's unique 'cranked' wing design was immensely strong, which was necessary to withstand the regular high g forces involved in dive-bombing.

Australian service ▶
This Vengeance Mk II, diverted to the RAAF from a British order, flew with No. 12 Squadron in 1943.

▲ Bombing Burma
In June 1943 No. 45 Squadron Vengeances started striking back at advancing Japanese forces in Burma. Attacking communications and troop positions, they combined accuracy and reliability with a low loss rate.

FACTS AND FIGURES

▶ Like the Ju 87 Stuka, the Vengeance began as a twin-tailed design, but flew with a single tail.

▶ The initial contract price for the RAF was $17,042,640 for 200 aircraft.

▶ A Vengeance 'warbird' has been restored to flying condition in Australia.

▶ The Vengeance had a unique 'cranked' wing shape which enhanced its dive-bombing capability.

▶ Total Vengeance production was 1931 aircraft, including 1529 built in Nashville.

▶ Heavy control surfaces resulted in one pilot calling his aircraft the Flying Cow.

PROFILE

Wreaking vengeance in the Far East

Vultee designed the Vengeance dive-bomber initially for France's Armée de l'Air, which was seeking an equivalent to the dreaded Junkers Ju 87 Stuka. As the war progressed, the Vengeance flew for Britain, India, Australia, and the US. After production began in Downey, California, most Vengeances were built at the maker's plant in Nashville, Tennessee.

In the US, some Vengeances were used to train dive-bomber

pilots, but most simply languished at American bases, with little effort made to exploit their potential.

In the Far East, four RAF, two Indian, and five Australian squadrons operated Vengeances resourcefully under difficult conditions during the period May 1942–July 1944. The Indian-based squadrons saw action in Burma, while the Australians made perilous attacks on New Guinea and other islands until B-24 Liberators could take over the job at higher altitude.

Below: Despite early problems, mainly with the powerplant, the Vengeance had a distinguished career with the RAF as a low-level bomber and dive-bomber.

Above: The US judged the Vengeance unsuitable for front-line operations. Its duties included training in gunnery and dive-bombing.

The US Army experimented with improved versions of the Vengeance, including one model which had the same engine as the B-29 Superfortress. The Vengeance was used by both France and Great Britain as a gunnery trainer and target tug in the latter stages of the war.

VENGEANCE MK III

Although dive-bombers were dismissed by the British Air Ministry as unsuitable, Vengeances such as this example served with distinction with four RAF squadrons in the Far East.

Early problems with the Wright R-2600 engine were largely solved by a series of modifications on the British aircraft. French machines without these modifications were judged to be unreliable and uneconomical.

The pilot was protected by 8-mm thick armour plating covering an area of 1.35 m² (14½ ft²). The gunner was protected by bullet-proof glass shields. The pilot was provided with a stainless steel 'relief tube' for long sorties.

The wing structure comprised a very heavy skin reinforced with U-shaped stringers, allowing a large space for the bulletproof fuel tanks. Large perforated dive-brakes made of aluminium alloy gave the aircraft excellent stability when dive-bombing.

After tests the British found the American 12.7-mm (.50-cal.) machine guns unsuitable, and modified all their aircraft to carry 7.7-mm (.303-cal.) Browning machine guns. Up to 907 kg (2000 lb) of bombs could be carried beneath the wings.

Although aileron controls were light, pilots found that rudder and elevator controls were extremely heavy, especially when recovering from a dive. However, the large flying surfaces gave the aircraft good stability, which is vital for accurate bombing.

Built in three sections, with crew and bomb-bay in the deep forward section, the fuselage was riveted together on final assembly.

FB922

Vengeances around the world

■ **FREE FRENCH AIR FORCE:** This A-35B of GB I/35 served briefly as a pilot and gunnery trainer in North Africa before economy and reliability problems led to early retirement.

■ **ROYAL AUSTRALIAN AIR FORCE:** After retiring as bombers, a number of Vengeances were converted for use as target tugs. This example served with No. 7 Operational Training Unit in 1944.

■ **US ARMY AIR FORCE:** Most A-35s intended for US Forces were exported and few saw operational duties. This example was used as a station 'hack' in the UK during 1944.

A-35B Vengeance

Type: two-seat dive-bomber

Powerplant: one 1268-kW (1700-hp) Wright R-2600-13 Cyclone 14-cylinder radial engine

Maximum speed: 449 km/h (279 mph) at 4115 m (13,500 ft)

Cruising speed: 370 km/h (230 mph)

Range: 3701 km (2300 miles)

Service ceiling: 6800 m (22,310 ft)

Weights: empty 4672 kg (10,300 lb); maximum take-off 7439 kg (16,400 lb)

Armament: four fixed forward-firing 7.62-mm (.30-cal.) or 12.7-mm (.50-cal.) machine guns in wings plus two flexible rear-firing 7.62-mm machine guns in gunner's position; two 227-kg (500-lb) bombs in fuselage bay and two 113-kg (250-lb) bombs under the wings

Dimensions:
span	14.63 m (48 ft)
length	12.11 m (39 ft 9 in)
height	4.67 m (15 ft 4 in)
wing area	30.84 m² (332 sq ft)

COMBAT DATA

MAXIMUM SPEED

As an early version of the P-51 Mustang powered by an Allison engine, the Apache was faster than the purpose-built A-35 and Ju 87 dive-bombers, which traded speed for strength and bombload.

A-35B VENGEANCE	449 km/h (279 mph)
Ju 87D-1	410 km/h (255 mph)
A-36A APACHE	499 km/h (254 mph)

ARMAMENT

Able to carry a far larger bombload than the two US designs, the Ju 87 delivered its ordnance with great accuracy. However, its lack of speed and armament made it more vulnerable to enemy fighters.

A-35B VENGEANCE	6 x 7.62-mm (.30-cal.) machine guns 680-kg (1500-lb) bombload
Ju 87D-1	3 x 7.9-mm machine guns 1800-kg (3968-lb) bombload
A-36A APACHE	6 x 12.7-mm (.50-cal.) machine guns 454-kg (1000-lb) bombload

RANGE

The Vengeance's impressive range made it ideally suited to the vast Pacific theatre. The Ju 87 and A-36 could only operate fairly near to the front line and generally flew close air support missions in co-operation with ground forces.

Ju 87D-1	1535 km (954 miles)
A-35B VENGEANCE	3701 km (2300 miles)
A-36A APACHE	499 km (310 miles)